# Christian Gnosis

# Christian Gnosis

Christian Religious Philosophy in Its Historical Development

FERDINAND CHRISTIAN BAUR

*Edited by* Peter C. Hodgson

*Translated by* Robert F. Brown

Translation of Ferdinand Christian Baur, *Die christliche Gnosis oder die christliche Religions-Philosophie in ihrer geschichtlichen Entwiklung.* Tübingen: C. F. Osiander, 1835.

CASCADE Books • Eugene, Oregon

CHRISTIAN GNOSIS
Christian Religious Philosophy in Its Historical Development

Copyright © 2020 Peter C. Hodgson and Robert F. Brown. All rights reserved. Except for brief quotations in critical publications or reviews, no part of this book may be reproduced in any manner without prior written permission from the publisher. Write: Permissions, Wipf and Stock Publishers, 199 W. 8th Ave., Suite 3, Eugene, OR 97401.

Cascade Books
An Imprint of Wipf and Stock Publishers
199 W. 8th Ave., Suite 3
Eugene, OR 97401

www.wipfandstock.com

PAPERBACK ISBN: 978-1-5326-7739-7
HARDCOVER ISBN: 978-1-5326-7740-3
EBOOK ISBN: 978-1-5326-7741-0

*Cataloguing-in-Publication data:*

Names: Baur, Ferdinand Christian, author. | Hodgson, Peter C., editor. | Robert F. Brown, translator.

Christian gnosis : Christian religious philosophy in its historical development / Ferdinand Christian Baur ; edited by Peter C. Hodgson ; translated by Robert F. Brown.

Description: Eugene, OR: Cascade Books, 2020. | Includes bibliographical references and indexes. Translation of Die christliche Gnosis oder die christliche Religions-Philosophie in ihrer geschichtlichen Entwiklung.

Identifiers: ISBN 978-1-5326-7739-7 (paperback). | ISBN 978-1-5326-7740-3 (hardcover). | ISBN 978-1-5326-7741-0 (ebook).

Subjects: LCSH: Gnosticism. | Theology, Doctrinal—History—Early church, ca. 30-600.| Christianity. | Religion—Philosophy.

Classification: BT1390 B38 2020 (print). | BT1390 (ebook).

Manufactured in the U.S.A. JUNE 23, 2020

# Contents

*Editor's Foreword* | xiii
*Baur's Preface* | xxvii
*Baur's Introduction*: *The Topic of This Investigation and How it Has Been Treated: Massuet, Mosheim, Neander* | xxxi
*Abbreviations* | xxxvi

## Part One: The Concept and Origin of Gnosis, the Division of Gnosis as to Its Various Principal Forms, and Their General Determination

1   The Concept of Gnosis | 3

    The Lack of Specificity in the Most Recent Determinations of the Concept and Essence of Gnosis: Neander and Matter | 3

    The Relation of Gnosis to Religion: Religious History and Religious Philosophy as the Essential Elements of Gnosis | 8

    The Components of Gnosis from the History of Religion Are Derived from Three Main Forms of Religion: Paganism, Judaism, and Christianity | 11

    The Actual Character of the Religious Philosophy Organically Connecting These Historical Elements | 14

2   The Origins of Gnosis | 19

    The Initial Elements of Gnosis Were Constructed in the Historical Arena: Alexandrian Philosophical Religion; Philo; the Septuagint Version of the Old Testament; the Old Testament Apocrypha; the Therapeutae and the Essenes; Two Kinds of Judaism | 19

    Christianity as a New Element | 25

    Expansion of Religious Horizons via the Religious Systems of the East | 26

    The Relation of Gnosis to the Basic Character of Pagan Religion, as Presented to Us in Its Main Forms, and Particularly in Buddhism | 28

    Elucidation of the Main Teachings of the Buddhist Religious Systems That Are Pertinent Here | 30

    Owing to Its Speculative Character, Pagan Religion Differs from Jewish and Christian Religion; and in Virtue of Its Principle, It Is therefore Religious Philosophy | 34

    Gnosis Originates from the Consciousness of the Unity and Difference of the Religions | 36

    Justification of the Preceding Explanation for the Origin of Gnosis, in Response to the Most Recent Dissenting Views | 37

## Contents

        Matter's View | 37
        Möhler's View | 40
    The Meaning of the Word γνῶσις in the Linguistic Usage of that Time, Demonstrated from the Epistle of Barnabas, from the First Epistle of the Apostle Paul to the Corinthians, and from Clement of Alexandria | 46
        The Epistle of Barnabas | 47
        First Corinthians | 49
        Allegory and Clement of Alexandria | 52

3  Classification of the Gnostic Systems | 55
    Mosheim, Neander, Vater, Gieseler, Matter | 55
    The Lack of a Firm Principle | 59
    The Three Main Forms of Gnosis, Which Depend on the Circumstances of the Historical Elements of Gnosis: How the Three Main Forms of Religion—Paganism, Judaism, and Christianity—Relate to One Another | 61

### Part Two: The Various Principal Forms of Gnosis

1  The Form of Gnosis Linking Christianity Closely to Judaism and Paganism | 71
    The Systems Belonging in This Class and Their General Character | 71
    1. The Valentinian System | 72
        The Development of Valentinianism's Main Ideas | 72
        The Platonic Foundation of This System | 82
        The Idea of Syzygies | 86
        The Three Principles: Pneumatic or Spiritual, Psychical, and Hylic or Material | 93
        The Concept of Matter | 94
    2. The System of the Ophites | 100
        Development of the Main Ideas | 101
        How the Christian and Pre-Christian Elements in the Ophite and Valentinian Systems Are Related | 115
    3. The Systems of Bardesanes, Saturninus, and Basilides | 121
        Bardesanes | 121
        Saturninus | 121
        Basilides | 122
    How These Systems View the Relationship of Christian and Pre-Christian Elements | 132
    The Symbolic, Mythic, and Allegorical Form of All These Systems of the First Main Form of Gnosis | 135

2  The Form of Gnosis Separating Christianity from Judaism and Paganism: The System of Marcion | S141
    Marcion's Antinomianism as Related to Judaism | 141
    The Imperfect Nature of the Demiurge | 141
    Christ the Revealer of a Completely New, Unknown God | 145
    The Antithesis of Law and Gospel; Christianity as the Religion of Love | 146

The Jewish Christ and the Christian Christ | 149

Marcion's Docetism in Relation to Paganism (According to Marcion, Christ's Manifestation Is Mere Appearance) | 151

The Significance of Gnostic Docetism as Such | 153

Christianity as the Religion of Freedom from Matter | 158

Marcion's Dualism; His Doctrine of the Primal Being | 163

The Subjective Nature of This Standpoint | 168

Marcion's Importance for His Time, and His Reforming Tendency | 174

3 The Form of Gnosis Identifying Christianity and Judaism, and Setting Forth Both of Them in Opposition to Paganism: The Pseudo-Clementine System | S178

The Form and Character of the Clementine Homilies | 179

The Anti-Marcionite Aspect of the Pseudo-Clementine System | 184

Recognition of What Is True in Marcion's Dualism with Regard to the Old Testament | 187

Opposition to Marcionite Dualism, with Reference to Two Principles: The Relation of Matter to God; The Origin of Evil | 189

The Positive Aspect of This System | 192

Monotheism: God Is the World's Creator; The Doctrine of God's Nature and the Image of God, and the Human Being's Ethical Relation to God, Which Rests Upon It | 193

The Gnostic Content of This System; the Doctrine of the Syzygies; True and False Prophecy | 199

Polytheistic Paganism Is the Religion of Error and Sin | 204

    The Demonic Origins of Paganism | 204

    Paganism Is No Ethical Religion | 208

Refutation of the Reasons for Upholding Pagan Religion | 212

Monotheistic Judaism Is the True Religion and Is, As Such, Identical with Christianity | 213

    Identity of Persons: Adam and Christ | 214

    Identity of the Contents | 215

The Difference between Judaism and Christianity: Christianity Is the Reform That Purifies and Enlarges the Judaism That Is Adulterated and Limited | 216

    Practices and Institutions Renewed by Christianity | 220

The Influence of Paganism on Judaism as Reformed by Christianity: Ordinary Gnosticism as a Pagan Form of Christianity, or as a New Form of Paganism | 223

    Gnosticism Is Polytheism | 224

The Demonic, Pagan Nature of Docetism | 227

The Concept and Nature of Prophecy | 229

General Assessment of the Gnostic Standpoint of This System: It Stands Intermediate between the Objectivity of the Systems in the First Form of Gnosis and the Subjectivity of the Marcionite System | 236

The Goal of Gnosis Is Clear Self-Consciousness | 238

Cerinthus, a Representative of the Judaizing Form of Gnosis | 240

Apelles, a Follower of Marcion | 241

Concluding Remarks about Part Two | 246

## Contents

**Part Three: The Conflict of Gnosis with Neoplatonism and with the Teaching of the Church; the Further Development of Gnosis in Virtue of This Conflict**

Introduction: The Pagan and Christian Polemic against Gnosis | 249

1   The Polemic of the Neoplatonists against the Gnostics | 251
     Plotinus' Polemic against the Gnostics | 252
          The Gnostic Doctrine of the Principles | 252
          The General Gnostic Worldview | 254
          The Distinctive Conceptions on Which the Gnostics Seek to Base Their Worldview | 257
          The Gnostics' Claims about, and Moral Principles for, Engaging in Practical Life | 259
     Who Are the Opponents at Which Plotinus Directs His Polemic? | 262
     The Doctrines of Plotinus and Those of the Gnostics Are Internally Related; The Relationship between Plotinus' System and That of the Valentinians | 272

2   The Polemic against Gnosis by the Church Fathers: Irenaeus, Tertullian, and Clement of Alexandria | 278
     The Main Arguments of Irenaeus against the Valentinians | 279
          The Supersensible World and the Sensible World Are not Related to Each Other as Archetype and Image | 279
          The Pleroma Cannot Contain within Itself the Principle of the Finite World | 280
          The World's Creator May not Be Separated from the Absolute God | 281
          The Gnostics Ascribe Human Affects to God | 282
          The Gnostics' Effrontery and Inconsistency with Regard to Knowledge of the Absolute | 283
          The Valentinian System Is Composed of Pagan Elements | 284
     Tertullian's Polemic against Marcion | 286
          The Marcionite Contempt for the World Is Already Refuted by the Pagan View of the World | 286
          Refutation of Marcionite Dualism: It Conflicts with the Christian Consciousness of God's Oneness | 287
          Being Unknown Is Incompatible with the Concept of God | 288
          We Cannot Think of Goodness as God's Essential Attribute If We Take It in the Sense in Which Marcion Assigns Goodness to God | 290
          The Concept of the World's Creator That Is Worthy of God, Set Forth by How the Concepts of Justice and Goodness Are Mutually Related | 292
          Refutation of Marcionite Christology, Especially Marcionite Docetism | 294
          How Can Marcion Set Himself above Christ? | 296
     Clement of Alexandria as an Opponent of the Gnostics | 296
          The Gnostics' Failure to Appreciate the Moral Freedom of the Will and Human Beings' Relationship to God, Which Rests On It | 297
          The Gnostics' Contempt for the World, and Their Rejection of Marriage | 300
     Clement of Alexandria as a Gnostic | 306
          Clement's Concept of Gnosis: Gnosis as Absolute Knowledge | 306

The Gnostic Is not Merely a Knower, but Is Also Perfectly Wise in Practical Matters | 308
   Clement's Christology | 312
   The Relation of Clement's Gnostic System to the Systems of the Gnostics | 314
  How Clement Sees Christianity as Related to Judaism and to Paganism | 315
   Christianity's Relation to Judaism | 315
   How the Christianity That Is Identical with Judaism Is Related to Paganism | 317
   The View That Pagan Philosophy Is from God via the Logos | 317
   The Contrary View: That Philosophy Has a Demonic Origin and Comes from Thieves and Robbers | 322
   Reconciliation of These Two Views | 326
   Clement's System as a Whole: Christianity as the Uniting of All the Separate Streams of Truth; Clement's Gnostic Standpoint | 327
  Part Three in Retrospect | 330

## Part Four: Ancient Gnosis and More Recent Religious Philosophy

1  The Transition from Ancient Gnosis to the More Recent Religious Philosophy | 335
   Manicheanism | 335
   The Augustinian System | 337
   Medieval Scholasticism | 338
   The Reformation | 338
   Catholicism and Protestantism as Related to Gnosis | 339
   The Split between Theology and Philosophy since the Reformation | 341

2  The More Recent Religious Philosophy | 343
   The Theosophy of Jacob Boehme | 343
    The Duality of Principles in the Basic Idea of the System | 344
    The Trinity | 347
    The Seven Source-Spirits | 348
    The Angels | 350
    Lucifer, His Fall, and His Significance in Ethical and Physical Contexts | 351
    The Dualism and Monism of This System | 359
    The Finite, Created World, as a Third Principle, Originates from the Interaction of the First Two, Eternal Principles | 360
    The Three Worlds as Three Forms of the Relationship of the Principles | 365
    The Human Being, the Conflict of the Principles in Him, and His Fall | 366
    Redemption: The Virgin and Christ | 370
    Boehme's Mystical Theosophy as a Higher Way of Knowing God | 375
    The Relation of Christianity to the Mosaic Law | 378
   Schelling's Philosophy of Nature | 379
    Presentation of Schelling's Position | 379
    Its Relation to Gnosis and the Connection of Its Speculative Ideas to the History of Religion, to Paganism and Christianity | 382

## Contents

- Opposition to Schelling's Dualism | 386
- Schleiermacher's *Glaubenslehre* | 389
  - Its Task and the Subjectivity of Its Standpoint | 389
  - The Relation of this Position to Pantheism | 392
  - Christianity Is the Definitive Form of the Feeling of Dependence Developing Itself in the History of Religion, and As Such It Is the Absolute Religion, or the Religion of Redemption | 393
  - The Concept of the Redeemer: the Distinction between His Archetypal and His Historical Aspects; Understanding the Archetypal Aspect as Something not Utterly Supernatural Is in the Interest of the Philosophy of Religion | 396
  - The Archetypal and the Historical Factors, the Idea and Historical Reality, Are not Completely Unified in the Person of the Redeemer | 400
  - Schleiermacher's Antinomianism | 407
  - Comparison of Schleiermacher's Glaubenslehre with Kant's Religion within the Limits of Reason Alone | 409
- Hegel's Philosophy of Religion | 414
  - Schleiermacher's Subjective Standpoint and Hegel's Objective Standpoint | 414
  - General Overview of Hegel's System as a Whole; Its Relation to the Gnostic Systems | 415
  - The First Form of Absolute Spirit, or the Absolute, Eternal Idea of God: God in the Element of Pure Thinking | 418
  - The Second Form: God in the Element of Consciousness and Representation | 420
  - The Third Form: Spirit in Its Return to Absolute Spirit, in Its Reconciliation | 421
  - The Idea of the Process in Hegel's Philosophy of Religion, as in Ancient Gnosis | 422
  - Further Development of the Major Moments of the System | 423
  - The Triune God in the Three Forms of His Self-Revelation | 423
    1. The Kingdom of the Father | 424
    2. The Kingdom of the Son | 426
       - Finite Spirit, or Human Being and Nature, as the Revelation of God | 426
       - The History of Religion as an Integral Part of Hegel's Philosophy of Religion | 428
       - The Revelation of God in Finite Spirit: God's Incarnation | 430
    3. The Kingdom of the Spirit, or, the Idea in the Element of the Community | 432
  - The Main Factors in Assessing the System | 435
    1. The Idea of the Process, the Views of Its Opponents, and Their Assessment | 435
    2. The Relation of Hegel's Philosophy of Religion to Historical Christianity. The Three Moments of Hegel's Christology; the Separation of the Historical Christ from the Ideal Christ; the Historical Christ | 440
  - How Hegel's Philosophy of Religion Locates Christianity in Relation to Paganism and to Judaism | 447
  - Assessment of Hegel's Concept of Paganism: Paganism or Nature Religion Is Religious Consciousness Mediated by the Consciousness of Nature | 448
  - Assessment of Hegel's Concept of Judaism: Judaism Is Religious Consciousness Mediated by the Consciousness of the People and of the State | 451

Christianity Is Religious Consciousness Mediated by the History and Person of an Individual | 455
Concluding Remarks | 455

*Index of Persons* | 459
*Index of Subjects* | 463

# Editor's Foreword

BAUR'S *DIE CHRISTLICHE GNOSIS* appeared from the same publisher (Osiander in Tübingen), and at the same time (June 1835), as David Friedrich Strauss's *Das Leben Jesu, kritisch gearbeitet*.[1] In fact a notice of Strauss's work is bound into the back of *Gnosis*. The furious controversy that immediately erupted over Strauss's critique of the gospel narratives[2] completely eclipsed his teacher's monumental study, and only gradually has it come out of the shadows and received the recognition it deserves. Baur published another book in 1835, *Die sogennanten Pastoralbriefe des Apostels Paulus*, which was as revolutionary in Pauline studies as *Die christliche Gnosis* was in the history and philosophy of religion. It demonstrated that Paul could not have been the author of the epistles to Timothy and Titus, and it anticipated Baur's later conclusion that only four epistles (Galatians, 1 and 2 Corinthians, and Romans) can be regarded as assuredly written by Paul.

Baur's interest in Gnosticism arose from his early studies in the history of religions, specifically his inaugural dissertation of 1827–28, which examined the idea of Christian Gnosticism and compared it with Schleiermacher's theology, and his 1831 monograph on the Manichean religious system.[3] But the specific motivation that led to the present book is the dispute that arose in the period 1832–34 between Baur and his colleague on the Catholic theological faculty, Johann Adam Möhler, over the doctrinal differences between Catholicism and Protestantism.[4] Möhler had argued in a lengthy

---

1. See Volker Henning Drecoll, "Ferdinand Christian Baur's View of Christian Gnosis, and of the Philosophy of Religion in His Own Day," in *Ferdinand Christian Baur and the History of Early Christianity*, ed. Martin Bauspiess, Christof Landmesser, and David Lincicum; trans. Robert F. Brown and Peter C. Hodgson (Oxford, 2017), 116 n. 1. (The German original is *Ferdinand Christian Baur und die Geschichte des frühen Christentums* [Tübingen, 2014].) Drecoll's chapter (pp. 116–46) provides an excellent introduction to the book and helped motivate the translators to provide an English version.

2. For details see Ulrich Köpf's chapter on Baur and Strauss in *Baur and the History of Early Christianity*, 3–44, esp. 10–22. Strauss's book was translated into English by George Eliot in 1846 as *The Life of Jesus Critically Examined*.

3. *Primae Rationalismi et Supranaturalismi historiae. Pars I. De Gnosticorum Christiani ideali. Pars II. Comparatur Gnosticismus cum Schleiermacheriane theologiae indole* (Tübingen, 1827). *Das manichäische Religionssystem nach den Quellen neu untersucht und entwickelt* (Tübingen, 1831).

4. On this dispute see Notger Slenczka's chapter on Baur's interpretation of the Protestant principle in the controversy with Möhler, in *Baur and the History of Early Christianity*, 46–66. See also below,

treatise that Protestantism represents a Gnostic inward turn that rejects historical Christianity, and Baur had responded with an equally lengthy defense of Protestantism and its turn to the subject against false charges of subjectivism. Evidence suggests that *Die christliche Gnosis* was written very hastily in response to various pressures of publication and academic dispute. Baur was establishing himself as a New Testament scholar and as a historian of the Christian church and theology, so there was a lot on his plate in the mid-1830s.[5] The German text of *Gnosis* contains a number of flaws—typesetting mistakes, erroneous citations of primary sources, and the like—that are not recognized in the Errata at the end of the volume. The translation silently corrects these flaws wherever they were noticed, but has not attempted to verify the accuracy of Baur's citations of pagination in the secondary sources he discusses.

The work as a whole has an uneven quality. The section on Boehme (the least helpful part of the book) is largely a string of long quotations interspersed with brief interpretative comments. This is true of other sections as well, but to a lesser extent. Baur often directly quotes his sources, noting them but sometimes without providing quotation marks, a common practice at the time. His method of citations is erratic. Sometimes he uses footnotes, but at other times sources are indicated in-text. Sometimes he provides publication information, other times not. We have attempted to make the notation style more uniform and to provide more complete bibliographic information. Interspersed with Baur's notes are quite a few editorial notes, designated as [*Ed.*]. Brief editorial insertions are marked by square brackets, or in some instances italics. We have referred to existing English translations of ancient texts, using the abbreviations *ANF* to designate *The Ante-Nicene Fathers* and LCL to designate the Loeb Classical Library.[6] There are a few major headings in the text itself, but Baur introduced detailed headings into the table of contents. Some of these are sentences rather than normal headings. We have put all these headings into the text and have broken up the long paragraphs, which often run for several pages without a break. Baur sometimes adds lengthy footnotes in or near the end of a section, as though he has thought of more that needs to be said, and he even provides additions through the Index and the Errata. The work has the feel at some points of being made up as it goes along. In its original form it is difficult to read, and unfortunately a critical German edition of it has never been published.

Despite all of this, *Die christliche Gnosis* is a brilliant book and a true tour de force. It reveals Baur's remarkable grasp of the history of religions, the history of Christianity, the philosophy of religion, and philosophical theology, ranging from ancient sources

---

Part 1, n. 51 and the following text.

5. *Die christliche Gnosis* completed the first phase of Baur's work, the religio-historical phase. In the next phase he turned to the history of doctrines and New Testament studies, and in the final phase he addressed church history. However, essays on all these topics appeared throughout his career.

6. *The Ante-Nicene Fathers: Translations of the Writings of the Fathers down to A.D. 325*, ed. Alexander Roberts and James Donaldson, 10 vols. (Edinburgh, 1867–73); reprinted many times. *Loeb Classical Library* (Cambridge, MA, 1911–).

to the nineteenth century. This range is a hallmark of all his scholarship, and it is first revealed here. Despite a few earlier works, *Die christliche Gnosis* is Baur's first major scholarly presentation, and his first major engagement with the modern thinkers who deeply influenced him, Schelling, Schleiermacher, and especially Hegel. Hegel was the most recent, Baur having assimilated his ideas very quickly after the posthumous publication of Hegel's *Lectures on the Philosophy of Religion* in 1832. For these reasons, this book is foundational for Baur studies.

The word *gnosis* is written the same way in Greek, German, and English, and simply means "knowledge," especially religious knowledge or (esoteric) knowledge of spiritual truth. "Knowledge" in English comes from the same Indo-European root as *gnosis*, namely ĝnō. We capitalize the term in this translation because Baur uses it to refer not only to the concept of Gnosis but also to the movement known as Gnosticism (for which he also employs the term *Gnosticismus*). The more customary term for "knowledge" in German is *Wissen*, which (along with English "wise" and "wisdom") derives from a different root. *Wissen* forms the basis for *Wissenschaft*, which means scientific or scholarly knowledge. In Baur's day academic theology was regarded as a *Wissenschaft*, along with other human sciences (*Geisteswissenschaften*). Writing about the goal of Gnosis as "clear self-consciousness" (in the section on the Pseudo-Clementines), Baur says that Gnostic systems assumed an identity between being and knowing such that "being can only be for knowing, that it can only be 'being as thought and known.'"

As the subtitle of Baur's book indicates, his usage of the term Gnosis goes beyond ancient Gnosis to designate the concept of "Christian religious philosophy" (*christliche Religionsphilosophie*) in its historical development. The term *Religionsphilosophie* poses a problem for translators.[7] On the one hand it can refer to "philosophy of religion" in the sense of a philosophical analysis of the concepts and shapes of various religious traditions without the philosopher necessarily sharing any convictions with these traditions other than a recognition of their importance. This is the modus operandi of most current Anglo-American philosophy of religion. On the other hand, the term can apply to the work of a religious believer or sympathizer who uses philosophical concepts and methods to describe and/or construct the belief system of a specific religion—Christian religion (and its antecedents) in the case of *christliche Religionsphilosophie*—as well as to defend it against criticism. This practice might be called "religious philosophy" or "philosophical religion" or even "philosophical theology," and it is the one followed by Baur in this book. He also reads Schelling and Hegel as "religious philosophers," and he interprets Schleiermacher's *Der christliche Glaube* (*Christian Faith*) as containing a religio-philosophical aspect because it intends to be a *science* (*Wissenschaft*) of faith. When *Religionsphilosophie* occurs in the section on

---

7. For a fuller discussion of this issue, see the Editor's Foreword to Baur's *Christianity and the Christian Church of the First Three Centuries*, ed. Peter C. Hodgson, trans. Robert F. Brown and Peter C. Hodgson (Eugene OR, 2019), xxi n. 24.

Hegel, we translate it as "philosophy of religion" because the reference is to what Hegel himself called *Philosophie der Religion* in his lectures on the topic and elsewhere. These distinctions are of course not hard and fast.

Gnosis as used by Baur involves a theory of *religious history* as well as of religious philosophy or philosophical theology. Religious history is concerned with the relations among three major forms of world religions: paganism, Judaism, and Christianity. Baur devotes a great deal of attention to this matter in Part 2 and offers a classification of the Gnostic systems based on how they construe the relationships. The first major form of Gnosis links Christianity closely to both Judaism and paganism, and includes the systems of Valentinus, the Ophites, Bardesanes, Saturninus, and Basilides (Part 2.1). The second major form separates Christianity from both Judaism and paganism, and is represented only by Marcion (Part 2.2). The third major form identifies Christianity with Judaism, and opposes both of them to paganism (Part 2.3). Baur finds a historical exemplar of the latter in the Pseudo-Clementine system (the *Recognitions* and the *Homilies*). Volker Henning Drecoll points out that this is a logical rather than a history-of-religions construction of religious history, and that a fourth major type is conceivable in which Christianity is linked to paganism while rejecting Judaism.[8] Baur can find no historical representation of this final form because a Christianity "reduced to the same level as paganism" would be a contradiction of the singular character of Christianity, and thus does not appear in the history of Gnosis (although aspects of it are present in Manicheanism).

There are two major drawbacks to Baur's theory of religious history. One of them is summarized by Drecoll, who explains that Baur's portrayal of Gnosis

> sets out from the concept and then goes on to classify the phenomena. Baur certainly does know his sources, and he develops his concept in such a way that he can order the phenomena accordingly. All the same, his procedure is altogether deductive. It would therefore be unthinkable for him to have a loose structure of categories based on common features, or even a "typological model," of gnosis . . . This procedure does not take into account the full spectrum of types of Gnosticism (nor, accordingly, the extensive new discoveries of the twentieth century, since Baur's definition of gnosis can seem no longer serviceable today).[9]

The logical character of Baur's typology is revealed when, in turning to his third type, he writes: "The self-advancing concept of Gnosis has not yet run through all the moments in the course of its development." He was convinced that logical patterns are displayed in historical events, but he analyzes the events (and writings) themselves in strictly empirical fashion. Religious history draws on philosophical and theological ideas at the macro level, but on the micro level it is historical-critical.

---

8. In his essay in *Baur and the History of Early Christianity* (n. 1), esp. 126. See below, Part 1, n. 83.

9. Ibid., 145. Baur acknowledges in his Preface that he does not cover all the branches of Gnosticism.

*Editor's Foreword*

The other drawback concerns Baur's use of the category of "paganism" in his account of the historical trajectory of world religions, moving from paganism to Judaism to Christianity. This is in fact a very traditional typology going back to early Christianity.[10] The issue comes up in an interesting way when Baur offers a critique of Hegel's organization of religions in the second part of his *Lectures on the Philosophy of Religion*.[11] Hegel does not employ the category of "paganism" at all but speaks rather of "determinate religion" (*die bestimmte Religion*). In the edition of Hegel's *Philosophie der Religion* available to Baur, Determinate Religion is divided into two main parts: nature religion, which includes the religion of magic, Hinduism, and transitional religions (Persian and Egyptian); and the religion of spiritual individuality, which includes Judaism, Greek religion, and Roman religion. Baur by contrast wants to expand the category of nature religion to include all the so-called pagan (non-Judeo-Christian) religions, and to distinguish Judaism from them because it reorients divine mediation away from nature to history. Hegel finds a progression within Determinate Religion itself toward "spiritual individuality," including Greek religion as well as Judaism, each of which contributes important elements to Christianity. Roman religion is a retrogressive form of spirit and provides the immediate context for the birth of Christianity. Hegel's scheme is more innovative, but it relativizes Judaism; Baur's scheme is more traditional, but it requires use of the negative category "paganism," under which the majority of world religions are lumped. Both schemes are hierarchical, placing Christianity as the "absolute" or "consummate" religion at the top. The critical edition of Hegel's *Lectures on the Philosophy of Religion*[12] points out that Hegel was constantly experimenting with the organization of Determinate Religion and could never arrive at a satisfactory arrangement. In fact, his final effort in 1831 gave nature religion a very minor role and distinguished the Asian as well as Near Eastern religions from it—just the opposite of the direction advocated by Baur.

Baur's attitude is ambivalent in that, while using the negative category, he says that paganism has been given "a less restricted role" in the more recent philosophy of religion (Schelling and Hegel). "In paganism, nature is regarded as the mediatrix who envelops the spirit that, in the realm of nature, is rising to the stage of religion[13] but of course is cloaked with nature's veil woven from so many colorful images, while at the same time also graphically setting forth in this veil the models or typology of the

---

10. See Part 1, n. 9.

11. This is found in a section called "assessment of Hegel's concept of paganism" (see Part 4, n. 185 and surrounding text).

12. See Part 4, n. 141. See the Editorial Introduction to vol. 2 of the ET of this edition, 88–89.

13. Already in Part 1 Baur says that in nature religion the absolute substance becomes subject and rises to consciousness of itself. See Part 1, n. 11. A few pages later he writes: It "is one and the same [absolute] spirit that mediates itself with itself, and comes to consciousness of itself, in all the pneumatic or spiritual beings, when they become conscious themselves that the life of the concrete individual is related to, and identical with, the highest principle of spiritual life. The task of Gnosis is to comprehend and explain this point."

## Editor's Foreword

gods." The epistemological mode of paganism is a way of seeing or perceiving things in nature (*Anschauung*). It is foundational for and is taken up into the reflective understanding (*reflectirender Verstand*) of Judaism and the reason (*Vernunft*) of Christianity. What remains externally related in nature becomes reflectively assimilated in Judaism and then through Christian rationality grasps the inner connection of things.

Part 3 of *Christian Gnosis* discusses the conflict of Gnosis with Neoplatonism and the teachings of the early church. Baur points out that this conflict played a decisive role in the historical development of Christian dogma, especially by Irenaeus and Tertullian, and that Clement of Alexandria was both a critic and a proponent of Christian Gnosticism. "Clement concurs with the Gnostics above all on the fact that there must be a Gnosis as knowledge of the absolute. Historical faith cannot suffice. Belief must be elevated to knowledge if Christianity is said to be the absolute religion." This Gnosis is not only theoretical but also serves as practical wisdom. At the beginning of Part 4, Baur provides a very brief survey of the role of Gnosis from Augustine to post-Reformation theology before arriving at more recent religious philosophy (Boehme to Hegel). We pass over these parts of his religious history.

"Gnosis," Baur writes, "is a matter of religious history (*Religionsgeschichte*) only inasmuch as it is at the same time religious philosophy (*Religionsphilosophie*), such that we gain a proper concept of the essence of Gnosis from the distinctive way in which these two elements and orientations—the historical and the philosophical aspects—have become intermixed in one totality." Our attention now turns to religious philosophy. In a key passage early in Part 1, on the concept of Gnosis, Baur writes:

> The philosophical perspective ... catches sight of an organic whole in which one and the same living idea moves forward in its concrete configuration, through a series of forms and stages of development. In the idea of religion, all religions are one; they are related to it as appearance or form relates to essence, the concrete to the abstract, what mediates to what is immediate or unmediated. The entire history of religion is none other than the living concept of religion, unfolding and advancing itself and, in so doing, realizing itself ... For the idea of religion, the history of religion is not merely the history of divine revelations, for these revelations are at the same time the process of development in which the eternal essence of deity itself goes forth from itself, manifests itself in a finite world and produces division with itself in order, through this manifestation and self-bifurcation, to return to eternal oneness with itself ... Gnosis is the remarkable attempt to grasp nature and history, the entire course of the world, together with all that it comprises, as the series of moments in which absolute spirit objectifies itself and mediates itself with itself.

One should not be surprised that this concept of Gnosis, which can be extracted from its ancient history, is also strictly analogous to the most recent religious philosophy. Baur thus anticipates Part 4 of his book, where he takes up Jacob Boehme's theosophy, Friedrich Schelling's philosophy of nature, Friedrich Schleiermacher's *Glaubenslehre*, and G. W. F. Hegel's philosophy of religion. Boehme's theosophy stands in the Protestant mystical tradition and is characterized by a duality of principles posited within the divine nature itself and carried over to the created world. It is still couched in mythic and symbolic categories, and Baur does not do much with it other than to quote long passages. His presentation of Schelling is rather brief and idiosyncratic, describing his relation to Boehme (as shown by his treatise *Of Human Freedom*, which also in part uses figurative terminology), his relation to Gnosticism (his concept of God as becoming, which involves identity, difference, and return), and his nature-spirit dualism.

Our interest in this final part focuses on its treatment of the relationship between Schleiermacher and Hegel, and the movement from the former to the latter. Schleiermacher emphatically insisted that his *Glaubenslehre* does not contain a philosophical grounding for Christian faith. Baur, however, begged to differ.

> While the contents of the Christian faith should hardly be based on philosophy, a *science* (*Wissenschaft*) of the Christian faith . . . can only be accomplished in a philosophical way by the use of philosophical methods and certain philosophical elements, those which theology takes up within itself and works with. But this scientific procedure is completely the same as the one we have already become specifically acquainted with as religious philosophy, in other words, Gnosis.

Schleiermacher's great work in dogmatic theology is not simply *Glaube* but *Glaubenslehre*, the doctrine of faith or teaching about faith. (*Glaubenslehre* is a shorthand expression used by Schleiermacher himself for *Der christliche Glaube*.) The "doctrine" part includes a theory about human subjectivity and how the objects of religious faith (such as God and Christ) are modifications of religious consciousness. Christian faith also requires Christian knowledge—knowledge of a *wissenschaftlich* character.

From what Baur says about Schleiermacher at the beginning of his treatment, we gain the impression that, despite their obvious differences in character and content, his own book, *Die christliche Gnosis*, is intended as a supplement to and corrective of *Der christliche Glaube*. This certainly comports with his view, expressed throughout this book and elsewhere, about how faith and knowledge, *pistis* and *gnosis*, are intrinsically connected.[14] As the Apostle Paul expressed it in First Corinthians, a knowledge (*gnosis*) that is not "puffed up" is a knowledge that is engaged in practices of love and is congruent with faith. At the same time it is a knowing by which faith in something

---

14. See his discussion of First Corinthians in Part 1 and Clement of Alexandria in Parts 1 and 3. One of his clearest statements about the relationship of faith and knowledge is found in an article published a year after *Gnosis*, "Abgenöthigte Erklärung gegen einen Artikel der *Evangelischen Kirchenzeitung*," *Tübinger Zeitschrift für Theologie* (1836), no. 3, 179–232.

historically given is "raised up" to the true concept of what is given. Faith is based on subjective conviction or certainty, while knowledge provides rational backing for it.

As for the transition from Schleiermacher to Hegel, Baur is tracking his own intellectual journey when he writes that "Schleiermacher's subjective standpoint—that of an absolute feeling of dependence without an absolute that has objective content—involves of its own accord the necessity of proceeding on to the Hegelian standpoint of objectivity." If the feeling of dependence is "absolute," if it refers to an "absolute causality," the mind finds itself propelled toward this absolute itself. While Schleiermacher assumes that philosophy can have nothing to do with faith, "Hegel insists on nothing more emphatically than recognizing that it is philosophy's task to bring religion to the true concept of itself and to elevate faith to knowledge, since philosophy and religion coincide as one and religion's object, like that of philosophy, is the eternal truth in its own objectivity: the absolute, or God." Subjectivity and objectivity are unified when it is understood that the mind's journey to God is at the same time God's self-knowledge returning to itself—that finite and infinite spirit are connected in the act of knowing. This connection is what the figure of Christ is all about.

Hegel distinguishes three moments in the doctrine of Christ: the moment of history (a nonreligious perspective),[15] the moment of faith (a religious perspective), and the moment of knowledge (a philosophical perspective). Baur describes the transition to the philosophical (or "spiritual") perspective as follows:

> This faith [in Christ] must therefore now first be elevated to knowledge. The spiritual content must be raised up from the element of faith into the element of thinking consciousness, where it is no longer based on the historical account as of something past and done with, but instead becomes justified by philosophy or the concept, as truth existent in itself, as absolutely present reality. For the truth existent in itself is absolute spirit, God as triune, the identity of the human being with God.

Where Hegel is heading is summed up by Baur:

> From the standpoint of speculative thinking,[16] God's becoming human is no solitary, one-time, historical event. Instead it is an eternal determination of God's being in virtue of which, in time, he becomes human (in each individual human being) inasmuch as God is human from eternity. The finitude and the painful humiliation Christ suffered as God incarnate is something God endures as human in every age. The reconciliation Christ accomplished is his deed occurring in time. But God reconciles himself with himself eternally, and Christ's resurrection and ascension is none other than spirit's eternal return to itself and to its truth. As human, as the God-man, Christ is human being in its universality. Not a singular individual, he is instead the universal individual.

---

15. See Part 4, n. 177.
16. On the meaning of the term "speculative," see Part 1, n. 41.

Baur, however, wants to descend from these abstract heights of speculation and "go once again to the lower sphere in which the difference between the historical and the ideal fittingly applies," that is, to the sphere where "Christ retains a standing and importance no one else can share with him." Here "Christ" refers to Jesus of Nazareth, the one who was believed to be the Christ. In accord with the usage of the day, it functions as a name as well as a title. Baur introduces a statement that establishes his own critical perspective on Hegel:

> Hegel's philosophy of religion regards Christ as God incarnate only as this relates to faith, and without speaking specifically about which objective features of Christ's appearing faith in him actually presupposes. But how would faith in Christ as God incarnate have been able to arise unless he was, in some way or other, what faith took him to be? In any case the necessary presupposition is that the truth existent in itself, the unity of the divine nature with human nature, had become concrete truth, become known self-consciously, for the first time in Christ, and had been expressed and taught by him as the truth. This is also therefore the distinctive prerogative or preeminence of Christ.

This statement raises the question as to who the historical Christ was and how he in fact was what faith took him to be. Baur himself investigated the teaching and activity of Jesus and established on that basis a connection between history and faith.[17] The idea and historical reality can never be completely identified in any single individual; rather the idea can fully actualize itself only in an infinite series of individuals. But the non-identity of the ideal and the real can be reduced to a minimum in a single individual, and this is in fact the case with the individual through whom the idea of divine-human unity enters into the consciousness of humanity at a specific point in time.[18] In this sense history provides a foundation for faith, but only faith can affirm that *God* is present in Christ.

Hegel recognized that the teachings and sayings of Jesus are couched in the language of faith and representation, not that of speculative knowledge, and it was Hegel who established the famous distinction between *Vorstellung* and *Begriff*, representation and concept. But only the *form* differs, not the *content*. The content concerns the oneness of divine and human spirit, and this is articulated by Christ in his own way, through teachings, parables about the kingdom of God, and his own messianic self-consciousness. Because the form differs, there must be a distinction between the historical Christ and the ideal Christ, but not, in Baur's view, a separation or disjunction. Baur summarizes his own view as well as that of Hegel when, in a section just preceding the conclusion to the book, he says that Christianity is the mediation of

---

17. See Baur's *Christianity and the Christian Church of the First Three Centuries* (n. 7), 21–35; and *Lectures on New Testament Theology*, ed. Peter C. Hodgson, trans. Robert F. Brown (Oxford, 2016), 94–128.

18. See the passage quoted in Part 4, n. 182, from Baur's *Die christliche Lehre von der Dreieinigkeit und Menschwerdung Gottes in ihrer geschichtlichen Entwicklung* (Tübingen, 1841–43), 3:998–99.

religious consciousness, not in the form of nature (paganism) or the theocratic state (Judaism), but as "the history and person of a single individual." However, "this single individual is at the same time the human being as such or in itself (*der Mensch an sich*)." Only Hegel's philosophy of religion can "make this connection between this form, the history and person of God incarnate as a single individual, and truth existent in itself." Thus Hegel's philosophy of religion must be distinguished from the docetic and dualistic tendencies that were everywhere present in ancient Gnosticism, especially in the system of Marcion.[19]

In his "Concluding Remarks" Baur says that "Christianity had to leave behind it all that is polytheistic and dualistic, the many different versions of the antithesis of spirit and matter, of a higher and a lower god, and the whole figurative, symbolic presentation of religious and speculative ideas." In place of all that it inherited from paganism and Judaism, "the idea of absolute spirit—which took shape in all these forms so as to manifest its own proper nature in them, and through this mediation to grasp itself in its own eternal truth—is what first had to become conscious [of itself] in its freedom and purity." The idea of absolute spirit could only develop on the basis of objective Christianity, and this same objective Christianity serves as a check on religio-philosophical speculation.

Baur's *Christian Gnosis* was written in 1835. Over a hundred years later, in 1945, a trove of fifty-two hitherto unknown Gnostic writings was discovered buried in a jar near Nag Hammadi in Egypt. Different literary genres were represented: gospels (like the "sayings source" used by Matthew and Luke), apocalypses, prayers, and non-Christian writings. These were Coptic translations of more ancient manuscripts, which date to the second century but may contain traditions older than the New Testament gospels. Scholars who have written about the find, such as Elaine Pagels, draw upon the Gospel of Truth, the Gospel of Philip, the Apocryphon of John, and the Apocalypse of Peter, among others, plus some of the ancient sources, especially Valentinus. Prior to Nag Hammadi, in 1896, the so-called Berlin Codex was also discovered in Egypt, containing the Gospel of Mary, the Secret Writing of John, the Wisdom of Jesus Christ, and The Acts of Peter.[20] Obviously none of these mostly gospel-type writings were known to Baur, whose information was based strictly on ancient Christian sources critical of Gnosis as a heresy. If nothing else, the new discoveries confirm that Gnosticism, in its great diversity of forms, was a massive presence in early Christianity.

Pagels makes a point of the fact that these writings were regarded as heretical, and that early church theologians together with the ecclesiastical hierarchy did everything in their power to suppress them. Her history of modern research on Gnosticism starts with Adolf Harnack, who shared the consensus view that the Gnostics propagated

---

19. See Baur's analysis of various types of docetism in the section under Marcion called "The Significance of Gnostic Docetism as Such."

20. See Elaine Pagels, *The Gnostic Gospels* (New York, 1979), xvi–xvii; and Christoph Markschies, *Gnosis: An Introduction*, trans. John Bowden (London, 2003), 43–58.

false, hybrid forms of Christian teaching, which he called the "acute Hellenizing of Christianity."[21] She does not mention Baur, for whom the category of "heresy" had an entirely different meaning. Heresy simply designated for him teachings and viewpoints that did not prevail in early controversies over the meaning of Christian faith.[22] These controversies were essential to the formation of Christian doctrines, and the victors in these struggles designated everything that did not conform to their point of view as heterodox or heretical. They tried to suppress the rich diversity of conflicting viewpoints and practices in early Christianity, a diversity that Baur attempted to recapture in his historical studies. So in this respect recent Gnostic studies share a common interest with Baur's monograph. In other respects, however, his discovery in Gnosticism of a Christian religious philosophy that came to modern fruition in the philosophies of Schelling, Schleiermacher, and Hegel would likely leave contemporary Gnostic scholars astonished and unengaged. They regard Gnosticism in religio-historical rather than religio-philosophical categories, and its modern significance lies in the diversity of religious practices it discloses, as well as its interaction with Judaism and other religions.[23]

Another point made especially by Pagels is that the Gnostics used an abundance of female symbolism to describe the nature of God, the creation of the world, the hierarchies in the world, and the redemptive figure.[24] This reflects the fact (in part) that in its earliest years the Christian movement was remarkably open to women; but by the second century patriarchal authority had become entrenched and suppressed gender as well as other forms of diversity in the Christian movement, driving it underground. Baur recognized and described in detail the female imagery in Valentinian and other Gnostic systems; but he attributed it to the influence of paganism, which gave a much larger role to female forces and figures than did Judaism (despite the fact that certain key words in Hebrew such as "wisdom" and "spirit" are feminine in gender). In all the pagan systems there was a strict hierarchy between male and female, with the female occupying the lower level. Yet "the primal being is male-female, inasmuch as

---

21. Pagels, xx–xxx.

22. Baur notes in his Introduction that researchers of Gnosticism preceding him had to deal with the inherited prejudice that it was just "the random play of an intoxicated fantasy." They did this in part by tracing its origins to Platonism and "Oriental philosophy."

23. In addition to Pagels and Markschies (n. 20), a few other modern studies confirm this point: Robert M. Grant, *Gnosticism and Early Christianity* (New York, 1959); Michael A. Williams, *Rethinking "Gnosticism": An Argument for Dismantling a Dubious Category* (Princeton, 1996); Karen L. King, *What Is Gnosticism?* (Cambridge MA, 2003); Birger A. Pearson, *Ancient Gnosticism: Traditions and Literature* (Minneapolis, 2007). An exception is Hans Jonas who, in his classic study, *The Gnostic Religion* (Boston, 1958), turned from historical to philosophical questions and argued that Gnosticism arose from a sense of existential alienation. The Gnostic worldview was a philosophy of pessimism combined with an attempt at self-transcendence, and finds modern parallels in Heidegger. This is of course a very different philosophical perspective from that of Baur.

24. Pagels, chap. 3. This is part of her argument for the contemporary religious significance of Gnostic themes.

the thought still enclosed within the most profound silence of his essence... is distinguished from himself." The female is the principle of distinction and separation, thus giving birth and vitality to what would otherwise be a solitary lifeless male monad. Sophia (or Achamoth) is both a mother to and a consort of Christ, a role assumed by Mary in canonical theology.[25]

In her final chapter Pagels addresses a theme that aligns her to some degree with Hegel and Baur. The way to the knowledge of God is not through external revelations and authorities but through knowledge of oneself. By turning to the "light within," one discovers the light that enlightens the world. The Gnostics taught that the relation between God and humanity is reciprocal, each creating the other. Humans discover from their own inner potential the revelation of truth. "Many Gnostics then," she writes, "would have agreed in principle with Ludwig Feuerbach... that 'theology is really anthropology.'... For Gnostics, exploring the *psyche* became explicitly what it is for many people today implicitly—a religious quest." The religious quest is for *knowledge* because it is *ignorance*, not sin, that creates suffering (a motif central to Buddhism). "Both Gnosticism and psychotherapy value, above all, knowledge—the self-knowledge that is insight."[26] The question then becomes what prevents theology from simply *being* anthropology? Why call this a religious quest rather than a psychotherapeutic quest? Hegel and Baur were very clear that theology is not simply anthropology, that it is *God* as absolute spirit who overreaches the difference between the infinite and the finite, incorporating the finite into Godself as a differentiating moment, and returning to Godself as the true or genuine infinite. Hegel worked this conviction out with a philosophical rigor that could be beneficial for those who want to retrieve Gnostic themes today. Baur showed how the ideality of divine-human unity must be actualized in concrete historical events and figures, and how that ideality has progressed through history from Catholic orthodoxy to a modern Protestantism that stresses both the turn to the subject (Schleiermacher) and the objectivity of God (Hegel).

Cyril O'Regan, a Catholic theologian, has written the best (and virtually the only) study in English of Baur's *Die christliche Gnosis*.[27] His thesis, using tools of literary and

---

25. In commenting on the mythic and symbolic form of the Gnostic systems, Baur writes: "As soon as the myth has created its own personae via the personification process typical of it, myth also cannot fail to involve sexual relationships and sexual activities. We need not elaborate on how deeply this sensuality makes inroads into the essential nature of the Gnostic systems, and the significance that marriage and procreation, and the kinship relations resting upon them, have even in the highest regions of the spiritual realm."

26. Pagels, chap. 6, esp. pp. 122–24.

27. Cyril O'Regan, *Gnostic Return in Modernity* (Albany: SUNY Press, 2001). Earlier O'Regan demonstrated his masterful hermeneutical skills in *The Heterodox Hegel* (Albany: SUNY Press, 1994). Corneliu C. Simuț, a Romanian scholar, published in English his book, *F. C. Baur's Synthesis of Böhme and Hegel: Redefining Christian Theology as a Gnostic Philosophy of Religion* (Leiden, 2015). It is mostly a descriptive analysis of the influence of Boehme and Hegel on Baur. Appearing a couple of years earlier was his *God and Man in History: the Influence of Jacob Boehme and G. W. F. Hegel on Ferdinand*

philosophical analysis, is that the "Gnostic return" in modern Protestant discourses represents a third option in addition to orthodox and liberal Protestantism. O'Regan believes that "Gnostic ascription" is superior to other forms of heterodox Christianity: apocalyptic, Neoplatonic, and Kabbalistic. But the line from Boehme to Hegel calls into question the Christian biblical narrative, substituting for it another, ontotheological narrative, rooted in ancient Gnosis, which argues that God as trinitarian is "not given but becomes, . . . through the economy of creation, incarnation, redemption, and sanctification, in which the pathos of the cross has an essential place."[28] An extension of this model is found in post-Hegelian thinkers such as Berdyaev, Soloviev, Altizer, Tillich, and Moltmann.

O'Regan criticizes this model from the same perspective as the Catholic Tübingen School in the nineteenth century, recalling the debate between Möhler and Baur. He regards the Gnostic return as both "haunting" and "deranging," and he calls it a "fabulous catastrophe." It is fabulous because "the narrations are magnificent in their speculative adventurousness and their aesthetic appeal," and because they offer an "alternative to both the dead letter of Christianity in the post-Reformation period and the death of Christianity in the post-Enlightenment period." But it is a catastrophe because the biblical narrative "is systematically disfigured."[29] The "grammar" of biblical narrative is briefly described by O'Regan as constituted by classical versions of the central Christian doctrines: Trinity (Father, Son, and Holy Spirit as determinate personal entities), creation (the world as radically distinct from God), fall (through disobedience to the rule of God), redemption (through Christ as the incarnate Son of God), resurrection, and consummation.[30] This is the consensus view from Irenaeus to the Reformers and Protestant scholastics.

In response, we may point out that, for one thing, the biblical narrative is not as sui generis as this distinction makes it sound. It too is embedded in its historical nexus and draws upon non-biblical sources. But more importantly, modernity has uncovered tensions in the story that cannot simply be papered over—historical, logical, metaphysical, psychological, scientific tensions. History is violated by repeated supernatural incursions into it and by mistaking myths and legends as historical fact. In its literal form the story is riddled with logical contradictions, and it is based on a static metaphysics for which God is regarded as an unchanging entity beyond the world (the "supreme being") rather than as a spiritual process interacting with, suffering in, and being enriched by the world. The story can be illuminated by what has been learned about human beings from the psychological and social sciences, but if construed literally it conflicts with a scientific understanding of nature.[31] Baur belonged to a

---

*Christian Baur's Philosophical Understanding of Religion as Gnosis* (Piscataway NJ, 2013).

28. O'Regan, 33.

29. Ibid., 236.

30. Ibid., 162.

31. The classic statement of these contradictions is found in David Friedrich Strauss's *Die christliche*

generation of early nineteenth century theologians and philosophers who attempted to render the Christian metanarrative intelligible once again by rethinking central Christian doctrines, drawing upon repressed resources from the tradition, and employing bold speculative ideas. Whether they failed or succeeded, and to what degree, has been debated ever since.

---

*Glaubenslehre in ihrer geschichtlichen Entwicklung und in Kampfe mit der modernen Wissenschaft dargestellt* (Tübingen and Stuttgart, 1840–41). It has never been translated. In English the title reads: *Christian Dogmatics* (or *Doctrine of Faith*) *in Its Historical Development and in Conflict with Modern Science*. From Baur's perspective, Strauss's work was purely negative and destructive, but a necessary step. See his discussion of it in *Church and Theology in the Nineteenth Century*, ed. Peter C. Hodgson, trans. Robert F. Brown and Peter C. Hodgson (Eugene OR, 2018), 371–74, incl. n. 122.

# Baur's Preface

THE FIRST PART AND the main contents of this book involve a new examination of the ancient Gnostic systems. Given the well-known, recent studies that have so successfully advanced the investigation of this topic, it might seem to many people that mine is a rather superfluous undertaking. With all due respect and gratitude for the work of my predecessors, I cannot share this view. At this very time, after the previous inquiries have made so much progress, I believed that an even further step needed to be taken. In that pursuit, may this present book—one resulting from many years' study and which I present for public evaluation—prove its worth in the eyes of qualified experts.

As in my previous historical investigations, here too in the present one my main effort has not been merely to grasp the object being investigated as an external phenomenon. Instead I have sought above all to grasp it in its internal coherence, in the particular inner movement of its concept and the totality of its elements. It seems to me that the primary and most indispensable task for every new worker on this topic is to determine the concept of Gnosis[32] more precisely and more comprehensively, and from this concept itself to develop the various major forms of Gnosis as regards their origins. For these are the respects in which the results of the previous investigations can prove least satisfactory.

The initial plan for this book was first of all limited to the aforementioned goal, to those points now discussed in Part One. Nevertheless I soon became convinced that the more precise way I sought to determine the concept of Gnosis had to have a significant influence on the presentation of the individual Gnostic systems, in their development, so I believed I must part ways with previous portrayals by others on a number of points, and that only by doing so could my task be accomplished clearly and completely. Furthermore, since within the actual scope of these previous investigations there had been no inference to a main form of Gnosis—and without it there

---

32. [*Ed.*] *Gnosis* is used in Greek (γνῶσις), German, and English and means "knowledge," especially religious knowledge or (esoteric) knowledge of spiritual truth. "Knowledge" comes from the same Indo-European root as "Gnosis," namely *ĝnō*. We capitalize it in this translation because Baur uses it to refer not only to the concept of Gnosis but also to the movement known as Gnosticism (for which he also employs the term *Gnosticismus*). Some modern scholars (e.g., Christoph Markschies) prefer the term γνῶσις to γνωστικός for both the concept and the movement.

can be no understanding of the concept of Gnosis itself in the totality of its elements—my original plan underwent an expansion to include what is now elaborated in Part Two of this book.

Thus the present volume contains a presentation of the Gnostic systems that also goes into individual instances. Except the reader should not expect it to be the kind of presentation, even of those individual systems, that views them as only less significant modifications of one of the various major forms. The completeness I aimed at could not have been an edition that traces out the large family of Gnostic systems in all of its branches. Instead it was to present only those main forms of Gnosis that must be regarded as essential elements of the concept of Gnosis, and to do so from this perspective. I have intentionally passed over other matters not directly connected with the main purpose of this book, such as a more exacting and detailed discussion of the often asked question as to whether the beginnings of Gnosis are already perceptible in the New Testament. I have become convinced that this question is to be answered very differently than in the usual way. Based on these investigations, what I have to add to these discussions, and as a contribution to answering that particular question as such, I will seek to elaborate on in my forthcoming, critical treatise on the Pastoral Epistles of the Apostle Paul.[33]

Nevertheless, as I did in my depiction of the Manichean religious system,[34] I thought I must take particular account also of the polemic against the Gnostics, from both those in the church and those outside it. If we are to recognize the full meaning and importance of Gnosis, then it does not suffice to take it as merely an individual, free-standing phenomenon. The presentation of the Gnostic systems belongs to a *history* of Gnosis only if it follows up, as much as possible and in its full scope, on what Gnosticism has set in motion. Hence if Gnosis, indeed within its own sphere, is not understood to be a historical phenomenon in the true sense—even though the individual systems emerge as the elements necessarily conditioning themselves reciprocally, elements in which the concept of Gnosis unfolds itself in its inner, living movement—this movement must also be made the object of a historical examination in the wider sphere to which it extends, in the polemic that was directed against Gnosis and that was simply a continuation of the movement originally arising from Gnosis itself. This polemic, in itself no less valuable, deserves to be more fully appreciated. It is even the necessary point of contact (*Vermittlung*) if all those issues Gnosis was so long and so seriously occupied with resolving (as no one can deny), are said to be of innermost concern throughout the following ages and even extending to the present day.

---

33. [Ed.] *Die sogenannten Pastoralbriefe des Apostels Paulus aufs neue kritisch untersucht* (Stuttgart and Tübingen, 1835). Baur argues that the heretics mentioned in the Pastorals were Gnostics, probably Marcionites, and that therefore these epistles must date from a post-Pauline era.

34. [Ed.] *Das manichäische Religionssystem nach den Quellen neu untersucht und entwikelt* (Tübingen, 1831).

In the section about Plotinus pertinent to this matter, I very much wanted to be able to utilize the source cited on p. 253 n.1. But I faced difficulties presented because the works of this writer are still so inadequately edited or critically reconstructed. Of course the renowned master of Germanic philology has long since completed his work on them. But the new Oxford edition from abroad is continually delayed and thus unavailable.[35]

Given my standpoint regarding the determination of the concept of Gnosis, my horizon of course had to reach beyond the domain of ancient Gnosis, which heretofore marked the boundaries of this kind of investigation. I employed the concept of Gnosis that is none other than the concept of religious philosophy or philosophical religion (*Religionsphilosophie*). Doing so makes the more recent religious philosophy the natural fulcrum for this whole series of investigations and the place to find the most meaningful appearance of Gnosis. I willingly acknowledge that the more recent religious philosophy has in turn been an essential tool for correctly understanding the internal organization of the Gnostic systems and for having a more profound appreciation of them. In this way the history of Gnosis, which was supposed to be the first and principal topic of these investigations, quite naturally goes on to become a history of religious philosophy. My wish is for the present volume to be seen first and foremost from this perspective. The title itself indicates as much.

In my view a history of religious philosophy, which until now has been lacking, is not possible unless we look back to the phenomena that ancient Gnosis has engendered on its own very fruitful soil. For if we once take hold of this standpoint in its full scope, and with the concept of Gnosis also gain the concept of religious philosophy, then this standpoint directly enables us to see a related series of similar phenomena in which the very same concept moves forward via the internal connection of its developing elements or moments. Just as each single component within such a nexus is conditioned by all the others, so too an encompassing historical examination, of the kind at least attempted here, can be a history of religious philosophy in which the ancient part appears mediated by the modern part, and the modern by the ancient. I believe this allows each part to illuminate the other part. It also serves to support a more accurate grasp and appreciation of the most recent religious philosophy and its relation to theology.

It is of course appropriate to include a discussion of Schleiermacher's *Glaubenslehre*[36] in a book on this topic. At the same time it is my way of taking up again an earlier

---

35. [*Ed.*] Presumably Baur is referring to Georg Anton Heigl, whose edition of Plotinus (*Plotini ad gnosticus* . . . [London, 1832]) he cites on the indicated page. Baur had to rely on a review of this work by F. Creuzer in the *Theologische Studien und Kritiken* (1834) since it was not yet available to him in Tübingen.

36. [*Ed.*] Literally, "doctrine of faith" or "dogmatics." A shorthand expression for Schleiermacher's *Der christliche Glaube* (1821, 1830). Note the formal similarity in titles between Schleiermacher's *Christian Faith* and Baur's *Christian Gnosis* (or *Christian Knowledge*).

critical endeavor I had long felt I must return to, although my view is unchanged.[37] It is occasioned by the well-known *Sendschreiben* of this revered man, who is now removed from the sphere of his earthly influence.[38] A new critical analysis of the essential elements of the *Glaubenslehre* now comes forward together with another critique of it: Heinrich Schmid, *Über Schleiermacher's Glaubenslehre mit Beziehung auf die Reden über die Religion* (Leipzig, 1835). It has not been possible for me to include a comparison and consideration of it here. Likewise I could not yet utilize August Ferdinand Dähne's *Geschichtliche Darstellung der jüdisch-alexandrinischen Religionsphilosophie* (Halle, 1834), in its two initial parts, which would have been the first place to make comparisons. For it, and others too, I took the occasion to make a few additions (some in the index, some in the list at the end of the book).

Works such as those I have mentioned, as well as numerous others, attest to the lively interest in such investigations. Also, religious philosophy has become very important, in particular because of the work of Hegel.[39] While I am well aware of the difficulties facing someone who takes on this task, if doing so even partially satisfies the expectations of science, perhaps the present volume will be favorably received.

---

37. [Ed.] See Baur's *Primae Rationalismi et Supranaturalismi historiae capita potiora*. Pars II. *Comparatur Gnosticismus cum Schleiermacheriane theologiae indole* (Tübingen, 1827). Baur argued in this work that Schleiermacher's *Glaubenslehre* is a form of *Religionsphilosophie*.

38. [Ed.] Schleiermacher had died in the previous year, 1834. He responded to the criticisms of Baur and others in his "Sendschreiben über seine Glaubenslehre, an Dr. Lücke," *Theologische Studien und Kritiken* 2 (1829), 255–84, 481–532.

39. [Ed.] G. W. F. Hegel's *Vorlesungen über die Philosophie der Religion* was published posthumously by Philipp Marheineke in Berlin, 1832. Baur came under its influence shortly thereafter.

# Baur's Introduction
## *The Topic of This Investigation and How it Has Been Treated: Massuet, Mosheim, Neander*

THERE IS HARDLY ANY other topic in church history that has been more repeatedly and thoroughly examined than the extraordinary phenomenon referred to by the general terms "Gnosis" and "Gnosticism." This phenomenon became prominent in various forms within the setting of the early church and, with its various orientations, it cut across the church by being pointedly and hostilely antithetical to the prevailing dogma.

Since the onset of a more penetrating and more independent form of research in the broad area of church history, scholars have also turned to investigations of the Gnostics. These investigations were partly into the many branches of Gnosticism, taken as a whole, and partly into its individual components as such. They never ceased but were always renewed, by relying on what diligence and erudition, a sagacious and ingenious combination, had to offer. These investigations sought to penetrate the mysterious darkness, which, although illuminated at a few points, was all the more enticing to the spirit of inquiry owing to its glimmering light. The researchers set out from very diverse perspectives and, although they did not exhaust the topic, the results they gained seemed to be at least a contribution of lasting value toward the achievement of the larger goal.

Massuet, Mosheim, and Neander are the prominent names associated with the three epochs in the history of the lengthy series of these investigations. The guiding interest has always aimed at finding how those foreign and abnormal aspects, which seem to mark the entire phenomenon of Gnosticism, have points of contact with what makes a general understanding of Gnosticism possible, with what locates it within the given historical context of the pre-Christian history of religion and philosophy, and makes it explainable on that basis.

Massuet[40] at least tones down the ancient abhorrence of this class of heretics, an abhorrence that is the heritage from the era of those who first challenged them.

---

40. [*Ed.*] René Massuet (1666–1716) was a French Benedictine patrologist. His edition of Irenacus, *Contra haereses libri quinque* (Paris, 1710), was later included as the Irenaeus text in Migne,

These critics had regarded Gnosticism as a willful perversion of, and an intentional contradiction to, Christian truth. The early church fathers seemed to assign Gnosticism's ultimate source to a deep-seated opposition to the Christianity of the Catholic Church. Instead of this, it was now located in an unfortunate mental aberration, and the Gnostics were considered to be, at the least, fanatics who can be compared to similar manifestations of crazed enthusiasm in other eras.[41]

Massuet, as the editor of the five books of Irenaeus' *Contra haereses* [Against Heresies] (Paris, 1710), was a distinguished contributor to the historical interpretation of the Gnostic systems. He is meritorious for his exacting and learned demonstrations (in his *Dissertationes praeviae in Irenaei libros, Dissert. 1. de haereticis, quos libro primo recenset Irenaeus, eorumque actibus, scriptis et doctrina*) of how Gnostic teachings are linked with Platonism. However, inasmuch as the entire phenomenon of Gnosticism could hardly be satisfactorily derived from this source alone, and especially from Massuet's knowledge of how to make use of it, that had to leave a considerable excess of eccentric and abnormal material that could only come under the heading of fanatical foolishness. Hence the next step forward could only come from expanding and extending as much as possible the horizons within which one operated in grasping and evaluating the phenomena of Gnosis, so as to create a wider scope for what one could produce by doing so. Then one would not have to seek in the Gnostic creations themselves, however much their own peculiar features might involve it, just the random play of an intoxicated fantasy, devoid of reason.

This is what Mosheim[42] aimed to do when, dissatisfied with merely presupposing Platonism, he believed that he could find the actual source of the Gnostic systems simply in what he referred to as "Oriental philosophy." Indeed this term directly expressed the call for those investigating this topic to transfer their attention to a new and distinctive sphere. They would have to bring with them a quite different measuring stick than our usual Western one for gauging reason and fantasy, to deal with the speculation presented in Gnosticism. Despite Mosheim's great effort to construct a system of "Orientalism," and despite the fact that we undoubtedly have to thank him for his more exacting research into the internal nexus of the Gnostic systems, it is nevertheless well-known how he hardly ever wanted to fall in line with the idea of an Oriental philosophy that has a solidly historical basis and bedrock. Thus however

---

*Patrologia Graeca*, vol. 7. His 1710 work also contains his own "dissertations on the heresies impugned by Irenaeus," from which Baur includes quotations below.

41. In his dissertation on the Valentinian Gnostics (*Dissert. praeviae*, p. xlvi in the 1710 edition), Massuet ends by drawing a parallel between the extravagant views of the Valentinians and the foolishness and craziness of the fanaticism present in his own times in various European countries. [*Ed.*] This statement sums up the lengthy text in Latin from Massuet, which Baur quotes in full in this footnote.

42. [*Ed.*] Johann Lorenz von Mosheim (1694/5–1755) was a wide-ranging historian and theologian at Göttingen. [*Baur*] The principal works by Mosheim pertinent here are: *Institutiones historiae christianae majores, saeculum primum* (Helmstädt, 1739); *Versuch einer unpartheiischen und gründlichen Ketzergeschichte*, 2nd ed. (Helmstädt, 1748); *De rebus Christianorum ante Constantinum Magnum commentarii* (Helmstädt, 1758).

often Mosheim came back to this theme, it was always just reiterated as that "round dance about the altar of an unknown god—the eternal circle of Oriental philosophy revolving within itself, with no footing or standing," as Herder, with clever and not wholly undeserved ridicule, characterized Mosheim's "Orientalism."[43]

That idea always remains a lifeless abstraction devoid of any concrete concept. This is especially evident from the fact that it hardly serves as a satisfactory and natural basis for sorting out and classifying the various Gnostic systems. Indeed Mosheim has still not even disengaged himself from Massuet's notion of a Gnostic fanaticism. To him the Gnostics seem at times to be not so much fanticizers as they are metaphysicians afflicted with a fanatical pestilence.[44] Notwithstanding this, Mosheim's idea of Oriental philosophy expressed the presentiment of an internally and externally magnificent nexus of Gnostic systems, a presentiment truly confirmed by subsequent investigations.[45] What other result than this can there be from the investigations of learned and discerning researchers who returned our attention to this topic, such as Neander,[46] Lewald,[47] Gieseler,[48] Matter,[49] and others? These works appeared after a lengthy interim period in which people had simply been content to augment

43. Johann Gottfried Herder, *Aelteste Urkunde des Menschengeschlechts*, Part 3.4, *Morgenländische Philosophie*. In *Sämmtliche Werke: Zur Religion und Theologie* (Stuttgart and Tübingen, 1827–30), vol. 6, pp. 206, 215. The only question is what right Herder has to spew forth his ridicule of Mosheim, and to demean this gifted man himself, in contrast to how Walch (n. 50) treats him (p. 208). Or do Herder's interpretations shed significant light on this issue? See, for instance, p. 200, where he says: "Gnosis was a deluge of ancient, obscure wisdom that, even with its prolonged, foul stagnation, inundated and ensnared, and thus became sufficiently detestable on, the soil of every region, everywhere from Bactria to Arabia and Egypt. Could it have looked the same everywhere in Asia and Africa? Could the vessel have changed something in the muddy water that was not yet stagnant? Now what results is the Gnostics' great hatred of the Jewish religion and Moses . . . They had a different and higher authority! . . . Their gnosis was the fount of truth, the oldest religion of the world, delivered by a hundred prophets"; and so forth.

44. "I think they were not stupid and outrightly lazy people. Still, they were not of a sufficiently sound mind. In short, they were fanatical metaphysicians, infected with pestilence." *Institutiones majores* (n. 42), 147.

45. In the *Theologische Zeitschrift*, ed. by F. Schleiermacher, W. de Wette, and F. Lücke, vol. 2 (Berlin, 1820), see the article on pp. 132–71, by Friedrich Lücke, "Kritik der bisherigen Untersuchungen über die Gnostiker, bis auf die neuesten Forschungen darüber von Herrn Dr. Neander und Herrn Prof. Lewald." The article, which dealt with just part of the topic, only discussed Mosheim.

46. August Neander, *Genetische Entwicklung der vornehmsten gnostischen Systeme* (Berlin, 1818). [*Ed.*] Neander (1789–1850), a convert from Judaism, was a Lutheran theologian and professor of church history in Berlin from 1813 until his death. He represented a very different approach to history than that of Baur, who, while appreciating his study of Gnosticism, in later years became critical of his partisan spirit.

47. Ernst Anton Lewald, *Commentatio ad historiam religionum veterum illustrandam pertinens de doctrina gnostica* (Heidelberg, 1818).

48. See especially J. C. L. Gieseler's extensive evaluation of the two aforementioned works by Neander and Lewald, in the Halle *Allgemeine Literatur-Zeitung* 104 (April 1823), 825 ff.

49. Jacques Matter, *Histoire critique du Gnosticisme et de son influence sur les sectes religieuses et philosophiques des six premiers siècles de l'ère chrétienne*, 2 vols. (Paris, 1828). German translation from the French, by C. H. Dörner (Heilbronn, 1833).

Mosheim's investigations with Walch's kind of diligence and mentality.[50] Or else they were content with Semler's audacity in coupling the even more serious suspicion of a cunning popular deception with the ancient prejudice that Gnosticism was reckless fanaticism.[51]

What sets this period we are discussing apart is that many elements had to combine of their own accord in order to cast a new light on this segment of the early history of the church. These elements included: more extensive geographical and ethnological information; the discovery of so many new sources that threw ever more light on the ancient Orient; the now so very successfully initiated research on the symbolism and mythology of ancient peoples; the general progress of science, and of critical historiography in particular. In the process what then appeared was the recent era's own critical tendency, which stood directly opposed to Mosheim's orientation.

Based on the general statement that he himself had constructed, Mosheim sought to study closely the special character of Gnosticism; whereas Neander in the main almost wholly bypassed the general question and turned directly to researching the internal origins and construction of the various Gnostic systems. Although that general question could not be dismissed, to simply avoid Mosheim's vague lack of specificity the researchers were far more inclined to draw narrower boundaries in place of overly widely horizons. The two contemporary scholars, Neander and Lewald, did so in the most striking way. Neander focused in a one-sided way on the Platonism of Philo, while Lewald just sought to identify the roots of Gnosis in Zoroastrian dualism. The continuing investigations by Neander[52] had the evident tendency to increasingly compensate for the one-sidedness of his earlier standpoint, by tracing Gnosis back to both Alexandrian Platonism and Persian dualism, as the two predominant elements behind it. Other scholars, in contrast, are noticeably inclined to adopt a standpoint either far too limited in scope, or else far too extensive and indefinite.

So as not to anticipate what follows below, I refrain here from engaging in a broader critique of the current status of the investigations of the Gnostics. However,

---

50. C. W. F. Walch, *Entwurf einer vollständigen Historie der Ketzereien*, vol. 1 (Leipzig, 1762), 217ff.

51. In the introduction to Siegmund Jacob Baumgarten's *Untersuchung theologischer Streitigkeiten*, vol. 1 (Halle, 1771), 158: "Valentinus had devised such a system that its mysterious and weighty contents consequently were able to cause a great sensation among simple-minded, fanatical people. Doubtless he himself found it amusing that people so readily believed in the reality of such notions." But Semler has a different verdict (p. 119): "In fact one can only with difficulty avoid the verdict that many of the so-called heretics of that time, Gnostics especially and Manicheans, were the same sort of theosophists as Boehme, Dippel, and similar writers of our day . . . In short, the Gnostic kind of teachings that Irenaeus informs us about one can very well learn how to envisage for oneself in Boehme's writings, teachings one elsewhere looks upon as much too erudite and wholly false." Our own investigation later in this book will show how accurate this comparison with Boehme's theosophy is (although in a different sense than Semler supposed). [*Ed.*] Johann Salomo Semler edited this book of his teacher Baumgarten, writing a preface, a brief "history of Christian doctrine," and a historical introduction.

52. *Allegemeine Geschichte der christlichen Religion und Kirche*, vol. 1, pt. 2 (Hamburg, 1826), 627 ff.

what even here indeed deserves mention, as the most illuminating point of Neander's elucidation of this topic, is his division of the Gnostics into two groups, Jewish Gnostics and anti-Jewish Gnostics. This provides for the first time something more specific to hold on to as we look more deeply into the inner organic structure and principle of Gnosticism, rather than merely exhibiting and arranging the Gnostic systems in the colorful multiplicity of their mutually intersecting features. Yet although this division attests to Neander's historical acumen, we can hardly overlook or pass over in silence the halfway measures with which he comes to a halt. Simply consider that the same distinction and dividing line that Neander drew with regard to Gnostic Christianity's relation to Judaism must also hold good in relation to paganism. This is the completion of Neander's standpoint that is needed. Yet at the same time it would have to essentially change our entire view of Gnosis as such.[53]

In short, Gnosis must be treated from the perspective of a history of religion encompassing all three religions: paganism, Judaism, and Christianity. While what is distinctive and striking about it formerly seemed to be accounted for only via the concept of Oriental religious philosophy, I maintain that, in the end, Gnosticism can only be accounted for, conceptually, as religious philosophy itself. That is because, in its essential nature, religious philosophy itself has forever after taken the same path that ancient Gnosis had already taken.

---

53. I initially suggested this view, and the classification of Gnostic systems resting on it, in my inaugural dissertation, *De Gnosticorum christianismo ideali* (Tübingen, 1827), 33ff.

# Abbreviations

*ANF*  *The Ante-Nicene Fathers Translations of the Writings of the Fathers down to A.D. 325*. Edited by Alexander Roberts and James Donaldson. 10 vols. Edinburgh, 1867–73

*LCL*  Loeb Classical Library. Cambridge: Harvard University Press, 1911–

*LPR*  G. W. F. Hegel, *Lectures on the Philosophy of Religion*. 3 vols. Edited by Peter C. Hodgson. Translated by R. F. Brown, P. C. Hodgson, and J. M. Stewart. Berkeley and Los Angeles: University of California Press, 1984–87. Reprint, Oxford: Oxford University Press, 2007

# PART ONE

The Concept and Origin of Gnosis,
the Division of Gnosis as to
Its Various Principal Forms,
and Their General Determination

# 1

# The Concept of Gnosis

## The Lack of Specificity in the Most Recent Determinations of the Concept and Essence of Gnosis: Neander and Matter

IN SURVEYING THE PREVIOUS investigations into Gnosis and the various Gnostic systems, it is in fact not easy to form a clear concept of how the essence of Gnosis originated.

Mosheim and his immediate successors have been criticized and found wanting for having no better way to characterize the essence of Gnosis than by employing the general and indefinite idea of an Oriental philosophy. With our present knowledge of the Orient, it is in any event quite possible to differentiate the various Oriental religious systems that have influenced Gnosis. As a result of more recent investigations we now know what in fact is to be added to Mosheim's description and conceptual determination when it comes to the essence of Gnosis as a whole, and to gaining as clear and definitive a concept of it as it is possible to have. So, might the more correct and more well-grounded approach, the more advantageous one—as Neander for instance prefers—be to speak not of an "Oriental philosophy," but instead of an "Oriental theosophy"?

The consensus is that the Gnostic systems inherently have a predominantly Oriental character. Yet as soon as we ask for a more specific feature that is recognizable as Oriental, no one feature can be pointed to that fits all the Gnostic systems, that can be viewed as a general and essential feature or indicator of Gnosticism. If the doctrine of emanation is said to preeminently express the Oriental character of Gnosticism, then right away comes the significant reservation that the very Gnostic whom Neander considers to be the main representative of a distinctive class of Gnostics, namely Marcion, completely excluded from his system the doctrine of emanation and the doctrine of Aeons that depends on it. Equally so, one cannot take the dualism of Gnostic systems, the antithesis of a good principle and an evil principle, to be a basic Oriental element common to all Gnosticism. That is because not all Gnostic systems are comparably dualistic in nature, and also because the simple antithesis of spirit and matter, something on which all Gnostic systems agree, has nothing about it that is essentially Oriental. Finally, the docetism that one thinks of here is in any case not common to all the Gnostic systems, and in those where it is undeniably recognizable it appears with very different modifications. Docetism presents only a single and rather subordinate aspect of Gnosticism. When it is supposedly traced back to a specific Oriental religious doctrine where it seems to be ultimately rooted, namely Indian religion, there is largely disagreement as to how far one might go in accepting its influence on Gnosticism's origins and configuration.

From this we indeed see how the general designation as "Oriental" is hardly suited for providing an appropriate and specific concept of the essence of Gnosticism. Nevertheless we want to give somewhat closer consideration to the interpretations of Gnosticism made by more recent researchers.

In explaining how the most prominent Gnostic systems originally developed, Neander has placed the most weight on Philo, by locating him at the head of the series of Gnostics.[1] Philo is the one who provides the most material for seeking out the elements of Gnosis in the Alexandrian religious philosophy.[2] For this purpose the following principal theses exemplify the way Neander explains the connection between the Gnostic systems and the teaching of Philo:

1. Philo's distinction between the spirit and the letter, in other words, between certain higher truths and the shell or husk in which they are contained or expressed in the scriptures and formal religious practices of the Old Testament, involves the beginning of a polemic, not against Judaism as such, as divinely instituted, but instead against a misunderstanding of Judaism by a multitude attuned to matters of the flesh.

2. Philo distinguishes a sublime essence of the deity, which is hidden, self-enclosed, incomprehensible, beyond every description and depiction, from God's revelation as the initial crossing over to the creation as the basis for the unfolding of all life. Revelation is most closely connected with Philo's doctrine of the divine powers that go forth like rays from the transcendent deity as the original source of all light.

3. The human spirit, which is itself the image and likeness of the heavenly and eternal revealer of the hidden deity, of the eternal Logos, of the highest, divine reason, also has this same character of revealing God, of receiving divine life within itself and disseminating it from itself.

4. Philo's perspective on religious knowledge is twofold. There is perfect knowledge, which God himself reveals through himself, and there is imperfect knowledge, coming to human souls via spirits or angels as God's representatives, knowledge that guides and saves them.

---

1. [*Ed.*] August Neander, in his *Genetische Entwickelung der vornehmsten gnostischen Systeme* (Berlin, 1818), devotes the introduction (pp. 1–27) to "Elements of Gnosis in Philo." Baur summarizes this material below.

2. [*Ed.*] Philo of Alexandria (c. 20 BC–AD 50) was a Hellenistic Jewish philosopher. He used allegory to harmonize Jewish scripture with Greek (Stoic, Platonic) philosophy. His method was more important for Christian and Gnostic thought than for Rabbinic Judaism.

5. According to Philo, the individual peoples and individual human beings in the sacred history are, as such, only appearing as symbols and visible representatives of universal spiritual forms of humanity, as certain eternal qualities or characteristics. Thus the people Israel is the symbol by which to contemplate the most highly dedicated spirit. While the other peoples only have higher spirits, God's angels, for their overseers, the Jewish people is the lineage directly overseen by God.

6. With Philo we already find the seeds of the view, based on the occurrence of theophanies and angelic appearances in the Old Testament, that God and higher spirits reveal themselves concretely to our human senses in apparently sensible forms that have no real existence.

Thus it is hardly deniable that all these ideas recur in the Gnostic systems and are to be viewed as a not-inessential foundation of Gnosticism as such. On the other hand, we can hardly overlook the fact that we find these ideas in a very different form in the case of the Gnostics, and that is why they cannot fully suffice for a comprehensive explanation of the essence of Gnosticism. What a great distance there is between the allegorical interpretation of the Old Testament, by rejecting reliance on the letter of the text, and the manifest polemic that so many Gnostics present in opposition to the entirety of Judaism. What a great distance one has come from drawing a distinction between the absolute God and the Logos mediating God's revelation, to the idea of a supreme God who is utterly foreign even to the Demiurge [world creator or artisan] that hostilely strives against him, a Demiurge who gets identified with the God of the Jews simply in order to demote both Demiurge and Jewish God to the lowest level. While all that we behold in the Gnostic systems and in Philo's religious doctrines is of course definitely related, at the same time these are two quite different phenomena. So that weighs against any sufficiently satisfactory derivation of the one from the other. If we wish to understand the very broad domain of Gnostic systems and ideas as being based on the limited standpoint of Philo, taken simply in its own terms, then we will forever encounter too large a gap between them, one that is unbridgeable, a striking mismatch between cause and effect.

As another discerning researcher in this domain has maintained, a full understanding of Gnosis comes from considering it to be a new development of Philonic Platonism via its combining with the Christianity that, in Syria, had been modified by Persian dualism.[3] Thus the essence of Philonic Platonism had, first of all, to be reduced to its pure form and reiterated from a general perspective, in order to gain the true concept of how Gnosticism arose from this Platonism by being a new development of it. However, in concert with singling out Philo, Neander reminded us that, in pursuing this investigation, we always have to consider the fact that Platonism was the foremost thing in Philo's mind, and that he often treated the received doctrines of Jewish theology as just allegorical versions of Platonic ideas; whereas for the Gnostics, in contrast,

---

3. J. C. L. Gieseler, review of works by Schmidt and Matter, *Theologische Studien und Kritiken* (1830), pt. 2, 378.

their predominant interest was in Oriental theosophy. Neander says that they used this theosophy to shed light on Platonic philosophy and to fill in its gaps; that they sought to give this philosophy greater impetus and vitality, for they contended that Plato did not have an in-depth understanding of the spirit world. Accordingly, this would simply be to dismiss the general and indeterminate concept of Oriental theosophy, so as to fill out completely the sought-for principle of explanation that one still failed to find in Philo. This is the very same Oriental Gnosis that Neander sets forth for us in his new presentation of Gnosis and Gnostic systems in his church history,[4] a presentation comprehensive in many respects and one in which Philo now moves into the background.

Neander reminds us of the remarkable era of fermentation from which the Gnostic systems emerged, and the lively and extraordinary exchange of ideas that took place between the peoples of East and West. He reminds us of the ardent desire with which the unsatisfied spirit mixed many different religious elements together by drawing upon Greek mythology and the answers provided by the Greeks' philosophical systems, and sought to reassemble from all this the fragments of a lost truth. Hence in the Gnostic systems, with their elements of ancient Oriental religious systems (in particular, Persian, but also surely East Indian ones), Jewish theology, and Platonic philosophy, all blended together, one can at the same time detect a distinctively animating principle that invigorates the majority of these components. Not only has the time at which they emerged given them a stamp all their own, the basic tenor of an unsatisfied longing they would fulfill, but also the idea of salvation or deliverance, which forms the distinctive essence of Christianity, has been attuned to this basic tenor or longing. What we get from this depiction [by Neander] of the character of the Gnostic systems is the concept of a religious syncretism linked to Christian ideas.

Matter's characterization of Gnosis[5] does not go any further than this. Matter explains that, in joining the Christian religion, the Gnostics did of course sincerely intend to renounce their previous beliefs. However, owing to this syncretism they were, so to speak, molded and swayed by habits of heart and mind that were stronger than their new convictions. Initially and unconsciously, with some reservations, and in the end quite eagerly, they mixed the new with the old, religion with philosophy, exoteric church teaching and esoteric traditions. Gnosis is none other than the attempt to introduce into Christianity all the cosmological and theosophical speculations that have shaped the greater part of the ancient religions of the East, and have also been accepted by the Neoplatonists in the West. However these speculations have not merely been copied, as a kind of mosaic. It would be a serious misunderstanding

---

4. Neander, *Allgemeine Geschichte der christlichen Religion und Kirche* (Hamburg, 1825–31), vol. 1, pt. 2, pp. 627ff.

5. [*Ed.*] Jacques Matter, *Histoire critique du Gnosticisme et de son influence sur les sectes religieuses et philosophiques des six premiers siècles de l'ère chrétienne*, 2 vols. (Paris, 1828). Matter (1791–1864) was a professor of church history in the Protestant Theological Faculty at the University of Strasbourg.

of the human spirit if one wanted to compare its endeavors with ordinary mechanical processes, and could, not incorrectly, pass judgment on Gnosis as though one considered it from this perspective—as has simply been the case for too long a time.

Gnosticism is perhaps the most original of all the systems that antiquity has produced. At least it is the most copious one of them all. What in fact constitutes its spirit, the predominant feature in its ideas, sets Gnosticism apart from every other kind of teaching precisely because Gnosis owes its origins to a wholly distinctive need or desire. This need in fact results from spirit's unbridled striving to finally break through the confines of the sensible world. The ancient mysticism of Asia had doubtless had an entirely analogous orientation, but it only drew upon the existing mythology. In contrast Gnosis, by at most adopting a few ideas providing the main foundation for the ancient mythologies, at the same time discarded all their forms and traditions. By avoiding on the one hand all the anti-philosophical features of mythology, and on the other hand all the anti-dogmatic features of philosophy, Gnosticism adopted a few of the most robust doctrines of Christianity. In five or six articles of faith it created a system, or rather systems, that extended over all that the human spirit might embrace. These articles furnished a series of dogmas linked together in the most remarkable way.[6]

Oriental theosophy, syncretism, unbridled striving on the part of spirit—these and similar designations for the essence of Gnosis are obviously very general and tenuous indicators that can give us no clear and satisfactory concept. In part these terms are attached to features that do not even seem to be mutually compatible. If Gnosis is simply a blend of cosmological and theosophical speculations from the ancient religions of the East, then how can it at the same time be called the most original of all the systems of antiquity? And if this originality is located in the unbridled striving on the part of spirit to break through the confines of the sensible world, cannot this same originality also indeed be ascribed to the ancient religions of the Orient themselves, the ones from which Gnosis is said to have acquired its content? What concept of the essence of Gnosis are we supposed to form if, of course on the one hand, it is mainly related to the ancient, mythic mysticism of Asia, and on the other hand, however, it is said to have discarded all those forms and traditions? Furthermore, one must also remember here that all these features either do or do not exactly fit one of the noteworthy Gnostic systems, or at least do so only very imperfectly. However, the Marcionite system is so negatively related to everything pre-Christian that, because of this it does not share in the Oriental theosophy or the syncretistic character of the other Gnostic systems. Also, it is in any event quite free of the unbridled striving to break through the confines of the sensible world. However, all the major Gnostic systems must themselves include the features said to make clear the essence of Gnosticism as

---

6. Matter, *Histoire critique*, vol. 1, p. 12. See vol. 2, p. 191: "It certainly bears repeating that the Gnostics are not theologians, nor moralists, nor philosophers. They have much higher aims than these do. They are theosophists in the more exclusive sense that one can give to this term."

such. One of these systems that is distinctive and noteworthy as such can hardly be disregarded in determining the general concept of Gnosticism.

## The Relation of Gnosis to Religion: Religious History and Religious Philosophy as the Essential Elements of Gnosis

Of all the characteristic features that Gnosis presents to us, none stands out more clearly or lets us see, at first glance, more deeply into the essence of Gnosis, than does its relation to religion. Religion is the topic Gnosis is in fact dealing with, although this is not first of all religion as abstract idea but instead is religion in the concrete shapes and positive forms in which it has objectified itself historically at the time when Christianity appeared.

Paganism, Judaism, and Christianity are the integral elements that constitute the material contents of Gnosis in all of its main forms. However negatively and harshly the individual Gnostic systems may see their relation to one or another of these religious forms, the task they have is always to spell out how these three religious forms are mutually related in terms of their character and their intrinsic value. The Gnostic systems do this critical comparison as their way of arriving at the true concept of religion. Hence if, as so often happens, the essence of Gnosis is located in philosophical or theological speculation, this specification is directly emended to saying that we are not to regard the subject matter of Gnosis as what is speculative in and for itself, in the way that philosophy takes up the business of speculation. Instead its subject matter is speculation only to the extent that speculation is something given via the contents of the positive religions to which it attaches itself.

It is from this perspective that we can readily evaluate the accuracy of the contention—already found in ancient writers, and often repeated by more recent ones who follow their precedent—that the actual problem Gnosis was attempting to solve is the question about the origin of evil.[7] It is true that the contents of the Gnostic systems can for the most part be traced back to that question. Since the Gnostic understands evil not merely in the moral sense but most especially in the metaphysical sense, such that evil is the finite that is distinct from, and separated from, what is absolute, the issue comprises none other than the major problem as to how the finite comes forth from the absolute, or how the world proceeds from God. And since the descent or

---

7. See Tertullian, *Prescription against Heretics*, ch. 7: "The same subject matter is discussed over and over again by the heretics and the philosophers; the same arguments are involved. Whence comes evil? Why is it permitted?" [ANF 3:246]. Also, *Against Marcion* 1.2: "Marcion (like many persons now, and especially heretics) broods about the question of evil: What is its origin?" [ANF 3:272]. In his *Ecclesiastical History* 5.27, Eusebius speaks of "the problem of the source of evil, so much traversed by the heretics" [LCL *Eusebius*, 2:514–15]. In *Against Heresies* 24.6, Epiphanius says, in speaking of the sect of Basilides: "This evil doctrine originates with the inquiry into the origin of evil; the kind of evil that is displayed in the whole of one's own life. The doer of evil is in truth a purveyor of evil and does nothing good. As it is written, 'Do no evil, and evil will never overtake you' (Ecclesiasticus 7:1)."

falling-away from the absolute cannot be conceived of without a future turning-back to, and reacceptance into, the original principle of being, that single question embraces both aspects of the sphere within which all the Gnostic systems operate, whether describing a larger or a smaller orbit.

But if this were the only principal issue that prompted the quest for a solution by the Gnostic systems, then their inherent character would lack a satisfactory explanation. Since this very question that occupied them is a purely philosophical question, it had to give them far more the shape of philosophical systems, and thus one could not rightly conceive why, for such a purpose, they had to locate themselves so specifically in relation to the positive, historically given religions. They could support this way of answering the question only if they considered these systems from a more general perspective, as the necessary mediation of what is said to be recognized as truth in philosophy and religion.

Sufficient attention has been given to the fact that the three forms of religion existing in mutual contact at the time when Gnosticism came on the scene are elements constitutive of the acknowledged foundation and material contents of Gnosis. So in this sense we have to consider Gnosis from the perspective of the history of religion. But this is only one aspect of the essence of Gnosis, and it must be linked to another aspect essentially belonging to Gnosis. That is to say, Gnosis is a matter of religious history (*Religionsgeschichte*) only inasmuch as it is at the same time religious philosophy or philosophical religion (*Religionsphilosophie*),[8] such that we gain a proper concept of the essence of Gnosis from the distinctive way in which these two elements and orientations—the historical and the philosophical aspects—have become intermixed and combined in one totality. Each Gnostic system contains pagan, Jewish, and Christian elements. Yet in each system these elements at the same time appear to us as mutually related in a specific way, such that the nature of the religious form to which they belong is determined by the position given to them in the arrangement of the whole system.

Over and above the merely historical way of considering these systems there stands the philosophical or reflective perspective, which, in the combination of components from the historically given religions, catches sight of an organic whole in which one and the same living idea moves forward in its concrete configuration, through a series of forms and stages of development. In the idea of religion, all religions are one; they are related to it as appearance or form relates to essence, the concrete to the abstract, what mediates to what is immediate or unmediated. The entire history of religion is none other than the living concept of religion, unfolding and advancing itself and, in doing so, realizing itself. In other words, by doing so, religious knowing first becomes an absolute knowing, a knowing about the absolute religion, so that it is also self-aware of its own mediation. This is the perspective from which Gnosis considers the historically given religions in their mutual relationships. But at

---

8. [*Ed.*] On the translation of these terms, see the Editor's Foreword.

the same time the idea of religion fully unites with what it has for its essential and necessary content, with the idea of the deity (*Gottheit*). Hence for the idea of religion, the history of religion is not merely the history of divine revelations, for these revelations are at the same time the process of development in which the eternal essence of deity itself goes forth from itself, manifests itself in a finite world and produces division with itself in order, through this manifestation and self-bifurcation, to return to eternal oneness with itself.

This is the explanation for the strict antithesis found in all the Gnostic systems, the antithesis between the absolute God and the self-revealing God. The more abundantly the deity manifests itself in its unfolding life, and the more varied is the series of divine powers into which the eternal one spreads out, the greater too is the effort to hold fast to the idea of the absolute in its purely abstract character. The Gnostics have insufficient expressions to designate the self-enclosed and concealed essence of the deity, what is nameless and unnamable, what utterly transcends every conception and description. Yet if the deity is supposed to be characterized as going outside itself, then one must be able to conceive of the determinative cause for this. The cause is matter, and the antithesis between spirit and matter is therefore the factor that conditions and determines the divine self-revelation in its various moments.

The entire divine revelation and world-development becomes a struggle of two mutually opposed principles, one in which the supreme task of the deity, or of the absolute spirit, is to overcome, and put an end to, the antithesis owing to matter. Matter can of course be related to God in different ways. Matter can be thought of as outside God, as an eternal principle equal to deity. Alternatively, matter can be posited within the divine nature itself. Or else matter is not in fact anything substantial, but is only the negative principle that—as soon as the deity reveals itself and establishes the antithesis of infinite and finite—cannot be separated from the finite world in which the deity reveals itself, for it functions as what limits and confines the complete expression of the divine essence. Yet even in the latter case, where the concept of matter is reduced to this more minimal factor, the antithesis between spirit and matter remains, in itself, completely the same. If matter is conceived of as an independent principle over against God, then God can only reveal himself in a contest that limits his absolute being and subjects it to finitude. Thus, although matter does not stand over against God as an independent principle, that nevertheless leaves us with the deity as forever having the not-further-explainable tendency to go outside itself and reveal itself in a world where the completeness or perfection of the divine essence can only present itself as something limited and finite. The same higher necessity that sets matter over against God also holds sway because the deity cannot withstand the inner pressure of its nature to reveal itself in a world that can only be a material world, a world with matter.

However if, in the creation of the world, we might even conceive of matter as in this way having control, so to speak, over God, as a principle negating the absoluteness of the divine being, this is nevertheless just always a negation that is in turn itself negated and must be canceled out. For the moment of redemption, and of the return of the finite to God, stands over against the moment of world creation through which God makes himself finite. The spirit given over to matter and held captive by matter must be freed and delivered from its power. The divine self-revelation turns back once more to that from which it has gone forth, although in doing so the end is not completely the same as the beginning. For, since spirit once again resists the domineering influence of matter, spirit has gathered itself within itself and withdrawn itself from matter, and is now, for the first time, truly conscious itself of its independence from matter, of its absolute power. Even if matter, as an independent principle, stands over against spirit, with the two principles resuming their former positions (the Gnostic ἀποκατάστασις, the complete restoration, or return of all things), there no longer exists the same relationship as before. Instead, the outcome of the struggle is spirit's newly-born consciousness of their true relationship. So these are the principal moments of the self-revelation of the divine being, and of the world's development, the moments through which all the Gnostic systems, with all their variant forms, make their way.

When we consider Gnosis in this way, it appears with the higher meaning that in almost all cases had to be recognized in it if one could form any clear concept of the distinctive nature of Gnosis. Gnosis is the remarkable attempt to grasp nature and history, the entire course of the world, together with all that it comprises, as the series of moments in which absolute spirit objectifies itself and mediates itself with itself. This is all the more remarkable since, in the entire history of philosophical and theological speculation, there is nothing more related to, and analogous with, Gnosis than the most recent religious philosophy [Boehme, Schelling, Schleiermacher, Hegel].

## The Components of Gnosis from the History of Religion Are Derived from Three Main Forms of Religion: Paganism, Judaism, and Christianity

There are two questions we have to consider first of all, with regard to the two elements to be distinguished in the essence of Gnosticism: the historical and the philosophical elements, or the historical-religious aspect (*Religionsgeschichte*) and what we call religious philosophy or philosophical religion (*Religionsphilosophie*).

First, what components in the material contents of the Gnostic systems are traceable to the individual forms of religion that constitute the historical-religious aspect of Gnosticism?

Second, what is the inherent nature of the religious philosophy overarching the historical elements and interrelating them in a specific way?

The answer to this first question directly presents us with the three principles that, in addition to the supreme and absolute principle of the deity, all the Gnostic systems share: matter, the Demiurge, and Christ. From this it is self-evident how these three principles relate to the three religions in question here. Since Christianity is represented by Christ and Judaism is represented by the Demiurge, only matter is left for the pagans. These pairings fully correspond to the successive stages or levels assigned to these three religions. Christianity stands higher than Judaism, and Judaism is acknowledged to have undoubted precedence over paganism.⁹ On this view, the well-known Gnostic classification of human beings into πνευματικοί, ψυχικοί, and ὑλικοί or χοϊκοί (people of spirit, of the psyche, and of matter or earth respectively)—which is analogous to the trichotomous division of human nature into πνεῦμα, ψυχή, and σάρξ (spirit, psyche, and flesh or body)—also carries over to the followers of the three religions. This is the sense in which Valentinus and Marcion, for instance, explain that the Jews are the realm of the Demiurge, the pagans are the realm of matter or of Satan, and the Christians, as people of spirit, are the people of the supreme God.

Since pagan religion stands at the lowest level, matter forms the most extreme antithesis to the deity. Indeed the concept of matter itself wholly belongs in principle to pagan religion, and simply stems originally from it. There are numerous reasons why it cannot be deemed inappropriate to look upon matter as the principle pagan religion represents in the Gnostic systems. They include the facts: that the idea of a God creating by the power of his word remains completely foreign to pagan religion; that paganism has everything issuing forth from a primordial chaos wildly driven by blind forces; that most of the pagan deities are just personifications of the material elements and forces of nature, or of the sensuous urges dominating human life; and moreover, that the idea of Satan, which in the Gnostic systems is so closely linked to the idea of matter, with Satan as the prince of darkness and the ruler of matter, is in any event an idea belonging to pagan religion certainly inasmuch as Zoroastrian dualism is simply one of its various forms. This makes it obvious that, with such a way of looking at things, where one is only dealing with the most prominent and characteristic concepts, and can fix one's eyes only on the extreme position without regard for intermediate cases and nuances, there must always be a certain one-sidedness. So it is only in this one-sided sense that matter, the most extreme concept from which pagan religion proceeds, can be regarded as the signature concept belonging fundamentally and pre-eminently to it.

While the pagans occupy the lowest place, Christians belong to the highest one. Hence Christianity stands at the level of humanity's course of religious development where the idea of a redemption, consisting of purification and liberation from everything of a material nature, is not merely something one is conscious of, but is

---

9. [*Ed.*] It is difficult to avoid the negative connotations of "paganism" or "heathenism" (German *Heidentum*, the term used by Baur). Jews and Christians used these words to distinguish their own religion from non-Jewish, non-Christian, and mostly Eastern religions. The word "pagan" comes from the Latin *pagus*, "country," with its Indo-European base *\*pak-*, "to join, enclose, fasten." "Heathen" is traceable back to a Gothic root meaning "heath." Perhaps a more neutral version of the term would be "indigenous religion." Baur includes under this category Greek religion, Pythagorean-Platonic philosophy, Indian religious systems (Hindu and Buddhist), and Zoroastrianism.

also realized. Therefore, however freely and arbitrarily the Gnostics might proceed in determining the true content of Christianity, they see it as the religion having the absolute truth about, and knowledge of, the return from the world of antithesis and estrangement, and back to oneness with God. This exalted status and significance had to be ascribed to Christianity if, as the more perfect and consummate religion, as the religion of the pneumatic or spiritual people, it was said to be the successor to the subordinate levels at which the still-so-imperfect religions stand, the limited and one-sided religions of paganism and Judaism. Accordingly, everything the Gnostic systems embody concerning the idea of redemption, all the teachings related to it, all the practices and institutions the Gnostics have introduced among themselves supposedly for the purpose of realizing the idea of redemption—all this is either directly borrowed from Christianity or else modeled after Christianity. In any event all this shows what influence Christianity had on Gnosticism, and what an essential contribution it has made to the material contents of Gnosticism in its various forms.

Judaism is the intermediary or intermediate form of religion between paganism and Christianity. In the series of Gnostic principles, the Gnostic Demiurge occupies a comparable position. Since the Gnostics generally understood the Demiurge to be the God of the Jews, it quite clearly indicates the element of Gnosis deriving from the Jewish religion and, as such, points to the position that Judaism itself has within the context of the system. The various predicates the Gnostics assign to the Demiurge, by portraying it sometimes in more brilliant terms and sometimes in darker tones, as befits the twofold nature of such a being, are by the same token judgments about the inner worth of Judaism and its religious laws and institutions. However, with all their disparaging depictions of the Demiurge's essential nature and all the even more petty notions they therefore harbor about Judaism itself, for all of the Gnostics the main idea—as the idea that had to be made known to religious consciousness first of all by Judaism—forever remains the idea of a world-creator and a world-ruler. [As inferior to Judaism,] pagan religion had never actually risen above the concept of matter, because all of its divine figures, which paganism conceives of as arising in unruly confusion from the obscure, dark fermentation of chaos, can still always fall back again into chaos, for none of them can gain an existence and consistency that is independent of chaos. Yet at the same time the concept of matter itself, as a principle distinct from divinity and standing independently over against the divine, spiritual principle, had for the Gnostics a truth and reality, so that there was also no mistaking the intrinsic religious value belonging to pagan religion. Likewise, because of its distinctive idea of redemption, Christianity maintains a position in the Gnostic systems that gives the most convincing testimony to the inner power of its religious truth. Thus Judaism too lays claim to a recognition that even no anti-Jewish Gnostic could have denied or wished to deny, in virtue of the idea Judaism first brought to consciousness and expressed, the idea of a world-creator transcending matter and working, or creating, according to specific ideas and purposes.

So each of these three religions has its own place in the process of religious development that humankind has to pass through on the path prescribed for it by the history of religion. The three principles that indicate the stage and sphere of each religion are the most essential and necessary moments through which the concept of religion progresses in order to attain its true significance and inclusive specificity, such that a prior moment is the necessary presupposition for the one that follows it. However, this is also the reason why the subordinate moments must have their own immanent truth.

## The Actual Character of the Religious Philosophy Organically Connecting These Historical Elements

The three principles we have traced back in this way to the three religions to which they belong, initially are not reciprocally related in the way they appear to us in the Gnostic systems. They first acquire this interconnection from the religious philosophy added or applied to these elements from religious history. But what is the character or nature of this religious philosophy itself when we subject it to closer examination?

It soon becomes evident that, howsoever subordinate the position of pagan religion with matter being assigned to it, it plays a very important part in the philosophy that links those elements and pervades them with its spirit. This philosophy proceeds from the same outlook that still always makes pagan religion the foundation in the same way—that is, pagan religion in its various principal forms, although with different modifications. God and world are conceived as mediated by the elements of a process, one embodying more or less the characteristic of a natural process conditioned by physical laws. The main difference here concerns that process or sequence being either from above to below or from below to above, either from what is perfect or complete to what is less so, or from the imperfect to the perfect. The downward direction can generally be called "emanation," and the upward direction "evolution."

The evolutionary view posits an imperfect state as the first and original condition, one that does indeed contain within it all the elements for a higher development. But this state or condition is only the foundation for a higher spiritual life, one that can only develop via a series of configurations in which the material principle is conceived of as in an ongoing struggle with the spiritual principle. This is the standpoint of Greek religion, which for that reason has a theogony instead of a cosmogony, and only at the highest level has free, self-conscious spirit soaring above the material world.

The view proceeding from the concept of emanation is typical of the Oriental religious systems that posit the purely independent spirit as the first principle, and have the material world initially resulting from the fact that spirit comes into contact with matter via a series of potencies and natures issuing from spirit like rays of light, but whose inner power diminishes the more distant they become from spirit as the original or primordial light, and that give way to the eclipsing power of a dark principle within them. In any event the term "emanation" designates this view only imperfectly and in a one-sided way, since it embraces quite different modifications of this position. Above all, the cosmogonies of the Indian religious systems cannot be assigned to the emanation idea as legitimately as can the Zoroastrian doctrine of Ormazd and the beings of light in which he reveals himself. However, we may always regard the most essential and universal point here as the fact that the mediation or interaction between spirit and matter, between the two antithetical principles, takes place in some way based on, or arising from, spirit. The eternal, absolute spirit objectivizes and individuates itself. It lets a part of its own essential nature go forth from itself and come under the control of matter. Here we also find the conception that higher spirits, the souls of human beings, as the result of their falling from the higher region, the spirit world, have descended into the sensible world and become enclosed in material bodies just like in a prison. Caught in these bodies, they groan under this burden and long to be freed from them. This is the Pythagorean-Platonic perspective, which opposes the ideal world to the real world and considers this real world to be the dim, shadowy reflection of that ideal world. We clearly recognize that this Platonic perspective is related to the religious teachings of the East.

It is now easy to see on which of the two sides that we have distinguished we are to place the Gnostic systems. It is the Oriental standpoint from which they proceed. The doctrine of the Aeons, which occupies such an important place in most of these systems, directly shows how justifiable it is to designate their way of representing the relation of the finite to the absolute in terms of an emanation doctrine. A series of Aeons proceeds from the absolute spirit, which is itself the Primal Aeon. The more numerous and manifold the classes and levels of Aeons, the stages marking the descent from the intelligible world to the sensible world, the more assuredly are the Aeons said to mediate the transition from spirit to matter, from the ideal to the real. This is that aspect of Gnosis in which the Gnostic systems are organized in the most diverse ways and display their productive energy most abundantly, in their competitive wrestling to solve the problem of mediating an antithesis that inherently can never be mediated. Whether their solutions involve expansion to a system of thirty Aeons, or concentration in the concept of a Sophia as a mere power and property of the Supreme God, it is always the same attempt at mediation.

While this aspect of those systems takes the route from above to below with the two outermost components of the antithesis being God and matter, a philosophical examination can distinguish different perspectives on this antithesis. Since the eternal, absolute being or essence puts an end to the inexpressible stillness—the ἄρρητον (secrecy), σιγή (silence), ἔννοια (thought)—in which it is pure self-identity, and fully proceeds to thinking of itself, and opens out from the unfathomable, self-enclosed depths (βυθός) to the unfolding of the seeds of life hidden in it, to the configuration of a particular existence, this is its transition from the abstractness of its essence to its concrete determinacy. It then becomes for the first time a concrete, self-conscious spirit. We can only understand it in this sense when the Gnostic systems, and especially the Valentinian system, which is the most thoughtful and thorough one, has the Νοῦς (Reason) or Μονογενής (Only-Begotten) coming forth from the absolute essence as the first emanation, and together with it also the Logos. It is in this way that the absolute God,remaining inconceivable in pure identity with himself, first gains the concept of his own essence or being.[10] The absolute *substance*, existent in itself, becomes the *subject*[11] when the divine essence steps forth vis-à-vis itself and makes itself the object, in the Νοῦς or Μονογενής. Hence this is the genesis of the divine self-consciousness, which, in the first Aeon coming forth from the divine substance, is presented in a manner analogous to the form of human consciousness. That is why the church fathers, for good reasons, faulted the Gnostics for assigning human forms and conditions to the divine being.

However, the divine ideas are also these same Aeons in which the divine substance becomes the subject, the ideas according to which the world is formed and structured. By the divine essence being revealed to itself, it also reveals itself in the world. The Aeons, descending level by level from the ideal world to the real world, are at the same time the bearers of the archetypal forms and are their conveyers to the material world. However subordinate the level at which the Demiurge falls in the series of Aeons, as the one who directly makes the world, he nevertheless can impress on the world, which is his work, no other forms than the kind he himself has received from above, as conveyed to him by the higher orders of being.

But the concept of emanation, to which we must stick closely here, also ultimately involves the fact that what is emanated diminishes in reality and perfection to the degree that it becomes farther away from its original source. This too is a perspective from which the doctrine of Aeons is to be considered. The farther down the series of Aeons descends, the more power the dark principle gains over the principle of light. Spirit has gone down into the domain of matter, and already here there begins the suffering and distress of Sophia-Achamoth, the last one of the Aeons, which the

---

10. See Epiphanius, *Against Heresies* 31.5.3–4, which introduces a statement from a Valentinian text: "the Self-Engendered contained in himself all things, things which were in him and were not known." The ἔννοια or thought is also called the σιγή (silence), "since Greatness [τὸ μέγεθος, *das Absolute*] completed all things through a concept without speech" [ET: *The Panarion of St. Epiphanius, Bishop of Salamis: Selected Passages*, trans. Philip R. Amidon, S.J. (New York and Oxford, 1990), 111]. See Irenaeus, *Against Heresies* 1.1.1. (ch. 10 in Epiphanius), where he says about the Sige or Silence: "... becoming pregnant, she gave birth to Nous, who was both similar and equal to the one who had produced him, and was alone capable of comprehending his father's greatness." And, in 1.1.2, he writes: "They proceed to tell us that the Propator [the pre-existent Aeon] was known only to the Monogenes [Only-Begotten] who sprang from him; in other words, only to the Nous, while to all the others he was invisible and incomprehensible" [ANF 1:316–17].

11. [*Ed.*] Italics ours. One of the main themes of Hegel's philosophy is that the absolute must be comprehended "as *subject* no less than as *substance*" (*Phänomenologie des Geistes*, ed. Johannes Hoffmeister [Hamburg, 1952], p. 19 [¶ 17 in *Phenomenology of Spirit*, trans. A. V. Miller (Oxford, 1977)]).

Valentinians in particular depict so vividly. So it is always in turn the same idea of emanation that is presented to us from different perspectives.

In any event all this just involves one side of the Gnostic system. For there must be another side corresponding to the emanation and going-forth from God: the returning, and being taken up once more, into the oneness of the divine being. In between these two antithetically juxtaposed sides then lies the entire course of the suffering-filled circumstances in which the spiritual principle is confined and constrained, and increasingly overcome, by material being. The suffering of Sophia-Achamoth, the entire period of rule by the Demiurge, and even the earthly appearance of Christ, are moments belonging to this entire course, which is wholly characterized by allowing this contest between the two principles to unfold in such a way that we can clearly see all of its more important aspects.

The world of the Demiurge has its counterpart in Sophia-Achamoth, who is suffering and downcast because of how clearly she is conscious of her descent from the spirit world. The unending sorrow of being overcome by matter is a more unfree and more unclear condition in the case of the Demiurge standing far below her. In this latter world the Demiurge no longer is very aware of his spiritual element, although at this lowest level of its self-alienation the spirit has not ceased working its way through all the obstacles and contrary influences presented by matter. At last, by gathering together all the forces of light in a unitary consciousness, spirit breaks forth all at once with a brilliant ray and ascends on the upward path to the realm of light—overcoming the final crisis in which the struggle between the two principles gets all the more fiercely aroused the more the moment of their decisive separation has arrived. In all those in whom the divine sparks of light are not completely extinguished, the longing for redemption and liberation from the bonds of matter is reawakened, and they are led upward on this path.

It is obvious that this whole domain within which the Gnostic systems operate—the twofold path they describe here, with one path downward from the spiritual world to the material world, down to the most extreme limitation and eclipse of the light principle by the material principle, and the other path upward from this extreme point to the highest region of the realm of light—has its type or model in all those forms of ancient religion that present us with deities of light and sun gods as the foundation for all the religious insights of antiquity. These religions have so many analogous shapes of the gods, of different contrasting conditions, the oppositions of light and darkness, of life and death, of struggle and conquest, as well as involving that whole series of transformations that the life of nature undergoes in its annual cycle. The basic idea and basic insight is always the same, although what appears to us in so many myths of the old religions, sticking to the narrowly confined sphere of the annual cycle of natural life, was similar or comparable to the lofty speculative standpoint of the Gnostic systems, to the great antithesis encompassing the highest principles and the antitheses of God and world, spirit and matter, good and evil, sin and redemption, fall and return.

However, what calls for special emphasis here is the identity of the spiritual principle that the Gnostic systems presuppose as present in all those beings said to mediate or connect spirit with matter, and then in turn matter with spirit. Just as the eternal, absolute spirit objectifies itself in the Aeons initially standing with it, so too all those remaining beings, said to mediate the antithesis between the two principles, are only different forms and shapes in which spirit veils itself according to the various aspects of its relationships to matter. Spirit does this in order that, by the whole series of these mediating elements in which it has to carry out its self-revelation on this broad path, it will return to absolute oneness with itself and then for the first time attain full consciousness of itself. We must necessarily have a misguided view of the Gnostic systems if we regard the kind of beings that are the turning-points of the system—beings such as Sophia-Achamoth, the Demiurge, and Christ—as simply individual beings in their own right, and if we regard them merely as contingently and externally related to one another. Just as it is one and the same antithesis and struggle between spirit and matter running throughout the entire system, so too it is one and the same spirit appearing here as the suffering and downcast Achamoth, there as the limited Demiurge who acts unconsciously, and then in turn as Christ who, with the most brilliant light of spiritual consciousness, enters into the order or system of sensible reality. This is one and the same spirit that mediates itself with itself, and comes to consciousness of itself, in all the pneumatic or spiritual beings, when they become conscious themselves that the life of the concrete individual is related to, and identical with, the highest principle of spiritual life. The task of Gnosis is to comprehend and explain this point. Even in the kind of Gnostic systems that, like Marcionism, with their predominant dualism, seem to completely dismantle this bond of identity, running through all of them, it still cannot be entirely overlooked, as will later become evident.

# 2

# The Origins of Gnosis

**The Initial Elements of Gnosis Were Constructed in the Historical Arena: Alexandrian Philosophical Religion; Philo; the Septuagint Version of the Old Testament; the Old Testament Apocrypha; the Therapeutae and the Essenes; Two Kinds of Judaism**[12]

IF THE CONCEPT OF Gnosis is spelled out as I have sought to do so here, then the question as to the origins of Gnosis can be understood and answered in a simpler and more specific way. As we have seen, Gnosis takes its material contents from traditional historical religions. So in fact the concept of Gnosis involves investigating and specifying how those historical elements are related to one another. From this it naturally follows that Gnosis can only come about on the kind of soil where elements of various religions have already come into mutual contact.

Therefore in researching the origins of Gnosis, and inasmuch as the Christian content of Gnosis is only an individual element of it, not an essentially necessary element, when we can go back beyond the Christian period the concept of Gnosis itself points us instead to the historical terrain of the Jewish religion. Hence the first elements of Gnosis could have only taken shape where the Jewish religion came into the kind of contact with pagan religion and philosophy where people felt compelled to recognize an immanent principle of truth on each side. Because of this people saw their task as making a definite, inner connection between what they acknowledged on each side as being true, and tracing it back to a single principle. As we know, this took place among those Jews who, living outside their native land, found themselves in circumstances where, while of course always remaining Jews, they at the same time had to de-emphasize and temper much that belonged to the uncompromising, strictly enforced nature of Judaism elsewhere. They saw themselves in a setting where they

---

12. [*Ed.*] We have slightly modified some of the headings in this section from how they appear in Baur's table of contents.

could not help but be receptive to the influence of new ideas and views, however that was said to weaken slightly their great respect for the religion of their fathers.

In order to account for the origins of the phenomena of Christian Gnosis, people therefore quite rightly gave special importance to Philo as the truest representative of the Alexandrian philosophy of religion. The ideas and views of Philo already emphasized above, based on Neander's presentation, could be set alongside much else from the writings of Philo, especially if one wanted to go into individual points, and that would furnish the clearest proof of the close relationship between the respective standpoints of Philo and the Christian Gnostics. However, we can locate the actual cause of this circumstantial relationship simply in the fact that, as a Platonist, Philo adopted, from the ideas of pagan religion and philosophy, those ideas that for him had to let the Jewish religion appear, in so many contexts, in a wholly different light than it appeared to ordinary Jews.

The Platonic idea of deity as absolute spirit or intellect is the idea of the being or nature that transcends, is infinitely distant from, all that is finite and humanly limited.[13] The doctrine of the Logos is closely tied to it and is formed from Platonic

13. This idea, together with the Platonic theory of ideas, is the means for the impact Platonism had on Gnosticism, via the intermediary role of the Alexandrian religious philosophy. It is the idea that the supreme deity cannot be directly related to what is finite. All those intermediary beings that the Gnostics have appearing in such great numbers, in the broad expanse between God and the created world, have their rationale and their origin in this idea. In his *Timaeus*, Plato himself therefore made this idea the basis of his teaching about the creation of human beings in particular, so that in the references to this idea in several Gnostic systems we actually see just a copy of the Platonic presentation. Pertinent here is *Timaeus* 41c–d, where Plato has the highest god, the Demiurge and Father, speaking to the deities: "In order, therefore, that they may be mortal and that this World-all may be truly All, do ye turn yourselves, as Nature directs, to the work of fashioning these living creatures, imitating the power showed by me in my generating of you. Now so much of them as it is proper to designate 'immortal,' the part we call divine which rules supreme in those who are fain to follow justice always and yourselves, that part I will deliver unto you when I have sown it and given it origin. For the rest, do ye weave together the mortal with the immortal, and thereby fashion and generate living creatures..." [LCL, *Plato*, vol. 7 (trans. R. G. Bury, 1961), 88–91.] See also *Timaeus* 69c–d: "He Himself acts as the Constructor of things divine, but the structure of moral things He commanded His own engendered sons to execute. And they, imitating Him, on receiving the immortal principle of soul, framed around it a mortal body, and gave it all the body to be its vehicle, and housed therein besides another form of soul, even the mortal form, which has within it passions both fearful and unavoidable..." [LCL, *Plato*, 7:178–79.] One could have found it very tempting to assume an even greater agreement between the Platonic doctrine as it is presented in the *Timaeus*, and the Gnostic systems: God the primordial father, intelligence (νοῦς), the souls with their twofold natures traceable back to the Pythagorean number and the unity-duality opposition, and matter, all of which appear to be the same principles in both these systems and seem to form the same spirit-matter antithesis. But the two concepts—spirit (or mind) and matter—do not have the same meaning in Plato's case. As we understand matter, the Platonic god is not spirit utterly antithetical to matter, but is instead a world-creator operating self-consciously according to specific concepts and purposes—as he is very much to be understood if, following P. A. Böckh on the depiction of the world-soul in Plato's *Timaeus* (in *Studien*, edited by K. Daub and G. F. Creuzer, 3 [1807]: 1ff.), Plato did not conceive of matter as something independent, and fully included an explanation of how the body gave rise to the material element. For, although the idea of a nature conceived of as a personal being is more a feature of mythological portrayals, the opposition between spirit (or mind) and matter is nevertheless defined differently, with the two not being hostile powers

interpretation had elicited in its role as the artificial mediatrix of what is speculative and historical by exercising this dominance over people's minds, what instead had to happen because of this change was the downgrading of Judaism to where it could only be regarded as a subordinate and imperfect form of religion, just an interim form, preparatory for another. On the basis of Philo's standpoint, this is what we arrive at as the explanation for the genesis of Gnosis.

But of course the presence of allegory in Philo's case points back to the time prior to Philo, a time where we also encounter other phenomena that present very noteworthy elements. Indeed the Alexandrian translation of the Old Testament [i.e., the Septuagint], this oldest document of Alexandrian-Jewish culture, in many passages where it strikingly deviates from the Hebrew text, is evidence of an outlook presenting God in a different way from how God operates in the Hebrew Old Testament. Instead of God working visibly and directly in the sensible world, the Septuagint regards God as altogether invisible and supersensible.[14] At that time, accordingly, the influence that foreign ideas had gained over Alexandrian Jews must have already prompted their effort to idealize, as much as they could, their Old Testament conception of God's essential nature. The necessary consequence of this was that, to the extent that they saw God's being as remote, to that same degree emphasis fell upon the [subordinate] divine forces and higher spirits that were agents of the divine efficacy. Hence there is also the Alexandrine notion, familiar from New Testament passages, that even the law was not directly from God himself but only became revealed by angels as intermediaries. We find more specific backing for this constantly strengthening and developing school of thought in the Old Testament Apocrypha, above all in the wisdom books.

The old Hebrew representation of God simply excluded all speculation concerning God's relation to the world, by locating the supreme principle of the divine efficacy in the absolute commands of God conceived of in personal terms. People could no longer be content with this exalted, albeit simply naïve, way of representing God as soon as they felt the need to make God's relation to the world the object of careful reflection. God's will, commanding and bringing things about sheerly through his mighty word, at least had to be conceived of as mediated by the ideas of the divine mind in determining and conditioning God's activity. So what took shape was the idea of a divine wisdom prior to the world, a wisdom attendant on the deity in all it does, an intermediary for all of the deity's activities and operations. We already find this feature in Proverbs, the Old Testament book that largely portrays the incipient activity among the Hebrews of the reflective intellect, as the principle and instrument of God's world-forming activity.

For the Alexandrian Jews, this idea also now became central to all the speculative ideas they found it suitable to introduce. They quite naturally attached to it what they adopted from the Platonic philosophy prevalent in Alexandria and believed they

---

14. See A. F. Gfrörer, *Geschichte des Urchristentums*, vol. 1, *Philo und die alexandrinische Theosophie* (Stuttgart, 1831), 8ff.

elements, as the necessary instrument of all divine revelation. Philo strictly maintains the antithesis of the two principles that determine and condition his whole view of the world and of life, the antithesis of spiritual and material aspects, of the ideal and the real. These ideas pre-eminently structure the contents of a philosophical religion as opposed to which Judaism, in the usual outward sense, seems to be only a subordinate stage from which one had to rise higher in order to properly be in step with the newly-won religious consciousness.

Allegory is where people found the balance between these two elements, the philosophical elements and the historical ones. Taken together, they constituted the essential contents of the religious consciousness at this new standpoint. Allegory was the ingeniously chosen means for infusing rigid scriptural literalism with a new spirit. It took what initially seemed to be the subject matter itself and converted it into merely a pictorial form in which the ideas one could no longer disavow—but which one still believed could only be regarded as genuinely possessed by holy scripture as their transmitter—were themselves reflected in scripture as its authentic, spiritual contents. Hence this resulted in a twofold Judaism, a higher and a lower Judaism, a spiritual version and a sensuous version, one esoteric and the other exoteric.

The unity of the two forms of Judaism was said to consist in the fact that they are related as spirit and letter, as soul and body, as content and form. But they were also said to differ, and that had to have further consequences. As soon as allegory fell into disfavor, and when people could no longer have the same concern to treat the Jewish religion as the absolutely true religion, and whereas the very ideas that allegorical

---

where one of them dominated and imprisoned the other. Instead they are conceived of as two collaborating forces, which is why the world is regarded as an artistic production, wholly in contrast to the Gnostic view. See *Timaeus* 68e: "The Artificer of the most fair and good took them over at that time amongst things generated when He was engendering as the self-sufficing and most perfect God; and their inherent properties he used as subservient causes, but himself designed the Good in all that was being generated" [LCL, *Plato*, 7:176–77]. Compare the concluding statement of the *Timaeus* 92c: "And now at length we may say that our discourse concerning the Universe has reached its termination. For this our Cosmos has received the living creatures both mortal and immortal and been thereby fulfilled; it being itself a visible Living Creature embracing the visible creatures, a perceptible God made in the image of the Intelligible, most great and good and fair and perfect in its generation—even this one Heaven sole of its kind" [LCL, *Plato*, 7:252–53]. Already here we have the same opposition with which Neoplatonism later confronted Gnosticism. The meaning given to the idea of freedom as such has an equally anti-Gnostic import, in conjunction with the idea of a free world-creator. See *Timaeus* 41e: ". . . the first birth should be one and the same ordained for all, in order that none might be slighted by Him" [LCL, *Plato*, 7:90–91]. Also 42d: "When He had fully declared unto them all these ordinances, to the end that He might be blameless in respect of the future wickedness of any one of them, He proceeded to sow them, some in the Earth, some in the Moon, others in the rest of the organs of Time" [LCL, *Plato*, 7:92–93]. Thus even with this relationship to Platonism, we may not attribute to Platonism any direct influence on Gnosticism as a whole. In other respects Platonism does involve ideas that modify the view found in the *Timaeus*. When Platonism is considered from this other angle it does seem to be more closely related to Gnosis. Although matter is not the principle of evil, it nevertheless has a burdensome, obscuring, and corrupting influence on spirit. While the idea of a fall on the part of souls hardly emerges in the *Timaeus* too, it is no less a Platonic notion. The more particular impact of Platonism can first be demonstrated in the case of individual Gnostic systems.

could link with their Old Testament religious teachings. Now the doctrine of the divine wisdom, in other words the divine Logos, gained the same position in Alexandrian-Jewish religious philosophy as the theory of ideas occupied in Platonic philosophy. This divine Logos functions as the vital sum and substance of all the divine ideas, as the support of the ideal world, as the instrument of all the divine activity, the principle on which the superiority of spirit over matter depends in the world in general, as it does in human life. One can of course see how this idea of the Logos is connected with the genesis of the Gnostic systems, from the fact that all the higher Aeons proceeding from the essence of the self-revealing and self-objectifying deity are in principle none other than a detailed explanation or filling-out of the original Logos-concept.

But what calls for special examination at this point is the distinctive way in which wisdom already appears here, in the struggle with a hostile principle contending against it. Based on the oldest accounts of the human race and of the people of Israel, the writer of The Wisdom of Solomon indicates (in this passage from 10:1–11:1) how the divine wisdom operates:

> Wisdom protected the first-formed father of the world [Adam], when he alone had been created; she delivered him from his transgression, and gave him strength to rule all things. But when an unrighteous man (Cain) departed from her in his anger . . . and when the earth was flooded because of him, wisdom again saved it, steering the righteous man [Noah, through flood] by a paltry piece of wood. Wisdom also, when the nations in wicked agreement had been put to confusion, recognized the righteous man (Abraham) and preserved him blameless before God, and kept him strong in the face of his compassion for his child. Wisdom rescued a righteous man (Lot) when the ungodly were perishing; he escaped the fire that descended on the Five Cities . . . Wisdom rescued from troubles those who served her. When a righteous man (Jacob) fled from his brother's wrath, she guided him on straight paths; she showed him the kingdom of God, and gave him knowledge of holy things; . . . in his arduous contest she gave him the victory . . . When a righteous man (Joseph) was sold, wisdom did not desert him, but delivered him from sin. She descended with him into the dungeon, and when he was in prison she did not leave him, until she brought him the scepter of a kingdom and authority over his masters . . . A holy people and a blameless race wisdom delivered from a nation of oppressors. She entered the soul of a servant of the Lord, and withstood dread kings with wonders and signs. She gave to holy people the reward of their labors; she guided them along a marvelous way, and became a shelter to them by day and a starry flame through the night . . . Wisdom prospered their works by the hand of a holy prophet.[15]

---

15. [*Ed.*] We have replaced Baur's German text with the NRSV translation. Most of the parenthetical insertions are from Baur; we have provided the references to Adam and Noah.

Here wisdom is engaged with the historical development of humankind from one generation to another, from one period to another, as a preserving and redeeming presence. In the same way too in the Gnostic systems wisdom is the principle understood as being in constant struggle with the power of evil yet always completely victorious everywhere. Wisdom upholds a spiritual lineage throughout all the vicissitudes of the antithesis between light and darkness, something for which the writer of The Wisdom of Solomon extols her in 7:22 ["wisdom, the fashioner of all things"], because "in every generation she passes into holy souls and makes them friends of God, and prophets" (v. 27). Although in her ongoing opposition to the resistant power of evil, where wisdom has to struggle and contend with evil in the history of the patriarchs and the people of Israel, which is quite different from the suffering and distress wisdom has to endure as Sophia-Achamoth, in the hostile conflict between the two opposed principles of spirit and matter in the world coming into being, the fundamental type is always the same. It is a duality of principles where, in their antithesis, what is good and pure can only develop via struggle and contention.

Everything that was connected in this fashion with Old Testament ideas and teachings, and that subjected the simple theocratic course, taken by the history of Old Testament religion, to assumptions about development—with speculation playing a greater or lesser role in this process—constitutes to that extent a transition to the phenomena of Gnosticism, wherein Judaism now first receives a quite different form and content. The more Alexandrian Judaism set itself apart from conventional Judaism, the more it became similar to the Gnostic religious philosophy. Hence in Philo's case we already see Alexandrian Judaism contrasting with conventional Judaism in a way entirely analogous to how, in the Gnostic systems, the speculative element sets itself above the historical element.

However, that is no reason to merely stop with what we find in the writings of Philo and in the Apocrypha. An even more striking sign of the transformation Judaism had already undergone is provided by the two remarkable sects of the Therapeutae and the Essenes,[16] which had no doubt already existed for quite some time and in any event pre-dated Philo. They of course espoused the Jewish religion and even revered Moses, God's great lawgiver, in a quite pronounced way. They were most fastidious in observing certain practices instituted by the religion of their fathers, for instance, the sabbath rest and the ritual of circumcision. On the other hand, however, they rejected most decidedly all animal sacrifice and the temple cultus connected with it, and that gives us a quite distinct concept of how, as Jews, they formed a contrast to conventional Judaism.

---

16. [*Ed.*] The Therapeutae were a Jewish sect, including both men and women, who lived near Alexandria and other parts of the Diaspora of Hellenistic Judaism, prior to and at the time of Philo, who described them in his *Contemplative Life*. The Essenes were likewise a sect of Second Temple Judaism, referred to by Pliny, Philo, and Josephus. The Dead Sea Scrolls were discovered in an Essene library.

Yet what we encounter here, as the internal or basic motivation for this deep-seated attitude contrasting with conventional Judaism, is the Pythagorean-Platonic view that pervades all these religious phenomena whose circumstances we now seek to determine. This philosophical outlook is the all-pervasive spiritual element that effects an inner and deeper coherence, and does so for the Therapeutae and the Essenes as well. Their characteristic positions include: the exalted, exuberant idea of the deity as the invisible, incomprehensible, absolutely pure being or essence of light; the doctrine of certain intermediate beings said to fill in the great gulf between God and world, in some way or other (as the Essenes placed particular importance on the doctrine of angels); the strictly maintained antithesis between spirit and matter, together with the conceptions and practical precepts related to this antithesis.

In the case of Philo, allegory appears as a weak link for holding together the two camps into which Judaism had now divided, the speculative, spiritual camp, and the historically traditional and literalist camp. Things could be no different with the Therapeutae and the Essenes, although for them the gap between the two camps seems to have been even greater. In holding consistently to their views about sacrificial offerings, they apparently had to consider a large part of the Mosaic institutions as alien elements, as a falsifying of the authentic religion of their fathers that only came about over the course of time. It is not unlikely, with their views about true and false Judaism, about the relation between tradition and scripture, that they already anticipated positions we find later among the Ebionites.[17]

## Christianity as a New Element

But if the original view of the essence and character of Judaism had been handed down for a long time in such an essentially different form, even though doing so just cast doubt on, or directly denied, the claim to divine origin of a part of the Mosaic tradition, then why was it so easy to completely downgrade Judaism to the level at which the Gnostics customarily put it in the course of humankind's religious development? Doing so had to be the necessary consequence of Christianity, as the newly-arrived element in this religious development. For the more people were already inherently inclined to venture beyond the limited sphere of traditional Judaism, they had to be very interested in taking up a religion that had announced itself as the completion and fulfillment of what Judaism had left still imperfect and unfulfilled.

The speculative religious philosophy already linked to Judaism contained a great deal to which Christianity's own distinctive doctrines could attach themselves in a very satisfying way. It was simply a matter of taking features drawn from Christianity's

---

17. [*Ed.*] The Ebionites were a Jewish Christian sect in the early centuries of the Christian era who accepted Jesus as the messiah but rejected his divinity and virgin birth. They placed an emphasis on voluntary poverty, from which their name derives. While adhering to the Hebrew Gospel of Matthew, they rejected the Apostle Paul.

distinctive contents and giving them the kind of form and shape that expressed the antithesis of the two principles, spirit and matter, as governing the whole—while uniting this expression of those features with the rest of Christianity as spelled out according to the same basic model.

In any case this was the natural course to take, since the contents of the ideas, thought of abstractly, did not change, and it was only in their concrete appearance or presentation that they took on different shapes. Alexandrian allegorical interpretation had already been immersed in the hues of Judaism, and so now it bore the stamp of Christianity. However, in its contents, the more concrete configuration was simultaneously also allegory's further development.[18]

## Expansion of Religious Horizons via the Religious Systems of the East

The new additional element in Christianity of course significantly expanded the horizons within which people endeavored to understand the religious course of humankind's development as an interconnected whole, in a series of successive moments or elements. This had to induce people to look to the higher spirit world in a more extensive way, a world from which Christ, as the savior Aeon, had descended in order to go back there once more. This raises the further consideration that, in the era between Philo and the emergence of the first Christian Gnostics, and mainly also because of how influential Christianity had become, there seems to have been a widespread and active religious movement, one that often intermingled elements from extant religions.

The Gnostics are evidence of the fact that this same linking of speculative ideas with Judaism, which constituted the essence of the Alexandrian-Jewish religious philosophy, was not just confined to Egypt and centered in Alexandria, but had also made inroads into neighboring lands, into Syria in particular. Christianity itself could not have initially given rise to this speculative religious philosophy, although Christianity must have been drawn directly into its orbit everywhere that it encountered it. It

---

18. The sect the Apostle Paul contends with in the Epistle to the Colossians is indeed an example of this kind of circumstance, where an already existing religious doctrine made its way into Christianity. The main juncture where the teaching of this sect could attach itself to Christianity was doubtless its angelology. The philosophy or theosophy we come across in Col 2:8 ["empty deceit . . . according to the elemental spirits of the universe"] and 18 ["self-abasement and worship of angels"] mainly involved angels. But it could give such great importance to angels only because it ascribed to them a mediating and salvific role in relation to human beings. The Christian faith presupposes that this very activity the sect ascribes to angels is entrusted to Christ. The dangerous error is then that its angelology always in turn conflicted with Christianity's own christology, or even displaced it. Only from this perspective can we comprehend the emphatic declarations of the Apostle in this epistle about the wholly distinctive, entirely incomparable, dignity and office of Christ. I think it most likely that this sect belonged to the Essenes. If so, then we also see in it an example of how Essenism in particular combined itself with Christianity, but in this combination just generally produced a new form of Gnosis.

was a matter of course that, in lands adjacent to Persia, this speculation assumed the character of Zoroastrian dualism rather than the Platonic form native to it in Egypt [Alexandria]. Yet since Christianity itself gave new fodder and a new impetus for this speculative orientation, and opened up so many new avenues for it, Christianity itself was conducive for bringing Zoroastrian dualism too into even closer ties with the other elements of Gnosis. And when, partly based on general historical factors and partly owing to individual and particular features, even an influence from Indian religious ideas is at least a possibility, that makes it all the easier to explain how, from these given elements, the systems of the Christian Gnostics increasingly evolved and took shape, grand systems in a wealth of forms and with such a wide scope.

Here we have: the lofty standpoint of the religious systems of the East, proceeding from the idea of the absolute; the great issue they seek to resolve in explaining the emergence of the finite from the absolute and the return of the finite into the absolute; the strictly defined cycle in which the Zoroastrian religious system in particular has the antithesis of the two principles developing from one period to the next; the particular significance in how higher beings and divine founders of religions enter into the world at decisive turning points in its course. These and other elements are just so many points of contact between the religious systems of the Orient and the Gnostic systems. Although there was not said to be specific proof of a historical connection between the East and the Gnostic systems, it is nevertheless not an arbitrary assumption that the religious ideas and outlooks of the more exalted East doubtless had, overall, a direct or indirect influence at that time. In an era so active and so receptive to the exchange of ideas, the East also influenced the lands of the West in a stimulating and lively way. It evoked and elaborated the fundamental religious outlook that we see pervading the Gnostic systems.

Thus the antitheses of spirit and matter, of the light and dark principles, of an ideal world and a real world, oppositions we of course find in the Pythagorean-Platonic philosophy, rest on the age-old foundations of Oriental ideas and outlooks. In Philo's case the antitheses are mainly concentrated in the narrow sphere where, in human consciousness, the sensible domain stands over against the spiritual principle; and on the larger scale, they comprise the antitheses of God and world, fall and return, sin and redemption. In the process of development where the eternal spirit objectifies itself and accomplishes the entire course of the world, the antitheses then structure the fundamental concepts around which the Gnostic systems revolve, the concepts of matter, the Demiurge, and Christ. There these concepts and forms then also structure the basic forms in which the idea of religion realizes itself, those of paganism, Judaism, and Christianity, according to their mutual relationships both externally and internally.

Part One: The Concept and Origin of Gnosis

## The Relation of Gnosis to the Basic Character of Pagan Religion, as Presented to Us in Its Main Forms, and Particularly in Buddhism

As I remarked already, in order to explain the origin of Gnosis we will first of all return to an area of religion where Judaism came into contact with pagan religion and philosophy. This is not yet Christian Gnosis, for, in order to grasp Gnosis in its true nature and principle, we must, by separating what is essential in it from what is less essential, distinguish various moments in the arising of Gnosis itself. Therefore, even though Christian Gnosis is the completion of Gnosis, the Christian element of Gnosis is nevertheless nothing so essential that Gnosis would not always have been Gnosis even without this element.

However, just as we can set aside the Christian element, we can go even farther than this and also consider the Jewish aspect as not directly an essential element of Gnosis. For although, inasmuch as Gnosis belongs to the history of religion, it assimilates Judaism and Christianity as historical elements, nevertheless the principle unifying the given historical elements is always just that religious philosophy standing over and above the history of religion, and whose origin is neither Jewish nor Christian. As we have already shown, according to its principle Gnosis belongs instead to the domain of pagan religion and philosophy, could only have arisen from this domain, and is itself to be regarded as the most distinctive characteristic by which pagan religion sets itself apart from the Jewish and Christian religions. For nothing else is so deeply embedded in the essential natures of these religions as is the distinction between a God transcending matter and the world in a free, ethical personality and positing the world simply by a free act of will, and the kind of God so caught up in the antithesis of spirit and matter that this God cannot be envisaged at all apart from this antithesis. We have already indicated the moments in the process of revelation and development directly involved in this Gnostic antithesis.

Given this close relationship between Gnosis and the basic character of pagan religion, it is therefore quite natural for the main forms of paganism, viewed as a whole, to have an inherent character very much analogous to Gnosis. We can expand upon what we already noted in this regard, and here is the place to call greater attention to this relation of Gnosis to pagan religion. That is because, with phenomena presenting us with just internal affinities and analogies, we can be easily and directly led to see an external, historical connection as well. Here we need only recall the relation of Gnosis to Zoroastrian dualism in order to understand at once how close is the contact between Gnosis and paganism. The major elements of the Zoroastrian religious system—the antithesis of the two principles; the course of the world, which unfolds and moves onward in the struggle between the two of them, carrying itself out in a specific time period; the final victory of good over evil—provide a vision of the same large-scale portrait of the world that is foundational to the Gnostic worldview.

The Gnostic Demiurge only differs in degree from the Zoroastrian Ormazd, who is subordinated to a higher principle and limited to the extent that he faces a hostile opposing power, such that, as world-creator, he can only bring into being a world that is finite, imperfect, and intertwined with evil.

Gnosis is similarly related to the Indian religious systems. Different as the forms in which Brahmanism portrays the relation of the deity to the world may be, here too, according to the prevailing view, the world is a manifestation of the deity in which the eternal, absolute spirit objectifies itself, in other words beholds itself, in the mirror image of maya (*māyā*), the principle of appearance and semblance, where all finite and real-world being is a mere semblance or make-believe (the Gnostic docetism).[19] If we may believe an established scholar,[20] even the Indian Trimurti, the triad of the three supreme Gods (Brahma, Shiva, and Vishnu) would be traceable back to three moments or elements (the supreme spiritual substance; the reason in nature, or the understanding that brings forth all things by transformations; concrete reason, in virtue of the freedom of spirit), in other words to the moments of what is existent (*Seiende*), what is non-existent (*Nichtseiende*), and what is immaterial or spiritual (*Geistige*).[21]

19. P. von Bohlen, *Das alte Indien mit besonderer Rücksicht auf Aegypten*, 2 vols. (Königsberg, 1830), 1:165.

20. Othmar Frank, *Vjāsa: Über Philosophie, Mythologie, Literatur und Sprache der Hindu, Eine Zeitschrift* (Munich and Leipzig), vol. 1, no. 3 (1830) 135.

21. Another point especially worth mentioning here is the analogy between these three Indian attributes or qualities and the Gnostic division of human beings into three classes as described above on pp. 11–12. As Wilhelm von Humboldt describes it in his exhaustive and ingenious treatise, *Über die unter dem Namen Bhagavad-Gītā bekannte Episode des Mahā-Bhārata* (Berlin, 1826), p. 29, the first of these three qualities is that of being (*Sein*), in the sense in which being is completely real and thus free from any lack or non-being (*Nichtsein*) as to the knowledge of truth or virtuous action. It is the quality of substantiality (*Wesenheit*), as Humboldt renders the Indian term *sattva*. The enchantments of the second quality (i.e., *rajas*), the earthly features, the love of all that is grand, mighty, and flashy, but also runs after appearances, are caught up in the colorful diversity of the world and even called impure in order to indicate the captivity that the worldly-minded soul is unable to escape from. Enterprise, fiery passion, and rash decisions are features of this quality. Kings and heroes possess this quality, but it is always mixed in with something bringing one down to earth, to reality, and that sets it apart from the calm and pure greatness of *sattva* or substantiality. The third and lowest quality, *tamas*, is characterized as obscurity, as darkness. Whereas the substantial aspect in all creatures simply sees the one undivided being in the separate beings, only their manifold individual separateness appears in their earthly aspect. For the clouds of darkness attach to them without entering into their foundation, in essentially limiting the way things are known, to what is individual, and these individuals are taken to be all there is. It is quite obvious how these three Indian qualities closely correspond to the three classes of the spiritual, psychical, and material persons in the structure of the Gnostic systems. The difference is only that the Indian view designates these three qualities as natural. [*Ed.* Baur has been discussing the three qualities called *gunas* in the Sāṃkyha school of Hinduism. The pertinent point here is that everything physical or mental that exists has each of the three to some degree. So the "difference" from Gnosis in virtue of their being "natural" is that the three are present everywhere in the universe; that the qualities are not limited to, or mainly about, different types of people as in Gnosticism.] They are the qualities of the eternal nature, equivalent to the deity, which bind the spirit as it aligns itself to them. That is, they draw human beings away from thoughts solely directed to the deity and, by doing so, hinder them from attaining the ultimate goal, the supreme peace. In the same sense what is noblest, for instance knowledge, can take hold of the spirit. See also Bohlen (n. 19),

## Elucidation of the Main Teachings of the Buddhist Religious Systems That Are Pertinent Here

From what I have written elsewhere, about the relation of Buddhism to Manicheanism,[22] one can indeed judge how many parallels and analogies Buddhism offers with the Gnostic view of the world. The same scholar we have to thank for his fundamental investigations into the religious teachings of Buddhism has also directly called attention to the kinship of ancient Gnosis with these teachings.[23] The more our knowledge of Buddhism grows, the less doubt there can be about this relationship.[24]

Just as Gnosis moves entirely within the antithesis of spirit and matter, so too "the entire system of Buddhism" rests on "the dualism operative through spirit (or mind) and nature (or matter), a dualism revealing itself in the phenomena of the world's formation.[25] The purpose of Buddhism's teaching is to overcome (*aufheben*) this dualism by liberating the spirits caught up in the bonds of nature and by ultimately uniting the multiplicity of the spiritual realm in the oneness of the absolute spirit.[26] Yet Buddhism's whole outlook on the world is inherently so marvelous and colossal that, in comparison, the Gnostic systems appear to be just poor imitations of the Buddhist view, sketched out on a much smaller scale. Whereas the Gnostic systems usually suppose several worlds and different spiritual realms, what heights of abstraction the Buddhist teaching about the three worlds leads to! The first one is the world of abstract intellect or mind, and the conceptual locus of true being; the second

---

1:174ff., on these three gunas, fundamental forces, or qualities, through which nature operates, and how they relate to human beings, determining how people conduct themselves in their earthly lives.

22. *Das manichäische Religionssystem nach den Quellen neu untersucht und entwickelt* (Tübingen, 1831), 434ff. [*Ed.*] In this book Baur draws upon works by Bohlen (n. 19) and Schmidt (n. 23) as well as other sources.

23. Isaak Jacob Schmidt, *Ueber die Verwandtschaft der gnostisch-theosophischen Lehren mit den Religionssystem des Orients, vorzüglich dem Buddhaismus* (Leipzig, 1828).

24. See in particular Schmidt's more recent investigations of Buddhism: "Ueber einige Grundlehren des Buddhaismus," in the *Mémoires de l'Académie impériale des sciences de St. Petersbourg. VI Série. Sciences politiques, Histoire, Philologie*, vol. 1, bk. 2 (1830), 89–120; bk. 3 (1830), 221–62. See also "Ueber die sogenannte Dritte Welt der Buddhaisten, als Fortsetzung der Abhandlungen über die Lehren des Buddhaismus," in vol. 2, bk. 1 (1832), 1–39. Also "Ueber die tausend Buddhas einer Weltperiode der Einwohnung oder gleichmäßigen Dauer," in vol. 2, bk. 1, 41–86.

25. [*Ed.*] The discussion of Buddhism that follows here refers to the doctrine of emptiness (German *Leer*) and to the fact that there are multiple Buddhas. This makes it apparent that the account of Buddhism Baur relies on from his German secondary sources has to do with a version of Mahayana Buddhism. These Buddhists routinely use the term "mind" to designate the center of one's personal existence or being. So while Baur pretty consistently sticks with the German word *Geist* (and occasionally includes *Intelligenz*, or "intellect," as well), we frequently render *Geist* as "mind" (while sometimes also rendering it as "spirit" to reflect Baur's wish to link the Buddhist notion with the wider world of "things spiritual in nature," a sense Baur has in mind when he parallels Buddhism as he understands it with Manicheanism and Gnosticism, where "spirit" functions as the preferred term). Also, in Baur's discussion of *Schicksal* in Buddhism, he is clearly referring to the Buddhist doctrine of karma; hence we simply translate *Schicksal* as "karma."

26. Schmidt, "Ueber die tausend Buddhas" (n. 24), 51.

is the world of revelation in bliss and glory; the third is the world of appearance in matter. The Buddhas manifest their efficacy in the three worlds, in order to end the seeming existence of these worlds and to lead all the bits of mind, which are scattered throughout these worlds, back to the Universal Intellect or Mind that is completely free of matter.[27]

Most Gnostics identify the concept of mind or spirit with the concept of light, so that the two seem almost entirely overlapping. In contrast, Buddhism strictly distinguishes them and in no way regards light as non-physical. Yet for it light is also the vehicle for spirit's appearance in matter. Mind as linked to matter derives from light that is veiled or concealed. Here the light-stuff is increasingly diminished, and can ultimately be so obscured or darkened that the mind sinks down to become completely devoid of consciousness.[28] Hence what occurs is the transition to the arising of the world in the threefold region of light (which is called the second *dhyāna*), and which contains mind in its multiplicity, in addition to containing the seeds of nature.[29]

But the most important point where Gnosis and Buddhism intersect is always the strict antithesis between spirit and matter. The fundamental view of Buddhism is that spirit or mind is the only thing that is eternal, substantial, free for its own sake; that there is nothing higher and more essential than the free spirit, which for Buddhism appears to be the only true existent. Spirit is free because it wills, and is conscious of, itself. It is unfree only within the bonds of nature, as long as it is subject to nature and allows itself to be drawn and held fast by the forms of matter, and in doing so it more or less loses consciousness of its own nature, the consciousness that is its freedom.[30]

This is the very point of the antithesis between nirvana (*nirvāna*) and samsara (*samsāra*). Nirvana is a completely non-material and absolute state that is in no way involved with, or affected by, matter. Nirvana is the state first attained by mind or spirit when it has made a complete break with the course of nature and, in ridding itself of all material forms, has freed itself from all ties to matter.[31] The material world is samsara, the world of rebirth, the constantly undulating ocean in which the cycle of metempsychosis carries on ceaselessly.[32] Upon leaving samsara behind and entering into nirvana, one's cyclical rebirth comes to an end, according to the laws of the consequence of one's acts (karma). Only in nirvana is the mind therefore at peace, for in the life of this world no eternity is possible, nor is any lasting, uninterrupted peace conceivable.[33]

27. Schmidt, "Ueber einige Grundlehren" (n. 24), 233.
28. Ibid., 247.
29. Schmidt, "Ueber die tausend Buddhas," 47.
30. Ibid., 48–49.
31. Ibid., 50.
32. Schmidt, "Ueber einige Grundlehren" (n. 24), 108, 223.
33. Schmidt, "Ueber einige Grundlehren," 240; and "Ueber die sogennante Dritte Welt" (n. 24), 22. On the meaning of the two Sanskrit words *samsāra* and *nirvāna*, see his treatise *Ueber die*

However, this is just an apparent antithesis. The fundamental view Buddhism has of the absolute spirit-matter antithesis also incorporates the basic idea that there is no difference between samsara and nirvana. In other words, all three of the worlds are empty. This amounts to saying that nothing exists besides the intellect or mind dispersed in all three worlds, mind that is eternal, non-material, and hence empty of material concepts.[34] This is so because the forms this mind can attach itself to have no permanence, so they count for nothing and consequently count as empty. Then samsara, or the cycling through all the stages and shapes of material existence, by the mind held captive, must come to an end. Then the mind that persists as indeed captive, but unaware of being so, is finally liberated and returns to its origin. Thus samsara, the adversary of this mind, only seems to be distinct from nirvana when it seeks to keep the mind bound, by means of the terminology of the sensible world, and to deprive it of the awareness that it belongs to nirvana. With the awakening of this awareness, the mind strives to free itself, and it enters into a state all its own, that of nirvana, by doing so either in stages or directly, depending on the level of knowledge it has achieved. In that case samsara loses the merely apparent existing being (*Dasein*) that it has for mind and reverts to being nothing.

Therefore, all three worlds are empty, that is, there is nothing in them besides the non-material and non-perceptible mind. The existing being of these worlds, conditioned by samsara, is only something apparent. With its cessation, there is only one [reality], or rather there is no world at all. That is because once those dispersed and individualized minds form a confluence in the grand oneness, there can no longer be talk of any world.[35] Here we have a docetism determinative of the view of the world and the view of life; a docetism that seems to be just a feebler and more obscure reflection of the Gnostic docetism and everything related to it.

The unmistakable relationship between Gnosis and Buddhism presented here becomes more amazing the further one pursues it. Just as the Gnostics assigned justice to the Demiurge as his preeminent predicate, and therefore also considered the law of justice to be the dominant force in the world ruled by the Demiurge, so too in Buddhism it is the concept of justice that gives the material world its distinctive character. The Buddhists' "destiny" or "karma" is none other than the concrete concept of justice, realizing itself in the constant and necessary connection of wrongdoing with punishment. As long as samsara endures, the karma that is a product of one's acts, one's deeds and thoughts, and is not forgiven [i.e., not counterbalanced by good acts], does not neglect its due, but instead makes it always mandatory. Guilt for wrongdoing is what

---

*Verwandtschaft* (n. 23), 11. Samsara refers to the world of transitory phenomena, and the cycle of metempsychosis. Nirvana refers to eternal bliss, complete liberation from matter and rebirth in the material world, and union with deity.

34. "Ueber die tausend Buddhas" (n. 24), 50. What is empty is what is completely non-material. This calls to mind the Gnostic concepts of the πλήρωμα (pleroma) and the κένωμα (void).

35. "Ueber einige Grundlehren" (n. 24), 223.

the Buddhists call karma, and it dictates the law of karma both for nature as a whole and for its smallest part or member. The intellect or mind that is not yet free, in other words has not yet entered into nirvana, is unconditionally subject to this law of karma.

Hence even the region of light is no place of peace, for everything here involves circumstances inescapably belonging to matter and still subject to strict consequences. This is just the gathering place for guilt in its most transparent state, guilt that must be atoned for. The still unsatisfied demands of karma are the basic cause for every new world-creation. Only in nirvana does the reign of karma come to an end.[36] This point is naturally related to the idea of liberation or deliverance, and of an activity of deliverance proceeding from the higher world, an idea substantiated in similar fashion in both Gnosis and Buddhism.

The Buddhas appear in human bodies, in other words in incarnations best suited to the various circumstances and conditions of various times, making use of light and of maya, or supernatural power and magic, and with complete control of matter. The purpose of these appearances is deliverance from the ever-fluctuating ocean of samsara, from the cycle of metempsychosis. They appear in order to liberate the beings dwelling in the third of the worlds who, as a result of their past actions, are inexorably banished to places of punishment and ordeals. They lead these beings on the path where they can head toward complete deliverance. In short, the Buddhas arrest the inherent continuation of the creation in this world by freeing the mental components, dispersed within the world, from the bonds of samsara.

A revelation of this kind cannot take place except by linking a Buddha, or even just a part of his mind, with matter. It occurs by the decision or choice to assume some sort of apparent body, or by the usual route of being born. However, despite the otherwise unlimited, absolute power of the Buddhas, they are not in a position to act contrary to the operations of the irrevocable laws of the karmic force, as these laws affect one's actions. The entire cosmogony is a work or an outcome of this karma, so the Buddhas cannot operate directly. They can only call to the attention of beings endowed with reason, that one's karma is inescapably conditional upon one's actions; and, on the one hand, to point out to them the punitive consequences that each unjust act committed in this life inevitably has for one's subsequent rebirth, just as, on the other hand, to hold out to them the future rewards that grow from meritorious actions and efforts.[37]

It may be appropriate, in concluding this discussion, to remark briefly on the position that Buddhism and Gnosticism respectively assign to human beings within the world as a whole. It is true that the two highest ranking groups of the third Buddhist world, the gods and spirits, far surpass the human group in splendor, excellence, and other good qualities. Yet in the Buddhist scriptures the human group is everywhere regarded as the noblest one, because it indeed has, above all else, the merit of being

36. "Ueber die sogenannte Dritte Welt" (n. 24), 25ff.
37. "Ueber einige Grundlehren" (n. 24), 108 and 99; 241, 247, 249.

preeminently receptive to the idea of what is non-material, and so the drive to be aroused from the bonds of samsara is most easily awakened in it. The more content the gods and spirits are with their current condition, the less receptive they are to the heights of nirvana. Of course as long as the mind is still imprisoned in total darkness, in the various bodies of unreasoning animals, it simply must make amends for earlier misdeeds, until the karma of its actions allows it to take on a human body once more, as a result of some previous merit on its part. But if this happens, then the mind dwelling in a human body is awakened to self-consciousness. Then it can recognize the wretchedness of its condition, owing to the overriding dominance of sin and, in consequence of its previous wrongdoing, having to be imprisoned in such a body. Thus it becomes completely overcome by the dominance of sin; or indeed it sinks back wholly into rebirth as an animal; or else, by doing battle with the senses and amassing a treasury of meritorious works, it withdraws from the sensible world and, by continuous efforts of that kind, it comes ever closer to nirvana and ultimately comes to share fully in it.[38] Here too, as in the Gnostic systems, a human being accordingly stands at the most momentous level, where the mind attains consciousness of itself. Upon regaining this consciousness, it is also given the assurance of complete liberation from the bonds of matter, and of its return to the absolute.

## Owing to Its Speculative Character, Pagan Religion Differs from Jewish and Christian Religion; and in Virtue of Its Principle, It Is therefore Religious Philosophy

We can only establish in more specific terms how encompassing and well-substantiated the relationship and analogy indicated here is in its essential features, on the basis of a closer examination of the individual Gnostic systems.[39] First of all we will sketch

38. Ibid., 248.

39. I would hope the foregoing discussion has at the same time more firmly established, and set aside the reservations expressed concerning, the view about the relation of Manicheanism and Buddhism that I set forth in my treatise, *Das manichäische Religionssystem* (n. 22). Herr Dr. J. C. L. Gieseler (in *Theologische Studien und Kritiken* [1833], p. 1213) states that the antithesis in Manicheanism is entirely different from the antithesis in Buddhism, for the Manicheans do not set spirit over against matter, but instead oppose good to evil; and they also recognize an evil spirit and a good matter. But I am not convinced that this contention is correct. Manicheanism only recognizes a good matter because its concept of spirit and its concept of light coincide. Yet for it the evil spirit, the prince of darkness standing over against the light-principle, is basically conceived of as matter itself in the way they expressly speak of it. As I have shown in my own treatise (p. 39), the Manicheans' portrayal of it as an evil spirit, or as the prince of darkness, in the final analysis can simply be regarded as a way of personifying matter as a self-acting operative principle. In any event the antithesis of good and evil is a substitute for the antithesis of spirit and matter. For since the most general category, the one comprising all the other antitheses, is the antithesis of spirit and matter, this makes it undeniably clear that all the contents of the Manichean system revolve around two ideas—the domination of spirit by matter, and the freeing of spirit from the power of matter. These same two ideas are also the main elements of Buddhism. This agreement between the two systems would remain completely incomprehensible if they were nevertheless radically different as to their principles. Buddhism understands the concept of

here, in its broad outlines, just the general perspective we must adopt in order to correctly understand and evaluate the Gnostic systems.

In the first place, the way I have juxtaposed these positions nevertheless by no means involves the contention that there is a specific external, historical connection between Gnosis, Manicheanism, and Buddhism. In any event such a connection can only have occurred via a series of intermediate factors, one still occupying the attention of historians. Whatever the outcome of this historical intermediation may be, the main thing for us is their obvious internal affinity or relationship, and the resulting recognition of the truth that the basic character distinctive of pagan religion in general, in all its main forms, also belongs to the essential nature of Gnosis.[40]

Inasmuch as pagan religion always takes the antithesis of spirit and matter, a duality of principles, as its point of departure, it embodies an essentially speculative element and is, for that reason, in principle a philosophical religion or religious philosophy.[41] In contrast to the speculative character of pagan religion, the Jewish and Christian religions have a character that is in part ethical, and in part positive. For instance, they are ethical inasmuch as, apart from the antithesis of spirit and matter, they have to do with a human being's moral relationship to God. But they are positive religions in that their contents are given by a revelation ultimately grounded simply in a free act of will on the part of the deity. The revelation of the deity is the content and the object of each religion. But while pagan religion only has the deity revealing itself because the spirit cannot engage in activity or display its inner life otherwise than as mediated by matter, in the Jewish and Christian religions the purpose of revelation is simply to make God's will known to human beings. Revelation in the latter sense

---

evil in the same way Manicheanism does, for the primordial evil is considered to be wholly the origin of all existence, in other words, the crossing-over of spirit, or mind, into matter. See Schmidt, *Ueber die Verwandtschaft* (n. 23), 8ff. It is therefore just as implausible to present, as a radical difference, the fact that the Manichean antithesis is eternal and immutable, whereas the Buddhist antithesis has come about and is something that vanishes. This is just the same discrepancy we have already spoken about above, on p. 10. The more definitively Buddhism locates all substantiality of being in mind or spirit, the less it can regard matter as also something truly substantial. In a certain sense Manicheanism does see both spirit and matter as having substantiality, although in it we also still see the same antithesis everywhere. In this regard the whole difference between Manicheanism and Buddhism is no greater than the difference between the Valentinian and the Manichean systems.

40. It simply makes clear both the actual kinship of Gnosticism with Manicheanism, as well as the kinship or affinity of both with Buddhism, even if a historical connection of Gnosticism with Manicheanism should turn out to be just as indemonstrable as it is with Buddhism.

41. [*Ed.*] The sense in which Baur uses the term "speculative" can be puzzling. Here it functions in contrast to the terms "ethical" and "positive" ("historical"), and means something like "philosophical" or "theosophical" or "spiritual." More generally, the Latin term *speculum* means "mirror," and "speculative" entails for Baur (as for Hegel) a double mirroring—a mirroring of the objective by the subjective, and of the subjective by the objective. Speculation involves self-knowing and God-knowing, an intellectual or spiritual envisioning of how things relate to and reflect each other. Through Gnosis a speculative element enters into (or is drawn out of) Judaism and Christianity, interacting with the ethical and positive aspects. This interaction generates conflict and thus development in Christian theology.

rests on a free divine act of will, while in the former sense it occurs out of a necessity that can only be thought of as natural necessity. Thus inasmuch as it is philosophical religion, paganism also is typically a philosophy of nature.

Ethical religions operate within the antithesis of guilt and punishment, of sin and grace, without seeing themselves needing to go beyond it. However, to the extent that this antithesis is situated within the larger and more general antithesis involving the concepts God and world, spirit and matter, and the initial antithesis is mediated by that other one, this decidedly subordinates the ethical domain to the speculative domain. Then a person is no longer a free, self-determining being; then one is just regarded as something located within a large system, a component within the general order of nature, dependent on it and determined by it. This is a feature shared by the Gnostic systems and everything analogous to them. Yet when the ethical domain is internally connected with the speculative domain, then the ethical element is readily transformed into the speculative element. Nothing illustrates this more clearly than with the idea of redemption (*Erlösung*), which, albeit essentially a Christian idea, is still no less also a feature of pagan religion. The simple reason for this is that, with all their differences, all religions are nevertheless always united in the concept of religion; so they also involve everything belonging to the concept of religion, both in the same way as also in different ways.[42]

## Gnosis Originates from the Consciousness of the Unity and Difference of the Religions

Gnosis must have originated from the consciousness of the unity and difference of the religions.

Gnosis first appeared in the setting of the Jewish religion. Then Christianity, the new arrival, made people aware of the same relationship of unity and difference, but within a wider scope and in a more definitive way. Despite its ethical character, Christianity presented so many elements of truly speculative significance, ones naturally linking up with the speculative ideas of the pre-Christian religious philosophy, that Gnosis came about in the form it presents itself to us in the Gnostic systems, by apparently completing and becoming fully conscious of, the Gnosis that already existed.[43]

---

42. [*Ed.*] Redemption (*Erlösung*) and reconciliation (*Versöhnung*), according to Baur, constitute the concept (or "midpoint") of religion, despite the many differences among religions. See the Introduction to Baur's *Die christliche Lehre von der Versöhnung in ihrer geschichtlichen Entwicklung* (Tübingen, 1838), esp. 1–11.

43. Based on this standpoint, we can rightly appreciate Mosheim's perspicacity in investigating the essence of Gnosis [see the Introduction to this work]. Mosheim's procedure was to construct what were supposedly the sources of Gnosis, by isolating all the individual differences in order to arrive at the unity and common foundation of the Gnostic systems—thus constructing a theology, cosmogony, anthropology, redemption doctrine, and ethics of Orientalism, analogous to the Gnostic systems. People called this a circular procedure, since, in explaining the origin of Christian Gnosis, it took what was already at hand as its result. Friedrich Lücke, in "Kritik der bisherigen Untersuchungen über

## Justification of the Preceding Explanation for the Origin of Gnosis, in Response to the Most Recent Dissenting Views

I do not believe that significant objections can be raised against the procedure undertaken here for explaining the essence and origin of Gnosis. At least it is very easy to demonstrate the unsatisfactory nature of the attempts made in other quarters to strike out on a different course. So as not to speak further about ancient views, and about the one-sided derivations from Philonic Platonism and from Zoroastrianism,[44] I will confine myself simply to the most recent explanations.

### Matter's View

When the author of the critical history of Gnosticism[45] links his investigations quite rightly to Plato and Philo, but in dealing with Plato he directly calls to mind the Thracian, Samothracian, and Eleusinian mysteries, as well as the whole series of those hallowed poets one regards as followers of Orpheus, then here we obviously see ourselves

---

die Gnostiker" (Introduction, n. 45), p. 164, writes: "How could it escape this sagacious man that his so-called Orientalism was nothing more than a schema he concocted to organize the ideas common to most of the Gnostic systems? He did not overlook the fact that, with this schema just having some sort of historical semblance, it ought not involve the idea and the term 'Christian,' which necessarily belongs to the essence of Christian Gnosticism. However, he took up into his Orientalism an apparent figure or likeness of the redemption doctrine, in a way neither dualism nor the system of emanation was inherently able to construe it. For he just installed it using Christian ideas, and was able to create, configure, and set up a Gnosticism forced to blend emanationist and dualistic ideas, within or alongside the Christian Church. But in doing so Mosheim himself seems to have confused what he initially wanted to clearly separate. Thus he undeniably engaged in a historically circular procedure." In any event Mosheim followed this circular procedure inasmuch as he arrived at his Orientalism, which seems to him to be the presupposition for Gnosis, not so much from historical links but rather simply through abstract reasoning. Yet his ingenious way of looking into the essence of Gnosis is evident in his seeing that Gnosis must have as its presupposition something already containing the whole, just not in the same concrete way that it subsequently took shape in Christian Gnosis. Hence Mosheim was fully justified in also presupposing a pre-Christian redemption-idea, and that on no account would the Christian doctrine of redemption have become so important for Gnosis if that pre-Christian religious philosophy had not already contained a point of contact for this doctrine. The essential nature of Gnosis cannot be comprehended if one has it arising in just bits and pieces, and not organically. What it adopted from Judaism and Christianity always found a specific place prepared for its reception. That pre-Christian, speculative, philosophical religion just attached itself to positive and historical religion as the abstract does to what is concrete.

44. Concerning the position set forth by Lewald (see p. 106 in the work cited in the Introduction, n. 47), one can refer to p. 828 of Gieseler's review of it (Introduction, n. 48), which quite rightly reminds us especially of differences in the concept of matter. For Zoroaster, matter is in part good and in part evil, which is why there is a resurrection of the dead and a purification of matter by the great world-conflagration; whereas for the Gnostics matter is utterly evil and the source of all evil. Furthermore, Ormazd created the world in its original purity, whereas the Gnostics regard Aeons as the world-creators, thinking of them as equally weak and imperfect when they seem to betray their product, the creation.

45. [*Ed.*] Jacques Matter, *Histoire critique du Gnosticisme* (n. 5).

transferred into a sphere where we no longer have anything to hold on to that is firm and secure.

Based on Philo, Matter also goes back to the striking and remarkable syncretism that took shape between the splendid teachings of the Persians and of Palestine after the Jews were transplanted to the banks of the Euphrates and the Tigris. In order to seek out the origins of Gnosis in these momentous facts of Eastern history, he wishes to discover the elements of Gnosis nowhere else than in those Persian teachings brought to Alexandria by the Jews, and which the distinguished Jewish writers intertwined with their sacred scriptures and with the doctrines of Platonism. Matter also alludes to the exiled Jews having adopted the teachings and practice of magic from the Magi and the Chaldeans, and even to the Indians [Hindus], from which they were said to have become acquainted with individual teachings while they were in Persia.

Aside from how very mundane and unhistorical the notion is that, in the initial period after the Exile Parsiism had a direct and very significant influence on Judaism,[46] we must pose the question here as to exactly what teachings and ideas in Philo are supposed to so obviously manifest this influence from Parsiism. Philo knows nothing of an antithesis of two realms engaged in mutual combat. Matter speaks of a kingdom of darkness and the Logos doing battle against it, yet this notion is entirely foreign to Philo. There is just as little basis for the contention that the Philonic Logos would coincide with the Parsi Ormazd and the Gnostic Christ. Yet Matter also states that Zoroastrian ideas are intimated here and there in Philo; so in any event their impact is, on the whole, so unimportant that nothing can be gained by this route for the explanation of how Gnosis originated that is not already naturally present in Philo's relation to Platonic philosophy. Matter[47] also invokes The Wisdom of Solomon, from the Apocrypha, and the two sects of the Therapeutae and the Essenes, but without highlighting any elements from them that can be more closely linked to Gnosis.

In contrast, Matter greatly emphasizes the Kabbalah and even uses it to make still tighter the bond said to link Gnosticism with Parsiism. Matter contends[48] that the beginnings of the Kabbalistic doctrines trace far back before the Christian era. He says the Book of Daniel bears unmistakable traces of them, although the clearest proof is provided by the idea of emanation, which is in the same way the heart and soul of both the Kabbalah and Zoroastrianism. That is why these ideas could be familiar to the Jews simply via their close ties to the Persians. With this as the basic principle, the similarities and reproductions of a derivative sort in the Kabbalists' theories are so numerous that, placed next to Zoroastrianism, the Kabbalah seems to be just a copy alongside the original. There is also no denying that the Kabbalah is very closely related to Christian Gnosis. So one cannot avoid comparing these two both as whole

---

46. Gieseler's remarks about this in *Theologische Studien und Kritiken* (1830), pt. 2, p. 381, are incontestably correct.

47. In *Histoire critique du Gnosticisme* (n. 5), vol. 1, pp. 73, 91.

48. 1:94.

systems and in their individual doctrines, as Neander too has done in the appropriate places.[49] But if we consider the reasons Gieseler has briefly reminded us of in his assessment of Matter's work, then accepting a pre-Christian origin for the Kabbalah must be such a dubious affair that, at least from this perspective, the Kabbalah can be of no use for explaining the origin of Gnosis.

However, if we also allow for the Kabbalah's existence prior to Christianity, at least in the form we know it, as being independent, and we merely stick to looking at the Kabbalah and Gnosis as two parallel, closely-related phenomena, then doing so quite naturally requires the assumption that both of them proceeded from a common source. Then we are at the same time significantly backing the view that this same combining of speculative ideas—created partly from the Platonic theology and partly also from Oriental religious systems—with the religious teachings of the Old Testament, the combination we see in Philo making such a remarkable crossover to Christian Gnosis, was not something that just existed in Egypt, in Alexandria. Instead it was also present elsewhere, where Jews saw the opportunity to venture beyond the narrow horizons of Judaism.

If we put together all those elements the Kabbalah has in common with Gnosis, they thus consolidate into a shared foundation from which both Christian Gnosis and the Jewish Kabbalah were able to take shape, based on this same religious philosophy. They come into the most contact in what is actually the emanation part of the system, emergent in the aspect where, based on the absolute principle, the series and successive stages of the divine powers mediate the relation of spirit to matter. These powers then converge once more in the end point where the spiritual life that has emanated from the deity is said to return into it and be taken up once again into the oneness of the supreme principle. These philosophies are most divergent in the intervening parts of the system, in all those doctrines in the Gnostic systems related to the Demiurge and Christ, naturally for the reason that this is where the Gnostic view of Christianity's relation to Judaism had to take hold, as well as the idea of redemption that the Gnostics adopted from Christianity.

In order to justify the assumption of a pre-Christian origin for the Kabbalah, Matter therefore contends that, had the Kabbalah arisen at the same time as Christianity, or only later than it, then the Kabbalah would have been something quite different than it actually is. In doing so he refers to the Neoplatonists, who did indeed set their system over against Christianity yet adopted the most magnificent and certain truths from Christianity. To the contrary, we should note that, just as the Neoplatonists did not appropriate anything from Christianity that would have required them to forsake their Neoplatonism, so too the Kabbalists always still had to remain Jews. For any further rapprochement to Christianity would have placed them in the same relation to Christianity as that occupied by the Gnostics, and then they would no longer have been Kabbalists but would have been Gnostics. Accordingly the Kabbalah

---

49. In his *Genetische Entwickelung* (n. 1), esp. 225ff.

points very much to Judaism as the fertile soil on which such products of the religious spirit sprang up at that time, and so provides no more definite anchor for explaining the genesis of Gnosis.[50]

An additional point to note is that Matter precedes this by presenting the two main classes of Gnostic sects, Syrian and Egyptian, a portrayal of Syrian-Phoenician and Egyptian religious teachings. This serves to set forth the elements the Gnostics may perhaps have utilized for their systems (which simply omits the more specific demonstration—certainly difficult to provide—of how this utilization actually took place). All this just goes to show the adequacy of the verdict we already reached—that here we are drawn into a sphere that is overly broad and far too vague, one where every characteristic means for tracking down the origin of Gnosticism has vanished.

## Möhler's View

We have seen the sphere within which we have to seek the beginnings of Gnosis as too broadly drawn. In contrast to this another researcher, who has briefly made this issue the topic of a new investigation of its own, has drawn the bounds too narrowly.[51]

Möhler opposes the conventional view, which can be summarized as follows. According to it Gnosis proceeded from a purely theoretical interest, from the need to orient oneself speculatively concerning the world and its phenomena; the need to comprehend the facts of Christianity and its historical, positive nature, in general terms as idea, as pure truth of reason, and in the context of all its parts. For after people who subscribe to an Oriental-Platonic philosophy have converted to Christianity, they do not give up their philosophizing mental outlook and exchange it for the practice of Christianity. Instead they do the opposite. In contrast to this way of looking at things, Möhler contends that Gnosis proceeded quite immediately and directly from Christianity, and indeed from a practical impulse, so that only in the course of its history did it adopt a speculative orientation.

---

50. For particular opposition to the derivation of Gnosis from the Kabbalah, see Massuet, *Dissert. praeviae* in his edition of Irenaeus (Introduction, n. 41), p. xx; and Lewald (Introduction, n. 47), 88ff.

51. J. A. Möhler, *Versuch über den Ursprung des Gnosticismus* (with his *Beglückwünschung Seiner Hochwürden dem Herrn D. Gottlieb Jac. Planck, zur Feier seiner fünfzigjährigen Amtsführung am 15ten Mai 1831, dargebracht von der katholisch-theologischen Fakultät zu Tübingen*) (Tübingen, 1831). [*Ed.*] Johann Adam Möhler (1796–1838) was on the Catholic Theological Faculty at Tübingen in the early 1830s and founder of the Catholic Tübingen School. He and Baur became involved in a bitter controversy over the doctrinal differences between Catholicism and Protestantism through books published by Möhler in 1832 and Baur in 1834. This controversy tapped into Baur's interest in Gnosis because Möhler said Protestantism represented a Gnostic inward turn and world-rejection. See Notger Slenczka, "Ethical Judgment and Ecclesiastical Self-Understanding: Ferdinand Christian Baur's Interpretation of the Protestant Principle in the Controversy with Johann Adam Möhler," and Volker Henning Drecoll, "Ferdinand Christian Baur's View of Christian Gnosis, and of the Philosophy of Religion in His Own Day," in *Ferdinand Christian Baur and the History of Early Christianity*, ed. Martin Bauspiess, Christof Landmesser, and David Lincicum; trans. R. F. Brown and P. C. Hodgson (Oxford, 2017), 48ff. and 118.

As spelled out more precisely, this new and distinctive view of Gnosis holds that, after the spirit's long and deep preoccupation with the external world and with earthly striving, Christianity turned the spirit inward, into itself, in such a powerful and forceful way that the new focus within, and the pull heavenward, expressed itself in many Christians in a wholly overexcited, excessive, unhealthy fashion. The physical world filled them with infinite loathing, and an inner, profound disgust (βδελυρία) accompanied all their contacts with it. The painfully aroused, deeply offended feeling, the disgusting pressure, the sense of the world as contemptible, still struggled for a term expressing the dark working of the spirit and, by giving it a name they brought it to consciousness. It went as follows: the visible, external world is itself what is evil, and its substance is not from God, for spirit and body are absolutely opposed to each other.

What developed from this exclusively practical concern, among all those people who needed for reason to come to the aid of feeling, was a singular kind of speculation, one now raising all those questions that, together with their given answers, constitute the more specific contents of the Gnostic systems. These questions from which Gnosis took shape could not have existed at the outset, but are to be regarded as the second moment in the history of Gnosis. What now happened was that, in order to ground the vagaries of the life of feeling in a speculative fashion, all that the ancient philosophies, theosophies, and mythologies had to offer got utilized for this purpose. That is also what gave rise to the striking analogies Gnosis has with the Zoroastrian, Kabbalistic, Platonic, and other theologumena. In addition to what else got deployed as further grounding for this Gnostic outlook, special emphasis rested on the fact that, when people looked around in the world contemporaneous with the era of the first Gnostics, one question posed the greatest difficulty: Where were the Gnostics supposed to have gotten, as such a stimulating, vital principle, the dualistic conception that undergirds everything else in Gnosticism? All the inspiration, all the power of the Gnostics, flows from this dualism, and without it there could be no explanation at all for Gnosis as the phenomenon that caused such a huge stir in the church. It does not suffice to regard the Zoroastrian system, or Platonism, or Alexandrian-Jewish idealism, or the Kabbalah, or Neoplatonism, as the source of Gnostic dualism.[52]

In assessing it, we can locate its truth simply in the fact that Gnosis shares with Christianity a deep and vitally stirring religious feeling, owing to the idea of evil. However, as soon as we analyze this feeling and its content, the idea of evil, we see that the Gnostic idea of evil distances itself from the Christian idea of evil to the same extent as Gnosis points us back to the pre-Christian world as its homeland. It is of course true that Christianity redirected the human spirit inwardly and drew it away from the external world. But this surely happened only because Christianity led human beings to find their deepest and innermost antagonism to God in the consciousness of sin it awakened in them. Christianity knows of no other concept of evil or of sin than simply the purely ethical or moral one, which considers evil to be just a human being's

---

52. See Möhler (n. 51), 4–8 and 16ff.

own ethical or moral act. But if one considers the powerful impact Christianity had on the Gnostics to have only resulted in the Gnostics being disgusted by, and tired of, the world—and their expressing this sense of contempt for the world in the view that the visible, external world is itself evil, that its substance or material is not from God, and that spirit and bodily being are absolutely opposed to each other—then one does not correctly see how Christianity is said to have played such an intimate part in this Gnostic worldview. For what can be more in conflict with Christianity than a view setting aside the purely moral concept of evil and, in place of the free moral act of a human being, tracing evil back to matter and a human being's physical or material body? That view could not possibly have been derived from Christianity itself. It could only have been the consequence of a misconception that, as is undeniable, could easily have been linked to Christianity.

However, the cause of this misconception, one linked to their understanding of Christianity for just one group of Christians, is also then simply to be sought for in other circumstances external to Christianity. But these circumstances can be none other than the very ones in which people had for a long time endeavored to locate the beginnings of Gnosis. While a direct derivation of Gnosis from Christianity can hardly be satisfactory, the demonstration supposedly showing that Gnosis could not have arisen outside of Christianity is just as unsatisfactory.

Of course the basic view from which the latter approach proceeds is extremely one-sided. The contention, by using a negative designation of the character of Gnosis, is that Gnosis is the demonization or condemnation of nature. For that reason it is not a reaction, on the Christians' part, against Judaism and the Jewish spiritual orientation. It is just the countering of a phenomenon characterized by the divinization of nature, which is something found only in paganism, not in Judaism. In paganism, spirit is merged into nature and submerged in it, for paganism has divinized nature. But as a Christian offshoot, as hyper-Christianity, Gnosis has then striven to withdraw entirely from nature, and it demonizes nature. While paganism has never become clearly (and generally) conscious of the opposition between spirit or mind, and body, and has treated the two as one, Gnosis gave these contraries the form of an absolute contradiction. Yet dualism is by no means just a phenomenon peculiar to Gnosis. We of course also find dualism in the ancient religions, and can rightly say, with regard to the familiar phenomena pertinent at this point, that these religions did not merely divinize nature, but also demonized it. This point is obviously connected with the other factors supposedly further undergirding this view as to the origin of Gnosis. [Such is Möhler's position.]

We concede that neither the Kabbalah nor Neoplatonism has played a part in the origin of Gnosis. However, it is very untenable to maintain the same verdict about Persian dualism, Platonism, or Alexandrian Judaism. The objection to Persian dualism being a foundation for Gnosis is that it is very difficult to comprehend how this system in decline, at the time of its greatest weakness, is supposed to have exercised such a vital influence on the Christian Church. Yet it is far more comprehensible that it would have been enlivened once again through Christianity, in those persons in whom it lay buried as a footnote to a bygone history, and come to be newly appreciated, so that it was therefore simply employed as a welcome historical support by the kind of persons who were transposed by Christianity into a wildly enthusiastic movement. If we are also allowed to go further, with the assumption being correct that the Zoroastrian system was at that time just a footnote to bygone history (for such designations are always very subjective in nature), then this in any case nevertheless points to the fact that a dualistic worldview was present long before Gnosis. So all the line of argument introduced proves is just that Gnosis did not take its origin directly from Persian dualism, and that fact in any event also makes other bases for it likely.

A further contention is that the deepest foundation of Gnosis, its distinctive dualism, is even less so to be derived from Platonism than it is derivable from the Zend system. If this statement is at first quite apparently true, it is nevertheless true only in a limited sense. We should differentiate two separate views of the Platonic *hylē* or matter. In what seems to be the more correct understanding it is, so to speak, the irrational element in God himself; it is what acquires form and structure via Nous and makes its appearance in individual beings. The difference in views is that, for Plato, spiritual and bodily existence derive from one and the same source, whereas for Valentinus the pneumatic or spiritual aspect comes from the essence of deity, but the bodily aspect takes shape from the matter that is alien to, and opposed to, deity.

The usual conception is that God has fashioned a material present outside himself, and existent because of him, into the world.[53] The Valentinian teaching, where possible, deviates from this view. The cause of evil is hardly to be sought in the *hylē*, as the utterly formless material that is also able to be shaped endlessly and is totally lacking in resistance. Rather, the pre-existing souls first brought this *hylē* with them into bodily existence, in that, in a previous state they acquired a guilt they must atone for by their imprisonment in a body. That is because the Gnostics resisted with all their might the very idea that evil developed, in some way or other, from God's doing, from spirit. A further huge difference is that, for Plato, the world as created is perfect from the outset, is sound and free of defects; whereas for the Gnostics, in contrast, it is a wretched, deplorable, contemptible thing. Finally, Plato's Nous shapes the world of spirits and of bodies, while the Gnostics' Nous just shapes the pneumatic or spiritual beings. In any event it is certainly undeniable that the Platonic antithesis between God and matter is not the same as the Gnostic one.

Yet when we look even more closely at the Platonic concept of matter, then we see the enduring feature all these views have in common, the fact that in some way matter

---

53. [*Ed.*] Here Baur treats Plato's creation account in the *Timaeus* as affirming that the deity actually created the world in time, in the steps described in this dialogue. Some Platonists would say, in contrast, that this creation story recounted by the astronomer Timaeus instead serves Plato's purpose as a literary version of the timeless metaphysical relationships existing among the various levels of spiritual and material kinds of being. That is, Plato is not in fact a "creationist."

forms a certain antithesis to the pure essence of the deity. Although Plato definitely does not consider and designate matter as the locus and principle of evil, and he does straightforwardly call the world complete and perfect inasmuch as it was formed and arranged by God, at the same time Plato sees the material principle as an obscuring, darkening, and disuniting factor as soon as it comes into direct contact with what is spiritual and forms an organic unity with it, as matter does in the human organism. This is how Plato sees matter, given the Platonic antithesis between the ideal and the real, and its well-known view of the body as the prison of the soul, as well as his view of the imperfection and misleading nature of sense perception. The fact that Plato accepts a fall of the soul while in its pre-existent state does not prove that he in any respect considers matter to be the cause of evil, since every dualism can allow that souls are defiled by the evil of matter simply by their already having an inherent disposition to be defiled by it.

Indeed one cannot even maintain that, according to Plato, minds and bodies are formed by the same principle. The supreme God is the world's creator only in that he imparts the divine element in the human being, one's soul. For God relegates to the gods, to the immortals, the task of adding the mortal element. These gods occupy the same subordinate and intermediate level, between God and matter, that the Gnostics' Demiurge occupies, just as the Platonic principle, that the divine has no direct interaction with what is mortal, is entirely in keeping with the Gnostic worldview.[54] What is otherwise involved in how the Platonic concept of matter relates to the Gnostic concept of matter can only be determined more specifically from a closer investigation of the individual systems. In each case the question as to what influence Platonism may have had on the emergence of Gnosis calls for considering not merely what one was justified in finding in Plato for his own sake, but also what one believed could be found there and was inclined to find there. Once the antithesis of spirit and matter was up for consideration, it was able to be understood and elaborated on in various ways.

In what way does the Platonic matter already appear quite different in Philo? According to Philo, matter is definitely a stuff existing apart from God before the creation of the world. The divine activity of creating merely functioned as a shaping or formative activity. This pre-existing matter was not merely without form, for it was also utter confusion and disorder. Just as God is the principle of life, and most especially the principle of the spiritual life, so matter is lifeless; and just as God alone is freedom, so matter is blind necessity. But should one nevertheless have thought it requisite to assume that there is a very great difference between this concept of Philo's and the Gnostic concept of matter, it is quite befitting to consider that, while Philo did indeed intensify the Platonic concept of matter, so too the Gnostics, even apart from other additional factors, quite naturally went even farther in that direction. As a rule each new phenomenon of this kind had features of its own that it elaborated into a specific form, using the previously existing foundation.

54. See n. 13.

From this vantage point, accordingly, we will simply refer back once again to Philo. He forever remains the most remarkable intermediary between Platonism and Gnosticism, however much even Möhler contests, from a new angle, this relation of Philo to Gnosis, based on the standpoint of a Judaism that Philo professed and to which he was devoted, even as a Platonist—assuming the customary view of Judaism. Möhler of course concedes that there are very striking affinities between the Alexandrian-Jewish idealism and Gnosis. But at the same time he contends that, since Gnosis has an absolute dualism as its foundation—a dualism not to be found in more refined Jewish theology, either in its ideal form or in the Kabbalah, which are the two forms of this theology—there can therefore certainly be no talk of Gnosis proceeding from this theology. Generally speaking, it is exceedingly difficult to conceive of a transition from Judaism to heretical Gnosis. Möhler writes that:

> The Jews never stood so far away from the true God. From time immemorial the Jews were altogether reliant on the tenets of an ethical religion. They were far too familiar with the purer religious conception of nature for acquaintance with Christianity to have been able to evoke such a wholly perverse, spiritualistic extreme [as Gnosticism] in them. The more akin one's religion is to Christianity, the less, because of this, one runs the risk of becoming converted to eccentric sentiments. The greater risk instead lay in failing to adopt Christianity, as we then observe this also in the case of Jews. Given all the misconceptions about Judaism in each of the Gnostic systems, one must be more cautious about having Gnosis emerging from Judaism, especially since those phenomena seeming to form a transition between them in fact do no such thing.

A series of propositions in fact cannot increase the likelihood of the proposed view. If the Jews were too closely associated with the true God for them to become Gnostics, why should the same not also hold good for the Christians? If Gnosis is said to be just a direct product of Christianity, but at the same time the closer someone's religion stood to Christianity the less would have been the risk of becoming converted, by this proximity, to eccentric sentiments, or to becoming a Gnostic, then what follows from Möhler's position is that only the abruptness and suddenness of the changeover from paganism to Christianity could have given rise to the Gnostics. What speaks against this position is the fact that, in all likelihood, nearly all of the first Gnostics were Jews. One can only find a bridge from Judaism to Gnosis to be unlikely if one posits the essence of Gnosis as being an absolute dualism, and will not acknowledge what is indeed undeniably present in Philo, the bridge connecting Philo with Gnosis.

If, in addition, we also include other seeds that demonstrably prepare the way for Gnosis, both in Philo and also in the Septuagint and the Apocrypha—as well as how notably Jewish sects such as the Essenes and the Therapeutae had already gone beyond the bounds of conventional Judaism, in the way they had related Gnosis to their own speculative ideas—then surely nothing is more natural than the view that the shortest and most direct bridge or transition to Gnosis was based on Judaism. The seeds of Gnosis were already present as soon as people began to philosophize about the Jewish religion in the way we have indicated, notwithstanding Judaism's positive and historical character.[55]

## The Meaning of the Word γνῶσις in the Linguistic Usage of that Time, Demonstrated from the Epistle of Barnabas, from the First Epistle of the Apostle Paul to the Corinthians, and from Clement of Alexandria

The accepted definition for correctly understanding the essential nature of Gnosis came from distinguishing a philosophical factor and a historical factor, and proceeding from the relation between these two elements. That the very meaning the word γνῶσις was given in the linguistic usage of the time prior to the actual emergence of the Gnostics might not have been so very unusual. Matter[56] designated a few passages in the Septuagint translation (to which can also be added chaps. 10 and 11 in The Wisdom of Solomon), and ones in the New Testament, where the word γνῶσις already would seem to have a meaning more closely connected with the essence of Gnosticism. I might have given no weight to that, although the choice of this word, to which people seem to have forever linked the concept of a purer, more perfect, more exalted speculative knowledge, in general a more profound knowledge, is in any event noteworthy. The following discussion might be more closely related to the main concept we are dealing with here.

---

55. Among the more recent investigations into the essence and origin of Gnosis, we might also mention here Friedrich Lücke's *Commentar über die Schriften des Evangelisten des Johannes*, 1st ed., 3 vols. (Bonn, 1820–25), 1:160–214. Lücke provides a brief history of the contrast between πίστις (belief) and γνῶσις (knowledge), from its origin to its fuller development in the Alexandrian school. He recounts how it unfolded by starting with the Fall and expanding this investigation into truth and error among the peoples of the earth and the people of God, to include true and false Gnosis, the difference between Pauline and Johannine Gnosis, the opposition of the church fathers' Christian Gnosis to actual Gnosticism, the origin of Gnosticism in Persia and India with regard to the systems of emanation and dualism (as distinguished by Friedrich Schlegel), and the circle of error and confusion in the systems of Basilides and Valentinus, of Marcion and Carpocrates, where Gnosticism, albeit in Greek forms and because of all-pervasive dualism, developed from a system of emanation right up to its conclusion in materialism and pantheism. With full appreciation for the ingenious ideas presented here, it is nevertheless often said—especially since in the more recent, second edition of the commentary this entire section is no longer to be found—that even here one seeks in vain for a more precise definition and delimitation of the concept of Gnosis.

56. In his *Histoire critique du Gnosticisme* (n. 5), vol. 1, pp. 119 and 125.

## The Epistle of Barnabas

Neander[57] has, correctly and in general terms, called attention to the meaning that the word γνῶσις has in the epistle attributed to Barnabas, in connection with the contention that the Jews have completely misunderstood the entire ceremonial law, by looking at it externally instead of just seeing in it an allegorical portrayal of universal and moral truths. According to the writer of this epistle, Gnosis alone threw light on its true sense. This point now calls for a somewhat more detailed explanation.

Right at the outset of his epistle (in chap. 2) the author says to his audience: "In understanding, we progress little by little, so that with our faith we completely come to possess knowledge too."[58] Thus the writer wants to lead them from πίστις (faith or belief) to γνῶσις (knowledge). However this knowledge can only be understood as being the main contents the epistle is dealing with, that to which it directly transitions in what follows, the spiritual understanding of Old Testament teaching and commandments. This is made even clearer in the following passage from chap. 10, where the writer cites the Mosaic commandment in Leviticus, chap. 11: "Moses said, 'You shall not eat the swine, nor the eagle, nor the hawk, nor the raven, nor any fish that does not have scales.' He embraced three doctrines in his mind ... Moses spoke with reference to spiritual matters."[59]

What then follows is an allegorical interpretation, according to which we are to understand the animals mentioned as indicating human beings with impulses and inclinations expressing the attributes of those animals. So the writer continues:

> Moses then issued three doctrines with a spiritual significance concerning meats; but they (the Jews) received them according to fleshly desire, as if he had merely spoken of meats. David, however, comprehends the knowledge of the three doctrines, and speaks in like manner: "Blessed is the man who has not walked in the counsel of the ungodly," as the fishes go in darkness to the depths of the sea, "and has not stood in the way of sinners," like those who profess to fear the Lord, but go astray like swine, "and has not sat in the seat of scorners," like those birds that lie in wait for prey. Take a full and firm grasp of this spiritual knowledge.[60]

---

57. In his *Allgemeine Geschichte der christlichen Religion und Kirche* (n. 4), vol. 1, pp. 628 and 653.

58. [*Ed.*] This is our translation of the Greek cited by Baur. There is nothing like it in the *ANF* translation of ch. 2 of the Epistle of Barnabas. However, in ch. 1 the author says (according to *ANF* 1:137): "I have hastened briefly to write you, in order that, along with your faith, you might have perfect knowledge." This must be the passage to which Baur is referring. There are both Latin and Greek texts of this epistle. The *ANF* translation of the first four-and-a-half chapters is based on the Latin version. The epistle was written in Greek between about 70 and 132 AD.

59. [*Ed.*] Barnabas, ch. 10 (*ANF* 1:143).

60. [*Ed.*] Barnabas, ch. 10 (*ANF* 1:143). The words attributed to David are from Psalm 1:1: "Happy are those who do not follow the advice of the wicked, or take the path that sinners tread, or sit in the seat of scoffers."

It is clear that the word γνῶσις here means none other than the allegorical interpretation and understanding of the literal, verbatim sense of the scripture passage.

The word γνῶσις has the same meaning in chap. 9 of Barnabas. Here the topic is circumcision, and the author demands that his reader grasp circumcision indeed in its deeper sense.

> Abraham, the first to enjoin circumcision, in looking forward in the spirit to the Son (Jesus), practiced that rite, in that he set down the teaching in three letters. For scripture says, "And Abraham circumcised 318 [10, and 8, and 300] men of his household." What then was the knowledge imparted to him? First notice what the 18 signify, and then the 300. As for the 18, the 10 is denoted by iota, the 8 by epsilon, and so you have [the beginning of] the name "Jesus" [i.e., IH]. And because the cross was said to express grace, by the letter tau [i.e., T], there are said to have been 300 (in addition to the 18). Thus the writer has pointed to Jesus with two letters, and to the cross with one letter. The person who knows this is someone who has placed within us the instilled gift of his teaching.[61]

So here too the word γνῶσις signifies the secret, mystical, allegorical sense linked to the external signs of the letters.

Accordingly, we also see here, precisely in the linguistic usage of the word γνῶσις, the origin of the concept linked to it. Just as Jewish-Christian Gnosis has its most ancient roots in the allegorizing that sought to go beyond the sheer letters and to give spiritual meaning to the externally given contents of the Old Testament scriptures, this spiritual knowledge, imparted via allegory, also has the name "Gnosis." So from the outset people linked to the word γνῶσις the concept of such a spiritual orientation, which of course proceeds from what is historically given but does not stop with it. Instead it seeks to understand the historically given in its true sense, from the standpoint of higher ideas, in the very elements that the divine spirit, as the actual author of the scriptures, initially placed into them although at the same time they were concealed in the outer husk of the words. Hence the allegorical feature that constitutes the essence of Gnosis is also the pneumatic or spiritual feature.[62] When the Gnostics consider themselves to be pre-eminently the "pneumatic ones"—while this of course involves additional meanings (just as, in the same fashion, Gnosis is most certainly not only limited to allegory)—we do also see in this expression the same conceptual connection.

In the entire contents of the Epistle of Barnabas, allegory is the key for the author. This key unlocks the correct understanding of scripture. (Chap. 10: "We then, rightly understanding his commandments, explain them as the Lord intended. For

---

61. [*Ed.*] Barnabas, ch. 9 (*ANF* 1:142–43).

62. Therefore the statement above, that "Moses spoke with reference to spiritual matters" is directly saying that "Moses spoke allegorically."

this purpose he circumcised our ears and our hearts, that we might understand these things."⁶³) This key makes clear to Christians what is hidden to the Jews. (Chap. 8: "And on this account the things which stand thus [types, allegories] are clear to us, but obscure to them, because they did not hear the voice of the Lord."⁶⁴) Even in the kind of passages where Gnosis and allegory do not occur so directly together, the word γνῶσις nevertheless still always involves the concept of something directly given, to which something else must still be added as its more specific and more exalted sense. Thus the writer says in chap. 18 that he wants "to pass to another sort of knowledge and doctrine." He then says that "there are two ways . . . , the one of light and the other of darkness."⁶⁵ To describe the way of light, the writer says, "The knowledge given to us for the purpose of walking in this way is the following."⁶⁶ Then follows a series of moral commandments and tenets that provide more specific meaning to, and a clear awareness of, the more indefinite sense of "the way of light." All this is important for how the concept of Gnosis developed.⁶⁷

## First Corinthians

Yet perhaps we can go back farther and take up a concept already present in the New Testament that is very closely related to Gnosis. What seems in fact pertinent to me is the meaning the word "Gnosis" typically has for the Apostle Paul in a few passages of his First Epistle to the Corinthians, but especially in 8:1ff.

Here the Apostle is speaking to those members of the Corinthian congregation to whom the epistle is principally addressed, about eating food sacrificed to idols. In the first verse he says that he shares with all of them the awareness that, as Christians,

63. [*Ed.*] *ANF* 1:144.

64. [*Ed.*] *ANF* 1:142.

65. [*Ed.*] See *ANF* 1:148.

66. [*Ed.*] Ch. 19; *ANF* 1:148. The image is one of "traveling to the appointed place."

67. The Epistle of Barnabas contains much that, on the whole, is noteworthy as a transition to Gnosis proper. For the author, with his allegorical standpoint, Judaism, together with its religious institutions, must have seemed on a very low level. Hence the complaint about the blindness of the Jews clinging to the letter. But the writer goes back farther and derives this status of the Jews from a principle of deep-seated hostility. At all events in ch. 9, where he speaks of the circumcision that the Jews have also just understood literally, not spiritually, he says: "He has circumcised our ears, that we might hear his word and believe, for the circumcision in which they trust is abolished. For he declared that circumcision was not of the flesh, but they transgressed because an evil angel deluded them" [*ANF* 1:142]. There is no major difference between this "evil angel" who is the cause of the Jews' blindness, of their complete lack of any spiritual understanding of their own religion, and the Gnostic Demiurge, who is himself of course the author of Judaism but who at the same time, unawares, planted spiritual seeds in Judaism. In any case we see, in this same writer of Barnabas, how closely the allegorical perspective, so akin to Gnosis, borders on docetism. The writer speaks of Christ in rather docetic terms, having Christ appear in the flesh only because otherwise human beings could not have borne the sight of him. "He manifested himself to be the Son of God. For if he had not come in the flesh, how could human beings have been saved by beholding him? For, by looking upon the sun . . . which is the work of God's hands, their eyes cannot bear its rays" (ch. 5 [*ANF* 1:139–40]).

we know we all have a higher knowledge (οἴδαμεν, ὅτι πάντες γνῶσιν ἔχομεν). Yet he states at once that he must oppose the concept of γνῶσις to the concept of ἀγάπη (love), and reminds them that it is not merely a matter of knowing, but also of the way one knows [God] (καθὼς δεῖ γνῶναι, vv. 2–3). That is, it concerns the way in which one has applied what one knows to the given circumstances one ought to consider. Gnosis by itself is merely theoretical, whereas love first puts theoretical knowledge into practice. Gnosis by itself is unfeeling, one-sided, egoistic (ἡ γνῶσις φυσιοῖ—"knowledge puffs up," v. 2). Love first turns one to take into account the requisite consideration for the spiritual well-being of others (ἡ δὲ ἀγάπη οἰκοδομεῖ—"love builds up," v. 1).

In v. 4, Paul takes up, and answers in more specific terms, the issue raised in v. 1 about eating food sacrificed to idols [specifically, meat]. He says that, as Christians, we are certainly aware that these idols do not really exist in the world, and that "there is no God but one." For, if these so-called gods exist, whether that be "in heaven or on earth—as in fact there are many gods and many lords, yet for us [in keeping with our Christian convictions] there is [only] one God, the Father, from whom are all things and for whom we exist, and one Lord, Jesus Christ, through whom are all things" and through whose mediation we are (what we are through him as the redeemer).[68] However, not all of us have Gnosis. (Not everyone has the universal Christian consciousness as an active, clear, and specific knowing.) Instead there are many who, with the notion they have of an idol, still take the sacrificing of food to idols at face value. So, "their conscience, being weak, is defiled" (v. 7). That is, with the sacrificing of food to idols they link the concept of something defiling, the concept of sin. Therefore, when they eat such flesh themselves, they must see themselves as defiled by doing so, and thus actually incurring the sin of lapsing into paganism, or at least of straddling the fence between paganism and Christianity. "We are no worse off if we do not eat, and no better if we do. But take care that this liberty of yours does not somehow become a stumbling block to the weak. For if others see you, who possess knowledge, eating in the temple of an idol, might they not, since their conscience is weak, be encouraged to the point of eating food sacrificed to idols? So by your knowledge those weak believers for whom Christ died are destroyed" (vv. 8–11).

It is certainly not by chance that the Apostle repeatedly uses the word γνῶσις here. We surely see that the meaning it has here is no new or unusual one; instead the meaning has already entered into general linguistic usage. For, as we see, based on the affirmative οἴδαμεν ("we know") in v. 1, based on the term the Apostle adopts in the missive to the Corinthians, they wanted to designate with this term something expressing itself in their consciousness, something issuing directly from it. That it designates, on the whole, a higher knowledge, a spiritual knowing, an enlightened way

---

68. [*Ed.*] The parts of this sentence within quotes come directly from 1 Cor 8:5–6. With the mention of "many gods and many lords," Baur interpolates within our text the qualification: "in this sense—to the extent that they are said to be gods (θεοὶ λέγονται) or recognized as existing (νομίζονται εἶναι)."

of thinking, is evident in part from the passage's overall contents, and in part from the Apostle's concluding words to chap. 7, in v. 40: "And I think that I too have the Spirit of God." With these words the Apostle is already making the transition to what he has to say about Gnosis in chap. 8.

However, in order to gain an even firmer grasp of the concept linked to the word γνῶσις, the surely noteworthy point is that we are dealing here with religious notions, and with antithetical views where one side believed it has the true concept of the matter whereas the other side occupies a lesser standpoint from which it is most difficult to disengage itself. Gnosis belongs to those who, as Christians, have become clearly and firmly aware that the gods the pagans believe in are not only no gods but have no true reality as such. With this awareness, these people also can have no reservations about eating food sacrificed to idols because, with [these supposed] beings having no reality at all, that also leaves the food offerings dedicated to them as entirely just food for its own sake; so this food in reality involves no relation to these idols and accordingly can have no defiling effect. Such doings become a matter of indifference for them once they have this awareness, because they cannot come into any real connection with beings they are convinced do not exist.[69]

What we have here as well, with the word γνῶσις, is a kind of religious knowing by which something at a lower, inferior level, something still linked to deficient and limited notions, gets raised up so one has the true concept of it; a knowing by which someone aware of the circumstances of something in religious belief that is historically given, becomes conscious of the true concept of the matter—in other words, also becomes conscious, in a more general sense, of how various historically-given religions are related to the idea of religion itself. Therefore in the case of Gnosis, and according to the linguistic usage linked here with the word "Gnosis," we are dealing with both a given object and a specific knowing of that object. In the passage in Paul, the given is the belief in the pagan gods, how the pagans hold it from their religious standpoint. Here this belief becomes the object of Gnosis when one becomes distinctly aware of the reality of this belief, its religious value, by looking at it from a higher standpoint, the Christian standpoint. In doing so, therefore, how paganism relates to Christianity, in other words how these two religions relate to the idea of religion itself, also gets spelled out at the same time. Gnosis is the knowing of this relationship.

---

69. The later Gnostics also regarded the eating of food sacrificed to idols as a matter of complete indifference. In characterizing them, Irenaeus writes in *Against Heresies* 1.6: "They make no scruple about eating meats offered in sacrifice to idols, imagining that they can in this way contract no defilement. Then again, at every heathen festival celebrated in honor of the idols, these men are the first to assemble" [*ANF* 1:324]. Irenaeus of course traces this practice back to the Gnostic principle that those of a pneumatic or spiritual nature are unaffected by such practices and so incur no fault in doing so. It is all the same, whatever one's motives. Eating food sacrificed to idols always seems to be a matter of indifference simply from a standpoint where one disregards the distinction adhered to in the usual view.

## Allegory and Clement of Alexandria

The same relationship holds good when Gnosis equates to allegory. Allegory's object is the given that first calls for a spiritual interpretation. When Christians, from their higher standpoint, are able to take what the Jews, from their inferior standpoint, can see in the Old Testament in simply verbal and literal terms, and regard it as just symbols and types of a higher meaning, and convert the externally given into something spiritual, then the Christians occupy the higher standpoint of Gnosis. They possess a higher knowing, through which they become conscious of the true relationship of Judaism to Christianity. No doubt the word γνῶσις has no other meaning than this, even in 1 Cor 12:8 and 14:6.

According to the most probable explanation, λόγος γνώσεως ("utterance of knowledge," 1 Cor 12:8) is essentially a declaration focused on the relation of the Christian economy of religion to that of the Old Testament. It declares that what is in the Old Testament can only be understood and known in the correct light on the basis of Christianity, and indeed it also sought to illuminate it with the aid of allegorical interpretation. If we may assume that these Greek words, λόγος γνώσεως, involve this concept [of the relation of the two Testaments], a concept more plausibly associated with this term than are any other expressions to be found here, and assume that it is the concept to be rightly anticipated in this context, then we see directly from this passage—which also includes many other related terms and concepts—just how much this distinctive meaning is linked to this concept. Instead of elaborating further upon this point, I simply make the following observation. The elements of this concept that I have identified here are also prominent features in the writings of the very church father who assimilated Gnosis in its purest and most far-reaching sense, and whom we can count as witness to the most current linguistic usage regarding the term "Gnosis," Clement of Alexandria.

It is in fact typical of Clement, as it is on the whole typical of the Alexandrians and of the Gnostics themselves, that the concept of Gnosis has its distinctive meaning only in contrast to the concept of πίστις, or belief; that γνῶσις always presupposes [the existing] πίστις. For, based on this entire development so far, what else do we see as the most essential feature in the concept of Gnosis but the distinction between a historical element and a philosophical element? For Gnosis, all that simply belongs to belief constitutes its historically-given objects, the doctrines and institutions Gnosis takes from the historical religions lying before it. Gnosis takes the idea of religion from them. It evaluates them as to their inner religious worth; it distinguishes essential from nonessential features. It sets forth what, according to these religions' outward form and appearance, is simply inadequate and unsatisfactory. Gnosis spiritualizes religion by relating it to a higher idea, and in this way as such it determines the relationship of the historically-given religions to the absolute religion. Thus the content of πίστις is always just what is immediate; and by negating it γνῶσις presses on to the true concept. That is the reason why it is evident in so many contexts, especially with Clement too, that in its essence Gnosis is itself the concept [of religion], in its movement through the various moments by which it has to be mediated or transmitted.

For Philo, the mediator between πίστις and γνῶσις, between the historical faith and philosophical knowing, was of course allegory, the wonderful, mysterious art that transforms the rigid form into something fluid, by making the literal components of the text a transparent medium for spiritual ideas. Allegory relegates the historical faith to being just the mere husk for these spiritual ideas. That is why the concept of allegory was most closely connected with the concept of Gnosis, and why, for those who were real Gnostics, allegory for the most part retained its ancient significance to a greater or lesser extent. Thus, for Clement of Alexandria too, allegory was an essential element of his Gnosis, and the principal medium by which, as a Gnostic, he came to understand how Judaism is related to Christianity. The entire contents of his *Stromata*, with its diverse, colorfully-woven texture, also exhibits the principle of its unity chiefly in the typological and allegorical way of looking at things that pervades the whole text. Hence even Clement expressly considers allegory to be a Gnostic feature.[70]

To be sure, the use made of allegory had to be of a different kind [for Clement], a somewhat more limited use of it one always more or less negatively determined in keeping with the relation of the historically-given religions to the absolute religion. Gnostics who placed Judaism in a closer relation to Christianity, in seeking to find, already in Judaism, what first in fact belonged to Christianity, also had to give more scope to allegory than the kind of interpretation that drew a sharper boundary between Judaism and Christianity. But this is all of a piece with the topic of our further investigation. Here we stick first of all to the fruits of our previous inquiry. Thus, in order to spell out the basic concept linked with the word γνῶσις, we can now set the object of γνῶσις apart from the contents of [all other] knowing and look exclusively at the form of this particular knowing.

Even just formally considered, γνῶσις is still always a knowing that presupposes a different kind of knowing and is first mediated by that other kind of knowing. In other words, Gnosis is a knowing in which one is conscious both of the distinction within the object and of the oneness of what are set apart, that is, the elements by which the concept of the object is mediated. This knowing becomes absolute knowing only because of its being conscious of its own mediation—which brings us to the final point we arrive at in our investigation of the concept of Gnosis. The final point is Gnosis as absolute knowing as such, the very meaning of the word γνῶσις that it always has in philosophical parlance, at least insofar as philosophers wanted to use this word to designate no other knowing than the highest and most perfect knowing. Hence the systems we are speaking of here are of course also properly called "Gnostic" because they have to do throughout with an absolute knowing, a knowing conscious of its own

---

70. See *Stromata* 6.11: "From the scriptures the Gnostic knows ancient things, and he likens them to the things to come" [*ANF* 2:501].

mediation. The more definitively this mediation is considered to be, and portrayed as, grounded in the object of knowing itself (that is, in the historically-given religions with which Gnosis is dealing, and in the idea of religion itself, but in the final analysis grounded in the essential being of God), then the more definitively the general concept of Gnosis takes on its shape in the concrete concept of Gnosis, which forms the foundation for the Gnostic systems.

# 3

# Classification of the Gnostic Systems

## Mosheim, Neander, Vater, Gieseler, Matter

THE DIVISION AND CLASSIFICATION of the Gnostic systems is an equally important topic for a general investigation concerning the essence of Gnosis as such. Ever since people had endeavored to understand them as internally and organically connected systems, they also sought to tackle this other task in various ways, but always found it a very difficult problem. That is quite naturally the case, since the correct principle for dividing them up can only be provided together with the correct concept of Gnosis itself. Without a definition of the concept of Gnosis itself, the division of the systems could also hardly be successful; and correspondingly, a simple and natural division, encompassing the main forms and allocating to each one its own proper place within the whole arrangement, must also be regarded as the best test for the correctness of the definition provided.

Mosheim made the first attempt to classify the Gnostic systems according to a principle for dividing them according to their internal properties, instead of just lining them up historically and chronologically, as people had usually been content to do.[71] The shortcoming of Mosheim's effort at classification lay in the same one-sided perspective that almost all who followed him could not rid themselves of.

Neander was the first one to shed light on this matter by distinguishing Judaizing Gnostics from anti-Jewish Gnostics, by making this the basis of his *Genetische*

---

71. On this point see Lücke, "Kritik der bisherigen Untersuchungen über die Gnostiker" (n. 43), 116ff. In his *De rebus Christianorum ante Constantinum Magnum commentarii* (Helmstädt, 1758), Mosheim divided the Gnostics into two classes, with regard to the dualism in their principles. On p. 410 Mosheim says that "they share a major interest with other sects of the ancient East, the doctrine of two things from the beginning complete and unconnected. Each is removed from the other. Separate and mutually foreign, they are complementary." All the Gnostics assume a god distinct from the world's creator. "Those native to Syria and Asia designate a special lord of eternal matter, whether one who is self-existent or one born of that matter. That is, to the good principle they also add evil, a material principle that nevertheless differs from the world's creator. Those who are in fact born and educated among the Egyptians—Basilides, Valentinus, and others—do not know of this lord of the material world."

*Entwickelung der vornehmsten gnostisichen Systeme* (n. 1). But even Neander himself hardly knew how to appreciate the true significance of this new perspective. We see this clearly from the fact that Neander did not see himself further obliged to vindicate his own division, when he remarked in passing (p. 229) that an enemy of Judaism and the Jews would have readily derived a different view of the God of the Jews from the same basic idea those Gnostics attaching themselves to Judaism took as their starting point. That is, this enemy could have envisaged God as not merely ignorant of the highest world order, albeit unconsciously guided by it and, upon its revelation, submissive to it, but instead have seen God as a limited, arrogant, tyrannical being, hostile to what is above it. In addition to Marcion and his school, Neander places the so-called Ophites and Saturninus in this class of anti-Jewish Gnostics.

Those who were dubious about this division include Vater[72] and Gieseler.[73] In an otherwise not very clear discussion, Vater called attention to Neander's vacillation regarding the stance he ascribed to individual Gnostics. For instance, Neander puts Basilides in the category of Judaizing Gnostics, and yet he at the same time admits[74] that Basilides belonged to neither the set of Judaizing theosophists nor to the thoroughly anti-Jewish Gnostics. As for the anti-Jewish Gnostics, he does in any event correctly emphasize the animosity the Ophites inherently harbored toward the Jewish God, as well as Marcion's total opposition to the God of the Jews, while he also still sees no vast difference between Marcion's notions about the God of the Jews and those held by the Judaizing Gnostics. Similar thinking with a different turn to it could support not separating the Gnostics into an anti-Jewish group and a group attaching itself to Judaism.

Gieseler certainly does not overlook the fact that Neander's division derives from a relationship that, if understood and spelled out in a different way, undeniably had to have an important impact on the entire arrangement of the Gnostic systems. For what had to be front and center in all the parts of a Gnostic system is whether the Demiurge was considered to be an instrument or an antagonist of the supreme God, and whether Judaism was thought of as containing a few higher revelations, albeit in a veiled form, or was utterly to be rejected. Notwithstanding these distinctions, that way of dividing up the systems is inadequate because it still does not base itself on how the Gnostic systems are fundamentally related. However much the view of the Demiurge and the view of Judaism had to influence the various parts of a Gnostic system, one of these

---

72. J. S. Vater, "Ueber die neuesten Eintheilung der Gnostiker in an das Judenthum sich anschliessende und antijüdische, über den damaligen Zustand der Kirche und ein *Evangelium Ponticum*," in *Kirchenhistorisches Archiv*, ed. Stäudlin, Tzschriner, and Vater (1823), 1:97–113. [*Ed.*] Vater (1771–1826) was an Orientalist, linguist, and church historian who taught in Halle and Königsberg.

73. In his assessment of the writings of Lewald and Neander (Introduction, n. 9). [*Ed.*] J. K. L. Gieseler (1792–1854) was a professor in Bonn and Göttingen (as successor to G. J. Planck) and author of a multi-volume *Lehrbuch der Kirchengeschichte*, which was translated into English and became a popular textbook in the latter part of the nineteenth century.

74. *Genetische Entwickelung*, 62.

systems still could cross over from one class to another without making any radical changes. Quite often that actually occurred. Whereas Basilides himself belongs to the class of Gnostics attaching itself to Judaism, his later followers move into the class of anti-Jewish Gnostics. The Valentinian system is so similar to the Ophites' system that there is no mistaking their common origin; yet the Valentinians belong in Neander's class attached to Judaism and the Ophites belong in the anti-Jewish class. Now since that plays havoc with this arrangement of undeniably correlative and related systems, it makes it equally clear, on the one hand, that the basis for this arrangement could not be derived from a fundamental relationship, and on the other hand, that this arrangement undermines a pragmatic presentation of Gnosis.

Furthermore, there are such small steps from one class or group to another that, in the case of a few systems it is in fact hard to determine to which class they must be assigned. To be sure the Ophites regarded Ialdabaoth, the founder of Judaism, as a being engaged in a hostile struggle against the higher order of things, so that, considered from this angle, they are to be reckoned among the anti-Jewish Gnostics. Despite that, from Judaism's revelation they extracted a great deal that, contrary to the will of Ialdabaoth, Sophia conveyed to the prophets. For the Ophites, Judaism taken as a whole also contained more profound disclosures about the light-world, so that to this extent one might also say that the Ophites attached themselves to Judaism.

Gieseler himself proposed, as the most suitable way of dividing up the Gnostics, that we trace them back to the lands where they made their appearance: Egyptian Gnostics; Syrian Gnostics; the schools of Cerdo and Marcion as a third and special class. This method not only preserves the natural historical ties among the various factions, together with their further local features; for it also finds its justification by exhibiting a specific, distinctive, fundamental character possessed by each of these classes.

Enthusiastic speculation predominates among the Egyptian Gnostics, while the Syrian Gnostics are enthusiasts for asceticism. Emanationist views are more pronounced with the Egyptians, while the Syrians incline more toward dualism. Of course a certain dualism pervades all the Gnostic systems, because all the Gnostics regard matter as the source of evil, and as being co-eternal with the deity. But the Egyptian and the Syrian Gnostics differ in their further characterizations of matter. The Egyptians think of matter prior to the creation as merely disorderly stuff originally lacking any life of its own, such that life first gets activated in it through contact with the realm of light. Hence the dualism of the Egyptian Gnostics does not go beyond that of Philo. In contrast, dualism is much more far-reaching with the Syrians. For them, *hylē* or matter already has within it an independent life-principle, before having any contact with the realm of light, a principle that, as the primordial evil, continuously battles in the creation with the realm of light.

Whereas Neander's earlier depiction of this matter was marked by more general standpoints and perspectives, in his new treatment of it,[75] he was persuaded, mainly by the weight of the aforementioned reasoning, to modify and enlarge his earlier division of the Gnostics. Following Gieseler, Neander then elaborated more on individual cases, by finding the element of Greek speculation, or the influence of Alexandrian Platonism, more prevalent in one of his classes, and the element of Oriental ideas, or the influence of Syrian Parsee views, prevalent in the other one. Thus he said that, going by their most essential and influential differences, the most natural way is to divide the Gnostics into: those recognizing the connection between the visible and invisible orders of the world, between God's revelation in nature, in history and, within Christianity, the links between the Old and New Testaments as one entire theocratic development; and those sects severing this connection and this linkage by making Christianity into just one isolated fragment within human history. A brief summation could be: those Gnostics attaching themselves to Judaism, and those sects hostile to Judaism. What this division has to recommend it is that only in this way would Marcion's own distinctive system, which in one respect necessarily would belong in the series of Gnostic systems, be able to maintain its rightful place among them. Aside from Marcionism, however, Neander also counts in the class of anti-Jewish Gnostics the Ophites, as well as the Pseudo-Basilideans, the Sethians and Cainites, Saturninus, Tatian and the Encratites, and the eclectic, antinomian Gnostics, which include in particular Carpocrates and Epiphanes.

The most recent writer about the Gnostics is Jacques Matter.[76] In his critical history of Gnosticism, Matter has no compunction about declaring outright that the way Neander seeks to justify his earlier classification, by dividing the totality of the Gnostics into Judaizing, anti-Jewish, and eclectic sects, is the most deficient schema of them all. Matter says it would be impossible, in the first five centuries of the Christian era, to find Gnostics who were wholly foreign to Judaism. Because of Christianity's intermediary role, all are on good terms with this teaching. While, as we know from eighth-century monuments, the Sabeans were essentially marked by a hatred for Judaism, a hatred expressed far more decidedly than it was in Marcion's case, who among us favors the view that they originally had the same orientation? Not one Gnostic sect merits the label "eclectic." What these sects all avow is syncretism, not eclecticism. Likewise no one of them merits the label of a "Judaizing" sect. Not one of them purely and simply accepts the Mosaic revelation, and not one of them adheres to the additions to it by later Judaism. Still more: the feature setting Gnosticism apart in all its branches is its denial that the supreme being is the creator. It does so in order to assign creating to a lesser agent, to the Demiurge or to even lower spirits, in contrast to the essential character of Judaism, which ascribes the creation to the supreme being—a principle setting Judaism apart from all other Eastern teachings. That is why all the

75. In his *Allgemeine Geschichte der christliche Religion und Kirche* (n. 4), 1:602ff.
76. [*Ed.*] See n. 5.

Gnostic sects merit the label "anti-Judaizers," and it leaves no single one to which the term pre-eminently belongs, for all of them can to some degree be brought into connection with Judaism.

The examples of Valentinus and the Ophites strikingly demonstrate how unsuitable this division is. Valentinus sets out from a few Jewish principles, while the Ophites, who adhere so strongly to individual Valentinian teachings that they just form a branch of Valentinianism, are the declared opponents of Judaism. Accordingly, what would have followed from the method of division advanced [by Neander] is that at least one ought not place in the same category sects that are mutually divergent. The only correct historical method would be the one that indicates the sequence of events, and the proper division of sects is the one based on the schools to which they belong. These two very simple principles are interconnected.

The major schools that collectively embrace all the Gnostic sects are the schools of Syria, Egypt, and Asia Minor. The Syrian school is obviously the oldest in historical terms as also the oldest inasmuch as its theories are much simpler and more moderate than those of the Egyptian school. According to Gieseler and Neander, there is less difference between these two schools than there is between them and Marcion's school, which, regarded as in the third category, marked an offshoot from the Syrian and Egyptian schools yet set itself apart from them by its more practical orientation, and by a kind of aversion to purely metaphysical speculation. Like the Egyptian school, Marcion's also in turn split into several branches, something scarcely avoidable since, from its roots in Syria and Asia Minor alike, it took shape in Rome and spread from there to Egypt, Syria, Palestine, and other regions. That is why Matter is inclined to prefer calling this school that is sporadic, scattered here and there, the "Italian" or the "Asia Minor" school.[77]

Thus according to Matter's classification Saturninus and Bardesanes belong to the Syrian school, Cerdo and Marcion belong to the Italian/Asia Minor school, and all the rest are placed in the Egyptian school. This means that the Egyptian gets assigned not only Basilides and Valentinus together with their numerous followers, but also the Ophites that Neander grouped together with Marcion, and the Sethians, the Cainites, and the school of Carpocrates.

## The Lack of a Firm Principle

This overview certainly makes very clear what it is intended to show: that all these classification systems are extremely unreliable, uncertain, and arbitrary. It shows that the one invalidates, and declares to be nonessential, what the other wants most especially to affirm. It shows the same system placed now in this class, now in that one.

---

77. *Histoire critique* (n. 5), 1:244; cf. 344.

## Part One: The Concept and Origin of Gnosis

If we want to start off from an internal, fundamental relationship among the systems, then we have Neander's division into Judaizing and anti-Judaizing Gnostics. However, for the reasons given in the foregoing overview, we cannot find Neander's template fully satisfactory, either in itself or in the way he proceeds to apply it to the individual Gnostic systems. Except that, on the other hand, the opponents of Neander's classification are in error if they wish to conclude, from its shortcomings, that in general it is not possible to classify the Gnostic systems according to an internal principle of division. For one must also concede that there is a common thread running through all the systems, and that there are only minor gradations in crossing over from one of them to the other. And yet there is no mistaking the fact that in no way do these systems inherently have the same character throughout; that instead, with all their analogous features, they are nevertheless organized in very different ways.

Hence one might want to shed light on the issue by turning to a simple division of the Gnostics according to the lands where they first appeared. But this is a purely external way of viewing them, a way that, for anyone who wants to understand this entire phenomenon in its deeper context, is so unsatisfactory that people have not been able to stick to it. That simply explains why the same scholars who embraced this method nevertheless saw themselves in turn obliged to couple an internal principle of division with the external one. No sooner was a division proposed on the basis of lands of origin, in contrast to Neander's classification, as the most suitable one, than it was also commended because its justification rested on pointing to a specific and distinct basic character for each of these classes. So now one speaks about the different forms that dualism has had among the Egyptian and Syrian Gnostics. It is only on this basis, by linking an inner element with the external one, that Matter can speak of different schools underlying the sects, in addition to the factors of temporal sequence and lands of origin.

But this is then what gives rise to all the disadvantages that must be attendant on a division illogically wavering this way and that, vacillating between different perspectives. If one divides the Gnostics into Egyptian and Syrian varieties, according to the different forms of their dualism, then one cannot possibly set aside from these two classes the schools of Cerdo and Marcion as a special class. For it must be shown that Cerdo's and Marcion's Gnosis is to be assigned to either the Egyptian or the Syrian form; or else that it presents a new form of dualism all its own; or that, if even this is not successfully demonstrable, the consequence is that the whole division proceeding from the Gnostics' dualism is a misguided approach. And what should one make of "a scattered or sporadic school" if it has previously been substantiated that underlying the sects of the Egyptian and Syrian Gnostics are schools whose character has been determined by the religions of their respective lands? Is this notion of a "sporadic school" anything other than a vague "and so forth," as if one now wanted to retreat from any further classifying?

Gieseler[78] does indeed approve of what Matter, in following Gieseler's own procedure, has said about the difference between the Syrian and Egyptian Gnostics. However, Gieseler says it is incorrect to hold that the Demiurge of the Egyptian Gnostics is a being of better character than the Syrian Demiurge; that the Egyptian Demiurge is the instrument of a higher will, whereas the Syrian Demiurge is hostile to all that is higher. That is to say, were Matter correct in what he states about this, then surely Neander's division into anti-Jewish Gnostics and Gnostics attaching themselves to Christianity would wholly coincide with the division into Syrian and Egyptian Gnostics. Yet Matter himself certainly recognizes that Saturninus' world-creating angels are nothing less than evil angels and, by comparison, he depicts the Ialdabaoth of the Egyptian Ophites as a proud and malignant being.

But once one resorts to an internal principle of division, there is not much more to say about the external element of the different lands, and it is not so utterly evident why one should not maintain that the difference in character of the Demiurge is just as valid a distinction regarding the different forms of dualism as is one's appeal to matter in this respect. Yet it is surely striking that, once dualism is said to be the principle determining the diverse character of Gnostic systems, the very same systems that are most dualistic in their view of matter do not also maintain their dualism with regard to the Demiurge. The only conclusion one can draw from this is that Gnostic dualism in general, at least in the sense adopted by Gieseler and Matter, is just something nonessential and of lesser import, and that still does not let us see into the deeper basis for how these systems are organized.

## The Three Main Forms of Gnosis, Which Depend on the Circumstances of the Historical Elements of Gnosis: How the Three Main Forms of Religion—Paganism, Judaism, and Christianity—Relate to One Another

If we want to classify the Gnostic systems according to an internal principle of division, the natural course is first of all to take into consideration the three principles: matter, the Demiurge, and Christ. These three principles are common to all the Gnostic systems, and they undergo various modifications within each system, although these modifications do not display any consistent pattern. The stricter dualists when it comes to matter are not also comparably dualistic regarding the Demiurge. Although docetism generally goes hand in hand with stricter dualisms, this is not always the case; for example, there is less difference between Basilides and Marcion as to their respective dualisms, and a greater difference between them when it comes to docetism.

How the various modifications of the Gnostic systems relate to those three principles they have in common first becomes more important in a specific sense when we

---

78. In *Theologische Studien und Kritiken* (1830), 2:390.

## Part One: The Concept and Origin of Gnosis

resort to a higher vantage point, one from which we can grasp more reliably what, in these Gnostic systems, is more or less essential in them, that is, what is incidental or is of enduring significance. This higher perspective arises of its own accord from what has been shown in our investigation into the concept of Gnosis, from the distinction between a historical and a philosophical element in Gnosis without which one cannot correctly grasp the concept of Gnosis itself. By starting out from this distinction we will find it entirely befitting the subject matter that what determines the character of an individual Gnostic system, much more than anything else, is how the historical elements that particular form of Gnosis involves can be mutually related. In each of the Gnostic systems this concerns the three, historically-given forms of religion: paganism, Judaism, and Christianity. Each of these systems first of all wants to discover the true concept of religion pervading these forms, but each kind of system does this in a different way. Although they always locate the absolute religion in Christianity, both how Christianity is related to Judaism and paganism, and how Judaism and paganism relate to each other, is spelled out now in one way and now in another.

In this regard it is indisputable that the perspective from which Neander starts out is the only correct one. That is because it fixes its attention not merely on one individual, secondary feature, but instead takes hold of a fundamental relationship pervading the whole. But, in doing so its shortcomings appear right away. First, it confines the issue it deals with merely to the relationship between Christianity and Judaism, and secondly, it does not consistently and clearly carry out the idea it put forward. First let us address the inconsistency. It is manifestly just as inconsistent as it is disruptive for this entire way of looking at things, to place the Ophites next to the sects classified with them, and then furthermore to assign Saturninus and Carpocrates to the anti-Jewish sects. The reason for this placement of the Ophites can only be that the Demiurge of the Ophite doctrine is described as a being hostile to the supreme God, in a way he does not seem to be in the Valentinian system. But if one is not speaking about how Judaism relates to Christianity, then the issue is not merely whether the Demiurge behaves in one way or another vis-à-vis the supreme God. Instead the issue is whether, already in the pre-Christian era, especially in the sphere of the Jewish religion at that time, there was something analogous to Christianity, a revelation of God anticipating and mediating Christianity itself; or else that what is true and godly is so very much confined to the orbit of Christianity and cut off from Judaism that, even in Judaism itself, one can only behold a gulf separating the pre-Christian world from the Christian world.

With this way of posing the issue, the Demiurge is no longer the exclusive focus. For what at once becomes clear is that, despite any reaction on the part of the Demiurge, the divine principle was able to be already at work prior to Christianity, as a glance at the Ophite system also shows; for Sophia, who stands higher than the Demiurge, was very active in opposition to him, in fostering the development of what is divine. Seen in this way, there can be no doubt about shifting the Ophite system closer to the Valentinian system in the same degree to which it becomes distant from the Marcionite system; for whereas the Ophites have Sophia playing an active role in the world order prior to Christ, the Marcionites regard the entire pre-Christian world as a dark domain not yet illuminated by any ray of light.

Furthermore, we hardly see any sufficient reason for placing Saturninus among the anti-Jewish Gnostics, since his world-creating angels are not beings hostile to the supreme God. But if the reason supposedly lies in the imperfection of these angels, or else in the fact that Saturninus counterposes a realm of darkness to the realm of light and with the figure of Satan sets an independent evil principle over against God, he does so from an entirely different perspective; and according to his system, neither of these factors prevents Saturninus from also affirming that the divine already communicated with humanity in the pre-Christian era. If one wishes to stick firmly to this perspective, then one should not confuse the more or less dualistic view of matter with the more or less dualistic view of Christianity's relation to Judaism. Hence I can in no way join Neander in recognizing a distinctive strain of the Gnostic systems in the teaching of Saturninus.[79] In any event Saturninus, like Bardesanes, belongs instead in the line of Judaizing Gnostics. Later on we will see how things stand with Carpocrates.

And now I return to the main point that seems to me makes Neander's classification deficient. It is confining the issue he is dealing with solely to the relation between Judaism and Christianity. After having enlarged on all the preceding points, we can therefore have no doubts about the legitimacy of this objection. The Gnostics certainly did not borrow the elements with which they constructed their systems solely from Judaism and Christianity; they took them from paganism too. In pursuing their concept of religion, the Gnostics took the path of religious history, and paganism also fell within their horizons. Each of their systems also included a specific verdict about paganism, as it did about Judaism and Christianity. Hence it is just as proper to distinguish between a greater and a lesser attachment to paganism, and between adopting a closer or a more mutually repellant relationship of paganism and Judaism, as it is proper to distinguish between Judaizing and anti-Judaizing Gnostics. If a system such as Marcion's was even less able to recognize a divine revelation in paganism than it could in Judaism, then that indeed makes it likely, on the other hand, when we come to the general relation of Gnosis to the Alexandrian religious philosophy, that there were also Gnostic systems placing paganism in a closer relationship with Judaism, and so also with Christianity. The most important Gnostic system, that of Valentinus, cannot be appreciated to the fullest extent if we do not see it as a system mediating paganism with Christianity as well as mediating Judaism with Christianity.

As confirmation of his classification system, Neander[80] cites a passage in the *Stromata* of Clement of Alexandria (6.6), where this writer calls Valentinus the κορυφαῖος τῶν πρεσβευόντων τὴν κοινότητα, "the leader of those who accept a common source"

---

79. Neander, *Genetische Entwickelung* (n. 1), 269; and *Allgemeine Geschichte* (n. 4), 1:759.

80. *Allgemeine Geschichte*, 1:662.

for the revelation of the divine in humanity, and do not deny Christianity's connection with all earlier revelation of God. However, at the same time this very passage serves as proof that, for this class of Gnostics, one ought not understand "all earlier revelation of God" as referring solely to Jewish revelation. In connection with this passage Clement says that, in addition to the Jewish people, each pagan people that turns to the Lord is holy to the Lord. He continues by quoting from Valentinus' book, περὶ φίλων: "Many of the things that are written, though in common books, are found written in the church of God. For those sayings which proceed from the heart are vain. For the law written in the heart is the People of the Beloved [of the redeemer]—loved by him and loving him."[81] Clement adds that Valentinus might understand the "common books" as being the books of the Jewish scriptures, or the books of the philosophers. In any case Valentinus sees the truth as something they have in common (κοινοποιεῖ τὴν ἀλήθειαν).

Neander himself holds[82] that the interpretation according to which Valentinus, in speaking of pagan literature, says that the pagans also share in the truth, is more compatible with there being an inner connection [between paganism and Judaism.] If Valentinus—like Isidore, the son of Basilides, as reported directly after this in Clement's text—may have regarded the truth of pagan philosophy as derived from the writings of the Hebrew prophets, then in this sense we also have the truth as something possessed in common; and that is simply a more novel proof that, with this class of Gnostics, we have to assume in general the same view of the relationship of paganism to Judaism as we have with the Alexandrians.

The main thing following from our discussion thus far, the only suitable perspective from which we can classify the Gnostic systems as things now stand, is for us to examine the mutual relations among the three forms of religion the Gnostic systems are dealing with.[83] As a general principle, the Gnostics always regarded Christianity as the religion more or less identical with the absolute religion. Therefore Christianity always had to stand in a certain antithesis to the other two religions. But whether or not this was thought of as a harsh antithesis, the important thing is that Christianity's overall relation to Judaism and to paganism was spelled out in dualistic terms. The result was two main forms of Gnosticism. With Christianity being related to Judaism

---

81. [Ed.] Clement of Alexandria, *Stromata* 6.6 (*ANF* 2:492). *ANF* gives the title of the book as *The Intercourse of Friends*.

82. *Genetische Entwickelung*, 137.

83. [Ed.] Baur identifies four logically possible types of relationship of Christianity to the other religions: Christianity linked to Judaism and paganism (Valentinus, Basilides, the Ophites), Christianity rejecting both Judaism and paganism (Marcion), Christianity linked to Judaism and rejecting paganism (the Pseudo-Clementine Homilies), and Christianity linked to paganism and rejecting Judaism (no historical examples because this type contradicts Christianity and dissolves into philosophy, but compare Manicheanism). Thus he arrives at the three main forms analyzed in Part 2. See Volker Henning Drecoll's discussion of Baur's classification scheme, and his diagrammatic representation of it, in "Ferdinand Christian Baur's View of Christian Gnosis," in *Baur and the History of Early Christianity* (n. 51), 124–27.

on the one hand, and to paganism on the other hand, one form sees an affinity between Christianity and the other two religions, and the other form sees Christianity as repelling them.

The great majority of the Gnostic systems, and the oldest ones, belong to the first main form. It includes the systems of Basilides and Valentinus and the numerous followers of Valentinus, as well as the Ophites and those belonging to correlative sects, those of Saturninus and Bardesanes. The fact that some of them spell out the relation of matter and of the Demiurge to the supreme God in a more dualistic way—and likewise think of Christ in more docetic terms—than the others do, does not constitute an essential difference. These are modifications that certainly merit attention; and inasmuch as they have their basis in the separate lands where the Gnostics appeared, the distinction of Egyptian Gnostics from Syrian Gnostics, in this limited sense, does not seem inappropriate. However, this distinction has altogether no influence on the fundamental relationship we have seized upon here, since all these Gnostics agree that the pre-Christian era, in both Jewish and pagan circles, is closely linked to Christianity and in many ways has introduced, and prepared the way for, Christianity. On the whole, these Gnostics stand on the same foundation and soil where we find the Alexandrian-Jewish religious philosophers such as Philo standing, as well as Alexandrian church fathers such as Clement and Origen. Surely the Gnosis of these latter two figures can even be considered to be another possible modification of the same basic form. So we accordingly see in it too a new confirmation of the view that the way of thinking already prevalent in Alexandria for such a long time, and so significantly influencing Christianity itself, has played a part in the whole phenomenon that we designate by the term Gnosis in the narrower sense.

The second main form of Gnosis has its only representative in Marcion, who had a system all his own, one that invariably had to be recognized as strikingly different from all the others. Its most noteworthy property always had to be seen as his placing Christianity in a harsh and repellant relation to Judaism. Naturally Marcion also included the same verdict about paganism in the one he delivered regarding Judaism, except that he was even less able to recognize anything related to Christianity in paganism than he could find as such in Judaism. Therefore here Christianity's relation to Judaism and to paganism is understood, for the most part, from a dualistic standpoint. I of course freely concede that, when the dualistic outlook once appears in such a characteristic way, even just in one respect as we find this to be the case with Marcion, it would naturally also influence the characterization of the relation of matter and the Demiurge to the supreme God, as well as influence a docetic view of Christ's person. The result would certainly be that Marcion's Gnosis, seen as a product of history, stands far closer to the Syrian form of Gnosis than it does to the Egyptian version. Yet if we ought to hold firmly, in its pure form, to the principle for classifying the systems, then we must carefully distinguish the main thing in Marcion's dualistic view, what only can refer to Christianity's relation to the other two religions, from lesser features that concern only individual points of the system.

Alongside the two main forms of Gnosis, characterized as I have indicated, our principle of division still leaves us with the possibility of a third main form of Gnosis. As soon as we understand that a more dualistic view is the basis for Christianity's relation to the other two religions, we can have this dualism applying in a comparable way to both Judaism and paganism, as Marcion does; or we can limit its application to just one of them, whether that be paganism or Judaism. Whereas Marcion coupled Judaism and paganism in order to set both of them over against Christianity in a dualistic way, a different Gnostic (as a first possibility) could have coupled Judaism with Christianity, by having these two religions appear as equally opposed to paganism. In fact it must have been surprising when, given Gnosticism's such ample productivity, this form, which the prevailing way of considering Gnosticism portrayed as a possible form, did not in fact even appear. From the usual portrayals of the Gnostic systems one ought of course to have supposed that there was no position representing this alternative.

But that is not actually the case. We must attribute this apparent absence chiefly to the still apparently deficient and unsatisfactory character of the portrayals of Gnosticism up until now. Only the dubious nature of the entire perspective from which people have set out to understand Gnosis as such, and from which they classified its various forms, could have allowed them to almost completely overlook one of its main forms, at least to the extent that it was not recognized as an independent form and given its due place. Of course Cerinthus belongs here. In his *Genetische Entwickelung der vornehmsten gnostischen Systeme* Neander completely overlooks Cerinthus, and only in his *Allgemeine Geschichte* did he present Cerinthus, as belonging in the same class with Basilides and Valentinus and others. As we will show later on, he is in any event a Gnostic in a different sense than those customarily assigned to the Judaizing class.

However, even if there are doubts about Cerinthus, it is nevertheless undeniable that the system peculiar to the Pseudo-Clementine Homilies inherently has a Gnostic character throughout, whereas it cannot be made compatible with any other class of the systems customarily specified as being the main forms of Gnosis. One of the outstanding merits of Neander's *Genetische Entwickelung* is that it recalls our attention to the remarkable contents of the Homilies, although it does so only in an appendix just intended as a contribution to the history of the Ebionites. Neither in Neander's *Allgemeine Geschichte*, nor in any of the more recent presentations of the Gnostic systems, has this form of Gnosis, the Cerinthian and Ebionite form, been allocated the place that belongs to it in the series of forms in the development of Gnosis.

The distinctive character of this form consists, overall, in its identifying Judaism and Christianity as much as possible, while establishing a very sharp antithesis between these two religions on the one hand, and paganism on the other. In doing so it essentially sets itself apart from the other two forms. That then raises the question: Is the only remaining possible form, one linking paganism to Christianity and setting these two over against Judaism, detectable in any one of the Gnostic systems? This calls to mind the teachings of Carpocrates and Epiphanes, who placed a Pythagoras, a Plato, an Aristotle, among the pagans, in one class together with Christ, and glorified all of them for having risen to the highest way of thinking by their own power (*die Kraft der Monas*). This appears to count paganism and Christianity as equals, and expresses their antithesis to Judaism. Thus the highest way of thinking, which Jesus attained in virtue of his especially pure and robust soul, they ascribe to him because he freed himself from the restrictive laws of the Jewish God and negated the religion stemming from this God.

But if Christianity is placed on the same footing with paganism in this fashion, instead of with Judaism, and if all the historical religions are so profoundly devalued as opposed to the absolutely solitary individual (*der Einen absoluten Monas*), so the religious insight these historical religions have becomes a matter of complete indifference, then Gnosis is at the point where it leaves behind not merely the realm of Christian Gnosis, but that of actual Gnosis as such. For the concept of Christian Gnosis always involves acknowledging the distinctive worth of what is Christian. If in this regard a certain identification of Christianity with Judaism is of course possible, it nevertheless contradicts the nature of Christianity to reduce it to the same level as paganism. However, if at the same time one declares that one is equally indifferent to all religions whatsoever, then there can no longer be a contrast or an antithesis between one form of religion and another, and there is no longer any connection between Gnosis and the history of religion, inasmuch as Gnosis can no longer be involved in arriving at the absolute concept of religion by mediating the historical elements of religion.

Like the Gnosis of all those who are indifferent to merely religious matters, especially to practical matters, and no longer count religious Gnosis as an authentic form of it, the Gnosis of a Carpocrates is simply a purely subjective, philosophical way of thinking.[84] The main forms of Gnosis, the only ones we can recognize as such, thus rest, according to the preceding analysis, on the more or less dualistic view of the

---

84. Inasmuch as some among the Gnostics sought to elevate belief to knowledge, they expressed a bolder self-confidence, a confidence in the comprehensive, commanding power of thinking and rational knowledge. We see this confidence in the followers of Carpocrates, in the presumptuous arbitrariness of a dismissive subjectivity that abandons historical objectivity for a procedure making the individual phenomena of the newer rationalism its equivalent. Irenaeus has a very significant statement about them in *Against Heresies* 1.25.2: "The soul, therefore, which is like that of Christ, can despise those rulers who were the creators of the world, and, in like manner, receives power for accomplishing the same results. This idea has raised them to such a pitch of pride, that some of them declare themselves similar to Jesus; while others, still more mighty, maintain that they are superior to his apostles" [*ANF* 1:350]. See also Tertullian, *On the Soul*, ch. 23. In 1.25.6 Irenaeus says: "They call themselves Gnostics." Actual Gnosis could only be the result of thinking, whereas, apart from the thinking that this result presupposes, they sought to have acquired this result by a priori arbitrariness.

relationships among the three forms of religion with which Gnosis is concerned. In light of this dualism or antithesis, Gnosticism takes two main forms in relation to these religions (even though we may consider them to be different stages of religion). Dualism is always the foundation, inasmuch as two of these religions are always juxtaposed to the third one [i.e., Christianity], which rejects them or is open to them. If it is open, then that can be openness to both of the religions in addition to Christianity, or to just one of them. For this reason the more dualistic of the main forms in turn subdivides into two subordinate forms.

On the whole, however, there are three essentially different forms of Gnosis. We can even regard them as coordinate forms, in that each of them involves a distinctive assessment of a specific form of religion. The first form (in the main, the Valentinian form) also wants to give paganism its rightful place alongside the other two religions. The second form (Marcionism) has to do chiefly with Christianity. The third form (in the Pseudo-Clementine Homilies) has a special affinity for Judaism.[85] What is characteristic of the three main forms of Gnosis that I have identified is therefore also determined by the character of these three religions. In order to comprehend these systems on their own as well as in their relations to one another, we must always refer back to the religions corresponding to them. But given how it appears to be grounded in these factors, this view of how the main forms of Gnosis are related also lends itself to elaboration in historical terms, and that must lead to closer examination of the individual major systems.

---

85. I differ from Neander as to both the first and the third forms, since I regard only the third form as in fact a Judaizing form. The second form is the only one where I concur with Neander, although here too I depart from him in that I see paganism, and not just Judaism, as antithetical to Christianity, and that I regard Marcion as the sole representative of this form.

# PART TWO

The Various Principal Forms of Gnosis

# 1

# The Form of Gnosis Linking Christianity Closely to Judaism and Paganism

## The Systems Belonging in This Class and Their General Character

THE MOST IMPORTANT SYSTEM representative of the first principal form of Gnosis is indisputably the Valentinian system, which was set up in part by Valentinus himself, and further elaborated in part with various modifications by several of his sagacious followers. Since here we are only dealing with the system as a whole, and only with its essential or basic features, for our purposes it is not necessary to differentiate its original form strictly from the shapes it assumed later on.[1] The Ophite system is the one most closely connected to the Valentinian system. Deserving special mention in addition to these two are the systems of Basilides, Saturninus, and Bardesanes.

Our contention is that the distinctive character of all these systems is determined first of all by paganism; that, next to Judaism, paganism is pre-eminently what asserts its rights in them; that everything here said to be adopted from Christianity must take a path via paganism. From this contention it is self-evident that we not merely have to adhere to the explicit statements found in these specific systems about Christianity's relation to paganism and Judaism, for we must consider most especially the form and makeup of these systems themselves. When we compare the systems of this class with other Gnostic systems, what must strike us in this regard as their most distinctive feature, and dominant perspective, is that they are dealing with the relation of the real, objective world to God as the absolute principle. According to their main

---

1. The original system of Valentinus himself can hardly be separated from his followers' modifications. In Irenaeus' presentation of the Valentinian system he introduces particular like-minded followers of Valentinus, such as Ptolemaeus, Marcus, and several others, and always speaks only of Valentinians but not of Valentinus himself. [*Ed.*] Valentinus (c. 100–c. 160) was born in Egypt and received a Greek education in Alexandria, where he became conversant with Middle Platonism and Hellenized Judaism. Later he became a prominent Roman Christian and a candidate for bishop of Rome.

contents they are cosmogonic systems. The major topic occupying them is the attempt to explain how the existing, finite world, and human beings as part of it, came to be. Everything else besides this issue that they take over from the contents of religious consciousness is for them in principle important only to the extent that it is related to this main issue, is a function of it and is shaped by it. Hence when for them Christ is the redeemer, he is the redeemer merely because the emergence of the finite world from the absolute also, of its own accord, includes the return of the finite to it, since when the creation is thought of as the disruption of an original harmony, one must also envisage a reinstatement of that harmony.

Previously we spoke of the spirit-matter antithesis as the domain all the Gnostic systems share and operate within, and which most especially finds its application in them. They very conspicuously devote all their efforts to having those two principles intertwine most closely and repeatedly, so that, by this intertwining of a network to be followed out in all directions, they provide a very vivid picture of a world that, in virtue of the law of opposites, simply consists of the mixture of opposed principles, of relationships forming and dissolving. What we have in the cosmogonic and cosmic character of these systems is, in general terms, an accurate picture of the ancient Eastern worldview. For the more we look at the individual systems in detail, by seeking to analyze their synthetically articulated, organic structures, and see what they are up to, the more strikingly we find the confirmation of this general perspective.

## 1. The Valentinian System

Among all the Gnostic systems, the Valentinian system is the most Platonic in its tenor. We encounter its Platonism directly in two fundamental ideas that unmistakably and inherently bear a Platonic stamp, and are deeply embedded in the internal, organic nature of the system itself. One of them is the idea of a falling-away (*Abfall*), resulting in the finite world coming to be. But since this falling-away has its origin in the spiritual world, its ultimate basis can only lie in the actions of spiritual beings. The other Platonic idea concerns the antithesis, or sharp distinction, between the ideal and the real.

### The Development of Valentinianism's Main Ideas

Although the finite world simply comes into being because of a falling-away, the finite world is nevertheless a reflection of the spirit world, just as in general terms the ideal is reflected in gradations within what is real.

According to Valentinus,[2] the falling-away that calls the finite world into being already begins at the highest level of the spirit world. When the supreme, absolute

---

2. The main source is Irenaeus, *Against Heresies* 1.1ff. [quoted and paraphrased by Baur below]. The others—Tertullian, *Against the Valentinians* (see also *The Prescription against Heretics*); Epiphanius,

being decided to reveal himself and to display or develop himself, Nous or Mind came forth through the mediation of Bythus and of Ennoia (also called Charis and Sige). Nous is also called Monogenes or the Only-Begotten, the father and the beginning of all things. Nous is just as perfect as the one from whom it proceeds, such that it alone can comprehend the Father's greatness. It alone could make known the primal being (*Urvater*), who was invisible and incomprehensible to the other Aeons. Since Nous enjoyed the greatest pleasure in contemplating the Father and considering his immeasurable greatness, it wanted to communicate to the other Aeons too the Father's greatness, his absolute being as without beginning, beyond comprehension. But, in keeping with the Father's will, Sige or Silence restrained Nous because it wanted to lead them all to the thought of the Father and the desire to look into his nature. That is why, just secretly and silently, they harbored the desire to investigate the one who had issued forth his offspring, and to learn of their timeless roots. Here we already have the origin of the great divide separating the finite from the absolute.

The Only-Begotten's desire is just as natural and legitimate as it is excessive and overstepping the proper bounds. The activity of spiritual beings, the innermost striving grounded in their spiritual nature, can only be directed to the absolute in which they themselves have the ground and root of their own being and knowing. Yet inasmuch as each being is not itself what is absolute, or is not identical with the absolute in the way that the Only-Begotten is, it can only grasp and know the absolute in a way suited to its own being. Hence whenever such a being wishes to apprehend and know the absolute, it must always be directly aware as well of how incongruent it is with the absolute; that is, conscious of a mismatch that forestalls any oneness between its own being and the being of the absolute. There always remains an ἀχώρητον or disparity, and the basis for it lies in the being that cannot grasp the absolute because it is not equipped to do so. It becomes conscious of the negativity of its own nature, because of which it stands over against the absolute. That is the reason why the desire of the Only-Begotten had to be countered by Sige, according to the Father's will, for Sige can never allow the unfathomable being of the Father to be made known.

This desire is the initial deviation, and it appears already at the first stage where a distinction is posited by the absolute's self-objectification in the Only-Begotten. It has no further consequences in that the mere admonition of Sige was sufficient, and the Aeons just silently harbored the desire aroused by their spiritual being, in not allowing its expression. This account simply serves to explain that, the higher the level

---

*Against Heresies* 31; Theodoret, *Heretical Tales*, 1.7—follow Irenaeus more or less word-for-word. Only Epiphanius, in an account more typically his own (chs. 1–7), in fact also provides his own Valentinian fragment (chs. 5–6). The *Excerpta ex scriptis Theodoti et doctrina, quae orientalis vocatur, ad Valentini tempora spectantia, epitomae*, which relies on the writings of Clement of Alexandria and is customarily also used for presenting the Valentinian system, can serve for elucidating individual ideas. But we can only learn from Irenaeus details about the internal organization of the system as a whole. The few fragments that Clement of Alexandria conveys from the writings of Valentinus himself are especially valuable.

or stage at which spiritual being becomes conscious of a certain boundary or limit it has in relation to the absolute, the weaker is its consciousness of the negativity of its own nature in this context. Although something negative becomes apparent here in this being, the positive element in its nature is nevertheless so preponderant, the closer it stands to the absolute, that the negative factor is only initially present in a minimal way, and it does not obscure that being's consciousness of the absolute. Yet while the divide becoming evident in embryo is also readily alleviated—since the Only-Begotten willingly follows Sige's signal, he is himself the upholder of the natural order—it is nevertheless by no means nipped in the bud nor so thwarted that it could not emerge all the more intensely from a different angle.

As the distance from the absolute grows, with the series of beings emerging from the absolute,[3] the negative aspect comes more into play and they are increasingly and necessarily compelled to be conscious of the negativity of their nature. That is why, according to Irenaeus,[4] Sophia (Wisdom), the last and youngest of the Aeons, rushed forth whereas the others kept their desires to themselves. Separated from her consort Theletos (Will), she suffered a passion that had already first arisen in the sphere of Nous and Aletheia, but now broke out more intensely in this last of the Aeons. Her temerity was a striving, based on the fact that, unlike Nous, she was not in communion with the perfect Father. Hence her passion was the desire to search into the Father and comprehend his greatness. But she undertook something impossible for one of her nature and that caused her to be extremely distressed, since the Father's nature is endlessly deep and unsearchable, whereas she felt a great love and longing that ceaselessly drew her to him because his nature is so attractive. In this striving she would have been swallowed up and absorbed into the universal substance had she not been restrained by the power that supports and watches over everything outside of the infinite being, by Horos (Boundary), who held her back and pointed out the limits of her nature. In turning back to herself and having been convinced that the Father is beyond comprehension, her previous intention vanished and with it also the passion that had been driving her.

The divide had indeed become wider, but there was still more to come. Sophia was of course brought back again to herself, and the syzygy[5] from which she had torn

---

3. The total number of Aeons is thirty, divided into an Ogdoad (eight), a Decad (ten), and a Dodecad (twelve). Those forming the Ogdoad are: the Proarche (Bythus) and Thought (Ennoia, or Sige); Nous (also called the Only-Begotten) and Truth (Aletheia); Logos and Life (Zoe); Humankind (Anthropos), and Church (Ecclesia). [*Ed.* Baur's shorter version is filled in here with details from Irenaeus, *Against Heresies* 1.1.1 (*ANF* 1:316).] Logos and Life bring forth ten others, and Human Being and Church produce twelve additional Aeons. All of these concepts, hypostatized as Aeons, are the categories by which the absolute being must be conceptualized, in other words are the logic of the divine thinking itself.

4. *Against Heresies* 1.2.1. [*Ed.*] This and the following paragraphs paraphrase passages from the initial chapters of Irenaeus.

5. [*Ed.*] A syzygy is a pair of things, especially a pair of opposites. Baur's presentation of the Valentinian system makes it sound a bit like a macro version of quantum entanglement theory! Everything

herself loose was restored. This could only have happened through a new potency, which the Father for this reason produced by means of the Only-Begotten (Monogenes), namely the aforementioned Horos, who is also called Stauros (the Cross), Lytrotes (the Ransom), Carpistes (the Fruit), Horothetes (Boundary Setter), and Metagoges (Repentance). All of these names are supposed to designate the separate and exclusive attributes of this potency: holding fast (στηρίζιν, to make fast, as attribute of σταυρός, the Cross); restoring; leading back; setting bounds to each.[6] So that what happened in the case of Sophia would not be repeated with any other Aeon, the Only-Begotten, acting in accord with the Father's providential will, caused a new syzygy, Christ and the Holy Spirit, to come forth in order to fortify and strengthen the Pleroma, a syzygy influencing all the Aeons to maintain their perfection. For Christ instructed them about the nature of the syzygies and about the essence or nature of the Father: that his being is inaccessible and incomprehensible, and cannot be seen or heard by anyone other than solely through the mediation of the Only-Begotten; that the Holy Spirit plays this intermediary role equally for all of them, and imparts to them a state of true repose, so that, in the complete Pleroma, now brought to a state of rest, what prevailed was the most blissful delight in, and glorification of, the Father.

In this blissful feeling the whole Pleroma of the Aeons, with the concurrence of Christ and the Holy Spirit, and with the Father's approval, resolved that they all would unite the most beautiful and most excellent thing that each of them had, thus producing, for the honor and glory of Bythus, a perfect beauty, a shining star, the most excellent fruit, namely Jesus, whom they also called Soter or Savior, and Christ, and Logos, and Everything, because he is from all of them. Only in this way can the unity and harmony of the Pleroma itself be secured. While the Pleroma disperses into a series of beings, there must be a counterweight to this force expressing itself via emanation, that is, another force guiding what is emanated back to unity, reconnecting the Aeons

---

constituting the Pleroma is paired with its opposite, and these pairs collectively point back to the absolute oneness. Stated in very oversimplified terms: Quantum entanglement involves pairs or groups of particles, which interact and cannot be described independently of each other. They comprise the quantum system as a whole. Viewed in this way, Gnostic speculation does not seem quite so far-fetched: it mythologizes the categories of foundational reality (n. 3). See further below on Platonic aspects of the system (next section), Pythagorean number theory (n. 44), the Ophites' view of Nous as a serpent-like "entwining" of things (n. 90), and the symbolic, mythical form of these systems (last section of Part Two).

6. See August Neander, *Genetische Entwickelung der vornehmsten gnostischen Systeme* (Berlin, 1818), 111. With the Gnostic Horos recalling the Egyptian Horus, the son of Osiris, as it does for Jacques Matter, *Histoire critique du Gnosticisme* (2 vols., Paris, 1828), 2:134, we have one of those vague combinations so often encountered in the critical history of Gnosticism. In ch. 2 of the *Excerpta ex scriptis Theodoti* (n. 2), the activity of Horos is described in general terms as separating the world from the Pleroma. According to Epiphanius, *Against Heresies*, ch. 15, Horos has two activities: as Stauros, an inwardly strengthening activity; as Horos, an outwardly separating and dividing activity. Should this remind us of a related matter, it is Philo's statement about the Logos in *Who Is the Heir of Divine Things?*, that the Father who creates all things has given to the Logos, the archangel and most ancient word, as the most splendid gift, that of setting the boundary (μεθόριος στάς) between what is begotten and what is created.

to the oneness. Hence these similar beings—Horos, Christ, the Holy Spirit, Jesus—are additions to the already set number of Aeons but without going beyond these Aeons. That is because, just as the Only-Begotten certainly also unites in himself both the outgoing tendency and the returning tendency, these additions present, so to speak, just one particular aspect belonging to the nature of the Aeons, unity with the absolute. For the most secure bond of spiritual beings resides in their being clearly aware of their relation to the absolute; and for them all collectively it resides in a commonality adjusting the nature of each of them to the natures of the rest. There is indeed a reason for using distinctively Christian terms for these potencies who establish and secure the oneness of the emanated Aeons with the absolute; because in the big picture the main role of Christianity is to lead everything back to oneness or unity, and to bring about the consciousness of oneness with the absolute.

Accordingly, the principle of conscious oneness functions in this highest region of the spirit world in the same way as it does down here below. As all of this serves to perfect the Pleroma, so too Sophia is reinstated in her relation to the Pleroma. However, this reinstatement in fact only pertains to one aspect of her being, whereas the other aspect no longer belongs to the Pleroma. When Sophia sought, with unsuccessful and audacious efforts, to fathom the incomprehensible being of the primal Father, she gave birth to an amorphous substance, whereupon she felt grief and fear, and was in the most tormented state. This amorphous substance is none other than that negativity and imperfection of which Sophia was aware when she sought to become wholly conscious of the absolute; and what she experienced in doing so is the very natural expression of a nature become conscious of its own negativity. She was able to be upheld in unity with the Pleroma only by the cessation of her former desire and the passion bound up with it.[7] In other words, it was only because she held fast internally and more forcefully to the positive element expressing itself within her, and allowing her to know the absolute in a way suited to her own nature, that Sophia overcame within herself the negativity of her own nature.

Yet once that negative element had entered into consciousness, it could only be overcome but not eradicated. It simply did not harmonize with the relations among the Aeons, with the Pleroma where each of the Aeons was supposed, in its own place, to represent within itself the absolute being. Thus the negative element had to find a place suitable to it outside the Pleroma. That is why the Valentinian myth has the negative element relegated to being expelled like an aborted fetus, separate from the mother who bore it. This was indeed at the instruction of Horos, who—in the way he sets the limits for each being, also therefore the twofold aspects in the nature of each—separates the positive from the negative, the higher from the lower, the divine from

---

7. [*Ed.*] In the text Baur includes the Greek of *Against Heresies* 1.2.2, repeated in the 1.2.4 passage he is now paraphrasing: προτέρα ἐνθύμησις, her "earlier inborn idea." This *enthymesis* of Sophia is what needed to be expelled from her. It does not disappear but, according to Irenaeus, remains a "spiritual substance" that is nevertheless "amorphous."

the finite.⁸ Thus that product, engendered like it bubbles up from some boiling material, now lies in an empty, darkened place. It is spirit in its profoundest self-divestment and finitization, the finite spirit in which the negative, completely obscured spiritual life must gradually come out from the lowest level and return to consciousness.

But the Christ dwelling on high took pity on that formless being through the mediation of Stauros (that is, of Horos, inasmuch as Horos is the power securing the being of this substance), and gave it a shape, but only with regard to its being but not with regard to consciousness [or knowledge].⁹ Whereupon Christ withdrew his influence, so that Sophia's Achamoth,¹⁰ left to itself, felt her suffering, the result of separation from the Pleroma. This awakened in her a longing for better things, for she now had at least a certain whiff of immortality that had been left to her by Christ and the Holy Spirit. After she had gained a shape and become intelligent, but suddenly saw herself deserted by the Logos who had been invisibly present to her, that is, by Christ, she sought to take hold of the light that had forsaken her. But she could not reach it because she was prevented from doing so by Horos, who at that time first uttered the name IAO.¹¹ Since Horos rendered her incapable of carrying out her intention, she then just became immersed in her suffering and was left solely on the outside with her suffering-filled state in all its manifold forms. They were not merely, as with her mother, the initial Sophia, the Aeon, a series of changing emotional states. Instead they followed as wholly contradictory to one another. Sometimes she wept and lamented that she was left alone in darkness and destitution (κένωμα), and sometimes she burst out laughing. When she thought about the light that had forsaken her, she

8. In order to correctly understand the concept of this abortion (ἔκτρωμα), we should look especially to Irenaeus, *Against Heresies* 1.2.4: "For the enthymesis (or inborn idea) of Sophia having been taken away from her, along with its supervening passion, she herself certainly remained within the Pleroma; but her enthymesis, with its passion, was separated from her by Horos, fenced off and expelled from that circle. This enthymesis was no doubt a spiritual substance, possessing some of the natural tendencies of an Aeon, but at the same time shapeless and without form, because it had received nothing" [*ANF* 1:318]. The enthymesis (ἐνθύμησις), together with its passion (πάθος), is therefore what enters Sophia's consciousness with regard to the absolute; is what in fact disposes her negatively to the absolute; is incapable of grasping the absolute. This is also why the abortion, or the inborn idea, is something purely negative insofar as it is separated from the Sophia Aeon; it is spirit insofar as it is the negation of the absolute; it is divested of absoluteness and finds itself, as it were, outside of the absolute, hence is a formless and shapeless being. As such, it is not-knowing, "what has received nothing." See 1.4.1: "For she [the enthymesis] was excluded from light and the Pleroma, and was without form or figure, like an untimely birth, because she had received nothing [from a male parent]" [*ANF* 1:320]. The passage from 1.2.4 concludes: "And on this account they say that it was an imbecile and feminine production" [*ANF* 1:318].

9. [*Ed.*] Baur is paraphrasing Irenaeus, 1.4.1, and adding his own interpolations, including "consciousness" for the word γνῶσις in the Greek passage he provides within our text. The remaining sentences in this paragraph continue the paraphrase from this same passage (*ANF* 1:320–21).

10. [*Ed.*] Achamoth is a Hebrew equivalent of Greek Sophia. The Gnostics depict her as Sophia's daughter, and she has an important role for them in creating and managing the world, even becoming the bride of Christ.

11. [*Ed.*] The footnote in *ANF* 1:321 suggests that this likely is meant to correspond to the Hebrew name for God.

was struck with terror. She thought life too might abandon her like the light did, and she was dismayed and beside herself. She also shifted into a particular frame of mind where she gravitated toward the one who had imparted life to her.

In this state where she ran the gamut of suffering and could not rise above it, she turned in urgent supplication to the light that had forsaken her, to Christ.[12] Since Christ had already gone back into the Pleroma and did not wish to come out a second time, he sent the Paraclete, that is, Soter (the Savior). The Father gave all power to Soter and made everything subject to him. The Aeons did likewise, so that "in him all things in heaven and on earth were created, things visible and invisible, whether thrones or dominions or rulers or powers" (Col 1:16). So Soter came to Achamoth, accompanied by the angels, his companions. At first Achamoth modestly covered herself with a veil. But when she saw him nigh with all his endowments, she ran to him, and acquired higher power from his appearing. He then gave her the form of conscious intelligence and healed her from her passions, except that he could not completely divorce them from her, or remove them, as had been done for the higher Sophia, because they had taken deeper root with Achamoth. Yet in her case too a culling took place: incorporeal passion passed over into an incorporeal [unorganized] matter.[13] This matter congealed into body, from which there arose two substances, an evil one, from passion, and one subject to passion or suffering, from longing (ἐπιστροφή). The formative power of Soter brought this about. But when Achamoth was freed from her passion, her beholding the lights of Soter, that is, the angels accompanying him, filled her with such great joy that it made her fruitful and she brought forth a spiritual fruit in their image, the pneumatic or spiritual element as a third principle in addition to the material (*hylisch*) principle, the product of Sophia's passion, and the psychical principle arisen from her longing.

These three principles then had to be given form and shape. Because the pneumatic principle was of the same nature as Achamoth or this Sophia, she could not herself give it form. That is why the main object of her formative activity is the psychical element, and she applied to it what she had learned from Soter. First of all she formed from the psychical element the Father and King of the psychical domain, also called the right hand, as well as of the hylic or material domain, the left hand. Then he (the Demiurge) formed all of this, being moved, but unknowingly, by the mother. Thus he is also called "Metropator, Apator, Demiurge, and Father"—"Father" in relation

---

12. J. C. L. Gieseler has quite correctly shown (in his review of Neander and Lewald in the *Allgemeine Literatur-Zeitung* 104 (April 1823), p. 841) that Christ cannot be the product of the enthymesis, or of Sophia existing outside the Pleroma—as Neander (in *Genetische Entwickelung* [n. 6], 118) wants to have this regarded as Valentinus' original view, according to the *Excerpta ex scriptis Theodoti* [n. 2]), chs. 23, 31–33, and 39. The entire context of the Valentinian system obviously precludes that assumption.

13. [*Ed.*] The footnote in the *ANF* translation (1:322) refers to Baur's text here, as well as to the standard text of Irenaeus (Harvey). It also cites an emendation of the text that would make it read "corporeal matter."

to the right hand or the psychical domain, "Demiurge" in relation to the left hand or hylic domain, and "King" in relation to the whole.[14] Everything heavenly or earthly, everything hylic or psychical, everything of the right or the left hand, everything easy or difficult, everything mounting upward or sinking downward, is created by the Demiurge, such that Achamoth produced it but the Demiurge supposed that he is the creator of all this. He formed the heavens but was ignorant of the heavens; he formed human beings yet did not know them. He made the earth manifest without knowing the earth. In thinking altogether about what he created, he did not even know his mother herself. Yet he believed that he is all things and therefore had it proclaimed via the prophet: "I am the Lord and there is no other; besides me there is no god."[15] As we already stated, the Demiurge himself was made from the psychical element. Everything hylic or material arose from the three affective states of fear, grief, and perplexity, whereas the psychical element arose from fear and longing. Thus the Demiurge gained his existence from longing. The other psychical natures arose from fear. The corporeal elements—the souls of unreasoning creatures, of beasts and of human beings (to the extent that they are merely psychical beings)—came forth from dismay and perplexity, which are nevertheless ignoble affects. The latter, corporeal stage is the extreme point where spirit has completely divested itself of its nature and become rigid, completely tied to material being utterly devoid of consciousness.

Nevertheless, in the finite world created by the Demiurge the pneumatic principle also has at least some presence alongside the psychical and hylic principles. Of course spirit can increasingly divest itself of its own nature, can take on finite and bodily form in the psychical and hylic domains. However, the distinctive, substantial character of its nature, the pneumatic element, can never completely vanish. It always remains the positive factor, in relation to which the psychical and hylic elements are simply something negative.

This brings us to the creation of human beings in connection with the world's creation. The spirit struggles to rise up again from that lowest point at which its spiritual consciousness is obscured and has died down, as the negation of the Pleroma, and spirit must work its way upward. This is its coming to consciousness, and the separation of the principles, the setting aside of the psychic and the hylic elements, can only serve to concentrate the pneumatic element at a central point where the light of consciousness can dawn in it. This obviously makes clear what an important place the creation of the human being occupies in this entire process of spirit's development. Spirit is of course a creation of the Demiurge.[16] Yet only the hylic element and the

---

14. [*Ed.*] "Metropator" indicates that he proceeded solely from his mother, Achamoth. "Apator" indicates that he had no male parent.

15. [*Ed.*] Isaiah 45:5, reiterated in v. 6.

16. In ch. 2.8 of Clement of Alexandria's *Stromata* we find some special features concerning the creation of human beings, cited from a letter by Valentinus. It states that the created human being was the product of the angels, but they were terrified regarding their own work because the primordial human being presented itself in Adam. According to Irenaeus (1.5.5) the human being was indeed

psychical element (the breath of life, which the Demiurge breathed into him) and the sensible body (χιτὼν δερμάτινος) stemmed from him. He had received the pneumatic element in the proper sense from Achamoth. This is that spiritual product that made Achamoth fruitful upon beholding the angels accompanying Soter. Unbeknownst to the Demiurge, she secretly embedded it in the human being so that it imparted the soul created together with the human body. Implanted in the body like a seed, it grew and became capable of receiving into itself the fullness of reason. So unbeknownst to the Demiurge, Sophia thus implanted the spiritual human being with a mysterious, divine capacity or function, along with what the Demiurge breathed into it. Just as the Demiurge did not know his mother, so too he did not know her seed the church, the image of the church above. So a human being has a soul from the Demiurge, a body from the earth, flesh from matter, and spiritual humanity from the mother, Achamoth.

As the spiritual principle placed into human beings increasingly develops itself and takes shape as self-conscious life, the course of the world proceeds further toward its appointed goal. For its completion appears when all that is spiritual is formed and perfected by knowledge, that is, when all the pneumatic or spiritual persons have perfect knowledge of God and, as the Valentinians pride themselves for being, are initiated into the mysteries by Achamoth.[17] There is no special procedure of redemption, for what enters into the Pleroma is simply the offspring, the pneumatic principle that indeed was initially just a feeble seed but then attains its perfection.[18] What is from matter is hardly capable of salvation; and what is pneumatic can hardly be excluded from it, or be subject to destruction. As gold does not lose its beauty when immersed in filth, so too there is nothing a person does that can damage the nature of what is spiritual.

Nevertheless at a certain time this system has a redemptive activity playing a role in the world's course. That is because the actual target of redemption is the psychical element lying in between the material and pneumatic aspects, where it can incline to one of them or the other. The pneumatic element itself is sent out in order to take on a form linked with the psychical aspect, and is fashioned in a symbiotic relationship with it. Since this is the purpose behind creating the world, the Savior or Redeemer (Soter) also appears in order to rescue what is psychical and has free will. But the Redeemer himself had to have within him the first fruits of what he was said to redeem. That is why he received the spiritual element from Achamoth. The Demiurge invested him with the psychical Christ. By a special dispensation he was enclosed in a body of psychical substance, one organized with marvelous skill so that he could be

---

originally made from matter: "not taking him from this dry earth, but from an invisible substance, consisting of fusible and fluid matter" [*ANF* 1:323]. Only afterward was he enveloped in an animal exterior or body, so Valentinus doubtless assumed it was only as a consequence of falling from the higher region of paradise because of sin that the human being plunged down into this world.

17. Irenaeus, *Against Heresies* 1.6.1.
18. Ibid., 1.6.4.

visible and tangible, and be capable of suffering. He only lacked matter, for matter is incapable of redemption.[19]

But the fact, as stated here, that the Redeemer received what is spiritual from Achamoth, whereas the Redeemer himself awakened the spiritual life within Achamoth, doubtless gets explained by what Irenaeus introduces as just the opinion of a few,[20] but at the same time seems to express the more specific sense of the Valentinian system. It is that the Demiurge also sent a Christ [i.e., Anointed One] as his own son, but only a psychical son. The prophets have spoken about him, and he is the one who passed through Mary as water flows through a tube. When he came to be baptized, that Soter who was in the Pleroma, as the joint product of all the Aeons, descended upon him in the form of a dove—although the spiritual seed received from Achamoth was within him.[21] The Redeemer's effectiveness could only consist in his making people clearly conscious of the pneumatic and psychical aspects, of the spiritual character of their natures, of the spiritual world to which they belong, and of the primal Father, the original source of the spiritual life in all spiritual natures. The Redeemer could only awaken and elicit what was already inherent in every nature related to God but initially was still dormant in them as a hidden seed.

At the time when Soter, together with his angels of light, appeared to Achamoth in the depths of her suffering, he simply reawakened in her what could never have been extinguished in her as a daughter of the Sophia above. It is therefore the same Redeemer who caused those human beings, to whom Achamoth had imparted these very seeds of light, to have in them the clear light of self-conscious spiritual life. Then, when the original sparks of light that just lie dormant in the pneumatic natures, but can never be extinguished, shine forth again in this way and illumine their entire consciousness, what happens is that the Father who is called solely good, who freely works via the revelation of the Son, of the heart that solely via him can be pure and freed of every evil spirit, has mercy so that this heart is made holy and shines full of light.[22]

19. Ibid., 1.6.1.

20. Ibid., 1.7.2.

21. So Matter's statement (in *Histoire critique* [n. 6], 2:146) about the Redeemer on high, that he is the one who came into the world through the Virgin Mary as water flows through a tube, is incorrect. Epiphanius of course makes this statement (in *Against Heresies* 31.4) about Soter (= Jesus), although when he distinguishes Christ from Horos (= Soter) and identifies Horos with Jesus, and says about Jesus that he passed through Mary ὡς διὰ σωλῆνος (as through a pipe), Epiphanius fails to state that this can only be understood as referring to the psychical messiah of the Demiurge.

22. See Clement of Alexandria, *Stromata* 2.20, in the passage citing a letter of Valentinus [*ANF* 2:372]. Since the Redeemer just awakens the dormant consciousness, redemption itself simply consists in knowledge of the absolute. In Irenaeus, *Against Heresies* 1.21.4, the Gnostic teaching is "that the knowledge of the unspeakable Greatness is itself perfect redemption" [*ANF* 1:346]. Since falling away, and suffering, and ignorance have come about, this entire world-order based on ignorance can only be set right again by knowledge (γνῶσις). That is why Gnosis is the redemption of the inner person. Gnosis pertains neither to the transitory body nor to the soul that itself arose from the fall. Instead it is spiritual. The inner human being, the spiritual person, is redeemed by Gnosis, so that it is what gains its complete liberation through knowledge of the whole. This is true redemption.

The fact that the efficacy of the Redeemer is to be considered from this perspective is also made clear in Irenaeus[23] from what the Gnostics teach about his suffering. The pneumatic Redeemer was free from any suffering, since he who is invisible and imperceptible also cannot undergo suffering. That is why the Spirit of Christ who had descended upon him departed from him when he was brought before Pilate. Certainly not even the seed of light he received from the mother [Achamoth] suffered, for this is also incapable of suffering, since it too is of a spiritual nature and was not seen even by the Demiurge. Thus only the psychical Christ underwent suffering, as well as what, by a special divine dispensation, was linked to him in a mystical way. Yet this suffering had just typological significance. Through the suffering Christ, the mother Achamoth wanted to present an image of the Christ above, who displayed himself through [the figure of] Stauros, the Cross, and gave substantial form to Achamoth. For everything that took place here has a typological relation to what is above, on high.

They also speak[24] of the Lord appearing, in the last of the world's periods, to suffer in order to indicate the passion experienced by the last one of the Aeons, and to make known through his own end the ending of the process that took place in the Aeons' world. But the course of the world in time is ended[25] when all the spiritual seeds have fully sprouted. Then Achamoth, their mother, left her intermediate place and, entering into the Pleroma, received her bridegroom, the Soter who had arisen from the collective Aeon world. The two of them now form a syzygy. Talk of a bridegroom and a bride is to be understood as a syzygy, and the entire Pleroma itself is a bridal chamber. For when the pneumatic ones have set aside their souls and have become intelligent spirits, they are given as brides to the angels who stand around the Redeemer. The Demiurge then comes to occupy the place of the mother Sophia, the intermediate place that is also the place of rest for the souls of the righteous. That is because nothing of a psychical nature can enter into the Pleroma. When all this has taken place, then the fire hidden within the world will break out, and, when it has consumed all that is from matter, the fire itself will burn out, falling into nothingness (*Nichtsein*).[26]

## The Platonic Foundation of This System

In looking back at this system as a whole, it is certainly correct to say that, in general, its foundations are Platonic. As it unfolds this system traverses three main moments: absolute being, the fall, and the return. Of these three, the idea of the fall is the one that most points back to Platonism.

---

23. *Against Heresies* 1.7.2.
24. Ibid., 1.8.2.
25. [*Ed.*] Baur adds here in parentheses the Greek for: "the end or goal of the troubles among the Aeons."
26. [*Ed.*] This whole paragraph paraphrases Irenaeus, *Against Heresies* 1.7.1.

The difference from Platonism can be found simply in the fact that, in Platonism the fall directly involves individual souls and so is at once thought of in ethical terms, whereas here, in the higher speculative setting of Valentinianism, it concerns the essential nature of spirit itself. In Platonism, the souls sink down from the ideal world owing to their lack of higher spiritual power, and to their moral weakness of will. In the Gnostic system of Valentinus, the one reality divides itself up into the moments of differentiation of the self-dividing, absolute spirit itself. In considering the system as a whole, we must hold firmly to the fact that all those forces and natures emerging sequentially, and interacting in a specific way, are always just in turn the one primal being itself realizing its own immanent concept, via all of these reciprocally self-conditioning moments. That is especially true since we can assign the external form in which they appear simply to the pictorial and mythical form of the system.

What we are always presented with is the internal struggle in which spirit is engaged with itself when, as driven by its own essential being, it is said to go out from itself and yet remain in oneness and identity with itself. As long as this process of spirit takes place for its own sake, still within the Pleroma, the predominant feature remains chiefly the power of spirit staying in itself and adjusting each posited distinction again to the unity. This is where we envision the three potencies that stand on the same level and refer to the same concept: Monogenes (the Only-Begotten), Horos (the Limit), and Christ. However, once the unavoidable break occurs, separating the Sophia below from the Sophia above, spirit then goes out into its negation (out of the Pleroma and into the κένωμα, the destitution), and what commences is the whole labor and effort of spirit grappling with itself to do away once more with the negation set within it and, through all the moments of the mediation process, to press on to the negation of the negation.

That is why the Redeemer, Jesus, stands, so to speak, at the outermost limit of the Pleroma, as the product of the collective Aeons, representing and comprising within himself the entire Pleroma as a unity. He stands here as the guardian spirit guiding the process taking place outside the Pleroma in order to preserve the bond that links the spirit entering into finitude with the absolute, even in his emptying himself of his own proper nature. When he appears to Achamoth, together with his angels of light, he does so to renew in her the radiance of her own essential nature. At the end of the lengthy course in which spirit wrestles with itself and moves onward, in order to arrive at consciousness of its own self, Achamoth—as the unity of all the pneumatic natures that, together with her, strive upward from their labors and troubles—is wedded to Soter, who himself has lowered himself to her with the same urgency and imparted himself to her, just as the innermost longing drives her to him. When all this takes place the Pleroma becomes the bridal chamber, in which bride and bridegroom join together in the most blissful of bonds. Then everything finite and negative is done away with and spirit has overcome its own negation. Then spirit has realized the concept of its own essential nature, has run through the course of its own process of mediation, and has elevated itself to the absolute idea. This is then the region of spirit in which "there flows the River Lethe from which Psyche drinks, when she immerses all pain, forms all the troubles and darkness of time into an illusion, and transfigures it into the radiance of the eternal."[27]

If we proceed from the perspective I have indicated, then we can indeed rightly say that this system is basically modeled on Platonism. It is of course the same basic model that also recurs, with various modifications, in the other Gnostic systems. However, none of the others start out as closely related to Platonism as the Valentinian system is. For the very relationship of the Redeemer to Achamoth, and the passionate longing that in both of them is the bond mediating between the world above and the world below, and ultimately uniting the two as bride and bridegroom, quite clearly calls to mind the Platonic Eros, who in the soul never lets the drive toward eternal beauty rest, and thereby lifts the soul up to the eternal archetype of its own being.

However, what we should mainly look at, with regard to the Platonism of the Valentinian system, is the obvious influence the Platonic theory of ideas has had on its entire structure. The ancient writers themselves already emphasized this as a characteristic feature of the Valentinian system. In chapter 8 of *On the Soul*, Tertullian writes:

> For Plato maintains that there are certain invisible substances, incorporeal, celestial, divine, and eternal, which they call ideas, that is to say (archetypal) forms, which are the patterns and causes of those objects of nature which are manifest to us, appearing to our corporeal senses. The ideas (according to Plato) are the actual verities, and the objects are the images and likenesses of them. Well, now, are there not here gleams of the heretical principles of the Gnostics and the Valentinians? It is from this philosophy that they eagerly adopt the difference between the bodily senses and intellectual faculties—a distinction which they actually apply to the parable of the ten virgins: making the five foolish virgins to symbolize the five bodily senses, seeing that these are so silly and so easy to be deceived; and the wise virgins to express the meaning of the intellectual faculties, which are so wise as to attain to that mysterious and supernal truth, which is placed in the Pleroma. (Here then we have) the mystic original of the ideas of these heretics. For in this philosophy lie both their Aeons and their genealogies. Thus, too, do they divide sensation, both into the intellectual powers from their spiritual seed, and the sensuous faculties from the animal, which cannot by any means comprehend spiritual things. From the former germ spring invisible things; from the latter spring visible things, which are lowly and ephemeral, and which are obvious to the senses, placed as they are in palpable form. [*ANF* 3:197–8]

---

27. [*Ed.*] Baur quotes this passage without a citation, as if it is well-known. The story of Psyche is found in Apuleius, *Metamorphoses* (*the Golden Ass*), chs. 4–6, but the quotation does not seem to be from this source.

The account in Irenaeus not only expresses their basic view that the world below relates to the world above, the sensible finite world to the spirit world, as the image or copy relates to the archetype, or as what is real relates to what is ideal, as the reflection of the ideal.[28] He also explicitly states that the enthymesis (Achamoth), or rather Soter through her as intermediary, created all things in the image of the Aeons in order to honor them. Instead, and simply from this [Platonic] assumption, we could gain a clear picture of the whole system as it is organized according to Irenaeus. What the invisible Father is in the Pleroma, the enthymesis or Achamoth, completely unbeknownst to the Demiurge, is in the world outside the Pleroma. The Demiurge corresponds to the Only-Begotten, as the image representing him, and, in the world of the Demiurge, the archangels and angels he created are parallels to the other Aeons within the Pleroma.[29]

28. [*Ed.*] Within the text Baur gives the Greek of Irenaeus, *Against Heresies* 1.7.2 ("For they declare that all these transactions were counterparts of what took place above" [*ANF*, 1:325]), and of 2.7.1 ("They tell us that, outside the Pleroma, images were made of those things which are within the Pleroma" [*ANF* 1:366]).

29. This is doubtless the meaning of the otherwise obscure passage in Irenaeus, *Against Heresies* 1.5.1: "For they say that this Enthymesis, desirous of making all things to the honor of the Aeons, formed images of them, or rather that the Savior did so through her instrumentality. And she, in the image of the invisible Father, kept herself concealed from the Demiurge. But he was in the image of the only-begotten Son, and the angels and archangels created by him were in the image of the rest of the Aeons" [*ANF* 1:322]. [*Ed.* This passage, which Baur has already paraphrased in the text, appears in Greek in this footnote.] The noteworthy fragment from a homily by Valentinus belongs in this context; Clement of Alexandria presents it in his *Stromata* 4.13. After having quoted a passage from this homily of Valentinus, Clement says that Valentinus assumes there is a group who naturally become blessed. This race set apart has come down to us from on high to abolish death, for death has come about as the work of the creator of the world. That is why Valentinus also accepts the saying, "No one will see the face of God and live" [Exod 33:20], understanding it to mean that death came about because of the creator (therefore no one can see the face of God without having to die first, according to the law of the Demiurge). Valentinus has in mind this very god (the Demiurge) when he writes: "As much as the image is far inferior to the living face, so too is the world far inferior to the living Aeon. What is, then, the cause of the image? The majesty of the countenance that the figure presents to the painter is accordingly honored for its name, because the name augments what the likeness lacks. So too the invisible nature of God has the effect of producing belief in the likeness" [*ANF* 2:425]. Clement continues that Valentinus says about the Demiurge that, since he is called "god" and "father," he is an image of the true God and a prophet, while he understands the "painter" to be Sophia, whose work is to honor the image of the invisible one. For everything proceeding from a syzygy or pairing is a Pleroma, while what proceeds from the one is an image or likeness. But since what is mere appearance, something seen, is not from the one, and the soul is from what is intermediate; thus what is better, namely the infusion of the better spirit and in general what is breathed into the soul, arrives as spirit's likeness. (Here I am interpreting the Greek to mean that "they say it is different," so that the soul cannot be linked with the ψυχή or psychical nature, since ψυχή and πνεῦμα, or spirit, form an antithesis.) On the whole what they say about the Demiurge, to the extent he was created in the image (of God), was foretold prophetically by a sensible image in the things Genesis says about the creation of human beings—a likeness they also carry over to themselves—in their teaching that the Demiurge himself was not aware of the imparting of the better spirit. Accordingly the Demiurge and the world of the Demiurge are a mere imitation of the divine nature. But the mere image, in and for itself, is actually nothing. It only has reality to the extent that the archetype is seen through it, for what is visible calls to mind what is invisible. In other words, the world below relates to the world above as the psychical relates to the pneumatic. Thus in fact what is truly substantial in the world, within the psychical

As the Pleroma forms an Ogdoad in the region of the highest Aeons, the Demiurge likewise creates seven heavens over which he rules, and in virtue of which he himself is called Hebdomad. (These heavens are also thought of as angels, with the Demiurge himself as an angel like unto God.) The mother, Achamoth, is added to form an Ogdoad in order to faithfully correspond to the archetypal number, the primary Ogdoad of the Pleroma. She is also called Sophia, Terra or Earth, Jerusalem, Holy Spirit, and, with a masculine term, Lord. Her place of habitation is an intermediate one, where she is indeed above the Demiurge, but below the Pleroma and outside it, right up to the end of the world's course.[30] As close as she stands to the Pleroma in all these relationships, like the Demiurge she nevertheless belongs to the world found outside the Pleroma.

Like Monogenes, the Only-Begotten within the Pleroma whose likeness the Demiurge bears in himself, the Demiurge is the lord and king of the world he created. His mother, Achamoth, intentionally sought for him to regard himself as the head, and the principle or source of his own being, and as the lord of his entire creation.[31] However, it is evident how in this case the image stands far below the archetype, because the opinion the Demiurge has of himself rests on sheer error. For Monogenes is the true foundation and father of all, because he is not a mere image but is instead directly identical with the primal being itself. Just as the whole process of development manifesting itself in the world below ultimately must already have its prototype in the world above, so too, as already demonstrated in the foregoing presentation, a separation ensues here along with the emanation. Hence the emanating tendency, distancing itself from the unity, must involve a corresponding activity that preserves, sets limits, and restores the unity.

## The Idea of Syzygies

As one of the ideas deeply embedded in the organic structure of the Valentinian system, the idea of the syzygies also calls for special attention, for the whole world of the Aeons divides up into male and female Aeons.

The highest Aeons form the Aeon pairs: Bythus and Ennoia (who is also called Charis and Sige); Monogenes and Aletheia; Logos and Zoe; Anthropos and Ecclesia. Even the highest being takes part in this gender duality. According to Irenaeus,[32] they say that sometimes the Primal Father acts independently of the distinction between male and female (which is why they say about Horos that the Father had him issue forth "in his own image, without conjunction, not womanly"), but also in turn they have him form a syzygy with Sige. In the fragment from a Valentinian writing

---

element, is simply what is πνεῦμα or spirit, as the one and only principle of life.

30. Irenaeus, *Against Heresies* 1.5.3; Epiphanius, *Against Heresies* 31.4.
31. Irenaeus, 1.5.3.
32. *Against Heresies* 1.2.4.

Epiphanius cites,[33] the Primal Father, who encompasses all things and is self-enclosed in a state without consciousness, is the never aging, eternally young Aeon, who is also called male-female (ἀρρενόθηλυς). These three representations are in principle only slightly at variance. One could say the Primal Father is without gender if one simply held fast to the abstract concept of the primal being, and distinguished substance from person in the way that Tertullian does in speaking of such a distinction. He writes: "They call him indeed, as to his essence, Αἰῶν τέλειος (Perfect Aeon), but in respect of his personality, Προαρχή (Before the Beginning), Η Αρχή (the Beginning), and sometimes Bythus (Depth)."[34] The concrete representation makes Ennoia, Charis, or Sige the female Aeon linked with the Primal Father. However this is the same being both male and female, for these names are, in themselves, of course surely mere predicates that are to be regarded as one with the concept of Bythus, seen from an equivalent standpoint, as well as one with the primal being itself. Thus the primal being is male-female, inasmuch as the thought still enclosed within the most profound silence of his essence—that is, his blessed perfection, the Charis in which, however, the highest perfection is already thought of as something imparted—is distinguished from himself. (As Epiphanius, among others, puts it, Charis "has furnished the treasures of Greatness to those from Greatness."[35])

This idea then also corresponds to how the Valentinians describe the original self-revelation of the supreme being. After this being, Bythus, had spent endlessly long stretches of time just together with the one named Ennoia, Charis, or Sige, in the most profound silence and repose, and when he thought to have the principle of all things issue forth from him, he deposited this emanation (προβολή), like a seed, in the womb of Sige who was linked to him. She received it and, becoming pregnant, gave birth to Nous.[36] Epiphanius depicts this spiritual process in what are sensuous terms, in the fragments he presents. He states about Sige that "those who speak truly have addressed her as Silence, since Greatness completed all things through a concept without speech";[37] and that she sought to break through the bonds of silence. She awakened in the absolute being a desire for a female half or side of his own, in order to make Greatness womanish, by his desiring to lie with her. She had intercourse with him and so produced the Primal Father of truth, the one called Anthropos.[38]

33. *Against Heresies* 31.5.

34. Tertullian, *Against the Valentinians*, ch. 7 [ANF 3:506].

35. [Ed.] Epiphanius, *Against Heresies* 31.5.2. *The Panarion of St. Epiphanius, Bishop of Salamis*, trans. and ed. Philip R. Amidon (Oxford, 1990), 111.

36. Irenaeus, *Against Heresies* 1.1.1.

37. [Ed.] Epiphanius, *Against Heresies* 31.5.2 (Amidon, 111).

38. In his *Genetische Entwickelung* (n. 6), p. 209, Neander mentions a passage in Clement of Alexandria, *Who Is the Rich Man?*, that describes the supreme being's self-revelation and imparting of life in this same sense. But this "becoming womanish" (θηλύνεσθαι), this drive to impart oneself, which, as has already been pointed out, is itself indeed a passion (πάθος), is always thought of as an inclination linked to what is finite. Clement, in *Stromata* 13.93, says about Cassian, a follower of Valentinus, that

The emanation of the subsequent Aeons took place in the same way. Thereupon Sige produced the natural unity of light with Anthropos and revealed Aletheia (Truth), who rightly bears this name because she is in truth like unto the mother, Sige. Aletheia then awakens in her Father a desire for her, and they join together in immortal union, from which then proceeds a spiritual male-female tetrad as counterpart to the first tetrad, which consists of Bythus and Sige, the Father and Aletheia. The tetrad taking shape from the Father and Sige is formed by Anthropos and Ecclesia, Logos and Zoe. A decad and a dodecad then originate in similar fashion.[39] This all proves very clearly how the Valentinian system has hardly any reservations about connecting up with pagan religion itself in its ordinary polytheistic configuration. In the old religions the divine realm divided up into gods and goddesses, and the entire theogonic and cosmogonic system was structured by sexual relationships and the concept of procreation. Even the primal being itself was fairly often thought of as male-female. So that is how the Valentinians portrayed their world of Aeons.

However, this sexual dualism is consistent with the Platonism of the Valentinian system owing to the view that there can be nothing in the created, real world here below that does not have an archetype in the ideal world above. Hence the contrasting male and female principles appearing everywhere in the visible, natural world, and being all-pervasive throughout the entire, sensible universe in the most varied forms, cannot be at all foreign to the world of spirits. This arrangement must be supremely grounded in absolute being itself—in what is the universal, absolute principle of all existing being, simply because its influence is all-pervasive and it contains within itself the seeds, principles, and original forms or archetypes of everything.

But this sexual dualism has a still deeper significance, and is more closely connected with the Platonic theory of ideas in the way the Valentinian system appropriated it. In the theory of ideas, spelled out strictly according to the contrast or antithesis between the ideal and the real, what is ideal is alone what is substantial, and the real relates to the ideal only in the way the likeness or copy is related to the archetype existent in itself. Of course it is the nature of the idea that, in order to reveal itself, it reflects itself in an image of its own being. However, this reflection, this image, is always just a mere semblance of true reality, an appearance that is not itself the nature of the thing itself. The image has its being and substance only in dependence on something other than itself.[40]

---

"our brilliant friend must take a more Platonic view and imagine that the soul is divine in origin and has come to our world of birth and decay after being made effeminate by desire" [*Clement of Alexandria, Stromateis, Books One to Three*, trans. John Ferguson, Fathers of the Church (Washington, D.C., 1991), 315]. Plato himself, in this same sense, has those who live unjustly being changed from men to women upon their rebirth. See *Timaeus* 42c, 91a.

39. [*Ed.*] In the text Baur gives the Greek from Epiphanius, *Against Heresies* 31.5.8–9: "a dodecad of masculofeminine procreative powers . . . a decad of procreative powers who are also masculofeminine" (Amidon, 111).

40. The term ὑστέρημα (defect) is also said to designate this relation or disparity between the world

The contrast or antithesis between male and female in the Valentinian system has precisely this significance. What is female or "womanly" is what is dependent, imperfect, deficient, what has its support and subsistence only in what is male.[41] What is female just serves to allow what is male to come forward in the appearance according to a specific aspect of its being. The fact that the Valentinians conceived of the relation of the female to the male in this way demonstrates that they explain the initial set of eight Aeons in terms of its four male members. Irenaeus says[42] this "first-begotten Ogdoad is the root and substance of all things." He says it goes by "four names": Bythus, Nous, Logos, and Anthropos. "For each of these is masculo-feminine, as follows: Propator [the Primal Father] was united by a conjunction [syzygy] with his Ennoia; then Monogenes [the Only-Begotten], that is, Nous, with Aletheia; Logos with Zoe, and Anthropos with Ecclesia." Therefore this initial series of Aeons indeed forms an Ogdoad, although what in fact sustains the Ogdoad is the substantial element in it, which consists simply of the four masculine Aeons, as compared to which the feminine Aeons, who are of course covered by the masculine ones, do not come under consideration.

The number four leads us to a further point. Irenaeus himself remarks[43] that the Valentinians have called the first two pairs of Aeons—Bythus and Sige, Monogenes and Aletheia—the first and original "Pythagorean tetrad," and "the root of all things."

---

below and the world above. It refers to the Demiurge, or rather to the world he rules, inasmuch as it originated as the result of a fall (Irenaeus says, of a "defect," in 1.21.4). In 3.4.1–3 of *Against Heresies*, Epiphanius writes: "... which Deficiency they also call Almighty and Demiurge and creator of substances. They say further that a later Ogdoad, copied from the first Ogdoad, was created by Deficiency after seven heavens, it being in the Ogdoad and having made seven heavens after the Ogdoad. To this Deficiency they wish to join a virgin aeon which is without a female counterpart" [Amidon, 110]. The latter is Horus = Soter = Jesus. On account of this defect or deficiency, of the image always falling short of the archetype, the unity of the world above is divided and scattered into a multiplicity. This idea is best expressed in Irenaeus, 1.17.2, with reference to Marcus the Valentinian and his followers: "They declare that the Demiurge, desiring to imitate the infinitude, and eternity, and immensity, and freedom from all measurement by time of the Ogdoad above, but, as he was the fruit of the defect [of Achamoth and her fall], being unable to express its permanence and eternity, had recourse to the expedient of spreading out its eternity into times, and seasons, and vast numbers of years, imaging that by the multitude of such times he might imitate its immensity. [*Ed.* See the obviously similar-sounding statement in Plato, *Timaeus* 37d–e.] They declare further, that the truth having escaped him, he followed that which was false, and that, for this reason, when the times are fulfilled, his work will perish" [*ANF* 1:343–3]. Just as the one Primal Aeon fragments into a series of Aeons and this accordingly gives rise to a world, so at the end of the world these Aeons return again to the oneness of the Primal Aeon. Here we then have the wreath that, in the beautiful Manichean hymn (see my *Das manichäische Religionssystem* [Tübingen, 1831], 16ff.), encircles the head of the great king in the age of the Aeons.

41. Hence the previously-cited passage from Clement of Alexandria (*Stromata* 4.13) says: "The things which proceed from a pair (ἐκ συζυγίας) are complements, and those which proceed from one are images (εἰκόνες)" [*ANF* 2:425]. That is, the full reality of the Aeon is always just in the linkage of the female principle with the male principle; but where the female principle operates on its own (as it does in Achamoth), what arises is always an unsubstantial image.

42. *Against Heresies* 1.1.1 [*ANF* 1:316].

43. Ibid.

The Pythagoreans gave this same sacred meaning to the number four. For them it was the source and root of eternal nature.[44] So this points us back to the Pythagorean doctrine of numbers, and directly throws light on the only possible explanation for why the Valentinians also regarded just the four male Aeons as the substantial elements of the initial Ogdoad. When we put these four Aeons in the series with their female partners in the syzygies, the four form the number sequence 1, 3, 5, 7, which makes it clear that the well-known Pythagorean doctrine of the relations of odd and even numbers finds its application in the relations of male and female Aeons. For the Pythagoreans an odd number is complete and perfect, whereas an even number is incomplete and imperfect.[45] Indeed they themselves called the odd number male and the even number female. For them, right and left have this same significance.

This is very helpful in gaining a deeper understanding of the Valentinian system. Wherever we find the female aspect standing alongside the male aspect, she is the aspect turned away from the purity and substantiality of the idea, the innate propensity of the idea to go outside itself and manifest itself. Hence only the four male Aeons constitute the actual substance of the Ogdoad. They are the very ones whose role it is to keep the substantiality of being intact; to counter the fall from being into nonbeing; to assure that each nature is sustained in its existence. Horos does not have a female counterpart. The fact that the female Aeon's being is dependent and imperfect simply explains why she is always in turn conceptually linked with a male Aeon.

Irenaeus is explicit on this point:

> It is impossible that the thought (Ennoia) of any one, or his silence (Sige) should be understood apart from himself; and that, being sent forth beyond him, it should possess a special figure of its own . . . But if this be so, then

---

44. The Pythagoreans said about the number four (the τετράκτυς) that it is "the everlasting spring or source, containing the root of all nature." They also called this "holding the keys (κλειδουχός) of nature." See also: Massuet, *Dissertationes praeviae* to his edition of Irenaeus (Introduction, nn. 40–41), xxvii; the older work on this topic by J. Meursius, *Denarius Pythagoricus* (1631); A. Boeckh, "Über die Bildung der Weltseele im Timäos des Platon," in the *Studien* of K. Daub and G. F. Creuzer, 3 (1807), 54ff. In 2.14.6 of *Against Heresies*, Irenaeus himself calls attention to the connection of Valentinian teachings with those of the Pythagoreans: "As to the desire they exhibit to refer this whole universe to numbers, they have learned it from the Pythagoreans. For these were the first who set forth numbers as the initial principle of all things, and [describe] that initial principle of theirs as being both equal and unequal" [*ANF* 1:377]. Numbers are the principles of what is living and what is inanimate, of form and matter. "They further affirm that Hen—that is, One—is the first principle of all things, and the substance of all that has been formed. From this again proceeded the Dyad, the Tetrad, the Pentad, and the manifold generation of the others. These things the heretics repeat, word for word, with reference to their Pleroma and Bythus. From the same source, too, they strive to bring into vogue those conjunctions which proceed from unity. Marcus boasts of such views as if they were his own—the tetrad of Pythagoras as the originating principle and mother of all things" (Irenaeus, 2.14.6 [*ANF* 1:377–78]).

45. [*Ed.*] Presumably this is because an odd number cannot be evenly divided by 2 (this is its "purity" and "substantiality"), whereas an even number can be. An even number is dependent on its pair. This mathematical theory does not take into account that the male is dependent on its pair, the female, for reproduction, i.e., for its very existence.

> just like Bythus and Sige, so also Nous and Aletheia will form one and the same being, ever cleaving mutually together. And inasmuch as the one cannot be conceived of without the other, just as water cannot [be conceived of] without [the thought of] moisture, or fire without [the thought of] heat, or a stone without [the thought of] hardness (for these things are mutually bound together, and the one cannot be separated from the other, but always co-exists with it), so it befits Bythus to be united in the same way with Ennoia, and Nous with Aletheia. Logos and Zoe again, as being sent forth by those that are thus united, ought themselves to be united, and to constitute only one being. But, according to such a process of reasoning, Anthropos and Ecclesia too, and indeed all the remaining syzygies of the Aeons produced, ought to be united, and always to co-exist, the one with the other. For they think it necessary that a female Aeon should exist side by side with a male one, inasmuch as she is, so to speak, [the putting-forth of] his affection.[46]

Therefore the female Aeon takes a back seat, as merely a state or attribute of the other one (*affectio ejus*), as a mere accidental feature in the essential nature of the male Aeon's substance. This view had to be the result as soon as one sought to adjust the series of Aeons as much as possible to the idea of the absolute, and in each of them to catch sight of simply a new expression and reflection of the absolute.

Seen from this perspective, then, not only do the four female Aeons simply go hand in hand with the four male ones; also, three of the male Aeons—Anthropos, Logos, and Monogenes—just present themselves as different names for one and the same concept, that of the Primal Being objectifying himself in his own image or likeness. It is the very same aspect of the Pleroma in which Horos, no longer to be differentiated from Monogenes himself, most strictly sees to it that the absolute not go forth out of itself.

However, if we look to the other aspect of the Pleroma, where the absolute reveals itself, the idea has a reflection of itself, and the ideal is said to become something real, then we of course have Ennoia who stands beside the Primal Father as his own thought when she wishes to express the deep secret of uncommunicative Sige on the way to finitizing the absolute. As the system further unfolds, this is where there appear, in their full extent, the antitheses of finite and infinite, ideal and real, the higher and lower realms. When one contemplates these things there is always a female Aeon in the picture.

Hence it is Sophia, the last one of the female Aeons, who becomes the originator of the disharmony arising within the Pleroma itself. She plays this role simply in virtue of her separating herself from the male Aeon, Theletos, who is linked with her. This act also had to break the bond connecting her with the absolute, and only a female Aeon could have had such a fate as befell her daughter Achamoth—that she separated from the Pleroma and, vacillating between being and non-being, she had to establish

---

46. Irenaeus, *Against Heresies* 2.12.2 [ANF 1:371].

for herself a new realm in the world of appearance. Thus she stands at the apex of the real, finite world, and in contrast the male Aeon, Jesus—characterized as wedded to her yet now separated from her as long as time shall last—represents in himself the entire Pleroma. What the Valentinians did in calling the temporal, sensible world the female world, and the extra-temporal, supersensible world the male world, seems to be very much in the same context.[47]

In any case the contrast or antithesis between the πλήρωμα (fullness) and κένωμα (emptiness), as one speaks of the reciprocal relation of above and below, of ideal and real, of the supersensible and sensible worlds, can have no other meaning than this. For the Aeon or ideal world is fullness, true reality, and the sensible world is what is empty, is lacking in true reality,[48] in the same sense as the Pythagoreans called the odd, male number a full, perfect number, and the even, female number a deficient, imperfect number.[49] It was also not uncommon for the Neoplatonists to call the higher world πλήρωμα, that is, the world of the gods as opposed to the world dependent on that world, only acquiring reality through it and sensibly subsisting within it. Iamblichus states that it is the gods' prerogative "that they are not comprehended by any thing, and that they comprehend all things in themselves. But terrestrial natures possess their existence in the *pleromas* of the gods; and when they become adapted to divine participation, then prior to their own proper essence, they immediately possess the gods, which [latently] pre-existed in it."[50] In his *Platonic Theology*,[51] Proclus speaks of male and female deities, and thus also of being fulfilled and the need to be fulfilled. He says that fullness is prior to what is second, and thus stands as the fullness of perfection. The one begotten from fullness, by sharing in the power of what is best, itself comes to the perfection of what is first. Analogously, among the gods the Father is the monad, the number one, the cause of what is best. The Mother is the dyad, the number two, and the generatrix of beings. Thus in the Valentinian system too the mother Achamoth, as female ruler of the world found outside the Pleroma, certainly stands juxtaposed to the Primal Father, the supreme ruler of the Aeon world.

---

47. In the *Excerpta ex scriptis Theodoti*, the Theodotus who belongs to the Valentinian school (ch. 30), is also presented as stating (ch. 79), "First there is a female child, but then it becomes a man, son of the bridegroom."

48. See the passages from Clement of Alexandria cited above (nn. 29, 41) for the contrast between πληρώματα (what are full) and εἰκόνες (images), which amounts to the same thing as the contrast between life and death, or between πνεῦμα (spirit) and ψυχή (soul).

49. Plutarch, *De vita et poesi Homeri*, 145, tells us that Pythagoras said all things are made of numbers; that the even numbers are deficient and imperfect, while the odd numbers are complete and perfect. Censorinus, *De die natali*, ch. 20, says uneven numbers are complete.

50. Iamblichus of Chalcis, *On the Mysteries* (*De mysteriis Aegyptiorum*), ed. Stephen Ronan, trans. Thomas Taylor and Alexander Wilder (Hastings, UK, 1989), p. 33 (1.8).

51. *Theologia Platonis* (Hamburg, 1618), p. 68.

## The Three Principles: Pneumatic or Spiritual, Psychical, and Hylic or Material

The issue of the relationships among the three principles—pneumatic, psychical, and hylic—belongs in the context of the related concepts we are investigating here. They form a trichotomy that also attests to the Platonic character of the Valentinian system.

The pneumatic or spiritual aspect is the essential principle of the Pleroma, of the Aeons and the world of ideas. It is a distinctive domain of its own. What of pneumatic life is outside the Pleroma, in the created, sensible world, just stems from the Pleroma, from which it has come down through the agency of Achamoth. She imparted the seeds of the spiritual life and is called especially the mother of it. On the whole there is no life except inasmuch as it issues from the pneumatic principle.[52]

The psychical aspect attaches itself above all to the pneumatic aspect. The Valentinians' cosmogonic myth has the psychical aspect arising from the passionate, suffering conditions in which Achamoth finds herself, outside of the Pleroma. These are indeed the more noble sentiments in which a certain spiritual element still for the most part makes itself known. These sentiments gave existence to the psychical element. They are the longing for the lost light of the Pleroma. The psychical element is moved by them, as well as by the ignoble emotive states that rule over it. The Demiurge formed from this ψυχικὴ οὐσία (psychical being) is the true representative of the psychical element, and everything that typifies the Demiurge also furnishes us with the more specific concept of the psychical aspect. The psychical element is to be understood entirely as the intermediary between the pneumatic and the hylic elements, which is why they say that, as something inherently indifferent and undecided, it can turn toward either of the other two. The psychical is open to the pneumatic element, is inclined to take it up into itself. Indeed it is even the necessary agent through which alone the pneumatic element can appear outside the Pleroma and be active.

The psychical element appears to us with these attributes in the Demiurge, who is of course in complete submission to the direction of Achamoth. He is the instrument for the realization of her ideas, although he cannot rise up to become aware of that fact. We see the same thing in the Demiurge's relation to Christ. Already prior to Christ's appearing, the Demiurge had a special predilection for the souls that bore the seeds of Achamoth (were of a pneumatic nature). Hence the pronouncements of the prophets made an impression on him, although they were nevertheless beyond his ken. He knew not how to appreciate them or to infer what was their true source. So his state of ignorance lasted until the Redeemer came. But when the Redeemer had come, the Demiurge let himself be taught by the Redeemer, and attached himself to him without reservation, which is why the Valentinians saw in the Demiurge the

---

52. See Clement of Alexandria, *Stromata* 4:13, where he quotes from a homily in which Valentinus addresses the pneumatic ones: "You are originally immortal, and children of eternal life, and you would have death spread among you that you may exhaust and lavish it, and that death may die in you and by you; for when we dissolve the world, and you yourselves are not dissolved, you have dominion over creation and all that is transitory" [*ANF* 2:425].

centurion in the gospel who said to the Redeemer: "I too have under me soldiers and servants who do what I command" [cf. Matt 8:9].

Even after the appearance of the Redeemer, the Demiurge guides the course of the world up to its appointed time, and guides it in the interest of the church, however also with a view to the reward prepared for him, namely, that he could be replacing the mother.[53] His limited perspective would of course have been enlarged somewhat by Christianity (for, prior to the Redeemer's arrival, the Demiurge was ignorant of all that was to follow in the future, at the consummation of the world's course[54]). Yet it is only a narrow, egotistical interest that binds him to Christianity. Accordingly, the psychical element is indeed not lacking a sense for what is pneumatic, although it still always has just a partial grasp of the pneumatic aspect. This is the reason why the Demiurge cannot be taken up into the Pleroma as Achamoth was. Instead he is just advanced to the center of the place she vacated.

As the Demiurge himself has a psychical nature, everything that wishes to enter into his realm also must assume a psychical nature. That is why the Redeemer also had to appear in the covering of a psychical Christ, one with which the Demiurge clothed him—a representation in which the psychical element presented itself in this very way as the necessary compromise (*Vermittlung*) between the divine aspect in the Redeemer and his appearing as human. This is like the teaching of Origen about the human soul of Jesus, without which the divine Logos could not have become a human being. When we add in the concept of the hylic element, this just involves the possibility of greater specificity as to the concept of the psychical element having a twofold nature. The issue then is simply how the Valentinian system has defined the concept of matter, and that is not an easy question to answer.

## The Concept of Matter

Neander and Matter have not been very specific on this point, whereas Möhler[55] has been. He maintains that, in order to explain evil, Valentinus found it necessary to assume a matter existing eternally alongside God. But the passage Möhler cites,[56] and which attributes to Valentinus himself the statement, "Therefore I think what is called matter was together with him from the beginning, and evil seems to be from it," cannot count as proof. That is because the fragment Möhler cites in this text cannot, in light of Neander's critical remarks,[57] be attributed to Valentinus, and in general cannot be regarded as a source for the Valentinian system. Even the reference to Heracleon

---

53. Irenaeus, *Against Heresies* 1.7.3–4.

54. Ibid., 1.7.1.

55. Johann Adam Möhler, *Versuch über den Ursprung des Gnosticismus* (Tübingen, 1831), 27. [*Ed.*] On Neander and Matter, see n. 6.

56. *Dialogus de recta in Deum fide Opp. Orig.*, ed. de la Rue, 1:841.

57. In his *Genetische Entwickelung* (n. 6), 205ff.

the Valentinian does not prove what it is said to prove. For, according to Origen,[58] Heracleon said about the Devil that "his nature is not one of truthfulness, but rather is the opposite of truth, is from deceit and ignorance, from his own being as one of falsehood, by nature never able to speak the truth—from deceit and continual lying."

So the question, first and foremost, is how Heracleon sees the Devil in relation to matter. But nothing is said about that here. It only states that the essential nature of the Devil consists in "deceit and ignorance," or in "lying." But Heracleon could also have understood this same moral condition, what the Devil became by nature, as a moral attribute or state. In any event, according to Origen,[59] Heracleon indeed says that the Devil is "sharing wholly in matter," although he adds that "the world is altogether the domain of evil, the desolate home of beasts in which all one encounters are those apart from the law, and the Gentiles." Heracleon says of those alienated from God, that "they perish in the material depths of deceit, but the household of the Father are those who seek to worship the Father in his household."

According to these passages, one might not understand ὕλη straightforwardly as matter in the proper sense, for ὕλη κακίας and ὕλη πλάνης come to nothing more than κακία (evil) and πλάνη (deceit) themselves, and the word ὕλη just serves to circumscribe the moral concept of evil and deceit. In any case, therefore, we cannot derive anything certain about matter from these passages concerning Heracleon's teaching. But we can posit that he in fact assumed a matter existing from eternity, although it in no way follows that we must consider this teaching to be the original and general teaching of the Valentinian school.

If a concept such as that of ὕλη could be spelled out in different terms, if the Platonic teaching itself could have been understood in different ways, then it cannot be at all surprising if the Valentinian system originally took the concept of ὕλη in a purely negative sense. At least according to Irenaeus' portrayal, any other assumption seems unlikely. Irenaeus says nothing about the Valentinians having assumed an eternal matter. Also, he provides an explanation for the origin of the physical world that, while not precluding the prior existence of an eternal matter, makes such an assumption unnecessary. We have already seen how the Valentinians even had what is material and bodily emerging from the changeable emotive states into which Achamoth fell in her passion—from the very thing that, in her passion, set itself apart within her as what we could call the negation of her spiritual nature. All that is fluid originated from her tears, light from her laughter, all bodily elements from her sorrows and dismay. Gieseler[60] then indeed remarks, in agreement with Mosheim,[61] that this ought not be

---

58. *Commentary on John*, 20.22.

59. *Commentary on John*, 13.16 and 20.

60. In his review in the *Allgemeine Literatur-Zeitung* (n. 12), 834.

61. J. L. von Mosheim, *Commentarii de rebus Christianorum ante Constantinum Magnum* (Helmstadt, 1753). [*Ed.*] Baur gives the same page number, 834, as that cited for Gieseler, which seems unlikely.

misunderstood as saying that matter itself first came about in this way; although it surely does mean that life in previously lifeless and unorganized matter initially came from these sparks of light falling down out of the Pleroma. Therefore just as the vitality of Achamoth expressed itself in various ways, so too it has given rise to various forms of matter.

Yet according to the entire portrayal by Irenaeus it is difficult to understand what is said to have originated other than from the passion of Achamoth and still exists unrelated to it. Irenaeus[62] certainly does state that Soter, the Savior, "has commingled and condensed them, so as to transmute them from incorporeal passions into unorganized matter. He then by this process conferred upon them a fitness and a nature to become concretions and corporeal structures."[63] Is it not clearly stated here that what is incorporeal (the non-bodily passion) for the first time became corporeal or material in its passing over into stable bodies ("becoming concretions and corporeal structures")? In order to make clear this changeover from spiritual to material elements, the individual stages in the transition are also provided. Matter arises, so to speak, from solidifying or making concrete what is spiritual. But the "incorporeal passions" first become "unorganized matter," with the capacity and flexibility for receiving all possible forms. Since the process of solidifying takes a further course, solid bodies then came about from it for the first time.

Here, with the language about transmuting the passion arising in Achamoth into unorganized matter, we have precisely what Plato ascribes to matter—that it, without definite form and shape, would have the capacity to receive all possible forms. Therefore what Plato thinks of as matter is also what the Valentinians understand by matter, but with the stipulation that this ὕλη, initially as an unorganized matter and then as a compound become concrete in more solid bodies, would have originated from the incorporeal passion of Achamoth. Hence Irenaeus poses this objection to the Valentinian system: "And thus Enthymesis (Thought) was the passion; for she was thinking of things impossible. How then could affection and passion be separated and set apart from the Enthymesis, so as to become the substance of so vast a material creation?"[64] Irenaeus also certainly rebuts the doctrine of a pre-existing matter that the Valentinians have adopted from Plato. He writes: "Plato, for his part, speaks of matter, of exemplars, and of God. These men [Plato had included Democritus just before], following these distinctions, have spoken of the exemplars [Plato's ideas and archetypes] as images of things that are above. Through a mere change in terminology they boast of themselves as being discoverers and contrivers of this kind of imaginary fiction. Anaxagoras, Empedocles, and Plato expressed, before they did, their view that the

---

62. *Against Heresies* 1.4.5 [ANF 1:322].

63. Massuet correctly established the reading ἀσώματον (unorganized matter), by pointing to the Platonic concept of ὕλη, according to which matter, as ἄποιος (without a nature), as lacking in characteristics, as the abstract sum and substance of all possible forms, is also ἀσώματος.

64. *Against Heresies* 2.18.4 [ANF 1:384].

Creator formed the world out of previously existing matter."[65] He speaks in the same way[66] about the Pythagorean number theory, which the Valentinians have likewise made their own. Irenaeus says that the Pythagoreans' principles involve the even and odd numbers, and that "both things sensible and immaterial originated from these principles. They held that one set of principles gave rise to the matter [of things] and another to their form. They affirm that from these first principles all things have been made, just as a statue is made of its metal and has its special form. Now, the heretics have adapted this to the things that are outside of the Pleroma."[67]

However, what follows from this in any event is simply that individual adherents of the Valentinian system adopted the doctrine, foundational for Platonism, of matter in the aforementioned sense. It would be incorrect for us to presuppose that this same model is everywhere accepted in a school with so many offshoots and with respect to a teaching that inherently admits of different interpretations. According to the presentation of the Valentinian system in Book One of *Against Heresies*, one can only conclude that this system, doubtless portrayed in its original form here, knew nothing of an eternally pre-existing matter. This system locates all the reality and substantiality of being in what is spiritual, and has what is non-spiritual just coming about via negation of what is spiritual. Thus for it matter is the most extreme point at which all spiritual life passes over into rigidity, all consciousness into insensibility, all knowing into ignorance. From this perspective the corporeal world is accordingly the concept having become opaque to spirit in a state of finitude and negativity. The more knowledge of the absolute becomes for spirit a not-knowing, the more spirit's consciousness splits into the antithesis of the spiritual and the corporeal, the living idea takes on a material shell and appears over against spirit as a thick, solid mass that spirit's knowing can no longer penetrate.

This is the sense in which we must understand the view Irenaeus attributes to the Valentinians:[68]

> They confess that the Father of all contains all things, and that there is nothing whatever outside of the Pleroma (for it is an absolute necessity that [if there be such] it should be bounded and circumscribed by something greater than itself), and they speak of what is without and what is within in referring to knowledge and ignorance, and not with respect to local distance; but that, in the Pleroma, or in those things which are contained by the Father, the whole creation which we know to have been formed, having been made by

---

65. Ibid., 2.14.3–4 [*ANF* 1:377].

66. Ibid., 2.14.6 [*ANF* 1:377].

67. [*Ed.*] Baur's footnote here indicates the Greek equivalent Massuet correctly provides for the Latin of this sentence, which is given in English in our text. This might be of interest to Irenaeus scholarship, since the surviving text of Irenaeus is a Latin translation of the original Greek, only parts of which have survived as quoted in the writings of others.

68. *Against Heresies* 2.4.2 [*ANF* 1:363].

> the Demiurge, or by the angels, is contained by the unspeakable greatness, as the center is in a circle, or as a spot is in a garment. [Irenaeus enlarges on that view:] Then, in the first place, what sort of a being must that Bythus be, who allows a stain to have a place in his own bosom?[69]

Yet there certainly cannot be talk of a free-standing matter, existing independently of God, when there is said to be utterly nothing at all outside the Pleroma. What this statement presupposes is not a spatial separation between what is within the Pleroma and what is outside it, for the distinction only refers to knowledge as distinct from ignorance. Ignorance is a matter of the degree to which knowledge of the absolute is limited, negative, a not-knowing. In spirit's consciousness, "outside the Pleroma" is understood in spatial and real terms, whereas for absolute spirit and its absolute knowing there is only a "within the Pleroma," as opposed to which "outside the Pleroma" appears only as something minimal, as a vanishing point. In fact for what is absolute the finite does not actually exist. The finite only exists for the spirit that has become finite. In other words, awareness of the finite is just *secundum ignorantium* (lack of knowledge at lower level, or as a result). But this also fits with the fundamental idea of the system, according to which the passion of Achamoth, or the finitude of spirit, simply has its basis in the fact that Valentinian Gnosis posits a negative factor in spirit, one making it impossible for spirit to encompass the absolute with its own consciousness.

In conclusion, it seems to me there is a clear proof that the Valentinian system has no doctrine of an eternal matter. The proof lies in the fact that, ultimately, this system has everything material completely ceasing to be. That would have obviously contradicted what the opposing view presupposed, since an eternal matter, having no beginning, also cannot come to an end. The contention that what is material is ultimately annihilated gets repeated very specifically. Not only do they say that the world-conflagration breaking out at the end of things will "destroy all matter," and that matter and the fire as well will "have no further existence."[70] They also expressly designate the material element (among the three principles) as what "must of necessity perish, inasmuch as it is incapable of receiving any *afflatus* (in-spiration) of incorruption."[71]

---

69. On the antithesis of knowledge and ignorance, inasmuch as it coincides with the antithesis of spirit and matter, the contrast between things inside the Pleroma and things outside it, see also 2.5.2: "If they explain being within and without the Pleroma as implying knowledge and ignorance respectively, as certain of them do (since he who has knowledge is within that which he knows) then they must of necessity grant that the Savior himself (whom they call 'All Things') was in a state of ignorance. For they maintain that, on his coming forth outside of the Pleroma, he imparted form to their Mother [Achamoth]. If, then, they assert that whatever is outside [the Pleroma] is ignorant of all things, and if the Savior went forth to their Mother, then he was situated beyond the pale of the knowledge of all things; that is, he was in ignorance. How then could he communicate knowledge to her, when he himself was beyond the pale of knowledge?" [*ANF* 1:364]. See also 2.17.9.

70. *Against Heresies* 1.7.1

71. Ibid., 1.6.1.

In the future even the psychical element will, at least in part, share in the fate of what is material. That is because, in keeping with its twofold nature, it has a dimension inclined toward the material world. Only inasmuch as there is a better tendency within it, on account of its kinship with the pneumatic element, will that part find its resting place in the intermediate abode, in the place the Demiurge has occupied in times past. Since nothing psychical can enter into the Pleroma, what is pneumatic, what has been sown [in the world] by Achamoth, what has gradually grown and developed itself in the souls of righteous human beings, will be wedded as brides for the angels of the Savior (Soter) when these psychical ones have reached perfection. However, the souls they had will find their eternal rest in the intermediate abode together with the Demiurge.[72]

Hence the souls subdivide into good and evil souls, according to whether they are, or are not, receptive to the seeds of what is spiritual.[73] So it all just depends on the distinction between the pneumatic and psychical elements, although this distinction seems to be an everlasting one. As compared to the pneumatic element, the psychical element still has a certain semblance of worldliness (*Realität*). It is, so to speak, the shadow of the finitude that hovers around the light-world—that *macula in tunica* (spot in a garment) of which Irenaeus speaks in the passage quoted above. The spirit has of course overcome its internal negation that made room for the finite world, and for it the finite is no more. However, spirit would not have been conscious of the antithesis that was overcome, had it not been conscious of that negation of the absolute and the finite at least minimally, as the distinction between the pneumatic and the psychical in the sense indicated.

The hylic or material element can always be a reality only at the lower level of spiritual being, and there alone be as one with a unitary self-consciousness. Hence if the Redeemer was said to be the spiritual manifestation of what is human, then he could not have assumed a psychical or material body. Instead it was just something psychical. Yet since what is psychical for its own sake cannot visibly engage itself in the perceptible world, there had to have been some other special arrangement in place

---

72. In addition to the Demiurge, they also speak of a Cosmocrator (ruler of the world) and of evil spirits. Spiritual evil ("the wickedness of the spiritual ones") is said to have arisen from the sorrow of Achamoth. This is the origin of the Devil, whom they also call the Cosmocrator, as well as the origin of the demonic spirits and angels and the entire substance of spiritual evil. The Demiurge is a son of the Mother [Achamoth], and the Cosmocrator is "a creature of the Demiurge." The Cosmocrator knows what is above him because he is a spirit of evil, but the Demiurge does not know what is above him because he is of a psychical nature. "Their mother dwells in that place which is above the heavens, that is, in the intermediate abode; the Demiurge dwells in the heavenly place, that is, in the Hebdomad; but the Cosmocrator dwells in this world of ours" (*Against Heresies* 1.5.4 [ANF 1:323]). We see clearly that the Cosmocrator, together with his evil spirits, constitute merely an abstract notion, mainly from the fact that, unlike the Demiurge, he does not continue to exist after the consummation of the world's course in time. Thus he shares in the fate of the material element, and is himself none other than a personification of what is material according to its ethical aspect, inasmuch as matter holds sway as the moral perversity of the will.

73. Irenaeus, *Against Heresies* 1.7.5.

of the Redeemer's material body that would have made his appearing perceptible to people's physical senses. This is what made his manifestation an entirely unique and distinctive phenomenon. For every other human being has: a spiritual principle from the Mother, Achamoth; a soul from the Demiurge (from whom, therefore, the Redeemer likewise received his psychical element—the psychical Christ); a body from the earth and flesh from matter. This alone accounts for the prevalence of the three principles, and is the reason why the Valentinians affirm that there are three classes of human beings: pneumatic, psychical, and hylic or material. The three are represented, respectively, in the three sons of Adam: Seth, Abel, and Cain.[74]

The higher the position in life held by individuals, the purer and more spiritual is the function leading them to their ordained goal. That is why pneumatic individuals are carried into the Pleroma not by their acts or deeds, but only by the seeds they received as kernels but brought to ripeness. In other words, it is not by their πρᾶξις, their practice, but rather by their γνῶσις, their knowledge. As the Gnostics contended, this is what supposedly set them apart from the Catholic Christians. For what shapes these Catholic Christians and makes them secure in their Christianity are simply their acts or deeds, and their sheer faith. But they lack the perfect knowledge. Hence they stand only at the level of the psychical life and regard it as imperative to exhibit good conduct, else they will not be blessed. However, the Gnostics maintain about themselves that they do not become blessed by deeds. Instead they are blessed for no other reason than that they are pneumatic, or spiritual, by nature.[75]

## 2. The System of the Ophites

The Ophite system[76] is most closely associated with the Valentinian system. In each of them we find the same major concepts, the same terminology, and in general the same process of development.

---

74. See *Excerpta ex scriptis Theodoti* (n. 2), ch. 54. [*Added from the Errata*] See also Tertullian, *Against the Valentinians*, ch. 29. "Cain, and Abel, and Seth, who were in a certain sense the sources of the human race, become the fountainheads of just as many qualities of nature and essential character. The material nature, which had become unworthy of salvation, they assign to Cain; the animal nature, which was poised between divergent expectations, they find in Abel; the spiritual, foreordained for certain salvation, they discover in Seth. In this way also they make a twofold distinction among souls, as to the properties of good and evil—according to the material condition derived from Cain, or the animal condition derived from Abel, or the spiritual state from Seth" [*ANF* 3:517]. According to Philo, in an analogous way, the persons of the Mosaic earliest history portray different moral-religious states of the soul; see A. F. Dähne, *Geschichtliche Darstellung der jüdischen-alexandrinischen Religionsphilosophie* (Halle, 1834), 342ff. Yet from this we see at the same time a clear proof of difference between Philo and the Gnostics (as I indicated above on pp. 4–5 and 22). Thus Philo's "states of the soul" (τρόποι τῆς ψυχῆς) differ from those speculative or metaphysical principles of the Gnostics. On the whole, the Philonic and Gnostic standpoints are quite different, as are their antitheses regarding the spiritual and material principles, with reference to the domain of the human world.

75. Irenaeus, *Against Heresies* 1.6.7.

76. The main sources for the Ophites are: Irenaeus, *Against Heresies* 1.30; Epiphanius, *Against*

What sets the Ophite system apart is principally that it largely and inherently has a more realistic character, that it has a more dualistic tendency, and that it presents Sophia most especially as the principle active in the history of humankind's development. In what follows we will pay particular attention to the stance each of these two systems takes toward Judaism.

## Development of the Main Ideas

In the Ophite system too the highest principles are the Primal Father or Bythos, the blessed Primal Light, and the Primal Father's Ennoia, or thought. This Ennoia, however, is not so much linked to him and forming a pair or syzygy, as it is emanated from him. That is why, with the Primal Father himself called the Primal Human Being, the Ophites call the Ennoia the Son of Man, in other words the Second Man.

Following upon these two highest principles is a third principle, the Holy Spirit. A material principle standing over against it consists of four elements, called Water, Darkness, the Depth, and Chaos. Without a doubt these four are to be regarded as matter that is co-eternal with the supreme God. The Holy Spirit is the first female principle, and therefore it is called the Mother of all living things. Delighted and attracted by the beauty of the Spirit, the first two principles—the First Man and the Second Man, who accordingly also in turn form one and the same male principle—conjoin themselves with the Spirit. Christ issues forth from the conjoining of these two principles, the male and the female principles.

What then makes its appearance here in the Ophite system is the element designated in the Valentinian system by the passion of Sophia. When the First Man and the Second Man, the Father and the Son, conjoined themselves with the female principle, with Spirit as the Primal Mother, this conjunction could not completely receive into itself the fullness of the light streaming forth from them. The result was that a part of this light flowed over to the left-hand side. Thus Christ, together with his Mother, was indeed elevated directly into the eternal world of the Aeons, which is the true and holy church, as the unity of the Father or First Man and the Son or Second Man, the unity of the Primal Mother and her son, Christ. But "the part of the light that overflowed"[77] (called Sophia, Prunicus, the left-hand side, as opposed to Christ, the right-hand side; also male-female) crashed down into the waters of Chaos, which, previously unstirred, were then set in motion. The light-stuff that was in this part was the reason why it not only did not sink down into chaos, but also attached itself to all that is material.

However, the more this part became weighed down by matter, the more uneasy it grew in this condition. So it sought to escape the waters of chaos and to ascend to

---

*Heresies* 37; Theodoret, *Heretical Tales*, 1.14.

77. [*Ed.*] In a footnote Baur provides the Greek equivalent for this clause as it occurs in Theodoret and others.

its Mother. Yet it was prevented from doing so by the mass of stuff surrounding it. In order that the light from above still within it would at least not be allowed to fall under the control of the elements below it, by using its light-power as much as it was able to, it soared into the heights and, from the physical material surrounding it, it formed the heavens. By further developing its light-power, it succeeded in becoming even freer from that mass of stuff. Yet although now it no longer sank down into the depths, it nevertheless could not soar up above the material world once it had come into contact with matter, which held it back in an intermediate place.

In the state of weakness and ignorance in which it found itself,[78] it emitted Ialdabaoth. Since he was to be the father of others, the series of angels subordinate to him came from him in descending order: Iao, Sabaoth, Adoneus [Adonai], Eloeus [Eloi], Oreus, Astanphaeus. Thus the Ialdabaoth of the Ophites, together with his six angels, each at the head of his own sphere or heaven, form a Hebdomad.[79] So Ialdabaoth is like the Demiurge of the Valentinians, with the Mother, their Sophia, as Ogdoas [the eighth one], enthroned over the Hebdomad.

Ialdabaoth of the Ophites has a somewhat different character than the Valentinian Demiurge has, although he occupies exactly the same position in the system. The Ophites allow that something of his Mother's light-principle carries over to him, and he is not to the same extent lacking awareness of what is above him. This is why he sought to close off what is above him from the angels he created, and to conceal it from their eyes so that they will recognize nothing higher than himself. However, this is the very reason he also appears as a being reacting with a certain deliberate hostility. Since there is nevertheless another being under Ialdabaoth himself, one conceived of as still more decidedly opposed to all that stands above it, these various relationships involving opposition make it very difficult to get a clear understanding of this system, even irrespective of the muddled state of these accounts. One of the essential ideas of this system is the idea of a reaction in which the lower and imperfect principle is conceived of as opposed to the higher and more perfect principle, mainly in its egotistical intention to frustrate the aims of the higher principle, although in fact its strategy just results in these aims being most assuredly realized.

Hence as Ialdabaoth appears counter to his mother, Sophia, by presuming to be the independent and self-reliant creator and sovereign of the world entrusted to him, the controversy about this sovereignty thus also sets him at odds with the angels he created.[80] Here we have indeed what leads to the creation of the human being, which occupies a very important place in the Ophite system. When Ialdabaoth arrogantly

---

78. Epiphanius, *Against Heresies* 3.2: "It was cast into a state of feebleness, and ignorance of its own mother."

79. These are the planetary spirits. See Irenaeus, *Against Heresies*, ch. 7: "They want the sacred Hebdomad to be the seven stars that they call planets." For the prayers that must be directed to these planets by the souls seeking to pass through their realms, see Origen, *Against Celsus*, 6.31.

80. Irenaeus, *Against Heresies* 1.30.5.

boasted that he was lord of all that was under him, and declared "I am father and God, and there is no one above me," his mother, upon hearing this, cried out in response, "Do not lie, Ialdabaoth, for above you is the father of all, the First Man, and the Second Man is his son, the Son of Man."[81]

This surprising cry, and the term "Man" that had never before been heard, astonished the angels. (Since this Man is portrayed as a being superior in its own spiritual nature and destiny to these other spirits, the term "Man" could only have entered their consciousness from on high and become the leading idea of the work that they now undertook.) The angels asked: "Where does this new consciousness come from?" In order to distract them and draw them to himself, Ialdabaoth supposedly said: "Let us make humankind [i.e., Man] in our image" (Gen 1:26).[82] When the six angels heard this the Mother awakened in them the idea of the Man, so as to use him [the Man] to deprive them of the power of the light-world, which was within them. They collaborated in constructing a man immensely long and wide. But this huge bodily mass could not stand erect; it could only crawl upon the earth like a worm. When they brought this man to their Father, the Mother, knowing this, wanted to deprive Ialdabaoth once more of the divine power she had imparted to him (the moisture of the light); thus the power to bring it about that this spark of light would pass over to the Man together with the soul Ialdabaoth breathed into him.

The Man then had intelligence (νοῦς) and thinking ability (ἐνθύμησις). Right away he stood upright, rose in thought above the eight heavenly spheres, and recognized and praised the father exalted above Ialdabaoth without further bothering about the world's creator.[83] Ialdabaoth, angered by this, then thought to deprive the Man of his spiritual principle via the Woman. Ialdabaoth then produced the Woman from the *enthymesis* or thinking of Adam [the Man]. But Sophia, or Prunicus, secretly withdrew this higher power from the Woman.[84] Captivated by her beauty, Ialdabaoth's angels

---

81. Ibid., 1.30.6 [*ANF* 1:355].

82. [*Ed.*] Ibid., 1.30.6 (*ANF* 1:355).

83. See Irenaeus, 1.30.6; Epiphanius, *Against Heresies* 37.4.3.

84. This is where Mosheim and Neander have located great difficulties and contradictions in the Ophite system. I believe that in each instance they allow for easier and more gratifying solutions than is the case with my predecessors. First, we should consider Irenaeus, *Against Heresies* 1.30.7 [*ANF* 1:356], which says that "Ialdabaoth, being envious, wanted to empty the man by means of woman, and produced from his *enthymesis* a woman whom that Prunicus laid hold of unseen and emptied her of her power." Neander understands "his *enthymesis*" as referring to Ialdabaoth. Ialdabaoth has imparted something of a spiritual character (πνευματικόν) to Eve as he has to Adam. But this *enthymesis* cannot be the light principle Ialdabaoth would have received as imparted by Sophia. As Irenaeus states directly before this, "They say that by breathing into the man the spirit of life, he was secretly emptied of his power; however, the man thence has intelligence and *enthymesis*. Therefore Adam has *enthymesis*, and only from Adam could it have passed over to Eve. Hence the Latin translator should have rendered the Greek phrase not as *de sua* ("from his") but as *de ejus* ("from its"). Otherwise it would not even be conceivable in the context of the system, because Ialdabaoth's plan could only have been, by producing the woman from the man (doubtless so, given the text of Genesis 2:21–23), to have the spiritual element that was in Adam pass over to Eve, and accordingly through the sons that

begat sons with the woman Eve, sons who were angels like them. But Ialdabaoth's purpose, which was by this route to bring once more under his control the spiritual power that had passed over from him to Adam, could not be achieved.

There then ensued humankind's fall into sin. What the Mother, Sophia, did next was use the serpent to lead Eve and Adam astray. Eve willingly obeyed the voice that she took to be the voice of God's Son, and persuaded Adam to eat of the tree from which God had forbidden anyone to eat. The result of this partaking of the fruit was that they recognized the supreme power and authority that is exalted above everything, and renounced those who had created them. When Sophia saw that the creators of the world were defeated by their own creations, she cried out joyfully: "Thus the

---

Ialdabaoth's angels begat with her, to also pass it over to them, and thus at least the man would have been deprived of it once more. – A second point is Neander's contention (*Genetische Entwickelung* [n. 6], 262) that, in the portrayals of both Irenaeus and Epiphanius, there is a contradiction in saying the first man was directly aware of his origin, and raised himself up above Ialdabaoth, since supposedly he just became conscious of this for the first time through the fruit of the tree of knowledge. Presumably [Neander thinks] that in this case Irenaeus and Epiphanius have not correctly understood the Ophite system. However, the real contradiction lies rather in holding that merely eating the fruit would have given the man consciousness of God, since neither Irenaeus nor Epiphanius says that by then Sophia had already restored to the man the divine power she had withdrawn from him. For without the pneumatic principle the man cannot be conscious of the supreme God. This contradiction cannot be resolved except by making the textual change indicated above under the first point I raised. – A third point is that the passage in Irenaeus, 1.30.7, to which Mosheim has given so much attention (in his *Versuch einer unpartheiischen und gründlichen Ketzergeschichte*, 2nd ed. (Helmstädt, 1748), 161ff.), and has so very arbitrarily modified and expounded, admits of a simpler and more natural interpretation. Irenaeus says, "When Prunicus perceived that the powers were thus baffled by their own creature, she greatly rejoiced, and again cried out, that since the father was incorruptible, he (Ialdabaoth) who formerly called himself the father was a liar; and that, while the man and the first woman (the spirit) existed previously, this one (Eve) sinned by committing adultery." [*Ed.* Translation from *ANF* 1:356. Baur gives this passage in Latin, which is pertinent to what he says below in this note.] Here we doubtless have to understand *plasma* (their own creature) simply as Eve. For although Adam too was equally a creation of Ialdabaoth's angel, he nevertheless was not solely her work, since the idea of his nature had been passed down from on high, whereas Eve was produced solely from him. The words beginning with *Olim hic* [i.e., "he (Ialdabaoth) who formerly called himself the father was a liar"] can only refer to the proclamation by Ialdabaoth mentioned in the text above: "I am father, and God . . ." Hence the sense of the passage in 1.30.7 is therefore that Prunicus joyfully cried out: "The one who formerly called himself 'father'—whereas the [true] father is ageless—appears as a liar; and since the man and the first wife existed before, this one (Eve) has become an adulteress and sinner." (If the presence of *quoniam* in the text here is not due to an oversight, then it can only be the Latin rendering of the Greek ὅτι that stands redundantly before a speaker's words.) Ialdabaoth has been doubly defeated, with regard both to the eternal father and to the first man. As concerns the eternal father, the man has shown Ialdabaoth to be a liar by the man's acknowledging the primal father; but as concerns the first man, the beginning of sin did not take place with the primal man, who had been created according to the idea handed down from on high, but instead with the woman, whom Ialdabaoth, together with his angels and wholly as his own *plasma* (creature), set beside the primal man as the *prima femina* (first female creature). One ought not overlook the fact that, in the Ophite system, the woman is portrayed as the principle of sin. Understood in this way, it seems to me that this text calls for no alteration, although Neander declared that it is obviously altered from the original. In Matter's extensive presentation, *Histoire critique du Gnosticisme et de son influence sur les sectes religieuses et philosophiques des six premiers siècles de l'ère chrétienne*, 2 vols. (Paris, 1828), 1:207, which is, however, succinct on this very point, he not once gives prominence to the difficulty that is in question here.

one who called himself 'father' instead of the eternal father, has lied!" Ialdabaoth who, in his ignorance, had not intended all this to happen, then cast Adam and Eve out of paradise, because they had broken his commandment. "For he had a desire to beget sons by Eve, but did not accomplish his wish, because his mother opposed him in every point, and secretly emptied Adam and Eve of the light with which they had been sprinkled, in order that the spirit which proceeded from the supreme power might participate neither in the curse nor the opprobrium [caused by the transgression]. They also teach that, being thus emptied of the divine substance, they were cursed by him, and cast down from heaven to this world."[85] These words obviously confirm the previously-given account.

Ialdabaoth's intention, in seeking to have sons begotten of Eve, misfired because Sophia had taken away the spiritual principle passing over from Adam into Eve. Since both Adam and Eve were now deprived of this light-principle, the principle also was untouched by the curse that came upon them as the result of the Fall. But the most noteworthy point is that, even though the spiritual principle was taken from them, Adam and Eve now recognized the supreme being after they had fallen, and could rise above the world's creator. According to the Gnostics' teaching otherwise, this is only possible on the assumption that Sophia did not totally withdraw the divine power, that is, the light-principle, from them. For it is obviously necessary to make this assumption if the system is to be coherent.

Sophia's action is simply the mythical expression for what mediates the transition from the abstract idea of the human being to its concrete reality. The human being, in his original entry into existence, must also present himself directly in his very finest qualities, and must be thought of as having the ability to be conscious of the supreme God. But this is just the ideal human, the abstract idea of which must first be negated if this abstract idea is to become a concrete reality. For without this negation, and mediating transition from the abstract to the concrete that it enables, there can be no movement and development. That is why the Ophite system has the human being, who initially emerges with his completely spiritual consciousness, emptied in turn of his spiritual principle, and deprived of the awareness of it (because Sophia withdrew the spiritual power from him). This emptying is itself of course his fall, which presupposes a negating principle, a principle of weakness and of sin.

Hence his original spiritual power is withdrawn from the primal man in virtue of the woman proceeding from him. When she exists the light-force is extinguished, and she herself is Ialdabaoth's creation. The Ophite myth of Ialdabaoth's angels begetting sons with the woman serves to portray her even more specifically from this angle, as the sensuous principle alongside the spiritual principle. In the way she thus appears, as fornicator and adulteress, she herself is sin personified, the wife representing the sensuous world. However, since the spiritual principle withdrawn from the human being was not utterly taken away, but instead was just able to be tethered and restricted in its

---

85. Irenaeus, *Against Heresies* 1.30.8 [*ANF* 1:356].

influence, it also had in turn to find a way of expressing itself. Hence its development now first begins. But since there are now two principles, male and female, spiritual and sensuous, divine and demonic, the development can proceed only through the combined efforts of these two principles. Each moment of the development therefore has a twofold aspect, a good one and an evil one. Since the good or spiritual principle is the one still tethered, the impetus for development thus comes from the evil or sensuous principle. It is the disturbing, trouble-causing element; so the woman is the temptress who leads to the Fall.

Each new development makes the spiritual principle freer and more active. Thus as a result of the Fall, human beings' thinking now rises above the world's creator and they can become aware of their spiritual nature. But the awakening of this consciousness is only just the initial, feeble beginnings at freeing the spiritual principle operative in them, for it is still continually tethered, still a freedom withheld from them. Hence human beings are also still under the sway of the world's creator. Now they first start to become aware, instead, of the oppressive rule by which he holds them captive. The Ophite myth portrays this rule by the curse with which Ialdabaoth punishes their fall into sin. This is then the most suitable place to bring in the figure of the serpent, from which the Ophites are said to have taken their name.[86]

According to Irenaeus,[87] because the serpent had lured Adam and Eve to disobey the commandment given them, Ialdabaoth cast him down into the lower world. Here the serpent brought under his control the angels who resided there, and himself begat six sons, with the seven of them forming a Hebdomad said to be a copy of Ialdabaoth's Hebdomad. These are the seven world-spirits, the perpetual antagonists and enemies of human beings, because it was on account of the human beings that these seven were cast down into the depths.[88] As the serpent-demon in this way has dominance over a realm corresponding to that of Ialdabaoth, but belonging to a still lower region, he himself is thus a son of Ialdabaoth. According to Irenaeus,[89] Ialdabaoth had begotten him when his sons, lusting for power, rebelled against their father. Furious and in despair about this, Ialdabaoth looked down into the dregs of the matter lying below him, in which his own burning desire had objectified itself to him, such that this son had arisen from it. This son is Nous, twisted into the form of a serpent.[90] Irenaeus says

---

86. [*Ed.*] The Greek word for "serpent" is ὄφις.

87. *Against Heresies* 1.30.8.

88. See Origen, *Against Celsus*, 6.30, which describes the seven, there called "ruling demons."

89. *Against Heresies* 1.30.5.

90. See Irenaeus, *Against Heresies* 1.30.5. Designating what is evil and perverse by crookedness and being twisted in the form of a serpent calls to mind Plato's *Phaedrus*, 230a, where Socrates says: "I investigate . . . myself, to know whether I am a monster more entwined and more furious than Typhon, or a gentler and simpler creature, to whom a divine and quiet lot is given by nature." [*Ed.* Greek πολυπλοκώτερος refers to something like a wreath, which is made by entwining things.] It is striking that this "serpent-demon" is specifically called "Nous." It seems to indicate the view that evil, as the direct opposite of what is good, could simply be thought of as a spiritual principle. Like the Valentinian cosmocrator, the world-creator here has this demon as his son because evil, as what is negative,

that spirit, soul, and all worldly things stemmed from this Nous in serpent form, and from it also came all oblivion and wickedness, all hatred and envy, and death. As long as he was still with his father in heaven and paradise, he was mainly the one who, by his serpentine form, crooked and cunning, made the father even more perverse.

Epiphanius has him originating in the same way, although only after the creation of the human being when this one, ensouled by Ialdabaoth, has become conscious of the primal father and with this awareness rose above Ialdabaoth. "Then Ialdabaoth, taking it hard that the places far above him had been recognized, looked down in bitterness to the dregs of matter and engendered a power of serpentine appearance, whom they also call his son."[91] How then are we to think that this serpent-demon, as these writers tell us, was at the same time revered by the Ophites as an angel or spirit of light, as indeed an embodiment of Sophia and of Christ himself? Irenaeus writes: "Some of them assert that Sophia herself became the serpent, on which account she was hostile to the creator of Adam, and implanted knowledge in man, for which reason the serpent was called wiser than all others."[92] Of course only some of the Ophites said this. But it is still always the same sect that Irenaeus described as I have stated, and Epiphanius never expressed any qualifications but said in quite general terms that the Ophites revered the serpent as a deity.

The Ophites' serpent declares himself to be Christ. They attribute omniscience to their serpent, and say that, in the beginning it imparted knowledge to humankind. But they say Ialdabaoth did not want the Mother above or the Father to be remembered by human beings. Yet the serpent persuaded them and brought knowledge, and taught them the whole knowledge of the mysteries above. Because they imparted this knowledge to the human beings, Ialdabaoth cast the serpent down from heaven. This is why the Ophites call the serpent a king descended from heaven.[93]

Epiphanius also describes the reverence they customarily show for the serpent. They feed a real snake, which they keep in a basket. During their rites they place loaves on a table and invite the snake to the table. When it emerges from its opened basket, crawls up onto the table, and winds itself about the loaves, they count this as the most perfect sacrificial offering. They call it a eucharist. They break the bread around which the snake has wound itself and share it among themselves, and some of them even kiss the snake. Epiphanius is in fact justified when,[94] in light of all this, he accuses the Ophites of the greatest contradiction. He writes that:

> the Ophites refute themselves in their own doctrine when at one moment they revere the serpent as a deity, yet at other times say it led Eve astray by tempting

---

always has for its presupposition what is good, to which it is the opposite.

91. Epiphanius, *Against Heresies* 37.4.4 [Amidon trans. (n. 35), 131].

92. Irenaeus, *Against Heresies* 1.30.15 [ANF 1:358].

93. [*Ed.*] This paragraph paraphrases passages from Epiphanius, *Against Heresies* 37.2.6, 37.3.1, and 37.5.2–4. Likewise, the following paraphrases parts of 37.5.6–8.

94. In 30.6.5–6.

her; when in one breath they declare it to be Christ, yet they also say it is the son of Ialdabaoth who wronged his sons—for Ialdabaoth shielded his sons from the knowledge of higher things and showed disregard for the Mother and the Father who is above, by not allowing his sons to revere the Father on high. How can the serpent be a heavenly king if it rises up against its Father? How can it have imparted true knowledge if it is the one who led Eve astray?

Epiphanius has fully set forth this contradiction, and too little attention has been given to it in previous accounts of the Ophite teaching.[95] I believe the contradiction can be removed in a satisfactory way only by assuming that the Ophites split into different factions. The Sethians and the Cainites are generally recognized as such factions or parties. The ancient writers were misled by these names into just assuming that the names of these sects indicate what differentiated them. However, if we accept what is quite obviously the case, that the contrast between them went deeper than this and traced back to earlier pre-history, then it had to point most especially to the serpent in the story of the Fall.

By starting from the Cainites' [negative] view of the world's creator, and from the thesis that in the Old Testament good and evil are to be regarded as direct opposites, that those the world's creator is pleased with are to be looked upon as bad and those he hates and persecutes are seen as good, then it follows that the serpent could not have been thought deserving of the curse pronounced by the creator. On this view it is entirely consistent to maintain that the serpent is itself Christ or Sophia, and that, by enticing the human beings to disobey the creator's commandment, the serpent just intended what is best for them by guiding them to the true knowledge.[96] However, by

---

95. Most striking is the muddle in Matter's presentation, *Histoire critique* (n. 6), 2:202, where he compares the Ophites' serpent form first of all with the Persian Ahriman, the Egyptian Ptah (who also has a curved shape), the Feta-Hil of the Sabeans (which is also said to be the god Ptah, or El-Ptah), as well as with Phanes-Hephaestus and Heracles-Chronos of the Greeks. Thus the serpent form gets distinguished from a Spirit Ophis that Sophia sent, as her angelic spirit, to lure the human beings to disobey the commandments about envy and pride. Tossed into the abyss by Ialdabaoth, this Spirit Ophis became a second Satan, a Satan in microcosm, the likeness of the great Devil, the serpent form. Some Ophites have even confused these two beings, just as other Gnostics often mixed together the two Sophias, the two versions of Horos, or of Christ, or of the human being, the first and second one. (In any event, in Matter's presentation interchanges of this kind are not infrequent.) This duality of similar natures, albeit an afterthought, is something very noteworthy. With this mode of representation the Gnostics seem to have in view Plato's theory of ideas; or else, together with Plato, they formulated this view from the same source, namely the [Zoroastrian] doctrine of the *feruers* [*fravasis*, or pre-existing spirits]. – How is it possible to gain a clear picture of a system's internal coherence in this fashion? If one does not distinguish between different viewpoints, between factions, then there is no justification at all for distinguishing a Spirit Ophis from the serpentine form. For Irenaeus and Epiphanius explicitly state that this serpentine form itself is what enticed Eve to disobey. Given what we have seen, even Matter's remarks on p. 206, that no other system has brought the angelic spirit of evil into such close contact with the Demiurge, cannot be regarded as correct regarding the Ophites.

96. Portraying the serpentine formation of the human intestines as the life-engendering power of Sophia belongs in this context. [*Ed.*] Baur then includes a Greek quotation from Theodoret, *Heretical Tales*, 1.14, to this effect, and also refers to Irenaeus, *Against Heresies* 1.30.15, where it says, "By the

having a more favorable opinion of the world's creator, as we must assume the Sethians did, one is more inclined to regard the creator as a limited being rather than evil in nature. In doing so one could not have set out from the usual view that the serpent is a tempter to do evil, with that also being the reason why it is not unjust for the creator's curse to fall on that demon—indeed even more deservedly, since the serpent, as his son, directly sinned against his father.

Accordingly, in light of these factors, we have to view what has been taken to be the Ophite teaching as a whole simply as the Sethian doctrine. It is even very likely that the name Ophite itself originally belonged only to the sect whose view of the serpent contrasts the most with the traditional view; that therefore, as the Cainites saw it, the serpent is not an evil demon but instead is an angelic spirit of light.[97] Yet notwithstanding the fact that, even on this assumption, the Sethians held that enticement by the serpent led to the human beings becoming truly aware of their relation to the primal father, this does not count as an objection to the view I just stated. That is because this relationship is wholly in accord with the fundamental idea of the Ophite system, the idea that the subordinate, and more or less evil, powers must, against their will, serve the purposes of the realm of light. The demon in serpentine form (*serpentiformis et contortus Nus* [serpentine and twisted Nous]) above all just wanted to induce them to disobey Ialdabaoth's commandment; for doing so fit with his twisted nature (his *tortuositas*),[98] and with his perpetual feuding with spirits understood as being beneath him. Yet this was all under Sophia's control and a means for realizing higher purposes.

In the beginning Adam and Eve had light and bright bodies, or spiritual bodies, as the ones they were created with. But when they came down into this world they underwent a transformation; their bodies became more opaque, thicker and heavier, their souls slack and weak, since they had just received a breath of the world spirit from the world's creator. This is how Irenaeus[99] presents the Ophite doctrine, and we of course therefore see how it finds a place for the idea of a fall from the higher world into the lower world but without shedding any satisfactory light on the connection between this description and the Fall. There does not seem to be a sufficient reason given for why the higher consciousness awakened in human beings immediately disappears once more, or what basis Sophia could have had for rejoicing over the world's creator being overcome by his own creature if he still had it in his power in turn to thwart the purpose of Sophia that had scarcely been achieved. In any case we must assume

---

position of our intestines, through which the food is conveyed, and by the fact that they possess such a figure, our internal configuration in the form of a serpent reveals our hidden generatrix" (*ANF* 1:358).

97. This is why Irenaeus, 1.30.15, says: "For some of them assert that Sophia herself became the serpent" [*ANF* 1:358]. The names the Ophites gave to the serpent perhaps also relate to this twofold view of it. According to Irenaeus, 1.30.9, they say "the serpent cast down has two names, Michael and Samael. According to the rabbis, the latter is also a well-known name of the Devil" [*ANF* 1:356].

98. Irenaeus, *Against Heresies* 1.30.5.

99. 1.30.9. [*Ed.*] Much of what follows is a paraphrase of 1.30.9 and 10.

that, as things stand, this is the natural consequence of falling from the higher world into the world below; that Sophia's purpose was also achieved at least in part; that the world's creator was not allowed to have his own purposes be completely unsuccessful; and that all this must have taken place if the historical development of the world and of humankind is said to be advanced along the lines of this persistent antagonism.

In any event Sophia, or Prunicus, got directly engaged again in the interest of the human beings. She took pity on them in their state of need. She restored to them the pleasing aroma of the sprinkled light by which they became aware of their nakedness and recognized that they had material bodies. Of course they learned to feel the burden of their mortality, but they also saw themselves uplifted by the consciousness that this body will only be the shell enveloping them for a certain time. Sophia satisfied them with her means of sustenance, they mated, and they bore Cain, whom the serpent demon claimed directly as his own. He made Cain worldly and forgetful, plunging him into folly and arrogance so that he slew his brother Abel and brought envy and death into the world. After this, under the providential guidance of Sophia, Seth was begotten and after him Norea (i.e., Noah).

The ensuing human throngs plunged the lower world's Hebdomad into all sorts of evil, apostasy, idolatry, and impiety, whereas the Mother constantly and secretly offered resistance and preserved what was her own, the sprinkles of light. Ialdabaoth, exceedingly angry that human beings neither recognized nor honored him as father and God, released a deluge to destroy them all. Here too Sophia intervened in order to rescue those who were in the ark with Noah, via the sprinkles of light issuing forth from her, whereby the world was to be repopulated by humankind. From these people Ialdabaoth chose Abraham and made a covenant with him by promising to give him a land as an inheritance if his descendents would continue to serve Ialdabaoth. Later on Moses led the descendents of Abraham out from Egypt, and gave them the law.

Each of Ialdabaoth's seven angels, who formed the Hebdomad of the seven heavenly bodies [i.e., five planets, sun, and moon], chose for himself a herald from the Jews who was to glorify him and proclaim him as god, so that also others who hear this will render the same honor to those the prophets proclaimed as gods. The Ophites assigned the prophets individually as follows. Moses, Joshua, Amos, and Habakkuk belong to Ialdabaoth; Samuel, Nathan, Jonah, and Micah belong to Iao; Elijah, Joel, and Zechariah belong to Sabaoth; Isaiah, Ezekiel, Jeremiah, and Daniel belong to Adonai; Tobias [Tobit, Hosea?[100]] and Haggai belong to Eloi; Mica (?) and Nahum belong to Oreus; Esdras and Sophonias[101] belong to Astanphaeus. Each of these prophets glorified his own father and god. However, Sophia also spoke though them about the first human being, the eternal Aeon, and the Christ on high. She reminded human beings about the eternal light and the first humans, and taught them about the coming down of Christ. The princes [of this world] were terrified by, and marveled at, the new things

---

100. [*Ed.*] Hosea is the only prophet in the Jewish canon who is omitted.
101. [*Ed.*] *ANF* gives Zephaniah, but Sophonias suggests Wisdom (of Solomon).

proclaimed by the prophets. But Sophia, working through Ialdabaoth without his being aware of it, ushered in the appearing of two men, John [the Baptist] and Jesus.

In the Ophite system the appearing of the redeemer is driven by a sorrowful state in which the Sophia down below found peace neither in heaven nor on the earth, and cried out to her mother for help. This mother, the Sophia on high, had pity on the remorseful daughter and demanded of the primal human being that Christ be sent to her aid. This Christ descended to his sister and to her sprinkles of light and brought it about that John would announce his coming and that Jesus would be summoned into existence and prepared for him. When Christ descended, coming down through the seven heavens, he assumed the form of their head and drew their collective light-power unto himself. For he was united with his sister, and the two took delight in each other, like bride and bridegroom. Thus through divine power[102] Jesus was born of a virgin, and as a human being more excellent than all others owing to his wisdom, purity, and righteousness. United to Sophia, Christ descended upon him and so he then became Jesus Christ. Many of his followers did not recognize Christ's descent upon Jesus. But when Christ had descended upon Jesus,[103] he began to perform miracles, proclaimed the unknown father and openly declared himself to be the Son of Man.

Angered by this, Ialdabaoth, his father, with his angels, arranged for Jesus' death. When Jesus was led to die, Christ, together with Sophia, forsook him and the two of them ascended to the eternal Aeon. But after Jesus had been crucified, Christ sent to him a spirit from on high, which resurrected his body, yet only the psychical and spiritual aspects, for it left the mundane aspect in the world. That is why his disciples did not recognize him. For they were unmindful of the fact that "flesh and blood cannot inherit the kingdom of God" [1 Cor 15:50]. They supposed that he rose again in his worldly or earthly body (*mundiale corpus*). Hence this amounted to his being, after his resurrection, no greater than he was before his baptism. They say Jesus lived on for eighteen months after his resurrection. Sophia provided him with a clear knowledge of truth, which he conveyed to only a few of his followers, those he thought fit to receive greater mysteries. "He was then received up into heaven, Christ sitting down (*Christo sedente*) at the right hand of his father Ialdabaoth, that he may receive to himself the souls of those who have known them, Jesus and Christ, after they have laid aside their mundane flesh, thus enriching himself without the knowledge or perception of

---

102. And indeed born because of Ialdabaoth, who therefore is called the father of Jesus. See Irenaeus, *Against Heresies* 1.30.13 and 14. The Ophites have Jesus being born as a human being, from the Virgin Mary. See 1.30.11 and 12.

103. It is not entirely clear what moment the Ophites pinpoint for the uniting of the heavenly Christ with the man Jesus. Irenaeus says (1.30.14): "They strove to establish the descent and ascent of Christ by the fact that neither before his baptism, nor after his resurrection from the dead, do his disciples state that he did any mighty works, not being aware that Jesus was united to Christ; and the incorruptible Aeon [Christ] to the Hebdomad [which probably refers to Sophia as the head of the Hebdomad] . . ." [*ANF* 1:357]. [*Ed.* The words in brackets are Baur's.] This passage seems to require the conclusion that this uniting already took place prior to Jesus' baptism.

his father."¹⁰⁴ Whereas Jesus becomes more enriched by holy souls, his father must become diminished and poorer since, via these souls, all of the light principle still within him is withdrawn from him. For things must soon reach the point where he no longer has holy souls he can send down into the world. Instead he has only the kind who are of his own substance, who are made merely of his own breath or in-spiration; in other words, just psychical natures.

The consummation of the entire course taken by the world then occurs when all the seeds of light (the *tota humectatio spiritus luminis*) are gathered together and taken up into the Aeon of Immortality. In this final doctrine the Ophite system comes close to Manicheanism, with which it has on the whole many points of contact. In Manicheanism, Christ, as the angelic spirit of the sun, draws the scattered bits of light to himself, gathers them and takes them up into his oneness; so too in the Ophite system, the Christ who descends from on high, and works through Jesus, occupies this same place for the world as a whole.

This affinity is even more striking when we also include the sects Epiphanius¹⁰⁵ depicts and assigns the general label "Gnostic." These sects are very much like the Ophites, as is especially clear from what they taught about the serpent, who is said to have imparted its Gnosis to Eve, and about the seven princes of the world, who have almost the same names as those the Ophites give them and in any event have Ialdabaoth at their head. This makes it quite obvious that all those sects Epiphanius in fact introduces under various names—Gnostics, Sethians and Cainites, Archontics, as well as Nicolaitans—belong to one and the same main lineage, differing in part just in their names. For in each case they only vary to the extent that their differences are to be regarded as merely modifications of one and the same basic outlook.

This Ophite view of Jesus points to the idea that all those holy souls, or souls of light, that Jesus draws to himself and gathers together are simply parts of one and the same whole. We find this view expressed even more explicitly among the Gnostics Epiphanius writes about. He says¹⁰⁶ they had a gospel they called the Gospel of Perfection (τελείωσις), as well as the Gospel of Eve. In this gospel the following words are undoubtedly those of Sophia, or the world-soul: "I am you and you I, and wherever

---

104. Irenaeus, *Against Heresies* 1.30.14 [ANF 1:357]. Mosheim, *Versuch einer unparteiischen und gründlichen Ketzergeschichte* (n. 84), 190, and Neander, *Genetische Entwickelung* (n. 6), 267, both state that the words *Christo sedente* ("Christ sitting") are obviously an error, because only Jesus as Ialdabaoth's son could have sat at his right hand, whereas Christ could not have done so. I cannot agree. The words do not say what people suppose they do. Instead they say that Christ has taken his seat to the right of Ialdabaoth, the father of Jesus; that is, within the Pleroma, because the distinction is between the Pleroma (as the right side) and what is found outside it (as the left side). That is why Irenaeus writes in 1.30.2: "Christ, as belonging to the right side, and ever tending to what was higher, was immediately caught up with his mother to form an incorruptible Aeon" [ANF 1:354]. The reference in 1.30.14, to both Jesus and Christ, should be understood in the way these two are spoken about subsequently. Jesus is in fact the instrument or agent through which Christ works.

105. *Against Heresies* 26.

106. Ibid., 26.2.5–6.

you are, there am I, and I am scattered about in everything. And from wherever you wish, you gather me, but in gathering me you gather yourself."[107] This same world-soul is also said to be spread throughout the whole of nature. Epiphanius tells us[108] that is why, when these same Gnostics ate flesh (which, like the Manicheans, they regarded as something belonging to the archon) or vegetables or bread or other means of sustenance, they believed they were doing so in the interest of the creature, inasmuch as they gathered the souls from all of them and transferred them into the heavenly realm with themselves. That is the reason they ate all kinds of meat, for they said doing so was showing pity to their own kind. They maintained that the same soul is spread about in both domestic and wild animals, in the fishes and serpents, as it is in human beings, and likewise spread about in vegetables, in trees and grain.

A gospel this same sect attributes to the Apostle Philip, attaches these words to the soul that ascends to the light-world and does not wish to be held back by the heavenly powers, by those it must make its way through: "I have recognized myself and have collected myself from everywhere, and I have not begotten any children with the archon, the ruler of the world. Instead I have torn up his roots and collected the dispersed members. I know who you are, for I stem from on high."[109] All these ideas and doctrines are very closely related to those of Manicheanism,[110] even though there is no way of pinpointing how the two groups are externally related.

---

107. [*Ed.*] ET in Amidon (n. 35), 76.

108. *Against Heresies* 26.9.3–5.

109. Ibid., 26.13.2 [Amidon, 81].

110. The sect Epiphanius refers to as "Gnostic" has its docetism in common with the Manicheans. In 26.10.4–5, he has them speaking of "our Christ who came down and showed men this knowledge and whom they call Jesus. But he was not born of Mary, but shown through Mary. He did not take flesh; that was only an appearance" [Amidon, 79]. See also pp. 132–38 of my treatise, *Das manichäische Religionssystem* (n. 40). Indeed, Epiphanius in particular clearly assumes that much of what is purportedly Gnostic is actually Manichean. Yet on the other hand it is also quite likely that, as Manicheanism initially and willingly associated itself with related forms when it spread into lands to the west, by incorporating Gnostic ideas and doctrine it found there, Manicheanism gave itself the more specific form in which we know it. – The foundations of the Ophite system are very ancient. That may also be inferred from the fact that, unlike the other Gnostic systems, it is not traceable back to an individual who first created it and founded the sect. For the Euphrates whom, according to Origen's *Against Celsus*, 6.28, the Ophite sect was said to revere as its founder ("the Ophites boast of one Euphrates as the introducer of these unhallowed opinions" [*ANF* 4:586]) is such an obscure figure that he cannot be set alongside the known founders of other Gnostic sects. Doubtless all that constitutes the teachings the Ophites have in common with those sects belonging in the same class or category with them we have to look upon as the first, and more specific, form of Jewish and Jewish-Christian Gnosis. Hence it is also especially noteworthy how this system bears within it all the nuances of its Jewish origin. The close ties between Sophia of the Ophites and the Sophia (Wisdom) of the Old Testament Apocryphal books is most striking. (See above, pp. 23 and 110.) The Ophite angels and demons have Jewish names almost everywhere. Compare the angels' names on p. 110 above with those in Origen, *Against Celsus*, 6.32, where he writes: "They have borrowed from magic the names of Ialdabaoth, and Astaphaeus, and Horaeus, and from the Hebrew scriptures him who is termed in Hebrew Iao or Jah, and Sabaoth, and Adonaeus, and Eloaeus. Now the names taken from the scriptures are names of one and the same God" [*ANF* 4:588]. In 6.30 and elsewhere Origen says the names of their demons were Michael (in

## Part Two: The Various Principal Forms of Gnosis

What I have introduced here should simply serve to call attention to a difference between the Valentinian and Ophite systems. The Valentinian system also has everything pneumatic emerging from the Mother, Achamoth. Yet at the same time it holds more clearly to the idea of spiritual individuality, and does not identify the pneumatic element in human beings (the πνευματικοί or spiritual ones who, as such, are not by nature on an equal footing with their kinfolk but stand strictly apart from the ψυχικοί and the ὑλικοί, the psychical and material ones) in the same way as the Ophites do, with the light principle spread throughout nature. That is why the Valentinian system also knows of no Jesus who draws unto himself the souls, like rays of light. Instead it only speaks of a redeemer who enters into the Pleroma together with the pneumatic ones when they are perfected. The Valentinian system obviously has a more spiritual and idealistic character than the more realistically configured system of the Ophites.

---

the form of a lion), Suriel (as a bull), Raphael (as a serpent), Gabriel (as an eagle), Thauthabaoth (with the head of a bear), Erataoth (with a dog's head), Thaphabaoth or Onoel (with the head of an ass). The Ophites themselves adopted the Hebrew name of Naassenes, from the Hebrew word for serpent, as Theodoret tells us. There is no basis for the distinction Mosheim draws (in his *Ketzergeschichte* [n. 84], 21) between Christian and non-Christian Ophites, since nowhere do we find any mention of non-Christian Ophites. The passage he cites to make his case is Origen, *Against Celsus*, 6.28, where it says of the Ophites that they "are so far from being Christians, that they bring accusations against Jesus to as great a degree as Celsus himself; and they do not admit anyone into the assembly until he has uttered maledictions against Jesus" [*ANF* 4:586]. As Gieseler has very corrected noted (on p. 846 of his review that I referenced above [n. 12]), given the larger context, Origen cannot be speaking merely about one group of the Ophites. In his Commentary on Matthew, Origen himself groups the Ophites together with Marcion, Basilides, and the Valentinians, as "those who profess that they are of the church." It may well be that, in *Against Celsus*, 6.28, he only means they want to oppose the Catholic Christians, and just to say that they deplore the Jesus of the Catholic Church. In other words, we may assume that the later Ophites of Origen's day were the only ones to sharpen the antithesis, between the psychical Jesus and the pneumatic Christ, to such an extent that cursing the limited messiah of the psychical believers ultimately became a sign that one is a disciple of the higher Christ. (See Gieseler, as well as Neander, *Allgemeine Geschichte der christlichen Religion und Kirche* [Hamburg, 1825–31], 1:756.)—Given all this, it may very well be that there were Ophites prior to Christianity. Undoubtedly they sprang from the soil of the Judaism that was infused with Egyptian ideas. The significance they gave to the serpent is an ancient Egyptian theme, and we are likewise reminded of ancient Egyptian symbolism by the fact that their demons are figures with the heads of animals, and have their basis in an underlying animal symbolism. In this connection their Holy Communion, or mystery rites, where they set up a table with loaves of bread they break and share among themselves (Epiphanius, *Heresies* 37.5), even has a certain similarity to the mysteries of the Therapeutae (as described by Philo, in *On the Contemplative Life*). If we were to have a better understanding of the Ophites' rules for prayer according to Origen, and their so-called geometrical diagrams in the way the most recent research does (in particular, I think, how we are to understand the so-far-neglected arrangement of the planetary portals and spheres, which scholars have not yet fathomed), then that would surely let us point to even further agreement with ancient Egyptian religious ideas. Neander (*Genetische Entwickelung* [n. 6], 251) understands the "complete oblivion" (λήθη ἀπερίσκεπτος) in the first one of these rules for prayers (according to *Against Celsus*, 6.31) as the forgetting of higher things that precedes the descent of the soul, a forgetting the Ophites called the "forgetting of cosmic things" (λήθη κοσμική). In Irenaeus (1.30.9) there is at least mention, albeit in quite general terms, of a "mundane oblivion." In any event, however, the Ophites' entire representation of the planets is tied to the ancient doctrine about the wandering of souls. So Mosheim has correctly reminded us of the ideas about this that we find in Macrobius.

The more Gnostic idealism crosses over into realism, the more the spiritual principle is thought of as a world soul spread throughout nature, as a material principle of light whose dispersed parts must be collected and united in a physical way. And that makes it easier for Gnosticism to undergo that immoral degeneration it often experienced among the masses, through sects like the Ophites and others discussed by Epiphanius. It also led to a horror of provocative practices, a topic Epiphanius discusses at length in the chapter of his *Heresies* to which we have referred.

## How the Christian and Pre-Christian Elements in the Ophite and Valentinian Systems Are Related

After this presentation of the contents of the Ophite system, we have to consider the question as to how correct it is to classify it as I have done, by placing it alongside the Valentinian system. In doing so we also have to look back at the Valentinian system, in order to justify in more specific terms this placement of the two systems.

Based on its external form, the Ophite system seems to attach itself more closely to Judaism on the one hand, but also to position itself in an even more contrary relation to Judaism on the other hand. In the Valentinian system the Jewish element takes more of a back seat to its predominantly Platonic character; yet the result, on the whole, is that Valentinianism relates to both paganism and Judaism in the same way.

If we set out from the features people typically assign to the anti-Jewish character of Ophite teaching, then all those attributes the Ophites assign to Ialdabaoth and his spirits presuppose a very minimal concept of the religious value of Judaism. All the writers of the Old Testament scriptures have written under the influence of these lower spirits, and Sophia or Wisdom has made the higher wisdom known in just a few passages. Still, on this issue we ought not merely stop with the Sethians. The Cainites, who are their counterparts, also set out from the same principles and set themselves apart only by giving them an even more extensive application. They say that once the God of the Old Testament has been demoted to the level of Ialdabaoth, and the claims of Judaism to truth and godliness have been so severely contracted and contested, no further step was needed to arrive at the view that, in the Old Testament, such minimal truth proceeds from the Jewish God that one must instead locate truth in what is Judaism's direct opposite. As Epiphanius informs us,[111] the Cainites made this view into a basic thesis, saying that "they honor the wicked (those whom the Old Testament calls wicked), and they repudiate good people."[112]

---

111. *Against Heresies* 38.2.6 [Amidon (n. 35), 133–34].

112. According to Epiphanius (38.1) the world's creator, the maker of the vessel of all things, the vessel of the heavens and the earth, the Cainites call the ὑστέρα. In *Genetische Entwickelung* (n. 6), 249, Neander takes this word to be synonymous with ὑστέρημα (deficiency). But ὑστέρα just means *uterus*, which entirely fits with the other term for the world's creator here, since κύτος (vessel) amounts to the same thing as ὑστέρα. So this is what the Cainites called the world of the Demiurge, in order to designate it as the world of procreation and birth, as the world of birth and change (*Geburtswechsel*).

In keeping with the dualistic view prevalent especially in these Ophite sects, they assumed a constant antagonism between two hostile powers or forces, an antagonism that exists in general but was present, first and foremost, in the very earliest history; an antagonism between good and evil powers, between stronger and weaker ones. Cain stemmed from the stronger power, Abel from the weaker one. Each of these powers engendered its offspring with Eve. Adam and Eve themselves certainly stemmed from these same powers or angels. Thus the sons begotten from Adam and Eve also now quarreled, and the son of the stronger power killed the son of the weaker power. That is why each person must hold to the stronger power and keep apart from the weaker power, that is, apart from the power that created heaven, the flesh, and the world; why one must rise up to the highest regions by means of Christ's crucifixion. The reason Christ came from above is so that the stronger power would become fully present through him and would triumph by relinquishing the body.

Among the apostles, Judas was the one who best understood this. Since the rulers of this world (ἄρχοντες) were well aware that they will be increasingly stripped of their power by Christ's crucifixion, Judas hastened to turn Christ over to the Jews as quickly as possible, in order to become the author of our salvation by doing so. Irenaeus writes:[113] "They declare that Judas the traitor was thoroughly acquainted with these things, and that he alone, knowing the truth as no others did, accomplished the mystery of the betrayal. Thus he threw into confusion all things, both heavenly things and earthly things." So the very ones who, in conventional thinking, count as the most reprehensible figures, namely, Cain and Judas, accordingly formed a sequence of those who served the truth and acted as instruments of the higher principle.

While the Gnostics seemed to set what they regarded as the true religion, the one Christ revealed, in a harsh antithesis to conventional Judaism, they nevertheless accepted no such absolute antithesis between what was Christian and what was pre-Christian. On their view the pre-Christian period also already contained the elements of truth and a revelation of the divine. The only proviso was that one ought not seek all such things where people usually found them, in the sphere of Judaism proper. Hence what marks out this class of Gnostics always is what they taught about the operations of Sophia, already in the pre-Christian period. She was the one from whom all that is true and godly issued forth from the outset, and came to be received in the world in a vital and effective way. This is the same Sophia who, in the Cainite version, made into her chosen instruments Cain, Esau, and the Sodomites, as well as Korah and his followers;[114] whereas according to the Sethians she chose Seth and those belonging to his family line as her agents. Her purpose in doing this was to implant the divine sparks of light in the human race. The Cainites saw Cain as the progenitor of the pneumatic race, whereas the Sethians had Seth playing this role.

---

113. *Against Heresies* 1.31.1 [ANF 1:358].

114. [*Ed.*] Numbers 16 tells how Korah and a large group of his fellow Levites rebelled against Moses' leadership.

In the struggle with the angel who had created the world and produced Cain and Abel, after Abel had been killed the higher power deposited in Seth all that is pneumatic, so that through him, the pure and strong one, and his pure lineage, set apart from the world, the power of that angel would be destroyed.[115] But this struggle with the hostile powers, who sought to adulterate the godly race with the ungodly one, had to be constantly won anew. In order to maintain the holy and righteous race of Seth in its purity in the world, so that the higher race and the light-sparks of justice would develop from the lineage of Seth, Sophia resolved to eradicate the entire corrupt world by the Flood. However, the angel saw a way to insert Ham from its own race into the ark. That is why the old confusion, depravity, and impiety resumed after the Deluge. Nevertheless, Sophia's holy race was maintained because of her foresight, until finally Jesus Christ came forth from that race, or rather Seth himself reappeared in the world in an extraordinary way, in Christ.[116] Accordingly this points to an ongoing series of divine revelations throughout the entire pre-Christian period, due to the unceasing activity of Sophia, so that there now unfolded what had previously been present at least in the form of seeds, and could have only been consummated in Christianity.

This is entirely the same view of the relation between what is Christian, and what is pre-Christian, as that underlying the Valentinian system. The milder its verdict about the Demiurge was, the more it had to take the side of the Ophite factions that recognized divine truth was also handed down in the scriptures of the Old Testament itself. According to Irenaeus,[117] the Demiurge is even drawn to those pneumatic souls stemming from Achamoth; that he loves them more dearly than all the others, without knowing the reason why he does; that he supposes they have received this nature from him. Hence he assigns them to prophets, priests, and kings. These Valentinians maintain that it is through the influence of the light principle that the prophets expressed many things, since they have souls of a higher nature. They say the Mother also proclaimed a great deal about higher things, even doing so via the Demiurge himself and the souls created by him. This is why they draw distinctions among the prophecies according to whether they were uttered by the Mother, by the light-seeds, or by the Demiurge; just as in Jesus' case, whether what he says is spoken by the redeemer, by the Mother, or by the Demiurge.

---

115. Epiphanius, *Against Heresies* 40.5 [Amidon (n. 35), 136–37], presents the same thing as the teaching of the Archontics sect (Ἀρχοντικοί). They say that the Devil begat Cain and Abel with Eve. The quarrel and murder occurred because they were both in love with their sister. When Adam begat with Eve his own true son, Seth, the power above (ἄνω δύναμις) or Sophia came down, together with the angels of the good God, who were serving her, and took away Seth, whom the Archontics also call the "Alien" (ἀλλογενής). After Seth had spent a long time in the higher world, so that he would not be killed, he came down again into this world. Here he did not worship the world's creator, but instead acknowledged only the unnamable power and good God on high. They sought to publish books about this Seth, ones both about Seth himself and about his seven sons, for he has begotten so many, which the Archontics call "Aliens."

116. Epiphanius, *Against Heresies* 39.1ff.

117. *Against Heresies* 1.7.3.

We see even more specifically and clearly, from the important document Epiphanius has preserved for us,[118] how the Valentinians customarily distinguished among the various components of the Old Testament's religious teachings. It is a letter by Ptolemaeus, to a certain Flora, about the Valentinian teachings,[119] which are its main contents. Ptolemaeus sets out from the main antithesis in the existing view of the Old Testament.

> The Mosaic law cannot have been given by the perfect God and Father, for it is too deficient and so much in it is incomplete. It even contains commandments wholly in conflict with God's nature and will. Yet it is equally clear that the laws could not be attributed to the injustice of God's adversary. It cannot be the work of a pernicious God, for it can only be the work of a God who is good and hates evil. The two opposed views have their respective bases in the fact that one view (of those who assign the Old Testament to the evil demon) does not know the God of justice or righteousness, while the other view (of those who trace it back to the supreme God) likewise hardly know the Father of all, who has been revealed solely by the one who has come, the one who alone knew him. But whoever is familiar with both views is also the only one who can have the true concept of the law. Hence one must know that the entire law, contained in the five Books of Moses, is not from a single lawgiver, for it also has human commandments in it. Thus, according to the redeemer's teaching, the law is to be divided into three parts: 1. God's own legislation; 2. Moses' teaching when not decreeing as God's instrument but based on his own thinking; 3. the ordinances given by the elders of the people.

Ptolemaeus justifies this clear distinction between the divine commandment and Moses' commandment, based on what Jesus says in Matt 19:6–8.[120] We are not to forget that Moses did not arbitrarily deviate from the original law of God but did so because he had to, from consideration for the weakness of those to whom he gave his laws. However, in Matt 15:3–6 and Mark 7:3[121] the Savior says that traditions of the elders have also been mixed into the laws.

---

118. *Against Heresies* 33.3.1–33.7.10.

119. [*Ed.*] Ptolemaeus was the leader of a sect Epiphanius calls the Ptolemaeans, and was a follower of Valentinus, although he deviated somewhat from the master's positions. The entire text of the Letter to Flora is in Amidon (n. 35), 119–23. It is also found in *Ptolemée, Lettre à Flora*, ed., trans., and annotated by G. Quispel (Paris, 1966). But rather than relying on the existing English translation, we have decided to translate Baur's abbreviated German version as it stands, in the lengthy selections that follow.

120. [*Ed.*] Matt 19:6–8: "'what God has joined together, let no one separate.' They said to him, 'why then did Moses command us to give a certificate of dismissal and to divorce her?' He said to them, 'It was because you were so hardhearted that Moses allowed you to divorce your wives, but from the beginning it was not so.'"

121. [*Ed.*] Matt 15:3–7a: "'why do you break the commandment of God for the sake of your tradition? . . . So, for the sake of your tradition, you make void the word of God. You hypocrites!'" Mark 7:3: "For the Pharisees, and all the Jews, do not eat unless they thoroughly wash their hands, thus

Ptolemaeus in turn divides into three parts that portion of the law deriving from God himself.

> One part of the legislation is completely pure, is unmixed with evil. It is pre-eminently the law that the redeemer came not to nullify but to fulfill. For the law that he fulfilled cannot have been alien to him. Another part of the law is mixed with more inferior contents, and this is the injustice the redeemer annulled because it conflicts with his own nature. However, there is yet another part of the law, the laws that are figurative and symbolic in their function. The redeemer has transposed these laws from the sensible realm of appearances into what is spiritual and unseen. The pure and unmixed part of the legislation is the Decalogue. It involves what one must utterly refrain from doing, or what one must do. Yet this part of the legislation was also still imperfect because it needed to be completed by the Savior. The second part of the law, the part mixed with unjust elements, deals with retaliation on offenders, with recompense for evil (Lev 24:20).[122] But when the person retaliating does wrong it is no less wrong; the wrongdoer has a different place in the sequence, but the deed is the same. Such commandments may otherwise be just, but they run counter to the nature and goodness of the Father of all and can only be given as the result of a necessary concession to human weakness. That is why the Son had to abolish this part of the law, while at the same time acknowledging that it is from God. The figurative part of the law concerns everything that is an image of what is spiritual and higher. It includes the sacrificial offerings, circumcision, the Sabbath, the fasts, Passover, and the like. All these things, said to be just images and symbols, have a different character after the revelation of the truth. They are annulled with regard to their external and corporeal features but have an ongoing, spiritual meaning, such that the name remains the same but the things themselves have a different nature.

Following this discussion, Ptolemaeus continues:

> Since the author of the law can be neither the perfect God nor the Devil, it must have been given by another. This third one is the world's creator, who differs from the other two and is correctly located as intermediate between them. Neither good nor evil, he can only have a nature of a middling sort. What falls most especially to him is what is just and the administration of justice. He is inferior to the perfect God and not his equal in righteousness, since he begets and is not unbegotten (for there is only one unbegotten Father, from whom, in the highest sense, everything is and on whom everything depends). But he is above, is greater than and superior to God's adversary. In nature and substance he is as different from the one as he is from the other. The nature

---

observing the tradition of the elders."

122. [*Ed.*] Lev 24:20: "... fracture for fracture, eye for eye, tooth for tooth; the injury inflicted is the injury to be suffered."

of God's adversary is one of destruction and darkness, for matter and what is divergent are his domain, whereas the unbegotten Father of all is everlasting and light, what is unitary and whole. The intermediate being's frame of mind has produced a twofold power, although this world-creator is the image of what is higher.

In this remarkable letter Ptolemaeus only speaks about the legislation contained in the five Books of Moses. Nevertheless it is correct to assume that he would also have drawn the same distinctions regarding the various components of the prophetic scriptures. Hence we may, with justification, regard him as the main representative of those who of course strictly distinguished the Old Testament God from the supreme God, but at the same time related the two as closely as possible, and so also could not deny that the Demiurge has the attribute of revealing the divine.

This is where the Valentinians differentiate themselves from that group of Ophites who basically regarded the Demiurge as directly the principle of evil. Except that this distinction got offset in turn by the fact that what the one sect had being mediated by the Demiurge, the other one had all the more immediately from Sophia. The major consideration we therefore have to keep firmly in mind regarding this entire class of Gnostics is always their recognizing a sphere of divine revelation related to Christian revelation and already present in the pre-Christian era. This sphere of pre-Christian revelation of course then falls, first and foremost, in the domain of Old Testament religious history. (Even the Cainites found the agency of Sophia in the figures of the Old Testament.) What we are still missing is the additional and typical sign of this class of Gnostics, the fact that they do not confine this sphere merely to Judaism. It also extends to the domain of pagan religion. But although there are not comparably specific and explicit testimonies to this enlarging of the concept of revelation (κοινοποιεῖν τὴν ἀλήθειαν, or "making the truth for everyone," as Clement of Alexandria puts it), there is nevertheless the clearest evidence of it in the nature of these systems themselves. Everything in them that, as a result of their presentation and development, has been adopted from the Platonism of that era and from the theogonic and cosmogonic ideas of ancient religion, involves at the same time an indirect verdict about the religious worth of paganism in its relation to Judaism. These Gnostic groups could not possibly have given pagan religion and philosophy such an influence on the contents and form of their own systems, had they not been guided by the general view that the sphere of pre-Christian revelation comprises both paganism and Judaism, and that the seeds of light sown by a higher power have found a receptive soil in both places.

The fact that the creator of the world is thought of simultaneously as the God of Judaism cannot be the basis for any objections to this view, for, as the world's creator, he cannot merely be the God of the Jews exclusively. In any event he is himself dependent on Sophia, who stands above him. Sophia's superior status is, as such, the major concept on which what is distinctive about these systems concentrates. All those names or descriptive titles given to Sophia, in their multiple and changing forms—the Holy Spirit as a female being, the Mother, the Mother of all living things or the Mother of life, Prunicus, Barbelo or Barbero, the androgynous one, the left side, and so forth[123]—always indicate this same connection between pagan and Jewish representations, ones predominant here and taking their point of departure from that wisdom of course depicted in the Apocrypha and in the Old Testament. The syzygy formed by the female Sophia and the male Christ best makes vivid the relationship these systems assume exists between the pre-Christian religions, paganism and Judaism, and Christianity itself.

## 3. The Systems of Bardesanes, Saturninus, and Basilides

It will suffice to say just a few things about the systems finding their place here. That is because, especially in the fragmentary form they have come down to us, they are not inherently as significant as the systems we have already presented. Also because they are so closely related to those other systems that what is distinctive about these next ones and can be suitably emphasized is fairly obvious.

### Bardesanes

The Syrian Gnostic, Bardesanes, comes closest to the Valentinians and the Ophites. Here we find, without any essential modifications: the syzygies of the Aeons; Sophia, or Achamoth, plunging down into chaos; Christ the redeemer, descending to lift her up and unite himself with her; the Demiurge; and the entire process of development linked to this state of affairs.

The other two, Saturninus and Basilides, contrast with Bardesanes at least in that their systems do not speak of a Sophia or Achamoth. Instead they explain the origin of the world not so much as the result of a falling-away, but instead in dualistic terms; it arises from a hostile interaction of opposed forces or powers.

### Saturninus

The first issue is what we can say in more specific terms about this dualism, on the basis of our inadequate sources.

According to Epiphanius,[124] Saturninus spoke of angels, archangels, powers and authorities brought forth by the one, unknowable Father. He especially spoke of seven angels who made the world. Epiphanius also mentions a Satan. However, it is very unclear how this Satan may be related to the angels making the world, and how Satan is engaged in this creative process. Nevertheless, the teaching of Saturninus is so very

---

123. See *Das manichäische Religionssystem* (n. 40), 473.
124. *Against Heresies* 23.1.3; 23.2.5–6 [the next paragraph draws on 23.2.2–5].

similar to the Manichean doctrine that their having an analogous, dualistic foundation can hardly be in doubt.

The accounts about Saturninus in the ancient writers mainly concern his teaching about the creation of human beings. Indeed in this doctrine Saturninus agrees with the Manicheans.[125] The creation of human beings occurs as the result of a ray of light falling down to the angels standing far below and suddenly in turn vanishing, and an intense desire aroused within them, enticing them to make a likeness of that heavenly phenomenon. Except that these world-creating angels, with the Jewish God at the head of their group, are not the evil powers of the Manichean system but are instead the opponents of the Satan who battles against them. However, further doctrines are then wholly in the spirit of Manichean dualism. This teaching holds that in the beginning there were two human lineages, a good one and a bad one, and that with the help of the demons the bad lineage came to predominate over the good one, which made it necessary for the redeemer to appear. But this was a purely docetic appearing.[126] It holds that marriage and having children just prove to be the work of Satan, and that one must abstain from the pleasures of the flesh (ἐμψύχων).

What Saturninus said about the [biblical] prophecies[127] is that "some prophecies were made by the angels who made the world, and some by Satan." This statement certainly indicates his general view regarding the relationship of the good and evil principles in the world. A hostile, evil principle has of course taken hold in the created world. Yet at the same time, in the human being created according to the likeness of the divine light, there dwells by the same token a spark of light imparted from above, and it must be set free.[128]

## Basilides

Basilides was a contemporary of Saturninus (in fact Irenaeus and Epiphanius refer to both of them as students of Menander) and the two of them are often grouped together. It is even more difficult to determine the extent to which Basilides was a dualist.

According to Irenaeus and Epiphanius,[129] in Basilides' system too the angels who stood at the lowest level of the heavens that emanated from the primal being, as its image and counterpart, were the creators of the world. The violence with which the

---

125. See my *Das manichäische Religionssystem* (n. 40), 150.

126. [*Ed.*] Within the text at this point, in parentheses and in Greek, Baur quotes Epiphanius, *Against Heresies* 23.1.10, which states that "Christ himself came in human shape and appearance only, and did everything only seemingly: being born, walking about, being seen, and suffering" [Amidon (n. 35), 66].

127. *Against Heresies* 23.2.6 [Amidon, 66].

128. Ibid., 23.1.8–9: "The spark is the human soul. For this reason the spark is altogether saved, while all that is man perishes" [Amidon, 66].

129. Irenaeus, 1.24.4; Epiphanius, 24.1–2. [*Ed.*] Basilides taught in Alexandria from 117 to 138.

God of the Jews seized power for himself, and sought to make subordinate to him the other angels to whom the world was parceled out, provoked a war. Ultimately this caused such confusion in the world that the supreme Father had to send down Nous, his firstborn, to reestablish order. But he just came in an apparent form, and when the Jews believed him to be crucified, he indeed left the cross and took on the physical shape of Simon of Cyrene while giving the real Simon of Cyrene his own body. This was done so that Simon became the one crucified by the Jews, while he himself stood to the side, laughed at the Jews, and then rose up to the one who had sent him.

There is nothing actually dualistic about all of this. But since Irenaeus and Epiphanius are most likely just describing the teaching of later followers of Basilides, our only authentic sources for the teaching of Basilides himself are the random, fragmentary accounts found in Clement of Alexandria and in a passage of the *Acta disputationis Archelai*.[130] The *Acta* assigns Basilides[131] directly to the dualists and forerunners of Mani, and links his teaching to Persian dualism. This leaves no doubt about his being the same person as the Gnostic Basilides. In a passage the *Acta* introduces from Book 13 of the *Tractatus* by Basilides, he himself refers to the teaching of the Persians: "Those (foreigners) said that at the beginning everything consisted of a duality that they associate with good and evil (or bad). They say these were implanted; in other words, they were in principle light and darkness, which were themselves from seeds and were not said to have being." The two principles at first were by themselves. "Once each one has recognized the other, and the darkness has circumscribed the light, as they strove to acquire something better those elements pressed forward to intermingle."

If we now link with this passage what Clement of Alexandria says[132] about a τάραχός τις (confusion of each), and a σύγχυσις ἀρχική (original mixing together), which is the state of affairs according to Basilides' teaching, then this mixing together obviously fits very well with the intermingling (*commisceri*) spoken of by the *Acta*. Although the expression "original mixing together" is ambiguous—inasmuch as it can signify either a mixing together of the principles, the ἀρχαί, or an intermixing at the beginning [of the world-process]—that makes no difference, since a mixing together of two different principles is always presupposed. Gieseler remarks[133] that, in the context where Clement speaks of that original mixing together, this expression seems to refer, in the first place, to the human souls' initial fall into sin—something Basilides had to accept since, in keeping with his own strict theory about God's justice, he could not allow that human souls are caught up in the bonds of matter without any

---

130. [*Ed.*] A 4th c. anti-Manichean text traditionally attributed to Hegemonius. A Latin edition was published in 1698. Baur cites ch. 55.

131. Undoubtedly the same person as the well-known Gnostic Basilides; see my *Das manichäische Religionssystem* (n. 40), 84.

132. In *Stromata* 2.20 [*ANF* 3:372].

133. In *Theologische Studien und Kritiken* (1830), 396.

antecedent guilt on their part, without any freely-willed inclination toward matter and intermingling with it, an inclination whereby the lusts and desires, as προσαρτήματα (appendages of the flesh) that human beings have in common with the animals, are affixed to them, appendages by which humans are under the influence of matter. Yet even this remark of Gieseler's does not delimit the "original mixing," since in keeping with the general character of the Gnostic systems a "mixing together" with regard to souls always presupposes a mixing together of the principles as such.

The only question is therefore whether, regarding one of these principles, we are to simply think of an originally lifeless matter, or whether alongside it there is at the same time a being like the Satan of Saturninus and Mani, a being corresponding to the Persian Ahriman.[134] Since there are no attestations to this, one can only appeal to its being a plausible analogy. In this regard, I too cannot think of that "original mixing together" apart from some Ahriman-like activity, since it seems to me that the few reliable accounts of Basilides' teaching contain so many features reminiscent of the Zoroastrian system, ones that presuppose a closer relation between the two systems.[135]

Indeed the Ogdoad Basilides placed at the apex of his system is of a wholly different kind than the series of Aeons in the systems of the Valentinians, the Ophites, Bardesanes, and others. There is no mention here of syzygies, the conjugally linked Aeon pairs, and of all that pertains to them. This is certainly in the spirit of the Zoroastrian doctrine, which knows nothing of such symbolic representations. The Aeons that form the Ogdoad are potencies thought of abstractly, potencies that, even in name, partially remind us of the Amschaspands (Amesa Spentas) of the ancient Persians. According to Irenaeus and Epiphanius,[136] Basilides has Nous, or Logos, issuing from the supreme, unbegotten Being, Phronesis issuing from the Logos, Sophia and Dynamis from Phronesis, and from Sophia and Dynamis there issue the powers

---

134. In *Allgemeine Literatur-Zeitung* (1823), 835, Gieseler understands the teaching of Basilides, about the creation of the world, as follows: "Lifeless material (*Hyle*) receives just sparks of life from the last or lowest level of spirit coming in contact with it. As with all these levels, the more distant they became from the primal being, they more they not only became less perfect but also became closer to matter. In doing so, as each sought in turn to reveal itself in the way it was itself the revelation of the level just preceding it, the last and most imperfect stage of spirit, the one closest to matter, therefore had to stream itself forth into matter and reveal itself in matter. In this way matter became the limit or boundary of emanation, which otherwise would have gone on endlessly and would have produced ever more imperfect levels of spirit. This was also the means for bringing the emanations of light, which at each level were becoming increasingly distant from their original source, back to that source under the guidance of Nous." In any event this understanding of it is supported simply by the accounts in Irenaeus and Epiphanius.

135. [*From the Errata*] It seems to me that Origen points to such a relationship with the Zoroastrian religious system. See *Series veteris interpretationis commentariorum in Matthaeum*, 46. When Origen indicates here what is characteristic of the system of Basilides, as distinct from Marcion's doctrine and from the Valentinian tradition, he uses the expression *longa fabulositas Basilidis* (Basilides' drawn-out mythological accounts). This expression is very indicative of a system that, entirely on the model of the Zoroastrian system, draws out to a very great extent the mythically-presented struggle and conflict between two fundamental natures, throughout all its epochs and turning-points.

136. [*Ed.*] Irenaeus, 1.24.3; Epiphanius, 24.1.7.

(ἀρχάς), principalities (ἐξουσίας), and angels (ἀγγέλους). But suppose we replace these last three, which do not seem to fit properly here, agreeing with Neander and according to Clement of Alexandria,[137] where it says about Basilides that he "took up into the Ogdoad, Righteousness or Justice, and his daughter Irene or Peace, there to dwell forever," and then compare with these names and concepts the predicates given to the Persian Amschaspands by Plutarch:[138] "Oromazes created six gods, the first of Good Thought, the second of Truth, the third of Order, and, of the rest, one of Wisdom, one of Wealth, and one the Artificer of Pleasure in what is Honorable."[139] So it is rather striking that Basilides' Ogdoad and the Persian Amschaspands seem to be correlative, despite their slight conceptual differences.[140]

Even the distinctive representation of the so-called προςαρτήματα (appendages of the flesh), the passions (*Geister*) attaching themselves to the soul, seem to me to inherently bear a Zoroastrian stamp. Clement of Alexandria describes these "appendages of the flesh" according to Basilides in the same passage where he speaks of the "original mixing together," said to have been their origin. Clement writes:[141]

> According to Basilides there are in essence certain spirits attached to the rational soul, . . . and other spurious, heterogeneous spiritual forms in turn linked to them, forms of wolves, apes, lions, goats, whose properties hover about the soul as images, and make the desires of the soul correspond to the natures of these animals. For these spirits imitate the actions of the animals whose properties they bear. Not only do they take on in this way the impulses and forms of the irrational animals; they also are shaped by the movements and the beauty of plants because they even bear in themselves the properties of plants.

This is close to the Zend writings' notion of the Ahrimanic Daevas, who everywhere impinge on the good creation and attach themselves to it, covering themselves in various forms, especially in those of the most injurious animals, in order to harm human beings and entice them to do evil. In the Zend scriptures, everything arising in human beings' thoughts and desires of evil is certainly also an Ahrimanic influence, so to speak an evil demon attaching itself to people.[142]

---

137. *Stromata* 4.28.

138. *On Isis and Osiris*, 47.

139. [*Ed.*] Plutarch, *Moralia*, vol. 5, pp. 112–15, in LCL. The Artificer is a δημιουργός, a Demiurge.

140. Good Thought (εὔνοια) corresponds to Basilides' Nous as the principle of Truth (ἀλήθεια), while Wisdom (σοφία) is moreover the same in both cases, and Order (εὐνομία) combines in itself Righteousness or Justice (δικαιοσύνη) with Peace (εἰρήνη). The 365 heavens by which the spirit world descends to the created world likewise have for their model the entirety of the solar year, just as in the Zend scriptures the entire period of the battle between Ormazd and Ahriman is thought of as the great world-year.

141. *Stromata* 2. 20 [*ANF* 3:372].

142. The evil thoughts and desires in these "appendages of the flesh," as alien spirits, are to be distinguished from the human beings themselves. Compare with this the parallel passage in Clement,

On the whole these are "appendages of the flesh" attached to the rational soul. On this basis Basilides declares them all to be morally evil, in quite the same way as what in the Manichean system is called the double soul, the good and evil souls. Except that in a system [like Basilides'] that is not as decidedly dualistic as the Manichean system, the evil soul is considered rather to be the soul that is additional, or just attached, to the originally good soul. We therefore find that to be in fact the case. Isidore, the son of Basilides, wrote an essay of his own with reference to this doctrine, entitled περὶ προσφυοῦς ψυχῆς ("On the Parasitical, Evil Soul").[143] In support of it Isidore says:

> If you offer anyone a persuasive argument to the effect that the soul is not simple but that the passions of the corrupt appear by the force of the adventitious elements, then the scoundrels of humanity will have a marvelous excuse for saying, "I was compelled, I was carried away, it was not my fault, I acted unwillingly," even though it was they who took the initiative in setting their hearts on wrong, and who failed to fight against the force of the adventitious elements. We must use our greater strength through our possession of reason and be clearly seen to conquer the lower creation within us.

In other words, the evil is therefore something created in its own right within us, and so has a creator of its own, as does the good. Clement then adds his own remark: "Isidore further postulates two souls within us, like the Pythagoreans."

All of this harmonizes extremely well with the assumption of a dualism in a Zoroastrian form. However, it is less clear what position the Archon occupied in a

---

*Stromata* 2.20 [*ANF* 3:372], which quotes a letter written by Valentinus: "There is one good, whose presence is manifested by the Son. The heart can become pure by the Son alone, by the expulsion of every evil spirit from the heart. For the multitude of evil spirits dwelling in the heart do not allow it to be pure. Each of them performs his own deeds, insulting it with unseemly lusts. The heart seems to be treated like a caravanserai, one that has holes and ruts made in it, and is often filled with dung, with men living filthily in it and taking no care for the place as belonging to others. This is how the heart fares as long as no thought is taken for it, with it being unclean and the abode of many demons. But when the only good Father visits it, it is sanctified, and gleams with light. He who possesses such a heart is so blessed, that 'he shall see God' [Matt 5:8]." – Likewise in Buddhist scriptures, the body is compared to an empty house, with its empty rooms occupied by alien thieves or robbers who have unrestrained control of it, with each robber choosing his own course of action. These autonomous thieves are the senses. The Buddhists count six senses by adding to the usual five a sense of will or desire that is in a certain way the captain and leader of this robber band, because it seeks out circumstances only to be found in matter. This view is the basis of the entire Buddhist teaching about the conversion and liberation of a being from the dominance of the senses, which bring upon the world all the evils of sinful actions and their consequences for the present and the future. See Isaak Jacob Schmidt, "Ueber einige Grundlehren des Buddhaismus," in the *Mémoires de l'Academie impériale des sciences de St. Petersbourg* (Part 1, n. 24), vol. 1, bk. 3, p. 228.

143. [*Ed.*] Both the Greek and Baur's German indicate something that "grows upon" something else. The translation of this passage by John Ferguson, in *The Fathers of the Church*, vol. 85, renders the title as *On the Adventitious Soul*. The translation from Clement, 2.25, that follows is Ferguson's, in this volume, *Clement of Alexandria. Stromateis: Books One to Three* (Washington, DC, 1991), 231–32.

Basilidean system of this kind. Clement speaks of the Archon of Basilides in a passage[144] that is also noteworthy because of its other contents.

> In interpreting the divine words, "The fear of the Lord is the beginning of wisdom" (Ps 111:10; Prov 1:7), the followers of Basilides said the Archon himself, when he heard the words of the attendant spirit (the spirit active for the consummation of salvation), he was shaken by what he heard and saw, for, contrary to his expectation, the good news was being proclaimed. His dismay was called "fear," and became the beginning of the wisdom that distinguishes among the kinds of beings, that singles out, perfects, and restores or reinstates them. For the ruler of all now singles out, and sends forth (or sets free), not only the world but also the chosen ones.

As Gieseler has correctly pointed out,[145] this passage certainly does not say that the Archon served the higher world order from then on, even doing so joyfully. In any event it would only have been dismay and fear, before the self-revealing, higher level of spirit, that brought the Archon to decide to serve this higher world order. However, in doing so he would have shown evidence of a nature receptive to what is higher and related to the higher world order. Thus, unlike the world-creating angel of Saturninus, this Archon ought not be regarded as identical with the evil principle.

Yet it seems to me that, when we look more closely at this passage, it is even dubious whether that Archon's fear was for him the beginning of wisdom; in other words doubtful that it became his motive for wisely deciding to serve the higher world order. The passage can also just be saying that period of separation and restoration was only able to begin with the Archon's fear and dismay. That is because, in the very circumstances where the higher world order came about, the Archon had to see his previous realm in all the greater danger—that in fact the beginning of the higher realm was the end of his own kingdom.[146]

But what makes it even more apparent that this is the correct interpretation are other indications in Clement of Alexandria seeming to show that in fact Basilides regarded the Archon as a being hostilely resistant to the Christian world order, as the prince of the cosmos who now decided on his own (ἐκλογή) to constitute the opposition. Clement[147] attributes to Basilides the statement: "How is it not atheism to assign a place to the Devil?" Indeed I too might have agreed with Neander[148] on

---

144. *Stromata* 2.8. [*Ed.*] Cf. *ANF* 2:355 and Ferguson, 182–3. Baur's interpolations in parentheses.

145. In *Allgemeine Literatur-Zeitung* (1823) (n. 12), 836, in opposition to Neander.

146. The passage about the Archon hearing the proclamation of the good news does not state what Neander's interpretation (in his *Allgemeine Geschichte* [n. 110], 1:694) says it does. It only says the Archon was affected in a distinctive way by this wholly unexpected proclamation. So there is no basis for Neander's contention (p. 693) that the Archon, in worshipful dismay, freely subjected himself to the higher power, and from that time onward operated freely and consciously as an instrument of that higher power.

147. In *Stromata* 4.12 [*ANF* 2:424].

148. *Allgemeine Geschichte*, 1:683.

the notion of an autonomous evil being—although it is always a noteworthy phrase, since Clement can, for this very reason, accuse Basilides of divinizing the Devil, as Gieseler has rightly noted[149] in opposing Neander. I say this because Basilides regards the persecution of Christians, which Clement considered to be the Devil's efforts, as proceeding from divine providence, therefore as devilish activities on behalf of God. However, if we pair with that statement the subsequent passage in that same chapter of Clement[150]—"Providence, beginning, as is supposed, with the Archon ..."—as this relates to Basilides' view of the persecution of Christians, then this makes it very clear that Basilides ascribes these persecutions to the Archon. In the context of Basilides' general view that this suffering and persecution is deserved punishment, apparently just an instrument serving the purposes of divine providence that providence has, so to speak, set in motion, one in which providence takes the opportunity to express itself, then this just demonstrates the impotence belonging to the nature of evil, but not a good intention on the part of the Archon.

The Archon, as prince of the world, resisted the intentions of the good God and, in the suffering and persecution he decreed for Christians as the chosen race, also revealed his Ahriman-like nature. He introduced his darkness and obscurity into the light-world, which is why, in this same context where he contests the view of Basilides about persecution, Clement also depicts the same suffering in these terms: "Labor and fear are not, then, as [those around Basilides] say, incidental to human affairs, as rust is to iron, [but come upon the soul through its own will]."[151] Thus toil and fear befall all things, or human beings, from without, in the circumstances they find themselves, as iron becomes subject to rust. All the evil attaching itself to the soul, and all the soul itself commits, is, according to this authentically Zoroastrian picture, impurity added to it by the evil principle. The Archon is then this evil principle itself, or else is still to be distinguished from it. Clement believes this view of evil is contrary to Basilides' idea of divine providence, or of divine just punishment. But the higher unity of these two lies in the idea that punishment linked to the evil of the Archon's nature is at the same time the means for realizing the divine purposes.[152]

In returning once more to *Stromata* 2.8,[153] its other contents seem inherently to have the tenor of a dualism at least very similar to Zoroastrianism. Like the antithesis of fear (φόβος) and wisdom (σοφία), it therefore speaks of a distinguishing or separating (διακριτική) of races, of good from evil; setting apart (φυλοκρινητική) the children of light from the children of the world; a cleansing and perfecting (τελεωτική);

---

149. In *Theologische Studien und Kritiken* (1830), 397.

150. *Stromata* 4.12 [*ANF* 2:425].

151. Ibid.

152. This is the meaning of *Stromata* 4.12 [*ANF* 2:425]: "Providence, beginning, as is supposed, with the Archon, yet is implanted in beings at their origin by the God of the universe." The last part of this passage undoubtedly is said to express the teaching of Basilides.

153. [*Ed.*] See n. 144.

a restoration or returning by Sophia (ἀποκαταστατικὴ σοφία) of the two intermixed realms to their original conditions; an antithesis of the cosmos, dominated by the Archon, and the choosing (ἐκλογή) of the elect by Sophia. However, the mixing together of the two principles makes this dividing and separating necessary. According to Basilides, in whose system a strictly moral spirit prevails, this dividing has a profoundly moral basis, as it does in the Zoroastrian system too. This is clearly so, based on the view Basilides held according to the remarkable passages in Clement, *Stromata* 4.12.[154] There Clement states that, in Book 23 of Basilides' *Exegetics*, he writes this about those who are punished for being martyrs.

> I maintain that all those who suffer afflictions because they unknowingly transgressed in another way, will share in this blessing through the goodness of the One who has them partake of it, whereas they were accused on other grounds. This is so that they not suffer as those who are condemned because of acknowledged misdeeds, not as those held culpable of adultery or murder, but only condemned because they happen to be Christians. This consoles them in that they do not take this to be suffering. For although someone suffers who has done no wrong at all—which is seldom the case—yet such a person also does not suffer under mere authority, for he or she instead suffers like the underage child who seems to have not done wrong.

Further on Basilides says that:

> As then a child who has done no wrong, at least has done nothing in fact wrong although having within it the tendency to sin (τὸ ἁμαρτῆσαι ἔχων), when subjected to suffering the child experiences a blessing from which it very much benefits, an adult who has done no evil deed but suffers or has suffered, also suffers in the same way as a child. That is because the adult of course has the principle of evil (τὸ ἁμαρτικόν) within him but has done no evil because of there being no occasion to do so. Thus he is not to be accounted as having not sinned. For the one who wishes to commit adultery is an adulterer even though he has not actually done so. The one who wishes to commit murder is a murderer even though he cannot also carry it out. So of someone I say is without sin, when I see that he suffers even though having done no wrong, I will also say that he is evil because he has the will to do evil. For I will concede anything rather than ascribing evil to Providence.

Clement then adds that Basilides himself even applies this view to the Lord, since Basilides goes on to say:

> If someone wants to put me in the awkward position of saying about a certain person, "this one therefore has sinned because he has suffered," I will say, if you permit me, "he has of course not sinned, but he was like the suffering child." But if you press me more forcefully, I will say that everyone called a

---

154. [*Ed.*] For the following passages see *ANF* 2:423–24.

human being is human, and God alone is righteous. For, as has been said, no one is without blemish.

Accordingly there are sins attached to each human soul, and their origin lies far beyond the temporal consciousness of the individual. The basis of these sins can only be in that original mixing together (σύγχυσις ἀρχική) of which Basilides speaks elsewhere. He argues that, as surely as the imperfect, suffering-filled condition in which the soul finds itself in the present life cannot be the original condition, just as surely is the soul itself the author of sin, since every variation on sin that ensues with the soul can only be its own free act.

The principle that the will determines itself freely must have been a very important part of Basilides' system. Isidore says, in the passage previously cited, that the rational principle must predominate. In another passage he says: "What matters is simply that a human being wills what is good. Thus one will also be able to realize what one wills. It is just the will's own fault if it inclines toward sin."[155] This principle, linked to the idea of a moral retribution affecting the entire person of a human being, must ultimately have led to the assumption of an original fall of the soul, which—in the way one might have thought of the two principles as mutually related—could only have ensued because of an inclination toward matter awakened in the soul itself. This inclination drew the soul down from its originally pure and perfect condition, into the kind of state in which the predominance of matter obscured its light principle. Since this view mainly just amounted to presupposing a prior free act, but not also that the individual would have had a clear awareness of the connection between guilt and punishment, it shows how Basilides was able, at all the levels or stages of its natural life, to envisage this same soul—made opaque by matter and bound to it, in need of cleansing and liberation—struggling upward only with effort and in exigency.

Hence Basilides believed in the idea of the soul's transmigration, and believed he had even found a proof for it in the words of the Apostle Paul (Rom 7:9).[156] Origen[157] says about this passage:

> This Basilides should not understand the passage by turning from the law of nature and twisting the words of the Apostle into foolishness and godless fables. That is, by making them about the transfer of the soul into another being and another body, so as to construe these words of the Apostle as he wishes to. For Basilides states that the Apostle says, "When I was living without the law," that is, "before I came into this body, I lived in the kind of body that is not under the law, no doubt as a cow or a bird."

---

155. [Ed.] In our text Baur gives the passage in German, followed by the Greek text, from *Stromata* 3.1.

156. [Ed.] Rom. 7:9–10: "I was once alive apart from the law, but when the commandment came, sin revived and I died, and the very commandment that promised life proved to be death to me."

157. In his *Commentary on Romans*, bk. 5.

The higher these souls work their way up, in this transmigration, from a state devoid of consciousness to the consciousness of their own being, the more they must feel themselves strangers in this world, since their own being stems from a higher world. That is why Clement[158] has the soul of the true Gnostic saying, "I am a stranger in the earth, and a sojourner with you." In the same context he mentions Basilides as someone who holds this view too: "Hence Basilides says he understands that the elect ones are strangers to the world, being supraworldly in nature." The soul could only regard its elect status as something foreign to the world; in other words, see itself as chosen simply inasmuch as it is not of this world, because it has a supraworldly nature. (Clement himself does not grant this point to its fullest extent. He says: "This is not the case. For all things are of one God. And no one is a stranger to the world by nature, but they are essentially one and God is one. But the elect person dwells in the world as a stranger, knowing what to possess and what not to.")

The nature of the soul can be supraworldly only because what is spiritual stands higher than what is material. Therefore, as the soul becomes more aware of its spiritual nature, it increasingly withdraws from the world, the realm of the Archon. The result is the separation of principles, which makes the Archon fearful and terrified. Sophia intervenes with her sifting and cleansing activity, and those she takes away from the world now form her elect, the race she has chosen from the world. Thus in Basilides' system too, Christian salvation is all of a piece with the universal purification process that pervades the entire course of the world.

However, we do not know the details as to the way in which Basilides thought about this salvation and the divine activity manifesting itself to this end. The passages cited above show that he regarded Sophia as the actual principle of it, and that in this context he spoke of a separation (διακριτή), a perfecting (τελεωτική), and a restoration by Sophia (ἀποκαταστατικὴ σοφία). We see at once from this that Basilides places special importance on the appearing of the Spirit (the διακονούμενον πνεῦμα, the Spirit as messenger) at the baptism of Jesus in the River Jordan. This fits with Clement's statement[159] that the followers of Basilides celebrated the day of the Redeemer's baptism solemnly, and spent the preceding days in recalling it. In any case it is certain that Basilides had no part in the frivolous docetism of his later followers,[160] which did not square with the seriousness of his own system. Basilides regarded Jesus as an actual human being.

In connection with citing the aforementioned passages from Basilides' *Exegetics*, Clement reproaches him for speaking of the Lord as a human being, and also, like divinizing the Devil, for therefore daring, by comparison, to speak of the Lord as "a man subject to sin" (ἄνθρωπον ἁμαρτητικόν). In the passage where Basilides speaks of

---

158. *Stromata* 4.26 [*ANF* 2:440].

159. *Stromata* 1.21.

160. Clement of Alexandria remarks explicitly about how this movement deteriorated subsequently, also especially with regard to matters of ethics. See *Stromata* 3.1.

the principle that all suffering is the result of an antecedent guilt, he must in fact have wanted to absolutely rule out any exceptions, and so he was also necessarily thinking of Jesus. The passage also shows us that Basilides assumed Jesus actually suffered, although this must also consequently mean that, while Basilides hardly considered the man Jesus to be a sinless savior, he likewise could hardly have seen Jesus' suffering as having a real and direct connection with salvation. While Basilides was therefore hardly a docetist, for him the entire human phenomenon of Jesus had, on the whole, to be of little import.

Gieseler, in opposing Neander, has argued[161] that the followers of Basilides likely did not find the aforementioned celebration of Jesus' baptism as a rite already present in the Syrian church, and borrowed it from there; that instead they first celebrated it and provided the occasion for its introduction into the Catholic Church. Thus, Gieseler says, the interest they had in observing it can only have been from the fact that Basilides had already decided to especially emphasize the moment of Jesus' baptism in the River Jordan. If we may accept Gieseler's account, then Basilides wanted to fix such a moment in Jesus' life that most of all can show the man Jesus in his subordination to the divine principle active for the purpose of redemption (the διακονούμενον πνεῦμα, the Spirit as messenger, the Sophia; or else perhaps also, though it is not explicitly found in the sources, the moment that can show the Nous as the divine agent, as διάκονος).[162]

## How These Systems View the Relationship of Christian and Pre-Christian Elements

This presentation of the systems of Saturninus and Basilides by itself provides the justification for the place we have assigned to them. Throughout they seem to draw just a relative distinction between their Christian and pre-Christian elements. The fact that they have a more dualistic form, that Sophia or Achamoth does not play the same role in them as in the systems presented earlier on, changes nothing. The main thing is that they too see spirit making itself finite and objective in the material world in the same way, and having it in turn, in the endlessly many, dispersed seeds of light, pressing upward from its subjection to matter, toward the broad daylight of spiritual light and consciousness. The Christian element is simply a higher stage to which spirit elevated itself when it had passed through the pre-Christian period of development.

---

161. In the *Allgemeine Literatur-Zeitung* (n. 12), 836.

162. Basilides was hardly a docetist, and he hardly thought to utterly ban marriage. (See what Clement introduces in *Stromata* 3.1–3, including this statement from Isidore's *Ethics*: "sexual intercourse is natural but not necessary" (3.3 [Amidon (n. 35), 257]), which is the main, underlying principle.) Basilides sets himself apart from Saturninus in both of these respects. Except nothing follows from this that contravenes Basilides' system likely being a stricter dualism. It only amounts to Basilides being too level-headed and prudent to draw the harshest consequences directly from his principles.

Yet the elements of the spiritual life are so widespread everywhere in the pre-Christian world that there is no definitive difference between paganism and Judaism. At least no distinction of this kind gets drawn. One must instead assume that for paganism too, the claim that seeds of the spiritual life have developed from themselves, in a way analogous to how this happened in Judaism, ought not be accepted. At least so far as the system of Basilides is concerned, there is no lack of indications confirming this assumption. In *Stromata* 5.11 Clement says that Moses did not erect multiple sanctuaries, but only erected the one holy place [i.e., tent] of God, and in doing so did not merely acknowledge that the world stems from one being, as Basilides concluded from this, but also acknowledged what Basilides no longer concluded, that there is only one God.[163] We cannot take anything for our purposes from this passage, since it just speaks of the world's creator, which Basilides distinguishes from the supreme God.[164]

There is more to be considered in Basilides' statement, according to Clement, in *Stromata* 4.13. "We suppose one part of the declared will of God to be the loving of all things because all things are related to the whole, another part not to lust after anything, and a third part not to hate anything." If all things are related to the whole, and there is in the whole a Logos, a rational principle, then this factor must also carry weight when it comes to the relation of paganism to Judaism. What seems to shine through here is the Alexandrian idea of the all-pervasive Logos. The statement that belongs here most of all is the one we find in Clement, *Stromata* 6.6. Here Isidore, the son and follower of Basilides becomes, like Valentinus, reckoned among "the elders of the community." The first book of Isidore's *Expositions of the Prophet Parchor* contains these words:

> The Attics [those from Athens] maintain that Socrates had been apprised of many things by the demon [*daimon*] attendant on him. And Aristotle says that all people have *daimons* attending them during the time they are in the body. He has taken this teaching from the prophets, and he did not record in his writings whence he got it.

In the second book Isidore continues on this point:

> Let no one suppose that what we consider the distinctive property of the chosen ones has already been stated before by any philosophers. It is not something they discovered, for they have appropriated it from the prophets and have attached it to their own wisdom, which is actually no wisdom at all.

And he adds in the same book:

> It seems to me that those who wish to be philosophers may indeed learn what is the winged oak, and the variegated robe on it, and what the allegorical

---

163. [*Ed.*] There follows in the text the Greek that Baur has just paraphrased.
164. In *Genetische Entwickelung* (n. 6), 38, Neander surely concludes too much from this passage.

theology of Pherecydes[165] contained, which was taken from the prophecy of Cham.[166]

Isidore expresses here the well-known Alexandrian idea that what in the Greek philosophers is found to be true is only something coming from the wisdom of the Old Testament. To that extent the passage found in Celsus does not seem to prove what it is said to prove. Yet it is highly dubious whether Isidore understood the prophets he spoke of as being specifically the Jewish prophets, or whether, as Neander assumes, the tradition of secret philosophical teaching traces back to the biblical patriarchs. This is all dubious because, right after this Isidore calls Cham, who so detested the Jews, a prophet. Hence we are justified in supposing that Isidore considered that higher wisdom, upon which Pherecydes was said to have drawn in particular, as at least not the exclusive property of the Jewish prophets.[167] In tracing this wisdom back to the patriarchs, Isidore in any event thus shows that this Cham, who is also reckoned among the patriarchs (which perhaps presupposes a closer connection to Egypt and ancient Egyptian wisdom), did not restrict to a single people the teaching transmitted by the patriarchs, but instead held it to be a shared heritage. So the Greek philosophers are

---

165. [*Ed.*] Pherecydes of Syros (6th c. BC) was the author of a cosmogonic myth involving Zeus, Kronos, and Ge.

166. The oak tree, covered by the variegated mantle of Zeus, extending widely like spread wings (see *Stromata* 6.2), that is, the starry heaven, is incontestably a symbol of the world, as in Norse mythology Yggdrasil is the world-tree and the tree of fate. Maximus of Tyre (*Dissertationes* XXIX, ed. J. Davis [Cambridge, 1703], 304) emphasizes the same tree, alongside Ophioneus, the battle of the gods, and the robe, among the main topics in the poetry of Pherecydes. It is perhaps not by chance that Isidore appeals directly to Pherecydes. Maybe Isidore regards him as important especially because, like Basilides and Isidore, Pherecydes was mainly attuned to the dualism of the Zoroastrian religious doctrine. We see this from Origen, *Against Celsus*, 6.42. In his book directed against the Christians, in order to point to Christian teaching about Satan, Celsus also said about him: "Pherecydes, who is more ancient than Heraclitus, related a myth of one army drawn up in hostile array against another, and names Kronos as the leader of the one and Ophioneus leader of the other . He recounts their challenges and struggles, and mentions that they entered into agreements, such that whichever party should fall into the Ocean would count as vanquished, while those who repulsed and conquered them would be in possession of heaven" [*ANF* 4:592]. No one can fail to identify Kronos with Ormazd and Ophioneus with Ahriman, the serpent demon. The battle the two of them began as leaders of their armies, the negotiations they engaged in before their armies, and the consequences that the battle once begun had to have for them—are all indicated in the fragment of Pherecydes in a way so consistent with the portrayal in the Zend writings, that hardly any other testimony authenticates so decisively the great antiquity of these religious traditions. See my *Das manichäische Religionssystem* (n. 40), 83–87, where, regrettably, I failed to include, and make comparisons with, this fragment from Pherecydes. But, as we see from this fragment, if Basilides had specifically acknowledged the theology containing such teaching, would that not also have made more plausible the way we have to understand the phrase "original mixing together"? One could even have conjectured that Isidore's prophet Cham, who does not seem to rightly fit with these ancient Persian symbols and myths, is mistaken for the ancient Persian figure Hom (known to the Greeks as Ὠμάνης), the famous pre-Zoroastrian prophet.

167. In *Heretical Tales* 1.4, Theodoret says that Basilides held several named individuals "and other similar barbarians" to be prophets. The term βαρβάρους is of course ambiguous, but is most likely to be understood as in fact referring to non-Jewish prophets.

placed in a subordinate relation to that wisdom, which perhaps simply means that the ancients passed on to the Greeks all the higher wisdom from the East and from Egypt.

## The Symbolic, Mythic, and Allegorical Form of All These Systems of the First Main Form of Gnosis

The whole nature of the systems presented here incontestably points to their close relationship not merely to Judaism but also most especially to the main forms of pagan religion and to ancient religious philosophy. The principles on which they rest, and the ideas making up their essential contents, everywhere take us back to the nobler forms of antiquity. Evidence of that, and something deserving of special emphasis here, is the form distinctive of these systems and deriving from the ancient world's way of looking at things.

Symbols and myths, mythic configurations and personifications, certainly belong to the typical character of these systems. They share this feature with Pythagorean and Platonic philosophy. However, this philosophy itself attests that, in symbols and myths, it just has links to these ancient ways of thinking about things and envisaging them. So the Gnostic systems are attached far more to the ancient religious forms themselves. We find in the Gnostic systems the same need that marks the comparable level or stage of ancient religion, which is the need to express religious consciousness in the way it is conveyed via pictorial means, in symbols and myths. Hence it is quite natural to encounter with the Gnostics for the most part the same pictorial means the ancient religions use to make the ideas of the divine apprehensible, albeit with the Gnostics' various modifications and not in the same sensuous form. Absolute and finite, good and evil, spirit and matter—envisaged under the symbols of light and darkness—belong to the standard symbolism of these systems. Their mythic form is given religious, conceptual content via the personification everywhere prevalent in the symbolism.

However, as soon as the myth has created its own personae via the personification process typical of it, myth also cannot fail to involve sexual relationships and sexual activities. We need not elaborate on how deeply this sensuality makes inroads into the essential nature of the Gnostic systems, and the significance that marriage and procreation, and the kinship relations resting upon them, have even in the highest regions of the spiritual realm. Yet in other respects their entire organic structure can be explained principally on the basis of their symbolic-mythical way of looking at things. For their symbolism must have been more abstract on the whole than the ancient pagan form. Thus there are certain numerical relationships that especially draw our attention back to ancient symbolic conceptions.

We are familiar with the importance in Gnostic systems of the numbers eight, ten, twelve, and thirty. The number eight is most closely connected with the number seven, which had a very sacred meaning everywhere in the ancient world, one resting on people's view of nature.[168] The number ten also quite naturally had a very important place in these systems. According to Irenaeus,[169] the Marcosians belonging to the Valentinian school got to the number ten by adding to the seven globular bodies [which they also call heavens] the eighth heaven, which contains them, and then also adding the sun and the moon. This number ten was said to be the image of the invisible decad of Aeons that issued forth from Logos and Zoe. The number twelve is the dodecad of Aeons begotten by Anthropos and Ecclesia. The Gnostics relate it to the twelve signs of the Zodiac or the twelve months of the year, and the number thirty they relate to the thirty days in a month.

The religious significance of the planets and the signs of the zodiac in the ancient world also carries over into the Gnostic systems. This ancient nature symbolism will not only call to mind certain permanent numbers, for these essential natures of the religious outlook also appear to be mythically configured potencies or powers of the same kind as those were thought of in the ancient religions. According to Gnostic teaching, there is a destiny or fate linked to the stars or heavenly bodies, and mediated by them. The *Didascalia anatolica* (chs. 69ff.) declares about this fatalism that both those heavenly bodies that change positions (the planets) and those that do not (the fixed stars) preside over the invisible powers that in them govern procreation and generation. The heavenly bodies of course do nothing for its own sake. But they do indicate the influence of the powers governing in them, just as the flight of birds [as an omen] does not cause for its own sake what it indicates. So the heavenly bodies, as instruments and symbols of these powers, are [omens of a] twofold sort—some good and some evil, some of the right hand and some of the left—and everything born is jointly their product.

However, Christ is the one who has freed us from the conflict and opposition of these powers governing in the heavenly bodies—where one group of them assists us like soldiers while the other group attacks us like robbers—and Christ grants this freedom to us. Christ himself is the new, extraordinary star who has extinguished the ancient system of heavenly bodies (τὴν παλαιὰν ἀστροθεσίαν) by a new, unworldly shining light. This is then why, among those who believe in Christ, his providence has taken the place of ancient fate or destiny (*heimarmene*). The twelve signs of the zodiac are set over against the twelve apostles, who govern rebirth (ἀναγέννησις) as the heavenly bodies govern the birth (γένεσις) of earthly things.[170]

According to conventional Gnostic thinking,[171] those seven powers that, together with the Demiurge, formed his hebdomad, are the creators and direct rulers of the

---

168. On this point see my essay, "Der hebräische Sabbath und die Nationalfeste des mosaischen Cultus," *Tübinger Zeitschrift für Theologie* (1832), no. 3, 125–92. See esp. p. 128, as well as p. 166 on the number eight. They also spoke about the number ten in the same way.

169. *Against Heresies* 1.17.1 [ANF 1:342].

170. *Didascalia Anatolica*, ch. 25.

171. See Irenaeus, *Against Heresies* 1.30.9, for one example of this, from the Ophites.

material world, are the planetary powers. With Bardesanes the Gnostic we also find the notion, drawn from the mythologies of ancient peoples, that the sun is the father of all things and the moon is their mother; that the sun, as the masculine principle, imparted to the moon the fructifying seed of all natural life; that the moon received this seed and spread it throughout all of nature.[172] By utilizing perspectives and notions of this kind, and giving them significance, the Gnostics were standing wholly within the realm of the ancient, symbolic-mythic, nature religion. For them, as for the ancient peoples whose way of looking at things they followed, external nature provided their models for the divine.

But the Gnostics also joined hands with a newer realm of figurative perspectives—not merely ones in the Old Testament scriptures, to which they applied the same allegorizing methods as those of the Alexandrians, but also ones in the gospel story, which they knew how to utilize, typologically and allegorically, for their own ideas.[173] This is a phenomenon very typically indicative of the Gnostics. On the one hand, in keeping with the significance Christianity held for them, the Gnostics also had to give their ideas a Christian foundation. On the other hand, in their portrayal of Christianity they were still so dependent on the ancient symbolic-mythic form that they could not dispense with it as their medium. So they stuck with this same way of looking at things but transplanted it onto the soil of Christianity. Then Christianity itself, in the history of its founding, gave the Gnostics their figurative, intuitive forms, just as nature had previously provided them for ancient peoples.

In his portrayal of the Valentinian system, Irenaeus describes this distinctive feature of the Gnostics. He acquaints us with a series of such types and allegories, ones in which a very sensuous play of the imagination is unmistakable. He says[174] that, while Gnostic teaching is hardly as self-consistent as what the prophets, Christ, and the apostles taught, they nevertheless did endeavor to give an appearance of plausibility to their imaginative imagery based on the parables of the Lord, the declarations of

---

172. See Neander, *Genetische Entwickelung* (n. 6), 196. Also see the brief essay treating this topic by Kühner, *Astronomiae et astrologiae in doctrina gnosticorum vestigia*, Part 1, *Bardesanis gnostici numina astralia* (Hildburgh, 1833), 18. There is no basis, however, for drawing the further conclusion, from the position in our text, that in fact Achamoth is the planet Venus, Christ is the planet Jupiter, and the syzygies of the Aeons are conjunctions of the planets.

173. See in particular Irenaeus, *Against Heresies* 1.18. The Gnostics found the most meaningful numbers of their system especially in the Old Testament and with the same significance there. In 1.18.3 Irenaeus says: "In a word, whatever they find in the scriptures capable of being referred to the number eight, they declare to fulfill the mystery of the Ogdoad" [*ANF* 1:343]. Likewise in 1.18.4 regarding the number twelve: "As to the Dodecad, in connection with which there occurred the mystery of the passion of the ὑστέρημα or defect, from which passion they maintain that all visible things were formed, they assert that the Dodecad is to be found strikingly and manifestly everywhere in scripture" [*ANF* 1:344]. They assign a similar relation to New Testament numbers. [*Ed.*] Baur then says the sum of the numbers 1, 3, 6, 9, and 11 in Matt 20:1–16 equals 30, which points to the 30 Aeons. However, it is not clear to what in the parable itself he thinks these numbers correspond.

174. In *Against Heresies* 1.8 [*ANF* 1:326–29]. [*Ed.*] In this and the next paragraphs, Baur quotes and summarizes 1.8.1, 2, 4.

the prophets, and the teachings set forth by the apostles. Thus "they disregard the order and connection of the scriptures, and . . . dismember and destroy the truth." By recasting and moving things around, what they take from scripture they make out to be something quite other than it is. They carry on like someone who disassembled a likeness of a king already constructed by an artist from precious stones, and who, with the same stones and from the human figure of the king, made the likeness of a dog or a fox, and then maintained it is still the same beautiful likeness of a king because it is made of the same stones. Irenaeus then continues with a few more examples of this procedure.

That the Valentinian Gnostics found much in the story of the life of Christ that to them seemed to be typologically related to the ideas of their own systems is what one could have expected from their standpoint. Given how they generally considered Christ's suffering to be a revelation of the passion or suffering of Achamoth, they therefore found such a tie-in especially with Christ's statements in the course of his suffering. The pathos Achamoth underwent would have been indicated by the Lord's outcry on the cross: "My God, my God, why have you forsaken me?" (Matt 27:46). These words take us to the state in which Sophia found herself when she forsook the light and Horos prevented her from further striving toward it. The statement, "I am deeply grieved, even to death" (Matt 26:38), points to her sadness. The words, "My Father, if it is possible, let this cup pass from me" (Matt 26:39), point to her fear. The question, "Now my soul is troubled. And what should I say—'Father, save me from this hour?'" (John 12:27), points to her dismay. Bardesanes too has made the words of a psalm ("My God, my God, why have you forsaken me?" [Ps 22:1]) the basis for his portrayal of Achamoth as a woman lamenting her loneliness and calling upon God for help.[175]

Christ's statement (in Luke 15:4) that he has come to seek for the lost, wandering sheep the Valentinians understood as applying to Achamoth, inasmuch as she, wandering about outside the Pleroma, received form from Christ and was sought after by the Redeemer. They also related to Sophia the parable (Luke 15:8–9) about the woman who lights a lamp and sweeps the whole house searching for a lost coin. This is Sophia who lost her Enthymesis and then found it again after everything had been purified by the Redeemer's presence. So the Enthymesis had been reinstated in the Pleroma. In the twelve year old daughter of a leader of the synagogue, a girl Jesus restored to life (Luke 8:41–56), they saw a comparable image of Achamoth, indeed of that very condition in which Christ, by spreading his arms above her, gave her a form and restored to her the consciousness of the light she had forsaken. The fact that the Redeemer appeared to Achamoth when she found herself outside the Pleroma, like an abortion (ἔκτρωμα), is something Paul spoke about in 1 Cor 15:8. There he writes: "Last of all, as to one untimely born (ὡσπερεί τῳ ἐκτρώματι), he appeared also to me." A reference to the same moment when the Redeemer appeared to Achamoth, together

---

175. See Neander, *Genetische Entwickelung* (n. 6), 195.

with his attending angels, is the statement of the Apostle in 1 Cor 11:10: "For this reason a woman ought to have a symbol of authority on her head, because of the angels." Likewise the covered face of Moses signifies none other than the fact that, when the Redeemer came to Achamoth, she covered herself in a veil, from shame.

The Simeon who took the infant Christ in his arms and, praising God, said: "Master, now you are dismissing your servant in peace, according to your word" (Luke 2:29), was for the Gnostics an image of the Demiurge who, upon the coming of the Redeemer, acknowledged his own displacement and gave thanks to Bythus. They also state that Anna (of Luke 2:36–38), who the gospel says lived seven years with her husband and then spent the rest of her life as a widow until she saw and recognized the Redeemer, and spoke about him to everyone, without any doubt represented Achamoth, who, for only a short time had beheld the Redeemer and his attendant angels, and had then spent all of the remaining time in the intermediate place and waited there until he would come again and would restore their syzygy. This is also the well-known and oft-recurring image used to present the final uniting of Achamoth with Christ, of spiritual natures with angels (in other words the perfection of souls, their transfiguration into angels, since this too is indeed an image), as a marriage of bride and bridegroom, and to portray the Pleroma as a bridal chamber; or, as Bardesanes does, to portray this uniting as Sophia's banquet, to which all the perfected souls are invited guests.[176] All this likewise demonstrates the Gnostics' predilection for what is pictorial and allegorical. They applied their efforts directly to the New Testament in this way, so as either to take advantage of the pictorial elements they already found there, or else to create for themselves a new sphere of types and images by the meanings they gave to the contents of the New Testament.

In any event what we see in such types and allegories is, on the whole, just the same procedures applied to the New Testament as those the Alexandrians had for a long time routinely followed with reference to the Old Testament. Just as the Alexandrians were able to reconcile the ideas of their own religious philosophy with the words of the Old Testament via the medium of allegory, the Gnostics also thought it proper to adopt the same relationship to the New Testament, when they sought to make use of its factual contents on behalf of their own ideas. Yet when we especially consider how freely and arbitrarily the Gnostics otherwise dealt with the New Testament's contents, why could they be concerned to seek such a medium as allegory and attach some sort of value to it, if the pictorial way of looking at things would not have been looked upon as a typical feature of the entire standpoint they occupied?

Of course the very term "allegory" calls for a certain delineation or limitation of its application in this case. Here it just designates the procedure we can judge to be the original standpoint of the Gnostics themselves. The concept of allegory always presupposes the awareness that idea, and image or picture, certainly differ. It presupposes that we consider the factual and historical elements in which we find certain

---

176. See Neander, 195.

ideas expressed to be the external, perceptible, and more or less contingent form of those ideas. But then the very question we cannot find a way to answer is this: To what extent were the Gnostics themselves more or less clearly conscious of the difference between the idea in and for itself, and the pictorial form serving as its external framework? In the systems of the Gnostics in general we can simply behold a magnificent allegory in which ideas, whose profundity and speculative significance is undeniable, are packaged in a form to which they do not seem to us to be essentially and necessarily bound. At many places in these systems we rather strongly suspect and suppose that the Gnostics cannot possibly have identified form and idea in this way. We suspect that even to them the form could appear to be a mere image or picture, a poetic or mythic personification (as this manifestly seems to be the case especially with the syzygies of the Pleroma, with the passion of Achamoth, and in general with the entire role played by this being, Achamoth!). On the other hand, however, form and idea in turn nevertheless constitute a whole so indivisible that consciousness of their difference at least never becomes all-pervasive and enduring in the system. The concept always seems to just depend on the form in which it appears; to just enter into consciousness in this form. The whole system seems to lose its distinctive and independent meaning as soon as one divests its ideas of the form in which they are enveloped.

Here we have spirit's inability to understand, and hold firmly to, the concept in its purely abstract state. Spirit is caught up in the form that pervades all these systems, a form whose allure enabled these systems to take a strong hold on people's hearts and minds to such a great extent. This is the symbolic-mythic form, in part as it was basic to the religions of ancient peoples, and also in part as present in Jewish religion but not entirely assignable to Judaism, for in any event the allegorizing of the Alexandrians is just a related phenomenon. (In Alexandrian Judaism allegory emerges not in the larger context of a system, but instead only as a method of interpretation applied to the Old Testament scriptures.) So here we see how Gnosticism is related to the pre-Christian forms of religion. The relation lies in the great significance the pictorial or figurative element has as the form striving to convey or mediate religious ideas. The difference simply consists in the fact that, for the Gnostics, the pictorial form became the form of an entire system, and to those who made use of them, the individual figurative notions were drawn from the entire domain that, in this regard, opened itself up to the Gnostics in paganism, Judaism, and Christianity. Later on we will see to what extent docetism is linked to the pictorial character of the Gnostic systems, for docetism is a feature of Gnosticism that stays with us as we move on to the following category of Gnostic systems.

# 2

# The Form of Gnosis Separating Christianity from Judaism and Paganism

*The System of Marcion*

## Marcion's Antinomianism as Related to Judaism

OUR REPRESENTATIVE OF THE second class of Gnostic systems is Marcion.[177] What is distinctive about Marcion is the strict antithesis in which he sets Christianity over against paganism and Judaism. Here everything in the systems of the first class of Gnostics that seems to have Christianity converging with, and related to, both Judaism and paganism, now falls by the wayside. The boundary between what is Christian and what is pre-Christian now should be drawn as sharply as possible, no mediation between them is recognized, and the only thing in view is the wide gulf that separates them. This strict antithesis between Christianity on one side, and Judaism and paganism on the other side, is so very much the distinctive mark of the Marcionite system, that everything it otherwise has in common with other Gnostic systems shifts into the background and appears to be just the external framework on which the system proper is said to be erected.

## The Imperfect Nature of the Demiurge

Marcion agreed with other Gnostics in distinguishing the supreme God from the Demiurge, whom he identified with the God of the Jews. The Demiurge is of course no inherently evil being, for he stands intermediate between the good God and Satan, who rules over matter. Yet Marcion's efforts were very much directed toward depicting the Demiurge as a being whose attributes all place him far below what the true

---

177. [*Ed.*] Marcion of Sinope (c. 85—c. 160) was the son of a bishop. After he was excommunicated by the Roman Church, he returned to Asia Minor where he led congregations according to his version of the gospel, having published the earliest extant collection of New Testament books. His writings are known only through Tertullian's refutation, *Against Marcion*.

God is conceived to be. Since the Demiurge is the Jewish God who reveals himself in the Old Testament, the proof of his lower standing was to be that everything in the Old Testament Marcion found incompatible with the Christian concept of God as he understood it, presupposes an attribute in the Demiurge that is unworthy of the true God.

This proof was carried out above all in negative terms and showed that, according to the Old Testament, the Demiurge could only be regarded as an extremely weak, limited, and imperfect being. In *Against Marcion*, Tertullian says Marcion reproaches the Demiurge for his pettiness (*pusillitates*), weakness (*infirmitates*), inconsistencies (*incongruentiae*) and maliciousness (*malignitates*), and that Marcion sums up all these petty, weak, and disgraceful (*indigna*) features "to destroy the creator," in order to completely deny that the true concept of God fits the Demiurge.[178] A few examples Tertullian provides (mainly in Book 2) may give us a more detailed picture of this side of the Demiurge's nature according to Marcion.

Marcion turns, first and foremost, to narratives in Genesis, in order to disparage the Demiurge. According to Tertullian, Marcion argues as follows (based on Genesis, chap. 3):

> If God is good and foreknows the future, and is able to avert evil, why did he permit human beings—the very image and likeness of himself and, by the origin of the soul, God's own substance too—to be deceived by the Devil and fall from obedience to the law, into death? For if God had been good and thus unwilling that such a catastrophe should happen, and have foreknowledge so as not to be ignorant of what was to happen, and powerful enough to prevent from happening what should be impossible, given these three great divine attributes, it would never have occurred. But since it has occurred the contrary proposition is most certainly true, namely, that we must consider God to be neither good nor powerful, and also lacking in foreknowledge. As this could not have happened for a God reputed to be good, prescient, and powerful, and it has actually happened, he is not a God of this kind.[179]

In this same narrative Marcion finds it most unworthy of God that he first has to ask of Adam, "Where are you?" (Gen 3:9). And to Marcion it seems to be a further proof of God's weakness that God "must go down and see" (Gen 18:21) why there is an outcry against Sodom and Gomorrah, and how things stand there.[180] He opines that, when the Old Testament has God acting now one way and now another, this can only be caused by fickleness or shortsightedness. Tertullian says:

---

178. [*Ed.*] For these terms, see various passages in the five books of Tertullian's *Against Marcion*: 2.25, 2.27, 2.28, and 4.20 (all listed by Baur in the text).

179. Tertullian, *Against Marcion* 2.5 [*ANF* 3:300–1].

180. Ibid., 2.25.

You will have it that God is inconsistent in dealing with persons, sometimes disapproving when approval is deserved; or else lacking foresight by approving those who ought instead to be reproved, as if God either condemned his own past judgments or could not foresee his future ones.[181]

This explains the contradictions found in the Old Testament, when God overrides what he himself has commanded or forbidden. But Tertullian replies to Marcion: "You reproach God for being contradictory in his precepts, from fickleness and inconsistency."[182] Marcion cites the scandalous appropriation of gold and silver vessels from the Egyptians by the Israelites at God's command (Exod 12:35–36), the breaking of the Sabbath commandment by the order given before the walls of Jericho (Josh 6:15–17), and the worship of the serpent in the wilderness (Num 21:6–9) despite the strict prohibition of idolatry. In general, a God who is subject to human affections and passions lacks all the divine qualities. Tertullian has Marcion saying: "If God is angry, and jealous, and roused, and embittered, he must therefore be made worse and must therefore die."[183]

Since this procedure could only yield a negative concept of the deity, just the concept of an extremely weak and imperfect being, it was important, when the concept of the deity was said to apply to the Demiurge, that it be given a positive content by an attribute expressing not merely a deficiency but instead a perfection. This is the attribute of justice or righteousness, and Marcion used it to form the concept actually constitutive of the Demiurge. The Demiurge is not just the world's creator. As God of the Jews he is also most especially the lawgiver. The Old Testament revealed by him is the law as opposed to the gospel. But the law rests on the concept of justice. Hence there is no other attribute so essential to the Demiurge as that of justice or righteousness. But whatever positive feature this assigned to the Demiurge, it was at the same time a limitation, in that this positive attribute was hardly said to be anything of absolute importance.

The Gnostics' customary disparagement of everything falling under the concept of justice, and their strictly distinguishing this concept from those qualities that are the self-revelation of God's absolute being, are features most especially characteristic of the Marcionite system. Basilides appears to be an exception to this when he transfers δικαιοσύνη (Justice), together with her daughter εὐνομία (Good Order), into the Ogdoad.[184] The imperfection of the Demiurge gets expressed even in justice, which

---

181. Ibid., 2.23 [*ANF* 3:315].

182. Ibid., 2.21.

183. Ibid., 2.16.

184. Even according to the Valentinians, whoever is merely just cannot come into the Pleroma. According to Irenaeus, *Against Heresies* 1.7.1 and 5, the Valentinians teach that the souls of the righteous ones, together with the Demiurge, come to the intermediate place, for "nothing of the animal nature shall find admittance to the Pleroma" (the righteous ones therefore just belong in the psychical class). See p. 99 above, as well as p. 124 on Basilides.

is his chief attribute. Therefore justice certainly differs essentially from goodness, so there must certainly also be two essentially different Gods, expressing these two concepts. Tertullian challenges Marcion: "How will you separate your two Gods, separating one as distinctively the good God and the other as distinctively the just God?"[185] This separation is the reason why Marcion closely connects the concept of justice with the concept of strictness or harshness, and cruelty, albeit as imparted via the concept of just punishment.

As the God of justice, the Demiurge is also the judge. The judge's punitive role, which consists in imposing a certain amount of suffering on the violator of the law, makes the judge seem harsh and cruel. Hence Tertullian says about the Marcionites: "You designate God as judge, and reject as cruelty the judge's severity, which simply accords with the merits of the cases."[186] Hence the Demiurge, as strict judge, and the one who administers the law and justice, is also a stern and cruel God, an obstinate and warlike God, whereas in contrast to him, the attributes of goodness, love, and kindness belong, first and foremost, only to the true God.[187] For Marcion, the more those former attributes seemed to be related to justice, the more he had to directly exclude from the concept of justice all that conflicts with the concept of an absolute being and thus can only be attributes of a lesser being. So Tertullian asks: "Should God be regarded as a being of simple goodness, to the exclusion of all those other attributes, sensations and affections the Marcionites transfer from their God to the creator?"[188]

If the Demiurge, whose entire nature does not extend beyond the concept of justice, is so far beneath the concept of the true God, then the whole understanding of religion in the Old Testament could not have revealed the concept of the true God, for the true God remained completely foreign to Judaism. Thus a major thesis of the Marcionite teaching is that Christianity first made known the true God who before was completely unknown. Tertullian says:

> When I hear of a new god who was unknown and unheard of in the ancient world, and in olden times, and under the old god—a new god who for long centuries counted as no one, and of whom antiquity was ignorant, and whom a certain "Jesus Christ" and no one else revealed, a Christ they say who was

---

185. *Against Marcion* 2.12. [*Ed.*] Our text seems to call for adding the two sentences that follow in Tertullian: "Where the just is, there is also the good. In short, from the very first the creator was both good and just" (*ANF* 3:307).

186. Ibid., 2.27 [*ANF* 3:319]. [*Ed.*] Baur adds, in parentheses in the text, a statement from 2.11: "[After the fall,] God became a judge both severe and, as the Marcionites will have it, cruel" (*ANF* 3:306).

187. [*Ed.*] In our text Baur adds, parenthetically, Tertullian's remark in 1.6: "Marcion makes his gods dissimilar: one judicial, harsh, mighty in war; the other mild, placid, and simply good and the best" (*ANF* 3:275).

188. *Against Marcion* 1.25 [*ANF* 3:290].

new even though he was spoken of by the ancients—then I am grateful for this boasting of theirs.[189]

The Marcionites took the same antithetical stance toward paganism as they did toward Judaism. Paganism could not have made known the true concept of God any more than Judaism could. For the pagans the source of their knowledge of God is nature; for the Jews it is the law. The law or the Old Testament, inasmuch as it does not get beyond the concept of justice, cannot contain the true concept of God. So too, nature cannot disclose the true God, for nature only reveals the one who is the world's creator and whose work nature is. But the world's creator is not the true God, and that is so not merely because the world's creator is one and the same as the God of the Jews. It is also so because the world is a work unworthy of the true God, just as is the law or the Old Testament.[190] Marcion knew how to speak detrimentally about the Old Testament, and he likewise evaluated nature in a disparaging way. He refused to say that nature, as a work of the Demiurge, has any relation to the idea of God. Tertullian does not go into detail about his own objections to the conventional view of nature, but he does find the occasion to show that a human being is given an assured source for the true knowledge of God, both in external nature and in one's own consciousness.[191]

## Christ the Revealer of a Completely New, Unknown God

Neither nature nor the law, neither paganism nor Judaism, were consequently able to reveal the true God. Christianity is the first to unveil or disclose this God. The God of Christianity is, according to Marcion, a completely new and unknown God, one of which neither the pagan world nor the Jewish world had any inkling.

Because the revelation of God could not have been connected to anything related to it or preparatory for it, it found no intermediary in either Judaism or paganism. So, in virtue of Marcion's system, this revelation took on a character of its own, one Tertullian suitably describes in these words: "Christ appears suddenly, and John does too. This is how everything happens according to Marcion. Things are arranged entirely by the creator."[192] On Marcion's view of Christianity as disconnected from Judaism and paganism, the God who before was completely unknown could only reveal himself by his own action, or on his own. Tertullian reports that "the Marcionites say our God did not manifest himself from the beginning and by means of creation, but has revealed himself in Jesus Christ."[193]

189. Ibid., 1.8 [*ANF* 3:276].

190. [*Ed.*] In parentheses here Baur inserts in our text Tertullian's words in *Against Marcion* 1.13: "Marcion's most shameless followers turn to undermining the creator's works. Although they do say [ironically] that the world is a grand work and worthy of *a* God" (*ANF* 3:280).

191. Tertullian elaborates on this point in *Against Marcion* 1.10–14 [*ANF* 3:278–81].

192. *Against Marcion* 4.11 [*ANF* 3:360].

193. Ibid., 1.19 [*ANF* 3:284].

According to Marcion, the revelation of the previously unknown God, the unveiling of the true idea of God, began with Christianity, with the fact that, in the fifteenth year of the reign of Emperor Tiberius, Christ came down from heaven and suddenly, and entirely unexpectedly, appeared in Galilee, in the city of Capernaum.[194] As Marcion expressly maintained, it was completely unnecessary to prepare for his coming or to announce it ahead of time. When Christ revealed himself and revealed the true God, he testified to himself by what he said and did. Tertullian has Marcion saying: "Christ was to prove himself to be the Son, and the one sent, and the Christ of God, by his own deeds, by the evidence of his wondrous works."[195] For the previously unknown God could only have come forward in this way, through the Christ who revealed him, who is his *circumlator* (or "revealer," as Marcion apparently called Christ in this regard, as God's agent or instrument of revelation).[196] So nothing is more natural than for everything Christ revealed, the entire contents and form of Christianity, to appear as most decidedly antithetical to Judaism and paganism.

The view that there is no common ground at all between the two religious domains, between paganism and Judaism on the one hand, and Christianity on the other hand, is certainly the fundamental idea governing Marcion's whole system. Marcion could find no crossover point from Judaism and paganism to Christianity, because for him these two other religions, that is, the kingdom of the Demiurge, seemed to contain nothing worthy of the deity, nothing corresponding to the true idea of deity. So to Marcion everything from Christianity, all that Christianity comprised, therefore had to appear to be something completely different from paganism and Judaism. Where there is no common ground there can only be mutual resistance and hostility. So according to the basic viewpoint of Marcion's system, the view on in which it rests, Christianity arrived simply as the most decided opposition to Judaism and paganism; in other words, simply as the negation of both of them.

## The Antithesis of Law and Gospel; Christianity as the Religion of Love

In taking a closer look at this aspect of Marcion's system, we must pay attention above all to how he positions Christianity in relation to Judaism. That is because, from all we know about Marcion's system and the writings supporting and presenting it, what incontestably stands out is the fact that Marcion himself was most clearly conscious of the combative nature proper to his system when dealing with Judaism.

In the part of the system dealing with Judaism, where Marcion devotes all his mental efforts to delving into the depths of Christian consciousness, in order to understand the antithesis between law and gospel in its full intensity and extent, we have

---

194. Ibid., 1.19 and 4.7.
195. Ibid., 3.3 [ANF 3:322].
196. Tertullian 1.19 is the locus for this term *circumlator*.

## The Form of Gnosis Separating Christianity from Judaism and Paganism

before us what is actually the kernel and centerpiece of his system. The most important writings of Marcion that we still know of also bear on this very point. We may assume that, in compatibility with his system, Marcion's gospel was an altered gospel. This can hardly be in doubt, based on Tertullian and other ancient writers, and on the properties it must have had owing to its unanimity throughout. Thus Marcion's sole intention, in the only telling of the gospel story he recognized, was to follow through with the antithesis he thought existed between law and gospel.

Tertullian says:

> In everything he labored on [his gospel], and the drawing up of his *Antitheses*, he thought, in doing so, to establish a disparity between the Old and New Testaments, so that his own Christ may be separate from the creator and belong instead to the other God, and may be alien to the law and the prophets. It is also certain that he erased everything contrary to his own opinion and inspired by the creator, as if that had been added to the text by the creator's advocates, while retaining everything agreeing with his own opinion.[197]

Marcion's *Antitheses* had the same purpose as his gospel. The *Antitheses* is a supplement to his gospel, and its very title announces its purpose. Tertullian describes it as follows:

> To encourage belief [in his gospel], Marcion endowed it, so to speak, with a work composed of contrary, mutually opposed statements, entitled *Antitheses*, and compiled with a view to severing the law from the gospel. That would divide deity into two Gods, one for each instrument or, as it is usually called, testament. By such a means Marcion might defend belief in his gospel in accordance with the *Antitheses*.[198]

See also where Tertullian says about these antitheses that they "long to draw distinctions from natural qualities, whether as to law or virtue, and thus to sunder Christ from the creator, and what is best from the judge, the mild God from the cruel one, the salutary God from the destructive one."[199]

It is a pity that Tertullian does not more fully acquaint us with the contents of this work, since in rebutting the Marcionite concept of justice he thinks it unnecessary to go further into the details.[200] Hence we only know this much, that in the *Antitheses* the contrast of the world creator's justice with the true God's goodness, and the elucidation

---

197. *Against Marcion* 4.6 [*ANF* 3:351].
198. Ibid., 4.1 [*ANF* 3:345].
199. Ibid., 2.29 [*ANF* 3:320].
200. Just prior to the last passage quoted in the text, Tertullian writes (in 2.29): "I would have attacked Marcion's *Antitheses* more fully if a more painstaking demolition of them were required to defend the [true] creator as the good God and judge, after showing examples of both roles as befitting God. Since, however, these two attributes of goodness and justice together belong to the full concept of the divine being as omnipotent, I can be content with now having refuted his *Antitheses* in a brief way" [*ANF* 3:320].

of it, is treated via a series of mutually opposed statements taken from the Old and New Testaments. The antithesis of the just God and the good God is the most general perspective under which Marcion places everything that is in the same way characteristic of law and gospel, of Judaism and Christianity.

On the basis of this perspective, the doctrine of the free grace of God in the remission of sins therefore had to occupy a very important place in Marcion's system, as opposed to the doctrine of a justice simply calibrated to the measure of one's deeds, with some to be rewarded and some punished. Yet we are not given more precise statements about this matter here, and it is certainly of interest to know more specifically how Marcion understood, and spelled out, the Pauline concept of righteousness from faith (δικαιοσύνη ἐκ πίστεως). With the way he tied the concept of harshness and strictness to the concept of justice, for Marcion the essential attribute of the supreme God revealed by Christ was, on the contrary, pure goodness and love. That is why, in speaking of Christ, Marcion extolled nothing beyond his gentleness (*lenitas*) and mildness (*mansuetudo*),[201] and generally established, as the highest principle of religion, that it should completely exclude fear. According to Tertullian: "Marcion says his God is not feared; that a good being is not feared but a judge is, because the grounds for fearing—anger, severity, judgment, vengeance, condemnation—reside with him."[202] Or: "The Marcionites freely approach him because they do not fear their God at all. However, a bad one is to be feared, whereas a good one is to be loved."

Therefore Christianity is simply the religion of love, of forgiveness and grace, while Judaism is the religion of fear, of retaliation and punishment, of a justice resting on the principle "eye for eye, tooth for tooth" (Exod 21:24).[203] It is in this sense that Christ was said to be the founder of a new religion, in order to reveal the true God, the God of love and, as "the light of the new and grand religion,"[204] to come forward against the more impure, false religion whose author was the world's creator. Based on this perspective Marcion therefore placed special weight on all of those points at which the gospel story made known with special clarity its antithetical relation to the Old Testament understanding of religion and the spirit of it. These points include the fact that one of the apostles was a tax collector.[205] Also, Christ disobeyed the commandment regarding the Sabbath, and acted directly contrary to other laws of the God of the Jews,[206]

---

201. *Against Marcion* 4.9.

202. Ibid., 4.8 [*ANF* 3:355]. The following quotation is from 1.27.

203. [*Ed.*] Within parentheses in the text, Baur quotes Tertullian, 2.18: "the statute of retaliation, requiring eye for eye, tooth for tooth, stripe for stripe."

204. *Against Marcion* 4.17 [ANF 3:374].

205. [*In the text*] ("Marcion adduces the publican chosen by the Lord as proof that he was chosen as an adversary of the law and as unclean in Jewish eyes" [4.11 (*ANF* 3:360)])

206. [*Ed.*] The text cites Tertullian, 4.12, and adds parenthetically (from 4.20 [*ANF* 3:379]) the statement that "Christ acted as an adversary of the law; and therefore, while the law forbids contact with a woman having her period [Lev 15:19], he desired not only that this woman should touch him, but that he should heal her." Also Tertullian, 4.9: "as an enemy of the law, he touched the leper,

as we see in Luke 8:44 ["She came up behind him and touched the fringe of his clothes, and immediately her hemorrhage stopped"]. Also, he forbade his followers [i.e., the seventy] to take anything with them on the road [Luke 10:5], whereas the Demiurge commanded the Jews to take gold and silver from Egypt with them.[207] Also, Christ showed that he loved children, taught that one should "receive the kingdom of God as a little child" (Luke 18:16–17), while the Demiurge sent out bears to maul some boys in retaliation for their jeering at Elisha (2 Kgs 2:23–24).[208] Also, Christ rebuked his disciples for wanting to take revenge on a Samaritan village (Luke 9:52–55), whereas the Demiurge sent fire down in vengeance against the false prophets (1 Kgs 18:36–40), when Elijah demanded it. Also, Christ extended his hands simply to save the believers but not to turn away the unbelievers as Moses, the prophet of the world's creator did (Exod 17:9). Marcion set special stock on these and other antitheses, for they served his purpose of shedding light on the antitheses between law and gospel.

## The Jewish Christ and the Christian Christ

Since Marcion accepted the fact that the world's creator also proclaimed a Christ, this induced him to elaborate further on the general antithesis between Judaism and Christianity by speaking about the difference between the two Christs, the Jewish and Christian ones.[209]

The Christ of the world's creator could only have the same kind of character as the world's creator had. Therefore, because Marcion depicted the world's creator as a strict, vehement God animated by a warlike spirit, he could also think of the Christ this God proclaimed as inescapably having these same attributes. Tertullian remarks about this Christ that "he is held to be a militant, armed warrior."[210] On this basis Marcion believed that he could find nothing befitting his Christ in the prophecy of Isaiah, chap. 7, where it appeared to him that Christ was depicted simply as a warrior. Tertullian says: "Challenge us to consider Isaiah's description of Christ, which you contend at no point befits him [i.e., Marcion's Christ]. First of all you say that Isaiah's Christ will have been called 'Immanuel.' Then you say he takes the riches of Damascus and the spoils of Samaria against the king of Assyria. Yet [you say] he who is to come was not born under such a name nor engaged in any warlike enterprise."[211]

---

disregarding the precept of the law" (*ANF* 3:356).

207. Ibid., 4.24 and 5.13.

208. [*In the text*] ("this antithesis is imprudent enough" [4.23 (*ANF* 3.386)])

209. *Against Marcion* 4.6: "Marcion enunciated the position that the Christ who, in the time of Tiberius, was revealed by a previously unknown God for the salvation of all peoples, is different from the one the creator God ordained for the restoration of the Jewish state and is yet to come. He said there is a separation, a great and absolute difference between these two, as great as the separation between law and gospel, as great as the difference between Judaism and Christianity" [*ANF* 3:351].

210. Ibid., 4.20 [*ANF* 3:379] [as opposed to a "warrior against spiritual enemies"].

211. Ibid., 3.12 [*ANF* 3:330–31]. [*Ed.* Isaiah 8:4 seems to say the opposite: "the wealth of Damascus

Linked to this is the additional important difference Marcion points to, that the Jewish messiah is said to only lead the single people of the Jews out from its Diaspora, whereas the Christ of the Christians was sent by the God of love to free the entire human race.[212] Also that the loving God's kingdom is eternal and heavenly, whereas the Jewish Christian messiah only promised that the Jews would repossess their land, and rest in the bosom of Abraham after they die.[213] The rewards and punishments the world's creator proclaims to his own they could only have partaken of in the underworld; but the blessedness Christ imparts has its place in heaven. To this Marcion relates the parable of the rich man and Lazarus (Luke 16:19–31), in which he simply saw a description of the creator's underworld. He especially points to the words of v. 29 ("Abraham replied, 'They have Moses and the prophets; they should listen to them'"), which seem to him to be said to the Jews. Tertullian states: "Marcion says that the admonition of our God from heaven has commanded us not to listen to Moses and the prophets, but to Christ."[214] "Marcion is certainly thinking in different terms, and decides that both torment and ease are the creator's payment in the underworld for those who listened to the law and the prophets, while he says the heavenly bosom and haven truly belong to Christ and God."[215]

Since the difference between Christ and the Jewish messiah is so great, Christ also had to be unlike the world creator's prophets. In this context Marcion stresses that Christ accomplished his miracles by mere words alone. Tertullian says "Marcion finds it antithetical that Elisha required a material means by applying water, seven times over, whereas Christ brought about an instantaneous and permanent cure by his word alone."[216] Even John the Baptist took offense at Jesus' healing (Luke chap. 7, esp. v. 23) because he too, as one of the prophets of the world's creator, found in Christ someone entirely different from what he had envisaged.[217]

---

and the spoil of Samaria will be carried away by the king of Syria."]

212. Ibid., 3.31 [*ANF* 3:339]: "From this notion of yours you cannot derive a basis for differentiating the two Christs, as if the creator destined the Jewish Christ to restore this one people from its Diaspora, while the supreme God appointed your Christ to liberate the entire human race."

213. Tertullian has Marcion saying: "I hope for God's kingdom as an everlasting and heavenly possession—and this amounts to proof of the diversity of Christs. The Jewish Christ promises to the Jews their original condition, the recovery of their land, and after life is over, resting in Sheol in the bosom of Abraham. Oh, most excellent God! For, being appeased, he restores what he took away angrily ... You argue for a different Christ, because he announces a new kingdom" (3.25 [*ANF* 3:342, 344]). See also 4.14 [*ANF* 3:366]: "You suppose that the promises of the creator were earthly promises, but Christ's are heavenly promises."

214. Ibid., 4.34. [*Ed.*] In the text Baur refers to Luke 9:28–36, which is the account of Jesus' transfiguration, in which Moses and Elijah appear together with Jesus.

215. Ibid., 4.24 [*ANF* 3:406].

216. Ibid., 4.9 [*ANF* 3:356]. [*Ed.*] This refers to the healing of Naaman's leprosy by Elisha (2 Kgs 5:8–14) and Jesus' healing of a leper (Matt 8:2–3).

217. [*Ed.*] In parentheses in the text Baur cites Tertullian, 4.18: "But John is offended when he hears of the miracles of Christ, as of an alien God" (*ANF* 3:375).

## Marcion's Docetism in Relation to Paganism (According to Marcion, Christ's Manifestation Is Mere Appearance)

Marcion's docetism is what his antinomianism is in relation to Judaism, but in a still wider context, thus also in relation to paganism, that is, in relation to the whole world, both Jewish and pagan. Because Marcion's Christ opposed, and completely set aside, the law and the prophets, he could have no common ground with the God of Judaism. So, inasmuch as he is not merely the God of Judaism but rather is the creator of the world, the same repellent and hostile relation to this God was said to extend still further and find its fulfillment via docetism.

In order to completely cut Christ off from any ties to the world's creator and to his entire realm, Christ was not permitted to have any feature linking him in any way to external nature. Marcion therefore denied not only that Christ was begotten according to the natural law, but also that he had any kind of physical body, because everything physical and corporeal can have arisen only from the realm of the Demiurge, is subject to the Demiurge's laws, and is conditioned by them. Marcion's system stands out among the Gnostic systems in particular for its decidedly docetic nature.

In switching over to attack this docetism, Tertullian exclaims:

> Marcion vomits forth the virulence of his own mind when he alleges Christ to be a phantom. This opinion of his will surely have others of his precocious and addled Marcionites to maintain it, ones the Apostle John pronounced as antichrists when they denied that Christ came in the flesh (2 John 7). They did not deny it to establish the rights of the other God [which is what, according to Tertullian, Marcion also chiefly intended by his docetism]. They did so because they started by assuming that an incarnate God could not be a credible belief. The more firmly the antichrist Marcion had seized upon this assumption [that in order to be independent of the Demiurge Christ also should not have a natural body of any kind] the more prepared he of course was to deny that Christ had bodily substance, since he had introduced his God as being neither the author nor the resuscitator of the flesh, because he is altogether good and stands wholly apart from the creator's lies and deceits. Therefore, in order to avoid such lying and deceitfulness, and any notion that he belongs to the creator, Marcion's Christ was not what he appeared to be, and pretended to be what he was not—incarnate without flesh, a human without being one.[218]

Thus Christ's entire manifestation was mere appearance or illusion, although this illusion itself was not said to extend to everything belonging to the natural course of a human life.

Although Christ appeared publicly as an apparition and lived together with his disciples, teaching and operating as such a phenomenon, indeed even dying as a phantom being, he was nevertheless not said to be born in this apparent way. In order

---

218. Ibid., 3.8 [*ANF* 3:327]. [*Ed.*] The bracketed insertions are Baur's.

to stay as far away as possible from the assumption of an actual birth, he was also said to have not undergone an apparent birth. Tertullian even derives the entirely of Marcion's docetism from this point.

> Marcion adopted all these notions that Christ's corporeality was deceptive, with the intention of shielding his nativity from any attestation to his having human substance, so that all the statements about his undergoing a human birth, and being corporeal, would be assigned to the Christ of the creator instead.[219]

Marcion would not have utterly rejected Christ's having a human body if only one would not have inferred from it that he was actually born under, and in dependence on, the natural laws of the world's creator.

Marcion, and other heretics, found a very striking proof for this view in Matt 12:48, as enlarged upon in Luke 8:21.[220] In criticizing Marcion's gospel, Tertullian states about these passages: "We now come to the most persistently employed argument by all those who call into question the Lord's nativity. They say that the Lord himself testifies to his not having been born when he says, 'Who is my mother, and who are my brothers?'"[221] In order to free his Christ from "the utter disgrace or foulness of being born, from having to be educated, and from the vileness of the flesh,"[222] Marcion has Christ beginning his earthly existence with the aforementioned moment when he suddenly came down from heaven and entered the synagogue in Capernaum as a teacher comparable to the law and the prophets.[223] Tertullian designates this sudden, bodily appearance of Christ in these words: "In the fifteenth year of Tiberius, Christ Jesus proceeded down from heaven as the salvific spirit."[224]

With Marcion's Christ said to have had no part in human birth, this is also how he was said to have ended his earthly existence by suffering and death on the cross. This too could have just apparently taken place.[225] But for Marcion, this point was of even greater importance because of how it contrasts with Christ's distinctive entry into earthly existence. Also, since the Catholic Church already had Christ descending to the underworld after his death, Marcion was able, in agreement with this teaching,

---

219. Ibid., 3.11 [*ANF* 3:330].

220. [*Ed.*] Matt 12:48–49: "Jesus replied, 'Who is my mother, and who are my brothers?' And pointing to his disciples, he said, 'Here are my mother and my brothers!'" Luke 8:21: "But he said to them, 'My mother and my brothers are those who hear the word of God and do it.'"

221. Ibid., 4.19 [*ANF* 3:777]. See also Tertullian, *On the Flesh of Christ*, ch. 7.

222. *Against Marcion* 4.21 [*ANF* 3:382].

223. [*In the text*] (Luke 4:32: "They were astounded at his teaching"; also, Tertullian, 4.7: "From heaven straight to the synagogue" [*ANF* 3:352].)

224. Ibid., 1.19. [*In the text*] ("as solely spirit [πνεῦμα μόνον]," in the way Epiphanius speaks about this docetism in *Against Heresies*, ch. 42).

225. [*In the text*] ("It is false that he suffered, since he was an apparition," Tertullian, 3.11 [*ANF* 3:330].)

to have his docetism extending beyond Christ's earthly existence. As we see from Irenaeus and Epiphanius,[226] in Marcion's system there is explicit mention of Christ's descent to the underworld.

## The Significance of Gnostic Docetism as Such

While docetism does of course undergo various modifications in the different Gnostic systems, it is altogether typical of them. So we must address the issue of docetism's significance in these systems, and the place to do that is where docetism emerges so decisively and this issue is most pressing, namely in Marcion's system.

In general terms, docetism is the contention that Christ's manifestation (*Erscheinung*) as a human being is mere appearance or illusion (*Schein*) and has no truly objective reality. But spelling out this concept in more specific terms then depends directly on what counts as appearance and what counts as reality. If we set out from the orthodox concept of Christ's person as the Catholic Church affirmed it in principle from the beginning—that the divine element in Christ is just as really present as the human element; that these two aspects of Christ's being, as integrative elements, form the same personal unity as that in each human individual where spirit and body are joined in a personal, unitary being—then, as soon as the divine element in Christ becomes undeniable, there is a twofold antithesis. Either one denies that the human element in Christ is objectively real and declares that his human body is merely an apparent or illusory body; or else the human element is at least sufficiently separate from the divine element that there is no personal unity of the two aspects.

The first view is the purely docetic view, since according to it Christ is just apparently human. But the second of these views also shares with docetism proper at least this much, that it interprets the divine-human unity of the redeemer as merely an apparent unity. For, in distinguishing Christ from Jesus, it regards Jesus as an actual human being and has him being active, in a visibly human way, for the purpose of redemption. It is mere illusion when one regards Jesus as truly the person of the redeemer, as actually the subject performing the redemptive activity. Also, the first view admits of two different modifications, depending upon whether or not one holds strictly to the distinction between the pneumatic and psychical elements. If this distinction is downplayed, then Christ the redeemer is solely spirit, the salvific spirit (*spiritus salutaris*), whose human manifestation is just illusory. But if one differentiates the psychical element from the pneumatic one, and in turn separates the hylic, or properly material and corporeal, element from the psychical element, then one can assign a "psychical body" to the redeemer. However, in order to have this inherently invisible "psychical body" appearing in a visible, human form, one must then appeal to a special arrangement (οἰκονομία) whereby what is invisible becomes visible;

---

226. Irenaeus, *Against Heresies* 1.29; Epiphanius, *Against Heresies* 42.4

in other words, what is just "psychically corporeal" receives the form or appearance of a physical body. The psychical element therefore indeed conveys or transmits the manifestation, but the manifestation or appearing of the redeemer himself is no truly human manifestation but instead a merely docetic one. It simply has the apparent form of a human being, as in the first one of the aforementioned modifications.

Each of these three views [that is, the first one and the second with its two versions or modifications] has its own representative among the Gnostics. These three are Basilides, Valentinus, and Marcion. Basilides stands closest to the orthodox Christian view; Marcion is farthest from it; Valentinus has an intermediate position with his psychical Christ. Their views about Christ's nativity are the most telling indications of their differences. Basilides accepts an actual birth, albeit only the birth of the human Jesus. Valentinus says it was only an apparent birth. Marcion will not countenance associating Christ with any birth. That we juxtapose these three views for good reasons, and regard them as modifications of one and the same basic idea must result, more specifically, from the general significance that docetism has.

Docetism can only have emerged everywhere from a perspective that starts with a strict antithesis between spirit and matter. Its underlying idea is always that spirit absolutely rules over matter and is superior to it. Spirit alone is what is truly substantial and existent in itself, whereas matter is simply as different from spirit as accident is from substance or perfection is from imperfection. Matter in and for itself has no true and real being. It is, so to speak, non-being, what only appears to have being. In other words, even when matter encounters spirit as an independent being subsistent on its own, it still has such little absolute value that, in this regard at least, its relationship to spirit is one of the most complete subordination. Thus matter relates to spirit simply as what is impure relates to what is pure, or evil does to good. When matter is just the shell and form in which spirit must appear in order to objectify itself in the finite world, then matter is directly thought of as what is merely an accidental feature [of the spiritual substance]. Spirit "solidifies itself," so to speak, into a physical, corporeal world. However, in this crossing over of spirit into matter there must be a set point beyond which spirit may not go if it is to preserve the purity of its consciousness of its own absolute being.

Furthermore, on this view of spirit's relation to matter, if matter is always just spirit objectified, become finite, then inasmuch as the material aspect is set apart from the psychological aspect, it becomes an inert, lifeless stuff to which the free spirit is so harnessed that spirit's awareness of itself disappears in this circumstance. Therefore, if spirit is supposed to retain a consciousness of its own absolute nature, and of its absolute dominion over the material element, it must constantly be actualizing this mastery by breaking through the material form in which it appears. It must never allow its material form to become static and rigid. Spirit must instead rise above it, relate to it in a completely free way, and treat it as a form completely transparent to, and changeable by, spirit. Thus the perceptible form in which spirit appears is, in this sense, merely an apparent or illusory form, and it is only in such a form and no other that the redeemer can appear in the sensible world. For if in Gnosticism redemption consists in spirit once again becoming conscious of its absolute supremacy over matter, and by doing so gaining its freedom from matter, then in this sense the redeemer can only be the kind in which that consciousness had never been obscured by matter being superior to spirit. This is just how the redeemer, in the traditional Christian view, must himself be without sin if he is to redeem others from sin. Anyone in whom matter's scope has so grown that, as a thick stuff, a rigid body that a person can no longer penetrate with the free power of spirit, is himself in need of redemption. Therefore the principle of redemption for such a person can only be in another in whom matter has not attained such firmness and weighed down spirit in this fashion. This is what the Valentinians' docetism meant when they said that, while they could indeed grant that the redeemer was able to appear in a physical Christ, it was, however, only an apparent body and not a material body, lest the idea of the redeemer no longer apply to him.

Docetism accordingly expresses the principle on which redemptive activity depends, namely, freedom from matter. Nothing essentially changes on this view, although matter, in opposition to spirit, is considered to be an independent principle existent on its own. Then of course it is not the product of spirit, although it still retains the same relation to spirit. As opposed to matter, spirit alone has absolute worth and absolute reality. Matter itself, in and for itself, is without value and significance for spirit. If redemption is liberation from domination by matter, the redeemer therefore can have no association with matter, because any association with matter obscures spirit's purity, robbing it of its absolute superiority over matter. Hence the redeemer can only appear in a way that manifests at the same time his absolute independence from matter, spirit's essential difference from matter. If the redeemer had been linked in organic unity with a material body, the spirit in this body would have been dependent on its matter, would have seemed bound to it and constrained by it.

By the same token, however, the redeemer cannot express his redemptive activity apart from manifesting himself in a perceptible way in the material, finite world, for here alone are there individuals needing redemption. Therefore this redeeming can only take place in a form that, in itself, is not an actual human body but just appears to be one. In other words, the redeemer can in any case only become known in connection with an actual human being, in such a way that this human being merely serves as the redeemer's vehicle and instrument. Whereas the true redeemer, as the imperceptible idea, hovers above this being and the actual human himself just designates, as it were, the place in the sensible world where the redeeming activity is engaged. The human being is simply the sign of the redeeming activity; and one can say that, according to both Basilides and Marcion, the redeemer would have only apparently been a human being or just seemed to be manifest in an actual human body.

If we must find the significance of Gnosticism in this interpretation, then what is important here is not its deliberately and arbitrarily contradicting the factual basis of the gospel accounts. Instead it is that we see expressed in this view the basic idea of Gnosticism as to spirit's absolute freedom and independence from matter. This then further explains why the Gnostic systems have posited an absolute beginning in principle for the redeeming activity, a feature that is most striking in Marcion's case. Here we have the sudden, instantaneous factor in his system, that completely unexpected descent from heaven (*manare de coelo*). From the fact that the other two systems we are discussing now agree with it, we see that this is a major point we must pay attention to if we are to correctly understand docetism.

When Basilides and Valentinus too have that sudden descent coincide with the moment of Jesus' baptism, then the act of baptism itself is something nonessential and only contingently linked to a specific point in the gospel story, to an occurrence narrated in it. The main thing is the suddenness with which the redeeming activity begins, an activity for which the psychical Christ of Valentinus, and the natural human being Jesus for Basilides, had no significance at all. This is so despite the fact that both these figures serve as a prelude to the actual work of redemption, whereas Marcion's Jesus does not do this. In each case the redeeming spirit's entry into the world first takes place at that moment.

In this context the significance of docetism is that the principle of the redeeming activity, as the positing of an absolute beginning completely independent of the material world order and its development in accord with natural laws, is thought of as an engaging with the sensible world and the history of humankind in a purely supernatural way. It is only as something supernatural that the principle of the higher spiritual life can involve itself with human nature, just as, on the traditional view, Christ being without sin, simply because he does not originate in the sequence of human procreation, is an absolute beginning point. Yet we ought not just stop at this point. In the presentation of the Valentinian system we took special note of how the redeemer simply makes the pneumatic ones conscious of what is already and inherently present in their nature. The redeemer just indicates those stages of development that each spiritual individual must reach if he or she is to be aware of, and realize internally, the absolute superiority of spirit over matter. Without this point one will not understand the redeemer's relation to the individual, spiritual natures in need of redemption, in the other Gnostic systems too, even that of Marcion.

If we accept the fact that, in docetism it can simply be a matter of giving full weight to the moment at which the principle of redemption begins to be active, by treating it as an absolute beginning, then how can we also relate this point to the individual person in which the idea of redemption is said to be realized? The answer is that in this person there starts to be active a principle that, as purely supernatural, is not explainable from his or her entire previous existence or previous course of development, yet notwithstanding that fact it must belong to the sphere of human nature's capacity for development. Redemption is the moment of one's spirit becoming decisively free from its bondage to matter up to that point. It is the awakening of the higher self-consciousness, the pneumatic principle rising above and beyond one's psychical aspect.

But if redemption is in this sense merely an inner act taking place within each individual, why is there any concern to make it dependent on an external redeemer—on the story and person of someone appearing at a specific point in time? This concern is based, first and foremost, on the historical truth of Christianity; in other words, on the undeniable fact that Jesus was the first individual in which the redemptive principle actively emerged in this given sense. Yet while Jesus was the first individual of this kind in the series of individual human beings following after him, his story, albeit epoch-making, was nevertheless just the story of an ordinary man. Maintaining [that Jesus was] truly a redeemer first had to involve the additional concern to accept that, being first in the series, Jesus is also the archetype for the totality of human individuals falling under this concept of redemption; that he is the universal human being who simply individualizes himself, so to speak, in all the others and realizes in them the idea of his own being.

Yet if the archetypal Christ is separated from the historical Jesus, then the actual man Jesus could have had only the significance Basilides assigns to him. Then what one wanted to hold firmly to was just the pure idea of redemption, and the actual man Jesus simply designated the point and place in history where this idea first began to be active. In other words, one also wanted to understand the abstract idea concretely, and the human phenomenon Jesus then became the visible form in which, as its image, the personified idea of redemption mirrored itself. The docetic Christ is the freely dominant, archetypal human being, pure of any contact with matter and for that reason not permitted to have any direct ties to what is material and corporeal. But on the one hand what is just apparently a body, what is a corporeal illusion, an apparent form, is on the other hand something perceived visually and in which an idea presents itself, since the appearance is nevertheless always at the same time a shadow or reflection of the [redeemer's] nature itself.

Accordingly we also find expressed in docetism the inclination typical of Gnosticism in general, to make religious ideas sensible or symbolic by projecting abstract, conscious thoughts into a visually perceptible form in order to more effectively secure the objective reality of Gnosis itself. The historical Christ, Christianity itself, was said to have this significance in the Gnostic systems, at least a figurative reality, although the Gnostics believed they could not acknowledge the factual reality of the gospel story. The historical Christ had to give way to the archetypal Christ, although the archetypal Christ was at the same time said to be a figurative Christ or an image. The form in which the historical Christ appeared was said to be at the same time the evident glimmer, in the sensible world, of the objective idea of redemption.

So docetism is not merely a negative position; it also has very positive significance. The same Gnostic system—that otherwise in its disinclination for everything sensuous and pertaining to natural life, also seems mainly to disavow the Gnostic predilection for imagery, for symbolism and mythic personifications—had in this instance of docetism to at least follow the general train of thought in a very curious way. Tertullian correctly states about Marcion's docetism that "his Christ . . . was not what he appeared to be, and pretended to be what he was not—incarnate without flesh, human without being human." But when Tertullian draws from "a divine Christ" (that is, the God in Christ, the God revealed by Christ) "without being God" the conclusion "Why should he not also have conveyed an apparition of God?," this is a reversal of the image and the idea.[227] As a reappearing of the idea, the image is of course on the one hand something real, in that it contains the idea within it and shares in its being; while on the other hand the image exists within consciousness in that, as the mirroring of the idea, the image is a mere appearance whereas the idea itself can never be mere appearance, merely an apparition (*phantasma*). The latter is the case even though one abstracts the image from the reality of the external phenomenon in which it is envisaged.

As the results of this discussion show, the docetism of the Gnostics is most closely connected with both their purely real tendency and their efforts at sensuous imagery of the idea. Docetism directly shows how much this sensuous imagery belongs to the character of Gnosticism. This point alone can answer the objection Tertullian raises [about the Gnostic Christ not having real flesh]: "If God despises the flesh as earthly (and, as you say, filthy), why was he not also contemptuous of its image? For honor is not given to what is unworthy of it, nor to its image."[228]

## Christianity as the Religion of Freedom from Matter

Marcion's antinomianism, his rejection of the Old Testament law, provides his conceptual link to Christianity as the absolute religion. His docetism likewise leads to this same concept and enables us to have a keener and firmer understanding of it.

If, according to this antinomianism, Christianity is the religion of love that frees one's heart and mind from fear and from all the means by which the Demiurge, the God of the Old Testament law, dominates people, then according to Marcion's docetism, Christianity is the religion of freedom from matter and from the domination of one's spirit by matter. As Christianity increasingly makes one's spirit aware that it is superior to matter and thereby gains spirit's freedom from matter, the more fully the principle of redemption becomes realized. To this end Christ functioned as the redeemer, and the whole of his earthly appearing presents the religious task that each individual is supposed to carry out in one's own self. We have already noted that Marcion of course has his docetic Christ suffering and dying, but he does not have Christ being born. Tertullian charges Marcion with inconsistency in this regard:

---

227. Tertullian, *Against Marcion* 3.8 [*ANF* 3:327].
228. Ibid., 3.10 [*ANF* 3:329].

You are honoring your God under the cover of deception, since he knew he was something different from what he represented himself as being. In that case you might even allow the supposition that he was born . . . He wore the mask of his substance to act out the play of his fantasy from its earliest scene, while bypassing the origin of his flesh. You have of course rejected the sham of a nativity . . . After making all these things disgraceful, establishing that they are unworthy of God, birth will be no more unworthy of him than death, infancy no more so than the cross, the natural order of things no more so than punishment, the flesh no more unworthy than condemnation. If Christ truly underwent all things, then being born would be a minor affair. If Christ only appeared to suffer, as a phantom, then he could have also been born as a phantom.[229]

Nevertheless the distinction Marcion draws in this way, between Jesus' birth and his death, is very closely connected to Marcion's general view of his life.

On Marcion's view of spirit's relation to matter, he had to oppose not only everything restricting spirit from becoming free of matter but also whatever is the means for replicating the bonds of its captivity. He recoiled from the flesh, and the life of the flesh, with loathing and horror;[230] and everything manifesting the fullness and fecundity of natural life was for Marcion just the impure, vile, carnal pleasure of nature in its creating and producing activity—under the coarse control of material forces and impulses that delight in this detestable tumult, a workshop of carnal lust and the life of the flesh. Tertullian describes Marcion's view in these terms:

Complete your case against the most sacred and revered works of nature. Inveigh against all that you are, that is, destroy the source of the flesh and life by calling the womb of such a great animal a sewer, the sewer where a human being is produced. Elaborate on the detestable and shameful torments of labor, and then on the defiling, anguished spectacle of the birth itself.[231]

Hence Marcion naturally could also consider marriage and married life to be just a rule mandated by the world's creator, one by which this ruler, as God of the impure material life of nature, sought to ensure the preservation of his realm.[232] Marcion regarded marriage as a norm that cannot be recognized in Christ's true community if the one who honors the true God, the disparager of marriage, ought not to be at the

---

229. *Against Marcion* 3.11 [ANF 3:330].

230. [*In the text*] ("as you say, the flesh is earthly and filthy," Tertullian, 3.10).

231. Ibid., 3.11 [ANF 3:330].

232. Marcion's view of marriage here is especially characteristic of his own standpoint if we bear in mind that it is by no means the general Gnostic position. Clement of Alexandria expressly states that the Valentinians even held marriage to be a satisfactory arrangement, because of their teaching about the syzygies. "The sect of Valentinus justifies physical union based on heaven, deriving it from the teaching about the syzygies, and approving of it" (*Stromata* 3.1). Of course as Clement remarks, Basilides had a somewhat different view [i.e., based on Matt 19:10–12].

same time the servant of the world's creator. Tertullian rebukes Marcion[233] for his inconsistency in retaining in his mutilated gospel the passage for Luke 5:35 in which Christ is called "the bridegroom":

> Lo, you even impugn the law of your God. He does not join people in the bonds of marriage or, when contracted, allow it. He baptizes no one but a celibate person or a eunuch, and reserves baptism until death or divorce. Wherefore, then, do you make this Christ a bridegroom? Bridegroom is the designation for the one who united man and woman, not for one who separated them.[234]

Hence marriage ought not to be contracted in the Marcionite community, and those already married were either totally excluded, or else accepted only on condition of strict sexual abstinence. Tertullian says, in opposition to Marcion: "You put a stop to marriage by neither uniting man and woman nor allowing those who are married to be baptized or receive the eucharist, unless they mutually agree to repudiate the fruits of marriage and so the very creator himself."[235]

From all this we obviously see what must have made Marcion determined to not allow for the redeemer to be even apparently born. Even the sheer image of a real birth would surely have been an approval of the impure, material and natural life, of service rendered to the world's creator. On the other hand the redeemer's suffering and death, although merely in appearance but not in reality, fit entirely with Marcion's system.

Tertullian everywhere assumes that Marcion acknowledges Christ's death on the cross, and ascribes a distinctive religious meaning to it. He argues against the Marcionites:

> In your now believing that God took up a place in human form and all the circumstances of human nature, you no longer need to be convinced that God conformed himself to humanity, yet you remain bound by your own faith. If your God, from his loftier position, yielded the supreme dignity of his majesty to such submissiveness as to undergo death, and death of the flesh, why do

---

233. Tertullian also reproaches Marcion (in 4.17) for his reading of the phrase "you will be children of the Most High" (Luke 6:35) in his gospel. "What can be more shameless than for Marcion to be making us his children when, by forbidding marriage, God has not permitted us to make children of our own? How does God propose to give his followers a name that he has already eliminated? I cannot be the son of a eunuch! Especially when I have as my father the same great being who is the father of all things!" (*Against Marcion* 4.11 [*ANF* 3:373]). Marcion understood "you will be children of the Most High" as applying to the Christ of the world's creator. See Hahn, "Evangelium Marcionis in Thilo's *codex apocr.*," *N.T. Th.*, 1:444. [*Ed.* August Hahn (1792–1863) published *De gnosi Marcionis* in 1820–21. See below, n. 246. The citation in Thilo's vol. is pp. 401–86; Hahn's earlier work from 1820–21 was inserted into: J. C. Thilo, *Codex Apocryphus Novi Testamenti*, vol. 1, pp. 401–86 (Leipzig, 1832).]

234. *Against Marcion* 4.11 [*ANF* 3:361].

235. Ibid., 4.34 [*ANF* 3:405]. See 1.29 [*ANF* 3:293]: "According to Marcion the flesh is not to be baptized unless it be virgin, or a widow, or celibate, or else eligible by being divorced—as though those born of a marriage were themselves impotent. Such an arrangement no doubt amounts to forbidding marriage."

you not suppose that some humiliations are fitting for our God too, and are more tolerable than Jewish affronts and the cross and the tomb? Are these the humiliations that prejudice you against Christ (who is the target of human passions), while he is the divine one you reproach for sharing in human qualities? . . . You disdain such a God, and I do not know whether you believe, on faith, that God was crucified.[236]

For Marcion "the difference between the two Christs"[237] stood for the antithesis between the law and the gospel, in which antithesis the suffering and dying Christ also played a part. Hence Tertullian says:

> I suppose you try to introduce a difference of opinion about his death, simply because you deny that Christ's suffering on the cross was predicted of the creator's Christ; and also because you contend that it is unbelievable for the creator to expose his son to a death he had himself cursed. "Anyone hung on a tree is under God's curse."[238]

For what could the image of Christ's suffering and death have meant if it was not supposed to have concretely illustrated, and made one aware, that a Christian's supreme task in life is the duty to die to the world, to completely renounce all of life's material pleasures, all service to the world's creator? Only on this view was it possible to consider Christ's death on the cross as an occurrence that seemed to be a victory by the world's creator—given how it appeared and the current impression it made—but that in truth, and in its ongoing effects, had to contribute, more than anything else, to the downfall of the world's creator.

Marcion assumed that Christ's death on the cross was something arranged by the Demiurge (". . . that it is the Christ of the other God who was driven to the cross by the powers and authorities of the creator, so to speak by hostile beings"[239]). As the world's creator and as the God of the Jews, the Demiurge had every reason to do this. If the redeemer's entire activity was for the purpose of overturning the law and the prophets, and increasingly loosening the bonds tying human beings to material life and holding them fast in the realm of the world's creator, then the redeemer's life could only have been an ongoing struggle with the Demiurge. Even his descent to the netherworld was a continuation of the same struggle. For, just as he had come down from heaven to earth for the salvation of souls, so too he descended to the netherworld in order to snatch souls from the Demiurge and diminish his realm.[240]

236. *Against Marcion* 2.27 [ANF 3:318–19].

237. Ibid., 3.21 [ANF 3:339].

238. Ibid., 3.18 [ANF 3:336]. [Ed.] The quotation is from Deut 21:23. See also Gal 3:13: "Christ redeemed us from the curse of the law by becoming a curse for us—for it is written, 'Cursed is everyone who hangs on a tree.'"

239. Ibid., 3.23 [ANF 3:341].

240. Epiphanius, *Against Heresies* 42.4.2–3 [Amidon, *Panarion* (n. 35), 146]: "He says that Christ came down from above from the invisible and unnamable Father for the salvation of souls and the

## Part Two: The Various Principal Forms of Gnosis

After Christ's death the Demiurge carried on his struggle with Christ against the

refutation of the God of the Jews, the law, the prophets, and suchlike. The Lord descended to the netherworld to save those associated with Cain, et al." See also Irenaeus, *Against Heresies* 1.27.3. – It is most especially worthwhile to compare with this statement about Jesus' death the new and noteworthy source, from Armenian literature, for our knowledge of Marcionite teaching, published recently by Friedrich Neumann in Ilgen's *Zeitschrift für die historische Theologie* 4/1 (1834) 71–78, "Marcions Glaubenssystem, ... dargestellt von Esnig, einem armenische Bischof des fünften Jahrhunderts." Esnig [397—c. 478] contested the Marcionites in his major work, "Destruction of the Heretics," printed for the first time at St. Lazare in 1816. It attacks the errors of the pagans in general, the religious system of the Parsees, the views of the Greek philosophers, and the heretical theses of Marcion. The system of belief imparted is most extensive right where it concerns Jesus' death, and so we receive, at least partially, a desired expansion of the incomplete western account left by Luke. According to this account from Esnig (pp. 74ff. [Baur paraphrases Neumann's translation]), the God of goodness, the supreme God who dwells in the third heaven, moved by compassion for those people vexed and tormented by the evil of the lord of creation, and by matter, sent his son to redeem them. God said to him: "Heal their hurts, restore their dead to life, make their blind to see, and freely accomplish among them the greatest healing, until you face the God of the creation, who, having *become jealous*, will have you slain on the cross. After death you shall descend into hell and lead the dead out from there. For henceforth there will no longer be any hell among the living. The reason you shall be slain on the cross is *that you be seen* as a dead person, and for hell to open its maw to receive you. You will then go right in and empty it." [In following these instructions,] the Son of God was slain on the cross, went down into hell, and emptied it. He took the spirits, the very ones accompanying him from hell, and brought them into the third heaven, to his Father. The lord of the law was mightily enraged. In his wrath he tore his garment and the drapery of his palace; he darkened his sun and covered his world with darkness—and thus from vexation was in mourning for a long time. Jesus then came down a second time and appeared in his divinity before the God of the law, in order to remonstrate with him about his (Jesus') death. When the lord of the world saw the divinity of Jesus he therefore recognized that there is another God besides himself. Jesus said to him: "We have a matter to settle among ourselves, and there is no other to judge between us but your own laws, which you have written." When the law was then brought in, Jesus said to the lord of creation: "Have you not written in your laws, 'whoever kills someone shall die,' and 'whoever sheds the blood of the righteous, his blood shall in turn be shed'"? [Gen 9:7] He answered: "Indeed I have written this." Then Jesus said to him: "Then place yourself in my power so that I may kill you and shed your blood, as you have killed me and shed my blood. I am in fact more righteous than you are, and I have prepared the greatest blessings for your creatures." Jesus then began to enumerate all the blessings that he has shown to the creatures. When the lord of creation saw that he was overcome, he did not know what he should say, for he stood convicted by his own law. He did not know how to answer, for he was guilty of murder because of the death of Jesus. The lord of the law then withdrew into hell, and beseeched Jesus, saying: "Because I sinned, and unknowingly had you killed because I was ignorant of the fact that you are a God, and thinking you are a human being I unleashed that vengeance on you, I sought to afflict you where you always also are." Thereupon Jesus released him, betook himself to Paul, revealed the doctrines of the faith to Paul, and sent him out to proclaim the path we are to follow. Everyone who then believes in Christ will have switched over to this just and good way. – In my treatise on *Das manichäische Religionssystem* (n. 40), 61, I have called attention to the similarity, in the Manichean depiction, between the archetypal human being's struggle with the prince of darkness, and the way in which the earlier church fathers represented the redeemer's death. Here we then see how a different major conception of that ancient satisfaction theory [of the atonement] has originated with the Marcionite system. With its exposition in this passage from Esnig, compare the key section 5.1 in *Against Heresies* by Irenaeus, the earliest church father in whom we find the subsequent and very extensive elaboration of this theory, for it shows how closely the theory is related to the Marcionite system. The theory rests on the concept of justice, although the Marcionite system obviously has the particular application that so decisively validates this concept. Here too it was therefore the heretics who provided the initial impetus to the speculative development of Christian dogma. Yet the essential difference remains that, whereas the church fathers adopted this theory

disciples of Christ as well.²⁴¹ Since Marcion and his followers also had to trace the oppression they were undergoing as heretics, at the hands of the Catholic Church, back to the influence of the Demiurge—with the Christianity so closely intertwined with Judaism able to find his rule opportune and beneficial—it confirmed even more so their view that the true Christian's calling is to suffer, and to endure the world's hatred. This view was very clearly expressed when Marcion called his fellow-believers "companions in misery" (συνταλαιπώρους) and "associates in hatred" (συμμισουμένους).²⁴² Since they were subject to such suffering and to all those deprivations that their dread of sensuous pleasure, and their very strict moral teaching, imposed on them, the Marcionites were supposed to turn their minds all the more resolutely to the blessings and joys promised in the gospel. Thus Marcion, as well as many others who shared more or less the same way of thinking, believed they should be most especially entitled to apply to themselves those words of his gospel that are taken from Luke 6:20–26. As Tertullian says, these are "those ordinary precepts of his by which he adapts his own peculiar doctrine to his (so-called) edict of Christ: Blessed are the poor, for theirs is the kingdom of heaven, and so forth."²⁴³

## Marcion's Dualism; His Doctrine of the Primal Being

We still have not examined Marcion's doctrine of the primal being, which he assumes to be the principle of all existent being. What must already have caught our attention is that such a significant part of the Marcionite system was able to be expounded without engaging in a closer examination of this issue. It is certain that Marcion assumed, in addition to the supreme God, a matter that is co-eternal with God.²⁴⁴ The main question we have to address now is how Marcion locates the Demiurge in relation to these two primal beings [matter, and the supreme God]. There are two different ways to go here, and some authoritative support for each of them. The Demiurge either can

---

by giving absolute significance to the concept of justice, for Marcion it had only relative importance. That is because for him the concept just served to have the Demiurge, in his own obtuse state, yield to captivity. – In the conclusion of the passage one should not overlook the fact that Marcion knew how to connect this satisfaction theory closely with both his docetism and his Paulinism.

241. [*In the text*] (Tertullian, *Against Marcion* 3.22: "The apostles suffered all kinds of iniquitous persecution, from people belonging to the creator who was the adversary of the one about whom they were preaching" [*ANF* 3:340].)

242. See Tertullian, 4.9 [*ANF* 3:355], as well as 4.36: "Marcion, and all who are companions in misery, and associates in hatred with that heretic" [*ANF* 3:410].

243. *Against Marcion* 4.14 [*ANF* 3:365]. [*Ed.*] Luke 6:20–26 consists of four beatitudes followed by warnings to those who are rich, etc. Perhaps especially important for Marcion might be v. 22: "Blessed are you when people hate you, and when they exclude you, revile you, and defame you."

244. [*In the text*] (*Against Marcion* 1.15: "Marcion's sense of the creator is that he has fabricated a world out of some underlying matter that is unbegotten and unmade and contemporaneous with God" [*ANF* 3:282].)

be regarded as a completely independent principle, on a par with the other two, or else can be made dependent on one of them.

Megethius the Marcionite is represented as maintaining the following:

> I say that there are three primal powers or principles: the good God, the father of Jesus Christ; the creator [Demiurge]; and the other one, the bad one. The good power or principle is not the creator of what is evil, nor of what is born of woman, nor has he created the cosmos from himself, He is foreign to all that is evil, and to everything made by the Demiurge.[245]

The good principle rules over the Christians, the principle of the Demiurge rules over the Jews, and the evil principle rules over the pagans. These three principles have nothing in common with one another. They are of course unequal in power. The good principle is the most powerful, and the other two are subject to it. Nevertheless what these two bad or evil powers or principles do is not done in accordance with the will of the good principle. This is Hahn's authoritative basis for ascribing three fully independent principles to Marcion.[246]

But such a view is nevertheless always too contrary to reason for it to be assigned directly to Marcion himself without reliable testimony to that effect. Yet we cannot regard the aforementioned statement about Megethius as authoritative, because of observations we already made earlier, and must give the matter more thought before accepting this conclusion. For while Tertullian of course does expressly ascribe to Marcion the doctrine of a "matter contemporaneous with God," he indicates nothing to justify the assumption that Marcion assigned the same predicate to the Demiurge too.

Epiphanius also attributes the doctrine of the three principles to Marcion,[247] but does so in a very unclear fashion. Epiphanius says Marcion added a third principle to the two principles his forerunner Cerdo adopted, so that Marcion taught three principles. One is the unnamable and invisible one whom Marcion calls the good God and who has created nothing in the world. The second one is the visible God, the creator and Demiurge. The third is the Devil (διάβολος), who stands intermediate between the other two, the visible and the invisible ones. The Demiurge, the visible God, is also the God of the Jews and the judge. Especially unclear here is the position given to the Devil as "between the two." If Marcion is said to have accepted three principles, then the intermediate position can only be assigned to the Demiurge, and the Devil must go together with matter. Otherwise we surely get four principles, and we do not rightly

---

245. *Dialogus de recta in Deum fide*, sec. 1, introduction.

246. August Hahn, *De gnosi Marcionis antinomi*, pt. 1 (Königsberg, 1820), 11: "There is indeed no reason to doubt that Marcion established three principles to be respected (a good one, an evil one, and an intermediate one). They are called, respectively, the self-existent one (αὐτοφυῆ), the mean or contemptible one (ἀγέννητα), and the leaderless one (ἄναρχα). The intermediate one (the Demiurge) is neither produced from what is good, nor arisen from anything rational." See also pt. 2 (1821), 4.

247. *Against Heresies* 42.3.1–2.

see how the Devil, as a being in his own right, is supposed to fit with Marcion's system, since the Demiurge is the being with the role of opposing the good God.

If it is indeed more likely that Marcion accepted two principles rather than three,[248] then the Demiurge must be conceived as together either with the good God or with matter. Neander takes the former view, that Marcion did not regard the Demiurge as a being existent from himself, but instead as one who in some way derived his existence indirectly from the highest principle.[249] Neander believes this may be inferred from the fact that Marcion even called the Demiurge an angel, and that, according to Titus of Bostra,[250] Marcion called him an abortion (ἔκτρωμα). If Titus' report is correct, then according to it Marcion would have given his Demiurge the same position as Sophia, or Achamoth, had for Valentinus and other Gnostics. Yet one can hardly base such an inference on a single statement from a fairly late and solitary testimony. Just as little can we conclude with certainty from Tertullian (5.2) that Marcion called the Demiurge an angel. Other passages people appeal to in support of this conclusion do not make the situation any clearer. At the least, we do not know whether or not Marcion is being confused with one of his followers, specifically with Apelles.

The main basis of the supposition that Marcion derived the Demiurge from the highest being could only have been that he assigned justice to the Demiurge, as his essential attribute. For it hardly seems conceivable that Marcion would have separated this attribute from the idea of the good; that he would have conjoined justice with the concept of an evil being. Yet in light of Marcion's entire characterization of the Demiurge, I am dubious as to whether this view is actually so inconceivable. It may just be a matter of a more specific determination of the concept Marcion attached to his evil, primal being.

The church fathers concur that, in his teaching about the principles, Marcion followed Cerdo, the Syrian Gnostic he got to know in Rome. There is no doubt about Cerdo accepting just two principles. According to Irenaeus, Tertullian and Epiphanius,[251] Cerdo's teaching rested on the main thesis that the God proclaimed in the law and by the prophets is not the Father of our Lord Jesus Christ, for the one is known and our Father is unknown, the one is just and our Father is good. As Tertullian says, *unum bonum, alterum saevum* ("one is good, the other is fierce, or cruel"). Epiphanius puts it in even more specific terms: ". . . one who is the Demiurge and is wicked and known. He it is who spoke in the law, appeared to the prophets, and often made himself visible."[252]

---

248. [*In the text*] (Eusebius states, in his *Ecclesiastical History* 5:13, that Rhodo, an opponent of Marcion, reports that others agree with Marcion in "introducing two principles.")

249. Neander, *Genetische Entwickelung* (n. 6), 288. See also *Allgemeine Geschichte* (n. 110), 1:793.

250. *Contra Manichaeos* 3.5.

251. Irenaeus, *Against Heresies* 1.27; Tertullian, *Prescription against Heretics* 51; Epiphanius, *Against Heresies* 41.1.6.

252. Epiphanius, *Against Heresies* 41.1.6 [Amidon (n. 35), 143].

Since Epiphanius, supposedly by following Marcion, forthrightly calls the two principles Marcion accepted, "the invisible God and the visible God," one may justifiably assume, based on all these sources, that Marcion set out from the antithesis between the invisible and the visible as his main perspective. Accordingly for Marcion, matter was not directly the evil principle, but instead was simply the foundation of the visible world created by the Demiurge. Inasmuch as the created, visible world is the work and revelation of the Demiurge, the means by which he can be known, he is "the known God" who, in addition, has made himself known in many special ways of appearing, as the result of the Old Testament. The predicate of justice suitably applies to him both as the world's creator and as lawgiver, since the idea of justice is also the principle on which the order of the created world rests.

But the invisible stands over against the visible as the perfect does to the imperfect, as above does to below, and soul to body. The more the concept of the world's creator got determined more specifically, on the basis of the concept of the invisible, true God who was first revealed in Christianity, and the more one at the same time had to consider the hostile opposition Christianity experienced from Judaism and paganism, then the more natural it was to think of the world's creator not merely as an extremely limited and imperfect being, but also as an evil being hostilely opposing the good God. This is the way in which Marcion first arrived at the concept he had of his Demiurge as a ferocious, cruel God (*Deus saevus*), a concept also serving to fix his relationship to Cerdo. Thus Marcion started out from this same antithesis of the invisible God to the visible God, the unknown God to the known God.

However, this antithesis first acquired an intensity of its own, by Marcion carrying over to it all those concepts provided for him by the strict application of the opposition between the Old Testament and the New Testament.[253] Irenaeus confirms this view when, after mentioning Cerdo, he continues:[254] "Marcion of Pontus succeeded him, and developed his doctrine.[255] In doing so he advanced the most daring blasphemy against the one who is proclaimed God by the law and the prophets, by declaring him to be the author of evils, to take delight in war, to be infirm of purpose, and even to be contrary to himself." Surely this now gets us past the unclear position of Epiphanius and to a correct understanding of the διάβολος. It is clear that this

---

253. According to Tertullian's *Prescription against Heretics*, ch. 51, Cerdo had in principle already taught what Marcion is said to have taught, and had even defined the canon of scripture in the same way as Marcion did: "He (Cerdo) accepted solely the Gospel of Luke and not all of it. He took the epistles of the Apostle Paul but not all of them or all of their contents" [*ANF* 3:653, in ch. 6 of the Appendix to *Against All Heresies*, a spurious treatise]. According to Theodoret, *Heretical Tales*, 1.24, Cerdo had already constructed the same antithesis between the just God of the Old Testament and the good God of the gospel, and set up antitheses like Marcion did. Nevertheless the whole picture we get of Marcion does not fit with the assumption that he just made his own the teaching of someone else. However, in their hatred of this heretic, the church fathers may have been strongly inclined to deny him any originality.

254. *Against Heresies* 1.27 [*ANF* 1:352].

255. Eusebius says "increased the school," in *Ecclesiastical History* 4.11.2.

"Devil" Marcion supposedly added to Cerdo's two principles, indeed as "intermediate between the two others" (the "invisible principle" and the "visible God") is no proper principle but just designates the moral aspect of this relationship as something Marcion especially emphasized.

With the emergence of Christianity's own new principle, the Demiurge also had to take on a different character. The antithesis into which he was now placed for the first time naturally gave him a hostile stance. The Demiurge now had become the principle acting contrary to the good God. He was now the "cosmocrator," as Irenaeus called him, in the same sense people otherwise attached to this name.[256]

---

256. Irenaeus, *Against Heresies* 1.27.2. The Latin poet Prudentius (348–406 or later) is our confirmation for the fact that it was by no means unusual in the ancient church for the dualism identified above to be attributed to Marcion's system. The *Hamartigenia* ("The Origin of Sin") by Prudentius specifically attacks the erroneous Marcionite teaching. In this dogmatic poem, and induced by the doctrine of God's oneness (v. 56), Prudentius turns his attention to Marcion: "whose sectarian faith you condemn, divided the heavens among two Lords." According to Prudentius' portrayal, the Demiurge has so little in common with the good God that he instead belongs wholly with the evil principle. Prudentius depicts him as the world's creator (vv. 116–19): "As the world's creator, he created the earth, the sea, and the stars. He created human beings and added their filthy members, while in doing so, shaping what sickness consumes, what is defiled by many crimes, and the form that wastes away in the grave." Yet this same one is also the author of evil (vv. 155–56): "The one who in the beginning created evil, and who corrupted the good with depravity and stained what is bright and shining, with darkness, is said to be God." In authentically dualistic fashion, he is therefore to be thought of as the author of both physical (or natural) evil and moral evil. See H. Mitteldopf, "De Prudentio et theologia Prudentiana," in *Zeitschrift für die historische Theologie* (1832) 2.2, 146. – Thus the Marcionite system has great affinity with the Manichean system, except that the latter system assumes no event that first mingled good together with evil, for it says instead that the visible world is inherently a mixture of good and evil. The dualism of the Ophites is also utilized here, as we see with the sect of the Severians, among others. Epiphanius groups them above all with the Marcionites (*Against Heresies*, 45). The Severians themselves attested that they are connected with the Ophites, in that they sometimes called the evil principle Ialdabaoth, and sometimes Sabaoth [45.1.4]. Like the Manicheans (see my *Das manichäische Religionssystem* [n. 40], 251), because of its influence the Severians regarded wine as a product of the evil principle, for it stupefies the mind and leads to lustful desires; and they saw the serpentine form of the grapevine as a likeness of the serpent demon [45.1.6–8]. In the portrayal by Esnig, the Armenian bishop, the three basic principles are of course distinguished in the familiar way. But at the same time it is noteworthy that the Demiurge and matter are related to each other as man and wife, and thus in turn to be taken as a unity. They portray—as we also find this unity portrayed in the Manichean religious system (pp. 23ff. and 136ff. in my treatise)—the material productivity typical of the visible world and manifesting itself in procreation and birth. Esnig says ([see the article by Neumann cited in n. 240,] p. 72) that "he (i.e., Marcion) has the world and the creation coming into being as scripture teaches us. However, Marcion also adds that everything the God of the law made, he made through the agency of what is material, and that matter serves him as a female potency, as a woman for sexual union. After completing the creation, he (the God of the law) went into the heavens with his hosts, but matter and its sons remain on earth, and each of them rules in his own domain—matter on the earth, and the God of the law in the heavens." Therefore the Demiurge and matter form a pair joined in matrimony, like heaven and earth in ancient Greek mythology. Human beings came about in like fashion. Matter contributed something from its booty, and the God of the law then on his part provided the spirit. This account entirely fits with the Marcionite system as we understand it, and it is remarkable how other reports from eastern writers also agree with Esnig's account. Theodoret indeed states (*Heretical Tales* 1.24) that "the Demiurge, in presiding over evil, took hold of matter and out of it he fashioned the whole." But we find a statement from Ephrem the Syrian [c. 306–373] that is even

Part Two: The Various Principal Forms of Gnosis

## The Subjective Nature of This Standpoint

Accordingly, Marcion's dualism certainly has a metaphysical foundation, and one cannot maintain outright that he taught nothing of this kind about the metaphysical relation of the good God to the just Demiurge, for the other Gnostic systems had suggested such elements to him. Nor can one maintain that Marcion just stuck to the practical standpoint and set aside all merely speculative issues. Yet it is utterly unmistakable that Marcion's system stands apart in a distinctive way from the other Gnostic systems. So if we wanted to call this distinctiveness a practical standpoint, we would have had to doubt, and justifiably so, whether Marcion generally belongs in the series of Gnostics, since Gnosticism, by nature, can never have a predominantly practical orientation.

However, if we start out from the concept of Gnosticism we proposed, according to which the essential thing about Gnosticism is that it always just wants to arrive at the mediation of the pre-Christian religions with the true concept of Christianity as the absolute religion, then this gives us, of its own accord, the relation of the Marcionite system to the other Gnostic systems. In no other system is it as clear as it is in the Marcionite system, that the whole question the system struggles to answer involves working out how Christianity is related to the pre-Christian religions. Indeed it even seems that Marcion's system was the first one to become clearly aware that this is the task it is undertaking; whereas the other Gnostic systems just followed the general trend of the times on this issue, more or less unconsciously. Nevertheless, as one passed one's life within the orbit of ideas and outlooks belonging to the pre-Christian world, while at the same time recognizing that Christianity is the epoch of a new development in the religious life, and is itself the revelation of the absolute religion, how natural it was to suppose one could understand the essence of Christianity itself simply on the basis of that pre-Christian standpoint. But it was also just as natural to see Christianity in as close a relationship with paganism and Judaism as one could. Christianity seemed to be so closely related to both of these religions that what was fulfilled in Christianity had already been prepared for in the other two.

In Marcion's case, then, we must assume that, from the outset, he also stood within that orbit of religious ideas in which the other Gnostics operated. That he did is confirmed by the reports about his personal circumstances, his Christian origins and education. Or Marcion could not have had the same motivation and need to blend so

---

more consonant with Esnig. According to Ephrem's hymn about the Spirit that, according to Genesis 1, said "Be fruitful and multiply," the Marcionite representation was, as Ephrem put it, that "further multiplying was less laudable." See Hahn (n. 246), 2:6. – [*From the Errata*] We see at once from this that, while the Marcionite system wants to have hardly anything to do with the natural life in which myth has its origins, Marcionism still always involves a certain mythic element. With the Marcionite Demiurge himself being in the final analysis none other than a mythic personification, therefore, as his relation to matter shows, this even provides scope for mythic sexuality. Just as characteristic here, however, is the fact that Marcion locates everything mythic of this kind simply in that area from which he turns away altogether, with his total and typical abhorrence of the physical life of nature.

much that was pre-Christian into his own Christian religious system, for although a Gnostic (and he undeniably presented himself as being one) he hardly shared fully the standpoint of the other Gnostics. Marcion believed he could not form any clear concept of the essence of Christianity without having answered, first of all, the question as to how Christianity would relate to the pre-Christian religions and to Judaism in particular. Thus from his Christian consciousness, which had taken on a specific form, Marcion was led to the dualistic way of understanding the relation of Christianity to Judaism, and to the pre-Christian world in general, the view characteristic of his own system.

The deeper and more lively Marcion's consciousness of the distinctive essence of Christianity became, the greater the antithesis between what is Christian and what is pre-Christian, or non-Christian, had to appear for him. From the outset he had already taken up an authentically Gnostic standpoint, inasmuch as he grasped what is Christian simply as connected to what is pre-Christian and as mediated by it. Thus he had to have been readily inclined to adopt the kind of Gnostic ideas that served to support his dualistic view of Christianity's relation to Judaism, and that even seemed to be its necessary foundation. It is very indicative of Marcion's Gnostic standpoint that he is said to have adopted, from Cerdo the Gnostic, the very point on which the external form of his own system concurred most of all with the other Gnostic systems: the doctrine of the two principles forming the greatest antithesis. The distinctive elements of his system, everything with reference to the Christianity-Judaism antithesis, he had already built into his system before he fully completed it by adopting those principles at its apex.

Indicative of this same standpoint is the passage Luke 6:40–45,[257] which Marcion especially emphasized and placed at the head of his entire system as, so to speak, its motto. Tertullian called particular attention expressly to the significance this passage held for Marcion, only with the erroneous assumption that Marcion set out from the question about the origin of evil:

> The heretic of Pontus introduces two Gods . . . The unhappy man was first incited to his presumptuous idea by the simple passage [in Luke] in which our Lord pronounces, with reference to human beings and not divine ones, about the example of the good tree and the bad tree, that "the good tree does not bear bad fruit, nor the bad tree bear good fruit." . . . Marcion then applied to the creator of the world the statement about the bad tree bearing bad fruit, namely, moral evil. Then he presumed that there is another God, analogous to the good tree that bears good fruit. He finds in Christ a disposition of simple

---

257. [*Ed.*] This passage is an elaboration of Jesus' question in 6:39, "Can a blind person guide a blind person?" He describes people who see only the flaws of others, not their own flaws. Then he continues (vv. 43–45): "No good tree bears bad fruit, nor again does a bad tree bear good fruit; for each tree is known by its own fruit. Figs are not gathered from thorns, not are grapes picked from a bramble bush. The good person out of the good treasure of the heart produces good, and the evil person out of evil treasure produces evil; for it is out of the abundance of the heart that the mouth speaks."

and pure benevolence, which makes him differ from the creator, so he facilely argues that a new and foreign divinity is revealed in his Christ. Thus Marcion ferments the entire substance of the faith with his own acrid heresy.[258]

Marcion's essential point about this passage had to be the fact that it expressed the quite obvious antithesis between the features [of the two trees]; and on this basis, the reasons underlying their respective consequences, he pointed to their corresponding causes. In doing so Marcion indicated the overall course he had taken in elaborating his system.

We can therefore rightly say that, while the other Gnostics came to Christianity from a standpoint outside of Christianity, Marcion, in contrast, initially went from Christianity to the other Gnostics' starting point: he ended up where they began. Both groups thought they could take hold of the true concept of Christianity by just spelling it out in terms of Christianity's relation to Judaism and paganism. But whereas the others took account of the unity together with the difference, Marcion just held fast to the difference. The two mutually opposed principles that he set at the apex of his system were just supposed to serve to keep apart forever the two sides forming an irreconcilable opposition in his system. The other Gnostic systems, however, set out from these same principles in order to allow for the reconciliation of the opposition on a middle ground.

This sheds light on the profundity of Marcion's system as well as on its shortcomings. It is a bold and magnificent idea to understand Christianity simply from the perspective of an absolute antithesis in which it stands relative to all that is pre-Christian. If the Christianity to which our Christian consciousness bears witness is the absolute religion, then it can also be thought of as separated from everything pre-Christian not merely as a matter of degree, but instead only in virtue of an absolute antithesis. However, this absolute antithesis is of course just one aspect of this relationship, and it does not exclude the fact that, on the other hand, Christianity is in turn also more or less closely related to what is pre-Christian. Therefore such a system must get caught up in still greater conflicts when the purely religious antithesis gets explained in terms of a metaphysical antithesis and is tied to [the supposition of] two mutually opposed, fundamental beings, one of whom is said to be responsible for all that is created, visible, and material, and the other one for everything eternal, invisible, and pure in spirit. Yet for these two beings, so strictly separated, there must in some fashion be a meeting point at which they come together in the unity of one world. For how else could they have become one, were it not for the two of them falling within the sphere of one and the same consciousness, and being one at least within the unity of human consciousness?

Yet Marcion has done nothing to resolve all the difficulties relating to this issue, and Tertullian's polemic about this point has successfully exposed many weaknesses

---

258. Tertullian, *Against Marcion* 1.2 [*ANF* 3:272]. See also *Prescription against Heretics*, ch. 51.

in Marcion's system. We will come back to this polemic in another place. Here I just raise one issue. If human beings, as creatures of the world's creator, just belong to the world creator's realm, how can they have a need for redemption? In other words, how can they in any way be capable of assimilating the idea of the unknown, true God that Christ has revealed? The capacity for doing so presupposes a quite different principle than those the Demiurge could impart. For this reason the other Gnostic systems allow for the seeds indwelling the pneumatic life coming down from the realm of light into the realm of the Demiurge. That is also why it is not possible for them to maintain an absolute antithesis between what is Christian and what is pre-Christian.

There is of course one statement that could have made it appear that Marcion had once again drawn closer to the other Gnostics on this point. According to Irenaeus and Epiphanius,[259] Marcion is said to have taught that, in his descent into Hades, Christ blessed Cain and those like him—Korah, Dathan, Abiram, as well as Esau, the Sodomites, the Egyptians, and all those peoples to whom the God of the Jews was unknown. But Abel, Enoch, Noah, Abraham, and the other patriarchs and the prophets, and all who pleased the God of the Jews, Christ excluded from this blessedness, because they acknowledged the world's creator and obeyed his laws. However, no conclusion is to be drawn from this statement. Although Marcion regards as his own, as believers in the true God, those in the Old Testament proclaimed to be the most wicked ones, he in no way wants to maintain that they already had a knowledge of the true God before Christ appeared. For Marcion, the true God was utterly unknown before Christ, and given Marcion's anti-Judaism, he certainly could assume different degrees of receptivity.[260] However, the main question, as to what explains this

---

259. Irenaeus, *Against Heresies* 1.27.3; Epiphanius, *Against Heresies* 42.4.

260. According to the aforementioned Armenian account (n. 240), Marcion drew a certain distinction between paganism and Judaism, but one that favored the Jews. On p. 73 [of Neumann's translation] it states: "The God of the law wanted to distance Adam as much as possible from matter, and to unite fully with him. When, in its customary way, matter came to Adam in order to serve him, and saw that Adam did not heed it but proceeded to distance himself and not come near it, matter was quite astonished in its soul but recognized right away that the Lord of creation had deceived it. Matter said, 'Adam does not see clearly? What is going on? (*die Quelle des Auges ist durch ihr Wasser verdunkelt, was ist diess?*). Nevertheless, Adam has no children and I have already been deceived by that one [the God of the law] as to my being called a deity. Since he hates me and would not hold to the agreement with me, I will make a host of gods and fill the whole world with them so that when people seek the true God they will not find him.' Thereupon matter constructed many idols, called them gods, and filled the world with them. The name of God, of the Lord of creation, got lost among the plethora of gods' names, such that he could not be discovered anywhere. That is how the descendents of Adam took the wrong path and did not pray to the God of creation, for matter led them all to himself and did not permit even one of them to pray to the God of creation. Then the Lord of creation was furious that the whole lot of them had abandoned him and attached themselves to matter; and when they died, out of his anger he flung them all, one after another, into hell. Adam came to hell on account of [eating from] the tree, and so they were all in hell for 29 centuries." – From this account we see the sense in which the *Dialogus de recta in Deum fide*, sec. 1, assigns to the Marcionites the contention: "the bad principle (matter) is the ruler of the Gentiles." Thus Marcion thought so little of the Jewish religion that, for him, its monotheism, the relatively true and original religion as compared to pagan polytheism, could not be considered meritorious when compared to Christianity. For Marcion, from

receptivity for the idea of the unknown God, if human beings are just products of the world's creator, remains totally unanswered. If the world's creator is the creator purely and simply, then he has also created the souls of human beings, hence that receptivity cannot have been acquired from him. However, if he has not created the souls (and nowhere is this assumption suggested), then how should we think of them in relation to the supreme God? Marcion's system itself provides no answers to all questions of this kind, and we do not know how Marcion himself would have resolved such difficulties and contradictions.

In psychological terms, all we can say about the solution of this puzzle is that the general standpoint of Marcion's system can only be assumed to lie in the subjectivity of consciousness. When the idea of what is Christian has arisen in one's consciousness, then one sets what is Christian strictly apart from what is not Christian. Thus Marcion established this antithesis not merely as a way of treating Christianity and Judaism as antithetical, but also as an antithesis between the true God and the world's creator, between the unknown God and the known deity, between the invisible God and the visible one. This dualism had to lead to contradictions. Yet right when it was said to be apprehended in objective terms, these contradictions would vanish for Marcion because of the fact that he persistently retreated from the objective world and into the subjectivity of consciousness, by sticking utterly to the given facts of consciousness. Therefore, if an antithesis expresses itself with certainty in consciousness, the same antithesis must also be pervasive in the objective world. Yet for Marcion the unity of consciousness suffices as an established fact. For him, consciousness rests on itself and constitutes a unity, even when it contains antithetical elements.

This standpoint, based on the subjectivity of consciousness, also gets expressed elsewhere in Marcion's system. That antithesis between the visible and the invisible, and the basic insight on which it rests—that the invisible does not mirror itself in the visible, and the whole of external nature is no revelation of spirit, for only spirit itself can make spirit known—of course points back to a standpoint for which, in contrast to the objective world as the not-I standing over against the I or self, the true significance of being resides all the more in the inner power of self-consciousness.

Then look at the very idea of Christian revelation expressed here. Take that revelation of the God completely unknown beforehand, occurring without any advance preparation; that sudden *manare de coelo* (descent from heaven), as Tertullian designates this revelatory action; that becoming revealed in an external image, which is but the corporeal reflection of the invisible idea. What is it, other than the stream of thought breaking forth all at once from the darkness of consciousness and illuminating it? Tertullian has Marcion repeating the objection that the apparition of Christ's person would also make God himself into a mere phantasm, with Christ said to have been his *circumlator* (revealer). "Let us therefore take the very person of God himself,

---

the absolute standpoint of Christianity, paganism and Judaism are lumped together under the single concept of what is pre-Christian.

or rather his shadow or phantom as we have it in Christ." "Consequently, a divine Christ without being God! But why should he not have also borne the apparition of God? Can one believe him about the inner substance, one who was mistaken about the outer substance?"[261] But there is no basis for this objection once one bears in mind that, for consciousness, the idea [of something] has its reality directly in consciousness itself. Only from this perspective do we correctly understand the conception Marcion has of Christ's relation to the heavenly Father.

Neander supposes[262] that Marcion's christology was that of a Praxeas or a Noetus, and therefore it spoke of the same one God, only using different names with respect to different relationships or circumstances. He says that Tertullian's statements in *Against Marcion* 1.11, and particularly in 2.28 ("My God ordered another [*aliquem*] to be slain. Yours willed himself to be put to death"), shed light on the fact that Marcion, like the Patripassianists, whose view is best suited to his system and his way of thinking, drew no distinction between Christ and the supreme God.

Gieseler[263] simply wants again to see this as Marcion's aversion to metaphysical speculation. Nowhere do we find anyone going further into this topic. In his refutation of Marcion, even Tertullian is never led to compare him with Praxeas, despite the fact that he attacked Praxeas after first attacking Marcion. So it seems that Marcion too left this point undeveloped.

> Upon reflection, he had simply to maintain Jesus' moral unity with the good God. The good God has revealed himself to humankind in Jesus alone, and has influenced humankind only through Jesus. What he nevertheless was in himself, apart from this particular appearing in Jesus—whether personally separate from Jesus or not—lay beyond all human comprehension. From a moral standpoint, Jesus and the good God were one. In this instance too Marcion seems to have intentionally stopped at this point, and to have renounced all further speculation going beyond human beings' moral concerns.

Yet surely, in a system so decidedly favoring docetism, we ought not set very great store by an exclusive interest in morality and an aversion to speculation.

We will indeed state more correctly that, from Marcion's standpoint, from the subjectivity of consciousness, for Marcion Christ's relation to the supreme God could only have been as the self-revelation of the idea. The outward form, the appearance mediating God's self-revelation in Christ, is surely in fact just the reflection of the idea coming to the fore in consciousness. For Marcion the outward revelation could not have had the same significance as it had for a Praxeas or a Noetus. What we can hold fast to is already in turn just the "God revealed through himself," in other words,

---

261. Tertullian, *Against Marcion* 1.22, 3.8 [ANF 3:287, 327].

262. *Genetische Entwickelung* (n. 6), 293; *Allgemeine Geschichte* (n. 110), 1:796.

263. *Allgemeine Literatur-Zeitung* 104 (April 1823), 851. [*Ed.*] We assume the following quotation is from Gieseler.

the self-revealing idea. That is why Marcion's system lacks all objective specification about the essential being of God. All that the other Gnostics taught about the syzygies and the Aeons, and the associated relations of dependence with reference to God's essential being, could have no significance for Marcion, given the strict boundaries he drew between nature and spirit, between the visible and the invisible. Even that "descent from heaven" could doubtless be thought of without any reference to an emanation scenario. For Marcion, God is utterly spirit, the absolute spirit; and what God is *as* spirit, God is *for* spirit. That is why Marcion's entire system has for its object not what God is in himself, but instead only the fact of consciousness that God has revealed himself; in other words, that the previously unknown God has now become the known God. Tertullian says: "I know in what sense they boast about their new god, at any rate of their knowledge. For the one whom, by their knowledge, they present as new, they demonstrate as being unknown, prior to this knowledge."[264]

Of course the other Gnostics too have the supreme God first becoming fully revealed through Christianity, although none of them in Marcion's sense, because they accept an objective revelation of God in nature and history, already prior to Christianity. Thus what everywhere characterizes the relation of Marcion to the earlier Gnostics is the antithesis between the subjective standpoint and the objective standpoint.[265]

## Marcion's Importance for His Time, and His Reforming Tendency

In the strict antithesis Marcion set up between Christianity and all that is pre-Christian, and especially Judaism, we must at the same time see an intentional opposition to the current, and ever still very predominant, Judaism within the Christian church. One need only recall the this-worldly chiliasm widespread in Asia Minor, to be able to better explain how a system like the Marcionite system arose based on an antithetical stance toward chiliasm. While we ought not to lose sight of chiliasm and the reaction against it, this is still just one of the different factors keeping alive the issue of Christianity's proper relation to Judaism—at a time when Montanism and the differences over the observance of Easter had already attracted the attention of the public. In any event, in these current conditions there was indeed justification for Marcion heading

---

264. *Against Marcion* 1.9 [ANF 3:277].

265. A number of Marcion's other distinctive features can be related to the subjectivity of his standpoint. For instance, by appealing to Gal 6:6 ["Those who are taught the word must share in all good things with their teacher"], he did not acknowledge the usual distinction involving the catechumens (according to Jerome's commentary on this passage); and he even regarded the female sex as fit for the priesthood (Epiphanius, *Against Heresies* 42; Esnig [n. 240], 71; Tertullian, *Prescription against Heretics* 41). These examples show how, from Marcion's standpoint, religious consciousness was said to be significant simply in itself and independent of what is external and objective.

directly to Rome, whatever the circumstances behind his departure from Pontus may have been.[266]

Of course at that time an anti-Jewish tendency became prevalent in the Roman church. So here Marcion could not only be very well received; he could also hope for significant success in his opposition to Judaism. From Marcion's initial relationship with the Roman church[267] we are to infer that the hesitancy people subsequently felt about him might have been due not so much to his anti-Jewish tendency as it was to the Gnostic ideas he bound up with it. All that we otherwise know about Marcion lets us assume that he was a very important figure at that time. Many things attest to the great impact he had on his day: the considerable number of his closest followers; the equally numerous and significant opponents who stood up against him within the Catholic Church;[268] the extensive way in which the opponents refute his teaching; the bitter tone with which they speak about him. Marcion even continued to be influential long after his death.

In the *Dialogus de recta in Deum fide* (sec. 1) it not only says that Marcion himself was a bishop, for it states at the same time that, after his death, there were many Marcionite bishops. Before he goes on to describe Marcion's heresy, Epiphanius expressly calls attention to the great importance attained by this "great snake"[269] from his entry into the world. [Epiphanius says] that Marcion deceived a great many people and that, until the present day, this great school of deception continues to do so; that this heresy is still found today in Rome and in Italy, in Egypt and in Pontus, in Arabia and Syria,

---

266. Tertullian says: "After Cerdo there emerged a disciple of his, one Marcion by name, a native of Pontus, son of a bishop, excommunicated because of a rape committed on a certain virgin" (*Prescription against Heretics* 51 [*ANF* 3:653]). As opposed to this, Neander remarks (*Genetische Entwickelung* [n. 6], 280) that it scarcely fits the character of this man to have been dismissed from the congregation because of a moral transgression, and this report would not have come from a reliable informant. [He says] of course his opponents would have alleged that about him before this had there been some sort of basis for it. But next to Irenaeus, who in his main work touches only briefly on the heretic Marcion, Tertullian is the earliest church father dealing with Marcion, and we have no reason to discount his testimony so long as it is not improbable on internal grounds. Yet to me it seems that it is not improbable. For why should Marcion, who mainly appeared in so many respects to be of a truly Augustinian nature, not have lived like he operated in his teaching, in terms of harsh antitheses? So it then boils down to what Esnig, the Armenian, reports about this matter—a report all the more worthy of our attention because it is independent of the others. At the conclusion of his work, on p. 76 (n. 240), Esnig writes: "This Marcion came from the province of Pontus and was the son of a bishop. After he had assaulted a virgin his own father expelled him from the church. He ran away and went to Rome in order to receive absolution."

267. [*In the text*] (According to Tertullian, *Prescription against Heretics* 30, Marcion brought a monetary gift to the Roman community, not to the pontifical congregation—something Neander mentioned in *Genetische Entwickelung*, 280.)

268. See J. T. L. Danz, *De Eusebio Caesaria* (Jena, 1815), 97, concerning the authors opposing Marcion and his sect who are known to us merely from Eusebius' *Ecclesiastical History*. Also see Irenaeus, *Against Heresies* 1.27.4, where he only touches briefly on Marcion and says he intends to write something of his own against him. Irenaeus says, "This man is the only one who has dared openly to mutilate the scriptures, and shamelessly, beyond all others, to disparage God" [*ANF* 1:352].

269. Epiphanius, *Against Heresies* 42.2.1.

in Cyprus and in Thebais, indeed even in Persia and other places. What great evil he does among them with his deception! We see from Theodoret how numerous the Marcionites still were even in the fifth century, especially in Syria. Theodoret not only groups the Marcionites together with the Arians, Eunomians, and Apollinarians (in Epistle 145); he also affirms (in Epistle 113) that, in his diocese alone, he has converted some thousand Marcionites.

The impressive success that Marcion's activities had in this way obviously presupposes that, in his teaching, people found something that had its deeper foundation in Christian consciousness itself. In fact, if we take more general account of his tendency, then it is not merely polemical but has at the same time a reforming character. His antithetical stance toward Judaism is certainly supported by the fact that he could regard the Christianity still so intertwined in many ways with Judaism, as not being the authentic and original Christianity. Thus, on the basis of his own Christian consciousness, he sought to determine, in Christianity's scriptural documents, what is authentic and original, or else stems from Judaism.[270] Whether one calls Marcion's procedure critical or arbitrary, in any case he takes the criterion for authentic and inauthentic from the depth and inwardness of his own Christian consciousness.

Yet the more such a reforming-polemical tendency[271] belongs to the character of Christianity itself—belongs to what would preserve the purifying and cleansing power proper to it from the beginning, by seeking to break through all the forms continuing to adhere to it from outside, and to grasp it always purely in its innermost essential nature—the less surprising it can be that Marcion's efforts were approved and acknowledged to such a great extent. Marcion's teaching must have constantly gained new friends, from the conviction expressing itself in Christian consciousness that Christianity is something entirely different from Judaism, when combined with the very obvious fact in Christianity's early history that the Apostle Paul, whom Marcion counted as the only apostle,[272] elevated himself above the other apostles and even stood in a certain opposition to them. And from this same position, Marcion's original standpoint, even his Gnostic ideas, and accordingly the Gnostic dualism as such, provided ongoing support.

By grasping the phenomenon presented by Marcion, and his impact, from this perspective, we therefore see it taking hold in Christianity's historical development in a very vital and meaningful way. For the same opposition that Marcion posed to the Christianity of his day—in order, with an authentically reforming spirit, to go back to the original idea of Christianity and combat everything that lay between original

---

270. *Dialogus de recta in Deum fide*, sec. 2.

271. Tertullian, *Against Marcion* 1.20: "They [Marcion's adherents] allege that Marcion did not so much innovate on the rule (of faith) by separating law from gospel, as he did restore it after it had been previously adulterated . . . Now they say that Peter and the others, pillars of the apostolate, are blamed by Paul for not walking uprightly, according to the truth of the gospel" [*ANF* 3:285].

272. Tertullian, *Against Marcion* 4.34, has Marcion referring to Paul as "your own apostle" [*ANF* 3:405].

Christianity and the Christianity of his day, as a major degeneration and falsification of pure Christianity—had to relate to Catholic Christianity and Gnostic Christianity. The entire shape of his system shows how little the earlier Gnostic systems, in which Christianity still stood so close to Judaism and paganism, were able to satisfy his own Christian consciousness.[273]

Thus the Marcionite system not only presents us with a new form of Gnosis; it also marks a new epoch in the history of the development of Gnosis. As a new and distinctive major form of Gnosis, it can only be understood in its historical connection with the earlier Gnostic systems by which it is shaped. These others also apprehend Christianity as the negation of paganism and Judaism, for doing so is essential to the nature of Gnosis. However, these other systems seem to follow through with this negation in just an incomplete way. That is why for the Marcionite system Christianity is the pure, absolute negation of all that is pre-Christian, in virtue of Marcion's excluding all mediation with it. However, in what follows we show how even this understanding of the relation between what is Christian and what is pre-Christian calls forth another new form of Gnosis to which it has itself been just the transition. That is because the self-advancing concept of Gnosis has not yet run through all the moments in the course of its development.

---

273. [*From the Errata and Additions*] This difference of the Marcionite system from the earlier systems is also applicable to Origen's usage in his Commentary on Matthew (see n. 135), where, in speaking of the Valentinian system he uses the expression *traditiones Valentini* (Valentinian tradition), whereas he speaks of the *doctrina Marcionis* (doctrine of Marcion). As distinct from a "tradition," here "doctrine" is thought of as free-standing, a system not dependent on external authorities. In the final analysis, Marcion certainly has the actual principle of his system simply in his Christian self-consciousness. In contrast, because of its thoroughly mythic form, a system like the Valentinian one also has a traditional character. Furthermore, the Gnostics belonging in this class are expressly said to have appealed to more ancient authorities for their systems, as Valentinus himself appealed to Theudas [of Acts 5:36], a confidant of the Apostle Paul, and Basilides appealed to Glaucius, an interpreter of the Apostle Peter. (See Clement of Alexandria, *Stromata* 7.17 [*ANF* 2:555].) Marcion's rejection of allegory is also pertinent to his relation to the earlier Gnostics. That is because allegory is always at the same time the medium for linking what is new and one's own to what is old and traditional, and for conveying it via an already recognized authority. We see that Marcion rejected allegory not only because that is obvious from his view of the Old Testament, but also because Origen explicitly attests to that fact in his Commentary on Matthew, 15.3.

# 3

# The Form of Gnosis Identifying Christianity and Judaism, and Setting Forth Both of Them in Opposition to Paganism

## *The Pseudo-Clementine System*

WE HAVE ALREADY INDICATED how the two main forms of Gnosis presented thus far call forth yet a third form. Gnosis would not have completely run its course, would have still lacked a component needed to give the systems in which it is presented to us the unity of a compact whole, had history not also produced this third form. This form is contained in these *Homilies*, which, like a few other writings from the first century, have borne the name of Clement of Rome rather than the name of the actual author. The writer attaches this pseudonym to his own views, which are in part dogmatic and in part hierarchical in character.[274]

The system that we find in these *Homilies* is a very remarkable one for the history of Gnosis, as it is for the history of Christian dogma generally. It not only has a distinctive way of relating to the other Gnostic systems; it also provides the clearest evidence of the vitality that the Gnostic systems gave rise to and that positioned them vis-à-vis one another. We must hold fast to the fact that the *Homilies* have a thoroughly antithetical outlook, and that since this third form of Gnosis bears the characteristic stamp of Judaism, we are now in a domain where the antithesis is between Judaism and paganism.

---

274. [*Ed.*] The *Pseudo-Clementine Homilies* contain a fictitious narrative report purportedly written by Clement of Rome, the second (or third) successor to Peter as bishop of Rome, about discourses of the Apostle Peter and circumstances surrounding Clement's accompaniment of Peter on his travels. Baur believes that it reflects the views of Christian Ebionites who regarded the Apostle Paul as an apostate and attached themselves to Peter as the true representative of Christianity. An English translation is found in *ANF* 8.

Seen from the standpoint of this form of Gnosis, the other systems already presented appear to be merely forms of paganism. Of course this rebuff to Hellenism must most directly affect the kind of system that has been most pointedly antithetical to Judaism. Hence in this case we find opposition to everything in the Gnostic systems appearing to be incompatible with the principles of Judaism. So the Marcionite system in particular gets subjected to the strongest attacks, and its battle with Judaism is disregarded here.

## The Form and Character of the Clementine Homilies

So as not to leave this view, which first gives these *Homilies* their true significance for the history of Gnosis, without a foundation, we must preface the discussion here with a few remarks about their organization or structure.[275]

The circumstances in which the Apostle Peter encounters Simon Magus in Samaria, according to the Book of Acts, serves as an example of the *Homilies*' structure (Acts 8:9–24). The Apostle Peter saw this as the occasion to forcefully confront the false testimony of this magician who was leading the people astray. The *Homilies* has the same scene repeated in several different places, with the Apostle Peter constantly pursuing the itinerant magician from town to town and always engaging him in the same way, in order to challenge him, to oppose his teaching, and to counter the harmful influence he seeks to gain over the people, thus resisting Simon with the full weight of his apostolic office and function. Hence the main content of this homily depicts the debates between the Apostle and the magician, with one representing the true and authentic apostolic teaching and the other representing the erroneous teaching that opposes it.

This entire situation is just the further reproduction and simulation of that one scene in the Book of Acts. In similar fashion, the magician Simon in particular, in the way he is depicted here, should not be thought of as in any way an actual historical figure, nor should the teaching attributed to him be regarded as truly his own system. What is abundantly clear here is that ideas and tenets are placed in the magician's mouth that demonstrably belong most essentially to Marcion's system and for that reason cannot have been set forth in the same way by him. Seen in this way, however, it is clear proof that the Magus is made out to be the bearer of alien ideas and doctrines, and he is generally assigned the role of an opponent of the Apostle Peter in the same broad sense that the Pseudo-Clementine Peter himself is in no way the historical person known from the New Testament. So on this basis we must of necessity step back and can therefore also take other things ascribed to the Magus and consider

---

275. For the entire domain of relationships and factions in the very early church, a topic still receiving too little attention, see my article, "Die Christuspartei in der korinthischen Gemeinde, der Gegensatz des petrinischen und paulinischen Christenthums in der ältesten Kirche, der Apostel Petrus in Rom," *Tübinger Zeitschrift für Theologie* (1831), no. 4, 61–206.

them only from the perspective of the role given him here, at least when they surely trace back without great difficulty to other teachings of the Gnostics that we know about.

To be able to address this issue in a more definitive way, we must have more specific information about the person and teachings of the Magus from other sources that are independent of these *Homilies*. But we do not possess such sources. In the histories of the earliest heresies Simon Magus is frequently mentioned as the head and forefather of all the heretics, and in particular of the Gnostic heresy. According to a few testimonies it seems there can hardly be any doubt that he and his follower Menander left behind them a faction that continued to exist for some time. Given this, we can scarcely venture very far beyond the accounts provided in the Book of Acts, and the impression we get from a comparison of the major writers about him is the conviction that in any event he did not originally have the great historical importance usually assigned to him; that instead this only occurred later on.

If we take a closer look at Simon Magus from this perspective, then what is at least very understandable, in the first place, is how the very thing we must assume he initially did, according to the New Testament, could become the point of reference for what was subsequently said about him. According to Acts 8:9, Simon said "that he was someone great"; or, as the people of Samaria doubtless said about him, in the same sense: "This man is the power of God that is called Great" (v. 9), that is, an incarnation of God's supreme, substantial power. The first point I might bring to bear on this is the contention, repeated[276] in the Clementine writings, that Simon "wishes to be regarded as a supreme power, greater even than the God who created the world. And sometimes intimating that he is Christ, he styles himself the Standing One. He employs this epithet, which intimates that he shall always stand, and that he lacks any decay that would cause his body to fall."[277]

Clement of Alexandria[278] attributes this same contention to Simon's followers. Clement says that reason, remaining constant, the soul's guiding and ruling principle, is called the soul's pilot. For one has access to what is unchangeable only through something that is itself constant. So too the Simonians, as much as possible, become like the Standing One whom they revere. If it be the case that this is what Simon called himself, and if his followers simply wanted to use this predicate to specify what they had in mind by calling him the Standing One, then this term was, in the main, supposed to express what the Christians revered in Christ, namely the supremely divine principle through which all spiritual life, its existence and continuation, is received—life's immutable refuge, exalted above all that is transitory.

---

276. [*Ed.*] "Repeated" because the *Recognitions of Clement* 1.21 (*ANF* 8:96), says the same thing about Simon.

277. *Homilies* 2.22 [*ANF* 8:232–33]. [*Ed.*] After the Greek for "created the world," Baur inserts, parenthetically, "the supreme power, even exalted above the world's creator."

278. In *Stromata* 2.11.

This is the reason why Simon, as the "pilot," is also called Christ, and is generally designated under the same concept by the use of various terms for it, as we see from Jerome's *Commentary on Matthew*, chap. 24. He says a Simonian religious text includes these words attributed to Simon: "I am God's discourse, I am splendid, I am all-merciful, I am omnipotent, I am wholly of God." This is equivalent to the contention that Irenaeus attributes to Simon, that he is the same one who appeared in Judea as the Son, who came down in Samaria as the Father, and who has come to other nations as the Holy Spirit.[279] This was just a way of saying that, in and for itself, this is the same revelation of God although the names and forms are different. Thus, just as Christianity itself differentiates the revelation of the Son from the working of the Spirit although the essence of the revelation is the same, so too Christianity itself provides the justification for putting Simon alongside Christ and calling Simon Father, as representing the supreme God, just as Christ is called Son in the same sense.

If this contention must leave us very much in doubt as to what might perhaps apply to the Magus himself, some other things he is said to have taught leave us far less uncertain, for it was just one in a series of such statements about his relation to Helena as his consort. According to the *Homilies*, he himself said that Helena has come down into the world from the highest heaven, that she is the Lady, the Mother of all, is substance and wisdom; that the Greeks and barbarians fought over her, being deceived by an illusion of the truth since at that time the true Helena was with the supreme God (2.25 [*ANF* 8:233]). By including such allegorical fictions, embellished with Greek myths, and by many magical wonders of an astonishing kind, the Magus, in traveling around with Helena, sought to deceive people. We find a fuller account of this myth in Irenaeus and in Epiphanius.[280] In my book on the Manicheans[281] I have investigated the relationship of these different accounts and the main idea we have to assume is involved in their contents.

The result of this investigation shows that the Helena of Simon Magus is assigned the same features as those we previously became acquainted with in the case of Sophia-Achamoth, a major figure in the Gnostic systems. The different elements of Simon's relation to Helena—the syzygy the two of them form as the highest principles; Helena's deceptive descent to the world here below, by which the powers belonging to her first entered into existence; the appearing of Simon to free Helena, who had been held fast and brought so low by suffering and misdeeds of all sorts, and to lead her back again—are the same elements running throughout the Gnostic systems we previously examined. Hence it is clear that the very features we have taken from the Gnostic systems as a whole, as their most universal and most characteristic features, have been carried over to the Magus.[282]

---

279. Irenaeus, *Against Heresies* 1.23 [*ANF* 1:348].
280. Irenaeus, *Against Heresies* 1.23 [*ANF* 1:347–51]; Epiphanius, *Against Heresies* 21.2.2–21.3.3.
281. *Das manichäische Religionssystem* (n. 40), 467ff.
282. This is shown in the most striking way by the portrayal in Irenaeus, *Against Heresies* 1.23.2 [*ANF*

## Part Two: The Various Principal Forms of Gnosis

If there actually was a Simonian party or faction, one declaring allegiance to the

1:348], which on its own drives home this point. "Simon, speaking of Helena whom he leads around with him, declares that she was the first conception of his mind, the mother of all by whom he in the beginning conceived of making angels and archangels. This Ennoea, leaping forth from him and comprehending the will of her father, descended to the lower regions and generated angels and powers that he says made the world. However, after she generated them they detained her owing to their jealousy, because they did not want to be looked upon as the progeny of another being. They had no knowledge of Simon himself, but those powers and angels who had been generated by the Ennoea detained her. She suffered all kinds of outrages at their hands, so that she could not go back up to her father, but was shut up in a human body. She passed successively from one female body to another [on which, see p. 88 above], as from one vessel to another. For example, she was in that Helen because of whom the Trojan War was fought; the Helen for whose sake Stesichorus was struck blind because he cursed her in his verses, although he later repented and wrote what is called a palinode, singing her praises, and so had his sight restored. In passing from body to body and suffering outrages in every one of them, she finally became a common prostitute. So she was the 'lost sheep' (of Matt 18:12)." See also Tertullian, *On the Soul*, ch. 34. – One could have supposed that the tale of Simon and Helena, in the form we find it in Irenaeus and others, was first elaborated and put into circulation by the writer of the *Pseudo-Clementine Homilies*. But its essential features are also found in Justin Martyr's *First Apology*, which is doubtless earlier than these *Homilies*. In ch. 26 Justin writes: "Almost all the Samaritans, and a few even of other natures, worship him [Simon], and acknowledge him as the first god; and a woman, Helena, who went about with him at that time and had formerly been a prostitute, they say is the first idea (ἔννοια) generated by him" [*ANF* 1:171]. It is well-known that Justin was in error when he maintained (just prior to this) in the same passage that it was the same Simon of Samaria who came to Rome in the reign of Claudius and whom the Romans honored as a god by erecting a statue on an island in the Tiber River and bearing the inscription "To Simon the holy God." There is no doubt about this statue being dedicated not to Simon Magus, but to the old Roman god Semo Sancus [a Sabine deity], or else to Fidius [Jupiter]-Heracles (see Ovid, *Fasti*, 6.214). However, it is also quite natural to suppose that this confusion can be traced back earlier to Justin. The god Semo is also an ancient Eastern god who, in the lands of the Near East, in Phoenicia in particular and also in Egypt, was often the revered sun-god, Heracles. (Hence we have Sem = Phucrates as well as Heracles = Harpocrates. See Jablonski, *Opusc*, vol. 2, *Dissert. De terra Gosen*, 196; G. F. Creuzer, *Dionysus*, 141; and *Symbolik und Mythologie der alten Völker, besonders der Griechen* (Leipzig, 1810 ff.), 1.326.) From the Oriental name Sem we get the derivative name Simon or Simeon, and from the related Hebrew name we get Simson [Samson]. The Hebrew Simson is obviously the personified likeness of Heracles, even including the pillars; see Judg 16:25. These relationships thus explain quite simply the origin of most of the representations linked to the person Simon Magus. Simon had been revered as ἑστώς, the Standing One. This is the same predicate also assigned to Heracles when he was thought of as the pillar god. The pillar is known as the attribute of Heracles, indeed right in those lands with which Samaria has close religious contact. Herodotus reports as an eyewitness (*Histories* 2.44) that in the temple of Heracles in Tyre there stood "two pillars, one made of refined gold and one of emerald, a huge pillar that shone at night." (Perhaps the two pillars were symbols of the sun and the moon, of the cycle of day and night.) As Irenaeus, Tertullian, Epiphanius and others explicitly remark, Simon's consort Helena, who accompanied him, was from the city of Tyre. Because of her being related to the Helena of the ancient Greeks, she is the moon's woman. The *Pseudo-Clementine Homilies* state about this that she is said to be included in the number of the "thirty chief men" who represent the "moon's monthly reckoning," and to indicate that the moon's phases do not quite correspond with the thirty-day month. In the *Clementine Recognitions* (2.14) she is directly called *Luna*. Everywhere in those lands the moon was worshiped in addition to the sun. That female nature deity who was worshiped in Syria and Phoenicia under various names, in particular as Astarte (and by Greek writers called Here, Aphrodite, Artemis) was also principally a moon goddess. In *Goddesse of Surrye*, ch. 4, Lucian says he identifies Astarte with the moon. Since people thought of the sun and the moon as having sexual genders, and of the moon in particular as the principle of procreation and birth (on which, see Plutarch, *Isis and Osiris*, ch. 41) and thus also as a paramour like the notorious Pasiphaë (see Creuzer, *Symbolik und*

teachings ascribed to it, it could have simply copied its doctrinal framework from earlier existing Gnostic sects. However, a far more likely supposition might be that the part of its teaching involving Simon's relation to Helena was in any event a parody of Gnosticism originating in the Catholic Church, one especially intended to emphasize,

---

*Mythologie*, 4:96), they also saw fit to regard the Helena of the Magus as a paramour. Here we should also not overlook the prostitute of Judges 16:1 whom Samson patronized. Indeed even the wholly Gnostic predicate given to Helena when she is said to have been Simon's Ennoia perhaps has some connection with that Greek myth. Plutarch (in *Isis and Osiris*, ch. 41) at least distinguishes between the sun and the moon in this way: "They have a legend that Heracles, making his dwelling in the sun, is a companion for it in its revolutions, as is the case also with Hermas and the moon. In fact, the actions of the moon are like actions of reason and perfect wisdom, whereas those of the sun are like beatings administered through violence and brute strength" [Plutarch's *Moralia* in LCL, 5:100–101]. The moon is therefore intelligence, and the sun is power and strength, just as Simon is said to have called himself the Great Power. – From all this it seems to me very likely that Simon Magus, whoever he may originally have been (for I myself do not regard it as established that the Simon in the Book of Acts was clearly a historical figure), has become identified with the ancient god Sem (equivalent to Heracles) who doubtless would have been still worshiped at that time in Samaria by the pagan-minded sector of the people. As representative and as presumptive incarnation of the sun god, he was quite suited to be representative of the pagan religion with which the Christian religion came into contact in Samaria as its opponent and conqueror. Certainly Justin, a native of Samaria, is entirely credible when he, among others, says about Simon "almost all the Samaritans . . . worship him, and acknowledge him as the first god" (*First Apology* 26 [ANF 1:171]). This is simply the church father directly substituting the Magus for the national god. Acts 8:9–11 says: "Now a certain man named Simon had previously practiced magic in the city and amazed the people of Samaria, saying that he was someone great. All of them, from the least to the greatest, listened to him eagerly, saying, 'This man is the power of God that is called Great.' And they listened eagerly to him because for a long time he had amazed them with his magic." Can we not take this directly as a description of the prevailing cultus of that land? There assuredly were still very many pagans in the land of Samaria. It is expressly stated [by Justin] that Simon and Menander came from that land, Simon from the village of Gitto, Menander from the village of Capparetaea. The three Samaritans allegedly founders of the sect are forever in turn the same being. One falls when the other stands (*Pseudo-Clementine Homilies* 2.24), just as, in Egypt, Osiris, Typhon, and Horus alternate in ruling and falling. Doubtless this very idea of the sun god, revolving about the earth, roaming from morning to night, provided the occasion for the fiction that Simon would have preceded the Apostle Peter, the herald of the new faith, going from land to land in the distant West, into the city of Rome. As a representative of the old faith, now appearing to be false in light of the new faith, Simon could naturally be just a magician and wonder-worker. As there was a time when paganism, as a syncretism ostensibly indifferent to historical procedures, wanted to amalgamate with Christianity, we see it taking such a course partly from the Simon of the Book of Acts so readily bargaining with Christianity, and partly from the more specific doctrine concerning the Son in Judea, the Father in Samaria, and the Holy Spirit among the pagans, all having been one and the same deity. – However, if we are to rely on something from the church fathers about the sect in their day called the Simonians, as our source for the historical reality of the Magus, then we should just weigh what Irenaeus says in *Against Heresies* 1.27.4: "All those who in any way corrupt the truth, and do harm to the preaching of the church, are disciples and successors of Simon Magus of Samaria. Although they do not confess the name of their master, in order all the more to seduce others, yet they do teach his doctrines" [ANF 1:353]. This means there never actually was a sect of Simonians, but because there was at one time a Simon, the arch-heretic, so long as there were heretics there also had to be Simonians. We should understand in this same sense what Eusebius says about the Simonians and the Menandrians, in his *Ecclesiastical History* 2.1.10–12 and 3.26.1–4 respectively: that they stealthily sought to insinuate themselves into the church. In the view of the church fathers, the most abominable sects were a new form of the progenitor of all heresies, appearing in various guises.

in the most glaring way, the features of Gnosticism in which it made known most of all its oft-condemned relationship with paganism or Hellenism. In and for themselves these features of course provide a true picture of Gnosticism. However, they then had to make apparent, by the tenor in which they were expressed, how very strikingly they manifestly run counter to the spirit of Christianity. With Simon, as the Standing One, identifying himself with the supreme god, he was then said to be himself the forefather of the Gnostic systems. If, in keeping with the idea of the syzygies, one wanted to accompany him with a consort who united in herself all the attributes of Sige and Ennoia, of the Sophia above and the one below, all of which coincide in a single concept, there could have been no more fitting person chosen from the whole of Greek mythology than Helena. For in fact ideas in Greek mythology that point to an inner and deep-seated relationship between Gnosticism and Oriental-Greek religious teachings[283] are already linked with her. Finally, when Simon had even been made out to be the Greek Zeus, and when Helena would have been placed in the same relation to him as that of Athena to Zeus in the Greek myths, we can simply look upon this as a continuation of the same parody. Irenaeus says that "they also have an image of Simon fashioned after the likeness of Jupiter, and another of Helena in the shape of Minerva."[284] If Helena was said to be the Ennoia of the primal father,[285] then she completely resembled the Metis (Athena) who sprang from the head of Zeus.

## The Anti-Marcionite Aspect of the Pseudo-Clementine System

Now we come back to the *Clementine Homilies* and to the question as to what place the system they contain occupies in the history of Gnosis. This system evidently wanted to take a stance in opposition to Gnosis in general. We see this above all, and most unambiguously, in the role assigned to Simon Magus as Gnosticism's representative. Yet we do not find these homilies enlarging further upon this opposition to those systems we believe must be reckoned among the first main form of Gnosis. Instead we see clearly that this first form already lies outside the horizons within which these homilies operate. Instead they concentrate the full force of their opposition very much against the Marcionite system, in which, as all our references to it clearly show, the Gnosis of that time still seemed to be most vigorously alive and have its actual strength.

Therefore Marcion is the one the anonymous author of these homilies battles as his actual opponent, in a likewise anonymous way via the person of Simon Magus.[286]

283. [*In the text*] On which see my *Das manichäische Religionssystem* (n. 40).

284. *Against Heresies* 1.23.4 [*ANF* 1:348]. See also Epiphanius, *Against Heresies* 21.3.6.

285. Irenaeus, *Against Heresies* 1.23.2.

286. This is not to say that everything, without qualification, these homilies attribute to the Magus is to be regarded forthwith as authentically Marcionite. This applies specifically to the conceptions attributed to Simon by *Homilies* 3.2 and 18.4 that are not demonstrably Marcionite, but also not definitely identifiable as Gnostic, and indeed supposedly served the author of these homilies for letting the Marcionite doctrine appear even more polytheistic than it already inherently is. See *Das manichäische*

Accordingly, in approaching the Pseudo-Clementine system we must first of all fix our attention on its anti-Marcionite aspect, since this system could initially acquire a positive foundation of its own by overcoming and refuting Marcionite dualism. Hence in taking up this polemic we have to demonstrate at the same time that the contentions attributed to Simon Magus and contested by the writer of these homilies, in the figure of the Apostle Peter, are in fact Marcionite teaching.

The distinction Simon Magus repeatedly draws between the supreme God and the world's creator[287] is so generally accepted by the Gnostics we have been discussing thus far, that we can find a more specific connection to Marcion's system first of all in the arguments supporting this distinction. In this context the following points are unmistakably Marcionite in character.

First, there is the contention ascribed to the Magus, that the supreme God ought not be called "just" because the attribute of goodness pre-eminently belongs to him. In the main source treating this issue, according to the Magus, if the world's creator is also the lawgiver, then: as "lawgiver he is just; but if he is just, he is not good. But if he is not good, then it was another that Jesus proclaimed (Matt 19:17) when he said, 'There is only one who is good, the Father who is in heaven.'"[288] The lawgiver cannot be both good and just. In contrast, the figure of Peter seeks to show that the two concepts are not mutually exclusive. Goodness consists in bestowing, and one cannot say [as you, Simon, do] that God is then simply just when he has good people share in what is good, and evil people share in what is evil. When he imparts what is temporal or earthly to those who are evil in cases where they turn to him, and imparts what is eternal to those who are good, in cases where they persevere, then that would be his [true] justice, inasmuch as he gives to everyone—albeit when he grants his grace and, at the same time his goodness, to whose who distinguished themselves; and even more so when he absolves of their sins those who turned to him and, if they act well, assures them too of eternal life. "But judging at last, and giving to each one what he deserves, he is just."[289] As *Homilies* 4.13 says, the one God and creator of the world is both good and just, inasmuch as he absolves those who repent of their sins, and following their repentance, he forgives each one as his acts deserve. If, in agreement with Simon of Samaria, we would not concede that (the true) God is just, then there could not be any justice at all. That is because what is not at the root of all things also cannot be in the nature of the human being, as its fruit. For if there is no justice, or righteousness, there can also be no injustice, or unrighteousness (2.14).

---

*Religionssystem*, 343.

287. [*In the text*] In *Homilies* 2.22, and especially in 18.1 and 11: "I maintain that there is some unrevealed power, unknown to all, even to the Demiurge" (18.11 [*ANF* 8:327]).

288. *Homilies* 18.1 [*ANF* 8:324]. [*Ed.*] The added clause, "the Father who is in heaven," is a textual variant not included in the main text of Nestle.

289. [*Ed.*] This is the final sentence of Peter's foregoing argument in 18.2 (*ANF* 8:325). He then challenges Simon to refute it.

The second point concerns the antitheses between love and fear, which Marcion derived from the antithesis he assumed existed between goodness and justice. This is the contention that true religion consists not in fear but just in love. The polemic of *Homily* 17.11–12[290] relates to this point. The writer has his Peter figure stating this contention that one ought not fear God but instead ought to love God; yet adding that each one can accomplish this simply by the virtuous consciousness of having acted correctly, for acting correctly comes from fear. Some of course say that fear unsettles one's heart and soul; but I say fear is not unsettling, for it instead arouses and converts someone. Perhaps one could have rightly said that we ought not fear God if we human beings had not feared so many other things. Therefore whoever demands that we not fear God should free us from what we otherwise do fear. If he cannot do that then he should allow us our fear, since this one fear in facing justice frees us from a thousand other objects of fear. If, from fear, we do no evil in the sight of God who sees all things, then we can live in peace. If we are virtuously-minded servants of the true Lord, then we are free in everything else. If it is possible for someone to not sin who does not fear God, then he does not fear because it is love that does not allow him to do what is not fulfilling for him. "It is written that we should fear God; it is commanded that we should love God." These two, fear and love, are mutually related in a way suitable to how each person is constituted. "Fear God because he is just, but you must not sin, whether that be from fear or from love." Just as water extinguishes fire, so too fear curbs the desire for evil. Whoever teaches fearlessness is not himself afraid. But whoever is not afraid does not believe there is a judgment, and so allows his desires to become stronger.

The third point concerns Marcion's statements discrediting the world's creator, statements Simon Magus also repeated and ones to which Peter therefore replied. Marcion had said that the world's creator is a weak and limited, short-sighted being, lacking in character. In *Homilies* 3.38–39, Simon wants to demonstrate that the one usually called God is not the supreme, almighty Providence, for he certainly does not know the future ahead of time. He is imperfect, is not without defects and needs, is not good, and is subject to so many grievous passions.

> When this has been shown from the scriptures, as I say, it follows that there is another, not written about, who is foreknowing, perfect, free from defects and needs, good, and without any grievous passions. But he whom you call the creator is subject to the opposite evils . . . Adam, created initially in his likeness, was created without insight (*blind*), and is said to have had no knowledge of good or evil. He was found to be a transgressor, was expelled from paradise, and his punishment was being subject to death. After the dissolute behavior in Sodom, Adam's creator, whose sight does not extend to all places, said, "I must go down and see whether they have acted as the outcry coming to me

---

290. [*Ed.*] What follows in this paragraph is a close paraphrase of this passage. Baur frequently cites the *Homilies* in the text, and we do likewise whenever possible.

says they did; and if not, I will know" (Gen 18:21). So God showed his own ignorance. And in what he said concerning Adam—"and now, he might reach out his hand and take also from the tree of life, and eat, and live forever" (Gen 3:22)—the phrase "he might" shows God's ignorance, and the added words "eat and live forever" show God was envious. And when the scripture says "the Lord was sorry that he had made humankind" (Gen 6:6), this expresses both repentance and ignorance. Here God, not knowing what he wanted, reconsidered things in seeking to discover the outcome; in other words, he repented when things did not turn out as he wanted them to. Furthermore, when scripture says "the Lord smelled the pleasing odor" (Gen 8:21), this shows that he has needs, and that he enjoyed the aroma of the sacrificial offerings of flesh—it shows that he is not good. And the fact that, as scripture says, "God tested Abraham" (Gen 22:1), shows that he tempted, that he is evil, that he did not know the final outcome.[291]

Thus from numerous passages of scripture Simon sought to show that the God of scripture is a being subject to all possible weaknesses. Simon contends that, if what scripture says about the world's creator is true, then he cannot be the supreme God, and is instead a being subject to all sorts of wickedness.[292]

## Recognition of What Is True in Marcion's Dualism with Regard to the Old Testament

Comparison of these passages with Marcion's polemic against the teachings of Old Testament religion, as Tertullian depicts that polemic,[293] obviously indicates how all these arguments agree with the Marcionite polemic, some of them literally, and some of them at least by manifesting the same spirit. For a writer who, like the author of the *Clementine Homilies*, adopted the Old Testament standpoint as much as he could, refuting these arguments had to be as important as it was difficult. What is more remarkable then is that he quite decidedly brings to the forefront his attempt to establish an equilibrium between Old Testament or Jewish interests and those of a purely religious or Gnostic perspective.

In doing this the writer proceeds very methodically, in having his Peter figure at first remark, in opposition to Simon:

> If everything the scriptures contain about God being unworthy is true, it still does not follow from this that God is actually a being so extremely imperfect and wicked, because scripture also contains so much else that directly contradicts the passages introduced by Simon. Thus in any event only the one kind

---

291. *Homilies* 3:38–39 [*ANF* 8:245].

292. *Homilies* 3.41 [*ANF* 8:246]. [*Ed.*] In the text Baur then provides the Greek for the last part of this statement.

293. See p. 142 above.

> or the other kind can be true, and we can regard as true what in the text is compatible with the act of creation carried out by God—so that what clashes with it must be false. People say: "If Adam was created without insight, what was the point of God forbidding him to eat from the tree of the knowledge of good and evil?" If this is just to be understood as a lack of mental insight, it still is incompatible with the fact that, before eating from the tree, at the explicit instruction of his creator he gave all the animals their appropriate names (Gen 2:20). And how, if Adam did not know things about them in advance, could he have already given his sons at birth the names so entirely suitable to their future occupations? For he named his first-born Cain, that is, "envy," because later he slew his brother Abel out of envy; and he named his brother Abel, that is, "grief," because his parents later grieved for him as the first one to be slain. If Adam had knowledge of future things, how much more so would his creator have had such knowledge! Thus as a general rule all the passages of scripture that ascribe ignorance to God, or say anything else that is unworthy of him, have others that contradict them and state the opposite. But how can it be said, as the scripture does (in Psalm 18), that the God who abides in obscurity and darkness, and in the tempest, is he who, spanning the pure heavens, has created the sun to give light to all, and determined the invariable order in the courses of the innumerable stars? Thus the heavens show God's handiwork, the pure and never-changing spirit of the creator. So all the passages wrongfully accusing the creator of the heavens are invalidated by others contradicting them, and are refuted by the creation itself.[294]

This answer concedes that the opponent has raised real objections, and it recognizes that everything he maintains cannot be a component of the true idea of God.

But this can be a satisfactory answer only if one also has a reply to this directly pressing question: In places in the Old Testament where such contradictions occur, and given the fact that there are many such instances, by what right do we give preference to those that contain nothing unworthy of the deity? The answer provided by the writer of the *Homilies* shows still more clearly how, in fully opposing the Gnosis of his day, he nevertheless at the same time adopts a Gnostic standpoint himself. It involves the assumption that all those passages sounding unworthy of the deity "were not written by a prophetic hand."[295]

> The law of God, in unwritten form, was given by Moses to seventy wise men,[296] to be handed down to serve as the rule of conduct for succeeding generations. After Moses was taken up into heaven, it was written down by someone but

---

294. [*Ed.*] This lengthy combination of quotation and paraphrase consists of selected elements from *Homilies* 3.41–45 (*ANF* 8:246–47).

295. *Homilies* 3.46 [*ANF* 8:247]. [*Ed.*] The following passage, a combination of paraphrase and quotation, is from 3.47 (*ANF* 8:247).

296. [*Ed.*] A reference to the Septuagint, the Greek translation of the Hebrew Bible made in Egypt (third–second century BC).

not by Moses . . . But how could Moses write that Moses died? [Deut 34:5] About five hundred years after Moses died this law was found in the temple that had been built, and after five hundred more years it was in use, and it was burned under Nebuchadnezzar's rule. So it was first written down after Moses' time and often destroyed. This shows Moses' prescience, since in foreseeing its destruction he did not write it down. Those who did write it down, in not foreseeing its destruction, perpetuated their ignorance and therefore could not have been prophets.

One could take this to mean that scripture contains much that is untrue, that is unworthy of the deity. But if this is how things stand, if scripture is a mixture of truth and falsity, then we need a key for unlocking its truthful contents.

This question too does not go unanswered. But the answer hinges on the view put forward in these homilies concerning Christianity's relation to Old Testament religion. Here it suffices to see this puzzle solved in the same way that Marcion believed he could solve it simply by assuming two quite different deities, so that the contradiction only applies to the Old Testament. In other words, one acknowledges that, as a matter of fact, the Old Testament contains two quite heterogeneous components, ones the author of the Clementine writings believed he could hardly bring under a single concept any more than Marcion did with the two deities whose existence he deduced from the same phenomenon. So the reality of the phenomenon itself is recognized from two different angles, and only the conclusions drawn from this phenomenon are different. That is because on one view the contradiction has a purely objective basis, while on the other view it is simply found in the subjectivity of the Old Testament writers. The two views are in even further agreement. While Marcion, on account of the Old Testament, made the world's creator out to be an evil being, the author of the Clementine writings, in explaining the Old Testament's contradictions with the true idea of God, also reverted to an evil principle. The fact that, when the law according to Moses got written down, the scriptures incorporated so many falsehoods about God, the world's creator, is to be blamed on the guile that dared to do this. Given the Pseudo-Clementine idea of God, this is compensated for simply by the good intention with which it was done, or God let it be done. For it was done with proper forethought, so that one could recognize as such those who on the one hand ventured to welcome what is written unfavorably about God, and those who on the other hand, out of love for God, not only disbelieved such things but also never could abide them, even though they be true (2.38 [*ANF* 8:236]).

## Opposition to Marcionite Dualism, with Reference to Two Principles: The Relation of Matter to God; The Origin of Evil

In order to give his dualism a positive foundation, Marcion based it on the general antithesis of principles that form the Gnostics' starting point, the antithesis between spirit and matter. Thus the author of the Clementine writings would have only very incompletely solved his problem—how to refute Gnostic-Marcionite dualism—if he had not gone all the way back and taken a position on the spirit-matter antithesis that is the presupposition for the Marcionite antithesis between the supreme God and the world's creator.

If the interests of Judaism were what gave rise to this challenging of Gnostic dualism, then these interests could only be made secure by a purely monotheistic principle. The dualism could only be overcome by a system that also knew how to do so in some fashion when it was also a question of the way in which matter is related to God, and how evil originates. It must do this without having to rely on a principle independent of God. The author of the Clementine texts has by no means overlooked this point. Hence it is principally connected with the polemic directly aimed at Marcion, the one related to the concept of matter and the origin of evil. However, it is regrettable that the text we have has only survived in an incomplete form and breaks off suddenly right where it deals with this issue. So we hardly know the full context of the writer's teaching about these topics.

The way *Homily* 19 treats it gives us only a few indications as to how matter is related to God, for it tells us this only in the course of the writer's attending to the far more important topic of the origin of evil. When it comes to the largely divergent views about matter's relation to God—one regarding matter as existing independently of God's will, and the other one seeing matter existing as something willed by God—the author's view falls in between these two extremes. Matter of course exists apart from God but only because God wills this. Yet matter is not essentially different from God's own nature, for matter has proceeded from it.

This proceeding from God's nature can simply be the writer's conception, when he says "it is possible for God to have been the producer of the four substances, heat and cold, moist and dry," and that "the four substances were produced by God."[297] According to the usual meaning of the words προβάλλεσθαι, προβολή, and προβολεύς, the world, together with the substances that are its elements, is an emanation from God. These four substances form two antitheses—heat and cold, moist and dry—and so too there was originally just one and the same substance.[298] Originally one, so long as it was still within God, this substance was accordingly first when it proceeded forth from God, dividing twofold and fourfold. As various passages describe the process, the creation followed by God "combining those elements, making myriads of compounds from them, so that from these opposites and their mixtures what might proceed is the breath of life" (3.33 [*ANF* 8:244]).

---

297. *Homilies* 19.12 and 13 [*ANF* 8:334].

298. [*Ed.*] Baur gives the Greek for this last phrase, taken from *Homilies* 3.33, the first sentence of which reads: "He alone turned the one, first, simple substance into the four contrary elements" (*ANF* 8:244).

This same conception of an emanation, of something substantial proceeding from the being of God, seems to lead to the oft-used expression for the creation of the human being, when the text says he was "fashioned by the hands of God" (3.17 and 20). Therefore God, as it were, bore the human being within himself and gave birth to him from himself. The fact that this way of putting it does not refer merely to the formative act of creating, nor merely to the soul as, according to the Clementines, an immortal breath of the deity, is shown more specifically from the doctrine of the image of God.[299]

To the extent that we can pursue the issue of evil's origin, in the response of *Homily* 19, a response just present in fragmentary form, we find it understood there in a very multifaceted way. Without question this passage concedes that there is an independent principle of evil, but at the same time it points out that, when we think about the relation of evil to God, we cannot find fault with God himself because there is evil. This is the main perspective from which the writer set out.[300] He then sought to introduce the proof of a twofold thesis: that the evil principle neither is created by a power independent of God, nor is an uncreated being. In this still-extant part of the homily, the writer endeavors to show, if the evil principle did have a beginning, how it came to be, and by whom. In other words, to present its origin in such a way that God cannot appear to be the originator or author of evil, since God can only be the author of what is good.

The writer of *Homily* 19 is not satisfied with the notion of a being created as good and at one time having been good, but then becoming evil by its or his own choice. The writer believes he can only countenance an evil principle that becomes evil at its very origin, but with the evil as nevertheless his own deed. Hence the writer's own theory is that, when the four aforementioned basic substances had emerged from God and had become intermixed, a being originated from them that had the desire to corrupt or destroy the evil ones.[301] This being is from none other than God, for all things

---

299. It is most noteworthy that the Greek for "fashioning" in fact completely corresponds to the original meaning of the Hebrew word ברא. On this, see Johannsen, *Die kosmogonischen Ansichten der Inder und Hebräer* (Altona, 1833), 17ff. The verb ברא, from the same root as the name בר, or son, and itself cognate with the German *Gebären* (childbearing), actually means: bearing; bearing the embryo within oneself until it sees the light of day. "As a woman bears within herself the fertilized egg (*Samen*) of the child, and produces from out of herself, so too God bears in himself the seed of the being to be created. The action of creation consists in his having this seed come forth from himself and exist in a separate form or figure." – "The Hebrew expression, as in other languages (Indian *sridj*, Latin *producere*, German *Schaffen* and *Schöpfen*), conveys the view originally inherent in the mentality of various peoples, that creating is an emanating from the deity." All of this also explains the concept bound up with the word κυοφορεῖν, "fashioning."

300. [*Ed.*] In *Homily* 19 the "independent principle of evil" is discussed in terms of the figure of the Devil. This would not be immediately clear from the abstract way in which Baur commenced the discussion at this point. What follows in our text is drawn from *Homily* 19.5, which is a rather brief and terse exposition of the issues involved—perhaps what Baur has in mind when calling the response "fragmentary."

301. [*Ed.*] Baur elucidates this point in what follows, but some succinct comments might be helpful

are from God. However, its wickedness is not from God, but instead first comes about outside of, or apart from, God. Its evil nature is based on its own will, and from the basic substances mixing themselves together. Yet this does not occur contrary to God's will, and certainly not even apart from God's will. For no being, least of all one subject to God's authority and superior to a great many others, can come to be by chance (ἐκ συμβεβηκότος, *ex accidenti*), apart from God's will.

So we must therefore state the following points. What the will of the evil one willed took place according to the decree or resolution of what was mixed together. Hence evil is both something divinely necessary and something freely begun. While this view is a sufficient justification of God with respect to evil, this justification is also strengthened by more precisely spelling out the concept of evil—to wit, by showing that what is evil is not evil in every respect. The being that came about as described certainly has the urge to destroy the evil ones. (It could not have harmed those who are good, even if it wished to.) However, the destruction of the evil ones, which is the work of this wicked being, is a laudable business. Thus since evil essentially destroys itself, it is also in turn something good. People say, and theology acknowledges, that the evil one loves God no less than a good one does, except that the evil one engages in the destruction of evil by destroying the sinner, whereas a good one destroys evil by rescuing the sinner (19.12, together with 3.5).

## The Positive Aspect of This System

Despite his opposition to Gnosis, in this case the author of the *Clementine Homilies* also exhibits an authentically Gnostic tendency in his effort to comprehend evil as much as possible in its own deepest roots. If we leave out of account how he harmonizes the most extreme instance of evil with the principle of strict monotheism, then even his own monotheism inherently and fully embodies the character of Marcionite dualism. Just as Marcion's Demiurge is the God of the material world, so too, according to the Clementines' author, God has handed over to the wicked one (as we have described him) dominion over the present world when it comes to enforcing the law, that is, punishing those who do evil. Like Marcion's just God, this being accordingly exercises the judicial office of administering justice. Over against the "left hand" or power of God stands the "right hand," the good ruler of the world to come, that is, Christ (15.7). This Pseudo-Clementine dualism can become apparent in its true light in the following and fuller development of the whole system.

---

here. The larger context of *Homily* 19.12 is the consideration of "the wicked one," that is, the Devil. The four original substances are said to have "naturally directed their desire toward neither" good nor evil. But when they mixed together, the result was a living being with free choice, and from the very beginning of its existence this being, the Devil, freely chose evil. That is why he has "the desire to corrupt or destroy the evil ones," presumably those sinners who choose, and so become, evil under his influence.

## Monotheism: God Is the World's Creator; The Doctrine of God's Nature and the Image of God, and the Human Being's Ethical Relation to God, Which Rests Upon It

What has gone before sheds light on how the author of the *Clementine Homilies* has the nature of religion hinging entirely on the fundamental idea that the one supreme God is also the creator of the world. Once this idea has simply been established, and so the wide gulf with which the other Gnostic systems endeavored to separate the world's creator from the supreme God has been eliminated, then the Clementines' author has no compunction about taking the side of the Gnostics and making his own their way of thinking and looking at things. This fundamental idea is also then precisely what a further development of this system must mainly pursue if we are to become even more conversant with its positive aspects.

In this pursuit we constantly have to hold fast to the same two factors. On the one hand, all the emphasis lies on the idea of the world's creator as this idea is spelled out in the Jewish religion, where the whole spirit and character of the concept of God, and of God's relation to human beings, cannot be understood in metaphysical terms, but is instead simply an ethical concept. On the other hand, however, the writer of the *Clementine Homilies* is drawn to the metaphysical speculation of Gnosis in a way that gives his idea of God an essentially different form from that of a purely Old Testament or Jewish approach. Hence in this part of his system too there are two different elements to distinguish, and it is a matter of harmonizing them—the clearly Jewish or ethical element, and the Gnostic or metaphysical element.

As soon as the view is once established, that the world's creator is not a different being from the one true God, then this places the absolute God in the same close and direct relationship with the world he created and with human beings, as the Gnostics, and Marcion in particular, wanted to hold good just for the world's creator (as they conceived of him). That is why the Clementines' author, in contrast to Marcion's view of nature as godless, points with special emphasis to the creation as the work of God and as the basis for being able to know the Creator himself. So he calls the heavens "the handwriting of God," in which God himself has made known the features of his own being or nature.[302]

But the place where God himself is chiefly reflected is in the human being. The overall position given to the human being in this system in fact is what enables us to fully recognize for the first time the religious component in contradicting the Gnostic separation of the world's creator from the absolute God, and the ethical significance of the idea of God as the creator of the world.[303] That is why the doctrine of the im-

---

302. [*Ed.*] In the text Baur then gives the Greek for this passage from *Homilies* 3.45: "the handwriting of God—I mean the heaven—shows the counsels of him who made it to be pure and stable" (*ANF* 8:247).

303. This ethical-religious component is expressed in the strongest terms in *Homilies* 18.22, where the contention is that if the world's creator were distinct from the supreme God, and if he were himself

age of God (in a human being) occupies a very important place in this system, and why the distinctive ideas the Clementines' author sets forth about the nature of God seem to him, in a certain sense, just to serve for giving that teaching an even firmer foundation.

The writer declares in the following way what the teaching about God's nature involves, and how it is connected with the idea of the image of God.

> God has shape because he is the first and unique beauty. He also has every limb, and not for its utility. He has eyes but not so he can see with them, for he sees everything since his body is brilliant beyond compare, brighter than the seeing spirit that is within us and more splendid than every light, such that, compared with him the sun's light is darkness. He also has ears, but not to hear with, for he hears, perceives, moves, activates, and influences all things. He has the most beautiful shape on account of human beings, so that those who are pure in heart can see him and can rejoice because of what they have endured. For he has shaped human beings in his own image so that they would have dominion over all, and all would serve them. God himself is invisible, but the human being is his image, and whoever wants to honor God must honor his visible image, the human being. Whatsoever anyone does to a person, whether it be good or bad, is regarded as done to God. That is also why God judges each person as he or she deserves to be judged, for he avenges what is done to his own image.
>
> But suppose someone says that if God has shape then he also has a figure or form, dimensions, and has a spatial location; and if he is spatially bounded, he cannot be infinite, or omnipresent, because of having a form . . . The reply to this is as follows. The spatial location of God is the non-existent (*Nichtseiende*), although God is what is existent (*Seiende*). However, the non-existent cannot be compared with the existent. For how can there be a spatial location if there is not even an additional expanse that fills the emptiness of space? The emptiness is nothingness (*Nichts*), an empty vessel that, as a vessel, contains nothing. Hence everything existent can only be within what is non-existent. But what is non-existent is what people otherwise call spatial location . . . Yet although the spatial location is something, it is evident from the following example that what encloses is not directly superior to what is enclosed. The sun is a circular figure and is entirely surrounded by air. Nevertheless the sun is what illuminates the air, what warms it and shines through it, and as soon as the sun goes away the air is enveloped in darkness. The sun, in being surrounded, does all this by imparting its own being. Then why should God, as the creator and Lord of all things—even though he has figure, shape, and beauty—not have imparted his being endlessly? . . .

---

the most wicked of all beings, a human being's full reverence would nevertheless be due in any case to him alone, since one can have one's existence from him alone, and therefore one is also tied to him by the closest and most natural bonds.

The one true God stands before the whole in the most perfect shape, as the heart of everything in both directions, on high and here below, and as the center, the incorporeal, living power, he issues forth from himself all that is—the stars and the heavenly regions, the regions of air, water, earth, and fire, as a being extending immeasurably in the three dimensions of height, depth, and breadth, and in all these directions expanding its life-bestowing and rational nature. This endless streaming-forth on all sides must of necessity have as its heart the one who in his form is truly above all, who, wherever he be, is forever at the center of what is endless, and is the boundary of the whole. From him the six dimensions extend infinitely, to the heights and the depths, to the right and the left, to the front and the back. Looking upon this as upon a number equal on all sides, he completes the world in the six intervals of time [i.e., the six days of creation], for he is himself the resting-point [the seventh day] of all existence. Having his image in the infinite time to come, he is the beginning and the end of all things. For the six endless directions go back to him, and they all receive their extension to infinity from him.

That is the secret of the number seven, the hebdomad. It is the resting-point of everything, and whoever imitates on a small scale his greatness, he lets come to rest in himself... He is comprehensible and incomprehensible, is near and far, here and there, as the one [source of all]. Through the community of being, with the spirit infinite in all directions, the souls have life. If they separate themselves from their bodies and they have an indwelling longing for him, they will be borne along in his bosom like the mountain mists that in wintertime, drawn by the sun's rays, are borne immortally to him. What love must then awaken in us if we behold his beauty in the spirit! Otherwise it cannot be conceived, for it is impossible that beauty exist without shape; that one can be drawn to love it or suppose he has seen God if God has no shape. Hence it is wholly false, a contention lending support to evil, if, on the pretext of glorifying God, someone says God has no figure or form. For without shape and form God will be visible to no one, will be the object of nobody's longing. A mind or spirit not seeing the shape of God is also devoid of him. And how can anyone pray who does not know to whom he should go for refuge? To whom can he turn for support? For if one has no solid ground on which to stand, one is left with emptiness...

The eyes of mortals cannot see the incorporeal form of the Father or the Son, because its light is so great. It is not from envy but from God's goodness that he cannot be seen by a human being who is turned into flesh, "for no one shall see me and live" (Exod 33:20). The excess of the light destroys the flesh of one who sees him, unless by God's inexpressible power either one's flesh be transformed into the nature of light, so it is able to see the light, or else the substance of the light be changed into flesh, so it can be seen by flesh. The Son alone sees the Father directly, for the just ones do not do likewise until the resurrection of the dead when, in their bodies transformed into light, become like angels, they are able to see him. Indeed if an angel should appear to a human being, the angel must transform himself into flesh so that he can be seen by a being of flesh. For whoever cannot see a being without flesh cannot see just the Son, but also cannot see an angel.[304]

Of course it is not entirely clear how the Clementines' author conceived of the relation of the image of God to God's being or nature itself. For he says God is invisible by nature but calls a human being the visible image of God. He declares that God's essence is the purest brilliance of light, but he relates the image of God expressly to the human body.[305] Yet this much clearly emerges from this whole collection of related ideas: that a certain realism is held to be necessary when it comes to the idea of God. It is just that, if the being of God was conceived as having the specific concreteness of a real substance, then this specificity seemed so significant to human consciousness that it was able to be the basis for a truly vital relationship between God and humankind. In this case the entire relationship is understood as based far more on an ethical perspective than on a metaphysical outlook. Here God, in creating the world and humankind, does not reveal himself in the way other Gnostic systems portray it, in virtue of an inner necessity, belonging to God's own nature, to go outside himself and evolve in a series of emanations. Instead the reason why God reveals himself, imparts his own nature, and imprints his own image on human beings, lies instead in humanity itself. It is to realize, external to God himself, the idea of the human being as this idea is conceived of in the mind of God.

---

304. [*Ed.*] This long series of quoted passages consists of excerpts from Homilies 17.7–11 and 17.16 (*ANF* 8:319–23).

305. *Homilies* 10.6, says of people, "Ye who have his image in your bodies" [*ANF* 8:281]. See also 3.7, 11.4 ("The body of a human being bears the image of God" [*ANF* 8:285]), and 16.20. It seems that the writer has in mind the original human σῶμα or body as a shape of light, especially since in 17.16 he speaks of the human being as "turned into flesh." What deserves notice here is that the idea of a human being as the image of God is extremely important in the Gnostic systems closely connected with Judaism. While the Gnostics understood the being of God abstractly, it still seemed to them that if the human being was said to be the image of God, then also God had to be human in a certain sense. Irenaeus remarks about the followers of Ptolemy, who were a branch of the Valentinians: "They say that the Propator, or Primal Father of the whole, is called Anthropos; and that is the great and abstruse mystery, namely, that the power above all others and containing all in his embrace, is called Anthropos; and because of this the Savior speaks of himself as 'the Son of Man'" (*Against Heresies* 1.12.4 [*ANF* 1:334]). Tertullian maintains this about Valentinus himself, by remarking in opposition to Marcion: "I cannot see by what principle you, Marcion, can admit that Christ is the Son of Man . . . One thing alone can help you in your difficulty: boldness on your part, either to call your God the father of Christ, thus also human, as Valentinus did with his Aeon [Anthropos], or else . . ." (*Against Marcion* 4.10 [*ANF* 3:358–59]). Even the Ophites straightforwardly called the primal father "the first man," and the second principle "the second man." The same is true of the Adam Kadmon of the Kabbalists, as the first revelation of the deity and the oneness of the powers emanating from it. This is simply a further elaboration of the idea contained in the Old Testament passages of Gen 1:26 ["Then God said, 'Let us make humankind in our image, according to our likeness'"] and Dan 7:13 ["I saw one like a human being, coming with the clouds of heaven"]. However, it is very typical of the Gnostics' standpoint that they placed such importance on this idea, which set Judaism apart from paganism and mediated it with Christianity.

Here we have the reason why *Homilies* 16.19 says it is simply due to God's love for the human being (φιλανθρωπία) that God gives such a shape to the man taken from "the dust of the ground" (Gen 2:7). God's love taking the human being as its immediate object is the basis of the creation. That is also why there is no need in this system for any intermediary series of Aeons to get to the ultimate point at which human being can find its designated place in the series of moments of the divine evolutionary process. Human being is the immediate object and goal of God's creative activity. The entire creation preceding the creation of humankind is wholly with reference to it, because humankind and it alone bears within it the image of God. As *Homilies* 3.36 puts it:

> Someone who carefully considers all that God has made will find that God has created all this for human beings' sake . . . The animals serve human needs, the sun shines to divide the climate into the four seasons, and so forth . . . Whoever would have had dominion over the creation if it were not human beings? They have the wisdom to till the soil, to sail the seas, to catch fish, birds, and beasts, to observe the course of the heavenly bodies, to investigate the earth's interior, to cross the ocean, to found cities, to mark out kingdoms, to give laws, to administer justice, to recognize the invisible God, to know the names of the angels, to drive out demons, to heal sickness, to discover charms against poisonous serpents, to perceive antipathy? [ANF 8:245]

Hence as *Homilies* 16.9 observes:

> Although, as far as its substance is concerned, everything is superior to human flesh—the ether, the sun, the moon, the stars, the air, the water, fire and all else that has been made to serve human beings. Yet superior in substance, it all willingly serves what is inferior to it in substance because humankind has the shape of what is higher. For as those who honor the clay image of a king have honored the king himself, whose shape is the clay, the entire creation joyfully serves human beings made from the soil, because it looks to honor that higher being, God. [ANF 8:317]

So here we have the high status of human beings in this system. The image of God one inherently bears, as ruler of the entire visible creation, does not, however, merely designate the great privilege it bestows, for it also involves the whole sum and substance of the obligations a human being has in relation to God. Just as God has created human beings out of love, and has demonstrated his continuing love by drawing to himself, by his love, every religiously-minded soul, so too the whole of a human being's relation to God must rest on love. The love constantly aware of how great is God's benevolence is also salvific with regard to the world to come (3.6). Thus a person cannot commit any greater sin than being ungrateful and failing to love God (11.23). Proof of love for God, of the honor one owes to God, comes from doing what God has commanded and is according to God's will (11.27). This especially involves one's honoring God's image in others by loving them (11.4). Inasmuch as one must make oneself worthy of God's love by one's conduct, likeness to God is not the same thing as the image of God. Just as human beings bear the image of God in their bodies, they are also required to bear the likeness to God in their souls. Only by subjecting oneself to God's law does a person become human, for an irrational animal cannot be told, "Thou shall not kill, commit adultery, steal," and so on. Truly human nobility consists in obeying God's commandments. Those who become like God through good works thereby become God's children and, what they are supposed to be, the lords of all (10.6).

This obviously shows clearly how, on this understanding of a human being's relation to God, everything had to be vested in a person's free will. Thus in this part of the system no other doctrine is so important, in addition to the doctrine of God's image in human beings, as the teaching about freedom. It alone is the principle governing the possibility of authentic goodness. (The answer to the question, "How is it possible to be really good?," can only be "by one's own choice.") "For the one who becomes good owing to some other constraint is not truly good, because he is not what he is by his own free choice" (11.8 [ANF 8:286]). For freedom is entirely taken to be the ability to choose, because this system's teaching situated a human being between two opposed principles. The writer of the *Clementine Homilies* also demonstrates how important this doctrine is by explicitly taking into account the difficulties it faces. Since on this view the human soul is so inwardly bound to God that it is a living soul only by inhaling, so to speak, the spiritual power streaming forth from God (17.10), the direct objection to it had to be that everything we think and will would be fed into our souls by God. But the critic will dismiss this view as blasphemous because God would then have also become the author of evil thoughts and desires (11.8). Furthermore, if what is evil be necessary for the sake of what is good, in order to put goodness to the test, as Jesus says in Matt 18:7, then a human being would still be free to become an instrument of the evil ordained by God or not to do so.[306] Likewise the circumstances of a subsequent decision hardly detract from the freedom of a prior resolve. Although the subsequent decision is of course determined by the prior resolve, that would not cancel out the freedom if in fact the prior resolve was just made freely. Initially each one is good or evil through himself. The next goodness or evil comes about in keeping with one's prior act or resolve and through it, in someone's having, by the initial decision, made himself an instrument of the good or evil spirit (12.29–30).

---

306. [*Ed.*] Matt 18:6–7 concerns stumbling blocks, or obstacles, placed in the way of children. In v. 7 Jesus says, "Occasions for stumbling are bound to come, but woe to the one by whom the stumbling block comes!"

## The Gnostic Content of This System; the Doctrine of the Syzygies; True and False Prophecy

But if, as the *Clementine Homilies* teach, the supreme principle of religion is knowing and loving the world's creator as the one true God, then this principle follows of its own accord from how the religious system the *Homilies* contains stands in relation to Judaism. Owing to its monotheism, in other words to its theocratic teaching, Judaism is the true or absolute religion, whereas owing to its polytheism, paganism is for that very reason also the false religion. For, as the *Homilies* state, the essence of impiety is sticking with a religion that contends: "there is another God, whether superior or inferior, or who is in any way other than the one true God. The true God is just the one whose image the human body bears" (3.7 [ANF 8:240]).

Whoever believes that there are many Gods, not one, cannot have "a monarchic soul, and be holy."[307] However, since there is paganism as well as Judaism, the false religion in addition to the true one, and since false dogma also has so many points of contact with the scriptures—"for the scriptures say all manner of things" and one can prove from them whatever one wants to (3.10 [ANF 8:240])—we then face the question: Where do we find a sound principle for knowing the truth? The writer of the *Clementine Homilies* answers this question with his teaching about true and false prophecy.

First and foremost one must understand that the truth can be found in no other way than via the prophets of truth. The true prophet is the one who knows everything in its season, is aware of the purposes of everything, is without fault, and is clearly conscious of divine judgment. In contrast, there are also many false prophets and heralds of errors who are just as united in an evil principle as those pure prophets who, appearing in each season, are united as the prophets of truth (3.26). This makes even more pressing the question: What is the criterion for distinguishing truth from error? The answer lies in the doctrine of the syzygies.[308] This doctrine is deeply rooted in the entire Clementine system and in the distinctive view it presents about the relationships of the three religions: paganism, Judaism, and Christianity. Thus in this context we are led to all those teachings that constitute the actual Gnostic contents of this remarkable text. Like all the Gnostic systems, this one also considers those three religions to be essential moments of the great, developing process in which God's relation to the world and to humankind objectifies itself. Hence this system also has its point of departure in the creation.

As we already indicated, at first there was the simple substance of all things in God. Then God divided it in a fourfold way, into the shapes of heat and cold, moist and

---

307. *Homilies* 2.42 [ANF 8:237]. [Ed.] The ANF translator says in a footnote that the likely meaning is "a soul ruling over his body," not "a soul disposed to favor monarchical rule."

308. *Homilies* 3.16: "The chief cause of people being deceived is their not understanding beforehand the doctrine of the syzygies" [ANF 8:241].

dry, setting them outside himself and combining them. The basic stuff from which all individual being proceeds was therefore produced in this way. The Clementines call "wisdom" the active principle present with God. From eternity, God was blissfully in company with wisdom. Wisdom is God's own spirit, the soul most closely bound to him. Wisdom transmits God's creative activity, in that it proceeds from God as, so to speak, God's world-creating hand. By expansion and contraction the monad forms the dyad (16.12). This relationship of the monad to the dyad is the reason why the fundamental law of the universe is the law of opposites, in virtue of which the God who is one from the beginning first produces the heavens and then the earth, as right and left, and straight away all the other syzygies—day and night, light and fire, life and death.

However, beginning with human beings the order of syzygies was reversed. Initially the better one of the pair preceded and the lesser one followed, but now the worse one became first and the better one was second. Adam, the human being created in the image of God, was followed first by the unjust one, Cain, and only then by the just one, Abel. Likewise Noah, whom the Greeks call Deucalion,[309] first sent out the black raven and then the white dove, which are, respectively, symbols of impure and pure spirits. We see the same relationship with the sons of Abraham, with Ishmael, and Isaac who was blessed by God; also with Isaac's sons, godless Esau and pious Jacob; even with Aaron the high priest, and Moses the lawgiver. Adam himself had been created according to that initial divine arrangement. In the syzygy he formed with Eve, Adam precedes as the better member and Eve follows as the worse one.[310]

This is the reason why the writer of the *Clementine Homilies* has a very lofty conception of Adam's perfection.

> The prophet of truth is the one who knows all things. If anyone does not concede that the man fashioned by the hands of God had in him the great and holy spirit of the creator of all things, how would it not be the greatest error to ascribe this spirit to another human being born of impure seeds? Whoever does not honor the image of the eternal king sins against the one whose image the human being bears within himself. It is most pious to say that no other one would have the Spirit of God [or the Holy Spirit of Christ] but the one who from the beginning passed through the world under various changing names and forms, until finally, at the appointed time, anointed with God's compassion for the sake of hardships, he had gained eternal rest [Adam = Christ]. He was given the honor of ruling over and governing all things in the air, on the earth, and in the water. In addition, he had the breath [of God] that created the human being, as the inexpressible vestment of the soul that confers immortality on it.

---

309. [*Ed.*] In Greek mythology Deucalion, the son of Prometheus, built an ark to survive the flood Zeus caused in anger at people's sins.

310. [*Ed.*] Baur cites *Homilies* 2.26, but the likely reference is to 3.26–27.

As the one true prophet, and like its creator, he gave to each being the name that fits its nature. "Whatever the man called every living creature, that was its name" (Gen 2:19). How, then, did he still need to stretch his hand out to the tree, in order to gain the knowledge of good and evil? Only those who are lacking in judgment, who imagine that an animal lacking reason would be mightier than he who had created the first human being and everything else, could believe what scripture says about this.

Indeed alongside Adam a female nature was created as his companion (σύζυγος), someone far inferior to him and related to him simply as accident is to substance, as the moon is to the sun, as fire is to light. As the female ruler of the female-like present world, she is the first prophetess. But the other one, as the son of man, is the male ruler of the male-like world to come. So there are now two kinds of prophecy, male and female kinds. They are arranged according to the order in which the syzygies develop, with the female coming first, although at the same time as the prophetess of the present world, she wants her prophecy to be deemed the masculine kind. Therefore, by stealing the man's seed and covering it with the seed of her own flesh, she brings forth the fruit, that is the words, as wholly her own. So she proclaims earthly riches as her gift, and wishes to substitute slowness for speed, what is worse for what is better. She scarcely finds polytheism repugnant, and in fact believes she is a god. Yet with the hope of becoming what is contrary to her nature, she even loses what she has. Like a woman having her monthly period, she stains herself with blood from sacrificial offerings and makes unclean those who come in contact with her. When she conceives, she gives birth to earthly kings and stirs up many bloody wars. Those who wish to learn the truth from her she leaves forever seeking and finding nothing, even until death, by her constantly telling them contradictory things and making them do many things. For from the outset she leads blinded men to their death, since she deceives those who believe her, by her false, ambiguous, and misguided pronouncements. This is why she gave her first-born son the ambiguous name of Cain, which can mean both "possession" and "envy." . . . For he was a murderer and a liar and, being a sinner, he never wanted to be ruled or remain peaceful. Hence his descendents were the first adulterers, and makers of psalters, citharas, and weapons. That is why the prophecy about his descendents, as adulterers, and singers of psalms, secretly arouses one to war because of sensual pleasures.

However the other one [Adam], in whose soul the prophecy of the son of man is inborn and singularly present, as a male expressly proclaimed the world to come. He named his son Abel, which unambiguously means "grief." For Adam has his sons grieve for their deceived brothers. He does not deceive them when he promises them solace in the world to come. He knows only the one God. He will not speak of multiple gods, nor believe other people who do so. He tends to the good he has, and increases it. He hates sacrificial offerings, their bloodiness and libations. He loves what is holy, pure, and pious.

> He quenches the fires of altars, puts an end to warfare, teaches peace, enjoins moderation, expiates sins, sanctions married life, approves of temperance, and leads everyone to chastity. He also acts compassionately, enforces justice, places his seal on those who are perfect, carries out the doctrine of final rest, prophesies in explicit terms, expresses himself clearly, frequently reminds about the everlasting fire of punishment, constantly proclaims the kingdom of God, points to the abundance of heaven, promises unmistakable glory, and shows that sins are remitted by deeds.
>
> Put succinctly, the male principle is wholly truth, and the female principle is total falsehood. But whoever is born of male and female sometimes lies and sometimes speaks the truth. For the woman, in surrounding the white seed of the man with her blood, as with red fire, firmly supports her own weakness by bones not her own. Gratified by the temporary flowering of the flesh, and depriving the mind of its strength by ephemeral pleasure, she entices many to fornicate, and so lures them away from the splendid bridegroom yet to come. For each one is a bridge by receiving within oneself the white seed of the true teaching of the true prophet, and so becoming enlightened in mind and spirit. This is why one must heed only the prophet of truth, and must know that the bridegroom casts out of his kingdom every other seed of a teaching, because it leads to the sin of adultery. For those who know the secret know that adultery of the soul leads to death. If the soul receives other seeds into itself, it becomes forsaken by the spirit, as an adulterer and fornicator. The body divested of the soul dissolves into dust when the life-giving spirit is withdrawn from it. After the dissolution of the body, at the time of judgment the soul faces punishment commensurate with its sins, just as in human society someone caught in adultery is first kicked out of the house and then faces legal proceedings.[311]

This duality of the male and female principles thus corresponds to a twofold kind of prophecy. The two kinds are accordingly related as truth is to error, or as the world to come is related to the present world. The relation of the present world to the world to come is the type or model for the arrangement of the members of the syzygies.

> [For human beings God has changed the order of the syzygies.] What is lesser is first, and what is greater comes second, as with this world and eternity. The present world is transitory, and the world to come is everlasting. Ignorance comes first, then knowledge. So too is the order of the leaders of prophecy. The world now is female, and as the mother of children it bears the souls, whereas the world to come is male and, as a father, it receives the children. Thus even in this world there are the successive prophets who, as sons of the world to come, appear with the true knowledge. Had pious persons always known this secret, they would never have been led astray, into error.[312]

---

311. [*Ed.*] This very long quotation reproduces nearly all of *Homilies* 3.20–28 (*ANF* 8:242–43).

312. *Homilies* 2.15 [*ANF* 8:231, citation corrected].

In the *Clementine Homilies* we do not find this law of the syzygies applied in a thoroughgoing way to the epochs of world history and the history of religion, as regards their individual moments. The only historical application is that Adam is said to have reappeared at various times under different names, in Enoch before the flood, and after it in Noah, Abraham, Isaac, Jacob, and Moses, and ultimately in Christ. However the law of the syzygies is specifically mentioned in reference to Christ, and in this sense Christ is juxtaposed with his forerunner John, or Elijah.[313]

Just as the Lord had twelve apostles, which corresponds to the number in the twelve months of the solar year,[314] John thus had thirty men, which correlates with the moon's having thirty days in a lunar month. Their number included a woman named Helena, a feature that is not without significance. For a woman counts as half a man, so there are not fully thirty men, just as the moon completes its cycle of phases in less than a thirty-day month. The same feature repeats itself with Simon Magus and the Apostle Peter. (Simon was "the first and most esteemed" of the Baptist's followers, and after John's death, and after the foiled attempt by Dositheus [to succeed him], Simon took John's place.[315])

The author of the *Homilies* says, speaking in the person of Peter:

> By paying attention to these circumstances one can discern where Simon, who came to the Gentiles before I did, belongs in this sequence, as well as where I myself belong, for I am come after him. I followed him as light follows darkness, knowledge follows ignorance, healing follows sickness. Thus as our true prophet had said, first a deceiver must bring the false gospel, and only then, after the destruction of the holy place [the temple], can the true gospel be secretly spread to contradict the heresies to come. After this happens the Antichrist must arrive in turn, and only then does the true Christ, our Jesus, appear, whereupon, when the eternal light shines, all darkness will disappear. Since many do not know this law of the syzygies, they also do not know who Simon, my precursor, actually is. Had that been known about him, he would not have attracted believers. Because people did not know this about him, people gave him their undeserved belief. The one who does what hateful people do is loved; the enemy is taken to be a friend; he who is fire is regarded as light; the deceiver is listened to as the teacher of truth.[316]

---

313. *Homilies* 2.27. [*Ed.*] Matt 17:11–13 makes this identification of John with Elijah. In this footnote Baur also quotes the Greek of a statement from *Homilies* 2.23: "John, who was baptizing daily, was the forerunner of the Lord Jesus, according to the law of the syzygies" (*ANF* 8:233).

314. See *Excerpta ex scriptis Theodoti* (n. 2), 25: "The twelve apostles correspond to the Zodiac. As it governs the birth of things, so rebirth is subject to the apostles."

315. [*Ed.*] *Homilies* 2.33–34 (*ANF* 8:233).

316. *Homilies* 2.17–18 [*ANF* 8:232, correcting Baur's citation].

So the utmost criterion, the most universal criterion, the one by which the truth can be known and distinguished from error, is the rule of the syzygies that God has made evident to us in created nature.

## Polytheistic Paganism Is the Religion of Error and Sin

Judaism and paganism are the major results produced by true and false prophecy in human history, the phenomena in which these two kinds of prophecy have objectified themselves historically. Monotheistic Judaism is the religion of the only true God, whereas polytheistic paganism is the religion of error and sin.

### The Demonic Origins of Paganism

The author of the *Clementine Homilies* describes the origin of sin, and the predominance sin gained in the world because of the demons, as follows:

> After the only good God made all things as good, and after he had handed them over to the human being made in his image, this man, suffused with the divinity of his creator, lived as the true prophet who knew all things, in honoring the Father who had bestowed everything on him, and for the well-being of the sons born from him, as a true father does for his children. Filled with benevolence, he showed them the way leading to God's love, in order to love God and to be loved by God. He taught them what human actions will please the one God who rules over everything. He gave them an everlasting law that warfare does not eradicate, nor godless ones falsify, nor is kept hidden anywhere. Instead this law can be studied by everyone. As long as they obey this law they had everything in abundance, the finest fruits, long life, no sadness, no sickness, and the most undisturbed enjoyment of life together with the fairest changing of seasons.
>
> However, they still had no experience of evil, and were indifferent to the good things bestowed on them. They became ungrateful for this profusion of goods and this comfortable life, and took the view that there is no providence, since they had not gotten these good things by their own efforts, as the reward of virtue. Since they had not yet met with suffering or sickness, they disdained God, who was able to heal them. But their disdain directly resulted in the punishment that it naturally should incur, the removal of the benefits detrimental to them, and the introduction of ills as something salutary.
>
> The angels dwelling in the lowest region, who were displeased by human beings' ingratitude toward God, demanded that the spirits dwelling in the heavens allow them to come down into the lives of these humans in order to become human themselves and, by a better way of life, convicting those ungrateful to God by subjecting each one to the punishment he or she deserved. When their demands were met they transformed themselves, as godly natures

can do, into all possible shapes. They became precious stones, luxurious pearls, the finest purple robes, sparkling gold, and everything of the greatest value. They fell into the hands of some, onto the breasts of others, and willingly let people make off with them. They also changed themselves into four-footed animals, into snakes and fish and birds—into whatever they wanted to ...[317]

Having assumed these forms, they convicted thieves of their avarice and changed themselves into human natures in order, by living a holy life and showing its possibilities, to subject the thankless ones to their punishment. Yet because they were human in all respects, they also had human desires, and under their influence they had intercourse with women. As a result they lost their initial power and then were no longer in a position to change back to their own, originally pure, natures. The desires of the flesh in them were so overwhelming that their fire went out, so to speak. They plummeted on a godless path where they were now held fast in the bonds of the flesh, for they were no longer able to turn back to heaven. They also could no longer change themselves into precious stones and precious metals. So now, in order to please the women they loved, they pointed to things underground, to the metals and precious stones found in the earth. In doing so they instructed these women in various arts, teaching them magic, astronomy, herbalism, and other things the human mind would not have been able to discover. These included the arts of refining gold, silver, and other metals, and of dyeing garments in manifold ways. Everything serving for the adornment and pleasure of the female sex is something devised by these demons who are bound to the flesh.

The offspring of the demons' intercourse with women were called giants because of their enormous size [cf. Gen 6:1–4] ... God knew how brutish and coarse they were, and was well aware that a world created just to meet the needs of human beings would not have sufficed to satisfy them. So they would not have to resort to eating animals, which would be unnatural, God rained manna down to them. However, owing to their bastard nature they were not happy with [ritually] pure nourishment, but instead only desired blood [cf. Lev 3:17]. This is why they first of all required meat.

The people who were living alongside them soon followed their example ... When there were not enough beasts to eat, those bastard beings turned to eating human flesh. For it was but a short step to eating flesh like their own. So much shedding of blood produced foul air, which caused such sickness that people died early deaths. The earth was made so unclean that now, for the first time, it brought forth poisonous and noxious creatures. With everything going from bad to worse because of these brutish demons, God decided to do away with this evil leaven, lest the world to come be devoid of people who are saved, if each succeeding generation would be like its predecessors ...

---

317. [Ed.] This is an expression of the ancient Oriental idea that all the beings and forms of nature consist of spirits encased in them.

The consequence was the flood, with the righteous Noah [and his family] surviving. The souls of the giants who perished surpassed human souls, just as their bodies surpassed human bodies. These souls, being a new race, were called by a new name. They also received a righteous law that precisely defined their place in the world and how they should live . . . [The angel sent by the Lord said:] "Do not lord it over any human beings except those who, of their own free will, placed themselves at your service by praying to you, sacrificing and making libations to you, partaking at your table or otherwise doing something they ought not do, or shedding blood, or eating flesh, or consuming what is dead, strangled, or in some other way is unclean. You shall not have contact with those who hold to God's law. You shall flee from their presence. From the demons human beings shall put up with only what is just, what is the natural consequence of living as they do (ὁμοδίαιτος)." . . . If one does not pray to him, not even the prince of these demons can do anything contrary to God's law.[318]

[Baur's account continues, beginning with *Homilies* 9:3.]

After the flood Noah continued to live in harmony with his sons, as a king in the image of the one God. However, while monarchy produced unity, after Noah's death polyarchy made its appearance—war because one ruler cannot attack himself, but multiple rulers always have an excuse for fighting among themselves.. After Noah's death a number of his descendents strove to become dominant—one seeking to become victorious by war, another by deceit, and others by different means. One was from the lineage of Ham, who was the father of Mestren, from whom came the tribes of the Egyptians, and Babylonians, and the Persians.

Nebrod was born of this lineage. He was instructed in the traditions of the Magi, and was extremely resistant to God. The Greeks call him Zoroaster. He strove to gain supremacy, and by magical arts he compelled the world-governing star of the currently ruling evil principle to give him the supremacy. Since this star had the power to act on the one who had compelled him, he angrily poured down the fire of dominion in order to comply with the incantation, and to punish the one who had initially compelled him. The firestorm descending from heaven carried away Nebrod the magician, and owing to this event he then received the name Zoroaster. However, the foolish people at that time believed that, because of his friendship with God, his soul had been taken by the lightning flash. Because of this they buried what remained of his body, honored his grave in Persia by building a temple where the fire had come down, and worshiped him as a god. Following this example, the people there also buried others killed by lightning as those beloved of God, by honoring them with temples and with statues erected in their likeness. Local rulers then did the same thing. Most honored the graves of their favorites with temples

---

318. [*Ed.*] This very long quotation reproduces most of *Homilies* 8.10–20 (*ANF* 8:272–74).

and images, even if they had not been killed by lightning. They set up altars and commanded that these ones be prayed to as gods. As a result those who lived long after this time believed these figures were actually gods.

The one original kingdom divided fourfold in the following way. The Persians first took coals from the lightning that fell from heaven. They added fuel to the fire and honored the fire as the heavenly God. Their reason for doing so was that the fire first gave them the glory of a kingdom. According to them, the Babylonians stole coals from their fire, brought the coals to their own land, worshiped the fire, and then became rulers themselves. The Egyptians did likewise. In their own language they called the fire Ptah, who is the same as the Greek Hephaestus. Their first king also had this name. Local rulers likewise erected shrines and altars to honor fire, although most of these rulers lost their sway over the people.

Yet folk did not stop worshiping the images, for the magicians always knew how to keep people locked into this vain servitude. The magicians introduced festivals with sacrificial offerings and libations, with flutes and drummers. Being deceived, and now powerless, people did not forsake this cultus, since they found error far more congenial than truth.[319]

The cult of idols that came about in this way was at the same time also a cult of demons. The demons directed all their efforts to bringing human beings under their control because, as spiritual natures, they could only satisfy their desires through the medium of human beings (9.10 [ANF 8:277]). Thus the demons never showed their true nature. They always just used people's desires and passions for their own purposes, by linking themselves in this way to human souls. When demons have attached themselves to human souls and gained a controlling influence over them, these people take the promptings of the demons to be simply their own thoughts and desires (9.12ff. [ANF 8:277]). In order to deceive people, the demons take on various shapes as they like and then have themselves worshiped as gods by the credulous ones. They appear in people's dreams in the shape of gods; they terrify them, give them oracles, demand sacrifices, summon people to their feasts in order to devour their souls. For whoever sits at their table and gets caught up by their spirit, via food and drink, they make wholly subject to their will. To add to the error, in dreams they make such error visible in the shapes of their idols. For the idol lacks life and any divine spirit, so there is just the demon appearing and making use of such a shape. The supposed god is not appearing. Instead each person's soul constructs on its own the demonic shapes it sees, depending on how it is affected by its own fears and desires. That is why no such phenomena appear to the Jews. For of the prophecies and miraculous healings to which people appeal, some are sheer deceptions and others, to the extent they are the workings of the demons, are no proof of a truly divine power (9.14ff. [ANF 8:277–78]).

---

319. *Homilies* 9.3–7 [ANF 8:275–76].

## Paganism Is No Ethical Religion

The foregoing clearly shows the verdict about the religious worth of paganism, as seen from the standpoint of the Pseudo-Clementine system. The distinctive feature of this system as a whole is that it investigates, much more precisely and specifically, how paganism relates to Judaism and Christianity, a topic the other Gnostic systems never actually address directly. It is not satisfied merely to indicate the causes and principles lying behind the origin of paganism, for the Pseudo-Clementine system also seeks, from the consequences ensuing from paganism, to arrive, in a detailed way, at a general verdict about paganism, and to establish as precisely as possible the perspective from which to spell out paganism's relation to the absolute religion.

This issue forms the main contents of *Homilies* 4–6. Here, right at the beginning of the investigation of this issue, we find enunciated this general verdict: "I say forthwith that all the learning of the Greeks is a most dangerous fabrication by an evil demon" (4.12 [*ANF* 8:253]). The basis for this verdict is above all as follows:

> They have introduced many gods of their own, indeed wicked ones subject to every kind of propensity and passion, which is why someone who wants to act like them may do so shamelessly, since, as people typically do, he can of course take as his model the wicked, immoral habits of the gods of mythology. But whoever is shamelessly immoral also has no hope of repenting … Others have introduced the notion of fate (εἱμαρμένη), the so-called "genesis" (or original cause, the predestination dependent on one's hour of birth) by which everything a human being suffers or does is predetermined. This amounts to the same thing. For if someone believes that everything he suffers or does is predetermined, then he does not take sinning seriously, and when he has sinned he has no remorse or regrets, for he can excuse everything as something his origins compelled him to do. Because these origins cannot be changed, he has no cause to be ashamed of the sins he commits. Others introduce blind chance and maintain that everything just continues in its course without anything overseeing and governing it. This is the most pernicious opinion of all. For if no one stands at the head of the whole and makes provision for everything, and allows each person to share in what he or she deserves, then you can fearlessly and shamelessly do anything at all. It is implausible that those who think this way will lead a moral life, since they foresee no risk to themselves that could have moved them to change their ways or convert.[320]

Paganism accordingly attests to its demonic origin by the fact that it lacks any ethical motivation for one's conduct, and this of course seems to be the case. We may consider this feature of paganism according to its popular aspect or to its philosophical aspect.

As for the popular aspect, paganism as folk religion, it is sufficient to recall the immoral conduct of the gods so amply displayed in the Greek myths, the amours of

---

320. *Homilies* 4.12–13 [*ANF* 8:253–54].

Zeus, Poseidon, and so forth. Because of them such a religion proves to be totally unfit for peoples' moral upbringing. In whoever from childhood on is steeped in these myths, with their import, the godless acts of those supposed deities form such an ingrowth that in a person's mature years they bear their fruit as an evil seed implanted in the soul. They lay down such strong roots that they can no longer be eradicated from those who, when grown men, understand how pernicious they are, since people are certainly in the habit of sticking with what they got accustomed to in childhood. Therefore, since the force of habit is just as great as the force of nature, it is hard to internalize what is good when the basis for doing so has not been implanted in the soul from the beginning. Hence it is better by far to know nothing at all about the Greek myths, as we see from the rustics who, by not imbibing Greek culture also commit fewer sins (4.18–19 [*ANF* 8:254–55]).

However, suppose one appeals to the fact that all the things these myths recount about the gods did not actually take place; that instead it all has a properly philosophical meaning only knowable by means of allegory. "The wisest of the ancients, men who had by hard labor learned all truth, kept the path of knowledge hid from those who had no taste for lessons in divine things" (6.2 [*ANF* 8:262–63]). As the writer of *Homily* 6 says about this statement, what it shows is that the pagan religion can make no claim to having the features of a true religion. The allegorical view presupposes that the world arose from a condition of chaos; that in the beginning everything was disorderly and internally undifferentiated; that it surged hither and yon in blind motion until finally this disorderly motion had become orderly motion, the elements separated, and an organic nature took shape.[321]

If we think about the cosmos coming to be in this way, then Chronos and Rhea are time and matter respectively, Pluto is the sediment settling below, Poseidon is the moist substance floating above, and Zeus is the warm principle rising upon high in the purest ether, ruling over everything. The fetters of Chronos are the bonds holding heaven and earth together, and the severing of his sexual organs signifies the separation and segregation of the elements whereby all individual beings gain their own independent existence. Time itself no longer begets anything, because what it has begotten now takes its own natural course. Aphrodite, who emerged from the depths of the sea, is the procreative power of the moist element that arouses sexual desire and perfects the beauty of the world.[322]

The banquet Zeus held at the marriage of Thetis and Peleus portrays the world. The twelve deities are the twelve signs of the zodiac supporting the power of the Fates. Prometheus is the foresight or providence that gave rise to everything. Peleus is the

---

321. [*Ed.*] In this note Baur cites *Homilies* 6.4 and 6.12, and provides Greek that seems to combine wording from each of these passages: "The Demiurge surrounded the egg (or: surrounded it without breaking it). When it was broken the masculo-feminine Phanes leaped forth." Phanes, a bisexual Orphic deity, is the creator of all things. He was born from an egg produced by Chronos.

322. [*Ed.*] A paraphrase of *Homilies* 6.12–13 (*ANF* 8:265).

clay collected from the earth and mixed with the daughter of Nereis, that is, with water, to produce human beings. The first one of them came from the mixing of earth and water, and thus was not begotten. Instead he was formed as a grown man and was named Achilles. At a ripe old age, according to a dubious account, when his desire for Polyxena was aroused he died from a serpent's venom, although he actually died from a wound in the sole of his feet.[323]

The significance of Hera, Athena, Aphrodite, Eris, the apple, Hermes, and the judgment of the shepherd, is as follows. Hera is moral dignity. Athena is valor. Aphrodite is sensuous pleasure. Hermes is communication. The shepherd, Paris, is crude, irrational desire. When, in maturity, the reason that nourishes the soul is still crude (βάρβαρος) and, disregarding its own advantage, rejecting valor and decency, it just gives in to pleasure and prizes it alone, in order to gain its delights, this can only result in its own destruction and the ruin of what is its own. The outcome of bad judgment is the enjoyment of pleasure [for its own sake]. Eris is wicked contentiousness. Because of their opulence, the golden apples of the Hesperides signify riches that occasionally entice even prudent figures such as Hera, and lure even valorous ones such as Athena, to contentiousness about unseemly matters, and destroy the beauty of the soul as that happened to Aphrodite. As a rule, riches lead to evil controversies for everyone. That is why Heracles, the slayer of the serpent that was possessing and guarding riches, is the truly philosophical intellect that ranges about free from all the world's evils, indwells souls, and vanquishes those it runs up against, namely people, as Heracles vanquishes fearsome bears, or cowardly stags, or wild boars, or the many-headed Hydra. All the other narratives about the labors of Heracles are also symbols of the moral power of the mind or spirit.[324]

However, even if someone interprets the ancient myths allegorically in this fashion, he must above all be very curious as to why those wise and judicious men took what they could have presented piously and usefully, in an open and undisguised way, and instead portrayed it veiled in obscure symbols and indecent myths—ones that have led nearly everyone astray, as though these myths had been devised by an evil demon. Either these myths are not symbols and allegories but instead tell of actual sins by the gods, so then they should never have been given to human beings who would imitate such behavior; or the myths are sheer allegory, containing nothing about what the gods have actually done, so then their shortcoming is in any event that because of their immoral form these myths induce people to sin, and indeed to sin in a very disrespectful way against the gods whose existence they presuppose. For this reason it cannot have been wise men who concocted these myths to dress up what is intrinsically good conduct in such a despicable form. Instead it can only have been demons who did this, so those who wanted to take their betters as their model would imitate

---

323. [*Ed.*] A paraphrase of *Homilies* 6.14 (*ANF* 8:265).

324. *Homilies* 6.15–16 [*ANF* 8:265]. [*Ed.*] In the text Baur includes the Greek from 6.16, that all these examples are "hidden references to the mind's virtue (or valor)."

the deeds of these alleged gods—parricide; infanticide; incest with one's mother, daughter, or sister; adultery; and all the rest. Godless people believe all these stories are true, so they can be without shame when they do the same things. As opposed to this, respect for the gods demands that, even in cases where the gods had actually done what the myths say they did, one should cloak immoral behavior in some decent way instead of dressing up intrinsically good conduct in such an immoral form where its allegorical meaning must be hard to recognize. The price of allegory is that, while those who do recognize the meaning after much effort are preserved from error, those who do not understand it are led to ruin. Of course the allegorical interpretations may well be praiseworthy. Nevertheless it is more likely that the myths people tell about godless deeds have robbed the gods of their honor [6.17–18 (ANF 8:265–66)].

The poetical allegories never carry through in a consistent way. Thus the poet presents the world's creation as due to nature, but then to mind. The initial motion and mixing of the elements arose from nature, yet mind's foresight arranged it. If they say that nature brought about everything, they cannot explain the artistry of the creation and thus look for assistance from yet another principle, the foresight of mind. But this raises two questions. If the world has come about by chance, from natural causes, where did it get its orderly arrangement? That could only be the effect of an exceptionally superior mind. Yet if, as one must assume, it is mind that has mixed and arranged everything, how can it all have come about by chance? [6.19 (ANF 8:266)].

Those who have transformed the deeds of the gods into immoral-sounding allegories got caught up in a major difficulty, since their allegories did away with the gods as existing beings when they made the gods into substances of the world. Hence people say, with more plausibility, that their gods were evil magicians or godless human beings who, via their magical shapes, committed adultery and corrupted morality. Since the ancients were ignorant of magic, they took these magicians to be gods because of what they did. In various lands and cities people point to the graves of these so-called gods—for instance, in the Caucasus Mountains the grave of Saturn, a savage tyrant who killed his own children, in Crete the grave of Zeus, and so on. Manifestly these were therefore men who were accorded divine honors long after their death, just as a Hector also receives divine honors in Troy, and an Achilles does from those who live on the island of Leuce. Still today the Egyptians revere a human being as god even before his death. Most ridiculous is the worship of birds, serpents, and animals of all kinds. Thus most people think and act ignorantly. Yet nothing is more disgraceful than the scene where the father of the gods and of human beings is portrayed having intercourse with Leda [8.20–23 (ANF 8:266–67)].

The very concept of God itself makes it clear that the four original elements cannot be God, nor can the mixing or the engendering or the entire visible totality of things—not the sediment coalescing to form Hades, nor the water flowing above it, nor the fiery substance, nor the atmosphere extending down to us. For if they were separate these four elements could not have mixed together to produce a living being unless there were some great artificer. But if, on the other hand, they were always bound together, then even in this case there would have been a mind whose artistry produced the harmonious linkage of the members and parts that properly belong to an organic or structured being. For this great organic being that is the world also has everything that an organic being must have. Of necessity, therefore, there must be an unengendered artificer who either brought together the separate elements, or artistically blended the already combined elements to generate a living being, and so to bring about from all of this a perfect whole. For a work of wisdom cannot possibly be accomplished without there being a higher mind involved in it. Erotic life cannot be the artificer of all things, nor can desire or power or anything else of this sort, since these are all impulsive and subject to change. God, however, is not moved by anything else, is not altered by time or by nature, and is never reducible so as not to be.[325]

## Refutation of the Reasons for Upholding Pagan Religion

Pagan religion is hardly capable of satisfying human beings' religious concerns. Even if it rises above its polytheism, paganism still sticks to two equally pernicious worldviews, fatalism, and the doctrine of contingency [as opposed to providence].[326] The idea of an intelligent creator of the world is entirely foreign to paganism.

It is the Jewish religion's own idea. Hence this religion is consistent with the true idea of religion, whereas paganism is not. So there can be no doubt about the Jewish religion meriting unconditional precedence over paganism, since paganism lacks all the marks of true religion. All the same, certain reasons are advanced that supposedly serve to uphold pagan religion and to maintain its autonomy.

People make it a fundamental principle that it is the most godless thing to forsake the customs of one's fathers and adopt some others instead. But this cannot be held to unconditionally. The customs of one's fathers are only to be adhered to if they are religious in nature but are to be abandoned if they are irreligious. Otherwise the son of a godless parent who wishes to be pious would necessarily have not been allowed to be pious. There is a huge difference between truth and custom (ἀλήθεια and συνήθεια). Truth is found when one sincerely seeks for it. But once something has become the accepted custom, whether it be true or false, it automatically becomes unchallenged and people neither satisfy themselves as to its truth nor trouble themselves about its falsity. People base their belief not on actual findings, but on their preconceptions, since they trust in good outcomes from the opinions of their forefathers. One does not easily abandon the ways of one's fathers, even when their foolishness and absurdity are readily apparent (4.11 [ANF 8:253]).

---

325. *Homilies* 6.24–25 [ANF 8:267]. [*Ed.*] Baur simply has one citation at this point, *Homilies* 6.1–24, to cover this long section he has presented by paraphrasing and abridging these chapters, rather than subdividing it with multiple citations as we have done.

326. *Homilies* 4.12–13; 14.3 [corrected] and 5; 15.4.

In justifying polytheism, people often say that of course there is only one supreme lord, but the others are also gods, just as there is one Caesar, but under him there are procurators, consuls, governors, commanders of a thousand men, commanders of hundreds, and of tens. These are related to Caesar as those gods are related to the one great God. They are of course subordinate to him, but are gods ruling over us. However, this comparison directly proves how erroneous their entire conception is. One may not call anyone other than the real Caesar by that name. It is even less allowable to apply the term "god" to any other being, if one is not to insult the name given to honor the monarchy (10.14–15 [ANF 8:282]).

People also seek to defend idolatry in similar fashion. But whoever holds to the true concept of God knows that no other being can have a nature like that exclusive to God. What is exclusive to God is his being the creator of all things and the most perfect one; his power, because he has made everything; his greatness, because he is the infinite one, as opposed to what is finite; his form, because he is the most beautiful or most excellent one; his bliss, because he is the most blessed one; his mind and spirit, because he is the supreme one. Nothing created can compare with him. Not even the world can be God, because the world is created and is not absolute. Thus how much less so can parts of the world be given the name "god"?

Many of these defenders of idolatry then say that they do not include gold, silver, wood, and stone among the objects of religious worship, for they know that these things are simply lifeless material and the artistic products of mortal men. But they do call "god" the spirit present within these objects. Thus when they are convinced that what is visible does not suffice, they have recourse to the invisible. But how can one demonstrate that there is a divine spirit in lifeless images, since everything perceptible about them is evidence to the contrary? (10.19–24 [ANF 8:283–84]).

## Monotheistic Judaism Is the True Religion and Is, As Such, Identical with Christianity

All of this abundantly exhibits the falsehood and internal emptiness of pagan religion, and the absolute truth of the Jewish religion. This huge contrast has deep roots in the history of religion. It is evident throughout this entire domain, and in ever-recurring new forms.

Judaism and paganism stand, respectively, as truth and error, as do monotheistic religion and demonic-polytheistic religion. However, within Judaism itself there is true religion and false religion, and Judaism and polytheism have come into contact in many ways and become intertwined. What we said previously about the contrast between true and false prophecy also comes into play again here. Paganism is a consequence of false prophecy, as is false Judaism too. Everything typical of false prophecy in Judaism appears to be a pagan element that has made inroads into Judaism.[327] This antithesis between Judaism and paganism is also the setting for how the Pseudo-Clementine system sees the relationship of Christianity to Judaism. The great contrast between Judaism and paganism has its mirror image in the vast agreement between Judaism and Christianity. These two religions are even completely one when it comes to their actual essence and contents. The reason they differ is simply because of the influence paganism has exerted on Judaism. We have to consider the relation of Christianity to Judaism in light of these two aspects.

### Identity of Persons: Adam and Christ

The first light shed on the point that Judaism and Christianity are one comes from the identity of the persons who are the representatives and bearers of the two religions. Adam, the primal man created by God and filled with the breath of God, is also the original source of all religion and revelation. On this view each epoch in the series of antitheses that move the history of the world and the history of religion forward, by periodically obscuring the truth and in turn letting it re-emerge in its clear light, can only be a return to the pure, primal religion already revealed through Adam.

But the writer of the *Clementine Homilies* is not satisfied merely with this self-identity of the truth that emerges anew at different times. In order to give his identity an even firmer foundation, he also sees, in the persons who renew the primal religion and primal revelation, a reappearance of the same Adam who, as the primal man, was also the original instrument of the deity. The number seven, for the completion of the entire course taken by the world, is based in the nature of God.[328] So too there are seven pillars of the world (18.14), which are the bearers of the eternal truth extending throughout all the periods of the world. These are the seven prophets worthy of the most perfect favor of the just God. They include Adam who was created by God, Enoch who "walked with God" (Gen 5:22), the righteous Noah, Abraham the "friend" of God (Isa 41:8), Isaac, Jacob, and Moses.[329]

Christ attaches himself to these prophets, giving unity to the seven. In other words it is always just the same one true prophet, the man created by God and endowed with the Holy Spirit of Christ, who traverses the world's course from its beginning with the name of this figure changing from one period to the next, "until arriving at his own appointed time, and anointed with God's mercy for his efforts, he shall enjoy perpetual rest" (3.20 [*ANF* 8:242]).

---

327. In the true religion some sacrificial offerings are simply unacceptable, and the true prophet takes his stance by doing away with burnt offerings, bloody sacrifices, libations of wine, and fire altars. *Homilies* 7.3 and 3.26.

328. *Homilies* 17.8–9 [*ANF* 8:320]. [*Ed.*] Here the number seven gets its initial importance from the seven days of creation.

329. *Homilies* 18.13–14, 17.4 [*ANF* 8:327–28, 8:318–19].

## Identity of the Contents

The two religions are also the same when it comes to their contents. The most definitive expression of this view that Christianity is the same as Judaism is the contention that the essence of religion consists of one's conduct, of obeying the commandments given by God. This is a view most closely connected with the essence of Mosaic religion and its way of specifying a human being's relation to God.

The main passage addressing this point is *Homilies* 8.4–7:

> The fact that many are called is to be attributed not to those who are called, but simply to God, who calls them and causes them to come.[330] Because of this they have no claim to a reward, for it is not their own doing but the work of the one who has caused them to come. Yet if, after being called, they do what is good as their own work, then they will receive a reward because of it. For even the Hebrews who trust in Moses but do not heed what he commands are not blessed unless they do heed what he commands . . . Reward is rightfully given to those who do what is right. For there would have been no need for the presence of Moses or Jesus if people, on their own, had wanted to be mindful of what is in accord with reason. One cannot gain salvation by believing in teachings or calling someone "lord." That is why Jesus is hidden or veiled from those Hebrews who have received Moses as their teacher, and why Moses is hidden from those who believe in Jesus. Since the teaching of these two is one and the same thing, God accepts someone who believes in just one of these two teachers. However, the reason for believing in a teaching is doing what God commands . . . If the Hebrews, not knowing Jesus, just do what Moses has commanded them and do not hate the one they do not know, then he who has hidden Jesus from them does not condemn them for not knowing Jesus. Conversely, if those among the Gentiles, not knowing Moses, just do what Jesus has commanded them and do not hate the one they do not know, then he who has hidden Moses from them does not condemn them for not knowing Moses. One gains nothing from calling the teacher "lord" but not doing what someone who serves him has to do . . . Thus good works are altogether necessary. But if someone is granted the privilege of recognizing both Moses and Jesus, and has become aware that both of them have proclaimed one and the same teaching, then this person, regarded as a man rich in God, has come to see that, in time, what is old is new, and what is new is old.[331]

---

330. [*Ed.*] This is an allusion to Matt 8:11: "Many will come from east and west and will eat with Abraham and Isaac and Jacob in the kingdom of heaven." See also Luke 13:29. Baur's text then omits the next sentence of the homily, which quotes the textual variant added to Matt 20:16: "Many are called but few are chosen."

331. *Homilies* 8.4–7 [*ANF* 8:271]). [*Ed.*] In the text Baur also includes in parenthesis the Greek for the last part of this passage, from "as a man rich in God" to the end. He then adds that perhaps it is a play on Matt 13:52: "Therefore every scribe who has been trained for the kingdom of heaven is like the master of a household who brings out of his treasure what is new and what is old."

On this view, belief is an acceptance of the truth God communicates to human beings, but an acceptance that is in principle still ineffective by itself. Belief or faith is a person's passive relation to God working outwardly on him or her. One has a truly living relation to God only if one expresses in deeds what one believes and acknowledges as truth. Thus the substantial contents of religion are the commandments that make objective religion become subjective when one obeys them.

In this respect there is no difference between Jew and Christian, inasmuch as both obey the same divine commandments. This factor offsets what is otherwise a great contrast between the Jew and the Gentile. The Gentile who obeys the law is a Jew, and the Jew who does not obey the law is a Gentile, because the true worshiper of God is simply the one who does what the law enjoins (11.16). The writer of the *Clementine Homilies* of course saw Marcion's greatly emphasized antitheses between law and gospel, or justice and goodness, as annulled, and offset by the fact that, even in this regard, Christianity could not have taken any essential precedence over Judaism. *Homily* 4.13 says the religion of the Jews fully measures up to the true concept of religion, since it teaches that there is one Father and creator of this whole world, one who is good and just by nature, good inasmuch as he forgives the sins of those who repent, and just inasmuch as, after they repent, he rewards people as each one's deeds deserve.[332]

## The Difference between Judaism and Christianity: Christianity Is the Reform That Purifies and Enlarges the Judaism That Is Adulterated and Limited

Given this essential identity of Judaism with Christianity, what then sets these two religions apart? The answer is found in *Homilies* 1:18. This passage reads as follows:

> In various ways God's will has been unknown. Wretched instruction, perverse ways of life, deleterious societies, despicable customs, and false opinions all made for the prevalence of error. The results have been impunity, unbelief, lewdness, avarice, vanity, and a thousand other evils of this kind that have filled the world like a thick smoke filling a house and obscuring the faces of its inhabitants, not letting them look up that they may recognize God, the creator of the world, from its reflection of his nature, and so become acquainted with his will. That is why the friends of truth who are inside this house, must wholeheartedly cry out, with their truth-loving sensibility, so that someone within this smoke-filled house will approach the door and open it, to let the sun's light in and let the smoke from the fire out. This man who comes to their aid is the true prophet, who alone can enlighten people's souls so they can see the way to eternal salvation with their own eyes. (1.18–19 [ANF 8:227])

---

332. *Homilies* 4.13 [ANF 8:254]. See also 3.6.

Thus the prophet needs to appear, because the truth has been obscured.

The ultimate causes of this obscurity are the sins by which human beings make themselves servants of sin, thus becoming subject to all kinds of suffering and, consonant with God's righteous judgments, deprived of all that is good. This is why, from his superabundant mercy, God sent his prophets, so that, along with the initial goods we received, we would also share in the eternal life to come. His prophets teach us how to be of a right mind and how we must act, that is, how we have to worship the God who created the world (10.4 [ANF 8:280]). Hence although Christianity simply consists of the same worship of the world's creator as that already provided for in Judaism, Christianity is nevertheless a completely separate revelation of divine grace. Except that divine grace in the Christian system is merely a matter of a new imparting of truth, not the imparting of a new moral power and the creation of a new spiritual life, for people in a state of sin always retain free will.

Knowledge of truth must be imparted anew, since even in Judaism it had indeed become quite uncertain. If the scriptural attestations to the truth contain much that is false, is unworthy of the deity, then what is required, first and foremost, is a criterion for separating what is false from what is true. While scripture has become uncertain because truth and falsity are intermixed, divine providence nevertheless already provides, in the first book of the written law, a passage clearly indicating what in scripture is true and what in it is false. This passage is Gen 49:9-12. If we know the one who has come from the tribe of Judah, after a ruler's failure, one said to have been expected by the nations, one in whose coming is seen the fulfilling of the scripture containing this prophecy, and if we believe this one's teaching, then we can recognize what in scripture is true and what is false.[333] Therefore one must learn from him how to understand the scriptures.

He himself says that truth and falsity are mixed together in scripture, when, in Matt 22:29 and Mark 12:24, he answers the Sadducees: "You are wrong, because you know neither the scriptures nor the power of God."[334] The response that they do not know the truth of scripture presupposes that there is also falsehood in it. The expression, "Be ye prudent moneychangers,"[335] by finding counterfeit sayings alongside

---

333. [Ed.] This is a paraphrase of *Homilies* 3.49 (ANF 8:247), although Baur does not cite it. As such it is a reference to Gen 49:9-12, from a lengthy prophecy about what is to be anticipated from each of the tribes descending from the twelve sons of Jacob. Verses 10-12, which function for the *Homilies* to foretell the coming of Jesus, read as follows: "The scepter shall not depart from Judah, nor the ruler's staff from between his feet, until tribute comes to him; and the obedience of the peoples is his. Binding his foal to the vine and his donkey's colt to the choice vine, he washes his garments in wine and his robe in the blood of grapes; his eyes are darker than wine, and his teeth whiter than milk."

334. [Ed.] In the text and in a footnote Baur gives the Greek for this statement by Jesus, as it appears in Matthew. The passage in Mark says the same thing.

335. This is an alleged saying of Christ not found in our Gospels. See J.-B. Cotelier, in his edition of the *Apostolic Constitutions* 2.36; Heinichen, in his edition of Eusebius, *Ecclesiastical History* 3:389, Excursus IX ad Eus. H. L. 7.7. The quotation that follows this one in the text is also apocryphal. [Ed.] See *Homilies* 3.50 (ANF 8:247-48).

genuine ones, likewise proves this point, as does his statement: "Do ye not perceive that which is reasonable in the scriptures?" This is his way of referring to the understanding of those who sincerely are friends of truth. Notwithstanding the scriptures themselves, Jesus points to the scribes and teachers and says he must regard them as those who know the truth of the law.[336] However, the fact that he said "I have not come to abolish the law" (Matt 5:17), and yet manifestly did that very thing, proves that what he abolished did not belong to the law. And when he said, "Until heaven and earth pass away, not one letter, not one stroke of a letter, will pass from the law" (Matt 5:18), we see that what passes away before heaven and earth have done so cannot have belonged to the law.

As long as heaven and earth have endured, sacrificial offerings, kingdoms, the prophecies of those born of women, and other such things, as institutions and practices, not originating from God, have passed away. Thus we have the statement of Matt 15:13: "Every plant that my heavenly Father has not planted will be uprooted." This is why the true prophet says about himself: "I am the gate. Whoever enters by me will be saved" (John 10:9). It is because there is no other salvific teaching. Hence he calls out, "Come to me, all you that are weary" (Matt 11:28), that is, those who see truth for themselves and do not find it. And again, "My sheep hear my voice" (John 10:27); and "Search and you will find" (Matt 7:7), which shows us that the truth does not lie open before us. Also, a "voice from heaven said, 'This is my Son, the Beloved, with whom I am well pleased'" (Matt 3:17). As further proof, he says that the prophets they call their teachers have erred; that of course they longed for the truth but died without coming to know it (Matt 13:17). Also, he called himself the one Moses prophesied about (John 5:46; Deut 18:15).[337] So it is impossible to come into possession of saving truth apart from his teaching, even though one seeks it one's whole life long, where what one seeks is not to be found. It was, and is, found only in the teaching of our Jesus.

Since Jesus knew what in the law is true, he responded to the Sadducees about the question as to why Moses allowed marriage with seven widows: "It was because you were so hard-hearted that Moses allowed you to divorce your wives, but from the beginning it was not so. The one who made them at the beginning made them man and wife."[338] To those who believe, as scripture teaches, that God swears [takes

336. [*Ed.*] Matt 23:2–3: "The scribes and the Pharisees sit on Moses' seat; therefore, do whatever they teach you and follow it."

337. [*Ed.*] John 5:46: "If you believed Moses, you would believe me, for he wrote about me." Deut 18:15: "The Lord your God will raise up for you a prophet like me from among your own people; you shall heed such a prophet." These last two paragraphs are drawing on *Homilies* 3.50–54 (*ANF* 8:247–48).

338. [*Ed.*] Here Baur has run together two separate incidents and thus created a confusing text we have not tried to repair. He cites at this point Matt 22:23; 19:8; and 19:11. The incident about "seven" is in 22:23–32, where Sadducees, who deny any resurrection, refer to Deut 25:5ff., where Moses says a man whose brother dies shall marry the brother's widow. Thus the Sadducees try to trap Jesus by asking him about a hypothetical situation where a woman is married to seven brothers in succession,

an oath], Jesus says: "Let your word be 'Yes, Yes,' or 'No, No'; anything more than this comes from the evil one" (Matt 5:37).[339] To those who say that Abraham, Isaac, and Jacob are dead, Jesus says, "He is not God of the dead, but of the living" (Matt 22:32). To those who suppose that God tempts, Jesus says the wicked one is the tempter, the one who also tempted him. To those who believe God does not have foreknowledge, he says: "Your Father knows what you need before you ask him" (Matt 6:8; cf. 6:32). To those who believe that, according to scripture, God does not see all things, Jesus says: "Whenever you pray, go into your room and shut the door and pray to your Father who is in secret; and your Father who sees in secret will reward you" (Matt 6:6). To those who believe that God is not good, Jesus says, as scripture does: "Is there anyone among you who, if your child asks for bread, will give a stone? Or if the child asks for a fish, will give a snake? If you then, who are evil, know how to give good gifts to your children, how much more will your Father in heaven give good things to those who ask him!" (Matt 7:9–11). To those who maintain that God is in the temple, Jesus says: "Do not swear at all, either by heaven, for it is the throne of God, or by the earth, for it is his footstool" (Matt 5:34–35). To those who imagine that God is pleased by sacrificial offerings, God says, "I desire mercy, not sacrifice" (Matt 9:13 and 12:7), and that he desires knowledge of himself, not burnt offerings (Hos 6:6). To those who call him evil, because of the scriptures, Jesus says: "Why do you call me good? No one is good but God alone" (Mark 10:18; cf. Matt 19:17; Luke 18:19); and, "Be good and merciful, like your Father in heaven, for he makes his sun rise on the evil and the good, and sends rain on the righteous and on the unrighteous" (Matt 5:44–45). To those misled into supposing that there are many gods, he said, as the scriptures do: "Hear, O Israel: the Lord our God, the Lord is one" (Mark 12:29).[340]

Someone who examines the contents of scripture and is guided by these statements cannot regard as true anything of an irreligious nature that is said against God, or against the righteous ones mentioned in scripture. Thus we cannot believe that Adam, created by God, was a transgressor of the law; that Noah, found to be more righteous than all others, was drunk; that Abraham had three wives, since because of his moral stature he was blessed with many offspring; or that Jacob, the father of the twelve tribes, who made known the coming of our Lord, was someone with four wives, two of them being sisters; or that Moses was a murderer or learned from an

---

all of whom died with the last six having followed Moses' rule by marrying her in turn. The Sadducees ask: whose wife is she in the resurrection? But the question Baur has in the text is from Matt 19:8, followed by part of 19:4 (where the statement is "male and female," not "man and wife"). Matthew 19 is where Pharisees ask Jesus whether, and when, divorce is lawful. In doing this, Baur is paraphrasing *Homilies* 3.54 (*ANF* 8:248), which is responsible for the original confusion. But Baur should have pointed this out, rather than leaving the reader puzzled.

339. [*Ed.*] See Deut 23:5–7, on making a vow that God requires one to fulfill.

340. [*Ed.*] This last and lengthy compilation of New Testament passages reproduces the contents of *Homilies* 3.55–57 (*ANF* 8:248–49). Baur just has the single citation, *Homilies* 3.48–57, at this point, rather than having subdivided this part with multiple citations as we have done.

idolatrous priest how to administer justice—he who was God's prophet of the law for all time, and who was declared to be a faithful steward because of his real insight (2.52 [*ANF* 8:238]).

No matter how important this kind of discernment makes Christianity, it is not something belonging specifically and exclusively to Christianity. As we see from *Homilies* 3.28, it was also possible to separate truth from falsity in scripture before Christianity had appeared. That is why, in Matt 23:2, Christ himself says: "The scribes and the Pharisees sit on Moses' seat; therefore, do whatever they teach you and follow it." He says this about them as those who are entrusted with the keys of the kingdom, that is, with the knowledge that alone can open the gates of life through which alone someone can enter into eternal life. But he adds that, although they [the scribes and Pharisees] possess the keys, they nevertheless do not want to give them to those who wish to get in.[341] This is why Christ placed himself on the seat, like a father for the sake of his children, in order to proclaim what has been handed down from the beginning, secretly to the worthy ones. In order to extend his compassion to the Gentiles as well, and from pity for the souls of everyone, he did not spare his own blood. But what troubled him the most is that the very ones for whose sake, as his children, he took up the struggle, treated him in hostile fashion because of their ignorance. Nevertheless he loved those who hated him, wept for those who did not believe him, blessed those who reviled him, and prayed for those who were his enemies.

This accordingly constitutes the essential difference between Judaism and Christianity: the fact that what the teachers of the law who occupied Moses' seat had reserved as exclusively their own, became the shared possession of Jews and Gentiles. In other words, Jewish particularism expanded into Christian universalism.

## Practices and Institutions Renewed by Christianity

We should take note here of what the author of these Clementine writings teaches about several external practices and institutions said to serve for sanctioning and securing the relationship of human beings to God the creator, a relationship Christianity has renewed, just as Judaism portrays this relationship. They include the following.

1. *Baptism*. Baptism is the means ordained by God for renouncing paganism.[342] It is the necessary condition by which alone one can obtain forgiveness of sins and future blessedness. Indeed it is already an external, positive command of God that one be baptized. If one willingly subjects oneself to this command, then God regards sins previously committed as merely due to ignorance. However if one does not heed God's summons, or heeds it just hesitantly, then one yields to one's own will and resists

---

341. [*Ed.*] Matt 23:13: "Woe to you, scribes and Pharisees, hypocrites! For you lock people out of the kingdom of heaven."

342. *Homilies* 13.9 [*ANF* 8:302]. The means for renouncing Hellenism (ἀφελληνισθῆναι).

the divine will. Therefore baptism has religious value because it is commanded by God, and is a good work.

However, baptism also has an internal, rational relation to concomitant factors. Rebirth from water is a transformation of birth stemming from sensuous desire. That is why (according to John 3:5)[343] one cannot become blessed without it. For in baptism there is something compassionate from the beginning that hovers over the water and, by the threefold invocation of blessing, frees the person baptized from future punishment and, following baptism, offers the good works of the baptized person as gifts to God. Water is the only thing that can extinguish the force of the fire. Whoever does not want to be baptized still has the spirit that fears the water, which hinders one from approaching the living water for one's salvation.[344]

Just as water puts out fire, baptism is the powerful antidote to the fiery nature of the demons and to the spirit's lurking within people.[345] Thus baptism frees human beings from domination by demons, but also brings them into the closest fellowship with God. Water engenders everything but has its action initiated by spirit, while spirit originates with God the creator of all. So this quite naturally provides our conception of coming to God via baptism. Having been born again by the first-born water, we know our origins and are established as heirs of this parentage that has engendered us for immortality.[346]

2. *The Monarchal Understanding of the Church*. This understanding is supposed to serve as support for the worship of the one God. Monarchy brings about order and peace, whereas wanting all to rule and not subordinate themselves to just one is what leads to division and ultimately to complete dissolution. Because there are many kings all about the earth, there is continual warfare, for the wish to rule over the others

---

343. [*Ed.*] Jesus speaks of "being born from above" (John 3:3). He responds to Nicodemus' question about this baptism: "Very truly, I tell you, no one can enter the kingdom of heaven without being born of water and Spirit. What is born of the flesh is flesh, and what is born of the Spirit is spirit" (John 3:5–6).

344. *Homilies* 11.25–26 [*ANF* 8:289–90]. [*Ed.*] In the text in parentheses Baur follows his German for "water fearing," i.e., hydrophobia, with the Greek of the original: τῆς λύσσης φέρες πνεῦμα (rage-bearing spirit).

345. *Homilies* 9.11 and 19 [*ANF* 8:277, 279–80].

346. *Homilies* 11.24 [*ANF* 8:289]. The writer of the *Homilies* has very nicely interwoven into his historical presentation the idea that Christianity lets human beings recognize their origins; in other words, that it leads one to true self-awareness. The writer built this into his content by having Clement, following his baptism (11.35), rediscover and recognize his mother (12.23), his brothers (13.3), and his father (14.9), all of whom are now Christians too. Hence the title of this writing, Ἀναγνωρισμοί, or *Recognitions*, is not given to it by chance. Instead it designates something very essential, the idea that Christianity belongs to the very essence of human beings—that it mediates someone with him- or herself. According to these *Homilies*, the idea of recognition has deeply religious significance. "If separation (from each other) here is painful, how much more painful would it be to be separated after death?" *Homilies* 15.1 [*ANF* 8:309]. [*Ed.*] The *Clementine Homilies*, on which Baur draws, and the *Clementine Recognitions*, are two versions, with many identical contents, of the same original writing, or else of a longer original text. That is apparently why Baur feels free to introduce the term *Recognitions* here, when so far he has been speaking only of the *Homilies*.

gives each king an excuse for waging war. Accordingly, for those worthy of eternal life, in the world to come God appoints one ruler of everything so that the monarchal principle will establish perpetual peace.

So in the Christian Church also the oneness of God must be mirrored by having everyone follow one person as the leader. But the leader must know the way that leads to the holy city. If the church, like a city built on a high hill, is supposed to be constituted in a way pleasing to God, then above all the bishop, as the leader, must be obeyed in everything he says; the presbyters must carry out the bishop's orders; the deacons must busy themselves looking after the physical and spiritual needs of the fellowship and report all this to the bishop. The bishop sits on Christ's seat and is the representative of Christ himself. For this reason the respect or disrespect one shows to the bishop carries back to Christ and from Christ to God. Whoever disobeys the bishop's orders disobeys Christ; and whoever disobeys Christ becomes a target of God's wrath. That is why one must obey the bishop, completely respect him, and know that it is by the bishop that one is led to Christ, and by Christ to God. One must honor the throne of Christ. The command is to honor the seat of Moses, even if those who occupy it are deemed to be sinners.[347]

3. *Married Life.* It is also very closely associated with the monarchy of God. Married life is the finest and most vivid image of how human beings are said to stand in relation to God and Christ. The church is the bride of Christ (3.72), so each person also stands as a bride in relation to Christ.

This is why the violation of marital fidelity, any fornication or unchaste act, is in principle the same sin someone commits by being untrue to one's faith in the one God. It certainly parallels how, in paganism itself, the sin of fornication is most closely connected with polytheistic idolatry. The sin of fornication is second only to the sin of idolatry when it comes to sins the Clementine writings expressly warn people about. Fornication is the practical aspect of idolatry. The punishment set for fornication is the second-worst punishment, for the worst punishment is reserved for those who live in error, that is, in idolatry.[348] Fornication and adultery are even more terrible than murder, are a repeated murder committed on the soul, a defiling of the breath of God, which leads to the fire, to everlasting punishment.

A chaste wife who does God's will bears within herself a beautiful consciousness of the initial creation. She herself is aware that the one God has created one wife for the man. Her adornment is the Son of God as the bridegroom who clothes her with a holy light. Whoever is chaste also loves God and will be blessed by God.[349] Thus married life has its religious significance in the fact that, in the relationship of man and

---

347. *Homilies* 3.60–72 [ANF 8:249–51]. See also the Epistle of Clement to James, chs. 2, 12, and 18.

348. The greatest sin is "forsaking the sole Lord of all, and worshiping many who are no gods as if they were gods." *Homilies* 9.1 [ANF 8:275]. See also the Epistle of Clement to James, ch. 7.

349. *Homilies* 13.14–19 [ANF 8:303–4]. See also 3.28 [8:243], as above on p. 202.

wife, it portrays the same oneness as that on which rests the relation of a human being to God as the one creator of the world.

However, marriage is not said to be merely an image of this relationship. It also ought to facilitate this relationship in practice. That is why the Clementines' author considers marriage to be a means for thwarting the sensuous desire that results in fornication and adultery. This makes it the special duty of church leaders to urge the young and the old to marry, so that, by fornication and adultery, burning desire does not destroy the church like a pestilence. For to God the wickedness of adultery is an abomination surpassing every other sin, not only because it destroys the sinner himself or herself, but also because those who associate with the sinner likewise come to share in the same mania. Thus the presbyters and everyone else should see to it that marriage ceremonies are performed promptly, because marriage, being the means to protect the soul from unchastity, is a way of saving the soul (3.68 [*ANF* 8:250]). Thus the bride of Christ, the church, will be kept chaste. If the church's royal bridegroom finds it to be chaste, it is worthy of the highest honor.[350]

## The Influence of Paganism on Judaism as Reformed by Christianity: Ordinary Gnosticism as a Pagan Form of Christianity, or as a New Form of Paganism

From the perspective of this Clementine system, therefore, everything reckoned as belonging to Christianity's own essential nature gets regarded as a reform of Judaism, as a cleansing of Judaism from all the pagan elements that have attached themselves to the pure, primal religion and revelation originally set down in Judaism. In the ongoing struggle between Judaism and paganism, Judaism itself had become a Jewish-structured paganism. Therefore Judaism, as reformed by Christianity, also consequently met with a reaction from paganism, and there was even a pagan form of Christianity. This is the perspective from which the author of the Clementine texts understands Gnosticism in its general form as a phenomenon in the history of religion—a form determined of its own accord by the prior forms in which the relation between Judaism and paganism had developed in their own time.

The law or principle that antitheses underlie the course of development in the history of religion therefore entails that the purpose Christ's appearing was said to have achieved could not have been realized without the emergence of phenomena bringing on a new struggle between Judaism and paganism, between true and false religion. So whereas the Apostle Peter was ordained to carry on the work of Christ,

---

350. *Epistle of Clement to James*, chs. 7 and 8. The distinctiveness of each of the three different major forms of Gnosis is very typically expressed in its view of marriage. The Valentinians approve of marriage as something pleasing to God, and they even find it within their Pleroma, in their syzygies. However, the Marcionites regard marriage as objectionable, as something called for only in the realm of the Demiurge. The author of the Clementine writings of course allows for marriage, albeit only out of necessity, as the lesser evil compared to the greater evil of fornication.

paganism had to acquire its own spurious apostle and false prophet in the person of a Simon Magus.

We have already pointed out how the Clementines' author aims his polemic most directly at Marcionite dualism. This dualism could be overcome simply by applying the criterion taught by Christ as the prophet of truth, the criterion for distinguishing truth from falsehood in scripture, to the passages where it was already clearly valid to do so. This criterion deprives that dualism in advance of every foothold in scripture on which it relies for support. The only way to look at Simon Magus, that is, the Gnostics he represents, when they sought to set dualism over against the monotheism of the true religion in this fashion, is as paganism's attempt to reassert itself with renewed power. This is what we must take a closer look at, namely, the view the writer of the Clementine texts has of the essential nature of Gnosticism. Since we have presented this author's general ideas about the course of religious development, we can now comprehend in this larger context the fact that Gnosticism, in part as such and in part as the Marcionite kind in particular, is simply a new form of paganism and can take its place in the history of religion as a new member in the series of all these pagan settings.

## Gnosticism Is Polytheism

The Clementines' author presents Simon Magus everywhere as a herald of paganism.[351] *Homilies* 2.33 speaks of how the law or principle of opposites conditions all things: night precedes day, ignorance comes before knowledge, and illness precedes healing. So in human life too the truth can follow upon error just as the physician comes as a result of illness. Now, when the nations should become free from idolatry, evil as dominant has gained the advantage and sent out Simon Magus as a serpent to be its ally. As *Homilies* 3.3 says, the peoples have just barely conceived of accepting that their earthly likenesses of the gods are in fact not gods, when the Devil seeks to introduce yet another polytheism among them. He does this in order that, by dissuading them from the mania for polytheism (κατωπολυθεομανία), he can divert them to

---

351. Indeed inasmuch as Simon is a Samaritan, this writer counts him as a representative of paganism, for in the eyes of strictly orthodox Jews the Samaritans were pagans. This is the meaning of *Homilies* 2.22 when it says about the Magus: "He rejects Jerusalem, and substitutes Mount Gerizim for it" [ANF 8:233]. Hegesippus seems to have drawn a similar distinction, as Eusebius reports in his *Ecclesiastical History* 4.22.7. According to Eusebius, Hegesippus said: "There were various opinions among the circumcised, among the children of Israel, against the tribe of Judah and the Messiah (Χριστός), held by Essenes, Galileans, Hemerobaptists, Masbothei, Samaritans, Sadducees, and Pharisees" (LCL, 2:376–77). This somewhat obscure passage can only mean that Christians alone are the authentic Jews, are those who form the proper lineage of Judah. All the rest of them, even though circumcised, are sectarians. The Christians are related to the rest of the Jews in the same way as the orthodox [i.e., the true-believing] kingdom of Judah is related to the idolatrous, pagan-minded kingdom of Israel. The passage therefore also demonstrates that the earliest Jewish Christians, to which Hegesippus belonged, simply wanted to be authentic Jews.

an even worse deception as to the monarchy of God, so they will never have a chance to be worthy of divine mercy.[352]

This is the reason why Simon Magus appears with false scripture passages he does not hesitate to introduce as evidence against the true God, passages he takes from the prophets whom he himself does not believe. Of course he will not be successful with those whose forefathers have handed down to them the worship of the world's creator and the secrets of the scriptures that are able to deceive. But he will be very successful with those who do not know what is false in the scriptures, and who are inured to polytheistic notions from childhood on.[353]

> Thus since the wicked one sees how we are endeavoring, in the souls of those of the pagans who come to believe, to plant the love for the one God, a love that makes them immortal, that wicked one seeks to spread belief in many gods, or even in one god greater than the others. Thus by believing what they ought not believe, when these people die they will be cast out of the kingdom of God because they are guilty of adultery. (3.8 [ANF 8:240])

*Homily* 16 shows why it is justifiable to blame the Magus for doing this. It does so in an exchange between the Apostle Peter and Simon Magus, as to whether, according to the teaching of scripture, in addition to the one God who created the world, one may speak of other gods even just by name. The Magus appeals to such scripture passages as Gen 3:22 and 3:5, Exod 22:28, Deut 4:34, 13:6–8, and 10:17, Jer 10:11, Ps 34:10, and others. Peter counters with Deut 10:13, 10:17, 4:39, and similar ones. As can be expected, the author of the *Clementine Homilies* explains scripture's contradicting itself on the basis of his already-acknowledged assumption that the scriptural texts have been corrupted or falsified.

There is even more justification for Peter's position from the fact that, in this exchange with the Magus, he not only affirms his strict monotheism but also declares his opposition to the doctrine of Christ's divinity.[354] This issue is simply settled by the specific contention that Christ neither spoke of gods in addition to the world's creator, nor called himself God; instead he pronounced as blessed the one who called him the Son of God, the Son of the world's creator. Wanting to contend, to the contrary, that whoever is from God is therefore God, is to maintain an impossibility. The writer has Peter continuing as follows.

> The Father is unbegotten, whereas the Son is begotten. What is begotten cannot be comparable to what is unbegotten or begotten of itself, What are not the same in all respects may not be designated by the same name or term. What is begotten cannot have the same name as what is unbegotten, not even if the begotten one is of the same essential nature (τῆς αὐτῆς οὐσίας) as the one

---

352. *Homilies* 3.3 [ANF 8:239]. See also 3.59 [8:249].
353. [Ed.] *Homilies* 3.4 (ANF 8:239).
354. *Homilies* 16:15: "Our Lord . . . did not proclaim himself to be God" [ANF 8:316].

doing the begetting. Having come forth from God, and being likened to God, are hardly the basis for a claim to be called God. Thus while human souls have come forth from God and in a certain sense have the same essential nature as God, and are enduringly imbued with the breath of God, they nevertheless are not called gods. But if one wanted to call them gods, that would be only figuratively and only in the same broad sense in which Christ too was called God like all human souls. But then Christ would no longer be great, for he would only have what all have. Hence we only call God what in the supreme being is entirely peculiar to him and not imparted to any other. For instance, whoever is endless on all sides is called unbounded, and must of necessity be called unbounded because no other can be endless as he is. If someone says this is possible for another, that is wrong because two endless beings cannot coexist, for one of them would have been bounded by the other. Thus the unbegotten is one by nature. If he has a shape or figure, this shape is also one and incomparable, which is why he is called the Most High, because he is higher than all, and everything is subordinate to him. Yet if someone says that the term "god" would not capture the inexpressible essence of God himself, then why do people argue about the term? In any event the term is simply the one people conventionally use. But if this term is used for another being, then one must assign to this other being as well what one has not expressed. The expressed term or name opens the door to what is not expressed, and the misuse made of this term also carries over to what is not expressed.[355]

Thus the contention here is that the term or name "god" absolutely may not be applied to any being other than the one creator of the world. So it is clear that Marcion in particular, by speaking without hesitation about two gods, can hardly avoid the accusation of being a polytheist.

If every departure from the strict doctrine of the monarchy of God is polytheism, then dualism is also to be classified with polytheism. Dualism is set apart from ordinary polytheism only by its being a more refined, more sublime and more spiritual, form of polytheism. When the author of the *Clementine Homilies* speaks of an erroneous doctrine that does away with the monarchy of God, as an even more grave error than the "mania for polytheism," and speaks of a polytheism that, while of course not teaching many gods, instead teaches of one higher [than the other], then this statement is obviously about Gnosticism.[356] If, with the Clementines' writer, one affirms the idea of the world's creator, then ordinary polytheism, as "mania for polytheism," is as much beneath this idea as the one supreme, absolute God, to which (as that better one) the Gnostics subordinated their Demiurge, surpasses it. Then it all seems to be polytheistic in the same fashion, by wanting to set something else alongside the world's creator in one way or another. Yet inasmuch as the Gnostics gave the

---

355. [*Ed.*] This quotation incorporates most of *Homilies* 16.16–18 (*ANF* 8:316).

356. [*Ed.*] Baur includes in the text the Greek for the passage in *Homilies* 3.8 (*ANF* 8:240), about just two gods, one higher than the other.

Demiurge predicates incompatible with the true concept of God, and in doing so split the one true God into two beings with neither of them portraying in itself, purely and completely, the true concept of God, the Clementines' author was also able in turn to spot, in the Gnostics' Demiurge, the polytheistic element added to true monotheism.

This is the perspective from which to consider the discussion contained in *Homily* 16. The contention made there, that the one begotten from God is not himself God and ought not be called God, of course has no direct application to the Marcionite system, at least because this system knows of no Aeons emanated from God, and because it seems not to have set its Demiurge in such a direct relation to God. But it does have an indirect application, one that makes the contention into a line of argument aimed at the Marcionite system. If the name "God" itself is not to be given to the kind of being that has proceeded from God and is of a nature like his, then there is far less basis for giving it to a being that, like the Marcionite Demiurge, is so distant from the supreme God and according to its entire nature has nothing in common with the high God—a position Marcion doubtless adopted. Thus polytheism is destroyed at its roots and is deprived of any claim to religious truth, when it is denied the right to take the term "God" in any but the narrowest sense where it only designates the absolute being of God.[357]

## The Demonic, Pagan Nature of Docetism

The teaching of the Clementine texts sets what is demonic over against what is truly divine, false prophecy over against true prophecy. Thus if Gnosticism should be regarded as simply a more refined and more spiritualized paganism, then as so considered it must also inherently bear a pagan stamp and present itself as a simply demonic prophecy. The Clementines' writer places Gnosticism under this heading, if we may take what *Homilies* 17.13–17 says about visions, and the appearing of demons, in relation to Gnostic docetism.

Here the view attributed to Simon Magus is that communication through words is less than fully convincing, because we do not know whether or not the person we see before us is lying. But a vision, simply by its being seen, convinces the beholder that it is something divine. Peter states in rebuttal that whoever places faith in a vision, or in an apparition and a dream, has no certainty, and does not know in whom he believes. For it could indeed be an evil demon or a deceptive spirit misrepresenting what it is. If he asks who the one appearing is, the spirit could say to him whatever it chooses to. The spirit might remain as long as suits it, and could vanish like a sudden ray of light without giving the inquirer the desired information. In dreaming one could even be unable to ask what one might want to know, since the sleeper is not in control of his own mind. That is why, in dreaming, we are curious about many things

---

357. *Homilies* 16.18 [*ANF* 8:316], says: Where the name spoken (τὸ λεγόμενον ὄνομα) is one with the one not spoken (μὴ λεγόμενον), or goes unsaid (ἄρρητον).

but ask about something else, and why we learn things of no interest to us without asking about them; and when we wake up we are dissatisfied because we did not hear, or ask about, what was relevant to us.

Also, it is untenable to assume that only a righteous person would be able to see an authentic apparition; that an unrighteous person could not. We see that the opposite is the case from scripture passages in which godless people also have apparitions and true dreams. An example is when the godless pharaoh saw announced in a dream how fruitful or unfruitful the coming years would be [Gen 41:1–36]. Scripture tells us of similar examples involving the godless King Abimelech (Genesis 20) and the idol-worshiper King Nebuchadnezzar (Daniel 4). Therefore one cannot conclude from this that someone who sees a vision or an apparition, or has a dream, is in fact a pious person. Receiving external communications from visions and dreams is not, as a rule, the nature of revelation. Instead it is a proof of divine wrath, as it is indeed described in Num 12:6.[358] Or else, if one sees a vision, one must take into account that it might stem from an evil demon.[359]

As I have shown elsewhere, the theory advanced here—which traces everything back to social relations and personal development via instruction and example, and will not hear of a divine impact and awakening in a single moment—involves an obvious polemic directed at the Apostle Paul, one aimed at the vision (ὀπτασία) and revelation (ἀποκάλυψις) to which he appeals for verification of his apostolic office. Also, and just as I might have assumed, one can find in it a polemic directed at Montanism and disclosing, especially in its ecstatic prophecy, a relationship with paganism. This is a polemic in keeping with the overall standpoint on the basis of which the Clementines' author passes judgment on various phenomena of his day, according to their relation to paganism. However, it seems to me that, in the one instance or the other, we should not rule out a polemical relation to Gnostic, specifically Marcionite, docetism. Instead this circumstance makes it even more likely. For it is indisputable that docetism also presents an aspect based on which we can regard docetism as a pagan phenomenon.

If Christ's person is a mere apparition, then his entire appearing becomes a deceptive misrepresentation, like what we are accustomed to think of as the effects produced by demons. It is hard to understand how, on the docetic view, we can still hold fast to the concept of a personal activity and communication. Apparently one can only think of it as a series of visionary or unreal phenomena, and one does not know whether they are authentic or just illusory. Indeed this justifies the assumption that the Clementines' author saw Marcion's docetism simply as something demonic. *Homilies* 17 seems to point this out in more specific terms:

---

358. [*Ed.*] Num 12:6–15 tells how the Lord, being angry with the Hebrews, caused Miriam to get leprous spots.

359. [*Ed.*] This paragraph and the previous one draw on parts of *Homilies* 17:13–19 (*ANF* 8:321–24).

> When a person of flesh is said to behold God's essential being, either God's inexpressible power turns one's flesh into the nature of light, so that it can see light; or else the essence of light passes over into flesh so it can be seen by flesh. The Son alone can see the Father without undergoing any change himself... Even an angel sent to appear to a human being changes into flesh so as to be able to be seen by flesh. For cannot anyone see the fleshy nature not merely of the Son but also simply that of an angel? Yet someone who sees a vision should bear in mind that it could stem from an evil demon. [17.16 (ANF 8:323)]

The reference to Marcionite docetism is unmistakable here.

If the essential thing here is the contention that Christ was not tied to any fleshly nature, but that in the view of the Clementines' author a higher being cannot be seen without flesh, then it obviously follows that Christ's appearing visibly, something Marcion also affirms, cannot have been anything real but instead can only have been a demonic deception. If this demonic-docetic deception is also therefore the source from which Marcionite Christianity has come, then from this angle too, as it does in its polytheism, this Marcionite Christianity seems to be just a new form of demonic paganism. And when Simon Magus, as the representative of Gnostic docetism, is reported (17.13) as maintaining that someone could learn more from a vision than from an action or influence in reality, and Simon says he believes he is better informed about Jesus than Peter was, we see this contention as simply an instance of the clash between false and true prophecy.

## The Concept and Nature of Prophecy

This is the most appropriate spot to take up a topic that has not yet found its place in our elaboration of this system: the concept of prophecy according to the Clementine teaching. The foremost principle of the Clementine writings is that all knowledge of truth simply comes from prophecy. It is quite clear that this viewpoint is linked to the standpoint of purified Judaism adopted by the author.

Seen from this standpoint, all truth is divine revelation. The prophets are the instruments of divine revelation. According to the Clementines' teaching, the prophets themselves have their unity in the first prophet, that is, in the first human being God created who, as the primal human being, is also the original or primal prophet. For who should have had the Holy Spirit of Christ if were not the man created by God? (3.20). Hence prophecy is simply the principle of truth. The main passage about this is in *Homily* 2:

> If one does not know how great infallible prophecy is, one cannot attain what is supremely good. People may say what is supremely good is eternal life, enduring health, perfect understanding; or light, joy, immortality; or whatever else in the nature of existence is most excellent. Or they say that you cannot

attain the good without knowing in advance how things stand. Yet this foreknowledge cannot be gained unless you first recognize the prophet of truth. The prophet of truth is the one who knows utterly everything. He knows what has been, as it happened; what is occurring, in the way it does; what is to come, as it will transpire. This prophet is without sin, is compassionate, and is the only one to point the way to truth. Read and you shall discover the lot of those who believed they could find the truth on their own. It is the special feature of the prophet that he made the truth known, just as it is the special feature of the sun that it brings the day. So many have longed to know the truth but not had the good fortune to learn it from him. Seeking to know it, they died without finding it. For how is someone supposed to be able to find the truth, when he seeks it but just wishes to gain it through his own ignorance? Even if he were to come upon the truth he would pass by it as if it were not true, because he knows it not. Nor can he come to possess the truth via someone else who is ignorant but professes to know it. That truth has to be just the worldly wisdom to be gained from rational reflection, i.e., do not do wrong to others if you do not wish to be wronged by them.

That is why all those who have sought the truth by supposing they could find it on their own have been deluded. This is what happened to the Greek philosophers and the more persistent ones among the barbarians. In explaining the unknown by confining their speculation to the perceptible realm, they regarded what directly entered their minds as what is true. While still seeking the truth but acting as if they already knew it, they assented to some of the ideas that presented themselves to them and rejected others of them, without knowing what is actually true or false. Thus they established specific propositions as true, without considering that whoever seeks the truth by relying on his own misconceptions cannot know the truth. For, as we said, even if you have the truth before your own eyes, you cannot recognize it if you do not know it. Anyone who just seeks to know the truth by his own devices is guided by what pleases or satisfies him, not by the truth. Since what satisfies one person need not satisfy another, what is truth for one is not truth for the other. However, truth is what the prophet says is true, not what each individual finds satisfying. Otherwise if what is pleasing or satisfying were true, then these many things would be one and the same, which is not possible. This is why, with their speculations the Greek philologists, and not the philosophers, arrived at many, quite divergent, opinions. They took to be truth what followed from their own assumptions, without considering that if those assumptions are false, they will end up with a conclusion that is false too.[360] This is why one must disregard all else and trust solely in the prophet of truth. Even if we be

---

360. *Homilies* 1.19 says: "Each hypothesis [each philosophical proposition] is demolished and is constructed anew, and by dint of refutation it is held to be true and false. The hypotheses no longer appear to be as they are, for according to the refutations they appear to be understood as being, or not being, true or false" [*ANF* 8:227–28].

untaught and uneducated, we need only consider him alone to be able to judge whether he is a prophet. God has made provision for everyone, barbarians and Greeks alike, to be able to find him easily.

So here is how things stand: If someone is a prophet and knows how the world has been, and what is the case now, and what the future holds, then, as soon as something he foretold has actually come to pass, can we not also place our faith in him with regard to the future as something not merely known but also known in advance? Who should then have been so mentally deficient as not to see that we may have faith in him above all others, even with regard to the divine intentions, since out of all people he alone knows these intentions without first having to have learned them. Thus when it comes to such a person who, in virtue of the divine spirit within him, knows the future in advance, will we not accept that he knows the truth? Who else could we make that assumption about? Is it not the greatest proof of mental deficiency if one fails to ascribe to a prophet the knowledge one ascribes to someone who is not a prophet? It is clear that this is why we must above all seek the prophet with the help of the prophetic pronouncements; and why, having recognized him, we must obey his other teachings without any reservations. It is why we must live thereafter with confidence in the conviction that it is not the nature of someone who has said these things to lie. Even though something seems not right about other things he said, we must know that he did not speak erroneously. Instead, we simply have not understood what he stated correctly. Ignorance cannot competently judge knowledge, nor is knowledge itself truly capable of judging foreknowledge. Instead foreknowledge imparts knowledge to the ignorant.[361]

Compare these passages with *Homilies* 3.11–15, where this theory gets elaborated further and related to Jesus:

The true prophet knows all things, knows everyone's thoughts, is without sin, and is fully aware of God's judgments [about everything]. That is why we must conceive of his foreknowing as completely independent of all external factors. Physicians also predict many things by taking the pulse of sick people as an indicator, and other predictors rely on birds, sacrificial offerings, and other such things, now this one, now that one. They also prophesy, but they are no prophets. If anyone maintains that such predictions are equivalent to truly innate foreknowledge, he is quite mistaken. When any predictions of that kind turn out to be correct, they are just acknowledging present realities. But they do serve to prove that there is foreknowledge, although the foreknowledge

---

361. [*Ed.*] This lengthy quotation is comprised by *Homilies* 2.5–11 (*ANF* 8:229–30). [*Baur*] See also *Homilies* 1.19: "On this account the great need of religion is for a prophet of truth who tells us the way things are and what we are to believe about everything. So it is first necessary to examine all his prophetic signs and, after determining that he is a true prophet, to believe him in everything and not to sit in judgment over what he says" [*ANF* 8:228].

of the one true prophet does not merely refer to present reality. His limitless prophecy extends to the world to come and needs no external aids, because his prophesying is not obscure and ambiguous, so another prophet first had to explain what it means. Instead, his prophecy is clear and distinct. Thus in virtue of the ever-constant spirit dwelling in him, our teacher and prophet has always known everything. That is why he has spoken so confidently about future things, about specific events, times, and places. As the infallible prophet, he surveys everything with his boundless spiritual vision, and even knows what is hidden.

But we should be deceiving ourselves and misleading others if we were to think as most people do, that even the true prophet foreknows only when he has the spirit, and that sometimes he lacks it and so is ignorant or unaware of things. That is the case only with those who are transported, by a disorderly spirit, into an enthusiastic frenzy, who are drunken at the altars and have inhaled the fumes from the sacrificial offerings. Even when someone is found to be a liar and not to have possessed the holy spirit of foreknowledge, that is, someone who presented himself as being a prophet and was accepted as such, it is not easy to convict him of being a false prophet. If even a few of the many things he says turn out to be correct, people believe that he has the spirit, even though he speaks of what is first as last and what is last as first, or what has happened as future and what is future as already having happened; and though he makes disconnected utterances, saying things that are jumbled together and completely changed, are garbled, abrupt, unintelligible, ambiguous, improbable, unclear, and evidencing complete lack of awareness.

However, our teacher is no prophet of this kind. Instead, in virtue of the ever-constant spirit indwelling him, he knows everything all the time. He confidently and clearly spells out in advance the events, times, and places, and how everything will happen. For he prophesied about the temple, "You see all of these buildings, do you not? Truly I tell you, not one stone will be left here upon another; all will be thrown down" (Matt 24:2, 34). Also: "Indeed, the days will come upon you, when your enemies will set up ramparts around you and surround you, and hem you in on every side. They will crush you to the ground, you and your children" (Luke 19:43–44). He also announced just as clearly what was to follow, what we see with our own eyes, so that his words spoken to those they concerned would be backed up by the deed. The true prophet speaks in a way that those who hear his words can believe them.[362]

Therefore, given the complete subjectivity of all human knowing, truly objective knowing is only provided in prophecy.

Yet prophecy itself is not communicated via things seen, through dreams or visionary states; not as a rule through phenomena that do not have as their basis the full reality of a concrete, personal life. That is why for Jesus to function as a teacher he had

---

362. [*Ed.*] This lengthy quotation is drawn from *Homilies* 3.11–15 [*ANF* 8:240–41].

to spend an entire year in continuous engagement with those who were awake (17.19). Knowledge of truth is only authentically conveyed by personal interaction and the living word of communication and instruction. But even in the case of a prophet operating in this way, the gift of prophecy cannot be thought of as a momentary, variable, and transitory state. Instead it can only be conceived of as an immanent condition inseparably linked with the entire personal being of the prophet and his conscious identity. Thus the principle sign of the true prophet is the clarity and specificity of what he states, and as soon as such an expression has once proved successful from its objective result, when the prophecy has its attestation from the πρόγνωσις or foreknowledge (by which it must principally authenticate itself, in order to be recognized as γνῶσις or knowledge), it may quite justifiably be regarded as the principle and source of all knowledge of truth.

But however much this theory of the knowledge of truth seemingly amounts simply to dependence on an external, positive authority, it nevertheless strives, on the other hand, to gain for itself an inner, immanent basis of truth. So as not to posit the principle of truth merely in something momentary, contingent, and coming from outside, what makes a prophet to be one, according to this principle, is just his innate and everlasting spirit (ἔμφυτον καὶ ἀέννων πνεῦμα). Indeed this spirit is not ascribed to the prophet alone, since it generally belongs to all who are pious. Hence this theory ultimately transitions into a view positing an inner revelation in place of external revelation, one bringing a person to awareness of the external revelation. So this is already set down in the human mind as the seed and principle of truth. As *Homilies* 17.18 says in quite general terms, for the pious the truth wells up from one's indwelling, pure sensibility. In this same passage the Clementines' writer has his Peter say:

> Thus the Father also revealed the Son to me. So I know from my own experience the meaning of the revelation. For as soon as the Lord asked me (see Matt 16:13),[363] the answer rose up in my heart, I know not how, and I replied: "You are the Messiah, the Son of the living God" (Matt 16:16). The one who pronounced me blessed said to me that it was the Father who had revealed this to me. Afterwards I realized that revelation is something coming about within, apart from outward instruction, apart from visions and dreams. And so it is, for the truth God has sown within us contains the seeds of all truth. This truth is concealed or disclosed solely by the hand of God, since God works as he knows what each individual deserves. (Cf. also 18.8.)

We ought not regard this view as merely an outlier to the Clementine position. It has its deeper grounding in its connection with the christology of this system. If the same divine spirit that was in Adam also appears in Christ, then since the divine spirit that was in Adam also had to pass on to the human beings who are his descendents,

---

363. [Ed.] While Baur just refers to this passage, in parentheses, the text of *Homilies* 17.18 (*ANF* 8:323) quotes the question in v. 13: "But who do you say that I am?"

the divine principle in Christ is therefore not essentially different from what is divine in all other human beings—thus is nothing utterly supernatural. This is the same divine spirit of humanity (*göttliche Menschengeist*)³⁶⁴ that, in the "seven pillars of the world," pervades all the periods of world history and also indwells all human beings as their innermost principle. The only difference is that where Adam, as the primal man, comes forth in his substantial power and purity in that principle, it is more or less obscured in everybody else. Nevertheless in them too it is not so obscured and clouded over that it cannot always once more break through the darkness that conceals it and regain the full light of its self-consciousness, whether that be through the inner power of its principle, or through prompting from outside it.

This Adam-Christ is, so to speak, the male principle, which in individuals has been obscured and weakened simply by having attached to it a female principle that has gained the upper hand. The male principle is what is spiritual and rational, while the female principle is what is sensuous and weak, the side of human nature subject to error and sin. This is why the Clementine writings themselves, in the final analysis, trace the source of all those phenomena in which false prophecy, or demonic paganism, manifests itself, back to a principle present in human beings. Thus what Judaism and paganism are in relation to world history writ large, the two principles of reason and sensuality are in relation to individual human beings, and to human nature in and for itself. In both pictures, large and small, there is the same duality of a male and a female principle.

The principle of prophecy in no way makes human beings dependent on an external authority with regard to knowledge of truth, a point completely in accord with how important the principle of freedom is in this system. In seeking to be strictly consistent with its dualistic view of the world, it at the same says human beings, who stand in the midst of all these antitheses, have an unrestricted power of free will. Everything they can come to share in—knowledge of truth, immortality (16.10), the blessed life is said to be one's own free achievement. Everything that can lead people astray, into error and into sin, can be justified as providing the occasion for a person to discriminate between truth and falsity, good and evil, by his or her own investigation and self-determination (16.13).³⁶⁵

---

364. [*Ed.*] Here Baur includes parenthetically in the text the previously-mentioned Greek expression for this "innate and everlasting spirit," which he equates with the "Holy Spirit of Christ" and with "spiritual divinity."

365. [*From the Errata and Additions*] Here we still face the question as to how the Clementines' author conceived of his prophet of truth as entering into human life. Previously I believed I had to conclude that this occurred via a natural birth. See my treatise, *De Ebionitarum origine et doctrina ab Essenis* (Tübingen, 1831), 16, for the position I took there about his birth, based on *Homilies* 3.17: "God having made all things, if anyone will not allow that a man, fashioned by his hands, could have possessed God's great and Holy Spirit of foreknowledge, how is it not a great error to attribute foreknowledge to another who is born of spurious stock?" [*ANF* 8:241]. There I believed I must disagree with Neander (in his *Entwickelung* [n. 6], 409), who holds it was a supernatural birth, and instead conclude in agreement with Credner ("Über Essäer und Ebioniten," in Winer's *Zeitschrift für wissenschaftliche*

*Theologie* 2:253) that it was a natural birth. But now I must acknowledge that Schneckenburger is correct in his remarks made in his *Abhandlung über das Evangelium der Aegypter* (Bonn, 1834), 7, which has recently come into my hands. Assuming a natural birth would have eliminated the sinlessness and infallibility of the prophet of truth since, according to the *Homilies'* view of the relation of the two sexes in 3.27, no one born of a woman can be pure. It now seems to me that this passage hardly allows for such a conclusion, since the writer could also argue just polemically that, according to the usual Jewish view the Old Testament prophets said to have had the divine spirit were "of women born" (ἐκ μυσαρῦς ἀναγόνος, "from loathsome impurity"). Who then can deny this spirit to the man created by God? On this matter see Epiphanius, who says, in *Heresies* 30.28, that the Ebionites rejected the prophets from Joshua onward. [On a comparable relation of the prophets to Moses already found in Philo, see Dähne, *Geschichtliche Darstellung der jüdischen alexandrinische Philosophy*, 1:30.] Epiphanius also says, in 30.15, that "they abhor all the prophets." One should have thought it would have been more natural for the writer of the Clementines to have taken the same position, for we find the Ebionites, as presented by Epiphanius, otherwise in agreement with these teachings. Yet there are also exceptions. Epiphanius says (in 30.14, 16, and 34) that, wholly in keeping with the Gnostic way of thinking, the Ebionites distinguished the naturally-begotten Jesus from the Christ descending on him from above. Yet we cannot assume that our Clementine author does likewise. However, his set of ideas also does not include a supernatural birth from the Virgin Mary. For a writer who is wholly in agreement with the Ebionites, as Epiphanius presents them, and who locates David most especially in the series of vehicles of "female prophecy" (see the reference to "singers of psalms" on p. 201 above), cannot have been wedded to a descent from David. Also see *Homilies* 18.11, with reference to Matt 11:27 ["no one knows the Father except the Son"]. With this assumption, however, it seems to me just as decisive how, by accepting a natural birth, the view of the female sex is in conflict with the passage introduced above on p. 229, according to which a being lacking flesh cannot be seen, and that if angels themselves are to appear they must change themselves into beings of flesh. So this very passage makes it most likely that the writer presupposed the same thing about his prophet that he said about angels. The prophet did not appear because of being born either naturally or supernaturally, or even docetically. Instead he appeared because the substantial feature in him, the spirit of Adam, transformed itself into flesh. Even the Ebionites thought of the appearing of Jesus as the appearing of an angel. In *On the Flesh of Christ*, ch. 14, Tertullian says: "This opinion will be very suitable for an Ebionite, who holds Jesus to be a mere man, and nothing more than a descendent of David, and not also the Son of God; although he is, to be sure, in one respect more glorious than the prophets, inasmuch as he declares that there was an angel in him" [*ANF* 3:534]. Except that we ought not ascribe to our author the natural birth the Ebionites are said to have accepted. It seems to me, then, that what Credner has remarked about the supposition of a supernatural birth—and what accordingly must also count as the often-presented view, that this same kind of appearing must be assumed in the case of Moses and the patriarchs, in whom the same spirit of Adam was said to be appearing—no longer carries any weight. Not only can such a departure from the usual Jewish view fail to be conspicuous because it is otherwise so different; it also seems to me that it first appears because of its ties to this whole way of thinking. For on what basis could the Ebionites, who must have wholly shared this viewpoint with the Clementines' writer, have rejected all the prophets from Joshua onward, if they did not consider them to be instruments of female prophecy, as opposed to those instruments of male prophecy who were therefore also not "from loathsome impurity"? So this latter group were not prophets "born of women." This view of the appearing of Jesus, or of the Son of God, we can of course call "docetic," as Schneckenburger does, but it is still not the usual docetism. It is strikingly close to the view held by Apelles, a view we describe on pp. 242ff. as connected with docetism. I believe this explains why the Clementines' author, while emphatically contesting Marcionite teaching, nevertheless does not engage anywhere in a refutation of Marcionite docetism in the same scope and with the same earnestness as Tertullian does. This had to catch our attention, but it can only be based on the fact that he does not condemn Marcionite docetism unconditionally. He does at least concur with it in rejecting a human birth, although even here he certainly refrains from laying out more precisely his actual position on this topic as such (a topic on which, by the way, even the Ebionites must not have been of one mind—if only Epiphanius

## General Assessment of the Gnostic Standpoint of This System: It Stands Intermediate between the Objectivity of the Systems in the First Form of Gnosis and the Subjectivity of the Marcionite System

Our placement of the Pseudo-Clementine system within the series of Gnostic systems, and the general import we believe must be assigned to it in the history of Gnosticism, are adequately justified by the detailed explication of it that I have provided. In opposing Marcionite dualism, this system takes Judaism under its wing and therefore hardly concurs with the other Gnostic systems in their predilection for paganism. Here we may now indicate briefly, by a few more general and comparative remarks, the way in which this standpoint taken within Judaism also determines the Gnostic standpoint of this system.

Judaism is positioned between paganism and Christianity, and this gives Pseudo-Clementine Gnosis the character or role of a mediator. Marcionite dualism sets up a harsh antithesis between the Christian world and the pre-Christian world, and strictly repudiates both paganism and Judaism in the same way. Since the Pseudo-Clementines are unwilling to extend that antithesis to include Judaism, they position themselves instead on the side of those systems that consider Judaism to be the closest thing to Christianity. As we have seen, Marcion's purely Christian standpoint is at the same time that of the subjectivity of consciousness; whereas the Gnostic systems that, in contrast, still stick entirely to the pagan worldview, also therefore take up a clearly objective standpoint. In their contents these pagan Gnostic systems are cosmogonic systems, in the sense that the main feature of paganism's religious knowledge was always the cosmogony: teaching about how the world came to be; about the relations among the various fundamental forces and elements that form the cosmos or, in other words, the relations between spirit and matter. All the forms of Gnosis are dealing with how this antithesis is offset or accommodated. In the systems turned toward paganism, this accommodation is located wholly in the objective world. They confront the antithesis between God and the world, or that between spirit and matter, or else the antithesis of infinite and finite, inasmuch as, in its relation to matter the absolute spirit is conceived of as in a major bifurcation, as estranged or divided from itself.

This original and purely objective antithesis first gains subjective significance from the fact that, in the course of the world's development, the spirit that is intertwined with matter gradually comes to be conscious of itself. In contrast to this, in Marcion's system the same antithesis has its locus and point of departure in the subjectivity of consciousness. This is the antithesis of law and gospel, which is grounded

---

had not confused the issue). If the attempt made here to shed somewhat more light on this obscure point is not unsuccessful, then the new form of docetism it makes known to us serves at the same time to complete our presentation of the different forms of Gnosis by a new element. We see from it how even the Pseudo-Clementine system was not entirely able to divest itself of the docetism running throughout all the forms of Gnosis.

in Christian consciousness and given directly with it. In other words, it is the antithesis consisting of the relationship of the two concepts, those of justice and goodness.

How then is Pseudo-Clementine Gnosis related to this objectivity and subjectivity of the two other forms of Gnosis respectively? It maintains its mediating character in this context too. The antithesis from which it sets out is neither the purely objective antithesis of spirit and matter, nor the subjective antithesis in the sense in which Marcion separates law from gospel on the basis of his Christian consciousness. Instead it is the antithesis emerging in world history and human history, between true and false religion, between Judaism and paganism. That is why this Pseudo-Clementine system knows no antithesis at all between spirit and matter, since it transposes matter into the very substance of God, from which it has the other antitheses issuing forth freely rather than necessarily. These other antitheses include the antithesis between the present world and the world to come, and that between the two rulers of this world, one of which is good and the other is evil. These other antitheses are significant first of all because of how they relate to human beings. All the antitheses within the domain in which this system operates originate initially with the existence of the [first] human being and as his history unfolds.

Since the Marcionite system makes its Demiurge out to be in principle a personification of the idea of justice, and Sophia-Achamoth falls from the Aeon world,[366] what alone in this Pseudo-Clementine system is therefore comparable to the older Gnostic systems is the separation of the original one human being into the duality of a male principle and a female principle. This separation then provides the initial antithesis of the principles whose mutual relations shape the entire course of the world. In the other systems, the fall that occurred at one time is the external point from which commences the entire development serving to restore harmony to the antithesis resulting from it. Here too in the Clementine system a sudden and unexplainable fall is posited without further ado by the assumption that, from the first human being onward, the order of the syzygies has been reversed, so that while initially what is better preceded what is lesser, now the worse could be first and the better of the pair would come second. What this says is that what is worse initially went along with what is better, albeit as just concealed and subordinate, but from that human being onward what is worse became dominant and far more prevalent.

With the great significance this system gives to the idea of freedom as a moving force in the historical domain, the principle from which all the antitheses arise can only be the freedom of the will. All these antitheses are important only in the human world. However, what one is, as a moral being, one is only in virtue of one's own free self-determination (2.15 [*ANF* 8:231]). Hence the reason why the order within the syzygies was reversed from the human being onward is expressly posited in human freedom. In fact this freedom is none other than the same freedom by which

---

366. What in those other systems are outside of God, as the Sophia and the Demiurge, become here the Sophia as "the hand" in God "that fashions the universe" (*Homilies* 16.12 [*ANF* 8.315]).

the fall of Sophia-Achamoth took place. So it can hardly seem strange to us that this system, in being driven by the idea of freedom, also shares the common character of Gnostic systems to such an extent that it regards the human being as having a nature completely conditioned by the general cohesiveness of the cosmos. The antithesis of the male and female principles, and the order in the syzygies predetermined for the human world—in virtue of which the worse member takes the lead over the better member—is none other than a law of nature that, while of course not suspending the freedom of the individual, does make the course of development taken by the whole depend on a higher necessity with regard to its successive periods. Thus in nature there are indications of this law, as in *Homilies* 2.15.

This antithesis, the duality of a male principle and a female principle, is even carried over into the essential nature of God. The Sophia forever bound to God as a soul, the world-creating principle by which God goes forth from himself and the monad becomes a dyad—and by which also a female principle appears out of the one original man—is the same as what in the older Gnostic systems is the syzygy of the Primal Father and Ennoia. The only difference is that in the Pseudo-Clementine system this relation of genders is conceived of much more purely and abstractly, and is not presented in the unfolding of any series of Aeons. Just as the relation of the genders has an affinity with the Marcionite system's repudiation of everything of a sexual nature, so too it is quite similar to that system in that the Clementines see the law of the syzygies playing out in the entire course of the world. This is the perspective from which they consider how the present world is related to the world to come, and how individual human beings are related to Christ.

As I remarked earlier, the character of this system gets expressed in a noteworthy way in its view of marriage. While Marcion classifies marriage together with fornication, the Clementines' author commends marriage just as earnestly as he abhors fornication for being the greatest sin. Thus their views of fornication at least are the same, and marriage, as merely a measure to prevent fornication, is in principle simply a necessary evil. But if we wish to see this stance as strongly tending toward Gnostic dualism, then what counts in the Pseudo-Clementine system is the ethical character, since it bases its view of marriage not on a spirit-matter antithesis, but just on seeing in marriage the direct reflection of human being's ethical-religious relation to God, and in fornication, according to the familiar Old Testament depiction, the most grievous injury to that relationship.

## The Goal of Gnosis Is Clear Self-Consciousness

It is correct to say that, in the Pseudo-Clementine system, the general goal of Gnosis is, for the first time, to achieve completely clear consciousness. As we saw earlier, all the Gnostic systems are dealing with the relations among the three religious forms of paganism, Judaism, and Christianity; in other words, with how truly Christian consciousness is mediated through the forms that preceded Christianity in time.

In the systems of the first form the historical features of religion are so tightly interwoven with the cosmogony, and with the ideas about the relation of spirit to matter that are associated with the cosmogony, that Christian consciousness cannot appear in its purity. Christianity seems to be just an element of the general process of the world's development, a development thought of analogously with the ancient cosmogonies. The Marcionite system puts the cosmogony, and everything associated with it, wholly in the background, whereas it occupies itself too one-sidedly with just the relationship between Judaism and Christianity. The Pseudo-Clementine system is the first one to make the full range of religious history into the object of Gnostic speculation, such that all the moments of religious history serve to mediate or convey Christian consciousness.

This is what the Pseudo-Clementine system regards as its highest task and goal, by calling this goal "the knowledge of the things that are."[367] This goal comprises all knowledge of truth, and it can only be conveyed by the prophet of truth.[368] Because so much emphasis is placed on this quest for truth, Gnosis is what is uppermost in this system too. If Gnosis is conceived of as simply the kind of knowing that is linked to an awareness of how it is transmitted, then this concept of Gnosis is expressed more clearly in this system than in any other. The entire doctrine of the syzygies, which is so important for this system, has no other purpose than making one conscious of those factors by which knowledge must be conveyed so that, by the negation of ignorance, one arrives at absolute knowledge.[369] There is knowledge only inasmuch as not-knowing, or ignorance, comes before it; in other words, inasmuch as ignorance is negated. By this negation of ignorance one becomes conscious of the transmission of knowledge, and for the first time there is knowledge itself. Only in this sense can the law of the syzygies be the canon of truth, the rule that keeps us from error.

Only to the extent that this rule, expressing the necessity for the transmission of knowledge via the negation of ignorance, takes one back to a universal order of nature

367. *Homilies* 1.17 [*ANF* 8:227]: γνῶσις τῶν ὄντων, knowledge of beings.

368. *Homilies* 2.5 [*ANF* 8:229]. [*Ed.*] In parentheses in the text Baur includes the Greek for this statement.

369. This is clearly the contents of two major passages that express this point directly. *Homilies* 2:15 [*ANF* 8:231]: "Therefore the one God, in teaching human beings the truth of what exists, has distinguished all principles into pairs and opposites. As the sole God from the very beginning, he made heaven and earth, day and night, light and fire, sun and moon, life and death. Among these he made human beings alone to be self-controlling, able to be either righteous or unrighteous. God placed the likenesses of the syzygies before them, first small ones and then such larger ones as the world and eternity. The cosmos at present is transitory but the world to come is eternal. First there is ignorance, then there is knowledge." *Homilies* 2:33 [*ANF* 8:235]: "You must perceive the truth of the rule of the syzygies, for if you stick to it you cannot be misled. As we said, since we see all things in pairs and contraries—and as night is first and then the day; ignorance is first and then knowledge; disease is first and then healing—first we go astray in life and then the truth comes forward, as the physician does for disease."

ordained by God, can there be the fundamental assumption that knowing and being are one and the same. That is also why being, like knowing, can be elevated to what is absolute only via the moments through which it is transmitted or mediated. Accordingly this system also shows how it is an essential feature of Gnosis as such to proceed from the identity of being and knowing, in other words from the presupposition that being can only be for knowing, that it can only be "being as thought and known." In the individual systems themselves there is an awareness of this identity, to a greater or a lesser degree. But it is only from this standpoint that we are in a position to correctly understand the internal structure of each of them.

The Pseudo-Clementine system is the last phenomenon to be considered in the domain of Gnosis, the one in which the series of its developing forms, based on the internal unity of the concept, comes to a close. The Jewish element, detectable from the outset in the origin of Gnosis, has made itself felt in a most remarkable way in this system. But this same Jewish element can also be traced in a few noteworthy phenomena during the transition from that initial point to this end point. As Neander has shown, the contents of the Pseudo-Clementine system harmonize with what we know from Epiphanius as the Ebionite teaching, in such a striking way that we can simply regard them as the further development and elaboration of the teachings and perspectives found in the Ebionite sect. But even in the case of the Ebionites themselves an older form of Judaism can have simply been blended with Christianity in this fashion. According to the information contained in the—indeed very confused—account of Epiphanius, about the various Jewish sects, a connection between the Ebionites and the Essenes can therefore by no means be unlikely.[370]

## Cerinthus, a Representative of the Judaizing Form of Gnosis

We also have to mention Cerinthus here in this same context. In any event this teaching, like that in the Pseudo-Clementine system, points to a Judaizing form of Gnosis.

It does of course deviate from the Pseudo-Clementines by contending that the world was not created by the supreme God, but rather by a subordinate power that did not know him.[371] Alternatively, as Epiphanius says,[372] it was created by angels, to which Cerinthus also assigns the law and the prophets. This approximates to the teaching ascribed to Simon Magus in the *Clementine Homilies* (18.12), that the supreme God

---

370. I sought to demonstrate this point in more detail in my *De Ebionitarum origine et doctrina ab Essenis* (n. 365). No doubt also traceable back to this same source is the significance of the bride-bridegroom relationship so often depicted by the Gnostics, that is, traceable to the male-female choirs of the Therapeutae described by Philo. See my treatise, "Über die ursprüngliche Bedeutung des Passahfestes und des Beschneidungsritus," *Tübinger Zeitschrift für Theologie* (1832), no. 1, 76.

371. Irenaeus, *Against Heresies* 1.26. [*Ed.*] Cerinthus lived during the second half of the first century, and according to Irenaeus was educated in the Gnosis of the Egyptians. None of his writings survived.

372. Epiphanius, *Against Heresies* 28.1.2–3.

sent out two angels, one of whom was the world's creator and one the lawgiver. Nevertheless Cerinthus likely did not associate this teaching with a devaluation of creation and lawgiving. Instead he was surely just thinking analogously to how the Alexandrians had the law being handed down by angels, ones serving as intermediaries for the divine activity relating to the world. Else how, as Epiphanius himself remarks,[373] could he have declared that the law is a good thing and it is necessary to obey it? In doing so Cerinthus could only partially adhere to Judaism,[374] since Gnosis always characterizes itself by distinguishing authentic Judaism from inauthentic Judaism.

Yet wherever Cerinthus got the notion that Judaism is adulterated, the main thing is always that he upheld the law as continuing to be binding, so that he places Judaism in relation to Christianity in a way like that of the Clementines' author. Thus those who challenged the authenticity of the Book of Revelation agreed as to Cerinthus' completely reprehensible chiliasm.[375] One might justifiably take this as Cerinthus speaking in a figurative way about something his opponents simply interpret in sensuous and fleshly terms. Nevertheless Cerinthus was in any event able to be a chiliast simply on the basis of Judaism. Accordingly he is, like the Clementines' author, to be regarded as a representative of the Judaizing form of Gnosis, and his teaching followed from the same Jewish elements of Gnosis. However it does in fact deviate in many points from the Clementines' doctrines, in particular in its christology; for in this regard the Gospel of the Hebrews, which serves solely Ebionite interests, can demonstrate the connection between Cerinthian and Ebionite teaching.[376] This difference is to be explained from the fact that the teaching of the Clementines initially got elaborated in the form in which we find it in the *Homilies* because of having to distance itself as much as possible from the Gnostic dualism and docetism to which it is antithetical.

## Apelles, a Follower of Marcion[377]

The church of Rome fundamentally and energetically rejected Gnostic dualism, specifically the Marcionite dualism. This move ran counter to the remarkable writings that doubtless had originated there. It might be worth noting, in this regard, how the

---

373. *Against Heresies* 28.2.1.

374. Epiphanius also says this in 28.1.

375. [*Ed.*] Within the text Baur identifies these opponents as Gaius, Bishop of Rome, and Dionysius, Bishop of Alexandria, and he cites Eusebius, *Ecclesiastical History* 3.28, on which see the LCL volume, 1.262–67. Chiliasm is the doctrine that Christ would rule on earth for a thousand years after his Second Coming (on which see Rev ch. 20). Eusebius goes on to speak of the carnal indulgences the opponents ascribe to Cerinthus' expectations for this millennium. The LCL volume remarks in a footnote, 265: "It would appear that Gaius thought that Cerinthus was the writer of the Apocalypse."

376. Neander, *Allgemeine Geschichte* (n. 110), 1:675.

377. [*Ed.*] This heading is not found in Baur's table of contents, but it is clearly a separate topic from that of Cerinthus. Apelles (mid-2nd century Christian Gnostic) developed a modified Marcionism that allowed Christ to have human flesh but denied his nativity. His writings have not survived.

Clementine teaching relates to that of Apelles, the most important one of Marcion's followers. Yet it is regrettable that the indications and notices about this that Tertullian and Epiphanius in particular provide are far too scanty and disjointed.[378] According to Tertullian, Apelles taught that there is only one God:

> Apelles introduces one God in the infinite, higher regions, and states that he made many powers and angels. Beside him is another virtuous being, which he says is to be called Lord but which he represents as an angel. He wants this one to be seen as the originator of the world, in imitation of the higher world. A principle of repentance was to be intermixed with our world because he had not made it as perfect as the instituting of that higher world.[379]

Tertullian also writes:

> They (the followers of Apelles) mention a certain renowned angel as having instituted this world of ours, and after doing so, having repented for it ... The world must then be at fault because he instituted repentance, for all repentance is an admission of fault, because there is no repentance unless there is fault.[380]

Therefore the world was indeed created on the model of higher ideas, but because of the intermediary role of a spirit it was unable to fully realize these ideas. That is why the consciousness of self-annulling negativity (*poenitentia*, or repentance) is bound up with the concept of the world.

Tertullian opposes the view of Apelles' followers in this last passage by asking: "Could someone who had the mind and will and the virtue of Christ for such deeds have done anything that required repentance, since Apelles' followers also describe

---

378. Tertullian and Eusebius place Apelles in a singular relationship with a young woman, Philumene. Eusebius states, in his *Ecclesiastical History* 5.13, that Apelles "was persuaded by the utterances of a possessed maiden named Philumene" [LCL, 2:466–67]. Tertullian makes the same contention in his *Prescription against Heretics*, ch. 30, and adds that this was not a chaste relationship: "Forsaking the continence of Marcion, Apelles resorted to the company of a woman ... After some years ... he clave to another woman, the maiden Philumene (whom we already mentioned, in ch. 6), who herself afterwards became a notorious prostitute. Entranced by her, he wrote *The Revelations*, which he had learned from her." (See also ch. 51 [ch. 6 in *ANF* Appendix, 3:653–54].) This Philumene is no doubt merely a fiction, a personification of the higher world from which Apelles' own religious ideas seem to have come down to him. In the fantasies and pictorial language of the Gnostics the higher world takes shape for them, announcing its secrets to a woman divinely inspiring them. According to Irenaeus (*Against Heresies* 1.41.1), Marcus the Gnostic boasted in a quite analogous way that he was the instrument for revealing Sige. He says that the Tetrad itself has descended upon him in the form of a woman. Once the church fathers took such personifications to be actual female persons, then they were also directly inclined to regard them in the same way as they did the notorious Helena of the arch-heretic Simon.

379. *Prescription against Heretics*, ch. 6 [in *ANF* Appendix, 3:653]. Baur interpolates within this quotation, following "the infinite, higher regions" of the first line, this statement: "Of course this expression calls to mind the description of God's essential nature in the *Clementine Homilies* 17.9—being boundless, at the pinnacle, infinite, and so forth" [*ANF* 8:320].

380. *On the Flesh of Christ*, ch. 8 [*ANF* 3:529].

this angel using the parable of the lost sheep?"[381] This clearly shows that Apelles must have seen his "renowned angel" as an approximation to Christ, although when looked at more closely this term can hardly indicate Christ's relation to God. For of course Tertullian speaks here of "multiple powers and angels," and alongside them "another power," the "Lord" or world-forming angel, without mentioning Christ in this context. From the "renowned angel" Tertullian distinguishes a "fiery angel" as the "author of evil," when he calls him "Israel's God and ours."[382] Thus he seems to identify this "fiery angel" with the world's creator, the "renowned angel," or at least to set him alongside the creator.

While these relationships are unclear, they nevertheless do seem to justify the conclusion that Apelles did not want to transfer the concept and label of God to any other being in addition to God. Therefore he only spoke of a world-creating angel. Epiphanius does of course call this angel an "other God" alongside "the good God above."[383] But there is certainly no justification for this in light of what Tertullian says. Thus Apelles may generally regard those two angels, the "renowned angel" that coincides with Christ in some way or other, and the "fiery angel" that, as the "opposing spirit,"[384] takes his name from fire—similar to how the Clementines' author regards fire as the demonic element—and places them in the same relation to the one God as, for the Clementines, the two rulers, of good and of evil, or the right hand and the left hand, stand in relation to each other.

The Clementines' writer divides the matter proceeding from the essence of God into four elements, in two pairs of opposites. These are the same elements of which Epiphanius speaks in presenting the teaching of Apelles, dryness and dampness, heat and cold.[385] The body or the flesh with which Christ came down to the earth from the higher world consisted of three elements. "They say Christ borrowed his flesh from the stars and from the substances of the higher world."[386] These are therefore "the substances of the higher world" according to whose archetypes the world's creator, the "renowned angel," had fashioned the created world. Perhaps Christ is himself the creator of this higher world, and so, inasmuch as Christ is the direct transmitter of God's world-creating activity, is in fact God the creator of pure matter, Christ would then be, like the wisdom (σοφία) in the Clementines' system, simply the "creating hand" (χεὶρ δημιουργοῦσα).[387]

381. [Ed.] Ibid. The reference is to Luke 15:4–7.

382. *On the Soul*, ch. 23, speaks of "a fiery angel, Israel's God and ours" [ANF 3:203]; *On the Flesh of Christ*, ch. 8, speaks of "the fiery author of evil" [ANF 3:529].

383. Epiphanius, *Against Heresies* 44.1.4 and 44.2.1.

384. See Eusebius, *Ecclesiastical History* 5.13.2 [LCL, 1:466–67].

385. Epiphanius, *Against Heresies* 44.2

386. Tertullian, *On the Flesh of Christ*, ch. 6 [ANF 3:526]. See also *Against Marcion* 3.21: "a body of flesh . . . which he borrowed from the elements" [ANF 3:330].

387. See *Prescription against Heretics*, ch. 5 [ch. 6 in the *ANF* Appendix]: "Apelles does not affirm, like Marcion, that Christ had a phantasmal form, nor does he say Christ was in substance true body as

Marcionite antipathy to matter Apelles therefore confined to the flesh in the actual sense, and that is why he made its creator to also be the "fiery angel." Tertullian states that "earthly lures enticed our souls down from their super-celestial bodies by a fiery angel, Israel's God and ours, who then enclosed them firmly within our sinful flesh."[388] So Apelles was not a docetist like Marcion. According to Tertullian, Apelles maintained that Christ had "a solid body . . . a real body . . . flesh borrowed from the stars and from the substance of the higher world." Apelles and his followers appealed to the phenomena of the angels who are indeed appearing in a body, but not a body acquired by being born. "They set forth the flesh of Christ after the pattern of the angels, declaring that it is not born, and yet flesh for all that . . . The angels derived their flesh from the stars."[389]

In this context Apelles comes closer to the Clementine system. Thus he also seems to have adopted, along with it, the duality of male and female principles. Prior to their being bound to bodies, he divides souls into male and female souls.[390] Since Apelles affirms that souls fell because of their desire for the flesh, doubtlessly for him those souls who let themselves be banished into bodies of flesh by the fiery demon, the creator of the flesh, were female souls, and the male souls were those who kept themselves pure of all earthly, fleshly desire. Therefore the rule of that fiery demon extended as far as the desires of the flesh and the life of the flesh extended. This is probably why Tertullian made the adjustment of calling both the renowned angel and the fiery angel the creator and sovereign of the world. This readily suggests the following relationships: Christ as creator of the pure world above; the renowned angel as creator of the imperfect, material world; the fiery angel as creator of the sinful, fleshly world. This would be the Valentinians' trichotomy of the three principles, had Apelles not distinguished in a different way between matter and flesh; and especially since he also denied the resurrection of the flesh and contended that salvation by Christ pertains only to the soul.

Apelles' view of the Old Testament is also especially noteworthy. Tertullian directly states: "Apelles repudiates the law and the prophets . . . Besides, he has his own books, which he calls books of syllogisms, where he seeks to prove that whatever Moses has written about God is not true, but is false."[391] But with Apelles having found

---

the gospel teaches. Apelles says that, in descending from the higher regions, Christ wove for himself a flesh of a starry and ethereal nature, and that, as resurrected, in his ascent he restored to the individual elements what he had borrowed in his descent—so that the parts of his body dispersed, and in heaven he reinstated only his spirit" [ANF 3:653].

388. *On the Soul*, ch. 23 [ANF 3:203]. See also *On the Flesh of Christ*, ch. 8: "Apelles' followers greatly stress the shameful condition of the flesh, which they say has been furnished with souls tampered with by the fiery author of evil" [ANF 3:529].

389. Tertullian, *On the Flesh of Christ*, ch. 6 [ANF 3:526].

390. Tertullian, *On the Soul*, ch. 36. [*Ed.*] In the text Baur adds the Greek for this statement.

391. *Prescription against Heretics*, ch. 51 [ch. 6 in ANF Appendix, 3:653–54].

so much in the Old Testament that is false, mythical, and unbelievable,[392] he therefore had to draw a certain distinction. Epiphanius presents this as the teaching of Apelles:

> The savior truly appeared in the world and taught us the supernal knowledge. He taught us to despise the Demiurge and to deny his works, showing us in which book of scripture which things were really said by him, and which are from the Demiurge. For, Apelles says, in the gospel the savior said to become good moneychangers. Apelles says that he makes use of every book of scripture, choosing what is useful.[393]

It must not be surprising to see here a follower of the main foe opposed by the *Clementine Homilies*, applying to the Old Testament the same critical principles that these same *Homilies* affirmed as valid, in order to separate the authentic from the inauthentic, what is original and divine from what only got mixed in with it by the Devil. We certainly should not hesitate about accepting Epiphanius' account here, since Pamphilus (in his *Apology for Origen*) also ascribes to Apelles this same statement by Christ as the principle that he follows.

In light of all this information, are we to suppose that Apelles' teaching as a whole attests to the impression made by the Pseudo-Clementine system at that time? Tertullian himself describes a change that ensued in the view of Apelles: "He withdrew from Alexandria, away from the sight of his most abstemious master, and returning after some years, he was no better except that he was no longer a Marcionite."[394] Neander wants to credit this change to the influence of the Alexandrian philosophy and to Gnosis.[395] But why should one not, in this case, have looked upon the *Clementine Homilies* as the more specific source of this newly-acquired view (for the *Homilies* could certainly have become known very early on in Alexandria too)? When Apelles, in his advanced years and with an acquiescent spirit, expressed his view of Gnostic speculation, he considered the very teaching around which the whole system of the *Homilies* organized itself, as the fundamental teaching of all religion, the affirmation of one primal being, to be the essential thing to which faith must adhere.[396]

---

392. On this point see Origen, *Against Celsus*, 5.54: "Apelles, the disciple of Marcion, having become the founder of a certain sect, treated the writings of the Jews as fabulous" [*ANF* 4:567]. Eusebius writes in *Ecclesiastical History* 5.13: "Apelles—who says the prophecies are from an opposing spirit—uttered countless impieties against the law of Moses, and in many treatises blasphemed the divine words with no little zeal, as it seemed, for refuting and overthrowing them" [LCL, 1:466-67, 470-71].

393. Epiphanius, *Against Heresies* 44.2.5-6 [Amidon (n. 35), 162-63]. [On moneychangers, see n. 335.]

394. *Prescription against Heretics*, ch. 30 [*ANF* 3:257]. See also *Against Marcion* 4.17: "Apelles . . . a corrector of Marcion, although his disciple" [*ANF* 3:374]. See also 3.11: "Apelles and the other seceders from Marcion" [*ANF* 3:330].

395. Neander, *Genetische Entwickelung* [n. 6], 323.

396. See Eusebius, *Ecclesiastical History* 5.13.

## Concluding Remarks about Part Two

In looking back at all the contents of this part, we see these systems presenting both the internal and external development of Gnosis. The three main forms of Gnosis we have considered are, conceptually, the moments of the [internal] development. They likewise mark the three epochs of the external development of Gnosis, the epochs of its appearance as a historical phenomenon.[397]

In the sphere within which we see Gnosis operating, it completes its course of development in these three forms and epochs. Yet even within the scope delineated here, Gnosis is only relatively complete. The two forms of Gnosis following after the Valentinian form set themselves apart from it by the sharply-defined negation; whereas Valentinianism was not yet clearly and sufficiently conscious of the antithesis. Marcionite Gnosis negates both Judaism and paganism, while the Pseudo-Clementine Gnosis negates paganism. Therefore, whereas this third form has in turn eliminated the antithesis with, or opposition to, Judaism, paganism too can claim, with equal legitimacy, to not be reducible to the absolute negation of truth. Hence the point that must especially be emphasized more specifically, in the further development and explication of Gnosis, is the extent to which paganism too is not to be looked upon as the absolutely false religion; that paganism is to be viewed as one of the developmental elements by which the concept of religion realizes itself.

---

397. The main passage about the historical placement of Valentinus and Marcion is Irenaeus, *Against Heresies* 3.4.3: "Valentinus came to Rome in the time of Hyginus [in 140], flourished under Pius, and remained until Anicetus... Marcion... flourished under Anicetus, who held the tenth place of the episcopate [151–161]" [*ANF* 1.417]. (Valentinus also made his way to Rome, like Marcion. As one might suppose, both of them did so in the expectation that only in Rome could it be decided as to what form of Christianity would become predominant.) In *Stromata*, 7.17, Clement of Alexandria—in naming Basilides and Valentinus, who lived in the time of Hadrian and the earlier Antonine emperors, and were the founders of heresies—also says about Marcion that he "arose in the same age with them, living as an old man with the younger heretics" [*ANF* 2:555]. But this statement that Marcion was older than Basilides and Valentinus cannot be authoritative, since this passage calls for some sort of further explanation (that is, the natural modification [of skipping over "living as an old man with the younger heretics"], which gets in the way of the following and just as unusual statement, "And after him [that is, after Marcion] Simon heard for a little the preaching of Peter"). – Given how I define the concept of Gnosis, there cannot be intermediary systems of Gnosis in the sense in which this notion is set forth in Ludwig Baumgarten-Crusius, *Lehrbuch der christliche Dogmengeschichte* (Jena, 1832), 143. If the Valentinian system is said to be a mediation between Platonism and Gnosis, and the Marcionite system is supposedly a mediation of the gospel and church doctrine with Gnosis, that would make it difficult to say which system presents what Gnosis is in itself. In this same sense, then, the Pseudo-Clementine system would be a mediation of Judaism with Gnosis. Briefly put, my own view sets itself apart from this one in that I take Platonism, the gospel or Christianity, and Judaism to be each not what is mediated, but as what does the mediating. Gnosis was not mediated with Platonism, and so forth. Instead the concept of Gnosis mediated itself with itself, in doing so via Platonism or the others, that is, via the forms of Gnosis determined by them.

# PART THREE

The Conflict of Gnosis with Neoplatonism
and with the Teaching of the Church;
the Further Development of Gnosis in Virtue
of This Conflict

# Introduction
*The Pagan and Christian Polemic against Gnosis*

IN THE FOREGOING PRESENTATION we have already seen one system raise objections to another, one form of Gnosis versus another one. This is an ongoing and lively process in which one form conditions another, and in which all these forms together are exerting their greatest efforts in the contest for the one and only concept of the absolute religion. To arrive at this concept in its pure and perfect form, while challenging and supplanting one another, they seek, in the most rigorous and exacting way, to separate what is essential from what is nonessential, content from form, idea from image.

On its own turf, so to speak, Gnosis could just carry on with disputes and conflicts of its own. However, the actual battle it had to engage in emerged from outside, from the direction of those who were forming the church's orthodoxy and saw themselves obliged to oppose the interests of speculation with the interest of faith. They regarded the Gnostics as the original and principal heretics. In Gnosis as a whole they saw an orientation that seemed to stand most definitely opposed to the objective idea of Christianity as expressed in the religious consciousness of the overwhelming majority. There is scarcely any other phenomenon of the ancient Christian church that so moved people's hearts and minds, that gave rise to such literary activity, and evoked such a serious response. For those who were very much of one mind, as in this instance, it was a matter of the very essence of the Christianity that could not continue on a course befitting the development of its own idea if it had not, first and foremost, overcome the antithesis Gnosticism presented to it. This is the topic the most important [Christian] writers at that time were occupied with in their works. Given their intrinsic value and their significance for the era in which they appeared, these writings occupy an extremely important place in the historical development of Christian dogma. While the larger task they correctly assumed involved solving the problem of Gnosis, their efforts were rewarded by acquiring more specific knowledge of this remarkable conflict.

The arena for the conflict, moreover, was not confined to the Christian church. Neoplatonism was also a factor here, in a way that makes a very essential contribution to the picture we must form of this vital and phenomenal religious movement at that time. It is especially noteworthy how Neoplatonism, with all the distinctive features of an independent religious philosophy, on the one hand played a role in opposition to Christianity, while on the other hand it agreed with Christianity when it came to certain shared religious interests, and even supported Christianity in the conflict with alien elements Christianity sought to fend off. Hence, in the polemic contesting Gnosticism, we have to distinguish the pagan opponents of Gnosticism from the Christian ones. We wish to deal with the pagan opponents first, even though they were the ones who came forward later on. That is not only because they constitute a more isolated phenomenon, but also because, in the bigger picture, the pagan polemic against Gnosticism marks the most external point from which the anti-Gnostic polemic can proceed. At the same time, however, both this pagan polemic and the ecclesial-Christian polemic show us what we always have to hold fast to, and what the opponents of Gnosis always had to recognize, and presuppose, in it, namely, what the concept of Gnosis itself never entirely puts aside or lacks. Thinking spirit forever has the task of explaining what this is, albeit in a different form. Therefore we cannot be surprised to find that a church father, standing in the series of opponents of Gnosticism, is at the same time a Gnostic himself.

# 1

## The Polemic of the Neoplatonists against the Gnostics

PLOTINUS IS THE ONLY one I will introduce here as representing the pagan polemic against Gnosticism. For this great Platonist's ninth book of the Second Ennead[1] is devoted to this topic in such a distinctive and comprehensive way, that it sheds sufficient light on this aspect of the polemic against Gnosticism.

We have no hesitation about relying on Plotinus, even though he not once identifies, by their usual names, those he opposes, and that even the heading for this ninth book, "Against the Gnostics," derives not from Plotinus himself but was placed there by Porphyry, who prepared the *Enneads* of his teacher for publication. From the entire contents of this book we see quite clearly which opponents Plotinus is dealing with and, with his precise knowledge of the Gnostic systems, that he knew how to shed light on the relation of Neoplatonism to Gnosticism. I believe that the objections and rebuttals Plotinus poses to Gnosticism can be grouped under four general headings: (1) the Gnostic doctrine of the principles; (2) the general Gnostic worldview; (3) the distinctive conceptions on which the Gnostics seek to base their worldview; (4) how the Gnostics see their relation to Platonism, as well as their claims about, and moral principles for, engaging in practical life.

---

1. See especially *Plotini ad Gnosticos liber. Graece castigatias edidi . . .*, ed. G. A. Heigl (Ratisbon, 1832). See also G. F. Creuzer's informative review of this edition in *Theologische Studien und Kritiken* (1834), 337–80. [Ed.] We cite the English translation by A. H. Armstrong in the LCL edition of *Enneads* (7 vols., London and Cambridge, MA, 1966–88). Plotinus (c. 205–270) was the founder of Neoplatonism and greatly influenced early Christian theology. Details of his life are known mostly through his student Porphyry, who arranged his works in six groups of nine books, or *Enneads*.

Part Three: The Conflict of Gnosis with Neoplatonism and with the Teaching of the Church

## Plotinus' Polemic against the Gnostics

The Gnostic Doctrine of the Principles

The first point, concerning the Gnostic doctrine of principles, is the point of departure for Plotinus' polemic. He says (in chap. 1) that there can be no other principles than the three on which his own system rests: the Good, as what is utterly simple and is First; then Intellect (or mind, νοῦς); and then Soul.[2] This is the order corresponding to the nature of things, "and we must not posit more principles than these in the intelligible world, or fewer. For if people posit fewer, they will either assert that Soul and Intellect are the same, or that Intellect and the First are the same." But it has often been shown that these are different principles. However, if there are said to be more than three principles, then the question is what other principles there might be in addition to them.

There is no simpler and higher principle than the principle of the whole, of all things. Here one cannot differentiate potency or potentiality (δύναμις) from effectiveness (ἐνέργεια), for this distinction does not apply to what is sheer activity and nonmaterial. This same distinction does not even hold good for the following principle, since one cannot conceive of there being one Intellect at rest and the other in motion, or active. What then should a state of rest be for Intellect, and a moving or "going forth" (προφορά); in other words inactivity, and then in turn "acting"? Intellect is always "as it is." Its activity is an immanent activity.[3] Movement toward Intellect, and around it, is that of Soul. Even the reason (λόγος) that passes over to Soul and makes Soul intelligent does not involve positing another principle between Intellect and Soul. Nor can one speak of several Intellects because of course there is one Intellect but the others are self-conscious intelligences (νοεῖ ὅτι νοεῖ).

Plotinus goes on to say that the two cannot be separated, that it belongs to the essence of Intellect to be conscious of its own activity. As for the Logos or reason that people locate in between Intellect and Soul, they are depriving Soul of intelligence if it is said to have received its reason not from Intellect but instead from some principle standing in between Soul and Intellect. Then it would surely have just a likeness of reason and not reason or Logos itself. Soul would not know Intellect and not be intelligent as such. That is why Plotinus states (in chap. 2) that "One must not posit more principles than these, nor make superfluous distinctions linked to them; . . . that instead there is only one Intellect, unchangeably the same, imitating the Father as far as is possible; . . . that one part of [our] soul is directed to the intelligible realities,

---

2. [Ed.] Enneads 2.9.1.1–12 (LCL 2:224–27). In what follows in our text here, Baur is quoting from, and/or paraphrasing, the continuation of 2.9.1.

3. [Ed.] Baur includes in the text here the Greek from 2.9.1.30, for the statement, "Intellect is always the same, resting in a static activity" (LCL 2:228–29).

another to the things of this world, and another is in the middle, for this principle of Soul has many powers."[4]

Plotinus returned to this same topic in chap. 6, where he speaks of how the Gnostics have hardly understood Plato.

> They speak of one mind which, in a state of rest, comprises everything, another that is different from it and contemplates, and another that consciously thinks (νοῦν διανοούμενον) ... They speak of a number of principles of the intelligible world (πλῆθος νοητόν) and formed an image of it by having wholly examined the truth in this fashion. Yet by this very multiplicity they have taken what is intelligible and dragged it down to a likeness of what is sensuous and inferior. One ought instead to reduce those principles to the smallest possible number, attribute everything to the principle that comes after the first principle, and leave it that way. For this [second] principle is everything, is the first Intellect and substantial reality, and as such it is everything that already is in accord with the first nature or essence, whereas Soul is the third principle.[5]

It is self-evident that Plotinus could rightly object to the Gnostic systems, especially the Valentinian system, for having multiplied the highest principles excessively. A few of the key propositions in this quoted passage are perhaps even pointing to the Gnostic systems. When Valentinus designated the highest principle as Bythus (depth, βυθός), as unknown (ἄρρητον), as Silence (Sige, σιγή), and then in turn as Ennoia (ἔννοια), this could have given Plotinus the occasion for maintaining that a distinction could not be drawn between an intellect at rest and a self-moving intellect (a silent ἔννοια and an active νοῦς). The various designations of the same principle as Nous, as Only-begotten, as Horus, as Logos, could appear to be presupposing a multiplicity of intellects. In any event Plotinus admonishes Valentinus for placing the Logos between Nous and the Sophia who is the world-soul in this system.

The remark that such a multiplicity of principles would drag Intellect down to resembling what is sensuous and inferior perhaps refers mainly to the Gnostic syzygies. There may be good reasons for this and other points. On the whole, however, it must be conceded that there is not as significant a difference between Plotinus and the Gnostics as there seems to be at first glance. If the Gnostic systems are grasped according to how their ideas arose as internally connected, as we attempted to do above, then the first group of principles in the system, the only ones under consideration here, takes us back to the same three principles as those of Plotinus. We see right away, and there is no mistaking the fact, that Nous occupies the same place for these Gnostics that Intellect does for Plotinus. Also, that the Soul of Plotinus' system corresponds to the Sophia of the Gnostics; for, in contrast to Nous as immanent activity, these two latter principles designate the activity that is outgoing, that manifests itself in the world.

---

4. [*Ed.*] *Enneads* 2.9.2.3–7 (LCL 2:230–33).
5. Ibid., 2.9.2.20–35 [LCL 2:244–45].

And what essential difference is there said to be with respect to the first principle, whether we call it the One or the Good as Plotinus does, or by the terms the Gnostics use for it? In this very passage from Plotinus he indeed calls it Father, as the Gnostics do. As we might also say, it is what is utterly absolute, what is self-existent, what first passes over into Nous, into Intellect, into the distinction between what is thought and what is thinking, between object and subject, albeit within this distinction it is identical with itself.[6] But when we compare Plotinus with the Gnostics, the fact that he expressed this threefold nature of the principles consistently and definitively, and that he grasped it in a way that shows how closely the Christian Trinity is related to the Platonic trinity, then his system evidently and indisputably must be recognized as essentially superior to the Gnostic systems.

## The General Gnostic Worldview

The second of these points presents much greater difficulties. It involves the difference between the Platonic worldview and the Gnostic worldview. We also see that this is the main topic *Enneads* 2.9 is dealing with from a heading given to it in all the manuscripts. In addition to "Against the Gnostics" there is an alternative title, "Against Those Who Say that the Universe and Its Maker Are Evil."[7] The latter title is accordingly equivalent to the first one. It in effect expresses the main issue to be dealt with in investigating Plotinus' opposition to the Gnostics.

The main passage in which Plotinus expresses his own worldview in opposition to the Gnostics is *Enneads* 2.9.8:

> To ask why Soul made the universe is like asking why there is a soul and why it, the maker of the world, has created. It can only be a question posed by those who want to think of the Eternal as having a beginning. They then envisage the world's creator as having undergone a change, and believe they have found the cause of the world's creation. Hence they must be taught, if they are otherwise capable of being taught, how things stand with the nature of

---

6. Like the Gnostics, Plotinus also spoke of the self-dividing mind separating in the distinction of object from subject—of an overflowing. "The One, perfect because it seeks nothing, has nothing, and needs nothing, overflows, as it were, and its superabundance makes something other than itself. When this [otherness] has come into being, it turns back upon the One and is filled, and becomes Intellect by looking towards it" (*Enneads* 5.2.1.8–12 [LCL 5:58–59]). Thus Intellect—as the second principle, in which the first principle, the One, so to speak "overflows," but in doing so is reflecting upon itself—attains consciousness of itself. (See above, pp. 73–76 and 101.) In portraying the Ophites' teaching, Irenaeus speaks in this sense of a "being filled with a great light and it suddenly bursting out," of a "power from that sudden outburst" (*Against Heresies* 1.30.2–3). Except that Plotinus locates this overflowing in the absolute itself, and through it the absolute substance becomes absolute subject, whereas for the Gnostics it designates the inability of mind, already become conscious of the limits of its own subjectivity, to grasp the absolute as object.

7. [*Ed.*] Baur also gives the Greek of this title in the text. This alternative title occurs in Porphyry's *Life of Plotinus*, 24.56–57 (LCL 1:76–77).

these beings. That would stop them from disparaging, as they so often are inclined to do, what they should have honored and revered with religious awe. No one can rightly find fault with the order of the world, since it reveals, first and foremost, the greatness of the realm of Intellect. The life of the world is a coherent, expressive, multifarious life, extending everywhere and manifesting an infinite wisdom. Why should one not call it a living and noble image of the intelligible gods? If, as an image, it is not the very same as its archetype, that is entirely natural. Otherwise it would not be merely an image of it. It is a lie to say that the order of the world is a replica wholly unlike its archetype. It lacks nothing for being, as much as possible, a noble, natural image. There must necessarily be an image, but not as the result of it being a reflection or an artistic contrivance. Instead that is because what is intelligible cannot be the end point. For its activity must be twofold, an immanent activity and an activity extending to something else, which is why there still must be something after it. Only what is weakest of all has nothing below it, whereas there is a wondrous power at work here that has certainly made itself known. If another world is said to be better than this one, what should it be? If there must be a world and there is no other one, then this world alone has expressed the image of that intelligible realm above it. The whole earth is full of living creatures and immortal beings, and they fill everything right up to the sky. Why should the stars, those in the lower spheres as well as those in the highest ones, not be gods, since they move in the most beautiful, orderly way? Why should they not possess virtue, since nothing hinders them from acquiring it? The things here below that make people bad are not present up there, nor any obstacles to their bodily perfection. Why should they not possess the greatest insight, since they are constantly at leisure and with their minds they fully comprehend God and the other intelligible gods? Or is our own wisdom perhaps superior to theirs? Only a crazy person could say that. If the universal World-Soul subjects other souls to constraints, how could there have been any better compulsion than this? For [in this case] what is dominant in the soul is also what is better. However, if the souls reach this point willingly, why do you find fault with the place they have freely chosen, since they could surely abandon it in turn if it is not to their liking? If the world is such that one can have wisdom in it, and that those who find wisdom here can, by that wisdom, live in accord with that archetypal realm, how does this not show that the world depends on what is above?[8]

---

8. [*Ed.*] See LCL 2:250–55. The translation here is a hybrid of Baur's translation or paraphrase, and the Loeb wording, with modifications of both. This passage clearly manifests the hierarchical structure of Plotinus' ontology, with the eternal realm consisting of three principles (the One; Intellect, where the Platonic Ideas reside; and the World-Soul) in descending order, and the physical, temporal world deriving from, and depending on, the eternal realm.

Right after this (in *Enneads* 2.9.9) Plotinus points out that there is no reason to find fault with the world because some people are rich and others are poor, since that is not a factor in whether or not one lives an ethical life.

Plotinus' main aim, throughout all of *Enneads* 2.9, is to refute the Gnostics' contempt for the world. He goes on to say that whoever finds fault with the world does not really know what he is doing, nor where this presumptuousness takes him. The reason someone does this is that he has no concept of orderly succession, first to second to third, and continuing on to what is last. Thus one ought not disparage what is less perfect than what is first, but instead must calmly accept the nature of all things. One must direct one's gaze to what is first and cease to be concerned about those horrifying notions people often have of the cosmic spheres.[9] These higher levels simply serve human well-being and are not there to dominate us, for instead they produce beauty and order. We must not demand that everything be good, for that would not be possible. Nor should we find fault with the world and believe that there should be no difference between this world and that higher realm. We ought to regard evil as none other than what results from a lack of insight, and as a lesser degree of the goodness that diminishes as one goes down in the scale of being. It is as though one wishes to call the natural world evil because it lacks feeling, and to call what has feeling evil because it lacks reason. Otherwise one would have to call the supersensible world evil as well, because in the supersensible world Soul is lesser than Intellect, and Intellect is lesser than something else [The One] is.[10]

Anyone who has love for something must also grow fond of what is akin to the object of his affection, just as everyone has love for the children whose father he loves. But every soul stands in this kind of relation to the supersensible world and, to a far greater degree than our souls, the souls of the heavenly bodies are intellectual, are good, and are akin to the supersensible world.

> How then ought this world of ours, or the gods who are in it, be cut off from the supersensible world? We have already spoken of this, but now we must also say that they [the Gnostics], with their contempt for what is supersensible, have no concept of it whatsoever but just talk as if they do. For how should it be pious to contend that providence does not extend in the same way to this world of ours or to anything else? Is this not inconsistency on their part? For they state that providence affects themselves alone. Does this mean in the higher world, or here too? If it means when they were in the higher world, then how did they come to be down here? If it applies to this world, then why are they still here? Or, why is God himself not here? For how else

---

9. [*Ed.*] This remark alludes to the beliefs of some Gnostics, and of others in the ancient world, that in rising up to the world above one must pass through a series of portals in the spheres above the earth, domains ruled over by the spirits of the heavenly bodies and posing barriers to successful passage unless one knows the formulas or spells by which to open them.

10. [*Ed.*] Plotinus presents this extended argument in 2.9.13.

can he know that they are here, and that while they are here they have not forgotten him and have become evil? But if God knows those who have not become evil, then he must also know those who have, in order to separate one group from the other. Hence he is present to all, and is himself in this world in whatever way that may be. Therefore the world shares in God. But if he is distant from the world he is also distant from you, and you can have nothing to say about him and about what comes after him. Instead, whether there is a providence come down from above for you, or for whatever you like, this world is then the object of providence and it cannot be separate, nor at any time be separated, from God. Providential care and communication (*Gemeinschaft*) pertains far more to the whole than to the parts, and even more to that Soul (the World-Soul) as the being to which the rational nature of the world especially points.[11]

The main theses to which Plotinus' line of argument against the Gnostic worldview can be reduced are briefly summarized in the following passage.

> We cannot grant that the situation with the world is so grave because there are so many unpleasant things in it. Only those who want to give the world a higher status than it can have are able to make this contention. They demand that the world should be on a par with the intelligible world and not just an image of it. However, if it is just an image, what finer image of the intelligible world could there have been? What other fire is more comparable to the intelligible fire than the fire here? What earth is better than this one, in keeping with the earth there? What sphere is more perfect, more worthy of honor, more well-ordered in its movements, in accord with that sphere which the intelligible world comprehends within itself? What other sun is more excellent as compared to that one, than the sun we behold here?[12]

## The Distinctive Conceptions on Which the Gnostics Seek to Base Their Worldview

Closely connected with this polemic against the general Gnostic viewpoint are the objections with which Plotinus combats individual key ideas of the Gnostic systems that support this general perspective. These objections are mainly aimed at the Gnostic idea of a fall of the souls, or of the state of suffering in which Sophia-Achamoth found herself. Plotinus speaks repeatedly about this notion. He says:

> If they maintain that the Soul made the world when it "shed its wings" and plunged downward, the counter to this is that such a thing cannot happen to the Soul of the All. If they say that this Soul was guilty of a moral failure,

---

11. *Enneads* 2.9.16. [*Ed.*] The translation is a hybrid of Baur's wording and that in LCL 2:286–89.
12. Ibid., 2.9.4 [LCL 2:236–39].

then they should tell us what the cause of this moral failure is. When did the Soul fail? If it is an eternal failure, then this doctrine holds that the Soul forever abides in this condition. But if this condition had a beginning, why did it not come about earlier than that? We, however, contend that the Soul did not make the world because of its falling; instead it made the world in not falling. For if it fell, the Soul obviously forgot what is there in the intelligible world. But if it forgot this, how could it have made the world? For how can the Soul work creatively except according to what it has seen there? Yet if it works creatively, in the awareness of what is there, then it has not fallen at all. The Soul does not find itself with obscured vision; instead it orients itself to what is in the intelligible world so it will see clearly. If the Soul was left with even a faint awareness of it, why ought it not turn back to it? And what do they say Soul gained by making the world? It is ridiculous to say that Soul would have created the world so that it would be honored by doing so. Saying this just depicts Soul as like those who make sculptures. If it first occurred to Soul to make a world and doing so did not come naturally to it, although one assumes Soul has the power to do it, in what way can Soul have done it? Will it not also destroy the world? If Soul now regrets what it has done, why does it hesitate to destroy the world? But if it does not yet regret having created, perhaps that is because Soul is accustomed to the world and has for a long time been comfortable with it. If Soul is expecting [reunion with] individual souls, then it would no longer have allowed them to be reborn, since in their previous lives they have experienced the evils that are here and thus would already have left the world.[13]

The greatest absurdity (if absurdity is the correct term for it) Plotinus says is the Gnostics' teaching that, as they tell it, Soul sank downward as a certain Sophia.[14]

They say that Soul initiated the decline to what was below it, or that Wisdom (i.e., Sophia) was the cause of it, or else that the two of them are to be regarded as one and the same. They also maintain that the other souls came down with them, and are members of Wisdom, and assumed the bodies of human beings. But they say in turn that each individual soul came down because of Soul, that Soul itself did not come down, for it did not sink below. Instead Soul just had a ray of light fall into the darkness, from which an image came to exist in matter. And since now, through matter, they have an image arisen from an image, in other words a material quality or whatever they call it—now by one name

---

13. Ibid., 2.9.4. [LCL 2:234–37]. [*Ed.*] "Soul" is capitalized here and elsewhere when it refers to Plotinus' World-Soul or its Gnostic counterpart, but not when the reference is to individual souls.

14. [*Ed.*] The long series of quotations or paraphrases that follows consists of excerpts from *Enneads* 2.9.10–12 (LCL 2:264–75). They constitute an extended attack on the doctrine of the fall of Sophia-Achamoth from the higher world, as Baur discussed it earlier in his account of the Valentinians. The footnote in LCL 264–65 however suggests that Plotinus might have gotten his account of it from the older versions in a Sethian or Ophite form, while acknowledging that "Gnostic sects borrowed freely from each other."

and now by another, in utilizing many different terms to make their meaning obscure—they therefore introduce what they call the Demiurge, presenting him as fallen away from his mother. This is how they derive the world, as the most distant of images . . .

[Part 11 begins here.] If the Soul did not come down itself, but just illumined the darkness, how can one rightly say that it has sunk down? If something like a light has streamed from it, one cannot say it has declined. There must then have been something situated below it, to which it drew near in order to illumine that thing it came close to. However, if the Soul spread the light while remaining on its own and without doing something else, why did the light issue simply from it and not from what is mightier than it is? . . .

[Part 12] An investigation into this "illumination of the darkness" by the light will make them concede what truly causes the world to be. What was the point of this illuminating unless it was utterly necessary? The necessity is either a natural necessity or is contrary to the Soul's nature. If a natural necessity, then it must always be so. If it is contrary to the Soul's nature, then what is contrary to its nature must have its basis in the supersensible world. In that case there was evil already before the world existed, and the world is not the cause of evil; for what is here in the world depends on the supersensible world. Then the Soul does not depend on what is here; instead what is the case here depends on the Soul. Therefore reason must trace [the state of] the world back to the first principles. However, if matter is said to be the cause of evil, then the question is: Where does matter come from? They in fact say that the Soul who sank downward saw the darkness that was already present and illuminated it. Where did the darkness come from? If they say the Soul brought about the darkness when it sank down, then the darkness obviously was not already there as that to which the Soul could sink. And the darkness is not the cause of the sinking, but is instead in the nature of the Soul itself. But this just amounts to assigning it to a pre-existing necessity, so that the cause is found in the first principles.

Later on we will see how these objections from Plotinus presuppose that there is no actual creating of the world, that the world always is.

## The Gnostics' Claims about, and Moral Principles for, Engaging in Practical Life

Finally we take up the fourth and last of the aforementioned points, which concerns how the Gnostics see their relation to Platonism, and their claims about, and moral principles for, engaging in practical life. What comes to the fore here, based on what we have already seen, is how much Plotinus finds fault with the Gnostics on this topic too.

Plotinus states, in opposition to the pseudo-Platonism of the Gnostics, that because they have not understood the ancient wisdom of the Greeks, in constituting their own sects the Gnostics have concocted all sorts of innovations with their empty talk of being aliens (παροικήσεις) in the world, of their being resisters (ἀντίτυποι) to the world, and of their having changed their minds (μετάνοιαι) about it. These new ideas they introduced in order to establish their own philosophy are far from the truth. What they say about streams and rivers in Hades, about reincarnations, and about adding to the components of the intelligible world—by speaking of Being, of Intellect, of a separate Demiurge, and of Soul—they take from the wording in Plato's *Timaeus*.[15] But they have not understood Plato. They have no concept of the world's creation and impute much that is false to Plato. They distort this man's views. It is as though they alone have comprehended the intelligible world, while Plato and the other blessed ones have not. If they disagree, they might say so without envy and not by treating the Greeks scornfully and arrogantly when they seek the approval of their own audience. What the ancients have said about the intelligible world is far better and more intelligently presented and will be recognized as such by those who are not deceived by the humbug circulating among this crowd. For what they have added to what those ancient ones held is misplaced. In wanting to differ from the ancients, they introduce all sorts of initiatory and destructive factors. They find fault with the universe; they reproach the soul for being associated with the body; they disparage the one who governs the whole world by identifying the Demiurge with the Soul and ascribe to this (World-) Soul the same affective states as those of individual souls.[16]

According to Plotinus, the way in which the Gnostics saw their relation to Plato was due to their own arrogance and pretentiousness. It was a feature of their own particular character as such. In this context Plotinus refutes the Gnostics' charge against the world, by pointing to a justice that determines the lot of each individual according to his or her moral worth. He says:

> You must strive to become as good as possible, and not believe that you alone can become good—for if you think this you are not yet good. You must rather believe that other people can become good too; that the spirits (*Dämonen*) are good; still more so, the gods who are in this world and look to that other world, and look most of all to the leader or ruler of everything, the most blessed Soul. So one must go on to praise the intelligible gods, and the great king who is there, exalted over everything, and who reveals his greatness through the multitude of the gods.[17]

Plotinus continues:

---

15. [*Ed.*] Baur omits the following quotation from *Timaeus* 39e, 7–9, which Plotinus includes at this point (2.9.6.17–19): "The maker of this universe thought that it should contain all the forms that intelligence discerns are contained in the Living Being that truly is" (LCL 2:242–45).

16. [*Ed.*] In this paragraph Baur is paraphrasing portions of *Enneads* 2.9.6 (LCL 2:242–49).

17. [*Ed.*] *Enneads* 2.9.9 (LCL 2:258–59).

> But if you wish to disregard the others and exalt yourself as though you were no less important, then consider, first of all, that the better person is graciously disposed toward all things, toward people. Then consider that a person of dignity and quality, and free of tactless arrogance, must strive to the extent that one's own nature allows, with the conviction that there is also room for others at God's side, and not set oneself alone as next after God—as in a flight of fancy that just deprives one of the possibility of becoming a god to the extent that such is open to a human soul. The soul can do that insofar as the mind or reason (νοῦς) guides it. But setting oneself above mind or intellect is tantamount to forfeiting it. Foolish people are led astray as soon as they hear it said: "You are superior not just to all people but also to the gods." For people are very arrogant, and someone who previously was meek and modest, an ordinary person, puffs himself up when he hears it said: "You are the son of God, and the other people you admired are not God's sons nor the ones venerated from time immemorial. You are effortlessly more exalted than even the heavens themselves."[18]

The following passage also refers to this same egotistical exaltation of oneself by the Gnostics. As he does in 2.9.9, Plotinus sets over against it the pious humility that results from the Neoplatonic worldview, by not looking to the individual instance but instead to the whole, and therefore also willingly enduring everything arising from the world.

> They say that perhaps their teaching induces people to take flight from the body, even hate it, while our teaching holds souls fast in their bodies. But that is like contrasting two people living in the same fine house, with one of them finding fault with the structure and the builder yet staying there anyhow, while the other one has no complaints and maintains that the builder did everything most skillfully, and anticipates that a time will come when he has to leave it because then he will no longer need a house. The former person would have thought he is wiser and more open to departing, because he shrewdly says that the walls of the house consist of soulless stones and timbers, that it falls short of being a true dwelling place. But he does not consider that what sets him apart from the other person is just that he finds unbearable what he must accept, for someone quietly enjoying the beauty of the stones surely also does not pass it off with a discontented shrug of the shoulders. As long as we have bodies we must remain in these houses that have been prepared by our good sister Soul, who has sufficient power to work creatively and effortlessly.[19]

In a very serious tone Plotinus cautions us about the detrimental impact the Gnostic worldview has on one's moral life.

---

18. [*Ed.*] Ibid. (LCL 2:258–61).
19. Ibid., 2.9.18 [LCL 2:296–97].

Most of all we ought not overlook what influence this talk has on the souls of those who have listened to it and found it persuasive because of its contempt for the world and everything in it. There are two schools of thought about the highest good. One of them locates it in physical pleasure; the other in what is noble and virtuous, and the striving for which proceeds from God and leads back to God. After he had done away with providence, Epicurus was left with nothing but the precept to pursue pleasure and the enjoyment of it. The teaching of those people [the Gnostics] disdains, with juvenile insolence, the lord of providence and providence itself. This teaching has discredited everything said to hold good here, and exposed to ridicule the virtue and moral life recognized at all times. The result is that nothing any longer seems to count as good. This teaching has done away with morality and with the righteousness instilled in morals and perfected by reason and practice. On the whole it has done away with everything by which human beings become virtuous, so that this leaves nothing for them but pleasure and one's own self. They have withdrawn from fellowship with other people and have regard merely for their own needs, unless perchance one of them is by nature better than this teaching. For what others regard as fine and good is not so for them. Instead they strive for something different. Yet as "those who know," they were said to strive for that knowledge, and in their striving to seek first of all to uprightly maintain what comes from the divine nature. For it is good to set one's store by the divine nature. But the divine nature cannot make any impression whatsoever on someone who, by being contemptuous of physical pleasure, has no share in virtue. The proof of this is that these people do not have anything at all to say about virtue. They wholly lack any doctrine of virtue, and say neither what it is nor how many aspects it has, nor how much the teachings of the ancients contain about virtue—about how one can begin to be virtuous and acquire virtue, or how the soul is educated and purified. For the adage "look to God" (βλέπε πρὸς θεόν) can bear no fruit if you do not teach people how you want them to do the looking. For someone could say, "What prevents me from looking and yet not refraining from any pleasure nor controlling my anger, or from remembering the name of God and at the same time being in the grip of every passion and not seeking to get rid of any of them?" No, virtue, advancing toward perfection and abiding in the soul together with circumspection, is what points us to God. The name God, when spoken without true virtue, is a vacuous term.[20]

## Who Are the Opponents at Which Plotinus Directs His Polemic?

Before we seek to spell out in more specific terms how the Plotinian worldview, as expressed in the foregoing passages, is related to the Gnostic worldview, it is worthwhile

20. Ibid., 2.9.15 [LCL 2:80–85].

to take up the issue as to which opponents Plotinus in fact has in mind in the wholly polemical book *Enneads* 2.9, which bears the title "Against the Gnostics." This title of course indicates that it is aimed at the Gnostics. But Porphyry gave it this title, and it seems as though Plotinus intentionally avoided identifying his opponents this specifically.

Not once in this entire book do we find the term "Gnostic." Nor do we find the term for a different kind of opponent suited for this controversy. The relevant passage to consider on this issue is chap. 16 of Porphyry's *Life of Plotinus*. Here Porphyry states that:

> There were in his time Christians and many others, also heretics, who had abandoned the ancient philosophy: Adelphius and Aquilinus, who possessed a great many treatises of Alexander the Libyan, of Philicomus and Demostratus of Lydia, and who made public the revelations by Zoroaster and Zostrianus and Nicotheus and Allogenes and Messus and others of the same sort. They deceived themselves and many others, alleging that Plato had not actually fathomed the nature of the intelligible world. That is why Plotinus refuted them many times in his discourses, and also wrote the treatise I have entitled "Against the Gnostics." He left it to us to examine all the rest. Amelius ran to forty books in his refutation of the writings of Zostrianus. I, Porphyry, have assembled numerous proofs against the writings of Zoroaster, showing them to be entirely spurious and recent, concocted by those who produced heresies in order to convey the impression that these are doctrines of the ancient Zoroaster that they chose to honor.[21]

At first glance this passage seems to provide a helpful clarification, which is why Creuzer was chiefly occupied with it in the review indicated above.[22]

In this account, which is important for the history of philosophy and of the Christian church, Creuzer believes he has found a satisfactory explanation for why Plotinus composed this particular book, and for Porphyry's justification for entitling it "Against the Gnostics." I cannot share the good opinion he has of this passage for the simple reason that, as long as we must concede, as Creuzer himself does, that we do not know who all the people it names are, I do not see how it can give us any satisfactory information. The only datum we can extract from it with certainty is just the fact that Christians were circulating these so-called "Zoroastrian revelations," but because of their tendency to be incompatible with Neoplatonism, the Neoplatonists rejected them as demonstrably inauthentic. Yet that fact has no bearing on this text by Plotinus, since we find nothing in it that could be related to this point. Indeed the distinctive feature of Porphyry's remarks is that they not only do not provide the desired information, but also apparently wish to lead us astray, even if we utilize the

---

21. [*Ed.*] *On the Life of Plotinus and the Order of His Books*, ch. 16, in LCL 1:44–45.
22. [*Ed.*] See n. 1.

far more pertinent data offered by a comparison of Plotinus' text with reports from the church fathers about the Gnostics. For we do not know how that known information relates to this obscure passage.

Of course, Creuzer, in order to make as much use as he can from Porphyry's remarks here, has drawn from this mention of Zoroastrian revelation—in virtue of which, he assures us, these sectarians gave rise to Plotinus' polemic—what he believes to be an indisputable conclusion. Creuzer thinks that, although Porphyry's account does not explicitly mention the Manicheans, he conceives of the followers of Mani as included among the Gnostics. This account would then be evidence of the formal recantation in which the Manicheans crossing over, or going back, to the Catholic Church must have denounced those who said Zaradas (Zoroaster) and Buddha, Christ and Manichaeus [Mani], and the sun, are all one and the same being.[23] The objection to this is that Plotinus was dead by AD 270, so how could he have written in opposition to the Manicheans, who first appeared about 280? This objection is set aside by the observation that the doctrines called Manicheanism were of course already widespread in the Roman Empire before Plotinus made his entrance. It is unlikely that Platonism, which was so widespread, did not become intermixed with Manicheanism, especially in Alexandria where, at this time, recent developments in Platonic philosophy would have set people to thinking. Also, we are informed that Scythianus, a forerunner of Mani, lived in Alexandria and had read the works of Aristotle. But how could someone who immersed himself in Aristotle have been unfamiliar with Plato? This combination is so obviously fictitious that I can hardly take it to have any historical basis. Elsewhere[24] I have fully set forth the reasons why Scythianus, the forerunner of Mani, is hardly to be taken for a historical person. That does indeed undercut the assumption of a Manicheanism prior to Mani, something Plotinus would already have known about. However, the text of Plotinus also contains a few signs quite clearly incompatible with the assumption that he thought those he was contesting included Manicheans in particular. Plotinus describes his opponents as hostile to the natural world, and while that description does fit the Manicheans, they were not entirely hostile to it. Their dualism extends to all aspects of the visible nature of good and of evil, and their hostility to nature is least applicable to the sun, which was for them instead the seat and symbol of Christ the spirit of light (which is why, in the aforementioned formulation, Zaradas, Buddha, Christ, Manichaeus, and the sun are designated as one and the same being). However, Plotinus repeatedly mentions the sun in his polemic. Thus his opponents' contempt for nature must also have extended to include the sun.[25] Thus if one wanted to presuppose an already existing

---

23. [*Ed.*] Mani was a syncretist who said the "apostles of light" included Zoroaster, Buddha, and Jesus, who were thus all essentially one and the same.

24. *Das manichäische Religionssystem* (Tübingen, 1831), 459ff.

25. *Enneads* 2.9.4–5 states: "What other sun is there then, after the intelligible sun and before the visible sun? It is absurd that those who have human bodies, desires, and affects do not think modestly

link between Manicheanism and Platonism, this Manicheanism would not fit with the tenor Plotinus gives to those he is combating.

But suppose one ultimately extricates oneself from the difficulties involved in taking this course, by resorting to Creuzer's remark that "the name is certainly not what matters, and if one prefers to speak of a 'Gnostic dualism' rather than of Manicheanism, then I would not object to doing so."[26] This is indeed the only recourse open to us. But availing ourselves of it involves the concession that the established point, from which we thought we could set out, now looks to be untenable and must be abandoned. In fact whatever we might want to make of Porphyry's statement, it appears to be of no help at all, and it can only have originated from circumstances involving Porphyry himself rather than Plotinus. There can be no doubting the fact that Plotinus battled with no other Gnostics than those known to us from the writings of the church fathers. The accounts of the Gnostic teachings that we find in them adequately position us to explain Plotinus' polemic, even without our having to appeal for help from the Mani who is so remote from Plotinus. To demonstrate this in somewhat more detail, we must distinguish the Gnostic worldview as such from the individual doctrines and conceptions the Gnostics came up with. That is because we must observe that all of the points Plotinus upholds in making his case against the Gnostics do not apply in the same way to the various major Gnostic factions. An alternative title for *Enneads* 2.9 is "Against those who say that the universe and its makers are evil."[27] Plotinus remarks about the Gnostic worldview as such that this characterization holds good in a certain sense for any Gnostic system belonging to the first or second group as I have classified them. For, separating the world's creator from the supreme God and assuming there is a great difference between these two, makes the creator a highly imperfect being who is not fit for the idea of an inherent goodness. This reproach is at least applicable to the very system Plotinus elsewhere has in mind, the Valentinian system. Yet if it were to count simply against this system, he would have to have toned down his polemic quite a bit. Is it not far more correct to designate this Gnostic worldview—which for Plotinus "says the universe and its maker are evil," and for Clement of Alexandria "runs down the created universe and

---

of their powers, and attribute to themselves the ability to attain the intelligible realm while not wanting to concede that same ability to the sun. The sun stands higher and is less subject to passions and change, and has a better understanding than we have" [LCL 2:238–39]. Also, 2.9.18: "How can they greet the lowliest people as brothers but say it is wrong to call the sun and the heavenly ones brothers?" [LCL 2:296–99]. All this could not have been maintained against Manichean opponents, but it entirely fits the Marcionites. See Tertullian's statement about this sun in *Against Marcion* 2.2: "O human being, there is but one sun that rules this world, and if you ever do not think of him as what is best and beneficial, and see him instead as fierce and dangerous, or even as base and corrupt, yet he is true to his own principles. If you are unable to understand those principles, you would likewise be unable to bear the rays of any other sun, however great and good, if there be another one" [*ANF* 3:297–98].

26. Creuzer's review of *Plotini ad Gnosticos liber* [n. 1], 357.
27. [*Ed.*] See Porphyry's *Life of Plotinus*, 24.56–57 (LCL 1:76–77).

vilifies the body"[28]—as the view of the Ophites, of Basilides and Saturninus? And why should Plotinus not have directed his attention especially to the Marcionite system? The dualistic worldview was more widely disseminated by the Marcionite system than it was by any other. In no other system did dualism emerge in such a characteristic and harsh way. If we consider the external circumstance at this time, the Marcionite system is the most likely Gnostic position to have come to the attention of this Neoplatonic philosopher living in Rome, for, like the Valentinian system, it had many adherents in Rome.

Hence, as we for good reasons might anticipate, we in fact find a few passages in Plotinus that not only pertain very naturally to the Marcionite system, but cannot even be referring to any other one in the same way. When Plotinus finds fault with his opponents, as he so often does, he speaks of their "despising the universe and the gods in it and the other noble things" (2.9.16); of "insulting beautiful things [in this world]" (chap. 17); of "fleeing from the body, hating it from a distance" (chap. 18); of "hating the nature of the body" (chap. 17).[29] He says they "disapprove of this universe and blame the soul for its association with the body, and reproach the director of this universe" (chap. 6); he says about their doctrine that "it censures the lord of providence and providence itself still more crudely" (chap. 15).[30] What system do all these statements describe better than they do the Marcionite system? How explicitly they concur with the expressions used by Tertullian to describe the Marcionite system!

Chapter 15 goes on to say: "Their doctrine despises all the laws of this world, and the virtue that has been gained throughout all past time. It makes self-control something to laugh at, so that one sees nothing noble existing here below. It does away with self-control and the righteousness that is accomplished with one's character and is perfected by reason and training."[31] This of course refers principally to the context in which certain Gnostics derive their indifference to morality from their Gnostic antinomianism.[32] Here Plotinus can be thinking simultaneously of both Marcionite antinomianism and its typical disparagement of righteousness (for Plotinus as a rule juxtaposes related phenomena as often as he can). The statement in chapter 4 ("If he [i.e. Soul, an inferior being] is sorry he has made the world and is going to destroy it, what is he waiting for?"[33]) may also be a particular reference to Marcion's teaching, at least as it would have been modified by a few of his followers. One can hardly fail to recognize this, for it speaks of the World-Soul, or Gnostic creator of the world, in turn destroying the world he has made as the result of being overcome by remorse. In fact

---

28. *Stromata* 4.26 [ANF 2:439].

29. [*Ed.*] LCL 2:284–85, 294–95, 296–97, 290–91.

30. [*Ed.*] LCL 2:246–47, 282–83.

31. [*Ed.*] LCL 2:282–83.

32. [*In the text*] (What Clement of Alexandria refers to in *Stromata* 3.1 as disdain for the body, or misusing the flesh.)

33. *Enneads* 2.9.4.17–18 [LCL 2:236–37].

Apelles spoke of such remorse.[34] If, as Tertullian states in referring to Apelles' teaching, "the world must then be at fault because he [a certain renowned angel] instituted repentance,"[35] was Plotinus not very much entitled to pose the question, "What is he waiting for?"

No other Gnostic system, in addition to Marcionism, calls for consideration here to the extent that the Valentinian system does. We find the clearest indications of Valentinianism throughout Plotinus' refutation, indeed especially when it addresses the nature of the Gnostic system as such. As long as Plotinus is just dealing in general terms with the Gnostic worldview, his polemic presents, first and foremost, the Marcionite system. But if one also wants to weigh individual doctrines of the Gnostics' speculative theology, the Marcionite system, which restricted speculation as much as possible, is not equally suited for this purpose. The Valentinian system is the one that is especially given to speculation about the supersensible world, and that gives such broad scope to the relations between the supersensible world and the sensible world.

We have already shown how the Valentinian system is very much subject to the reproach of needlessly multiplying the principles of the intelligible world. Tertullian also criticizes it for this same reason. See, for instance, *Against Marcion* 1.5 [ANF 3:274]: "Valentinus is daring, for he conceived of two deities, Bythus and Sige, and poured forth a swarm of divine essences, a brood of no less than thirty Aeons, like the sow of Aeneas."[36] In one of his passages that goes into the greatest detail, Plotinus says:

> What ought one to say of the other beings they introduce, of their exiled beings, their antitypes, their repentant ones? For if they say these are affections of the soul when it has changed or repented, and antitypes when it is, in a way, contemplating images of realities and not the realities themselves, then this is a new jargon associated with their own school.[37]

Creuzer interprets this as based chiefly on the teaching of Basilides.[38] Together with Heigl,[39] he very appropriately refers back to the aforementioned statement from Clement of Alexandria.[40] All the same I prefer in this instance to keep in mind mainly, although not exclusively, the Valentinian system because of the larger context of this passage. It seems to me wholly fitting to understand the term "exiled beings"

---

34. [*In the text*] (In the passage cited above, pp. 242–43.)

35. [*Ed.*] See above, p. 243, in the quotation from Tertullian, *On the Flesh of Christ*, ch. 8.

36. See Virgil's *Aeneid*, 3.289-93: "When, by the flowing waters of a lonely river you find under some holm-oaks on the shore a great sow with a litter of thirty piglets she has farrowed, lying there on her side all white, with her young all white around her udders, that will be the place for your city" [*Virgil: The Aeneid*, trans. David West (London and New York, 1990), 59].

37. *Enneads* 2.9.6 [LCL 2:242–43].

38. In his review of *Plotini ad Gnosticos liber* [n. 1], 358.

39. *Plotini ad Gnosticos* [n. 1], 62.

40. *Stromata* 4.26.

(παροικήσεις) as referring to the World-Soul or Sophia living outside of the Pleroma—of her and the souls belonging to her having their temporary abode in the place the Valentianians called the intermediate place. As for the term "antitypes" (ἀντιτύπους), it refers to the Valentinians' view of "counterparts of what took place above."[41] In this sense it could have been considered as referring to the Sophia here below and the Demiurge as antitypes of the Sophia above. But it seems to me that Irenaeus' statement about the Valentinian cosmogony is especially pertinent here:

> They declare that this collection [of passions] was the substance of the matter from which this world was formed. For every soul belonging to this world, and that of the Demiurge himself, derived its origin from [her desire of] returning [to him who gave her life]. All other things owed their beginning to her terror and sorrow. For all that is of a liquid nature was formed from her tears; all that is lucent came from her smile; all the corporeal elements of the world are from her grief and perplexity.[42]

All these features and elements of the world, in which the various states of the soul are objectified, are images corresponding to the soul's own being.

The repentance (μετάνοια) of which Plotinus speaks also belongs in the series of these states. To me it seems to be none other than the same state that Irenaeus calls "returning" (ἐπιστροφή). After he has spoken of the sorrow (λύπη) of the fallen Sophia, of her terror (φόβος), of her embarrassment (ἀπορία), of her ignorance (ἄγνοια), he adds: "Another kind of passion fell upon her, namely, that of desiring to return to him who gave her life."[43] Plotinus could certainly speak of repentant ones (μετάνοιαι) in the plural, for the same state of returning, or restoration, was also ascribed to the Sophia above.[44] Anyhow it is unmistakably Valentinian when Plotinus speaks of a "soul shedding its wings," or a "moral failure" having been committed, of a "declining" or falling-away "from that place."[45] It is especially so when he says "the soul declined to what was below it, and with it some sort of wisdom (σοφία)," and speaks of the "other souls" that came down with it as "members of wisdom"; and speaks of the Demiurge who, as "an image of the image," is the likeness of Sophia-Achamoth that is itself an image of the higher Sophia; and that he "revolts from the Mother . . . to the ultimate of images."[46] Plotinus refers to a thought (ἐννόημα) that the Gnostics speak of,[47] and this

---

41. Irenaeus, *Against Heresies* 1.7.2 [*ANF* 1:325].

42. *Against Heresies* 1.4.2 [*ANF* 1:321].

43. *Against Heresies* 1.4.1 [*ANF* 1:321]. Also see the preceding remark, "she strained herself to discover the light which had forsaken her" [*ANF* 1:320], as well as the following statement in 1.4.5: "When the Mother had passed through all sorts of passions, and with difficulty had escaped from them, she turned herself to supplicate the light which had forsaken her" [*ANF* 1:321].

44. *Against Heresies* 1.2.3.

45. *Enneads* 2.9.4 [*LCL* 2:234–37].

46. Ibid., 2.9.10 [*LCL* 2:264–67].

47. Ibid., 2.9.11 [*LCL* 2:268–69].

is obviously none other than the Enthymesis of the Valentinians. He also mentions the Mother to whom they assign an image that is itself just an image of the image.[48] Also, the "waiting for each individual soul,"[49] in other words the doctrine that the world would last until all the pneumatic souls have come out of the world and into the Pleroma, is something Creuzer has rightly designated as being Valentinian.[50]

In contesting the Gnostic explanation for the origin of the world Plotinus asks, among other questions: "Whatever advantage did it (the Soul) think was going to result for it from making the universe?"[51] Here Plotinus is very definitely alluding to a well-known view of the opponent he is attacking. Heigl[52] quite rightly compares this to the Valentinian passage quoted above[53]: "What is, then, the cause of the image? The majesty of the countenance that the figure presents to the painter is accordingly honored for its name." Elsewhere too we find the view repeatedly attributed to the Gnostics that the visible world would have been created for the honor and glorification of the invisible world. On this point see the following passages from Irenaeus:

> These Aeons having been produced for the glory of the Father, and wishing, by their own efforts, to bring this about, sent forth emanations in the form of syzygies.[54] . . . This Enthymesis, desirous of making all things to the honor of the Aeons, formed images of them.[55] . . . These are images of those things that are within the Pleroma, the Savior having secretly labored that they should be so formed [by the unconscious Demiurge] in honor of those things that are above.[56] . . . While the Demiurge was thus ignorant of all things, they tell us that the Savior conferred honor upon the Pleroma by the creation [that he summoned into existence] by means of his Mother, inasmuch as he produced similitudes and images of those things that are above.[57]

See also Epiphanius' statement that the highest male Aeons "have acquired their names for the glory of the one who contains everything."[58]

The final point to mention is the Gnostic conception Plotinus rather fully rebuts, that the Soul did not so much come down itself as it just caused a ray of light to fall down, illumining the darkness. So this can of course simply be referring to

---

48. Ibid., 2.9.12 [LCL 2:270–71].

49. Ibid., 2.9.4 [LCL 2:236–37].

50. Review cited in n. 1, 369.

51. *Enneads* 2.9.4 [LCL 2:236–37]. [*In parentheses in the text*] See ch. 11: "How does it create for the sake of being honored?" (2.9.11 [LCL 2:268–69]).

52. *Plotini ad Gnosticos* (n. 1), 57.

53. In Part 2, n. 29.

54. *Against Heresies* 1.1.2 [ANF 1:316].

55. Ibid., 1.5.1 [ANF 1:322].

56. Ibid., 2.6.3 [ANF 1:366].

57. Ibid., 2.7.1 [ANF 1:366].

58. *Against Heresies* 31.5.9.

the influence the Valentinians see the Soul having on the Sophia existing outside the Pleroma or realm of light and based on it. This speaks of a ray of light that came down first from Christ, and then from Soter, into the darkness where Sophia was, a ray of light that both gave form or figure to Sophia herself and also was what made possible the creation of the world.[59] It is a way of speaking about a principle of light being active, in addition to Soul, in the creation of the world; it is like the Ophite system's depiction of Soul itself as some part of the light-principle that has fallen out of the Pleroma. This gave Plotinus the occasion to object that such views in fact involve the acceptance of two principles, one or the other of which is superfluous. In chap. 12, in a similar context, he raises the objection that one does not know whether the soul's falling already presupposes the existence of darkness, or whether the darkness is first produced by the soul's falling. This is of course obviously Plotinus replying to the traditional portrayal by the Valentinian system, for no other system could have been a target for this objection to such an extent. Of course Valentinianism does not regard darkness or obscurity, and matter, as independent principles, yet often enough it speaks of them in such a way that one could easily assume they are.

The indications I have provided are adequate justification for assuming that Plotinus is contesting no other Gnostic systems than the ones we know of from the writings of the church fathers. Frequently it is difficult to establish this in individual cases, mainly because Plotinus does not differentiate among the various Gnostic systems, nor does he ever draw more precise distinctions among the various principles that these systems have put in place. He just sticks mainly to those that have most bearing on the principles of Neoplatonic philosophy. A number of others receive no attention, in particular those the Gnostics designate with Christian names or terms. When considered in such a general way, much of this had in part to lose its own distinctive and original tenor, and to appear in a disjointed and ill-defined form that it does not have in the Gnostic systems themselves.

Related to this point is the oft-raised question, one Creuzer also poses, as to whether Plotinus has not aimed his book (2.9) at the Christians as such. This is an issue certainly meriting more attention than it has received thus far. Someone who pays attention to the course taken by Plotinus' polemic cannot, in many passages, help but think that he wants the reader to keep this prospect in the back of his mind. Hence much that stands out in this text might be satisfactorily explained by presupposing that its polemic, while of course not aimed directly at the Christians, is nevertheless intentionally so constructed that what it says first and foremost against the Gnostics also could apply to the Christians in general. Hence even Creuzer[60] does not wish to dispute the fact that in Plotinus' text we find statements containing a disguised opposition to the fundamental teachings of Christianity. For instance, in chap. 9 those who are unwilling to acknowledge multiple gods beyond the one God get reprimanded for

---

59. See Irenaeus, *Against Heresies* 1.4, and the discussion of this above on p. 59.
60. In the review cited in n. 1, 353; see also 369.

it. From whatever angle one wishes to look at it, this passage[61] concerns Christianity as such. It is one of the few passages that cannot be set aside or ignored. The rebuke to "contracting the divine into one," as opposed to "showing it in that multiplicity in which God himself has shown it," must be especially striking in a text directed against the Gnostics, since Plotinus also in turn reproaches the Gnostics for excessively multiplying the principles of the intelligible world: they "multiply natures" (9.2.1.26); they "make a plurality in the intelligible world" (9.2.6.14–15). This is the same characteristic feature of the Gnostic systems that the church fathers berate as pagan polytheism, pure and simple. However this very same major objection that Plotinus raises against the Gnostics' multiplication of principles might in fact be raised equally well against Christian doctrine as it is against the Gnostics.

Does not the following passage bring to mind the wording of the Christian Logos doctrine in its current, pre-Nicene form?

> It would be ridiculous to distinguish things existing actually and potentially, and so multiply natures, in things which exist actually and are without matter … One cannot conceive one intellect in a sort of repose and another in a kind of way in motion. What would the repose of Intellect be, and what its motion and "going forth," or what would be its inactivity, and what the work of the other intellect?[62]

The distinction current at that time, between an immanent logos (λόγος ενδιάθετος) and an expressed logos (λόγος προφορικός), completely fits the distinction Plotinus rebuffs, with regard to such principles, between existing potentially (δύναμις) and existing actually (ἐνέργεια), between in repose or at rest (ἡσυχία) and in motion (κίνησις) or "going forth" (προφορά). Even the expression "going forth" that he uses here (which is not very usual among the Gnostics, who make more use of the term προβαλή, or "putting forward," in this sense) might refer to this point. Moreover, what Plotinus asserts in opposition to the doctrine of the world coming to be, to a creation of the world taking place in time, applies to the Christians just as much as it does to the Gnostics.

The opinion he chastises in chap. 14, that diseases are evil spirits (δαιμόνια) people boast of being able to drive out verbally, so as to command the respect of the masses, was a view widespread not merely among the Gnostics but also among the Christians. They are presumptuous in finding fault with their opponents so often and in such strongly expressed terms, with the self-satisfied opinion they cherish that they

---

61. [Ed.] Enneads 2.9.9.34–39: "Then at this point one should go on to praise the intelligible gods, and then, above all, the great king of that other world, most especially by displaying his greatness in the multitude of the gods. It is not contracting the divine into one but showing it in that multiplicity in which God himself has shown it, which is proper to those who know the power of God, inasmuch as, abiding who he is, he makes many gods, all depending upon himself and existing through him and from him" (LCL 2:258–59).

62. Ibid., 2.9.1 [LCL 2:226–29].

alone are good, are children of God,[63] are the object of divine providence. They are contemptuous of everything that to the pagans seems to be worthy of reverence and divine in the world. They have the custom of greeting the worst people as brothers, provided that they just hold to the same opinions and tenets on this and other related points, even scorning virtue under the pretense that the only thing that matters is "looking to God" (that is, having Christian faith or belief). This all comes together in such a way that a pagan of that time had to believe he was seeing a picture of the whole Christian community and not merely one Christian sect. By taking all these factors together, one might even suppose it likely that the reason this entire text, as though intentionally, avoids putting a name to the opponents it is combating, is that Plotinus does not wish to confine his polemic exclusively to the Gnostics; that instead he wants to leave the reader free to see also how it could have been pertinent as such to Christians, to those whose general character seems to have found its specific expression in so many phenomena of Gnosticism.

## The Doctrines of Plotinus and Those of the Gnostics Are Internally Related; The Relationship between Plotinus' System and That of the Valentinians

The main question that remains to be answered concerns the internal relation between Plotinus' teaching and that of the Gnostics. We have already indicated that at many points the difference between them cannot be held to be as significant and essential as it seems to be at first glance. Since the Gnostic system Plotinus made the main target of his polemic, the Valentinian system, most definitely embodies a Platonic element, it is quite important to give our attention to what they have in common more so than to how they diverge.

If we go back to the original concept underlying Platonism, it is the view that the intelligible world is related to the world of the senses as the archetype is to its image or copy. At this point we see the two opponents, Plotinus and Valentinus, still on the same soil and foundation. Yet this is already also the point from which these two become forever divergent. The issue here involves the concept of an image. The image has two aspects from which it can be considered, a positive aspect and a negative aspect. As image, it is one with its archetype. However, as mere image, it is in turn something other than, and different from, its archetype. This simple distinction contains the key to explaining the origin of the entire difference existing between Plotinus and Valentinus as to the God-world relationship. Plotinus seeks to place the world on a par with God as much as he can, whereas Valentinus differs on this, and the other Gnostics belonging to this camp do all they can to separate the world from God by

---

63. Clement of Alexandria, *Stromata* 3.30: "Similar doctrines are expressed by Prodicus' school, who falsely claim the name of Gnostics for themselves, calling themselves natural sons of the primal god." [*Stromateis, Books One to Three*, trans. John Ferguson (Washington, DC, 1991), 274.]

the widest gulf. We do not need to elaborate further at this point on how they do so. The major teachings—about the disharmony brought into the Pleroma by Sophia, about the fall and suffering of Sophia-Achamoth, about the Demiurge standing so far below the higher world, furthermore about matter as the independent principle and the power of evil dominant in it, about the whole Gnostic dualism and what it involves—are all doctrines sharing the same tendency to separate the world as much as possible from God, and to follow through in all its rigor with the negative relation in which the world is placed vis-à-vis God. Yet if the created, sensible world is nevertheless to be called an image of the intelligible world, as Valentinus at least had to regard it, then it is just the kind of image in which the dissimilarity between the archetype and its likeness stand out to the fullest extent. In order to counterbalance this view in principle, Plotinus directly adopts a standpoint from which one should hold fast as much as possible to the unity of the image with its archetype.[64] The two must differ only to the extent that there is said to be a divergence between the archetype and its image or likeness. Thus as such there is not merely oneness but also an other or second one alongside the first, which is why Plotinus always comes back in turn to marvel so much at the beauty or excellence and the order of the universe, and at the divine imprint on it.[65] But the Gnostics look down on the whole visible world and despise it.

This difference then also sheds light on how Plotinus could hardly be of one mind not merely with what is in fact the dualistic teaching of the Gnostic systems, but also with all those who have the universe being subject to temporal change, who have the world coming into being and passing away. What weighs especially heavily against the Gnostics is the fact that they accept the principle of a Demiurge, one who could be actively creating by himself, undergoing change; also that they speak of "bringing about" and "doing away with."[66] Thus the doctrine of a fall of the Soul, which then posits a beginning of the world, is essential to the Gnostic systems; whereas in Plotinus' view the idea of the eternity of the world is necessarily the foundation.[67] One ought not ask why the world was made or how it began.[68] The world did not begin to be and it will have no end, for it is just as everlasting as the intelligible world is: "it always exists as

---

64. The fundamental perspective from which he sets out could not be expressed more specifically and more graphically than it is in ch. 8: "How should one not call it a clear and noble image of the intelligible gods? If, being an image, it is not that intelligible world, this is precisely what is natural to it; if it was the intelligible world, it would not be an image of it. But it is false to say that the image is unlike the original; for nothing has been left out which it was possible for a fine natural image to have" [LCL 2:252–53].

65. "Surely, what other fairer image of the intelligible world could there be?" (2.9.4 [LCL 2:238–39].

66. [Ed.] Within this sentence Baur includes in parentheses the Greek for these statements: "they think that the cause of the making was a being who turned from one thing to another and changed" (9.2.8 [LCL 2:253–54]); "they introduce all sorts of comings into being and passings away" (9.2.6 [LCL 2:246–47]).

67. That Plotinus takes offense at the Gnostic statement "in order that [the Soul] be punished" has its basis in their assumption that there must be a specific purpose for the world being created.

68. See the beginning of ch. 8.

long as the intelligible realities exist."[69] Because there is what is first, there must also be what is second, since it belongs to the nature of the first principle, inasmuch as it is what is absolutely good, that it imparts itself. In this context Plotinus says:

> If in the universe there are unlimited powers, how is it possible that there are these powers without anything sharing in them? Necessarily each being or nature must also share or participate in another. Otherwise the Good would surely not be the Good, or Intellect not be Intellect, or Soul not be what it is, unless after the initial life there is also a secondary life as long as the first life is. Of necessity, then, all things must always be, such that one follows upon another. But what has come to be has come about in that it is dependent on something other than it. Hence what we say has come to be has not come about absolutely but instead also always does so and will do so, and it will not also perish except as it can pass over into another. For what does not have an other into which it can pass over will not perish. If we say it passes over into matter, why should we not also allow that matter passes away? Yet if matter too passes away or perishes, what necessity was there for it to come into being? If we say it is necessary as a consequence [of higher principles], then it also necessarily exists now. Yet if matter is to be left all by itself, then the divine must not have been everywhere, but instead in a separate place and as though walled off by matter. However, if that is not possible, then matter must always be illuminated by the light the Soul itself has received and which it also spreads and imparts, so that what is here [in this world] is constantly held together and nourished by this light. What is living enjoys this light so far as it is capable of doing so, just as all things are warmed by a fire in their midst, although the fire occupies a limited space.[70]

According to this view there is no creation of the world if it means the idea that the world has a point at which it began to exist. If the world's being is posited conjointly with God's being, and if the world has its eternal subsistence in God, in the being of God himself, then in this system there also cannot be talk of any fall of the Soul, of an act or change of any kind as the Gnostics affirm that leaves the world separated from God, or the sensible world from the supersensible world, by a split as incurable as it could possibly be.[71] Yet on the other hand, the Plotinian system cannot

---

69. 2.9.7 [LCL 2:248–49].

70. [*Ed.*] Most of this long passage, which Baur encloses within quotation marks, is quotation or paraphrase from *Enneads* 2.9.3 (LCL 2:232–35). The last part, about the light and the fire, is perhaps Baur's own version of points mentioned in 2.9.4.

71. The idea of a fall on the part of Soul has roots in Platonic philosophy as also does the contrary view. This is apparent from the contrast between Plato's *Phaedrus* and his *Timaeus*. While a fall on the part of Soul [or souls] is more along the lines of Christianity, it is in the interest of Platonism, in contrast, to dismiss this idea to the extent that it can. Christianity, which does not start out from the idea of the absolute but instead sets up shop, so to speak, right amidst the moral and religious consciousness of human beings, can for this reason never be without the awareness of a split that separates people from God. So what takes shape is a noteworthy opposition to the Plotinian system on the part

avoid acknowledging the existing antithesis between God and the world, between the supersensible world and the sensible world, to the extent that it should have seen it as unnecessary to pinpoint more precisely the principle of this antithesis. The general basis for it is indeed the fact that what is second cannot be what is first, nor what follows be what precedes. But the pressing issue is always: At what point does this antithesis first emerge in its full significance, and what principle underlies it? That is why we see Plotinus, no matter how he expressly dismisses the Gnostic idea of the soul's falling, nevertheless agreeing with the Gnostics by locating the actual principle of this antithesis in the Soul, as he himself does not fail to explicitly emphasize. In chapter 2 he says:

> There is one Intellect, unchangeably the same and imitating the Father as much as it is able to. As for the Soul, one part is directed to the intelligible realities, one to the things of this world, and another is in the middle between them. Since the same principle has diverse powers, sometimes it withdraws into the best part of its nature and of existence, but sometimes the part of its nature that tends downward also takes the middle part down with it; but its entire nature can never be pulled down. This misfortune befalls it because it does not stay with what is finest, where Soul that does not share in this misfortune remains—and in which we too do not share. Here Soul allows the entire body to share in its nature, as much as the body is able to. The Soul effortlessly governs all things itself, without discursive thinking or need for improvement, but just by contemplating what lies before it, making it beautiful by its wondrous power. The more it dwells in this contemplative state, the more beauty and power it receives, in order to share it with what comes after it.[72]

So Plotinus too ascribes to the soul a πάθος or "misfortune" that draws it downward. It has an aspect of its nature in virtue of which it belongs not solely to the world above but also to the world below, and a downward pull it cannot resist. The cause of this lies in all that which distinguishes Soul from Intellect. For according to Plotinus the Soul, unlike the Intellect, is not an unchangeable, self-identical principle. Unlike Intellect, in which what is absolute beholds itself, the Soul sees existing being not in Soul itself but in the Intellect as a higher principle. Thus Soul's activity is no immanent activity like the activity of Intellect. Instead it is an outgoing activity whereby it brings forth something other, which is no longer something pure but instead already has an opaque being.[73]

---

of Origen's system, which does have a Platonic character but is entirely built upon the idea of a fall of the soul. That surely serves to explain the distinctive state of affairs in which Platonic philosophy was upheld by Plotinus and the Neoplatonists, where it posited an immanent relation of the world to God. This contemporary philosophy believed it had to oppose and confront the influence that Christianity, also especially in the Gnostic systems, began to exert on the spirit of the age.

72. *Enneads* 2.9.2 [LCL 2:30–33]. [*Ed.*] After "This misfortune befalls it," Baur inserts within parentheses the Greek for those words, and then specifies the misfortune with the Greek for "sometimes the part of its nature that tends downward also takes the middle part down with it."

73. See *Enneads* 5.6.4 and 6.2.22.

## Part Three: The Conflict of Gnosis with Neoplatonism and with the Teaching of the Church

At this point one rightly asks: In the final analysis, wherein lies the difference between Plotinus and his opponents, since on closer consideration any difference increasingly seems to vanish? Plotinus portrays the Gnostics' teaching as though they see the entire nature or being of the soul as sinking down below. This is why he replies to them that one ought not ascribe affective states to the universal World-Soul; that only particular souls could be subject to them. The reason the Gnostics do this in their systems is that, with their way of understanding things, they have not defined with sufficient rigor the sheer form of the idea by which they present this point. The fact is acknowledged, and cannot be denied, that the two Sophias, one above and one below, are, however distinct they seem, to be looked upon in turn as one and the same being. Hence the two of them are just two opposite sides of the same one being, mediating between the world above and the world below. That is why their attributes designate two divergent principles. Thus the Gnostics' Sophia is not essentially different from the Plotinian World-Soul with its diverse powers and orientations. Therefore, in the final analysis the main point on which they differ can also be found simply in the fact that the Gnostics give far more emphasis to the distinction and separation, whereas Plotinus, in contrast, holds more firmly to oneness and immanence. So the Gnostics follow through, to the fullest extent, with the negation [of oneness], whereas Plotinus considers the minimally-posited negation as already in turn abolished, in other words, as in principle never truly a factor. Hence while for the Gnostics the finite disengaging itself from the absolute, in order to seize upon its own apparent independence, also posits a temporal beginning for the world, for Plotinus this is just the eternal, accidental feature attached to self-same substance.

Accordingly the difference we are investigating here cannot be regarded as a fundamental difference resting on an antithesis of essentially dissimilar principles. Between systems that agree in so many respects, as the Plotinian and Valentinian systems do—on the Platonic paradigms they share, on the principles they establish, on their views of the relation between the sensible and supersensible worlds, on their doctrines about matter and evil, and so forth—there can be no greater discrepancy than there is between individual Gnostic systems themselves. Indeed, to some extent not even as great a difference.

The dualistic tendency by which the Gnostic systems set themselves apart from Plotinus' system has its principal basis in the Jewish and Christian element that these systems have internalized. It is characteristic of Judaism to keep the world separate from God, to locate it outside of the divine being and thus to regard it as something that has come into being and been created. Also, the idea distinctive to Christianity is that of redemption; and its true meaning necessarily presupposes recognizing that there is an antithesis or split between God and human beings, that the finite has fallen away from the absolute. The farther God and the world are separated in this way, the greater must be the number of beings and powers that get interposed between them as intermediaries partly in order to show how real is the separation conceived by the system, and partly in order to reinstate or restore the unity of God and world. Of course such a system had to embody a different organic structure than a system with a contrary tendency did. But this difference becomes even greater if that system, with its own instincts and inclinations, at the same time multiplies the principles it indulges in adding. This is why the typical form of its presentation involves personifying its operative ideas and making them out to be individual beings on their own, in the way the Valentinian system gives itself this particular character. In virtue of its strictly philosophical standpoint, the Plotinian system opposes such a propensity for mythic personification, a multiplication of principles in which the preponderantly external, nonessential form of portrayal threatens to become detrimental to the specificity of the concept.

Despite all this disparity, the two systems remain very much related, internally and essentially. Thus the system of Plotinus just presents the same basic form that constitutes the character of the Valentinian system, albeit in a purer and simpler structure. Earlier on we certainly had to characterize the Valentinian system as that form of Gnosis in which Platonism is by far the predominant element. Now that same Platonism appears to us in Plotinus, freed from all those modifications Gnosis had given it due to Jewish and Christian elements, and is thus elaborated as purely philosophical speculation from a distinctively pagan standpoint, unaffected by any Jewish and Christian concerns. We already see in the Valentinian system, more than in any other Gnostic system, the Jewish and Christian element put on a par with the pagan element, and even subordinated to it. Thus this pagan element emerges as exclusively in control in Plotinus, and the relation of this pagan standpoint to Gnosticism gets fully expressed by Plotinus in a characteristic way. For Neoplatonism wanted to attain its speculative goal only through the mediation of pagan religion, just as Christian Gnosis had its absolute religion being mediated simply by paganism, Judaism, and Christianity.

This is also why the traditional folk religion was able to gain its true significance here solely through speculation. Its divine beings counted simply as speculative ideas dressed up in mythic and allegorical forms. As Creuzer fittingly describes this characteristic feature,[74] Neoplatonism could hardly dispense with the personalities of the polytheistic national religion as necessary forms of its philosophical propaedeutic (Plotinus' mode of presentation is woven from below on the strands of Greek mythology), while nevertheless at the height of speculation this mythological apparatus, no longer needed, was freely demolished by the mind that had gained the knowledge and vision of the absolute. This is the very path that Gnosis has always taken. It cannot help being indebted to positive religion, although it always engages with it under the proviso that, as soon as positive religion has met its needs, Gnosis breaks out from it as what was merely an intermediary form.

---

74. In his review of *Plotini ad Gnosticos liber* [cited in n. 1], 352.

# 2

# The Polemic against Gnosis by the Church Fathers

*Irenaeus, Tertullian, and Clement of Alexandria*

IN TURNING TO THE Christian polemic against Gnosticism, what we now encounter is much the same as in the outcome of our investigation of the pagan polemic. As hostile as the Christian polemic sounds, and as harsh as the antithesis seems to be for the doctrinal system combating it, Gnosticism nevertheless repeatedly presents an aspect this opposition must involuntarily find congenial.

First and foremost among the Christian opponents of Gnosticism were the three great church fathers, Irenaeus, Tertullian, and Clement of Alexandria—very distinguished figures in many respects. The first two of them came forward against the Gnostics in purely polemical fashion, with Irenaeus most especially confronting the Valentinians and the offshoots of this main body, and Tertullian contending with Marcion and his school. Of course Clement of Alexandria contests the various Gnostic sects very zealously, although in his case we at the same time see heretical Gnosis become an authentically Christian Gnosis.

At this point we wish to examine somewhat more closely this more or less polemical relationship by disregarding what these church fathers affirm in opposition to the Gnostics based on Holy Scripture. That holds no further interest for our purposes, so we confine ourselves to the philosophical factors in their polemic. In doing so we will spell out more specifically how their standpoint set them apart from the Gnostics, and how they were able to dispense with the speculative issues that the Gnostics grappled with so very seriously and contentiously.

## The Main Arguments of Irenaeus against the Valentinians

In the first book of his work *Against Heresies* Irenaeus presents the Gnostics' teaching. Then in the second book he turns above all to the philosophical refutation of them. Irenaeus is a very skillful and sharp-witted opponent, and here we see right away that the Christian polemic is more penetrating, and that it arises on its own from a different standpoint than that of Plotinus. For Plotinus still shares with his opponents the Platonism or basic view that the sensible world is related to the supersensible world as image relates to its archetype. (He can make this the topic of his controversy with them inasmuch as it involves the issue as to whether both sides could be equally entitled to claim for themselves the same principle and the same authority, that of Platonism.) This is precisely the main point against which Irenaeus directs his strongest attacks, and he does this in different ways.

### The Supersensible World and the Sensible World Are not Related to Each Other as Archetype and Image

The main argument Irenaeus constructs against that view is this: the supersensible world and the sensible world, what is ideal and what is real, are so related to each other that it is in no way conceivable how the one can be the archetype and the other the image. For:

1. If the one (the archetype) is said to reflect and depict itself in the other (the image), then there is no longer anything primary and absolute, where we can come to a halt.[75]

2. The multiplicity and the manifold nature of the real, finite world do not lend themselves to explaining the self-enclosed unity of the ideal world.[76]

3. What is mental or spiritual, and is eternal, is set over against what is earthly and transitory, so that the one cannot be the archetype and the other the image.[77]

---

75. See *Against Heresies* 2.7.5 and 2.16.1 [*ANF* 1:367 and 380]: "If the creator of the world did not make these things from his own conception, but instead did so by using unrelated originals or archetypes, . . . why should we not affirm that these are, in turn, images of others above them, and those above these again, of others, and thus go on supposing innumerable images of images?"

76. "How then can those things, which constitute such a multiform creation, which are opposed in nature to each other and disagree among themselves, with one destroying the other, be images and likenesses of the thirty Aeons of the Pleroma, if indeed, as they declare, those possessing one nature are of equal and similar properties, and exhibit no differences [among themselves]?" *Against Heresies* 2.7.3 [*ANF* 1:367].

77. "But again, how can these things [below] be images of those [above], since they are really contrary to them, and can in no respect have sympathy with them? For those things which are contrary to each other may indeed be destructive of those to which they are contrary, but can by no means be their images—as, for instance, water and fire; or, again, light and darkness, and other such things can never be the images of one another. In like manner, neither can those things which are corruptible and earthly, and of a compound nature, and transitory, be the images of those which, according to these men, are spiritual." *Against Heresies* 2.7.6 [*ANF* 1:368].

Part Three: The Conflict of Gnosis with Neoplatonism and with the Teaching of the Church

## The Pleroma Cannot Contain within Itself the Principle of the Finite World

This argument already entails what Irenaeus affirmed as a further major argument in opposition to this Gnostic view. He elaborates on it with a series of additional objections.

If one wished to allow what has already been shown is not amenable to conceptualization, then one could only think about it in such a way that the concept of the absolute can no longer be linked with the Pleroma of the supersensible world. Accordingly one must abandon that way of thinking. For if the finite is said to be the image of the supersensible, then the supersensible must also contain within itself the principle of finitude. Yet in doing so it ceases to be what is infinite and becomes something finite itself. Hence Irenaeus says:

> If, again, they declare that these things below are a shadow of those above, as the Gnostics consider them when they maintain that what is below is an image, then one must also take what is above to be corporeal, for only what is corporeal can cast a shadow. What is spiritual cannot be thought of in connection with casting a shadow. However, if we grant to them what is not possible, that what is spiritual and is light also has a shadow, then the shadow of what is spiritual must be just as eternal and non-transitory as is the spiritual itself. On the other hand, if what is earthly is said to be transitory and changeable, then what is spiritual had to be like that too. However, if what is below is supposedly called the shadow of what is above simply as a way of designating the great distance between the one and the other, then what is above, the light of the Father, would be at fault for its shortcomings and impotence, as though it were in no position to be far-reaching, and too weak to fill the emptiness and dispel the shadow, although there is no obstacle to doing so. This presupposes something lacking in the light of the Pleroma, and no longer permits thinking of their Bythus, as the Pleroma, as being what is absolute.[78]

Such systems as those of these Gnostics always run up against the following alternative. Either the absolute, by having a principle of finitude or darkening within it or alongside it, is not truly what is absolute because it is constrained and delimited by such a principle; or, if that is not the way the absolute is, then the real world cannot be the shadow-side of the ideal light-world.[79]

---

78. *Against Heresies* 2.8.1–2 [ANF 1:368]. "It is, moreover, irrational and impious to conceive of a place in which, according to them, he who is Propator and Proarche, is Father of all and of this Pleroma, ceases and comes to an end" (2.8.3 [ANF 1:368–69]).

79. Irenaeus is especially emphatic about this alternative: "What is this vacuity or emptiness of which they speak? [*Baur inserts*: The κένωμα or void in addition to the πλήρωμα or fullness; the shadow in addition to the light-realm.] There will therefore be an absolute necessity, both that the Bythus and the Sige be similar in nature to a vacuum, and that the rest of the Aeons, since they are the brothers of vacuity, should also be devoid of substance. If, however, the vacuity is not something produced, then it is self-born and self-generated, and of the same age and honor as the one who is the Father of all" (*Against Heresies* 2.4.1 [ANF 1:363]). So for the Gnostics an image often has to take the

## The World's Creator May not Be Separated from the Absolute God

For the Christian opponent of Gnosticism, what follows closely upon these objections to the principle of the Gnostic worldview is the polemic against the Gnostics' customary separation of the world's creator from the absolute God. Here too Irenaeus asks first and foremost how this separation relates to the idea of the absolute. Are the two compatible or not?

Here is his answer:

> It contradicts the concept of God to set a higher principle above God, since God himself is what is absolute, is the fullness (Pleroma) of everything. As soon as something is outside God, then God is no longer the fullness comprising everything in himself. He becomes a being that is bounded and enclosed from without, and then one may think of the Pleroma and what is outside it as directly bounding each other, or else as separated by an endless space between them. In the latter case one gains a third principle that bounds and encloses the other two and hence must be greater than they are, for it bears the two of them in its bosom, so to speak, and thus there is no longer any resolution to the issue of what is bounded and what does the bounding. If that third principle begins above and ends down below, then it also must be bounded on the sides, and this bounding once again leaves us with the same situation, that our thinking can never just stick to the one God. But if we proceed beyond the concept of God, of the world's creator, then, with the same reasoning by which a Pleroma is posited as existing above the creator of heaven and earth, one Pleroma after another can be posited in an endless series.[80]

But by separating the world's creator from the supreme God, the Gnostics intended to shift the blame for the deficiency they attribute to the created world, from the supreme God to a being standing far below him. Therefore Irenaeus shows how this blame falls back once again on the supreme God.

---

place of a proof. So here they avail themselves of a pictorial comparison. "In the Pleroma, or in those things contained by the Father, the whole creation we know to have been made by the Demiurge, or by angels, is contained by the unspeakable greatness, as a circle contains the center or a garment contains a spot on it." But Irenaeus replies: "How can the Bythus allow there to be a spot in his garment? That would truly entail degeneracy in the entire Pleroma, since he would from the outset have been able to excise such a defect and those things that derived their origin from it. He would not have permitted the creation to form in ignorance or in passion or as defective. For he who can afterwards remedy a defect, and does wash away a stain, could have seen to it previously that there would be no such stain on what is his. If at first he allowed that the things made could not be otherwise, then they must continue always in the same condition. For how is it possible that things cannot be initially rectified, but can be rectified subsequently?" (2.4.2 [ANF 1:363]). As soon as one accepts into the Pleroma just one unilluminated point, it necessarily follows that the entire Pleroma will be something empty, misshapen, and darkened.

80. [Ed.] Although Baur places this statement within quotation marks, it is actually his abbreviated paraphrase of contents from *Against Heresies* 2.1.2–4 (ANF 1:359–60).

In *Against Heresies* 2.2.3 he shows that, while the world's creator, or the angels who made it, may be separated from the supreme God by an ever-so-long series of intermediate beings, the cause of what would have been created is still just to be sought in the one who willed to give rise to this entire series, or at least allowed it. Yet if we assume that the world would have been created without the consent and approval of the Father of all, that leaves us to consider whether or not the Father could have prevented it. If he could not, that would have been a proof of weakness and impotence. But if he could have prevented it, then he must have lacked a good will. Nothing can happen contrary to God's will, lest we want to do away with God's freedom and make him dependent on a necessity that stands above him. And of course at the outset he would have had to undercut such a necessity right at its source.[81]

## The Gnostics Ascribe Human Affects to God

We do not wish, at this point, to take up the individual arguments pertinent to the process in which the Gnostic systems evolved. They are too specialized for our purpose and also rest for the most part on an understanding that does not sufficiently distinguish the form from the content. However, an objection directed at the Gnostics' procedure as a whole—that they let the unity of the divine nature come apart in a series of activities that they hypostatize individually—very much deserves to be emphasized here, since these activities also relate to the concept of the absolute, and for that reason Plotinus also touched on this point.

In *Against Heresies* 2.13.3, Irenaeus says that when the Gnostics have Ennoia being sent forth from God, and Nous from Ennoia, and the Logos from Nous, then they are ascribing human affects, passions, and mental activities to God. They speak about the supreme Father in terms of what ordinarily applies to human beings. Yet they maintain at the same time that he is unknown to everyone and, so as not to imagine him as imperfect, they deny that he created the world. They assign to him human affects and passionate states, ones he must be thought of as transcending by far, since he is simple or onefold, not composite, and is wholly self-identical: wholly mind or spirit, wholly thought, wholly consciousness, wholly reason, wholly hearing, wholly sight, wholly light, wholly the source of all goodness, and because of that he is a being or nature transcending every conception of him. However, the emanations subject

---

81. "It would have been much better, more consistent, and more God-like, to cut off at the beginning the principle of this kind of necessity, than afterwards, as if moved by repentance, to endeavor to extirpate the results of necessity when they had gone so far" (2.5.4 [ANF 1:365]). Otherwise such a Father would surely have been no different from the Homeric Zeus, who says about himself, "I have freely granted it to you, but unwillingly" (2.5.4 [ANF 1:365]). Irenaeus remarks that no ignorance may be presupposed on God's part. "If he was really ignorant, then God will not foreknow all things ... But if he does know all things, and contemplated the creation which was to be in that condition in the future, then he himself made it that way because he formed it beforehand in his own mind" (2.3.1 [ANF 1:362]).

to him make him out to be a divided, composite, corporeal nature.[82] On the whole this is the same reproach expressed by Plotinus: "By giving names to a multitude of intelligible realities they think they will appear to have discovered the exact truth, though by this very multiplicity they bring the intelligible nature into the likeness of the sense-world."[83]

## The Gnostics' Effrontery and Inconsistency with Regard to Knowledge of the Absolute

Irenaeus is no less strict than Plotinus in censuring the Gnostics for their effrontery and arrogant self-confidence. But Irenaeus gives this censure a twist that Plotinus could not provide, without having to fear that the objection he raised could in turn apply to him too.

Irenaeus repeatedly puts to the Gnostics the question: By what right do they boast that they alone have knowledge of the absolute? He sharpens this objection by pointing out the contradiction involved in their ascribing to themselves a prerogative that they nevertheless deny to the creating being on whom they too depend.[84] Irenaeus finds the same contradiction between the opinion the Gnostics have of themselves and their contention that Sophia, by striving to force her way into the Pleroma and to comprehend the nature of the Father, was displaced into a state of ignorance and repeated suffering. The same striving, as one should have supposed, would not have resulted in perfection, passionlessness, and truth in the case of a spiritual Aeon, but instead the opposite. But Sophia, who is said to have occupied the position of those who are just human, strove to take hold of what is perfect and to know the absolute. Equally contradictory, Irenaeus further points out, is what the Gnostics teach about their so-called σπέρμα, the spiritual light-seed they say had been imparted to the Demiurge without his being aware of it.

Therefore the verdict had to come, in any event, from a standpoint that directly opposed a speculative position. For this very element, the speculative standpoint can always find its justification only by presupposing that absolute spirit arrives at its own consciousness in the knowing of what is absolute; and the moments by which it makes its way through itself are the mediating points through which it raises itself to itself, to its truth. In opposing this speculative standpoint, Irenaeus is fully entitled, from his own standpoint, to commend the simple and unquestioning belief in scripture, and

---

82. See *Against Heresies* 2.28.5.

83. *Enneads* 2.9.6 [LCL 2:244–45].

84. *Against Heresies* 2.6.3. "They show themselves superior to the creator ... It is as if foolish persons could learn from them something more precious than the truth itself! The statement [in Matt 7:7] 'search and you will find,' they interpret as expressing the view that they should find themselves to be above the creator, calling themselves greater and better than God, calling themselves spiritual but calling the creator animal" (2.30.2 [ANF 1:403]).

to accept the thesis that human beings must always be conscious of the limitations of their knowledge and of their great distance from God, who is what is absolute.[85]

## The Valentinian System Is Composed of Pagan Elements

When all is said and done, Irenaeus does not fail to view Valentinian Gnosis from the same perspective as the one we principally adopted in this investigation. He too considers it as related to paganism, Judaism, and Christianity, and his verdict is that the pagan element is predominant throughout.

In *Against Heresies* 2.14.1, Irenaeus first calls to mind the ancient comic poet Antiphanes, in whose *Theogony* Chaos is said to be produced from Night and Silence, Eros from Chaos and Night, Light from Eros, and with the rest of the first generation of gods proceeding from Light. Next he speaks of a second generation of gods and of the origin of the world. He tells how this second generation of gods created humankind. Irenaeus says that the Gnostics carry this whole account over into their system, while just changing the names. They substitute Bythus and Sige for Night and Silence, Nous for Chaos, and Logos for Eros (through whom all else had been set in order). The Gnostics model their Aeons on the initial and highest deities, and model the world of their Mother, outside the Pleroma, on the second generation of deities, which they call the second Ogdoad. They then portray the creation of the world, and the formation of humankind in relation to this second Ogdoad, entirely as that comic poet does. Thus they pass off as their own inscrutable arcanum what can be seen in any theater.[86]

The Gnostics treat the philosophers in a similar fashion. With their skillful dissembling they have stitched together the most colorful cloak from quite dissimilar bits of cloth. Their Bythus amounts to the same thing as the water that Thales made the principle of everything. Their Bythus and Sige form the same pair that Oceanus, as the "origin of the gods," together with the Mother Tethys,[87] are for Homer. Anaximander spoke of the Infinite or the Boundless as the principle that contains within itself the seeds of everything and the germ of endless worlds, and the Gnostics transferred this character to their Bythus and their Aeons. Anaxagoras "the atheist" taught that the animals originated from seeds that fell from heaven to earth, and the Gnostics attributed these seeds to their own Mother, maintaining that they themselves are these seeds. They have adopted their "shadows" and their "vacuity" from Democritus and Epicurus, who were the first ones to speak of empty space and of atoms; for the Gnostics called the atoms "what exists" and the shadows "what is nonexistent," with the former inside the Pleroma and the latter outside it. Their teaching that the sensible world is an image of the supersensible world is the doctrine of Democritus and Plato

---

85. *Against Heresies* 2.28.1ff.
86. [*Ed.*] Baur paraphrases this account, which can be found in *ANF* 1:376.
87. [*Ed.*] Baur has "Thetis," a different figure.

that they have made their own. Anaxagoras, Empedocles, and Plato likewise taught that the world's creator has formed the world from pre-existing matter. However, that each being would once again be reduced to the principles from which it has arisen, and that God is subject to this necessity such that he is in no position to grant immortality or imperishability to what is mortal or perishable but must allow everything to revert to its own substantial nature, is a general pagan teaching, especially that of the Stoics. In their distinctions among the three principles—pneumatic, psychical, and hylic or material—the Gnostics are following the Stoics.[88]

We see very clearly how much the Gnostics have taken from the Pythagorean number theory, in their system drawn up according to specific numerical relationships. Likewise one can hardly deny that the basic Gnostic thesis, that the nobility of the mental or spiritual principle cannot be sullied by any of one's outward acts, is derived from the Cynic school. Irenaeus also reminds us that the Gnostic redeemer [Soter], who proceeded from the collective Aeons as the sum and substance of the most excellent qualities that they have, is none other than a counterpart to the Pandora of Hesiod, and that the Gnostics themselves regard their twelve Aeons as the prototype for the twelve gods of the pagan pantheon.[89]

We can state without reservation that some of what Irenaeus has assembled does not actually fit in and some of it is only remotely relevant. But there can be no doubt about the correctness of the main idea Irenaeus is driving home: that a system especially like that of the Valentinians wholly embodies the character of pagan religion and philosophy, in keeping with all that has already been set forth on these issues previously and in different contexts. Irenaeus has quite correctly recognized this intermingling of what is Christian with what is pagan, as being the character of an entire class of Gnostic systems. Hence he has grounds for posing this alternative to his opponents: either all those aforementioned pagan poets and philosophers, the ones with whom the Gnostics are in full agreement, knew the truth, or they did not. If they knew it, then it was superfluous for the redeemer to have come down into the world. For why was he said to have descended? Was it perhaps to make the already-known truth known to people? But if those poets and philosophers did not know the truth, how could the Gnostics, while in such complete agreement with those who did not know it, boast about possessing a knowledge above and beyond that of all others, yet being in the same boat with those who do not know God?

---

88. [*Ed.*] These remarks about the philosophers thus far are taken from *Against Heresies* 2.14.2–4 (*ANF* 1:376–77).

89. [*Ed.*] See *Against Heresies* 2.14.5–6 and 9 (*ANF* 1:377–79).

Part Three: The Conflict of Gnosis with Neoplatonism and with the Teaching of the Church

## Tertullian's Polemic against Marcion

In his polemic against the Marcionites Tertullian had to take a different tack than Irenaeus had in his refutation especially devoted to Valentinians. However, these two church fathers also did have to follow the same course at many points.

Tertullian had a very important forerunner in the controversy with Marcionite teaching, the author of the Pseudo-Clementine writings. While he did not know of this text, he very often is in agreement with it. Also, in opposing the Marcionites, Tertullian even had to share the same view as Plotinus at least on one point.

### The Marcionite Contempt for the World Is Already Refuted by the Pagan View of the World

We begin with the last-mentioned point. For it cannot be surprising that even a church father was unable to accept the Gnostic contempt for the world that Marcion expressed most harshly, with the very great damage it does to the pagan philosophers. Tertullian even refers directly to the pagan worldview in his refutation to humiliate this Christian heretic.

Tertullian declares that:

> Marcion's most shameless followers attack the creator's works with haughty impertinence, in order to destroy them. To be sure, they say [just ironically] that the world is "a grand work, worthy of a god." . . . Yet how much more unworthy of him would it have been to create nothing at all! . . . Therefore to say something about the allegedly inferior quality of this world's makeup—which the Greeks speak of with distinction and refinement and not as sordid—these Greek experts in wisdom, whose cleverness inspires every heresy, have declared its element to be divine, as Thales did for water, Heraclitus for fire, Anaximenes for air, . . . and Plato for the stars.[90]

Consideration of the world's magnitude and power, its dignity and beauty, its permanence and harmonious regularity, has so impressed these philosophers of nature, or "physicists," that they suppose they can only regard these substances as gods, in the way the Magi of Persia do, as well as the Egyptian priests and the Indian gymnosophists. And when the ordinary pagan superstition in the myths becomes an embarrassment, then this superstition is indicative of natural elements and life, as Jupiter is indicative of fire, Juno of air, and so on.[91]

---

90. *Against Marcion* 1.13 [*ANF* 3:280]. [*Ed.*] Our text continues with an abbreviated paraphrase of what follows directly in Tertullian's account.

91. "Thus whenever Osiris is buried, and his revivification is anticipated and then celebrated, this is a sign of the regularity with which the fruits of the soil return, the elements recover their vigor, and the annual cycle continues. Also, the lions of Mithras [under the summer sign of Leo] express philosophically a link with an arid and torrid nature." Tertullian goes on to say: "It is enough for me that the placement and condition of these substances are more readily regarded as divine than as something

Tertullian continues with this point by emphasizing that the object of the Marcionite view of the world is the human being in particular; that the Marcionites' "better god" loved human beings so much that he came down from the third heaven, into these pitiful elements, and for human beings' sake he died on the cross in this, the world-creator's "little chamber." Also, the God who came down and was crucified for the sake of human beings certainly does not, with his sacraments, disdain the world's material elements. Only Marcion elevates himself above the master, so as to negate that for which the master longs. Yet even Marcion cannot escape from the creator's world and life within it, without relinquishing himself.[92]

Since this Marcionite worldview itself is based on Marcionite dualism, Tertullian had to make this dualism the foremost target of his polemic. So it is the main point that Tertullian attacks from all sides. We can divide the arguments he utilizes into two kinds, according to whether they bear on dualism in general, or on the special form dualism is given in Marcion's system.

## Refutation of Marcionite Dualism: It Conflicts with the Christian Consciousness of God's Oneness

At the head of his refutation of Marcionite dualism Tertullian places the general thesis, which is central to Christian consciousness, that God can only be thought of as one.[93] Human consciousness of God directly and necessarily thinks of God simply as what is absolute, and of all the attributes of God simply as particular forms of what is absolute. But if God is what is absolute, then he can also be simply one, because part of the concept of the absolute is that there can be no other equal to it.

If we wish to think of two absolute beings side-by-side, each within its own sphere as in two earthly realms, with each being having supreme power within its own domain, then this is a comparison that does not apply to God. Put differently, the comparison can only apply to a situation that nevertheless leads to a higher unity. For every multiplicity presupposes a unity, and we cannot think of two rulers side-by-side without the sole supreme power shifting to one of them as the mightier of the two. Moreover, Tertullian continues with a line of argument in which he concurs with the author of the Pseudo-Clementine writings, and which states that, inasmuch as dualism once abandons the unity, it even seems right away to be not essentially different from polytheism. If there are said to be two divine beings then one must ask, "Why

---

unworthy of God. But let us resort to lowlier matters. I presume that to you the proof of the creator's sorry state is that a single flower is inferior to a meadow, a shellfish from anywhere is inferior to one from the Red Sea, and the wing of a Moorhen is inferior to a Peacock!" (*Against Marcion* 1.13 [*ANF* 3:281]).

92. [Ed.] *Against Marcion* 1.14 (*ANF* 3:281).

93. "In principle, and consequently, the entire issue is one of number. Is it allowable to introduce two gods? . . . Christian truth has definitely declared that if it is not one, it is not God. That is because we properly believe that what is not as it ought to be does not exist" (*Against Marcion* 1.3 [*ANF* 3:273]).

not more?" And then "a multitude" would seem to be the preferable answer. But if this duality were to presuppose that there are two beings who, with each one equally absolute, are also fully equal to each other, then one would not grasp what significance there supposedly is in the mere number of them, unless the number is based on differences between, or among, the beings themselves. With this, Tertullian makes his transition to the refutation of dualism in the form in which Marcion has presented it.[94]

## Being Unknown Is Incompatible with the Concept of God

Since Marcion does not teach two equal gods but instead two essentially different gods, that opens the door to a new series of objections.

Tertullian's first rebuttal (in chaps. 6–7) is that differentiating the two gods by subordinating one of them to the other already does away with the concept of God as the absolute being. One may not appeal to the Old Testament practice of speaking of God by occasionally using different names or terms, since the concept of God can be determined not by the names used for God, but only by the nature of God. If, in considering the foundation of Marcionite dualism, one assumes that dualism in general, whether it be of two equal gods or of two different gods, seems to be completely untenable, then the first issue (in chap. 7) concerns the predicates Marcion wants to use in thinking about his two gods. There are two main predicates Marcion assigns to his supreme God. Marcion calls him the previously unknown God who first became known through Christianity, in contrast to the world's creator who is known through the visible world. Marcion also calls him the good God in contrast to the other one, the just God. Tertullian further elaborates these major concepts and opposes them with the full force of his polemic. His aim is to demonstrate that a single concept must embrace both that of the world's creator and that of the supreme God.

In chapters 9–11 of Book One Tertullian shows, concerning the concept of the unknown God, that being unknown conflicts with the concept of God. Since the world has been created, the one who created the world must also be known, because surely the direct purpose of the creation would be to make God known. The creator did not first become known through [the books of] Moses. Instead the idea of God expresses itself in a human being's immediate consciousness.[95] Of course Marcion sought to affirm this knowability with respect to the world's creator and not with respect to the

---

94. [Ed.] The argument in this paragraph is drawn from statements in *Against Marcion* 1.4–5.

95. "The soul existed before there was prophecy. From the beginning the soul is endowed with the knowledge of God. One and the same thing is true of the Egyptians and the Syrians and those in Pontus. For their souls call the God of the Jews their God ... Never shall God be hidden, never shall God disappear. He shall always be known, always be heard, even seen, in whatever way he wishes. God has this whole being of ours, this universe in which we dwell, as his witnesses. Thus he is proved to be both God and one, yet not unknown although another tries hard to prove it so" (*Against Marcion* 1.10 [*ANF* 3:278]).

supreme God that he sets apart from the creator. Thus Tertullian responds to him with the major thesis on which his argument turns: that one can be aware of God's existence insofar as God himself has revealed it.[96] Tertullian writes:

> Therefore the world's creator is God simply in virtue of the fact that everything is his work and his revelation, and belongs to him. For this reason there can indeed be no other god besides him, since the world's creator has already taken possession of the entire universe as his manifestation. Even the pagan world has acknowledged the general truth that God exists inasmuch as he manifests himself, in that the pagans declare to be gods only those who have made themselves known by some discovery and arrangement that is important and useful for human life.[97] For on what basis shall one affirm the existence of a god who produces nothing? The reason could only have been either that he cannot produce anything or that he does not want to. It is unworthy of a god to say that he cannot, but not a satisfactory explanation to assume he does not want to. For Marcion's unknown god did reveal himself at a specific time, and so must have had the will to do so. Therefore why did he not likewise reveal himself at the outset, and indeed in opposition to the one making himself out to be the sole creator of the world, in a way that would make the unknown God appear as fittingly transcendent over this other being? Whoever has no means by which he makes his existence known is himself nothing.[98]

Yet this principle, when put in such general and simple terms, could not stand in Marcion's way. Marcion's God was of course said to have revealed himself at a specific time and for a specific purpose. Thus Tertullian has the Marcionites making the claim that "One work suffices for our god, who has delivered human beings by his supreme and most excellent goodness."[99] The concept of redemption is just as distinctive to Marcion's supreme God as the concept of creation is to the world's creator. In order to undercut this tactic as well, Tertullian replies that a God who is said to have revealed himself as redeemer must have revealed his existence beforehand.[100] Here too the pressing question is: Why has he first revealed himself in what occurs later on and not already at the outset? How could there be no basis and no occasion for doing so at the

---

96. [*Ed.*] Baur adds here, within parentheses, the Latin for the well-known axiom that "one cannot prove a negative" (*satis est, nullum probare, cujus nihil probatur*).

97. "Marcion's god ought to have at least produced one chick-pea as his own, in order to be proclaimed as some new Triptolemus." [*Ed.*] In Greek myth, Triptolemus was from Eleusis where agriculture was said to have originated. Ceres sent Triptolemus to teach agriculture to the rest of humankind. See Ovid, *Metamorphoses*, 5:645ff.

98. [*Ed.*] This long passage, placed within quotation marks by Baur, is a mixture of quotation and paraphrase from parts of *Against Marcion* 1.11 (*ANF* 3:278–79).

99. *Against Marcion* 1.17 [*ANF* 3:283].

100. [*Ed.*] In parentheses in the text Baur gives the Latin for a subsequent statement in 1.17 (*ANF* 3:283): "The first thing to ask is, Does he exist?, and then, What is he like? The first is to be answered from his works [seen in the creation] and the second from his beneficence [in redeeming]."

outset, since from the very beginning human beings were the focus of redemption in the world, and they constantly needed the good God's support against the evil of the world's creator? Here too one would once again be driven back to the alternatives of God's being unable, or being unwilling, to do this. Both of these alternatives would seem unworthy of a God, and especially of the absolutely good God. This quite naturally leads to the second of the concepts mentioned, the concept of goodness, which Marcion assigns pre-eminently to the supreme God.

### We Cannot Think of Goodness as God's Essential Attribute If We Take It in the Sense in Which Marcion Assigns Goodness to God

Tertullian shows (in 1.22) that being unknown already inherently conflicts with the concept of God; thus it is still more contradictory to think of a God, whose essential attribute is said to be goodness, as not having been revealed. But goodness as such, in the distinctive and exclusive sense in which Marcion attributes it to his supreme God, is not to be thought of as the most essential attribute of this same God. This is the further line of thinking taken by Tertullian's polemic.

As is the case with all the divine attributes, God must be thought of in keeping with his own natural and likewise eternal nature. Accordingly these attributes are not to be regarded as something contingent, external, and temporal. So goodness too must be eternally in God and precede the reasons or occasions for expressing itself. Therefore why ought it not have already been active from the outset? A constantly-ongoing activity is a feature of God's nature. If, as Marcion maintains, God's goodness was ever inactive, then it also cannot be regarded as an attribute essentially belonging to God's nature or being. Then all the blame directed at the world's creator falls back on the one who withheld his goodness so as to allow the atrocities perpetrated by that creator to go unchecked.[101]

Just as everything in God is natural to him, so too everything in God is rational. The expression of goodness must also have a rational basis, for nothing can be considered to be good that is not also rationally good. However, this is why the goodness of the Marcionite God seems not to be a rational goodness. The human beings for whose salvation that goodness gets expressed are alien to God. If it is said that this salvation directly shows the love expressed toward such persons, as being all the more a free and voluntary love of those who do not deserve it, then that always puts love of one's enemy ahead of love of one's neighbor. With this reversal of the rational sequence it is natural, in referring to the goodness of the Marcionite God, to adulterate its rational character in yet another context. Its expression is bound up with the greatest injustice

---

101. [*Ed.*] This paragraph condenses Tertullian's argument in *Against Marcion* 1.22 (*ANF* 3:287–88).

and irreligiousness. For what can be more unjust and irreligious than snatching human beings away from the world's creator, who is their creator?[102]

Tertullian goes on to show, in 1.24, that the goodness Marcion assigns to his God is not once thought of as having the perfection that must be regarded as characteristic of a divine attribute. For how perfect is a goodness that has those it frees and redeems being far fewer in number than the Jews and Christians of the world's creator? If far more are lost than are saved, then surely what prevails is not goodness but its opposite quality, wickedness (*malitia*). Yet this goodness proves to be very limited even for those it redeems, since only the soul gets redeemed but not the flesh, which according to Marcion is not resurrected. What is the reason for this incomplete redemption but a deficiency of goodness that, imperfect itself, should have applied to the whole of a human being? If even Marcion's Christ is no actual human being, he has nevertheless assumed the appearance of being actually human, and was indeed for that reason also something indebted to the flesh. In any event, however, the flesh also surely is a part of human nature, and the redemption in which human beings are said to share thus cannot be limited merely to the soul.

In the contexts emphasized thus far, the goodness Marcion assigns to the supreme God is presented as an attribute that is not essential to God, one that is not rational or perfect. So this is a self-annulling concept, because it is separated from the other divine attributes, most especially from justice, in a way that is unworthy of God.[103] Marcion has removed from the concept of his good God all rigorous and judicial forcefulness (*severitates et judiciarias vires*); on the whole, everything that apparently must disturb his dispassionate, Epicurean-like calm, but for that very reason also deprives him of any moral seriousness. For how can the commandments of a God be upheld if he does not punish their transgression?[104] On this basis might fear not

---

102. "The character of Marcion's God is none other than this: swooping down into an alien world, snatching human beings away from the god who created them, the son from his father, the pupil from his tutor, the servant from his master, in order to make one impious toward his god, undutiful to his father, ungrateful to his tutor, worthless to his master . . . No one is thought more shameless than someone baptized to his god in water belonging to another; stretching his hands out to another heaven of another god; kneeling to another god on ground not belonging to that god; offering thanksgiving to his god with bread belonging to another god; distributing alms that belong to a different god for the sake of his own god. Who then is that god of theirs, so good that he makes human beings evil, and so gracious that he makes them angry toward that other god who is their proper lord?" (*Against Marcion* 1.23 [ANF 3:289]). [Ed.] This quotation concludes the lengthy argument of 1.23, which Baur has abridged in our text.

103. *Against Marcion* 1.25–26.

104. "I cannot tell how any system of discipline can be consistent for him . . . What is prohibited but not avenged is now tacitly permitted . . . No offense is taken . . . Or if he is offended, he ought to be angry; and if angry he ought to inflict punishment . . . But he inflicts no punishment, therefore takes no offense, and therefore his will is not violated. He did not want to have done what has been done, and he is now committed to acquiesce willingly because what does not go against his will is not a violation of his will . . . This will turn out to be an imaginary goodness, a phantom discipline, perfunctory duties, careless delinquencies" (*Against Marcion* 1.26–27 [ANF 3:291–92].

be separated from love?[105] After all, as justice can hardly be separated from goodness, likewise creation can hardly be separated from redemption, and the realm of the one God from that of the other one.[106]

This entire polemic is aimed at the concept of the supreme God that Marcion puts together, and it presents this concept in its untenability and futility. But this is only the negative aspect of this concept. If Marcionite dualism, that is, the separation of the absolute God from the world's creator, is to be completely refuted, that calls not only for dismissing the concept of that supreme god, but also for displacing the world's creator from the position Marcion reserved for him. This is the positive aspect that still had to be added to the negative aspect. It could only be added in a form setting forth a concept of the world's creator that is worthy of God and opposed to the accusation Marcion made against him. This is the main topic of the subsequent book of Tertullian's work. We only need to treat this topic briefly.

### The Concept of the World's Creator That Is Worthy of God, Set Forth by How the Concepts of Justice and Goodness Are Mutually Related

Tertullian first of all finds fault (in 2.2) with the audacity of the heretics in distinguishing a higher god from a lower god and daring to exalt themselves above the lower god. Whereas what they make the object of their reproof should simply make them aware of the human inability to know God. Nevertheless the main line of argument here too is dealing with the two concepts, goodness and justice.

In speaking of Marcion's unknown God, Tertullian sought to show that there is no firm ground and foothold for the goodness assigned to him. Thus he proceeded to demonstrate that goodness cannot be denied to the world's creator, and he does so by the use of analogy. The goodness with respect to the unknown God cannot have been allowed to remain unknown. So, by the same token, the first proof of the world creator's goodness must take into consideration the fact that he revealed himself and

---

105. [*Ed.*] In the text, within parentheses, Baur gives the Latin for Tertullian's question: "How do you love unless you be afraid of not loving?" (1.27 [*ANF* 3:292]).

106. Tertullian writes about this Marcionite deity: "Oh, what a god this is! . . . everywhere irrational . . . in whom I see no consistency, not even in the sacrament of his faith! What is baptism for, according to him? Is it the remission of sins? How is he seen to remit them if he is not seen to restrain them? He would restrain them if he acted as a judge . . . If it is deliverance from death, how could he who has not delivered *to* death, deliver *from* death? He would have delivered to death if at the beginning he condemned sin. If it is the regeneration of the human being, who can regenerate if he has not generated? . . . Baptism therefore removes the violation from one who has not violated, washes clean one who has never been defiled, and plunges the flesh that has no part in it into this sacrament of salvation . . ." [Later, with reference to Marcion's forbidding marriage, Tertullian says:] "How could he desire the salvation of a human being he forbids to be born, when he takes away the institution that leads to procreation? How will he have anyone on whom to set the mark of his goodness, someone who was not to have been born? How does he love someone when he does not love that person's origin?" (*Against Marcion* 1:28–29 [*ANF* 3:293–94]).

willed to have beings who know him.[107] The initial revelation of God is everywhere a revelation of his goodness, which is then first followed by the revelation of his justice, owing to the sins of human beings.[108] However, even on its own justice is so related to goodness that it cannot be separated from goodness. Everything just is also good, and what is not just also is not good. Hence goodness and justice can hardly be separated from each other, and by the same token there can hardly be two gods different in character because of these two different attributes.

From the beginning the creator has also revealed his justice, together with his goodness. His goodness has created the world and his justice has made it orderly. Indeed it is an act of his justice, working together with his goodness, that he decided to create the world in virtue of his goodness. Furthermore, it is a work of justice in that he declared the separation and distinction between day and night, between heaven and earth, between the waters above and the waters below, between the sea and the dry land, between the greater light and the lesser light—the light of the day and the light at night—and between man and woman, and so forth.[109] So justice, like goodness, is also accordingly an original and essential attribute of God—justice as governor of the world's operations (*arbitratrix operum*), and goodness as the originator of all things (*auctrix omnium*). Thus the concept of justice is not to be tainted by its being associated with evil.

Even after sin has become prevalent, goodness and justice work together in the closest way. Justice must give direction to goodness so that its gifts are bestowed only on worthy persons and are denied to the unworthy. Goodness and justice are most intimately interconnected, for each always presupposes the other. The divine perfection manifests itself in each of them, and every antithesis is in turn always mitigated in the idea of God. One and the same God smites and heals, slays and makes alive, brings down and raises up, produces evils and provides peace. But he does not bring about evil or misfortune in the way the heretics say he does. Instead he only does so as needed for human beings to distinguish the evil of guilt from the unpleasantness of punishment.[110]

We can let pass what Tertullian goes on to say in this part of his treatise, since it is in principle just a defense of the Old Testament. In order to rebut the heretics' trivial concept of the Old Testament God, Tertullian shows that the passages of the Old

---

107. [*Ed.*] Baur adds, within parentheses in the text, the Latin of: "For what is indeed so good as the knowledge and enjoyment of God?" *Against Marcion* 2.3 (ANF 3:299).

108. The first goodness of God is the goodness of his nature; his subsequent severity is in keeping with its causes. The former is inborn; the latter is accidental [a nonessential property].

109. [*Ed.*] This sentence, echoing parts of Gen 1:4–27, is found in *Against Marcion* 2.12. Baur then quotes, in a footnote, the passage that follows it in 2.12: "As goodness conceived all things, so did justice discriminate among them. With that determination, everything was arranged and set in order. Every location and condition of the elements—their motion and status, the rising and setting of the individual heavenly bodies—is decided by the creator" (ANF 3:307).

110. *Against Marcion* 2.11–14.

Testament to which they appeal, when correctly understood, do not actually contain such a concept, and also shows that consideration of human beings' moral freedom (in 2.5–7) would necessitate a certain limitation to be ascribed to God's being in itself.

## Refutation of Marcionite Christology, Especially Marcionite Docetism

Refutation of Marcionite dualism is at the same time the refutation of the Marcionite christology. Showing that separating the supreme God from the world's creator rests on vacuous assumptions, leads quite obviously to the fact that Christ cannot stand in relation to the supreme God and to the world's creator in the way Marcion understood that he does. The following two points merit emphasis here.

1. The entire way in which Marcion has his Christ appearing in the world, so suddenly and without preparation for it, seems to be incompatible with proper concepts of the divinely ordered world. Tertullian says: "This leads to the question: Ought he to have come so suddenly?"[111] If Christ is the Son of God, then the order called for is the Father announcing the Son, not the Son announcing the Father. The one doing the sending ought to have introduced the one sent by him, because no one coming on the instruction of another can prove his legitimacy by his own say-so.[112]

2. Above all it was the Marcionite docetism that had to conflict irreconcilably with Tertullian's view of the being and nature of Christ. In this context Tertullian exclaims:

> How can truth coexist with deception, light with darkness? If Christ's flesh is now found to be a lie, it follows that everything done by the flesh of Christ becomes a lie—his interactions with human beings, his living among them, the impression he made, even his miracles. When he touched people or let them touch him, when he healed someone from a disease, this cannot have truly

---

111. Ibid., 3.2 [*ANF* 3:320].

112. "Now Christ will neither be acknowledged as Son if the Father never pronounced him as such, nor be believed in if no sender gave him this mandate . . . Everything will be suspect if it violates this rule. In the first order of things the Father ought not be recognized after the Son, the sender after the one sent, or God after Christ. Nothing ought be acknowledged before its origin is recognized. Suddenly a Son, suddenly one sent, suddenly Christ! To the contrary, I daresay nothing comes suddenly from God, because everything is ordered and arranged by God. If ordered by God, why not also foretold, so that the foretelling proves it was ordered, and so is directed by God" (*Against Marcion* 3.2 [*ANF* 3:322]). See also 4.11: "Christ suddenly, and just as suddenly John! This is how things occur in Marcion's system. They take their own entirely special course. This is how the creator does them" [*ANF* 3:360]. (Compare *On the Flesh of Christ*, ch. 2: "Marcion will not brook delay, since he has suddenly brought Christ down from heaven" [*ANF* 3:522].) Also see *Against Marcion* 3.4: "I suppose Marcion's god disdained to imitate the arrangement of our God because it was displeasing to him, and was to be overturned. His god wished to come as a new being in a new way, a son coming prior to his father's announcement, someone sent prior to the giving of his mandate, so that he himself might propagate a most monstrous faith, one involving belief that Christ came before it was known that he existed" [*ANF* 3:323].

happened unless he truly had a body himself.[113] It is all just pretence. Then even Christ's suffering does not deserve our belief. For whoever has not truly suffered has not suffered at all. A phantom could not have truly suffered. Thus God's entire work is subverted and Christ's death, the whole import and fruit of Christianity, is denied—whereas the Apostle affirms that this is the foundation of the gospel . . . Besides, if his death is denied together with the denial of his flesh, then he cannot be truly regarded as having been resurrected; for if he hardly died, then he can hardly be resurrected . . . Likewise, if belief in Christ's resurrection is invalidated, then that undermines faith in our own resurrection. If Christ has no continuing existence, then neither can those for whose sake he has come.[114]

Tertullian draws further consequences from this point. In 3.15 he points out that, consistently with his view of matter, Marcion believed that his Christ would not be allowed to come into direct contact with matter. Thus it is contradictory to not also extend Marcion's contempt for matter to the likeness of matter. The image of something contemptible can have no greater worth than the contemptible thing itself. The response to this is that if Christ could not have been able to interact with human beings otherwise than through the intermediary of a phantom image of human substance, then one must have a meager notion of a God who could not let his Christ appear otherwise than in the phantom image of an unworthy thing that did not even belong to him. In other words, what value must one attribute to the flesh if even the supreme God was unable to do without it? Indeed he has surely honored matter by reproducing a likeness of it (*honoravit fingendo*).

This contradiction can only be resolved by either saying that Christ did truly and actually appear in the flesh, or resigning oneself to this flesh being merely apparent flesh. If Marcionite dualism does not consent to the former alternative then it is just left with the latter one, and for that very reason its docetism is fully equated with nihilism. However, if we let this docetism stand, together with its phantom Christ, then is not the idea of the God whom Christ revealed a mere phantom? Is someone deceived by the outer substance not deceived by belief in the inner substance? Inasmuch as deceitfulness is discovered in what is manifest, in what way is truthfulness to be had in what is hidden? What for Marcion seems to be sufficiently grounded in his own Christian consciousness and could not, for this consciousness itself, have also needed the external reflection in which it mirrored itself, appeared to Tertullian as completely vapid and meaningless as soon as it failed to rest on the broad foundation of the real world. God-consciousness no longer has any content for Tertullian if it does not get mediated via the external world.

---

113. [*In the text in Latin*] ("Nothing firm or solid can be accomplished by what is hollow, nothing full by what is empty.")

114. *Against Marcion* 3.8 [*ANF* 3:328].

Part Three: The Conflict of Gnosis with Neoplatonism and with the Teaching of the Church

### How Can Marcion Set Himself above Christ?

In Marcion's system there always remains a puzzling link between what is internal and what is external. Related to it is the following argument, which is not closely connected with his other arguments. We take up this argument here, as the simplest way to conclude our overview of Tertullian's polemic.

Tertullian asks: If Christian truth is to be found only with Marcion, then how is it that Christ of course appeared long before Marcion, but Marcion was the first one to reveal the true Christ?[115] Since the strict separation of law from gospel is the most characteristic of Marcion's undertakings, the God first become known because of this separation cannot have been known before it, and it is Marcion who revealed him, not Christ. The objection is especially noteworthy, for it goes hand in glove with a reproach directed at the most recent speculative theology. It is that, although Christianity might set itself very much apart from all other stages of human development leading to the absolute standpoint, because in Christianity the full content of the concept of absolute religion is indeed given, it is nevertheless always philosophy that first harmonizes this faith with absolute knowledge, and that, by taking a position above Christ, wants to show Christianity how to truly understand itself.

## Clement of Alexandria as an Opponent of the Gnostics

Clement of Alexandria stands alongside Irenaeus and Tertullian as a third partner in this same battle against the Gnostics, although he can scarcely be placed in a direct line with the other two. He is not an opponent of Gnosis as such, but only of the Gnosis of the Gnostics. So his polemic against the Gnostic systems is not as thoroughgoing and penetrating as that of these other two church fathers. Instead it just concerns itself with some individual Gnostic doctrines, viewpoints, and principles.

Of the points in contention for Clement, two stand out. One of them is the damage Gnosis does to human moral freedom and the ethical relationship human beings have to God that rests on this freedom, a topic the Gnostics seem to have a hard time dealing with. The other is the Gnostics' contempt for the world, to the extent that it resulted from the customary Gnostic rejection of married life.

---

115. "This impious heretic is from the time of Antoninus Pius. There is no doubt about that . . . The god of the Antonine period was not the god of the Tiberian period. Consequently, he whom Marcion preached for the first time was not revealed by Christ" (*Against Marcion* 1.19 [*ANF* 3:284–85]). [*Ed.*] Antoninus Pius ruled 138–161. Tiberius was emperor (14–37) during Jesus' adult life.

## The Gnostics' Failure to Appreciate the Moral Freedom of the Will and Human Beings' Relationship to God, Which Rests On It

The Gnostics draw distinctions among the different principles they establish and the different classes of human beings. Thus what makes the individual person capable of communion with God does not appear to be in principle the result of that individual's moral actions, but must have been just an effect of the self-developing spiritual principle within the overall cosmic setting. So the idea of moral freedom had to have taken a back seat very much to the view of a natural necessity determining the life of the individual.

Clement stresses this point in speaking about the followers of Basilides and Valentinus.

> The followers of Basilides regard faith as something natural, which is why they also ascribe to it a particular kind of choosing, as a kind of intellectual comprehension that finds truth apart from proof. Whereas the Valentinians ascribe faith to us, the simple folk, but maintain that they are the ones who are naturally blessed, because of the privilege of the seed setting them apart as those who possess knowledge; that there is supposedly an even greater difference between this knowledge and faith than there is between pneumatic and psychical persons. The followers of Basilides also maintain that faith and this choosing are adjusted to each level or interval (διάστημα) of the spiritual or intellectual world, with supramundane choice corresponding to the cosmic faith of each one's nature, and the hope of each one likewise paralleling the gift of faith that person possesses.[116]

For good reasons Clement replies to this position as follows:

> If faith is a natural prerogative, then it is no longer something freely willed. Someone who does not believe is not receiving his justifiable recompense, for his not believing is just as little assignable to him as believing is credited to someone who does believe. Proper reflection shows that here the peculiar thing setting faith apart from lack of faith is no longer the concept of praising or blaming, since it is all based on an antecedent natural necessity grounded in the omnipotence of the supreme being. If, like inanimate things, we are pulled through our natural actions as though by puppet strings, then willing freely is not essentially different from willing unfreely. I can think of no living being whose defining principle would be so moved by an external cause that it is totally a prey to necessity. How then are we to think of changing one's mind from a prior state of unbelief, such that it would result in forgiveness of sins? So too there is no longer any reasonable basis for baptism, nor for receiving the sign of blessing, nor for the Son or the Father. I suppose that instead God is for these Gnostics what constitutes the foundation of salvation as not

---

116. Clement, *Stromata* 2.3 [ANF 2:349].

being freely-willed faith, but rather the principle that imparts their natures to people.[117]

Clement later returns to this objection to Basilides and Valentinus for their accepting a kind of people who are saved owing to their nature (φύσει σωζόμενον γένος). See *Stromata* 4.13. Clement states that:

> If someone by nature knows God, as Basilides thinks, . . . then he cannot say that faith is the rational assent of a soul exercising free will. Hence the precepts of the Old Testament and the New Testament are superfluous if one is saved by one's own nature, as Valentinus would have it, or believes and is chosen by nature, as Basilides supposes. Surely then these natures could shine forth at one time or another, apart from the appearing of the savior. However, if one says the appearing of the savior is necessary, then these special prerogatives of their nature must fall by the wayside, and whoever is chosen becomes saved not by nature but by instruction, purification, and doing good works.[118]

This is certainly an effective rejoinder, whose main elements seize upon the antithesis to the views of these two Gnostics.

On the same basis, and in order not to concede that belief in moral freedom, and a divine foreknowledge consistent with it, could have invalidated it, Clement also thought he could not assent to Basilides' view of martyrdom, and to the concept of a necessary connection between guilt and punishment on which that view relies. According to Clement:

> Basilides says that the soul, having sinned before in another life, endures punishment in this life—the elect souls with honor by martyrdom, the others in being purged by appropriate punishment. How can this be true, for it depends on us whether or not we confess and suffer punishment? According to Basilides, when someone renounces his faith that happens because of providence . . . Where is the faith, if martyrdom takes place as the retribution for sins committed beforehand? Where is the love for God that endures persecution and suffering for the sake of the truth? Where is the praise for someone who bears witness to the truth, or the blame for someone denying it? What use is right conduct, the elimination of desires and the hatred of no creature? If, as Basilides himself says, we must, as one part of the divine will, love all things because all of them stand in a specific relation to the whole, and a second part is to not lust after anything, and a third part is to hate nothing, then it is impious to also think that the punishments [which we incur in the course of persecution] take place according to God's will . . . Yet does anything happen apart from the will of the Lord of the universe? So, to put it succinctly, we can only say that such things happen with God's permission (μὴ κωλύσαντος τοῦ

117. Ibid.
118. Ibid., 5.1 [*ANF* 2:444–45].

θεοῦ, "not as a hindrance to God"). In this way alone can God's providence and God's goodness be as one.[119]

This is a thoroughly ethical interest that Clement asserts in opposition to the Gnostic systems that see human beings as interwoven within the causal nexus of the universe. It is the idea of a purely ethical relationship of human beings to God, one seeming to lie for Clement just as much in a consciousness of the moral freedom of the will as it does in a correct concept of God's nature.

This interest is also expressed in the following passage:

> God has no natural or physical relation to us as the founders of the heretical sects maintain. He may have created the world out of nothing, or else formed it from an already existing matter. Since the former involves nothing at all, and the latter involves matter utterly different from God, then somebody had to venture to say that we are a part of God and have a being like his. But I do not know how someone who has a proper concept of God can bear to hear this if he casts a glance at our lives and considers how many evils they involve. Then surely a part of God's being had to involve sinning, although it is never permissible to say this. For parts are certainly parts of the whole and complete the whole. If they do not do so, then they are also not parts of it . . . We are not related to God in virtue of our being or our nature, or in virtue of some power indwelling our being. Instead we are related to God simply as creations of his will.[120]

This last point also involves the idea of moral freedom.

In *Stromata* 6.12 Clement answers the question put by the heretics: Was Adam created as perfect or as imperfect? They say that if he was created as imperfect, how can something imperfect, especially a human being, be the work of a perfect God? But if Adam was created as perfect, how could he have disobeyed God's commandment? Clement replies as follows:

> They shall hear from us that Adam was created as perfect, although not established as morally perfect but instead created as perfectly capable of taking up a virtuous life. For there is a difference between the ability to be virtuous and actually being virtuous. God wills that we become blessed by our own efforts, which is why it is the soul's nature to be self-determining. As rational beings our affinity is with philosophy, which has to do with reason. Yet this ability I speak of is not yet virtue itself, but is indeed a tendency to be virtuous. As the saying goes, all are by nature fit to be virtuous; but because of differences in training and practice, some are more apt to be virtuous than others. That is, a few attain perfect virtue, some are virtuous to a certain extent, but there are

---

119. Ibid., 4.12 [*ANF* 2:424].
120. Ibid., 2.16 [*ANF* 2:364].

## Part Three: The Conflict of Gnosis with Neoplatonism and with the Teaching of the Church

others who, although being naturally disposed to virtue, go astray owing to their own negligence and resistant attitude.[121]

### The Gnostics' Contempt for the World, and Their Rejection of Marriage

The second point in contention is the Gnostics' contempt for the world and the principles for one's practical life that are connected with it. Clement has spoken about this point in a very circumspect way, by fixing his attention especially on the moral concerns involved.

Clement declares:

> Those who disparage the creation and vilify the body are doing wrong. They do not see that a human being is made to be erect so as to contemplate heaven; that all our sensory organs strive to know; that all our limbs and bodily parts are created for excellent purposes, not for lust. That is why this body is the dwelling-place for the soul most precious to God; why it is dignified by the Holy Spirit through the sanctification of the soul and the body, and is perfected by the redeemer. In the Gnostic person who is engaged with the divine physically, ethically, and logically, the three virtues are most inwardly linked together: wisdom as knowledge of things divine and human; righteousness or justice as harmony among all parts of the soul; holiness as reverence for God. If someone wishes to disparage the flesh by appealing to the words of Isaiah (40:6–8), then one is also heeding what the Holy Spirit says through Jeremiah (13:24–27). There can of course be no doubt that the soul is a human being's nobler component and the body the lower part. But the soul is hardly good by nature and the body hardly evil by nature; and because something is not good by nature, that does not make it evil. For there are also things of an intermediate kind, and this group includes both things to be preferred and lesser things. This is why, in belonging to the sensible world, one must of course cope with life on the basis of different but not antithetical principles, given that a person is both soul and body. Good actions, as the better ones, are ascribed to the better principle, to the Spirit of the Lord, and lesser actions, leading in the direction of sensuous lust and sin, incline one to sin. The soul of the wise person, of the Gnostic, the one who exists as a stranger in the body, of course deals strictly with the body but not impulsively so, for one's bodily dwelling place will be abandoned only when the time for departure is announced. The soul says: "I am a stranger on the earth, a wanderer among you."[122] That is why Basilides says the Gnostics are the elect because they are strangers to the world, for they are otherworldly by nature. But that is not so. Everything without exception belongs to the one God and no one can be alien to the nature

---

121. Ibid., 6.12 [*ANF* 2:502].
122. [*Ed.*] An allusion to Abraham's statement to the Hittites in Gen 23:4 and to Ps 39:12.

of the world. There is one essential being and one God. The elect ones live as strangers in the world because they know that they possess all things and they possess nothing. The elect make use of the three things acknowledged as good by the Peripatetic philosophers.[123] However, the elect person travels widely in the body and stops at inns along the way. The elect one cares for worldly things and for the stopping-off places, but also quite calmly leaves behind the house and possessions made use of, and willingly follows the one who leads us out beyond this life, and without ever looking back with any regrets. The elect person is thankful for the accommodations, blesses the departure, and gladly welcomes the residence to come in heaven.[124]

Here we have the Gnostic worldview contested in general terms. Its practical application lies especially in the Gnostics' precepts concerning marriage. Therefore Clement takes this occasion to investigate in detail the bearing this view has on marriage.

Clement deals with this topic in part at the end of Book Two, where he speaks of marriage in the course of investigating the topic of how sensuous lust would relate to striving for virtue and godliness,[125] a discussion he continues over much of Book Three. Here the Gnostics' view of marriage is the most prominent one of the positions he presents. In 3.5 Clement distinguishes two classes of heretics: those who are completely indifferent to matters of right and wrong; those who are extremely strict and chaste, based on their godlessness and hostile hatred [of the world]. As Clement indicates in his rebuttal, the first group, those who promote sensuous lust as the supreme principle and whose antinomianism does away with all moral concepts—those who completely deny the dignity of human nature, its likeness to God, and any knowledge of God—do not concern us here because they are not closely related to the systems we are portraying. However, the second group is the class of those who, under the banner of chastity, act godlessly[126] against the creation and against the holy creator of the world, and against God the one ruler of all. They reject marriage and begetting children, because one ought not introduce others into the world to their misfortune, and ought not feed the cause of death (3.6). First and foremost among this second group are the Marcionites.

In *Stromata* 3.3 Clement describes the Marcionites as those who regard nature as evil because it originated from evil matter and is produced by the just creator of the world. In order not to populate the world produced by this world creator, they demand that people abstain from marriage. They oppose their creator and hasten to the good one who has summoned them, but not to the one whom, as they say, is a completely

---

123. [*Ed.*] The Peripatetics, or Aristotelians, held that a person consists of a physical body, a soul or principle that animates the body, and a mind that reasons.

124. Clement, *Stromata* 4.26 [*ANF* 2:439–40].

125. [*In the text in Greek*] ("Pleasure and lust seem to be included under the heading of marriage," *Stromata* 2.23 [*ANF* 2:377]).

126. [*In the text in Greek*] ("are impious by abstaining through self-control")

different kind of being. Because they do not want to leave behind them anything of their own, they are chaste not from their free decision but instead from hostility to the world's creator. They do not want to avail themselves of anything produced by him. Yet while they wage war against God with their godless mindset, they shun natural ways of thinking, and disparage God's forbearance and goodness. While not wanting to marry they do take advantage of created foodstuffs and inhale the world creator's air, for they are his own creations and abide in his world. And while, as they say, they proclaim a wholly new knowledge as their gospel, they nevertheless also should know to thank the Lord of this world that this is where the gospel has been proclaimed to them. In what follows, Clement shows that Marcion has wrongly taken from Plato the incentives for his strange precepts. But for his godless ingratitude toward the world's creator, he certainly could make use of much that the tragic poets have said about aversion for producing children.

But since Marcion, in opposing the world's creator, would not want to make use of worldly things, for him the cause of his chastity, if we may call it that, is the world's creator himself. Marcion believes that he has to oppose this hypothetical giant who battles against God, and for that reason Marcion is chaste contrary to his own will, and slanders the creation and God's work. Clement goes on to say, in chap. 9, that when these heretics appeal to Jesus' answer to Salome's question, "How long will there be death?" by replying, "As long as women give birth," they are incorrect in doing so. Here Jesus is not speaking of life and creation as evil, but only of death as the natural consequence of birth.[127] The law does not want us to abstain from everything that is unchaste and immodest. The law's purpose is to lead us from unrighteousness to righteousness, by our living in a virtuous marriage and having children. The Lord has not come to abolish the law, but to fulfill it. Human beings are not spiritual as long as they know no chastity and live just bodily. That is why the Lord also condemns adultery in thought.

> Well? Is it not possible to practice self-discipline within marriage without trying to pull apart "that which God has joined"? That is the sort of thing taught by those who dissolve the marriage bond. They bring a bad reputation to the name Christian. These people say that sexual intercourse is impure. Yet they owe their existence to sexual intercourse! . . . There are those who say openly that marriage is fornication. They lay it down as dogma that marriage was instituted by the Devil. They are arrogant and claim to be emulating the Lord who did not marry and had no worldly possessions. They boast that they understand the gospel better than others do . . . But they do not know the reason why the Lord did not marry. In the first place, he had his own bride, the church. Secondly, he was not an ordinary person who needed a physical

---

127. [*Ed.*] This exchange between Salome and Jesus is from the lost Gospel according to the Egyptians. See E. Hennecke and W. Schneemelcher, eds., *New Testament Apocrypha*, 2 vols. (Trowbridge, UK, 1966), 1:166–69.

partner. Furthermore, it was unnecessary for him to produce children, since he is eternal and God's only Son. He himself says: "Therefore what God has joined together, let no one separate" (Matt 19:6).[128]

Clement goes on to say: "Did not the righteous ones of past days share gratefully in God's creation? Some of them married and produced children while living a chaste married life." Also, did the apostles forsake married life? "Peter and Philip had children, and Philip gave his daughters away in marriage. Even Paul speaks of a wife he did not take with him on his travels (Phil 4:3)."[129]

In 3.9 Clement remarks that the aforementioned statement of Jesus to Salome is from the Gospel According to the Egyptians. Here the redeemer said, "I am come to destroy the works of the female." The "female" is sexual desire, whose works are birth and death. The text continues:

> So what are they to say? Has this world order been undone? They could never say that. The universe continues on in the same condition. But the Lord did not speak falsely. In fact he did away with the works of desire—avarice, controversy, awe, mania for women, and so on. The birth of these means the death of the soul, since we are "dead through our trespasses" [Eph 2:5]. So "female" means "lack of control." In the natural world, birth and death must occur in constant succession until the time of total dissolution and the bringing of the elect to their goal, so as to return to their own proper state the substances that are intermixed in the world ... How can these people do anything but stick to the true canon of the gospel, or even appeal to what follows in the words spoken to Salome? She said, "Then I have done right by not giving birth." The Lord replied that she has not understood birth as she ought to: "Eat each plant, but do not eat a bitter plant." This is telling her that it depends on us whether to abstain or to live as married, for there is no commandment dictating one's choice. He is also explaining that marriage is compatible with the creation. So no one should ever think that marriage in accord with reason is a sin ... It is up to each individual whether or not to have children ... One can understand the "two or three ... gathered in my name" [Matt 18:20], and in whose midst the Lord is present, to also mean husband and wife and child, because the wife is united with her husband by God ... Some of course want this statement of the Lord to be interpreted as follows: By the plurality he is speaking of the creator of the world as the god responsible for procreation; but by "one" he is speaking of the savior of the elect, the Son of a different God, of the good God. But this is wrong. God through his Son is with those who responsibly marry

---

128. *Stromata* 3.6 [Ferguson (n. 63), 285, 287)].

129. Ibid. [Ferguson, 288–89]. [*Ed.*] The reference in Phil 4:3 is to a "loyal companion" (γνήσιε σύζυγε) whom Clement of Alexandria assumes to be a woman, a "wife," perhaps because in 1 Cor 9:5 Paul speaks of being accompanied by a "sister as wife" (ἀδελφὴν γυναῖκα).

Part Three: The Conflict of Gnosis with Neoplatonism and with the Teaching of the Church

and produce children, and it is the same God who in the same way is with one who shows self-control in a rational way.[130]

In 3.11–12 Clement elaborates further on the rational rules suitable to the observance of chastity or moderation, and on how the principles of the heretics contradict the statements and teaching of scripture. He then gives particular consideration in chap. 12 to "the Syrian Tatian," and in chap. 13 to Julius Cassian, a student of Valentinus whom he calls "the founder of docetism." Both of them repudiate marriage and having children as something impure, sinful, diabolical, and leading to depravity. Tatian, in a way similar to Marcion, separated law from gospel, the old humanity of the law from the new one of the gospel. He regarded marriage as merely some ancient custom contrived by the law. Julius Cassian, drawing upon the Gospel according to the Egyptians, makes yet another contention based on Jesus' conversation with Salome: "When you trample underfoot the covering of shame, and when the two become one and the male is one with the female, there is no longer male and female." This was supposed to shed light on the fact that the distinction between the sexes is merely a feature of this world, and is not to be looked upon as originating from the God to whom we shall come. Clement's observation to the contrary is that

> the male impulse is temper, the female impulse, desire. When these are at work, repentance and shame are the result. So when a person refuses to indulge temper or desire, which in fact grow from bad character and bad upbringing, they overshadow and obscure rational thought. When one strips away this shell of darkness and in repenting feels shame, and integrates soul and spirit in obedience to the Word, then, as Paul says, "there is no longer male and female" [Gal 3:28]. The soul turns away from the shape consisting of the male-female distinction, and transforms itself into the oneness of being neither male nor female.[131]

But Cassian has supposed, in too Platonic a way, that the soul, being divine in origin, had become female because of desire and had descended to the world of birth and death, which is why Cassian "does violence to the Apostle in suggesting that Paul says our being born is simply a consequence of Eve's deception by the serpent, . . . for our being born is a work of the Almighty, who would never drive the soul down from a better home to a worse one."[132]

It is in this same context that Clement then (in chap. 16) rebuts what—based on the same Old Testament passages later used as major proof texts for the dogma of original sin[133]—was the consequence drawn at that time with regard to marriage and

---

130. [*Ed.*] This long passage consists of quotation and paraphrase from parts of *Stromata* 3.9–10 (cf. Ferguson, 295–98).
131. *Stromata* 3.13 [Ferguson, 314–15].
132. Ibid., 3.14 [Ferguson, 315].
133. [*Ed.*] These passages, listed in the text in parentheses, are Jer 20:14; Job 14:4–5; Ps 51:5;

having children, or for the thesis that being born (γένεσις) is an evil thing (κακός). If being born, or giving birth, is evil, then from this there follows the blasphemous contention that it was also evil for the Lord to be born and for the Virgin to bear him. On this basis we have the docetism of Cassian and of Marcion, and Valentinus' "psychical body." That is because, as they say, human beings share the attribute of sexuality with that of the beasts. If one says the serpent took the advice of the irrational animals and persuaded Adam to have sexual intercourse with Eve and, as some maintain, so to act differently than these first human beings otherwise would have done, then in that way the creation was maligned, and human beings descended below the level of the animals and had to follow their example.

But if, like the animals, nature impelled them to produce children, and they were sexually aroused earlier than they should have been while they were still too young, then God, in judging those who did not wait for his assent, judged them justly. Yet origination (γένεσις) is holy because through it the world is constituted, all its natures and beings—the angels, powers, and souls; the law, the gospel, the knowledge of God. How could the dispensation of the church achieve its purpose without the body? For "Christ, the head of the church" [Eph 5:23] made his way through the world in the flesh, "without form or majesty" [Isa 53:2], to direct our gaze to the unseen and incorporeal nature of the divine principle.[134]

Although Clement's polemic against the Gnostics confines itself to the points I have discussed here, it probes just as deeply into the inner character of the Gnostic systems as the rebuttals of Irenaeus and Tertullian do. The presentation of his main arguments demonstrates as much. Nevertheless we would have grasped his relation to the Gnostics in a very incomplete and one-sided way had we sought to stop with just this negative side of it. No other ancient church father stands as close to the Gnostics as Clement does. With none of the others do we see Gnosis and Catholic teaching in contact and interacting at so many points. Thus Clement is not to be viewed simply as an opponent of the Gnostics. Instead the system of teachings contained in his writings itself forms a new and important moment in the course of the development of Gnosis. That is why we can understand the true significance of his thinking only from this standpoint as well—his own relation to the Gnostic systems.

---

Mic 6:7. For instance: Jer 20:14 ("Cursed be the day on which I was born!"); Ps 51:5 ("Indeed, I was born guilty, a sinner when my mother conceived me").

134. [*Ed.*] These last two paragraphs paraphrase much of *Stromata* 3.17 (Ferguson, 320–22).

Part Three: The Conflict of Gnosis with Neoplatonism and with the Teaching of the Church

## Clement of Alexandria as a Gnostic

### Clement's Concept of Gnosis: Gnosis as Absolute Knowledge

Clement concurs with the Gnostics above all on the fact that there must be a Gnosis as knowledge of the absolute. Historical faith cannot suffice. Belief must be elevated to knowledge if Christianity is said to be the absolute religion.

As Clement defines the concept of Gnosis in *Stromata* 2.17, and sets it apart from other related concepts, it is the knowledge of the existent itself, the knowledge that harmonizes with the things themselves, the knowledge that is mediated by reason and cannot be overturned by some other rationality. It is the absolute knowing whose only purpose is this knowing itself. Clement states that:

> It is not fitting for the Gnostic to strive for the knowledge of God in order to serve some practical purpose, so that this thing may happen or that one may not. The reason he speculates is to possess the Gnosis itself (αἰτιατῆς θεωρίας ἡ γνῶσις αὐτή). I venture to say that he does not strive for Gnosis in order to be blessed, but chooses it for the sake of the divine knowledge itself. Through its exercise thinking becomes a perpetual thinking, and perpetual thinking remains the essential nature of the knower, as an uninterrupted process, an ongoing speculation, one's living substance (ἀΐδιος θεωρία ζῶσα ὑπόστασις μένει). If someone were to have the Gnostic choose between knowledge of God and eternal blessedness, assuming that these two are in fact separable, the Gnostic without hesitation would have chosen knowledge of God, being convinced that what is desirable for its own sake is having the property of raising oneself up beyond faith or belief, through love, to knowledge.[135]

Gnosis is not for gaining any kind of worldly success. It is simply for the sake of the knowing itself. Hence for the Gnostic, life has value inasmuch as a person's knowledge grows and one can attain Gnosis.

Clement describes Gnosis as follows:

> In its essence Gnosis becomes something enduring and unchangeable when pursued continually and without interruption. The Gnostic not only has grasped the first principle or cause and the second one proceeding from it, so that he holds firmly to this knowledge with his unchanging, unmovable thinking. He has also learned everything about good and evil, about all that is generated, in short everything about which the Lord has spoken, by gaining from the truth itself the most precise knowledge covering from the world's beginning to its end. He never gives preference over the truth itself to what is merely probable, or to what the Greeks present as seemingly necessary. What the Lord has said is clear and evident to him even though it be hidden from others. He has already acquired the knowledge of all things. For the oracles we

---

135. *Stromata* 4.22 [*ANF* 2:434]. See also 6.12.

possess (the prophetic scriptures) announce what exists as it is, the future as it will be, and the past as it has been. As one who knows, the Gnostic has his strength in knowing, discourses about the good, is always intent on intelligible things, and takes the norm for the management of human affairs from those archetypes above in the way that navigators follow the stars in guiding the ship . . . The Gnostic knows what is old from scripture and throws light on the future. He knows the full meaning of what is spoken there and the solutions to all puzzles. He is acquainted with omens and prophetic announcements, with the outcomes and events of which they speak.[136]

The following passage from *Stromata* 6.7 explains the sense in which Clement calls Gnosis, as absolute knowing, a prophetic knowing, one transmitted via the Old Testament prophets:

> If we call Christ himself Wisdom, and say that the effectiveness of the prophets' activity, by which we can learn the Gnostic tradition, is his activity, just as he himself taught the apostles when he was present, then this Wisdom would have been a knowledge and comprehension of what is, what will be, and what has been, as something passed down and revealed by the Son of God. And if the wise person's goal is speculation, then those who are still philosophers of course strive for philosophical knowledge. However, they do not attain it if they do not come to know the prophetic voice it elucidates and through which one understands what is, will be, and has been, in the way that it is, was, and will be. Gnosis itself is what has come down from the apostles to the few. It has come down to us as an unwritten tradition. Thus the practice of Gnosis, or Wisdom, must be a constant and unchanging contemplation [of this truth].[137]

All of these definitions and descriptions of the essence of Gnosis should just serve mainly to emphasize the concept of the absolute as the essential feature of Gnosis. Gnosis is knowing in the highest sense, is absolute knowing. But just as knowing, in order to be absolute, first requires being mediated by another knowing that is not yet absolute knowing, so too, according to Clement, Gnosis has to have faith or belief as its necessary presupposition. Faith (πίστις) and knowledge (γνῶσις) are most inwardly and reciprocally connected.[138] Faith is the foundation on which Gnosis rests, and it is just as necessary to the Gnostic as air is for someone living in the world. One cannot live without the four elements, and one cannot pursue Gnosis without faith.

---

136. [*Ed.*] Most of this passage quotes a substantial section of *Stromata* 6.9 (*ANF* 2:498). Baur identifies the last part as from 6.4, although it appears to be his own summary statement rather than a specific quotation.

137. [*Ed.*] *Stromata* 6.7 (*ANF* 2:494). Baur also inserts the Greek for several of these clauses.

138. "Neither is knowledge without faith, nor faith without knowledge" (*Stromata* 5.1 [*ANF* 2;444]). "Knowledge is characterized by faith; and faith, by a kind of divine mutual and reciprocal correspondence, becomes characterized by knowledge" (2.4 [*ANF* 2:350]).

Therefore faith must lead the way,[139] but it is just as necessary that Gnosis follows, because knowledge stands higher than faith. Gnosis is what first raises faith up to become full consciousness. Clement says:

> Gnosis is a perfecting of human beings as such. It is realized in the knowledge of divine things. It is in unison with itself and with the divine Logos. It perfects faith, for it alone makes the believer perfect. Faith is then a goodness established within one. Even apart from searching for God a person knows that God is, and praises God as the existent one. For now we start out from this faith and, by advancing in faith, we must, as far as possible, acquire the knowledge of God through God's grace ... Hence faith is, so to speak, a knowledge of what is necessary (σύντομος γνῶσις, concise knowledge) and is confined to what is universal. Gnosis is a firm and certain knowledge of what is received through faith.[140] It is the knowledge received from the Lord's teaching and built upon faith, and leading over to unalterable comprehension. The first salvific transformation is therefore that from paganism to faith, and the second one is from faith to knowledge, from πίστις to γνῶσις.[141]

When we combine these features, Gnosis is accordingly the faith that is elevated to knowledge; in other words, inasmuch as what is mediated in knowing is immediately present in faith, Gnosis is the absolute knowledge that is self-consciously aware of its own mediation. Clement indicates this distinction very precisely in particular by the expressions "necessary or concise (σύντομος) knowledge," "setting forth" (ἀπόδειξις), and others, since what is "set forth" is simply a kind of knowledge that is thoroughly acquired via the foundations and proofs on which it rests.

### The Gnostic Is not Merely a Knower, but Is Also Perfectly Wise in Practical Matters

What we have seen so far just concerns the extent to which people most readily think of Gnosis as a kind of knowing and cognition. However, Clement most especially apprehends Gnosis from a distinctive vantage point in which he gives equal weight, indeed even greater weight, to its practical aspects, rather than confining the concept of Gnosis merely to the theoretical side. For Clement the Gnostic is not merely a knower, but is at the same time someone perfectly wise in practical matters. The same ideal guiding the Stoics' thinking about their perfect sage appears in Clement's view of the Gnostic, enriched and exalted by all that Christianity was able to offer.

According to *Stromata* 2.10, Clement assigns three features to the philosophy he acknowledges as his own: 1) speculation (θεωρία); 2) carrying out the precepts

---

139. *Stromata* 2.11: "The Gnostic builds upon faith" [*ANF* 2:359].

140. [*Ed.*] Baur includes in the text the Greek for: "setting forth the mighty and established truths apprehended by faith."

141. *Stromata* 7.10 [*ANF* 2:538–39].

(ἐπιτέλεσις τῶν ἐντολῶν); 3) preparation or formation of good people (κατασκευὴ ἀνδρῶν ἀγαθῶν). These three elements, taken together, are what make people complete Gnostics, and the lack of only one of them makes for incomplete or imperfect Gnosis.[142] Accordingly, Gnosis must find its completion in practice, according to the idea of putting it into action that is found throughout Clement's *Stromata*. If we keep our attention on the highest level of attainment Clement's Gnostic can achieve in this way, then the following passage, in which the relation of this idea to that of the Stoic sage is clearly recognizable, can provide the best concept of Clement's position.

> The Gnostic has no other affective states but those that belong to our physical maintenance, such as hunger, thirst, and the like. In the redeemer's case it would have been ridiculous to hold that his own body as such would have had functions necessary for its maintenance. He did not eat for his body's sake, since it would have been kept whole by a sacred energy. Instead he just ate food so that his companions and others would not think him odd for not doing so; for later on some thought he did not eat and supposed that he had only an apparent (i.e., docetic) body. He was utterly impassible, without affective states. No such emotions could have gained entry to him, neither elation nor sadness. But the apostles overcame anger, fear, and desire in Gnostic fashion because the Lord trained them to do this. So they too were not liable to be affected even by those states counting as good ones, such as courage, zeal, joy, and desire. Those states could not do anything to disrupt the steadiness of their frame of mind, for the apostles continued to remain as they were trained to be, even after the Lord's resurrection.
>
> Even though those affective states be regarded as good ones to the extent that they are under the control of reason, they nevertheless do not belong to the perfect Gnostic, who has no need for courage because he is not in danger and regards nothing in life as perilous, and who allows nothing to remove him from God's love. He also has no need for a cheerful mind, never lapsing into sadness since he is convinced that all is for the best. Nor is he angry, for nothing can make him angry, since his love of God is constant and wholly directed to God, which is why he does not hate any of God's creatures. Also, he is not envious, since he lacks nothing for being like unto what is excellent and good. Nor does he love anyone in the ordinary way. Instead, through the creatures he loves the creator. Likewise the Gnostic is without any desire or longing, and, as far as the soul is concerned, he has no other needs, since he is already most inwardly bound by love to the Beloved One and feels blessed by the abundance of all that is good.

---

142. *Stromata* 2.10 [*ANF* 2:358]. The lack of one of them results in a crippled or ineffective Gnosis. See 7.1, where Clement sums up the entire essence of Gnosis in three main elements: "The three effects of Gnostic power are: the knowledge of things; the carrying-out of what the word or Logos suggests; the ability to deliver, in a way suitable to God, the secrets veiled in the truth" [*ANF* 2:524].

## Part Three: The Conflict of Gnosis with Neoplatonism and with the Teaching of the Church

For all these reasons he is obliged to be impassible like [Christ] his Teacher. For the Logos of God is purely intellectual or spiritual, which is why the image or likeness of mind is seen in human beings alone; and why the good person is, in his soul, like unto God and godlike in form. God is in turn human-like, for mind is the characteristic form of each of them . . .

But someone who objects that he who longs for what is excellent cannot be impassible, because every inclination toward excellence is bound up with a certain longing, does not know the godliness of love. For love is not longing by the one who loves. Instead love is a love-filled unity that restores in the Gnostic the unity of the faith, independent of time and place. But the one who by love is already in the place where one will be in the future, and who through Gnosis has previously been imbued with hope, is not striving for something for the first time, since he already, as much as possible, has the sought-after object. Hence by Gnostic loving he remains quite naturally in the one unvarying state and has no intense longing to become like what is excellent, for he already has excellence. As someone who through love has become united with the impassible God and through love has been enrolled in the number of God's friends, what more need should he have for courage and desire? Therefore we must look upon the Gnostic and perfect one as being free from all affective states of the soul. For Gnosis has practical consequences and its practice produces an enduring state and disposition—the kind of impassibility that is not merely moderation of affects, but impassibility as the fruit of the complete eradication of desire.[143] . . .

For it is impossible that he who has once been made perfect by love, and feasts eternally and insatiably, should delight in small and lowly things. For what reason could he have to turn back to the good things of the world after he has come to "the inaccessible light"? . . . He is at home with the Lord, through love for him, although his abode is still seen as being on earth. He does not withdraw from life, for he is not permitted to do so. But he has withdrawn his soul from affective states, for this is granted to him. However, as long as he lives his desire has died out and he no longer needs the body. He just continues bodily functions that are needed to keep it from breaking down . . .

His greatest wish is that as many as possible will become like him, to that glory of God which is perfected by knowledge. The one who becomes like the redeemer works redemptively himself, to the extent that human nature can receive within it the redeemer's image or likeness. One does this by obeying his commandments unerringly. That means honoring the divine by the true

---

143. Hence we have the statement about Gnostic martyrdom: "For the purification of those who plotted against him and disbelieved him, the Lord 'drank the cup' alone. The apostles imitated him, that they might in reality be Gnostics, and perfect; and they suffered for the churches they founded" (*Stromata* 4.9. [*ANF* 2:422]).

> righteousness of deeds and knowledge. But what is unchangeable cannot possibly gain firm footing and consistency in what is changeable.[144]

Compare with this major passage the following principal theses: "Attachment to intellectual objects naturally leads the Gnostic away from the objects of sense." "God is impassible." "The mystical Pythagorean saying is, 'The human being must become one,' since the high priest is also one and God is one, with goodness pointing immutably to God." "The human being, having through impassibility become like God, also becomes monadic."[145]

Hence the perfection of the Gnostic has no other highest goal than that of becoming like God oneself. The knowledge of the absolute is theoretical knowledge, but in practical terms it is the presentation of the absolute in one's sensibility, and one's life being a total orientation toward the absolute that is completely without affective states. For it is essential to Gnosis that its object is not merely the absolute in its purely abstract form; that instead Gnosis is also conscious of the mediation of the absolute, and lets it work its way through the moments of its mediations. For Clement too this is therefore the main perspective from which he considers his Gnostics.

The absolute element belonging to the Gnostic's own being is at first something coming to be in him. It first gains its concrete reality through a series of intermediate moments, indeed in such a way that the universe's overall process of development is reflected in the Gnostic's life. Just as the world and the whole of natural life moves within the cycle of the number seven,[146] so too the Gnostic first works his way to his absolute end via the hebdomad.[147] Clement writes:

> What the hebdomad also may refer to is a time that extends, in the course of seven specific periods, to its resting place, the Jubilee Year.[148] Or it may refer to the seven heavens in their ascending order. It may point to the fixed sphere that borders on the intellectual world, and is called the ogdoad. In any case the Gnostic must make his way up through the world of birth and sin. That is why the sin offerings are made for seven days and there are seven days of purification. For the creation of the world was consummated in this number of days . . . The perfect propitiation, however, is propitiation through the

---

144. [Ed.] This very long set of quotations is taken from the much longer ch. 6.9 in the *Stromata* (*ANF* 2:496–98).

145. [Ed.] Each thesis appears separately in *Stromata* 4.23 (*ANF* 2:437).

146. [Ed.] Baur inserts within the text here the Greek from *Stromata* 6.16 for the statement: "Now the whole world of creatures born alive, and things that grow, revolves in sevens" (*ANF* 2:513). This statement comes after Clement relates ancient numerology to the sixth and seventh days of creation.

147. [Ed.] Baur inserts here the Greek from *Stromata* 7.10 for this statement: "He makes his way into the ancestral hall, to the Lord's own mansion, passing through the holy hebdomad [of the heavenly bodies], to be a light that shines steadily and continues eternally, impassible in every part" (*ANF* 2:539).

148. [Ed.] The Jubilee is the fiftieth year, following the series of seven seven-year periods. See Lev 25:10.

merciful faith in the gospel received though the law and the prophets, and the purity gained through complete obedience, in combination with setting aside worldly things—where the soul gratefully returns its earthly abode after it has made use of it . . . The true Gnostic belongs among those who, as David says in Psalm 15:1, "Dwell on your holy hill." They find their rest in the church above where God's philosophers are gathered, the true Israelites who have pure hearts and are without guile.[149]

## Clement's Christology

This is then also where Clement's christology finds its place in his system; where we find its own proper import and where it engages with his other ideas.

In contrast to the absolute God who, in his abstract being-in-himself, transcends all knowledge of him,[150] the Logos is simply the mediating principle through which the idea of the absolute realizes itself, theoretically and practically. As Clement says (in 4.25), since God is not demonstrable he is not an object of knowledge. But the Son, being wisdom, is knowledge, truth, and all that they involve. Surely he is also open to demonstration and dialectical knowing. All the powers of mind or spirit ($\pi\nu\epsilon\tilde{\upsilon}\mu\alpha$) are as one and converge in the Son, for when it comes to each of them his power is infinite. He is neither one like the One, nor many like the components of something. Instead all these powers are "as one," which is why he is all of them. Because he is the set of all these powers as united, he is called the Alpha and the Omega. For in him alone the end becomes the beginning and the beginning the end, without some other factor in between, which is why there is so much to believe in him and through him, rather than his being monadic.

The classical text that ties all this together is *Stromata* 7.2:

> The Son, who is most closely connected with the Almighty One, is the most perfect, most holy, most principled and authoritative, most regal and most beneficent nature. He is the supreme leader who rules over all things in accord with the Father's will. He steers the whole universe in the best way, by influencing everything with his inexhaustible, indestructible power. He sees into

---

149. [*Ed.*] Baur introduces this quoted passage as being from *Stromata* 4.25. The first two of its three parts are taken from 4.25 (*ANF* 2:438), although they are not in the order in which Clement presents them. The third part is from *Stromata* 6.14 (*ANF* 2:505). The final sentence alludes to John 1:47, where Jesus says about Nathanael, "Here is truly an Israelite in whom there is no deceit!" Baur's own footnote at this point gives the Greek for the immediately following statement in 6:14: "They do not remain in the seventh place, the place of rest, but, owing to their likeness to the divine, they are promoted to the beneficence of the eighth level, and devote themselves to the pure vision of endless contemplation." The Greek for this "promotion" ($\dot{\epsilon}\pi o\pi\tau\epsilon\acute{\iota}\alpha$) was the term for the highest level of initiation into the Eleusinian mysteries. Also, at the conclusion of his footnote Baur says: See pp. 135–36 above, on the hebdomad and the ogdoad.

150. See especially the major passages on this point in *Stromata* 5.11 and 12.

the secret thoughts of those through whom he works. The Son of God never leaves his watchtower. He is never distracted, never detached, never looking from one place to another, always omnipresent, never bounded, ever mentally alert, a wholly natural light, all eyes, all-seeing, all-hearing, all-knowing, searching the powers with his own power. For the whole host of angels and gods is subject to him, the one who, as the Father's Logos, has received charge of the sacred household through those placed under him.

Therefore all of humankind is his, the ones who have knowledge and the others not yet so. Some are his friends, some are his faithful servants, and others are just his servants. He is the teacher who trains the Gnostics by mysteries, the believers by their hopes for good, and those who are hard of heart by a discipline affecting their betterment by sensory means. The holy scriptures of the prophets clearly teach that the one we call redeemer and Lord is a Son of God . . .

The truly governing and authoritative principle is the divine Logos and his providence, which has oversight of everything and does not let anything he has responsibility for get neglected. The ones who wish to belong to him are those being perfected by faith. He, the Son, by the will of the Almighty Father, is the author of all good things, the first principle of motion, a power not to be apprehended in a sensory way . . .

An attribute of the supreme power is his oversight extending to everything, even the smallest matters, one that connects everything with the supreme organizer of the whole, with the one who arranges the well-being of everything in accord with the Father's will. His oversight directs some to be above others in a higher order until it comes to the great High Priest. For what is first, second, or third depends on the one supreme principal figure who operates according to the Father's will. The blessed band of angels stands at the highest level of the visible world. Then ranging down to us in turn are levels below other levels that, by and through the one principal figure, both are redeemed and redeem.

Just as the power of magnetism, extending through many iron coils, moves the smallest bits of iron, so too those who have the gift of virtue are drawn by the Holy Spirit to be bound to the supreme, self-persistent principle (the πρώτη μονῇ).[151] The rest of the series extends down to the lowest level. But those who from weakness are evil, and find themselves in a habitual state of evil, are driven hither and yon by their passions, and they crash to the ground. For the rule from the outset is that being virtuous is something that is freely chosen . . .

---

151. [*Ed.*] The original text refers to the "Heraclean stone" (λίδος Ἡρακλεία) from Magnesia, whence comes the word "magnet." Baur apparently converts the reference into the image of the modern electromagnetic coil, for the relation between magnetism and electricity was a topic of great scientific interest at the time this book was published (1835).

> The solely good ruler of all brings about salvation through the Son, from eternity to eternity. But he plays no part in evil. For the Lord of all ordains everything for the salvation of the whole, both in general and in individual cases. Hence it is the business of salvific righteousness to lead each being to what is better and is perfect, insofar as that is possible.[152]

In this same sense Clement repeatedly calls the Logos the great High Priest, inasmuch as his mediating activity raises everything up to oneness with God.[153] The Gnostic too owes all that he is to this activity. The more completely the Logos is reflected in him and becomes one with him, the more perfectly the idea of the absolute comes to consciousness and to life in him. This is how Clement describes the Gnostic's relation to the Logos in the beautiful passage in *Stromata* 7.3.

> The soul of a righteous person is preeminently a divine image, like unto God. By obedience to the commandments it enshrines a sacred site and established seat for the one who is the king over all things mortal and immortal, and the producer of what is excellent and beautiful. He is truly law, system, and eternal Logos, the one redeemer for individuals in particular, and for all collectively. He is the true only-begotten one, the image of righteousness, of the universal king and almighty Father. He endows the Gnostic with perfect contemplation (θεωρία), according to his own image, as though with the imprint of a seal, so that the Gnostic is the third, the image made as much as possible like the principle, the second one, the true life. Through him we live the true life. This is our account of the Gnostic living within what is unchangeable and always equal to itself.[154]

## The Relation of Clement's Gnostic System to the Systems of the Gnostics

So Clement has his Gnostic undergoing a process of purification and growth similar to the one to which the Gnostic systems subjected their "pneumatic people."

The spiritual principle posited in both cases must pass through a series of stages until it attains pure consciousness of itself and the full reality of its spiritual life. In

---

152. [*Ed.*] These lengthy quotes are from Baur's German translation of *Stromata* 7.2, which differs at some points from the Greek text as translated in *ANF* 2:524–26.

153. For Clement, as for the Gnostics, the human dimension very much takes a back seat in the person of the redeemer, indeed because with the redeemer Clement mainly holds fast to the concept of the Logos. For the more exalted his concept of the Logos was, the less he could combine it with an authentically real human appearance. Hence he was inclined toward Gnostic docetism, as expressed in his *Exhortation to the Heathen*, ch. 10: "The Logos, assuming the visage of a human being, and fashioning himself in flesh, enacted the drama of human salvation" [*ANF* 2:202]. See the passage from *Stromata* 6.9, beginning with p. 309 above.

154. *Stromata* 7.3 [*ANF* 2:527]. See 5.12 and 13, and 6.1, which says: "Our knowledge and our spiritual garden is the Savior himself, and this is where we are transplanted" [*ANF* 2:480]. See also 8.12.

both cases Christ, or the Logos, is the principle guiding this process of purification and growth. Except that Clement apprehends this process initially in the moment at which the spiritual principle subject to the Logos raises itself from one stage or level to another; whereas according to the Gnostic systems the absolute itself has become something finite, in order to raise itself up again in turn from its finiteness to absolute being. The latter dimension lies outside Clement's horizons. In other words, he apprehends this process mainly in its ethical aspect and not as a cosmogonic process of the kind the Gnostic systems present it as being, one to which the ethical aspect is subordinated.

In the Gnostic systems the spiritual principle said to be elevated to oneness with the absolute appears in a state of negation, one to be gradually alleviated. But just as this negative state itself is to be seen as the status from the outset, Clement goes no further with the issue as to what preceded this negation, what did the negating. In any event, thus far we have considered this process, through which the absolute mediates itself with itself, simply with regard to the individual, to the extent that in the individual, as a Gnostic, πίστις or faith is raised up to γνῶσις or knowledge. However, in Clement's case this process is significant not merely for the individual; it has universal meaning. Each individual, with the idea of the absolute being realized in him, is given the principle of Gnosis only in Christianity. So Christianity as such is the absolute religion.

For Clement the absolute principle objectified in Christianity is of course not a cosmic principle as the Valentinians and other Gnostics generally understood it in relation to the world's overall structure. Instead it manifests itself in the world's history. Christianity has entered into the history of religion as the absolute religion, and has this significance in relation to both paganism and Judaism. Moreover, since the subjective standpoint of Marcionite Gnosis remained foreign to it, the Pseudo-Clementine system of Gnosis was the only one that could be very akin to the Christian Gnostic system. That brings us to the main question in investigating the close relationship of Clement's religious outlook to the Gnostic viewpoint. The previous discussion casts light on the fact that Clement thought of Christianity as the absolute religion and presupposes it everywhere. So how is Christianity, as the absolute religion, related to Judaism and to paganism?

## How Clement Sees Christianity as Related to Judaism and to Paganism

### Christianity's Relation to Judaism

What is most striking is the affinity Clement's standpoint has with that of the Pseudo-Clementine writings when it comes to Christianity's relation to Judaism.

Part Three: The Conflict of Gnosis with Neoplatonism and with the Teaching of the Church

For Clement, when it comes to their essential contents the Old and New Testaments, law and gospel, the prophetic scriptures and the apostolic writings, are so very much of a piece that there could only remain a formal distinction between them. We already saw this view expressed in *Stromata* 6.7, according to which Gnosis simply consists in Christ's elucidation for the apostles of what is contained in the prophets. This is just as clearly evident in the similar-sounding passage of *Stromata* 4.21, where Clement poses the question, "Who then is perfect?," and answers, "The one who can attest to abstaining from what is evil." He continues:

> This is the way to the gospel and to doing good. Gnostic perfection for the follower of the law (νομικός) is acceptance of the gospel, so that the person living according to the law (ὁ κατὰ νόμον) will become perfect. Certainly Moses, the man of the law (ὁ κατὰ νόμον Μωϋσῆς), foretold that one must heed it (Deut 18:15) so that, as the apostle says [Rom 10:4], we receive the end or fullness of the law, which is Christ. For in the gospel the Gnostic then already advances so as no longer to gain support merely on the basis of the law, but instead to also understand and comprehend, commensurate with the law, what the Lord, who gave the two testaments, handed down to the apostles.[155]

So the gospel is simply the elucidation of the law as correctly understood.

In Clement's system, however, this identity of the two testaments is mediated by the method of allegorical interpretation. For Clement this method has the same importance as it does for Philo, whose allegorical-mythic interpretations Clement quite often directly follows. Clement says:

> Neither the prophets nor the redeemer announced the divine mysteries directly, so that anyone could easily understand them. Instead they spoke in parables. The apostles explicitly state that "Jesus told the crowds all these things in parables; without a parable he told them nothing" (Matt 13:34). And if "All things came into being through him, and without him not one thing came into being" (John 1:3), then he also made the law and the prophets, and he spoke about them in parables. The scripture says, "They [the words of my mouth] are all straight to one who understands" (Prov 8:9), that is, to those who, in keeping with the church's rule, receive and observe the interpretation of the scriptures as it is given by the Lord. For the church's rule is that the law and the prophets concur and agree with the testament given by the Lord himself, when he appeared.[156]

The main purpose of allegorical interpretation is therefore to demonstrate the complete identity of the Old Testament with the New Testament, for their author is certainly the same Lord and Logos. Since the knowledge of this identity belongs to the

---

155. *Stromata* 6.7 (*ANF* 2:433). This is a direct continuation of the preceding passage as cited, although the reader might not realize it because the German text omits the initial quotation mark.

156. *Stromata* 6.15 [*ANF* 2:509].

very essence of Gnosis, the allegorical sense of scripture is thus related to the literal sense in the same way as Gnosis is related to belief.[157]

So regarded, Gnosis itself is none other than the interpretation of scripture and the understanding of its meaning. For only the Gnostic who has taken the trouble to understand scripture preserves the orthodox faith of the apostles and the church.[158] Clement and others criticize the capricious and outrageous way that the heretics deal with scripture. The scriptural interpretation of the Gnostics differs from that of the heretics because the Gnostics hold firmly everywhere, as their leading idea, to what completely suits and befits the Lord and Supreme God. They confirm everything proven from scripture by their use of scriptural analogies. By saying that this prevents subjective caprice, the Gnostics profess that they simply follow the rule or canon of the church, and the apostolic tradition. However, it is clear that their determination, as to what in scripture ought to be recognized as content truly worthy of God, was ultimately just their own speculation. That is why even the assumed identity of the Old and New Testaments, or of prophecy and Christianity, simply has its basis in the fact that Gnosis positions itself above both in the same fashion, and employs its own speculative ideas to mediate between them by using allegorical interpretation.

## How the Christianity That Is Identical with Judaism Is Related to Paganism

Since now Judaism is not to be separated from Christianity, the main issue is how the Christianity identical with Judaism is related to paganism. Is Clement taking the side of the Pseudo-Clementines' writer here, by agreeing with him in general terms about the relation of Christianity to Judaism?

Clement speaks about the relation of Christianity and Christian Gnosis to paganism, and to pagan philosophy, more often than he does about any other topic. Yet it is no easy matter to convey what is truly his own view on this issue, for we come upon two different and mutually contradictory contentions. One is that pagan religion and philosophy has an inner, independent and divinely-imparted truth. The other contention is that everything true in paganism is just something foreign to it, and is to be looked upon as finding its entry there through robbery and deceit.

## The View That Pagan Philosophy Is from God via the Logos

The first contention presents itself to us in the conviction that this philosophy has a propadeutic function. This view runs throughout all of Clement's writings and is expressed in very many passages.

---

157. Ibid.
158. Ibid., 7.16.

Hence Clement begins his *Stromata* by saying: "Like farmers, we wish to irrigate the land with the clear water of Greek philosophy, so that it may better receive and nourish the spiritual seed sown upon it."[159] This is his justification for utilizing philosophy. Clement states: "Before the advent of the Lord, the Greeks needed philosophy in order to be righteous. And now it is conducive to piety for those who want to have faith flourish to become knowledge . . . There is one way of truth, but many streams flow into it."[160] Philosophy is a preliminary training and preparation for wisdom. Clement expands upon this point by an allegorical interpretation of the two wives of Abraham, Sarah and Hagar. Sarah, who is wisdom, dwells with Abraham, the man of faith. She was initially barren, but as time went on she consented to Abraham having intercourse with Hagar, the Egyptian woman, the worldly education (κοσμικὴ παιδεία), after which Sarah gave birth to Isaac, who is a type or foreshadowing of Christ.[161] Later in this chapter Clement writes:

> Philosophy investigates truth and the nature of things, for wisdom is what the Lord himself speaks about when he says, "I am the way, and the truth, and the life" (John 14:6). The preparatory sciences train the mind, awaken the understanding, and produce the acumen that devotes itself to investigation by the true philosophy, the one that initiates possess after having found it, or rather have received it from the truth itself.[162]

Clement points out[163] that for the Gnostic the principal thing of course is Gnosis. Yet the Gnostic is also concerned with what prepares the way for Gnosis, since he takes from each science what it has to offer in the way of truth, by drawing upon music, arithmetic, geometry, astronomy, and dialectic. Many people have a childlike fear of Greek philosophy, as though it posed a danger to the truth. But the Gnostic must know a great deal, because it all serves him in distinguishing what is universal from what is particular. For error and false opinion reside in the inability to judge how things are associated with one another and are in turn distinct from one another. Hence the Gnostic cannot remain unfamiliar with the general sciences and with Greek philosophy. Except they will never be the goal as such, but are instead only a means to the goal.

Clement regards this as a preparation and education for the true philosophy, Christianity. As Clement expresses the point, although these disciplines are "not the

---

159. *Stromata* 1.1 [ANF 2:303].

160. Ibid., 1.5 [ANF 2:305].

161. [*Ed.*] See ibid., 1.5 (ANF 2:306). These statements in Clement draw upon Philo of Alexandria, *On Mating with Preliminary Studies*, 22–23. Clement attributes this same interpretation of Hagar as "worldly education" to Solomon. Baur inserts in parentheses the Greek for Clement's statement in 1.5.30 that here "Egypt is an allegory of the secular world."

162. *Stromata* 1.5 [ANF 2:307].

163. Ibid., 6.10. [*Ed.*] The rest of this paragraph is a summary and paraphrase of this chapter. See ANF 2:498–99.

whole extent of the truth," they do "prepare the way for the royal teaching, by enlightening the mind, shaping one's moral character, and strengthening someone who believes in providence to receive the truth."[164] On this account, although the value and uses of philosophy are initially just a kind of training, Clement also traces them back to God.

> Everything that is good comes from God, one good thing directly as the Old and New Testaments, another indirectly as philosophy. But also, perhaps philosophy was given directly to the Greeks at that time, before the Lord summoned them. Then, like a schoolmaster, it would have led the Greeks as well to Christ, as the law did the Hebrews. Philosophy is a preparation, since it paves the way that finds its fulfillment in Christ.[165]

In order to give this preparatory feature of philosophy its due, and to recognize its independent worth as a divine gift, Clement even refers to philosophy as the "testament" given to the Greeks:

> We shall not be mistaken if we say, about all things necessary and useful for life, that they simply come from God. Thus we might also maintain that the philosophy given to the Greeks as, so to speak, their own "testament," is the foundation of Christian philosophy—even though so many who philosophize in the Greek manner are oblivious to the truth, being contemptuous of the barbarian [i.e., Christian] voices or fearful of the deadly peril hovering over the believer from the laws of the state.[166]

Of its own accord the divine Logos, which is the author of both Testaments, presents itself to Clement of Alexandria as also the principle of revelation for pagan philosophy.

Hence Clement compares the Logos, as the universal reason imparting itself everywhere,[167] with the sower of the parable. He says that the sower who plants in the soil of our human earth is the one who comes down from on high, spreading the nourishing seeds from the beginning of the world and causing reason to fall down like rain in each age.[168] In the parable different times and places are said to have received the seeds. Whereas for Clement the conviction that divine providence extends to everything is certainly very important; so surely the divine truth must also be universally imparted. The Logos itself is this providence, for, as Clement states in *Stromata* 7.2, the truly ruling and preponderant principle is the divine Logos and its providence,

---

164. Ibid., 1.16 [*ANF* 2:318]. See also 1.20 and 5.3.

165. [*Ed.*] Baur places these sentences within quotation marks but does not identify a passage from which they come.

166. *Stromata* 6.8 [*ANF* 2:495].

167. Ibid., 1.7. See also *Exhortation to the Greeks*, ch. 6.

168. [*Ed.*] Baur is paraphrasing *Stromata* 1.7 (*ANF* 2:308), and at this point puts in parentheses in the text the Greek for "the Lord raining down reason."

Part Three: The Conflict of Gnosis with Neoplatonism and with the Teaching of the Church

which oversees all things and cares for everything. By drawing from one and the same source the Lord has given the law to one group and philosophy to the other one.

Hence Clement declares himself most emphatically opposed to the empty pretext that philosophy rests on an evil principle, and has been introduced into life by an evil contriver, simply to drag human beings down. Instead he wants to show in his *Stromata* that philosophy too is a work of divine providence.[169] He says that philosophy "does not give rise to falsehoods and evil actions, as some people say in disparaging it. Instead it is a clear image of truth and a divine gift to the Greeks. It does not draw us away from the faith as though it bewitched us by some deceptive artifice. Instead it endows the faith with a solid scientific standpoint."[170] He says "that according to some, Greek philosophy happened upon the truth accidentally and apprehended it just dimly and partially; that others contend it originated with the Devil; that others have the whole of philosophy being imparted by fallen spirits." However, philosophy in fact "prepares the way for the royal teaching."[171]

Clement speaks even more extensively about this point in *Stromata* 6.17.[172]

> It is not absurd to maintain that philosophy is imparted by divine providence as a preparation for the fullness [of truth] to be acquired through Christ, only with the provision that, as a pupil of barbarian Gnosis, philosophy is not ashamed to move on further to the truth. For if "even the hairs of your head are all counted" [Matt 10:30] as well as the smallest movements, then how shall philosophy be regarded as so meaningless? . . . From on high, divine providence extends down on everything, "like the precious oil on the head, running down upon the beard, on the beard of Aaron, running down over the collar of his robes" (Ps 133:2)—of the robes of the great High Priest "through whom all things were made and without whom nothing was made" (John 1:3). Not running down to ornament the body, since philosophy is external to the [Jewish] people like a garment [is outside the body] . . .

> Those who assert that philosophy did not come to us from God seem to regard it as impossible that God would also know particular things, and would be the author of all good things that are of a particular nature. Yet out of all there is, nothing exists apart from God's will. For if this is how things stand regarding God's will, then philosophy is from God, and it is as God willed it—in order that those who refrain from evil solely on account of philosophy would do so. For God knows all things . . . And he sees everything at a single glance, even

---

169. Ibid., 1.1. [*Ed.*] This first chapter concludes with the statement: "I shall show, throughout the whole of these *Stromata*, that evil . . . can never produce what is good, and that philosophy is . . . a work of divine providence."

170. Ibid., 1.2 [*ANF* 2:303]. [*Ed.*] This amounts to a quotation, although Baur does not present it as such. He includes in parentheses the Greek for the last sentence.

171. *Stromata* 1.16 [*ANF* 2:318].

172. [*Ed.*] What follows quotes parts of this lengthy chapter; see *ANF* 2:516–18.

though not everything happens because of his own direct action. For many things in human life of course happen due to human thinking, even though human beings are animated by God . . .

God arouses the thoughts of good people, for their souls have a certain disposition toward being so aroused. The divine will communicates itself to human souls, and those servants of God who are set above the individual play a role in such service. For individual peoples and cities are under the oversight of various angels, with some angels perhaps assigned to individuals.[173] So the Shepherd cares for the sheep, but those who most of all are objects of his oversight are the ones who stand out by nature and are able to be most useful. They are those skilled in governing and teaching. When God wants to do good things for human beings, by instruction, governance and guidance, these are the people through whom the workings of providence are most visibly manifested. For God always wills this, which is why he moves those who have the ability to work usefully in this way . . . How absurd then is it to make the Devil the bestower of philosophy, such an excellent thing, when one considers the Devil to be the author of disorder and injustice! For then the Devil surely had to have intended to make the Greeks better people than divine providence did.

Law and reason assign to each one what is one's own, what is fitting and appropriate to that person . . . No good person does what is evil, nor light produce darkness, nor fire make cold. Likewise, vice cannot do anything virtuous, for the activity of vice is evildoing, just as darkness confounds one's eyes. If philosophy, which educates for excellence, cannot be the work of wickedness, then it can only be from God whose work is what is good. Everything given by God is given well and is well-received. Furthermore, bad people do not make use of philosophy, for it was given to the best people among the Greeks. This makes it clear from whence philosophy came, namely, from the providence that imparts to each what one deserves. Therefore the Jews rightly had the law and the Greeks rightly had philosophy, until the Lord appeared. From then on there is the universal summons to a special people of righteousness, through the teaching that proceeds from faith. For the Lord, the one God of both Greeks and barbarians [non-Greeks], that is, the Lord of the entire human race, unites them as one. For I understand philosophy as being what in philosophy has come upon the truth, even though just in part.

---

173. [*Ed.*] See Deut 32:8 in the Septuagint version: "When the Most High apportioned the nations, when he divided humankind, he fixed the boundaries of the peoples according to the number of the angels of God."

## The Contrary View: That Philosophy Has a Demonic Origin and Comes from Thieves and Robbers

After all this there should be no doubt about what view Clement firmly held. It is that Greek philosophy contains an independent truth derived simply from the universal source of all truth, that of the divine Logos. Notwithstanding that, we also find in Clement an entirely different view, one coming quite close to the view he disputes in the last passages I cited.

This other view is incompatible with the contention[174] that, since the barbarians with their arts and sciences were largely the teachers of the Greeks, the Greek philosophers therefore simply borrowed from the Old Testament scriptures the best and truest things they found there. This other view holds instead that, if the philosophy of the Greeks is said to be the same as what the Old Testament was for the Jews, then in a sense the Greeks had in their philosophy a testament of their own and also their own God-given prophets.[175]

In support of the contention [that Greek philosophy is borrowed from barbarians], Clement shows, in *Stromata* 1.21–29, that the philosophy of the Hebrews is the most ancient philosophy, and that, even for the Greeks, [the books of] Moses are the sum and substance of all theoretical and practical knowledge,[176] in particular are the archetype of their entire legislation.[177] According to Plato, an Egyptian priest declared that the Greeks are just considered to be like children.[178] Thus very likely the ancient Hebrew wisdom could have made its way to the Greeks, since prior to the Septuagint there surely would have already been a Greek transmission of the Old Testament, one in fact utilized by Plato.[179]

However, according to Clement this transmission was by no means just a well-intentioned use of what was freely offered. Instead he repeatedly describes this appropriation of a foreign treasure as theft. In order to provide a striking concept of

---

174. Expounded in *Stromata* 1.13–16.

175. Ibid., 6.5.

176. [*Ed.*] In a general allusion to Gal 3:21–29, Baur cites *Stromata* 1.26 in giving the Greek for "the law makes alive, guiding one to Christ, the Logos or Word." *ANF* 2:338 has: "the law was a schoolmaster to bring us to Christ," a quotation from Gal 3:24.

177. Ibid., 1.26 [*ANF* 2:339].

178. [*Ed.*] Plato, *Timaeus* 22b: "One of the priests, a prodigiously old man, said, 'O Solon, Solon, you Greeks are always children: there is not such a thing as an old Greek . . . You are young in soul, every one of you. For therein you possess not a single belief that is ancient and derived from old tradition, nor yet one science that is heavy with age'" (LCL *Plato*, 7:32–33). Clement recounts this passage at the beginning of *Stromata* 1.29 (*ANF* 2:341).

179. [*Ed.*] In parentheses in the text Baur cites *Stromata* 1.1 and 1.22. In 1.22, Aristobulus is quoted as reporting: "And Plato followed the laws given to us, and had manifestly studied all that is said in them" (*ANF* 2:334). Also in 1.22, Numenius, the Pythagorean philosopher, is reported as writing, "For what is Plato, but Moses speaking in Attic Greek" (*ANF* 2:334–35). Baur's citation of 1.1 includes the Greek for a reference to Plato as "a knowledge from the Hebrews."

this "Greek theft or plagiarism from the barbarian philosophy,"[180] Clement sought to demonstrate precisely, with individual instances, in how many teachings, principles, and conceptions Plato, the Stoics and others, philosophers as well as poets, agreed with the philosophy of the Hebrews.[181] Also, the Greeks have not taken just dogma from the barbarians; they have also taken miracle. What the holy men have performed by divine power for the benefit of their own people the Greeks present as miracles in their own Greek mythology. We see clearly from those accounts—for instance, what they tell about the intercession of an Aeacus, about the sacrificial offering of an Aristaeus, and Empedocles as the "windstayer" (κωλυσαμένας)[182]—that the Greeks have appropriated from the Old Testament scriptures the belief that righteous ones can perform miracles.[183]

"The Greeks are called pilferers of all manner of writing."[184] The way they present themselves is testimony to their thievery. Their own writings bear witness to how inclined they are to thievery in their sayings and doctrines. There is constant borrowing. We need not speak about the philosophers, who owe their most important precepts to Socrates. As Clement shows by a lengthy series of examples, what is most striking in the case of the poets is how they copy one another, not just by borrowing and modifying individual sentences, but by having stolen entire passages word-for-word. The philosophers, historians, and rhetoricians have done likewise. At the conclusion of his long excursus Clement exclaims: "My lifetime would not suffice for exposing, in all the individual cases, the selfish plagiarism of the Greeks."[185] For Clement had already remarked previously that whoever does this with his own people and engages in such obvious thievery will hardly have shown any restraint when it comes to foreigners. So this is the clearest proof that, as the thieves they are, the Greeks have surreptitiously presented to their fellow countrymen truth taken from the Old Testament scriptures.[186]

However, the story of this thievery is not yet complete. The series of thefts the Greeks have carried out from their own is just a continuation of the massive thievery

---

180. Ibid., 5.14 [ANF 2:465].

181. In ibid., 5.14 to the end (see also 2.5), Clement wishes to go no further into the dogmas of philosophy. Demonstrated instead is the sense in which the Lord called the Greeks thieves, in such a way that in fact the entirety of the practical wisdom among the Greeks is taken from the barbarian philosophy. [Ed.] The last part of book 5 is about philosophical teaching, so these remarks properly apply to books 6–8.

182. [Ed.] Aeacus, a son of Zeus, ended a drought by his prayers to Zeus, and also besought Zeus to repopulate the island of Aegina following a deadly plague. Aristaeus, a son of Apollo, had offended the nymphs and placated them by sacrificing cattle to them, hence regaining his bee colonies that they had destroyed. Empedocles the philosopher was called the "windstayer" because he checked violent winds that were destroying crops (see Diogenes Laertius, 8.60).

183. Stromata 6.3 [ANF 2:486–87]. See also 2.1.

184. Ibid., 6.4 [ANF 2:489].

185. [Ed.] ibid., 6.2 (ANF 2:486). The earlier part of this paragraph also draws on 6.2.

186. Ibid., 6.2.

Part Three: The Conflict of Gnosis with Neoplatonism and with the Teaching of the Church

from the Old Testament. So this same thievery can be traced farther back, and Clement nevertheless seems again to agree with those who attribute an ungodly origin to philosophy. This is clarified by *Stromata* 1.17, where Clement refutes the opinion of those who derive Greek philosophy from fallen spirits or from the Devil. They even appeal to John 10:8, where Jesus says, "All who came before me are thieves and robbers." Clement continues:

> Therefore all who belong to the Logos, or Word, insofar as they lived before the Word became flesh, must be understood here in quite general terms. But the prophets, sent and inspired by the Lord, are no thieves but are servants, which is why the scripture says that "Wisdom has sent out her servant-girls, she calls from the highest places in the town" (Prov 9:3). But philosophy was not sent by the Lord, for instead, they say, it came stolen or was the gift of a thief. If it was a higher power or an angel who had learned something of the truth but did not abide in the truth, then this power imparted it and thievishly taught us. The Lord, who surely knew every outcome, what will be even before the individual has come to exist, simply did not prevent this from happening ... The Devil, who has free will and was able to change his mind or to steal, is the author of this thievery. The author is not the Lord, who did not prevent it ... The Devil is called "a thief and a robber" because he mixed false prophets among the true prophets, like tares among the wheat. Thus [John says] that all who came before the Lord did were thieves and robbers—not utterly all of them but instead all the false prophets, and all who were not directly sent by the Lord himself. Even the false prophets are called "prophets" (albeit dishonestly), for they are the prophets of the Liar ... So philosophy is stolen as though by a Prometheus [who stole fire from Zeus]; and the Greek philosophers can be regarded as thieves and robbers because, without acknowledging it and before the Lord had come, they took parts of the truth from the Hebrew prophets and appropriated it as their own teaching. They have falsified some parts, treated other parts ineptly with their sophistical art, and even fabricated other parts, for perhaps they even had a perceptive spirit.[187] Aristotle too concurs with scripture when he calls sophistry a theft of wisdom.[188]

It is clear that, although at first Clement introduces it simply as the opinion of others, here he concedes the demonic origin of philosophy far more than he rebuts it. This is the same Jewish notion that we already encountered with the writers of the *Pseudo-Clementine Homilies*, now applied here especially to the explanation for the origin of Greek philosophy. Tertullian also refers repeatedly to it.[189] This same view

---

187. [*Ed.*] Baur gives the Greek for this phrase (πνεῦμα αἰσθήσεως) as it appears in the Septuagint version of Exod 28:3.

188. [*Ed.*] Aristotle writes: "The art of the sophist is the semblance of wisdom without the reality, and the sophist is one who makes money from an apparent but unreal wisdom" (*Sophistical Refutations* 165a21–23 [*The Complete Works of Aristotle*, ed. Jonathan Barnes (1984), 1:279]).

189. *Apology*, ch. 35: "Arts made known by angels who sinned" [*ANF* 3:44]. *On Idolatry*, ch. 9:

must be presupposed when (in *Stromata* 6.8) Clement counters this very contention, that philosophy has its origin from the Devil, by just remarking that one must know that, according to scripture, "even Satan disguises himself as an angel of light" (2 Cor 11:14). And although we now find (in *Stromata* 7.2) the modification of this conception, such that the Lord gave philosophy to the Greeks via the inferior angels—since according to an ancient divine ordinance the angels are apportioned among the nations, with the Lord's own portion being the faithful—it follows that Clement was seeking to bring this in line with his own conceptions elsewhere. In keeping with the familiar Jewish interpretation of Deut 32:8, Clement too thought of the Logos as the leader of the people of God, but of the lesser angels, standing under the Logos, as leaders of the other nations, leaders who on the customary view were simply regarded as being fallen spirits or demons.[190] These angels or demons, leading the individual peoples or nations, were thought of as the representatives and principles of the spiritual or mental individuality of their people. Hence according to this idea one could see just a work of demons in paganism and its entire cultus. Thus from this same perspective pagan philosophy was also said to be regarded as a product of the same demons. From this perspective it is easy to see how, for Clement, in addition to recognizing the great value of Greek philosophy, there is always at the same time the verdict expressed that this philosophy is imperfect and internally untenable.[191]

---

"One proposition: that those angels, the deserters from God, the lovers of women [a reference to Gen 6:2?], were likewise the discoverers of this curious art, on that account condemned by God" [*ANF* 3:65]. *Prescription against Heretics*, ch. 7: "Doctrines of demons, products of prurient ears" [*ANF* 3:246]. [*Ed*. In fact only the last of these passages refers to philosophy as such. The other two pertain to astrologers, soothsayers, magicians, and the like.] See also *On the Apparel of Women* 1.2. In *Stromata* 5.1, Clement speaks of "the angels who had obtained the superior rank, having sunk into pleasures, told to the women the secrets they had come to know" [*ANF* 2:446]. See above, pp. 204–5.

190. [*Ed*.] Deut 32:8: "When the Most High apportioned the nations, when he divided humankind, he fixed the boundaries of the peoples according to the number of the gods; the Lord's own portion was his people, Jacob his allotted share."

191. See, for instance, *Stromata* 6.7: "So the philosophers copy the truth, in the way painters work. In each case their self-love is the cause of all their mistakes" [*ANF* 2:493]. According to *Stromata* 6.17, the Greek philosophers do not know God although they speak directly of him; for they do not revere him as God. Clement goes on to say here, in an especially apt statement, that God is the Lord of all things and is of course absolute. He says that "there are two ideas or forms of truth—the things themselves and the names for them. Some speak of the names, focusing on the beauty of the words, and these are the Greek philosophers. But we the barbarians focus on the things" [*ANF* 2:515–16]. This is also why the Lord had to appear in an unprepossessing form, so that no one would simply admire his beauty but be inattentive to his words; would just fixate on what is to be overlooked and be diverted from what is to be understood. We must therefore focus on the speaking, not on the outward sign. What is truly real is therefore only in Christianity. Paganism just amounts to the language that falls short of the substantial reality.

# Part Three: The Conflict of Gnosis with Neoplatonism and with the Teaching of the Church

## Reconciliation of These Two Views

The pressing issue now is how Clement was able to harmonize two so different and opposed views. To me the solution seems to lie simply in the distinction to be drawn here between what is false in a formal sense and what is true in a material sense.

Initially, of course, one should have thought that if philosophy owes its origins to a demonic act, then philosophy also cannot have any share in truth as regards its material contents. Yet Clement does not agree that there is such a connection between the formal aspect of philosophy's origins and its material truth. That is why Clement especially stresses (in *Stromata* 1.17) that the thievery committed does not occur without the Lord knowing about it even though he did not prevent it. For the robbery people successfully accomplished in this way served a purpose that was not what those who carried it out had intended but nevertheless was its result, since divine providence guided this audacious deed to produce the best outcome. Many people of course did not want to allow for this concept of [divine] permission (doubtless just with the intention of ruling out any divine involvement with this deed, as their way of being able to declare that philosophy is false and demonic also with respect to its material contents). However, the concept of free will requires it. Also the divine wisdom and power do not manifest themselves merely by doing good things, by doing what belongs to God's own nature just like it is the nature of fire to give warmth and the nature of light to illuminate. For his wisdom and power also especially act by guiding evil thoughts and intentions toward a good and useful goal, and making good use of what comes on the scene as something bad. So then, even in philosophy there is a spark, as though stolen by a Prometheus, which can, in a beneficial way, be stirred up into a flame of light—a trace of wisdom and a movement proceeding from God.

In this context Clement says (in *Stromata* 6.8) that, when the Devil takes the form of an angel of light and speaks prophetically as an angel of light, he must still also speak truly and beneficially, even though, notwithstanding this merely bogus activity, he is the epitome of apostasy. How then could he deceive if he did not utilize the truth as the means for drawing people to himself and luring them to falsehood? One must accept the fact that, although the Devil does not have the concept of truth, he at least is acquainted with truth. This, then, is also why philosophy cannot be false, although just like the one who is a thief and a liar, it speaks the truth only in a form adopted to seem truthful. The form of philosophy's origins does not annul the truth of its material contents, although, as we will see later, it does reduce the impact of these contents.

If this argument serves to harmonize the apparent contradiction, we still face the question as to the point of the assumption that the Greek philosophers and poets have robbed the Old Testament. For the truth found among the Greeks, and that can make likely their robbery of the Old Testament, is said to be due to an earlier robbery. But what is the point of a double robbery of this kind, when a single one seems to suffice? It is indeed not entirely clear how Clement thought these conceptions are specifically connected. Yet we cannot be wrong to assume that the second robbery is just a continuation of the first one, and that either one captured a feature typical of paganism, as indicating the externally appropriate semblance of truth.[192]

### Clement's System as a Whole: Christianity as the Uniting of All the Separate Streams of Truth; Clement's Gnostic Standpoint

In grasping Clement's system as a whole, there is no mistaking the fact that it inherently bears the character of Gnosis, with the same features we have brought to light previously as being typical of, and shared by, the various forms of Gnosis. It sets out from an absolute principle of truth, and posits a falling-away from the absolute, which of course replaces absolute knowing with finite knowing. But this fall is absolute knowing's necessary moment of mediation, since, by overcoming the antithesis posited in virtue of that falling-away, mind or spirit first becomes conscious itself of the mediation of its knowing.

Clement himself (in *Stromata* 1.2) very aptly designates the character of Gnosis when he says, about philosophy, that, by the antithesis, it sets the doctrine of truth in a clear light, one from which Gnosis first arises. He states there that philosophy did not come to exist for its own sake, but instead came from the advantages resulting from Gnosis, or knowledge. For we acquire a firm conviction of truth from the fact that what stands before us (*das Vorgestellte*) becomes something known.[193] Based on this perspective, therefore, Clement also will not countenance the utter condemnation of heresies. In distinguishing what is authentic from what is inauthentic, the heresies are even useful for a more secure recognition of truth. With all the self-love and conceit that is typical of the heretics, the heresies also have at the same time their own reason [for existing], in the fact that, faced with the vast and difficult task of finding the truth, people engage in different ways for investigating it.[194]

Clement locates absolute truth and absolute knowing in the divine Logos, the deity's supreme means of revelation, the sum and substance of truth. The perversion of truth into its opposite likewise occurs via a principle lying beyond human consciousness, just as, for the author of the Clementine writings, the sudden inversion

---

192. On the various sources from which Clement derives the truth of Greek philosophy, see August Ferdinand Dähne, *Commentatio historica theologica de γνώσει Clementis Alexandrini, et de vestigiis neoplatonicae philosophiae in ea obviis* (Halle, 1831), 48ff. As his main thesis Dähne affirms (p. 54) that, according to Clement's actual view the truth of Greek philosophy goes back to the Logos, that is, to human beings' natural capacity for knowledge, what Clement calls "the natural or innate reflection, the nature implanted by God." This still leaves unresolved the question at issue here. We know that the Alexandrian Jews also already held the opinion that the Greek philosophers have purloined a few meager bits of truth from the Old Testament scriptures and deployed them to their own advantage. On this point see Dähne, *Geschichtliche Darstellung der jüdisch-alexandrinischen Religionsphilosophie* (Halle, 1834), 1:78ff.

193. [*Ed.*] In parentheses Baur then presents the Greek for this sentence.

194. *Stromata* 7.15 and 17.

in the order of the syzygies is an act or a happening for which there is no further explanation. It is independent of human beings, taking place through the falling-away of those "inferior angels" who are set over the pagan peoples just as the Logos is the direct leader of the people of God and is their lawgiver. Truth and error, light and darkness, godliness and ungodliness, are mutual oppositions as represented by Judaism and paganism respectively, in the way they are in the Clementine system. But whereas the Clementine system sticks to this antithesis in an unqualified fashion, by regarding paganism as the utter antithesis of Judaism, and so also recognizes no truth at all in paganism, Clement restricts the antithesis in the way I have already indicated. The falling-away from the truth is of course an ungodly act in and for itself. Yet at the same time it is the means for imparting truth. Although truth has come to human beings simply by theft and treachery, via those "treasonous angels who defected," nevertheless truth itself is imparted. Judaism and paganism do not stand utterly opposed as truth and falsehood. Instead they just stand as the one, undivided truth that the Logos represents in its oneness, and the divided, so-to-speak fragmented truth that the angels convey here and there, according to the number and diversity of the peoples over which they are set.

Hence the constantly recurring idea for Clement is that paganism, in other words, pagan philosophy, recognizes the truth just partially and imperfectly, not fully and as a whole.[195] (That is why Clement locates the mental or spiritual character proper to paganism in this same way, whereas the author of the Clementine writings, in contrast, wants paganism to be judged not so much by its philosophy as instead by its mythical religion.) Therefore, according to the Clementines' writer, absolute knowing is transmitted via consciousness of the antithesis of truth and falsity, which is all-pervasive in the whole of world history and of the history of religion. Whereas for Clement the transmission resides in the fact that the Gnostics themselves of course everywhere recognize parts and elements of truth, but must at the same time constantly be aware that these are just individual, scattered pieces of a whole that is, in a word, a fragmented whole whose fragmentation is caused by something like a robbery—that everywhere error has attached itself to truth, the imperfect to the perfect.[196] Thus the

---

195. [Ed.] Baur adds in parentheses the terms from *Stromata* 6.7: "not perfectly (τελείως) but only partially (μερικῶς)" (ANF 2:493).

196. Thus the truth of paganism is indeed traceable back to the Logos as universal, objective reason. But inasmuch as the truth of paganism is just a particular, oft-divided truth, those angels function as the principle of paganism. The different principles to which paganism takes us back are therefore just the different aspects according to which paganism is to be considered. What the Logos is as the principle, the Old Testament is as the sum and substance of the truth revealed by the Logos. This twofold outlook presents itself in the relation of paganism to the Old Testament. The Greeks' robbery from the Old Testament is very indicative of Greek philosophy's agreement with the Old Testament contents, seen in the one-sided and deficient nature of the truth contained in Greek philosophy. All those various origins back to which Clement traces pagan philosophy and religion are thus merely different ways of considering it, inasmuch as one and the same subject matter presents different aspects to be examined. At the same time it sheds light on the close connection between Clement's Gnostic

more clearly the Gnostic himself is conscious of the endlessly divided status of truth on the one hand, and of the underlying unity of this multiplicity on the other hand, the more complete is his knowledge. That is why the Gnostic's supreme task is to work his way through to the one absolute knowing by examining, in the widest possible range, all the divisions of human knowledge.

Clement has suitably expressed this point in the following passage:

> The truth is just one, but falsehood involves endlessly many ways off the path. As the Bacchantes tore Pentheus apart and into pieces, the sects of the barbarian and Hellenic philosophies boast as though each of them, in having the truth given to them in part, would have possessed the whole truth. However, the dawning of the Light[197] casts light on everyone. All the Greeks and barbarians who have striven for the truth are proof of the fact that some have attained no small part of the truth and others only a very little bit of it.
>
> Eternity comprises within it the future, present, and past, in a single moment. But even far more so than eternity does, the truth is able to bring together as a unity the seeds belonging to it even though they have fallen on such different kinds of soil. In the opinionated teachings of the sects that have not become wholly barren and lost all connection with the natural order of things, much is to be found that, however mutually disparate it seems to be, still has certain ties to truth as such and, either as branch, or kind, or species, thus converges in a unity. The highest pitch and the lowest pitch of a musical instrument contrast greatly, but together they form a simple harmony. Even numbers and odd numbers differ, but both kinds go to make up arithmetic. When it comes to geometric figures, the circle, the triangle, the square and others, are all very different, and yet in the world as a whole all the parts, howsoever different they may be, maintain their proper relations to the whole. So then, the barbarian and Hellenic philosophies have the eternal truth in fragmentary form, not as fragments of the mythology of Dionysius but as pieces from the theology of the eternal Logos [*Baur*: so that the unity of the fragments lies not in the Dionysian mythology, but instead in the theology of the Logos]. For whoever brings the separated pieces together again and unites them will safely behold the Logos, the truth.[198]

Therefore only from the absolute standpoint of Christianity is it possible to unite what is fragmented and isolated as though one were uniting the limbs of a dismembered

---

standpoint and the eclecticism to which he confesses in *Stromata* 1.7. He writes: "By philosophy I do not mean the Stoic philosophy, or the Platonic or Epicurean or Aristotelian philosophy. I mean whatever is well-stated by each of these sects that teach justice or righteousness together with knowledgeable piety. I call this eclectic whole 'philosophy.' But I would never call 'divine' the human reason that is isolated and is just one's own" [*ANF* 2:308]. (It is proper that Clement mentions Stoicism first, for that is in keeping with how his system is presented, and according to the conclusive report of Eusebius in his *Ecclesiastical History* 6.13.2, Pantaenus, a Stoic philosopher, was Clement's teacher.)

197. [*Ed.*] Perhaps an allusion to John 8:12, where Jesus says, "I am the light of the world."
198. *Stromata* 1.13 [*ANF* 2:313].

body that belong together, and possible to envisage the original unity of what is separated. Even in the setting of Judaism, what in it inherently bears the marks of imperfection and narrowness, when taken literally, can be harmonized with Christianity as the absolute religion only by the allegory whose contents are spelled out on the basis of Christianity. Taking up this absolute standpoint seems to us, in Clement's case also, to be the task of Gnosis, that is, of religious philosophy. At the same time, however, we see how Clement gives its due and proper role not merely to Judaism but also to paganism. That is why he recognizes that the relationship established among these elements in the Pseudo-Clementine system is one-sided.

When we understand Clement's system as we have sought to do here, from the perspective to which it belongs based on its place in history, then we see very clearly how Gnosis in all its forms presents a fundamental problem whose inner significance is unmistakable, a problem that calls for a solution, inasmuch as reflection on the relationships among paganism, Judaism, and Christianity ought not stick to the simplest analysis. The more Clement inclined toward the standpoint of religious philosophy the less he could be satisfied with the purely negative results of a polemic just rebutting the Gnostics. While there was much he had to disapprove of and to reject in the Gnostic systems, Gnosis itself was for him still the utmost concern. Indeed his concurrence in using this label [for his own position] bespeaks a certain acknowledgment of the similarity of his standpoint [to that of the Gnostics]. This is how Clement essentially sets himself apart from Irenaeus and Tertullian. Here we will now return briefly to these other figures so that, after having surveyed Clement's relation to Gnosticism, we can spell out more precisely their overall relation to it as well.[199]

## Part Three in Retrospect

In looking back at the polemic of Irenaeus and Tertullian, at the course it takes and its results, there is no disputing the fact that it does not just contain many very appropriate and accurate points regarding Gnosticism's individual features. Also, with regard to at least one major point, their polemic has overcome most successfully the antithesis that had to be resolved here. All that Irenaeus and Tertullian did particularly to

---

199. Given Clement's close relation to Origen, one could have anticipated here a portrayal of Origen's system as well, for indubitably it is closely related to Gnosis. Nevertheless I believe it should be omitted here, since it provides nothing essentially new. On the whole it is a Platonism modified by Christianity, one having affinities with the Valentinian and Plotinian systems. Origen sets himself apart from these two systems mainly by the importance he gives to the will's moral freedom, and by the idea associated with it of a fall of the souls. What for Valentinus is the fall of the Sophia is for Origen the fall of the souls, although for both of them this fall takes place in the intelligible world, and the existence of the real or material world is itself initially a consequence of the fall. For Origen the Plotinian triad of principles corresponds to his three principles: God as what is absolute; the Logos; and the souls (as a multiplicity). Origen's thinking about the relations of Christianity to Judaism and to paganism is like Clement's. Allegory plays just as great a role for Origen, except that, when it comes to paganism, his Platonism emerges more decidedly as the foundation of his system.

oppose Gnostic dualism—inasmuch as it posits a duality of principles doing away with the absolute idea of the deity, and introduces an irresolvable contradiction into the view of the world and of life—we may justifiably regard as a gratifying result of their polemic, a result the philosophy of religion could not subsequently fail to appreciate.

These theologians scrutinized from so many angles the issues raised by the Gnostics as to God's relation to the world, the absolute's relation to the finite. The well-known forms of their positive solutions in opposing the Gnostics' speculation on these issues were the doctrines of the world's creation and the doctrine of the Trinity. The former doctrine was upheld entirely outside the domain of speculation, in the indefinite notion of a creation out of nothing. The Trinity was of course a speculative doctrine, but largely treated in such a way that, in this regard at least, there is no essential difference, grounded in the subject matter itself, between the speculative standpoint of the Gnostics and the standpoint of their opponents. In the doctrine of the Trinity the elementary notion of a relation of emanation and subordination got applied to the divine persons who constitute the threefold nature of the divine essence. In Gnosticism this notion was applied to the Aeons in which the self-enclosed essence of the absolute God manifested itself. The reason the church fathers did not want to allow their emanations to be more than three lay in the authority of scripture.

But these two church fathers still by no means grasped, in their truly speculative significance, those very issues that, in our general consideration of Gnosticism, must appear to be of far greater importance, namely, the issues concerning the relationships among paganism, Judaism, and Christianity. The Gnostics had sought to provide a positive, historical foundation for separating the world's creator from the absolute God by stressing the antithesis between the Old Testament and the New Testament. A fundamental refutation of that position forced one to identify Old Testament religion with New Testament religion. The means for demonstrating the full scope of this identity, and for finding one and the same contents in both Testaments, was partly via allegorical interpretation, which these two church fathers practiced, and partly via the most expansive concept of revelation and inspiration. However, in this same setting wherein Judaism and Christianity were put on a par, paganism was located below the other two and considered to be just the sphere of untrue, ungodly, demonic religion, as shown by Tertullian's well-known verdict on the perversity even of Greek philosophy as the source of all the still-so-awful heresies (although the direct, natural awareness of God that Tertullian expressly affirms conflicts with this view, so the one-sidedness of his better-known negative verdict should be pointed out.)

Yet even in recognizing Christianity as being the supreme divine revelation, in other words as the absolute religion, people apprehended Christianity exclusively in the immediate way it is presented in the scriptures of the Old and New Testaments and in the tradition of the church. In thinking that there is merely an external difference between Old Testament religion and New Testament religion, and in considering paganism to be in fact nothing more than a surviving, integral component of the history of religion in its entirety, people were not yet aware of an antithesis that religious consciousness is to overcome in order to have a fully concrete consciousness of the absolute religion, apart from the extent to which the heretics gave rise to singular antitheses or conflicts, ones to which people could not remain indifferent. The history of religion was still merely a history of revelation. However, this by itself was in principle no history, inasmuch as, in the unity of the revelation, the beginning, the progression, and the result of the development were treated so much on a par with one another that any mediatorial elements of a vital process of development had to be lacking. There was said to be just an external unfolding, over the course of time, of the ever selfsame revelation that does not admit of mediation via any real antitheses.

# PART FOUR

# Ancient Gnosis and More Recent Religious Philosophy

THERE WERE PERIODS OR phases through which Gnosis passed as the church fathers attacked it with their polemic. Yet the very issues that came into play, and were resolved in the various Gnostic systems in a way that was unable to satisfy the religious consciousness, were not permanently put to rest. They continued to be the topic of a religious philosophy striving to realize its own concept, a religious philosophy that, even in gaining a more specific awareness of its own task, also seemed increasingly to have to turn back to the standpoint of the ancient Gnosis. In order to see and understand the main moments of the relationship between ancient Gnosis and the more recent philosophical theology or religious philosophy, we still have to undertake a further part of our investigation.

The consequences of the Gnosis of the first few centuries, and of the battle concurrently waged against it, were felt for a long time. Indeed one may say that, on the whole the Gnostic perspective steadily persisted throughout the entirety of the Middle Ages, right up to the Reformation. In the time period directly after these early centuries there were two major phenomena of this kind: one very closely related to Gnosticism itself; the other one at least unable to remain unaffected by the consequences of the battle carried on against Gnosis. The former is Manicheanism, and the latter is the Augustinian system.

# 1

# The Transition from Ancient Gnosis to the More Recent Religious Philosophy

## Manicheanism

ALTHOUGH MANICHEANISM AROSE IN a domain of religion outside the one in which the Christian Gnostics operated, it is nevertheless a phenomenon thoroughly analogous to, and consistent with, Gnosis. Thus we see in Manicheanism simply a proof of how, in the history of religion, as soon as a new and distinctive development in religious consciousness calls forth a new form of religion, one that, by setting itself over against the already existing, historically-given religions, claims to be the absolute religion, the same phenomenon is repeated.

Mani[1] did something the Gnostics did not do, at least not in the same form. He put himself directly in Christ's place (inasmuch as he least professed to be the Paraclete as a proxy for Christ and completing the work of Christ). In doing so he simply expressed, more specifically and directly, that his religion is the absolutely true religion. This is why Manicheanism also placed itself in the same relation to the earlier religions as Gnosticism did. Of course for the same reason it had to be the dualistic form that was revived and further elaborated in Manicheanism. For the more decidedly Manicheanism appeared claiming to be the absolute religion, the harsher its relation to the earlier religions also had to be. Hence it is more like Marcionite Gnosticism than it is like the other Gnostic systems. Except it differs from Marcionite Gnosis in two ways. Marcion's subjective standpoint became a purely objective standpoint in Mani's case. Also, whereas in this context Marcion saw the visible realm and the invisible realm as mutually antithetical, Mani also of course located the antithesis within the visible realm itself as the antithesis between light and darkness.

---

1. [*Ed.*] Mani was a Persian born in 216 of parents who were reportedly members of a Jewish-Christian Gnostic sect. He composed seven major works that became the basis of Manicheanism, which spread very rapidly in the third century. Baur established his expertise on this subject early on with his *Das manichäische Religionssystem nach den Quellen neu untersucht und entwickelt* (Tübingen, 1831).

Both of these departures from Marcion are indicative of Manicheanism's close connection with the old nature religion. Valentinianism is the Gnostic system most akin to Manicheanism, as seen from this standpoint. Hence Manicheanism lies between the Valentinian and Marcionite systems. In other words, Manicheanism is rather the Valentinian system itself, reconfigured in purely dualistic fashion—clearly carrying out an objectively understood dualism—that indeed comes close to the system of Basilides but with the difference that in fact Manicheanism puts paganism directly in place of Christianity.[2]

Therefore quite naturally the polemic of the Christian church fathers called for renewed battle against Manicheanism, which was such a powerful enemy all around it. This was none other than the same challenge it had faced previously with Marcion—refuting the dualism paganism was presenting in a new form, by invoking the principle of monotheism, and salvaging the honor and worth of the Old Testament by opposing the bitter reproaches newly voiced against it. There is nothing essentially original about the way this took place. However, now too the Christian polemic was not able to overcome the emerging opposition to such an extent that the contested view did not constantly find new allies and commend itself to religious consciousness in the midst of the Christian church itself. So Gnostic and Manichean sects were pervasive throughout the entire Middle Ages. Although in them we encounter once again simply the old teachings and principles in a scarcely altered form, and they have not much new to offer that is of scholarly interest, they do nevertheless provide—by their sheer existence, by the vigorous and persistent battle the external authorities waged against them in every way they could, and by the major importance they had at this time in history—a remarkable testimony to how all those issues and problems the

---

2. Even Mani took Christianity to be the absolute religion, but only did so with the intention to lend a Christian character to his own religious system, which was essentially pagan in its contents and character. However, even with Christianity and Manicheanism supposedly being one and the same in the concept of the true religion, in Manicheanism we see Christianity identified with paganism in the same fashion as, in the Pseudo-Clementine system, we see Christianity identified with Judaism. In the classification of the Gnostic systems on pp. 66–67 above, we remarked that, although it is possible to identify Christianity with Judaism, it nevertheless conflicts with the nature of Christianity to place it on the same footing with paganism. The classification of the types of Gnosis there does leave room for the possibility of a form relating Christianity to paganism [although there it is an empty set]. But Manicheanism now realizes this possible form, and this naturally gives us a way of determining how Manicheanism is related to Gnosticism. Manicheanism is certainly to be placed together with Gnosticism under one and the same general concept. This is the concept of Gnosis or religious philosophy. Yet inasmuch as it is part of the concept of Christian Gnosis that it recognize the distinctive worth of Christianity, at least the concept of Christian Gnosis will no longer be applicable to Manicheanism. For this reason Manicheanism takes on a merely external relation to Christianity, one merely consisting of the transfer of certain [Christian] terms and forms to Manicheanism. Hence, despite its undeniable relationship to Gnosticism, people believed, for good reasons, that Manicheanism must at the same time always be distinguished from Gnosticism, as a phenomenon in its own right. [*Ed.*] It is apparent from this footnote, once again, that Baur is considering Gnosis exclusively as a phenomenon linked to Christianity, unlike more recent research into Jewish and other forms of pre-Christian and non-Christian Gnosticism.

Gnosis of the first centuries had initially raised, could never entirely disappear from religious and speculative consciousness.

## The Augustinian System

Augustine indisputably must be the foremost of the ancient opponents of Manicheanism. He carried on the combat with dualism begun by the earlier church fathers, doing so in the widest scope, and in the most penetrating and most versatile way. But he also deserves recognition here as the author of a distinctive system that had to have the most significant impact on the whole of Western dogmatics.

Augustine was the first to provide a positive foundation for the relationship the earlier church fathers had already been accustomed to posit between pagan religion and the religion of the Old and New Testaments. If the original sin of the human race obscured people's religious knowledge to the same extent that it robbed free will of any moral power, then the doctrine of inherited sin provides the reason why the pagan world could be thought of simply as the sphere of false religion, as the kingdom of darkness existing alongside the domain of biblical religion, which is illuminated by the rays of divine revelation and grace. But Augustine's approach also provided a firmer basis for the earlier view that had been affirmed in opposition to the Gnostics, and that could be grasped in its more specific ethical importance as a consequence of his system. The Gnostics always sought to derive the kingdom of darkness from a principle lying beyond the scope of human will. For the Gnostics it is a higher law of nature that spirit must work its way by stages in order to attain complete self-consciousness; that absolute knowing is conveyed via specific antitheses. They held that this knowing is grounded in a general antithesis of principles, and the process of development conditioned by them. That is why the church fathers set the idea of the will's moral freedom over against the Gnostic view of the individual being conditioned by the universal, natural nexus. In this same setting the Augustinian system also links everything to the sin of the first human being, inasmuch as it has all proceeding from that one's own freely willed act. For the reason why the whole of human life, in the way it plays out in the antithesis of sin and grace, as well as in the antithesis of error and truth, dependence and freedom, lies solely in this act of will and not in a higher order of things.

The more decisively the Augustinian system determined the view of the teaching methods of the subsequent ages, the less cause there was to expect, throughout the entire period of the Middle Ages, a return to the earlier standpoint of Gnosis. What prevailed was the general view of paganism's and Judaism's relation to Christianity that the earlier church fathers had established and that Augustine had firmed up in a more specific way.

## Medieval Scholasticism

While scholasticism gave a new and lively stimulus to the spirit of speculation, and while consciousness of the task of harmonizing faith and knowledge was all-pervasive, on the other hand scholasticism very much lacked a historical sense, so as to establish a vital link between speculation and the history of religion.

As the centuries passed everyone became increasingly distant from the time when paganism, Judaism, and Christianity were in direct, mutual contact and were activated by the deepest religious and speculative interests. Thus people stuck to the traditional dogmas of the church and just considered their contents to the extent this could be done piecemeal and in individual instances, without posing a challenge to the dogma as a whole. They engaged in dialectical reflection to mediate between dogma and religious consciousness. They just dwelt on the stability of the dogma and supported it. Reflection on how the dogma had come about, and on the moments in the ongoing development not only of the sum and substance of the church's dogma, but also of the religious life of the people itself in its historical context, still lay entirely outside the purview of an age that just held fast to the restricted domain of its own dialectical concepts.

## The Reformation

The Reformation presented a great contrast to this situation. The result was the separation into two wholly opposed systems of what heretofore had been a religious outlook and way of thinking headed in a single direction. This also had to have an impact on the standpoint from which people considered how Christianity is related to the pre-Christian religions. In this same setting wherein people broke free from the old axiom of the stability of the dogma, and acknowledged a historical movement or progression in the sphere of Christian dogma, that also had to awaken the inclination to gain a greater historical comprehension of the major phenomena constituting the contents of the history of religion.

In any event we see a remarkable demonstration of this point in the distinction of law from gospel that was asserted so emphatically by the Protestants right from the outset. Catholicism had located all moral merit and all salvific power in the performing of outward works. As opposed to this, Protestantism went back to what is innermost and is in the depths of the religious consciousness. In doing this Protestantism also had to adopt as its main orientation to the actual essence of Christianity, and to grasp as its focus, the fact that Christianity's entire principle of redemption consists simply in its being something entirely different from law. Hence strictly distinguishing law from gospel belongs utterly to the basic character of Protestantism. With that being what incited and motivated it in such a lively fashion in its initial phase, we naturally find Protestantism energetically expressing its awareness of this absolute value of gospel while also stating a low opinion of the law and contempt for it. Once this distinction was grasped people quite intentionally drew from it all the consequences it entails, and therefore what present themselves are phenomena that simply have parallels in the history of Gnosis in the first centuries.

The antinomianism of a Johann Agricola[3] and his followers is just as well-known as that of Marcion and his disciples. In order to devalue the law as much as possible in contrast to the gospel, and to place faith just as absolutely above works, in the way most Gnostics ascribed all salvific power simply to their Gnosis rather than to actions, the antinomians likewise now affirmed such propositions as the following. They said that the law has no bearing at all for believers and those who are reborn; that it is never worthy of being called God's Word; that all who associate with Moses must go to the Devil; that Christians with all their good works are of the Devil; that the best thing for Christians is to know nothing at all of the law; that Moses knew nothing at all about our faith and our religion; that the law, together with good works and the novel [religion of] dutifulness, belongs not in the kingdom of Christ but in the world, like Moses and papal rule, and so forth.[4] These are theses that lack nothing for being grounded in an authentically dualistic system, other than the tendency the Gnostics proper shared with their own time, namely, to also trace mutually contrary orientations back to mutually opposed principles and natures; in other words, to introduce concrete personifications into one's way of looking at things.

With such verdicts pronounced on the religious value of the law, it could hardly be regarded any longer as divinely revealed in the proper sense. The leaders of the Protestant church indeed made most zealous efforts to prudently and strictly head off extreme positions of this kind. Yet the old bond, by which one had previously sought to maintain the extensive identity of the Old and New Testaments as far as possible, was nevertheless dissolved by the Protestant concept of gospel and the redemption offered in it.

## Catholicism and Protestantism as Related to Gnosis

Phenomena such as this antinomianism, in connection with other Protestant teachings—in particular the doctrine of inherited sin, or the complete incapacity of human beings for spiritual goodness and the correlative doctrine of the efficacy of divine grace—have given Catholic writers of most recent times the occasion to present forthwith the contention that there is no religious phenomenon the system of the

---

3. [*Ed.*] Agricola (orig. Schneider) (1494–1566) was an early follower of Luther but later rejected by the Reformer because of his extreme antinomianism.

4. G. J. Planck, *Geschichte der Entstehung, der Veränderungen und der Bildung unsers protestantischen Lehrbegriffs*, 6 vols. (Leipzig, 1781–1800), 1:15ff and 61ff.

Reformers has more affinity with than Gnosticism. The Catholics say that, in its essential character, Protestantism is none other than a revival of ancient Gnosticism.[5]

In a different place I have indicated in which sense this contention is to be accepted, but also in what sense it is to be rejected.[6] If the concept of Christian Gnosis is just understood correctly, and one recognizes in it the purely ethical character that Protestantism ought never deny, then there is no reason to be ashamed of this comparison. In any case Protestantism shares with Gnosis a more profound awareness of evil, without having to face the reproach of being a Christian extremism, a hyper-Christianity, in the way that Gnosticism does. Indeed, based on this perspective, one can even extend that parallel further than those who originally stated it themselves have done. Certainly Protestantism wants to fully plumb the depths of the consciousness of sin simply in order, by this consciousness, to gain in its faith the true medium for the consciousness of redemption.

However, this very striving to become conscious for oneself of the absolute truth, simply by one also becoming conscious of its mediation, belongs to the distinctive character of Gnosis. Certainly for this reason Protestantism already stands more closely connected with Gnosis than is the Catholicism that is so content to just stick with the immediacy of the given, and makes no serious effort to penetrate the deepest, the innermost, elements of the mediation of the truth. But this consciousness also involves, of its own accord, the summons to recognize the same mediation process to which the individual's religious life has been subject, as also the perspective on the basis of which the course of development of the religious spirit, in the history of religion, is to be considered. In this context as well, Protestantism seems to be far more closely related to Gnosis than Catholicism is.

Whereas Protestantism strictly separates Old Testament religion from New Testament religion, via the antithesis between law and gospel, the effort of Catholicism is instead headed in the contrary direction, by understanding even the gospel as just a modification of law, as a new and more perfect form of the law. In the institutions

---

5. Johann Adam Möhler, *Symbolik, oder Darstellung der dogmatischen Gegensätze der Katholiken und Protestanten nach ihren öffentlichen Bekenntnisschriften* (Mainz, 1832); 3rd ed., 243ff. See also Thomas Moore, *Travels of an Irish Gentleman in Search of a Religion* (London, 1833), chs. 23–27. According to this wanderer's discoveries, Simon Magus is already authentically a Protestant (for according to Theodoret, *Heretical Tales*, 1.1, Simon taught that one does not become blessed "by doing good," but instead "by grace"). He also says that all the subsequent Gnostics are, in their true being, none other than Protestants. [Ed.] Möhler's thesis that Protestantism represents a modern form of Gnosis helped stimulate Baur's interest in the topic, leading to the publication of *Die christliche Gnosis* in 1835.

6. In my essay, "Der Gegensatz des Katholicismus und Protestantismus nach den Principien und Hauptdogmen der beiden Lehrbegriffe. Mit besonderer Rücksicht auf Herrn Dr. Möhler's *Symbolik*," *Tübinger Zeitschrift für Theologie* (1833), nos. 3–4, 1–438. See 367ff. Also compare 390ff. with what follows in the text. [Ed.] Published as a book in 1834. On the Baur-Möhler controversy, see Notger Slenczka in *Ferdinand Christian Baur and the History of Early Christianity*, ed. Martin Bauspiess, Christof Landmesser, and David Lincicum, trans. R. F. Brown and P. C. Hodgson (Oxford, 2017), 45–66.

of the Christian church, Catholicism sees only an extension and perfect fulfillment of the institutions of the Jewish theocracy. Indeed the Catholic Church gave its attention to smoothing over all the differences that posed a barrier to the immediate acceptance of its religious worldview. It even made its peace with paganism and gladly set Pelagianism in place of the Augustinian concept of inherited sin, by recognizing a natural light and instinct, a natural goodness (*bonum naturae*) in which paganism shared as well. By the Catholic Church taking these positions, it bridged as much as possible the ancient gulf between it and paganism on the one hand, and between Judaism and Christianity on the other hand.

So in the antithesis of Catholicism and Protestantism we see stability on the one side, motion on the other side; here a persistence in immediacy, there a struggling for mediation. In the entire domain of pagan religion Protestantism can only behold the dominance of sin with all its attendant consequences. According to the Protestant view the cause of the great antithesis running throughout the entire history of religion—in virtue of which the absolute power of religion must first break through the restrictive barrier of the darkening of spirit and the estrangement from God, by operating from below in the religious life of the individual—lies in the human being's original sin. Except that for Protestantism this sin, at least in the interpretation of Luther and Calvin, is no merely contingent act of human free will and subjectivity. Instead it is itself grounded in a higher divine arrangement conditioning the world order appearing in religious history.

However, we must always recognize the essential difference between Gnosticism's religious worldview and that of Protestantism, in that the supreme antithesis to which Protestantism takes us back can only be the ethical antithesis of election and rejection, of grace and sin, of the spirit and the flesh. It is not the metaphysical antithesis, the one from the philosophy of nature, the antithesis of spirit and matter, deity and world, absolute and finite.

## The Split between Theology and Philosophy since the Reformation

When theology and philosophy increasingly split into separate disciplines from the time of the Reformation onward, and each just thought to go its own way, this resulted in a greater remove from the standpoint of Gnosis. Philosophy just held to the abstract concept of deity, and what it called natural theology, in which it sought to reach an understanding about philosophy's relation to theology, was just an ill-connected aggregation of purely formal definitions.[7] Theology just thought to stand its ground from the standpoint of the creedal and ecclesiastical system.

---

7. There is hardly any greater contrast to Gnosis than Christian Wolff's natural theology. It of course wants to be a religious philosophy, but its God is just the abstract, intellectual concept of the *ens perfectissimum* or most perfect being. The distinction Wolff's theology posits in the divine being

As a result, when people grew indifferent to that old system and began to replace it with a new one, what emerged for the time being was a disconnected state, the negation of the previously-affirmed view. In putting aside the old concept of revelation, people saw the entire domain of religion and revelation as just a human product, as a series of religious notions and suppositions one believed one could evaluate simply according to the restricted norms of a reason confined to the narrow limits of one's own subjectivity, apart from any capacity for a wider vision of a cohesive and developmental process shaped by a higher divine necessity.

Although philosophy was conscious of its speculative task, the modern era initially had reservations about acquiring a pure and more lively concept of religious philosophy and of the religious history essentially bound up with it. Nevertheless, in moving on from the Reformation period itself, we see ancient Gnosis transitioning into the more recent kind of philosophy of religion. On this path we encounter, first of all, a phenomenon people regarded as simply lying far outside the domain of scientific knowledge, a phenomenon so peculiar that it ought not to have found a place at this point. I refer to the theosophy of Jacob Boehme. I cannot preface our consideration of it here in any better way than by reminding us of the influence that Boehme's ideas have had on Schelling's philosophy.

---

is simply the rigid, lifeless contrast—unmediated and dividing God's being into two completely different halves—of a God who is on the one hand recognizable by reason with all the evidential backing of Wolff's logic and metaphysics, and on the other hand unreachable by reason and knowable only through supernatural revelation. [Ed.] The German philosopher Christian Wolff (1679–1754) was a student of Leibniz and a popularizer of his philosophy. He wrote many books as the face of rationalism in the German enlightenment.

# 2

# The More Recent Religious Philosophy

## The Theosophy of Jacob Boehme

IT IS DIFFICULT TO perceive how Boehme's ideas are analogous to those of ancient Gnosis.[8] That is because Boehme endlessly repeats and varies the same main ideas,

8. Two major writings contain the purest form of Boehme's ideas. They appear as the first two volumes of the 1730 edition of his works. The first one is *Aurora, oder Morgenröthe im Aufgang*. (This "dawn" precedes the time of restoration when human beings on pilgrimage enter into the pure, luminous, and profound knowledge of God; see *Aurora*, 9.9 and 13.4.) The second work is *De tribus principiis*, which is a description of the three principles of the divine essence. – Given Protestantism's distinctively deep and inward understanding of the antitheses between sin and redemption, as the two principles around which all spiritual life revolves, it must also have involved a mystical element from the outset. In the early years this element made itself known in several noteworthy phenomena, but later on it was strongly suppressed by the supporters of biblical literalism and external authority. This suppression continued until an even stronger opposition to it emerged once again (and we see many indications of this in Boehme's case). If we direct our attention to Protestantism's natural mystical aspect, then it cannot seem out of place for a theosophical system such as Boehme's to emerge from Protestantism's original and basic instincts. Martin Luther and Johann Arndt had already warmly commended what also belongs to the mediating transitions then coming into view, namely a "German theology" (*Theologica Germanica*) in which, notwithstanding its very practical form, we also still see seeds of Boehme-like ideas and individual echoes of them. – [Ed.] Jacob Boehme (1575–1624). His first book, the *Aurora* (1612) was translated into English by John Sparrow (London, 1656) and republished as edited by C. J. Barker and D. S. Hehner (London, 1914; r.p. London, 1960). Boehme's second book, *Von den drei Principien Göttlichen Wesens* (1619) was translated into English by John Sparrow, as *Concerning the Three Principles of the Divine Essence* (London, 1648), and was reissued by C. J. Barker (London, 1910). Instead of quoting from these volumes in this section we have made our own translations from Baur's German in the lengthy excerpts he presents or paraphrases here. The standard German edition of Boehme's works is *Theosophia Revelata, Das ist: Alle Göttliche Schriften des Gottseligen und Hocherleuchteten Deutschen Theosophii Jacob Böhmens*, ed. J. W. Ueberfeld (Amsterdam, 1730). The facsimile reprint of it, ed. Will-Erich Peuckert in 11 vols., is Jacob Böhme, *Sämtliche Schriften* (Stuttgart, 1955–61). – The standard view is that Boehme's first four books contain early formulations that he later improved upon or ultimately discarded. So his mature and more consistent thought is to be found in the later works from 1620–24, most especially the *Mysterium Magnum* (1624). This position is well-established by the very detailed and still-definitive study of Boehme's authorship and thought: Alexandre Koyré, *La philosophie de Jacob Boehme* (Paris, 1929; r.p. New York, 1968). It raises the question as to how best to understand Baur's statement that the first two books "contain the purest form of Boehme's ideas." This can be problematic because Baur's discussion of the

343

and omits, or just indicates in part, so much that cannot be left out in the methodical development of a system. In fact his writings are, on the whole and inherently, in a form very inadequate for making everything into a coherent whole. In Boehme's case certain of his major ideas are so predominant that, in all the forms in which he presents them, they always have the same meaning for him, and this is the very, and somewhat surprising, point where we see the analogy with ancient Gnosis.

## The Duality of Principles in the Basic Idea of the System

The basic idea from which Jacob Boehme everywhere proceeds is the idea of a distinction presupposed within the divine nature itself, a duality of principles. It is the same dualism that defined the entire worldview of the Gnostics and the Manicheans, but with the difference that Boehme did not accept any principle different from, and independent of, God's own nature. Instead for him this duality of principles and powers is posited within the nature of God itself.

In the nature or essence of God itself there is an antithesis of darkness and light, of fury (*Grimmigkeit*) and gentleness (*Sanftmuth*), a duality from which proceed all the oppositions in the life of nature and of spirit, even including the antithesis of good and evil. It is a duality of principles, the former one of which, the dark, furious, acrid, and rigid principle (and whatever else it may be called) is of course not God in the highest sense, but is still also God or belongs to God such that it is the presupposition for God himself. In authentically Gnostic and Manichean fashion Boehme expresses his basic insight in the preface to the *Three Principles of the Divine Essence* as follows:

> As long as a human being then knows that he too is a twofold being, caught up in good and evil, . . . it is therefore surely very necessary that he come to know the following things for himself. What is his nature? What are the sources of his good and evil impulses? What is itself in fact the good and the evil in him? What brings it forth? What is in fact the origin of what is good and all that is evil? From what or by what does evil come about in the Devil and in human beings, as well as in all creatures? The Devil was a holy angel and the human being has also been created good. A repugnant state is to be found in all creatures such that everything is biting and comes to blows with itself, is repugnant, repressive, and antagonistic to itself. So there is an antipathy within all creatures, and every bodily being is discordant with itself. We see

---

*Aurora* and the *Three Principles* serves to set up his subsequent discussion of Boehme's influence on Schelling's treatise on human freedom; whereas Boehme's impact on that treatise clearly comes from his later works as well, and not just from the first two books. On this point see Robert F. Brown, *The Later Philosophy of Schelling: The Influence of Boehme on the Works of 1809–1815* (Lewisburg PA and London, 1977). Also see n. 88 below. Therefore perhaps the best answer to the question is that Baur likely regards the first two books as having the greatest affinity with the rather extravagant speculation of some of the ancient Gnostics, and that makes them the ones to examine in detail in a book on Gnosis. See what Baur says about Boehme below, n. 194.

that this is the case not only in living creatures but also in the heavenly bodies, in the elements, the earth, stones and metals, in wood, leaves, and grass, for there is poison and malignity in everything. This must therefore be the case, else there would be no life or mobility, nor would there even be color or virtue, no thickness or thinness, or any other sort of sensation or feeling. Instead it all would be emptiness, mere nothing. By regarding things in such a higher way one finds that all such is forthcoming by God and from out of God himself; and that it is God's own essential nature, what he himself is; and that he has therefore created out of himself; and that evil belongs to the process of generation and mobility, with goodness belonging to love, and strictness or antipathy belonging to joy.[9]

Compare with this the following passage from the *Three Principles*:

There is indeed no distinction within God. But when one asks whence evil and good come, one must know what is the primary and authentic fount of wrath, and then also of love, because they are both from one absolute origin (*Urkund*), from one Mother, and both are one thing. This is how we must speak in creaturely fashion if we would take hold of a beginning and make it into something that is known. For one cannot say that in God there is fire, or what is bitter or acrid, much less so that there is air, water, or earth in him. But one sees that these have been from that source. Also, one cannot say that in God there is death, or infernal fire, or sorrow. But we know that these have been from that source . . .

Thus we must investigate the source for the origins of things, for what is the *prima materia* or first cause of evil and is the same in both God's absolute origin and in creatures. For in the absolute origin it is all one thing, it is all from God, all made from his essence according to its threefold nature. The acrid, the bitter, and fire are in the absolute origin, within the first principle . . . It is the water-source; here, in keeping with the first principle, God is not called "God" but instead is fury, wrath, the severe source for the absolute origin of evil, of woeful deeds, of tumult and burning.[10]

See also *Three Principles*, chap. 4:

In the absolute origin we find the most frightful and most severe birth, all that is acrid, bitter, and fire. One cannot say here that this is God, and yet it is the innermost, primal source, which is within God the Father and according to which he calls himself an angry, jealous God. This same source is the first

---

9. *Three Principles*, Author's Preface, §§13–14.

10. Ibid., 1.4–6 and 8. [*Ed.*] The "threefold nature" is not the traditional Christian Trinity as such. Rather it is the three types present in everything: wrath or furious power, love, and the creative movement produced by the interaction of the other two. It is typical of Boehme that he also calls the three elements in the first principle—acrid, bitter, and fire—by the alchemical terms (capitalized): Sulphur, Mercurius, and Sal (in 1.7).

principle, and is God the Father in his absolute origin, from which this world itself originates.

In this principle there is nothing but just the most frightful gestation, the greatest anguish, the most hostile ecstasy, like a sulfurous spirit, and it is the very gates and abyss of hell, where Prince Lucifer remains, his light extinguished.[11]

In support of this view Boehme appeals to the natural world that manifests a twofold principle in every plant; to a second principle that is not the plant's stem or trunk itself and that originates from the light of nature (4.26–27). Among other things he appeals to human life, to the nature of the human temperament in which are found anger and evil as well as love and gentleness (10.34). In the same way he appeals to the universal natural law, the fact that no life is conceivable without a duality of principles and powers, nor also is the concept of God as a living being thinkable without the same antithesis. He says:

Might the mind [or temperament or disposition] not then have remained, as in sheer love, with one intention, like God himself? Here purpose and reason and knowledge are fixed. You see, if the will were of one nature then the mind would also have just one quality it would give to the will. Then the mind would be an immovable thing that would forever be still and do nothing further than always one thing—in which case there would be no joy and also no knowledge, no art, no science of various kinds and no wisdom. Everything is then emptiness and there would be no mind, no willing of something else, for there would be just the one thing. So we cannot say that the entirety of God, with the three principles, is in one will and essence. There is distinction or difference. Although the first principle and the third principle are not called God, and are not also God, this is nevertheless God's essence, since the light and heart of God is forever being born from eternity, and is one essential nature, like the body and soul in a human being. If there were not the eternal mind from which the eternal will issues, then there would be no God. But it is the eternal mind that gives birth to the eternal will, and the eternal will gives birth to the eternal heart of God, and the heart gives birth to the light, and the light to the energy [or virtue], and the energy to the spirit, and that is the almighty God who exists as one unchangeable will.

Behold now, the mind is in darkness and attaches its will to the light it is to bear, else there would be no will and also no birth. This same mind stands in anguish and in longing, and the longing is the will, and the will takes hold of the energy, and the energy fulfills the mind. Therefore the kingdom of God stands in the energy or virtue. The kingdom is: (1) God the Father, and the energy makes the light yearning for the will, and that light is (2) God the Son, for in the energy the light is forever born from eternity, and in the light

---

11. Ibid., 4.45 and 47.

proceeding out from the energy is (3) the Holy Spirit, who, within the dark mind, in turn gives birth to the will of the eternal nature or essence. Now behold, dear soul, ... what is the deity and contains within itself the other or intermediate principle. This is why God is solely good, is love, light, and power. Then consider that there would not be such eternal wisdom and knowledge in God if the mind had not stood in darkness.[12]

## The Trinity

Accordingly we have the eternal birth of the divine being, through which God himself realizes the eternal concept of his own essential nature. The moments of this eternal birth can be distinguished in various ways, based on whether they are considered in terms of the divine nature in and for itself, or else in relation to Satan, the world, and human beings. But even within the former context there are different perspectives under which the essential nature of God and his eternal birth get placed.

The light process in which it is initially possible to distinguish principles based on their operations within God's essential nature is one in which God becomes a trinitarian God. This Trinity is itself none other than the same eternal and necessary birth of the God giving birth to himself, apart from which God cannot be thought of as a living God. In the *Three Principles* Boehme says:

> In wanting to speak about the holy threefoldness, we must first state that there is one God, and he is called the Father and the creator of all things. He is almighty and is all in all. Everything is his, and everything is in him and comes forth from him, and remains in him eternally. And then (in the second place) we say that he is threefold in persons. From eternity he has given birth to his Son, who is his heart, light, and love; and they are not two natures but one eternal essence. Then (in the third place) we say, as scripture tells us, that there is a Holy Spirit who proceeds from the Father and the Son; and there is one essence in the Father, Son, and Holy Spirit. And that is therefore correctly stated. For behold, if (1) the Father is the absolutely original essence and origin of all essences or natures, and the other principle would not have come forth in the birth of the Son, then the Father would be a dark valley. Thus you surely see that (2) the Son, who is the Father's heart, love, light, beauty, and gentle benevolence, opens up a different principle in his birth. You see that the Son placates the angry fury (of the absolute origin, thus to be called the first principle) of the Father and makes him sweet and (if I may say so) compassionate. So the Son is a different person from the Father, for there is nothing in the Son's center but sheer joy, love, and delight. Now you surely do indeed see how (3) the Holy Spirit proceeds from the Father and the Son. For, if the heart or light of God is born in the Father, thus in the kindling of the

---

12. Ibid., 10.35–40.

> light in the fifth form there arises, from the water-source in the light, a wholly amiable, fragrant, and savory spirit. This is the spirit that, in the primal origin, was the bitter thorn or sting in the acrid Mother, and now, in the water-source (the gentleness) it makes many thousand (indeed endless and innumerable) centers, and this is all in the fount of water. Now you surely understand that the birth of the Son originates in the fire; and that his person and name are captured in the kindling of the gentle, wise, and clear light that he himself is, and that itself makes the sweet fragrance, taste, and gentle benevolence within the Father. The Son is properly the Father's heart and a different person, for he brings forth and opens up the other principle within the Father. His own nature is the energy and the light, because of which he is properly called the energy of God. But the Holy Spirit is not known in the absolute origin of the Father prior to the light. For when the gentle fount opens up into the light, as a stronger, more almighty spirit it therefore goes forth in great joy from the sweet water-source and the light, and is the energy of the water-source and the light. This spirit then produces forms and structures, and is the center within all essences, for the light of life originates in the light of the Son or heart of the Father. And the Holy Spirit for that reason is called a separate person, since he proceeds from Father and Son as the living energy, and confirms the eternal birth of the Trinity.[13]

The result of the duality of principles from which Boehme sets out is that in fact the Holy Spirit cannot stand in entirely the same relation to the Son as the Son stands to the Father. Instead the Holy Spirit is in the multiplicity what the Son is in the unity. So we take it in this sense when the Holy Spirit is called the forming and structuring principle, activating all the powers of the Father, opening up the immeasurable and innumerable centers in the birth of the Father's heart.[14]

### The Seven Source-Spirits

With the threefoldness actually being a duality, Boehme even has the threeness unfolding as powers that are seven in number, although the fundamental relationship still remains the same.

All power is in God the Father, and in his depths he is the source and fount of all powers.[15] In him are light and darkness, air and water, heat and cold, hard and soft, thick and thin, sound and tone, sweet and sour, bitter and acrid. Put somewhat differently, in God we find seven different qualities or source-spirits (*Quellgeister*). The first one is the acrid quality, that is, a quality of the pith or core, the concealed nature,

---

13. Ibid., 4.55–58.
14. See *Three Principles*, 4.74; also *Aurora*, 3.28, 12.109, 13.77.
15. *Aurora*, 8.4. [*Ed.*] In a number of cases our citations of Boehme do not correspond closely with Baur's. We are giving citations as the passages are numbered in the existing English translations, according to the on-line versions of Kraus House Publishers.

a sharpness, an attraction or coagulation quite sharp and acrid in the *Salliter*.[16] This quality produces rigidity and also coldness, so it is to be stirred up or inflamed. It gives birth to harshness as in the taste of salt (*Aurora*, 8.22). The next quality or next spirit of God in the divine *Salliter* or the divine power, is the sweet quality that works within what is acrid and mitigates the harshness so that it becomes wholly pleasing and mild; for it is an overcoming of the acrid quality. It is the source of God's loving kindness, which overcomes his anger (8.32–38). The third one is the bitter quality, an interpenetration or mastery of the sweet and acrid qualities that shakes, interpenetrates, and surmounts them (8.44). Everything that has form or shape depends on the power and control of these three main qualities; it has its shape because of them, and is even formed from their power (8.53).

The fourth quality is heat. Heat is the beginning of life as such and also the proper spirit of life. It ignites all the qualities. For if heat is at work in the sweet dampness it gives birth to the light in all the qualities, so that if the one sees the others, that seeing is the origin of the senses and thoughts. The lightning flash of life arises in this light (8.59ff., 10.12, 11.9–10). The fifth quality is gracious, genial, and joyous love. When heat goes up into the sweet quality and ignites the source of sweetness, then the genial love-light-fire in the sweet quality goes up and ignites the bitter and the acrid qualities. It gives them food and drink from the sweet juice of its love. It animates and illumines them, and makes them alive and enlightened. And when the sweet, bright power of love comes to them so they have a taste of it and take hold of their life, oh!, here there is a congenial harmonizing and overcoming, a congenial welcoming and great love, nothing but amiable and gracious kissing and affability: for the bridegroom kisses his bride.[17]

The sixth source-spirit in the divine power is sound or tone, so that everything sounds and resonates in it. What follows from it is language and the distinguishing of all things. The bells and the songs of the holy angels belong to it, as well as the forming of all colors and all beauty, and the joyous kingdom of heaven. For when the spirits wish to be active and to speak, the harsh quality must open itself up: the bitter tone bursts out with its own lightning flash, whereupon the tone issues forth and is pregnant with all the seven spirits, which differentiate the word in how it was enclosed in the center that is within the middle circle, for the word was still subject to the seven spirits. That is why the seven spirits of God created a mouth for creatures, so that when they sought to speak or make sounds they did not first need to get torn open. That is why there are all the blood vessels and powers or source-spirits in the tongue, so the sound or tone is uttered smoothly (10.1–2, 11–12, 15–16).

The seventh spirit of God is the *corpus* or body, which is born from the other six spirits. All the heavenly figures subsist in the *corpus* and everything has its shape

---

16. [*Ed.*] Boehme thinks of the qualities as interpenetrating one another organically, and uses the terms *Salliter* and *Salniter* for this state of interpenetration.

17. *Aurora*, 8.155–61. See also the beautiful passages that follow this, as well as 9.70.

and form in it. All beauty and joy proceeds from it. It is the spirit of nature proper; it is surely nature itself. It is the seat of comprehensibility, and all the creatures in heaven and on earth are formed in it. Indeed heaven itself is formed in it, and all that is natural in the whole of God is based in this spirit. So, in the absence of this seventh spirit there would also be no angel, no human being, and God would be an inscrutable nature that would simply subsist in its inscrutable power (11.1–3).

All these seven spirits then live and well up in one another. Taken all together, they are God the Father. For there is no spirit outside of the other spirits. All of the seven give birth, one to the other. So any one of them would not be if there were not also the others. However, the light is another person, for it is eternally born from the seven spirits, and the seven spirits eternally ascend into the light. The powers of these seven spirits eternally, in the splendor of the light, go out into the seven nature-spirits, and form and shape everything in these seven spirits, and this going-out in the light is the Holy Spirit (11.22–23, 32–37).[18]

## The Angels

The seven source-spirits are, in one sense, just the re-expression of the threefold character of the divine nature. The first four qualities most especially portray the nature of the Father. The fifth quality perhaps portrays the nature of the Son (for the light is the heart of the seven spirits and this light is the veritable Son of God) (*Aurora*, 11.38). The last two qualities, which give the spirits their specific and concrete form and shape, just as forming, confirming, and individualizing belong to the nature of the Holy Spirit, portray the nature of the Holy Spirit. This same relationship therefore also gets envisaged in a new, and more concrete, form in the case of the angels.

God created the angels from the seventh source-spirit, which is the basis of nature or of heaven above. In their welling-up and ascent, the spirits were self-activated by the concentration of God's nature, by the light within them, and by the spirit proceeding from them. The same thing also happened in the case of the creatures. Although each one of the angels of course had in itself the power of all seven of the spirits, in each angel one quality or another was strongest (12:1–10). But here the basic form conditioning this is once again the threefoldness of the divine nature, indeed in multiple senses. Each angel is created as being like unto the whole of the deity, as like a little God, because God created the angels out of, or based on, himself; and Father,

---

18. [*Ed.*] In this bewildering array of statements and descriptions in the preceding pages, Boehme is likely drawing upon terminology and categories from Renaissance nature-philosophy, alchemical speculation, and other sources, to make his points. In this section on the "qualities," the underlying idea is that God's nature is an eternal, interactive, and interdependent complex of elements and powers. That will then support the contention that the universe of creatures in space and time is grounded in, and in its own nature finitely reproduces, these same elements and powers. Boehme has no other way to envisage and characterize these elements and powers as they are in God, than to use concepts and terminology suited to the finite, everyday world of human experience.

Son, and Holy Spirit are everywhere (12.57–58). There is no difference between the spirits of God and the angels themselves, except for the fact that the angels are creatures and their corporeal nature has a beginning, although the power from which they are created is God himself (12.68).

However, the same threefoldness that is the nature of each individual angel also presents itself in the three angelic realms that the angels make up. Just as the threefoldness is the greatest and most prominent feature in God, in keeping with the supreme primacy of his threefoldness God has also created three archangels, each of which is assigned his own angelic host or natural place and is a natural lord over the regiment of angels of his place. Each is bound to God his creator as the soul is bound to the body (12.84, 103–6). The three angelic rulers are described as follows.

1. Michael is called the strength or power of God, and in fact goes by that name because he is the collective embodiment of the seven source-spirits, as a flowering of them. He then stands in God the Father's stead (12.118–19).

2. The one who is an outcast from the light of God is now called Lucifer. Whereas Michael was created according to God the Father's standing, nature, and properties, Lucifer was created according to God the Son's standing, nature, and beauty or excellence, and as a beloved son he was bound in love to God the Son. Lucifer's heart stood in the center of the light as though it were itself God, and his beauty or excellence surpassed all others, for what enveloped him, or was his foremost mother, was God the Son. And just as God the Father is bound to his Son in great love, so too King Lucifer was bound to King Michael with great love, as though they were one heart or one God. For the source or fount of the Son of God had reached into Lucifer's heart.

3. The third archangel, Uriel, has his name from the light or from the lightning flash, that is, from the outgoing of the light. He is formed according to the nature and standing of the Holy Spirit, and signifies God proper as the Holy Spirit.

These are God's three princes in the heavens. Then when the lightning flash of life, that is, the Son of God, rises up within the middle circle in the source-spirits of God and shows himself triumphant, and the Holy Spirit triumphantly surpasses himself, then in this ascending the Holy Trinity also ascends in the hearts of these three rulers and becomes triumphant and joyful; and in the deity there arises the wondrous and beautiful form of the heavens in all sorts of colors and ways (12:134–45).

## Lucifer, His Fall, and His Significance in Ethical and Physical Contexts

As with the Gnostics, in Boehme's case too we find the whole system and its main task driven by dealing with a transition from the ideal world to the real world, from the absolute to the finite. With Boehme's understanding of the spirit-world taking the form of a more specific and more concrete picture, his conception of how to deal with this transition also had to be very vividly concrete.

Boehme's solution for explaining the transition came partly through the idea of a falling-away (*Abfall*) and partly by presupposing an original duality of principles. On the latter point he concurred in particular with Manicheanism, yet with the essential difference that he located the crucial one of the two principles not outside of God but internal to God's own nature itself. For he dealt with the issue by establishing an equilibrium between the two theses, one in which evil has its ground and origin in God, and yet God himself is not the author of evil.

We encounter the idea of a falling-away especially in terms of the fall of Lucifer, an event Boehme very often mentions and describes. In doing so he seems above all to be simply expressing the Christian idea of the Devil as a fallen spirit. As we already noted, Lucifer of course was also originally one of the supreme spirits, one of the three angelic rulers. Boehme says:

> Lucifer's kingdom too was created in the glorious, lovely, and heavenly *Salitter*[19] of the divine qualities, without any greater stirring than in the others. For when Lucifer was created he was altogether perfect and was the fairest prince in the heavens, adorned and outfitted with the most splendid clarity of the Son of God. However, Lucifer was depraved in how he felt about the creation and thus would at no time have retained his perfection, beauty, and clarity. Instead he immediately became a more furious, more sinister devil and not a cherub.[20]

We should not overlook the fact that the perfection Boehme describes in this passage, and in others, as the kind Lucifer had actually already possessed, is also in turn portrayed as a merely hypothetical perfection, as merely a present possibility; in other words, as something Lucifer could have attained had he directed his heart toward God as the other spirits did.

The main passage pertinent to this point reads as follows:

> The seven spirits that are in an angel, that bear light and understanding, that are bound to the whole of God, are not said to denote anything other or higher or greater than God himself, but instead are said to be of one mode. They are just parts of the whole and not the whole itself, for God has created them out of himself so that, in such form and manner, they should befit God himself.[21] However, the source-spirits in Lucifer are then not of this kind. For since they saw that they sat in the highest primacy or rank, they therefore behaved acridly or harshly, so that the spirit to which they gave birth became very fiery and rose up in the source or fount of the heart like a haughty damsel.

---

19. *Salitter, Salniter*, actually saltpeter or *sal nitrum*, is for Boehme an alchemical-mystical designation for God's substance, the matter in God.

20. *Aurora*, 13.114–16.

21. [Ed.] Boehme utilizes the word-play between the qualities (*Qualität*) or features of the source-spirits that befit God because they are from God, and the fact of their therefore befitting (*qualificieren*) God.

## The More Recent Religious Philosophy—Boehme

Thus the source-spirits had been most delightfully befitting in how they acted before they had become creaturely, when they were still universally in God prior to creation. They even gave birth within themselves to a most delightful and gentle son, who was to be like unto the Son of God. Then the light within Lucifer and the light of the Son of God would have been as one, a single infusion of the qualities, a lovely embrace, heart and combination. Then the great light, which is the heart of God, would have gently and lovingly played with the little light in Lucifer as with a young son. For the little son in Lucifer was supposed to be the dear little brother of the heart of God. God the Father had created the angels with such a purpose in mind, that just as in his "love-play" the Father is manifold in his qualities and incomprehensible in his alterations, so too the little spirits or little lights of the angels, which are like the Son of God, were supposed to play before God's heart in his own great light, so that this might increase the joy in God's heart and might therefore be a holy sport or playing in God.

The light (to which the seven spirits had given birth out of themselves) was supposed to ascend to its gentleness in the heart of God and to be joyful in God's light, as though a child with its mother. Here there was to be heartfelt love and friendly kissing, certainly a gentle and lovely enjoyment. Here the sound was to mount up and resonate with the singing and ringing, the praise and jubilation. All the qualities were to joyously take part and each spirit to play its godly part, just like God the Father himself. All seven spirits were possessed of full knowledge, for they were in a state befitting God the Father, in that they could see, feel, taste, smell, and hear everything that God the Father did.

However, when the seven spirits exalted themselves in an intense conflagration they certainly acted contrary to the natural law, in acting otherwise than God their Father does; and that was an uprising or source contrary to the entirety of deity. For they ignited the *Salitter* of the *corpus* or body, and gave birth to an overweening son who, in the acrid quality, was harsh, severe, dark, and cold, and who was burning within the sweet quality, was bitter and fiery. The sound of it was a harsh, ostentatious resonance, and the love in it was a haughty hostility to God. The enkindled bride stood there within the seventh nature-spirit like a proud beast and presumed to be above God, to have no equal. The love grew cold and the heart of God could not have an effect on it, for there was antipathy between them. God's heart moved toward its heart, gently and lovingly, but this angel's heart was dark, harsh, cold, and fiery. The heart of God was to have infused (*inqualieren*) the heart of the angel, but that could not be. For it was a matter of harshness versus tenderness, sour versus sweet, darkness versus light, fire versus a lovely warmth, hard knocking versus a lovely singing. Hear this, Lucifer: who is then to blame for the fact that you have become a devil? Is it God, according to your lies? Oh no! It is you yourself, the source-spirits in the *corpus* that you yourself are, which in you have

> given birth to such a little son. You cannot say that God has ignited the *Salitter* from which he made you. Instead your source-spirits did it, after you were already God's prince and king.[22]

Also here, according to this account, Lucifer was called God's prince and king. Yet how could he have such an exalted perfection, with his heart standing in the center of the light, in the way this passage puts it, if there was born in him a son wholly different from the one who would have been equal to the Son of God? *Aurora* 13:128–31 likewise repeats the statement that the birth of a new son in the heart of Lucifer was all-pervasive in his *corpus* and was glorified and cheerfully welcomed by the Son of God who was outside the *corpus*. He was endowed with the greatest beauty of the heavens, in keeping with the beauty of God the Son, and it was in him as a beloved heart or attribute, one with which the whole deity had been infused. There now stands the beautiful bride, as a prince of God, to be the most beautiful of creatures, to be loved by God as a dear son of the creatures.

Notwithstanding the description of this birth in the foregoing passages, it cannot be envisaged as in fact a perfect birth. One ought not suppose that this is just one of Boehme's usual variations in the presentation of his ideas. As we will see subsequently, there is a more profound basis for it. In order to have a correct and overall understanding of Lucifer, the following passage from *Concerning the Three Principles of the Divine Essence* especially merits our attention.

> As well as the other angels, Lucifer was created from the eternal nature [of God], from the eternally indissoluble bond, and he stood in paradise. He too felt and saw the birth of the holy deity, the birth of the other principles: the heart of God, the confirmation of the Holy Spirit. His nourishment would also have been the Word of the Lord (*verbo Domini*), and he would have remained therein an angel. But because he saw that he was a prince, situated in the first principle, he despised the birth of the heart of God and its gentle and loving composition (*Qualificiren*), he meant to be a wholly dominating and terrifying lord within the first principle. He sought to constitute himself as a fiery force, he despised the gentleness of the Father's heart, and he was unwilling to see his place as being within[23] the Father's heart (unlike the other angels, in whose imagination or mind's eye the will of the holy threefoldness is within the deity). Therefore he could not be nourished by the Word of the Lord and his light went out. That is why he became right away something loathsome in paradise and he was vomited out, was thrust off his princely throne together with all the legions associated with him. And because he had now abandoned the heart of God, the other principle was closed off to him, and he therefore lost contact

---

22. *Aurora*, 13.44–58.

23. [*Ed.*] "Imagination" (the same in both German and English) is an important term for Boehme, but hard to work into the syntax here in the noun form. The German for the clause "he was unwilling to see his place as being within . . ." is: *seine Imagination wollte er darein nicht setzen*.

> with God and the heavenly kingdom, with all the paradisiacal esprit, delight, and joy. He remained within the darkest valley of the eternally attested four most anguished states.
>
> Thus he raised up his imagination and in it he ignited the source or root of fire. But the fire-root sought for the water as the true mother of the eternal nature. It found severe acridity and the mother in an alarming, deathly state. The bitter acridity formed the mother into a furious, raging serpent, coiling up in a quite terrifying way. In the indissoluble bond there was an eternal hostility, an internal antipathy, an eternal despairing of all that is good; the state of mind a crushing and stinging cycle, its will constantly rising up toward the fiery force and to the destruction of God, but never able to reach that point. For Lucifer is forever enclosed within the first principle as though in an eternal death. Yet he rises up evermore, presuming to reach the heart of God and to gain control of it. For the bitter sting in his birth therefore eternally mounts up in the fiery source and gives his will the expectation of having it all, while attaining nothing. His nourishment is the fount of water that is the mother, wholly in anguish, like the sulfurous spirit on which his indissoluble bond feeds. His delight is the eternal fire, the eternal coldness in the acrid mother, in the bitterness of eternal hunger, in the fiery source of eternal thirst. His ascent is his fall.[24]

According to this passage Lucifer's fall is first and foremost to be thought of as the fall of a higher spirit. This is the aspect of Lucifer's nature in which moral evil presents itself, inasmuch as his own self-will turns away from being united with the universal will of God, and apprehends itself wholly in terms of its own selfhood and selfishness. This is simply the ethical aspect, which is to be distinguished from the physical aspect, although both are inherently one and the same. Boehme's position is that moral evil and physical evil express one and the same concept. Evil in either of these senses is persistence in the first principle and being cut off from the second principle. It is the severing of the natural bond that unites the two principles, a bond that the second principle first illumines and clarifies. That is why Lucifer is forever locked up in the first principle; for in this principle there is nothing but just the most completely horrifying process of giving birth, the greatest anguish, an antagonistic ecstasy like a sulfurous spirit. Here there are the very gates of hell and the abyss (*Abgrund*). Here is where Prince Lucifer abides with his light extinguished. Here the soul (who is separated from the second principle, and in whom the light from the heart of God is extinguished) abides in the same infernal abyss.[25]

Regarded in this way, evil is indeed on the one hand not a principle distinct from God's nature but, on the other hand, as evil, it is not something brought about by God,

---

24. *Three Principles*, 4.67–71.
25. Ibid., 4.47.

inasmuch as the full concept of evil, in its truest and highest sense, is the turning-away from God. So God has not created evil.

> In its innermost or initial birth, the deity as a whole has, at its core, a pronounced and terrifying harshness, since the acrid quality is a terrifying confluence of acrid, hard, dark, and cold features, like wintertime when it is so fiercely cold that water freezes and it is completely unbearable. Within itself, in its innermost core, the acrid quality is of such a kind, and it exists solely for itself, outside the other qualities in God . . . This is therefore the very deepest and most inwardly hidden birth of God, according to which he is called a wrathful, jealous God, as we see from the Ten Commandments on Mount Sinai (Exod 20:5; Deut 5:9). Hell and eternal damnation reside in this acrid quality—eternal hostility, a den of thieves, and the kind of creature the Devil has been.[26]

This duality in the concept of evil is also expressed in the answer given to the question: Has God known and willed evil?

> God has indeed known evil according to his wrath, but not according to his love for which God is called God. No fury about, nor imagining of, evil plays a part in love; nor is there any inquiring about infernal creatures. When I say that, according to scripture, God knows no evil and God wills no evil, I understand this to mean that, in his love, which alone is the eternal goodness and is called God, there is apparent no hint of evil. Else if evil were apparent there the love would not be solely gentleness and meekness. However, inasmuch as God is called an angry, jealous God, and a consuming fire, and if he indeed knew this fire eternally, such that he himself would have been moved inwardly by it, he also knew that the same source would also have been something creaturely and not to be called God, but instead a consuming fire.[27]
>
> Therefore evil has no basis in the fact that God is also an angry God. The evil is the wrath of God himself, but Lucifer was the first to forcefully ignite the *Salitter* of God that had eternally been at rest and stood within God's gentleness, and which was indeed eternally at rest in concealment. It is from this igniting in this quarter that God now calls himself an angry, jealous God toward those who hate him.[28]

If God's wrath is none other than God's justice or righteousness, then Lucifer, or the Devil, is the instrument of the divine justice, inasmuch as it surely also reveals itself in the self-negating force of evil. Hence for the Devil, who has no authority for his own sake, if:

---

26. *Aurora*, 13.65–76.
27. Ibid., 14.45–47. See also *Three Principles*, 11.22.
28. [*Ed.*] This paragraph summarizes an important theme from *Aurora* 14. But Baur's individual citations cannot be linked to specific points found there.

everything depends on God's wrath, then the Devil is a hangman's servant and administers justice as a lackey; not a judge, but an executioner. He is the executioner in the kingdom of this world, the stars are the council, and God is the king of the land. Whoever are then sentenced by God, those who are sentenced in the council of the stars, go with many to the sword to murder themselves; they go with many to the noose or to drowning, for Lucifer is busy and is the executioner or hangman.[29]

The same fire that burns in the wrath of God also reveals itself in nature. All of nature is ignited and inflamed.

When Lucifer exalted himself and wanted to be alone God, he ignited the wrathful fire in nature. With his ignited, fiery spirit he roared into the nature of God, and the entire body within the nature of God was ignited in the full range of its dominion. But because the light available to him went out, he could not any longer, with his spirit, insinuate himself (*inqualieren*) into the two births—of the Son of God and of God's Holy Spirit. Instead he had to remain in the harshest birth of God and, with his fiery spirit, he was spewed out into external nature, where he has ignited the wrathful fire. This same nature is of course the body of God in which the deity gives birth to itself. But the Devil could not take hold of the gentle birth of God, which ascended into the light. For its body fades in the light and its source-spirits always give birth to themselves in the innermost strictness, according to the justice of the strict deity.[30]

Therefore after Lucifer's fall, when God creates this world, everything is created from the same *Salitter* in which Lucifer had his seat (*Aurora*, 15.93; cf. 21.127), and this fiery wrath of God is still present in this world, the body of God, until the end (15.69).

Because of this kindled fury the stars, together with the vanity, must therefore wane, rolling about until the Judgment Day (15.66).

In this kindling of the light in the stars and elements . . . nature stands in its sharpest, most austere and anguished birth, where the wrath of God shoots up without ceasing, like the fires of hell. If nature, with its sharp birth, had wholly transformed itself into love, according to heavenly justice, then the devils would have been once again in God's holy place. And so you can very well see and understand, in the horrific heat and cold, as well as in the poison of bitterness and sourness in this world, how everything stands with the birth of the stars, wherein the Devil lies captive. The stars are just the kindling of the great house, for the whole house is benumbed in death, as is the earth. For the outermost birth is dead and benumbed like the bark of a tree. But the astral

---

29. *Three Principles*, 17.66–67. There is the same concept of evil in the Pseudo-Clementine system (see above, pp. 192ff.), a passage that also calls to mind the Marcionite concept of justice.

30. [*Ed.*] Baur cites a passage in *Aurora* 23, but no compact statement could be found there that equates to this quotation. Pieces of it occur in *Aurora*, 23.99–102.

birth is the body, for life rises up in it. Yet in its body the birth is very sharp ... But when you behold the sun and the stars you must not think they are the holy and pure God ... for they are the kindled, austere birth of his body, for love and wrath wrestle with each other ... Heaven is the partition between love and wrath. It is the place where wrath is transformed into love ...[31]

Since all of God's creatures have been made from the same ignited *Salitter*, they formed themselves as bad and good, in the manner of the ignited qualities. This is the origin of the wild and vicious animals in this world. When Lucifer exalted himself and kindled his source-spirits, then the brutish spirit went forth in the tone, coming from all the bodies of Lucifer's angels and into the *Salitter* of God, as a fiery serpent or dragon, and shaped all sorts of poisonous and fiery forms and images, like unto the wild and vicious beasts. It was none other than as if a fiery thunderbolt went into the nature of God; or a furious serpent that raged and stormed there as if it wanted to tear the nature to pieces. This is why people call the Devil the ancient serpent, and also why there are vipers and serpents in this corrupted world; moreover all sorts of vermin such as worms, toads, flies and the like. Tempestuous weather—thunder, lightning, and hail—also has its original forms in this world ...[32]

All that is acrid, hard, thick, cold, dark, and the like, has its ground in Lucifer's fall. When the astringent quality compacted the *Salitter*, this was the origin of hard stones. The water in the *Salliter* also was condensed so that it became very thick, cold, and dark, the way the water now is in this world. Everything has become so hard and palpable; it was not so before the times of the angels. What is palpable in silver, gold, stones, fields, clothing, beasts, and human beings, is everywhere the wrath of God, otherwise it would not be hard and palpable. Therefore in his body (*corpus*) Lucifer has converted the sweet water into a sour sharpness, in intending in his haughtiness to rule over the whole of deity. He has brought things so far that, in this world, he reaches with his sharpness into the hearts of all creatures, into foliage and grass and into everything, as a king and prince of this world ...[33]

Now you will say that God should have resisted Lucifer and then things would not have come so far. Indeed, O blind one, it was not a human being or a beast confronting God; it was *god* against *God*, a strong one against another strong one. How was God supposed to resist Lucifer? Friendly love would not have succeeded. Lucifer was just contemptuous of love, and he himself wanted to be God. Should God then have met him with anger (which he did finally have to do)? If so then God had to kindle himself in his qualities in the *Salitter*, in which King Lucifer dwelled, and had to battle him forcefully and zealously.

---

31. *Aurora*, 24.45–49, 65–66, and 69.

32. *Aurora*, 15.70–81 (in part) and 91–92. See also *Three Principles*, 11.16–20.

33. [*Ed.*] Baur begins here with a summary statement and then quotes *Aurora*, 14.92, 94, 126, 130–31.

Owing to this battle, this kingdom of Lucifer therefore became darker, desolate, and evil, which made it necessary to have another creation.[34]

## The Dualism and Monism of This System

This is the point at which the relation of Boehme's system to Manicheanism is unmistakable. Most of the features in Boehme's entire description of his Lucifer remind us of the Manichean sovereign of this world and his prototype, the Persian Ahriman.

This is the same dualistic worldview, but differing only in that Boehme does not suppose he can make do with an original dualism by adopting a principle independent of God. Instead he seeks to conceive of the antithesis of the two principles itself as in turn a unity. However, despite this monism, the entire system inherently has a predominantly dualistic character. The two principles are of course embraced as one at the apex of the system. But as soon as they become active, each seeks to grasp itself in terms of its own distinctive nature. The dualism from which Manes sets out is itself the initial reality, and when Boehme has once posited dualism, his concept of the two principles is almost the same as that of Manes. One principle is the dark, material, corporeal principle but is also the sum and substance of all the powers that give natural life its sharpness, energy, and physical consistency. The other one is the intelligent principle that infuses the dark ground of nature with light, by overcoming the original hardness and stringency with love. The former of the two is the natural principle, and the latter one is the truly personal principle.

Boehme's system upholds its original monism in a way that at the same time makes recognizable the system's depth and distinctive character. It always makes the first principle the presupposition for the second principle, with the second one just developing itself on the foundation of the first. In virtue of this relationship between the two principles, the eternal deity gets conceptualized in the eternal birth of its own essential nature. The Son cannot be unless the Father is. But as soon as the Son is born, a higher stage of and potency of the divine life is given in him. In the Son, God first becomes truly God. Yet this same division of powers and principles, in virtue of which God manifests himself as Father and Son, also provides for the existence of Lucifer. The same principle that the Father is in his oneness with the Son, Lucifer is in this principle's being-for-self, in its complete antithesis to the Son.

However, this antithesis and difference that fully asserts its claim to power in Lucifer is also something that is eternally disaffirmed, is rejected. That is why the eternal, only-begotten Son directly takes the place of the fallen Lucifer. Our king now sits on the royal seat of Lucifer, who was expelled; so Lucifer's kingdom has become his instead.[35] From the same *Salitter* a different angelic host was to be set in the same

---

34. *Aurora*, 14.95–97.
35. See *Aurora*, 12.41, 80, 117.

place, in the locus of this world, a host to stand forever.[36] The disaffirming, antithetical factor is the Son, who for that very reason was fully equal to Lucifer as he was before his fall. The reality of the difference on the one hand, and the nullifying of the difference on the other hand, is the very point expressed by the aforementioned conception that Lucifer was not actually God's son but only potentially so (if he had not turned his imagination within and toward himself, had not dwelt on what was for himself, in other words had not fallen). Lucifer is disaffirmed or rejected *in himself*, as such, together with all the reality and autonomous self-reliance that the antithesis posited in Lucifer involves. For what exists as a possibility (a possibility Lucifer was free to choose) is now existent in itself. Hence there are two aspects to the first principle, two mutually opposed directions to be distinguished. Inasmuch as it makes itself the foundation for the Son, the first principle is the Father. But to the extent that the first principle fails to orient itself to the heart of God (as Boehme expresses this point) and instead strives against it—by turning away from the heart of God in order to persist within itself and to apprehend itself within itself, in its own selfhood—it is what is evil. What first appears at this point is dualism to the fullest extent: the antithesis between a dark, material, egotistical principle and a light, spiritual, universal principle.

### The Finite, Created World, as a Third Principle, Originates from the Interaction of the First Two, Eternal Principles

From this point onward, further development of Boehme's system can take no other course than the one Manicheanism also had taken.[37] Hence here too there can be no place for a creation in the proper sense, since that is certainly the case in Boehme's clearly expressed statement, introduced above, that the creation only ensued on the foundation of the divine *Salitter* to which Lucifer set fire.

What Boehme calls the creation is just the mixing and interaction of the two principles, the ongoing, hard struggle and contest in which the light principle seeks to illumine the dark principle, to break through and enliven rigid matter and give it a spiritual shape.[38]

> The kingdom of God and the kingdom of hell hang on each other as one body
> ... The earth has all seven source-spirits, for, by the Devil's kindling, the spirits of life are in the body together in death. They have, so to speak, been captured

---

36. See *Three Principles*, 10.8. [*Ed.*] Baur's sentence here also includes the phrase "in the human beings," which apparently refers to a subsequent statement in 10.8 about the image of God placed within the first persons (Gen 1:26–27).

37. In any event, however, its development does not, like Manes', begin with the dark principle attacking the light principle, and resulting in a mixing of the two. There is no basis for such an attack in Boehme's case, with the two principles co-existing from the outset and initially having to separate in an antithesis. However, in this antithesis they nevertheless mixed together in the way that, for Manes, first results from that attack.

38. [*Ed.*] The following quotations are from *Aurora*, 21.111, 21.104, 21.78, and 24.9–13.

> but not murdered . . . All the seven spirits of God are in the earth, and they give birth as they do in heaven. For the earth is in God, and God never died. But the outermost birth is dead, for the wrath rests in it. It is reserved for King Lucifer as a house of death and darkness, and as an eternal dungeon . . .
>
> The outermost darkness is in the house of God's wrath. The devils dwell in it and it is by rights the house of death, for in it the holy light of God is dead. Incomprehensible to the darkness, the body of this great house, which lies hidden under the shell of darkness, is the house of life in which love and wrath wrestle with each other. Now love forever breaks through the house of death and gives birth to holy, heavenly branches in the great tree that stands in the light. They spring up through the shell of darkness just as branches do through the bark of the tree, and they are a life with God. The wrath also springs up in the house of darkness, and it holds many a noble branch captive in death by its becoming infected in the house of fury. That is, in a nutshell, the contents of the sidereal or astral birth.

The sidereal and elementary birth of the stars and the [three] elementary kingdoms is what Boehme calls the created, finite world. Only inasmuch as this finite world has proceeded from the temporal mixing and interaction of the first two and eternal principles is it the third principle, the one that is fragile or corruptible.[39]

> God gave birth to, or generated, this third principle that he might be manifested by the material world. With the angels and the spirits having been created in the second principle, in the paradisiacal world, they therefore understood the eternal birth of God, as well as God's wisdom and omnipotence, in the third principle. They could be reflected in it, and could direct their imagination solely on the heart of God . . . Just as the heart of God in the paradisiacal heaven, in the immaterial heaven and birth, unlocks God's eternal power wherein eternal life perpetually comes forth and wherein eternal wisdom perpetually shines, so too the light of the sun, which has sprung up in the silent mother or womb (*matrice*) through the spirit simmering in it, opens up the third principle, that of this material world. This is the third and initiating principle, which in this form brings an end to the enumeration of principles. But it shall pass away, into its ether.[40]

Since the first two principles are reflected in the third principle, this physical world is itself just the copy of the archetypal world.

> The third principle is a similitude of the paradisiacal world, which is spiritual and is concealed in it. Thus God manifested himself. In seeing that the spiritual world of the angels is not enduring in this place, the physical world,

---

39. *Three Principles*, 4.3, 16.4.

40. *Three Principles*, 5.16, 5.10. [*Ed.*] Boehme's statement ends with an allusion to scripture, which Baur says is Heb 1:10–11, although the direct relevance of that passage is not apparent to the translator. But see 9.39, about passing away into its ether.

God has given to it another principle, wherein there is still a light and a lovely delight. God's purpose for it must endure, lest the first creatures had to remain in darkness.[41]

Compare this with the following passage in the *Aurora*:

> When you behold this world, you have a prototype of heaven. The stars signify the angels. For, as the stars must remain unchanged until the end of this world, so too the angels in the eternal time of heaven must remain unchanged forever. The elements signify the wondrous proportions and changing of the shape of the heavens. For as the region between the stars and earth is constantly changing in its own fashion—now bright light, now cloudy, now windy, now raining, now snowing, now deep blue sky, now greenish, now whitish, now dark—there are also changes, of various colors and shapes, to the heavens. But the latter are not of the kind that occur in this world. Instead they are all in accord with the mounting up of the spirit of God, and the light of the Son shines eternally in them. Yet there is a more pronounced mounting up at one time than at another, which is why the wondrous wisdom of God is incomprehensible. The earth signifies the heavenly nature, or the seventh nature-spirit, in which the images and forms and colors mount up. The birds, fish, and beasts signify the various shapes of the figures in heaven.[42]

That is why the eternal birth, by which the divine nature gives birth to itself, is constantly carrying on in the material, visible, comprehensible world as well.

> There shall be a continual birth through which the benumbed body of the earth shall give birth to itself anew. For such a new birth could be accomplished wholly apart from the Devil's will or consent. Thus the creator has given birth to himself in the whole body of this world in creaturely form, so to speak, in his seven source-spirits. All the stars are none other than the power of God. The whole body of this world persists in the seven source-spirits. All three persons of the deity are in this world in the full birth [of love, etc.].[43]
>
> Thus there is a strong will to give birth and to operate, and all of nature stands in great longing and anguish, constantly willing to give birth to the divine power, with God and paradise concealed in this willing. Nature gives birth according to its own kind and its own capacity.[44]

Nature is different in that its oneness disperses into an even greater multiplicity.

> The entire divine nature or essence stands in a continual and eternal process of birth or generation, like the human mind (although the divine process is unchanging). For thoughts are constantly being born from the mind, and will

---

41. *Three Principles*, 8.4.
42. *Aurora*, 12.165–69.
43. *Aurora*, 24.27, 29, 52.
44. *Three Principles*, 7.27.

and desiring are born from the thoughts, and the deed made substantial in the will is born from the will and the desiring. Then one's mouth and one's hands seize upon, and bring to pass, what has become substantial in the will. The eternal birth is like this . . . The mouth utters the *fiat* and the *fiat* makes the matter, and the spirit, going forth in power, separates the material into discrete beings. Because each is entirely discrete, there is the center (*centrum*) for the manifold of things, like the human mind is for the outflow of thoughts. But what is said to be born from this center? In the first place it is a spirit in such a birth and torment (as reported above) because of how the will is in anguish, and there is a desire in the will, and the desire produces the attraction, and the thought stands forth in the will, and in the thought is the mouth, and the mouth speaks the *fiat* with power, and the *fiat* produces the matter, and the spirit fragments the matter and forms it according to the thoughts. That is why there are so many different creaturely phenomena, like the eternal thoughts in the wisdom of God. The spirit has configured each species according to its idea in the eternal wisdom of God, and the *fiat* has given each one its flesh according to the essence of its idea, for the qualities are in the thought. This is therefore the birth and initial origin of all the creatures.[45]

Seen from an authentically Manichean perspective, this constantly occurring creation and birth in nature has its basis in the longing of darkness for the light.

The darkness longs for the light. The cause of this is that the spirit is reflected in the light and the divine power is manifest in it. But because the darkness has not apprehended the divine power and light, it has constantly and most desirously risen up toward the light until, from the radiance of the light of God, the darkness has kindled the fire-root in it. For the third principle has gone forth from the first principle, from the dark womb or mother (*matrice*), and made itself known by mirroring the divine power.

If there were no divine light and power, there would also have been no longing for it in the eternal darkness; there would have been no acrid desire that is the mother of eternity. Everything would have been an emptiness, nothing but an intense hunger, wholly barren, entirely as nothing, a desirous will. One should understand how the divine power appears in each thing and yet is not the thing itself; for God's spirit is in the other principle but the radiance is the thing, which therefore was from the desiring will. For the heart of God is in the Father, and the Father is the first desiring for the Son. The Son is the Father's power and light. The eternal nature has perpetually coveted this power, and thus, from the power of the heart of God, and in the eternally dark womb, the eternal nature gave birth to the third principle. Therefore this manifests God, otherwise the deity would have remained eternally concealed. But if the eternal nature becomes manifest by the longing for God's light, and if God's

---

45. [*Ed.*] Baur puts this whole passage within quotation marks and footnotes it as *Three Principles*, 9. 35ff. In fact it is a mixture of quotes and paraphrase (with Baur's additions) of 35–37.

> light is present and yet remains concealed to nature, then nature perceives just the power of the light, and this power is the heavens in which the light of God is concealed and [yet] shines in the darkness.[46]
>
> Thus the will (which is in the darkness, and bursts open the darkness, and abides within the light in the burst-open darkness from which the longing arises) now sets to work in the burst-open gates, so as to manifest its own wonders out of itself, as this is to be seen in the creation of the world and of all creatures.[47]

Everything created has its subsistence in the third principle. Yet as this principle itself had a beginning, so too everything created will come to an end. Yet even though it undergoes disintegration and ceases to be as a material thing, at least the idea of its being or nature remains as a shadow image.

> What has come forth out of the darkness, from the out-birth out of the center, has therefore been born in the will in time, and is not eternal. Instead it is fragile, transitory, like a thought. Now nothing makes it transitory but the spirit in the will, the body in the *fiat*. The figure of it remains eternally like a shadow, and this figure therefore might not be brought to the light and to visibility so that it would subsist eternally if it would not have been in the essence. But now it also cannot be transitory, for there is no essence in it. The center in the source[48] is broken asunder and has gone into its ether. The figure does neither good nor evil, but eternally remains [to manifest] God's wondrous deeds and glory, and to the delight of the angels. For if the third principle of this material world passes away and goes into its ether, then all the creatures as well as all growing things, and all that ever came from the light, remain shadows, including the shadows and figures of all words and deeds. They all become incomprehensible, not understood or known, like an emptiness or shadow over against the light.[49]
>
> This has been the purpose of the great, inscrutable God in his willing, and that is why he created all things. After this time there will be nothing but light, and the darkness in which the source or torment remains in each of them, as

---

46. [*Ed.*] Baur places this extensive statement within one set of quotation marks, and cites some passages in *Three Principles*, 7 and 9. Yet rather than specific quotations, it appears to be his own paraphrase of some of the recurring elements within Boehme's much longer, and rather confusing, repeated discussions of these issues in chs. 7 and 9.

47. *Three Principles*, 21.16.

48. [*Ed.*] The term here is *Quall* and suggests not only "quality" as a source, but also, as Boehme sometimes writes it as *Qual*, the "torment" at the center of nature (*centrum naturae*) from which the material world is produced.

49. See also *Three Principles*, 16.40: "The figure remains without the spirit. As long as, through the maiden of God's wisdom, the figure has beheld the eternal mind in the out-birth, as disclosing the wonders of God, then the eternal wonders and the figurative wonders must stand before it."

it has been from eternity, where each will not comprehend the others, as it has always been so from eternity.[50]

The creation of the world originally was a division or separation, but also an interpenetration, of the two principles. What thus ensues, when the light principle has increasingly separated itself from the dark principle, is ultimately a divorce of the principles. However, the ending is not to be utterly equated with the beginning, since everything that, in one principle or the other, has made its way to being a concrete life, can nevermore vanish.

> So everything in this third principle in turn remains in the first womb or mother. But what has been sown in this principle, and has its origin from the paradisiacal heaven and other principle—that is, a human being—remains eternally in that other mother. If in this time of one's life one has attained birth in that other principle, is born again in it, it is to one's good. But if not, one remains eternally in this womb or mother, but one does not see the light of God.[51]

## The Three Worlds as Three Forms of the Relationship of the Principles

In this system there are three distinct worlds, the world of paradise, the world of Lucifer, and the material world. But since neither of the two principles can operate apart from the other, in each of these three worlds both principles must always be thought of as operating concurrently. Hence these three worlds can simply be differentiated by how one principle has predominance over the other one.[52]

In the paradisiacal world the second principle, the principle of light and love, is predominant everywhere and the first principle is completely subordinate to it. The first principle is most decidedly predominant in the world of Lucifer. The two principles are both at work in the material world, and neither one is consistently predominant. Viewed in this way, the three worlds just stand externally related to one another and it is not apparent why the second principle is the ruling principle in the first of these worlds. But we must take the three worlds as three different standpoints from which one can understand the relation of God and world, of infinite and finite, of ideal and real. The paradisiacal world is regarded as the identity of the world with God; the God-world antithesis is regarded as inherently annulled. The world of Lucifer is the antithesis in its full scope and division; the difference between the principles is most

---

50. *Three Principles*, 9.37–40.
51. Ibid., 5.11.
52. [*Ed.*] Much of the previous discussion spoke of three principles, for the translation rendered Boehme's *principium* as "principle." That corresponded to the title of the frequently-cited book, *The Three Principles of the Divine Essence*. Those three principles would correlate roughly with what are now call the "three worlds." Here, however, where Baur speaks of "two principles" (*die beide Prinzipien*), he is referring to the principle of darkness, or evil, and the principle of light, or good.

fittingly expressed. The third world is in fact the return of spirit from this division, the freeing of the second principle from the bondage in which the first principle held it; the antithesis not something eternally annulled, but an antithesis suspending itself within time (by shattering the forms in which spirit is in contradiction with itself—which is why Boehme fittingly calls the third world "the shattered or broken world").

Since the principle of the self-annulling antithesis within time is Christ as the incarnate Son of God, according to Boehme Christ places himself over Lucifer and his world in the same way that, for the author of the Clementine writings, Christ, as ruler of the world to come, stands over the Devil as the ruler of the present world. Both these authors see, in Christ and Lucifer, the antithesis between God and world as a self-positing and a self-annulling antithesis. However, the annulling of the antithesis in its development within time is only possible because it is annulled in itself, a point Boehme expresses by the fact that, in the same moment when Lucifer falls, his place is taken by the Son of God. Yet for Boehme an incongruity always remains, in the fact that he makes the first principle the one positing the antithesis or the negation and to that extent he seems to begin with an absolute dualism, although this nevertheless can only be an apparent dualism, since both principles are posited in God himself.

## The Human Being, the Conflict of the Principles in Him, and His Fall

Like the Gnostics and like Manes, Boehme understands the human being—to whom the immediately preceding passage of course points—to be positioned within the whole, as the microcosm and as the clearly transparent, central point in which the great battle between the principles has its most intense and innermost significance.

Like the Gnostics and Manes, for Boehme it is the human being in whom alone the fall that occurred can, as it were, once more be set right, the existing great chasm once more be filled in. Hence Boehme too sees the creation of the human being as conditioned by the fall of Lucifer; the human being, created for the sake of the realm of light, is said to be a replacement for the spirits fallen into the realm of darkness.

> When God was angry in his outermost birth in nature, it was not his willful intention to be kindled, nor had he done that. Instead he pulled together the *Salitter* and prepared an eternal place for the Devil to dwell. For the Devil cannot be shoved away, beyond God and into a different kingdom of angels. There must still be a place for him to inhabit. So God also did not want to give the Devil the kindled *Salitter* as a place of eternal habitation, since the internal birth of the spirits was still hidden within it. For God had it in mind to do something else with the *Salitter*. King Lucifer was supposed to remain a captive until another angelic host would have come in his stead out of the same *Salitter*, and they are the human beings.[53]

---

53. *Aurora*, 16.90–93.

### The More Recent Religious Philosophy—Boehme

> The human being is and signifies the other host that God created from Lucifer's place, to replace Lucifer's ejected host.[54]
>
> Behold, when God created the third principle after the fall of the devils, when they fell from their glory (for they had been angels standing in the place of this world), he still wanted his will and intention to be upheld. He wanted to provide once again an angelic host in the locus of this world, one that would endure forever. And when he had then created the creatures whose spirits were supposed to remain forever, in keeping with the changing of the world, no creature was to be found who could take pleasure in it, and no creature was to be found who tended to the animals in it. That is why God spoke as he did.[55]

But since the human being is to be understood wholly as the microcosm, the same history ran its course in him as the chain of events we see in Lucifer. The only difference is that the possibility of redemption was posited in the human being together with the actuality of his fall. According to Boehme this human being even found himself originally in a state of ideal perfection, one from which, in his present state, he has descended very far.

> The matter from which God created the human being was a substance or fifth essence (*quinta essentia*)[56] from the stars and elements. It became earthly when the human being awakened the earthly center (*centrum*), and it at once belonged to the earth and to corruptibility. But this substance was from the heavenly womb, which is the root of the out-birth of what is earthly. Yet the heavenly *centrum* was supposed to remain fixed, and the earthly *centrum* should not have been awakened with such power. He (the human being) was a lord over the stars and the elements, and all creatures would have remained in awe of him and would have been incorruptible. He had in him the power and properties of all creatures, for his power was from the power of the understanding. Then he had to have all three principles, for he was said to be in the image and likeness of God. These three are: 1) the source of the darkness; 2) the source of the light; 3) the source of this world. Yet he was not supposed to live and act, or "qualify" in all three; instead just in one of them, the paradisiacal principle in which his life arose . . . His spirit was not supposed to mix in with the spirit of the stars and elements . . . Besides he had in himself the paradisiacal center (the paradisiacal breath, breathed into him by God; that is the spirit, the Holy Spirit), and he could have been able in turn to give birth

---

54. Ibid., 14.83.

55. [*Ed.*] This passage, from *Three Principles*, 10.8, then concludes with a reference to Gen 1:26–27, where God creates human beings in his own image and gives them dominion over all other living creatures.

56. [*Ed.*] The notion of a "fifth essence" (in addition to the traditional four—earth, air, fire, water—that in ancient philosophy were said to be the building blocks of all things) is found as early as the Pre-Socratics, persists in ancient and medieval philosophy, and is especially important in alchemy. This highest essence is what the heavenly bodies are made of. It permeates all of nature and is the purest, most perfect form of things—hence the term "quintessence."

or generate from himself, and to awaken the center, and thus to generate an angelic host in paradise, without need and anguish, and also without inner strife...

He was altogether perfect. He was not male or female, but as we will be in the resurrection—a proper and genuine image and likeness of God. In short, everything about this human being was heavenly, as we will appear on the day of the resurrection. For God's purpose endures; the initial image must be restored and remain in paradise.[57]

Nevertheless, struggle or tension was already a feature in Adam together with the presence of the three principles.

Because he was an extract from the eternal mind, drawn from all the essence of all three principles, he had to be temped as to whether he could remain in paradise. There was a threefold struggle within Adam, outside Adam, and in all that Adam saw. There were the three principles: the kingdom of hell as the power of fury or wrath; the kingdom of this world with the stars and elements; the kingdom of paradise that also wanted to have him. Now these three kingdoms were within Adam and also outside Adam, and in the essences there was a mighty struggle. They all pulled within Adam and outside Adam, and wanted to have Adam, for he was a great lord, drawn from all the powers of nature. The heart of God wanted to have him in paradise, and to dwell in him, for it said: "This is my image and likeness." The kingdom of wrath also wanted to have him, for it said: "He is mine, and has come forth from my fount, from the eternal mind of the darkness. I will live in him and he shall live in my might." The kingdom of this world said: "He is mine, for he bears my image and lives in me, and I in him."... The power in Adam toyed with all three of them... When the worm of darkness saw the command of God,[58] it said to itself: "I will not prevail, being spirit without body, whereas Adam is corporeal and I have but a third part in him; and besides, the command is an obstacle. So I will slip into the essences and toy with the spirit of the world and take on a creaturely form, by sending a legate from my kingdom clothed in the form of a serpent."[59]

Adam directed his imagination and lust to the kingdom of this world, and to the earthly fruit, and the pure paradisiacal soul became dark, and the spirit of this world seized him. Then he became blind as to God, and saw neither God nor the Virgin in his mind. Adam (with his mind) was not in God, but instead in the spirit of this world. He became feeble with regard to the kingdom of God, and so fell down and slept.[60]

57. *Three Principles*, 10.10–12 and 10.18.

58. [*Ed.*] Baur omits Boehme's explicit reference to Gen 2:16 concerning the command not to eat of the tree of the knowledge of good and evil.

59. *Three Principles*, 11.31–38.

60. Ibid., 11.41 and 17.54. Also 17.87.

Boehme therefore locates Adam's fall in the sleep into which he fell. Before sleeping, Adam was in angelical form. Afterwards he had flesh and blood.[61] The third principle, which held the human wholly captive,[62] clothed him with flesh and blood so that, in sleeping, Adam then became "hard gristles and bones."[63] In falling, in his sleep, [the image of] the Virgin escaped Adam's mind and, as opposed to it, Eve was created for him and for this corruptible life.

> She is the woman or wife of this world, and it could not be otherwise. For the spirit of this world, with its tincture, had overcome and possessed Adam, so that he fell down in sleep and could not generate from himself the Virgin image, as in beholding the noble and chaste Virgin of the wisdom of God, the one that had been espoused to him from the border (*limbus*) of heaven that was the mother in him. For in his overcome state there was given to him afterward the woman of the elements, that Eve who, in the spirit of this world's victory, was configured from Adam according to a bestial form.[64] . . . Therefore in his sleep God made the woman from him, the woman through whom he was to give birth to his kingdom.[65]

So with the principles that belonged to Adam's nature, he also already had a weak, feminine side, one inclined to fall. His falling resulted from his nature, which is why it too stands in the same relation to the divine will as Lucifer's fall does.

> God willed the fall. Indeed it is true, in keeping with the first principle, the abyss of hell, that God willed the human being's fall. But this is not called God's kingdom. There is yet another principle, and a firm line between them.

---

61. Ibid., 17.31.

62. In the third principle, in the kingdom of this world, the spirit of the stars and elements is in control. This is the same view according to which the Gnostics had the human being ruled over by the influence of the stars, above all by the signs of the zodiac, so long as he has not been reborn (gone from γέννησις to ἀναγέννησις). According to Boehme the heavenly bodies shape the child while it is in its mother's body. "We can state what has its basis in truth, that the constellations of the zodiac do not form a human being according to God's image and likeness. They do not have the might and understanding to do so. They just construct a beast with regard to how it wills, behaves, and senses. In willing to reach as high as it can, toward the image of God, what has been given birth here in the human being is an affable and crafty beast—nothing more than what it is in other creatures. Yet the eternal essences, which all human beings have inherited from Adam, remain in them with the hidden element in which the image is present yet altogether hidden unless there be a rebirth in water and the Holy Spirit of God. Therefore a human being, in the core of his brains and heart, with all five of his senses, is in the region of the stars—sometimes like a wolf, as intractable, crafty, strong, and voracious; sometimes like a lion, as stern, fierce, and magnificent in ferociously devouring its prey; sometimes like a dog, as cringing, shrewd, envious, ill-natured; sometimes like a viper and serpent; sometimes like a hare; sometimes like a toad." *Three Principles*, 16.20–21. See also 16.31: "The stars and elements, in controlling their captive human being, often give the human mind the nature of a lion, wolf, dog, serpent, and the like." This reminds us of what Basilides called "appendages of the flesh" (see above, p. 125), and which symbolically present this same idea.

63. *Three Principles*, 13.13.

64. Ibid., 17.10.

65. Ibid., 17.30.

> God is present in this other principle, and there God has not willed the fall. Everything is indeed all God's. However, the first principle is the band or shackle of eternity, and it makes itself.[66]

> The fall of the Devil and of the human being was of course beheld and seen in the eternal wisdom of God, before the creation of the world. The eternal Word in the eternal light knew very well that it would so manifest the fruit of the eternal birth that every form or shape of things would break out. But it was not the will of the love that is in the Word of light, that the form of wrath should have elevated itself above gentleness. But because wrath had such a mighty form, that is what happened.[67]

## Redemption: The Virgin and Christ

The human being has fallen.

> Henceforward his birth to life is in the third principle, in the realm of the stars and elements. He must eat of the fruit of this kingdom and live by its power. He then supposed that he was beyond recovery, that the noble image of God was shattered. The Devil continually pointed out his fragility and his mortality, and that was also all he could see for himself . . . However the gracious love, that is, the only-begotten Son of the Father (or, as I might convey the point—the gentle fount or source where the eternal light of God is born) sprang up and grew once more in Adam, in the center giving birth to his life.[68]

In the center of each one's birth to life there is also a center of rebirth in which the heart or Son of God must arise. This is the connection between fall and redemption, and we now have to take a closer look at it.

I have already remarked that Boehme describes the human being's fall as an escape or withdrawal of the heavenly Virgin originally linked to him. The main passage in which Boehme expands upon this image is as follows.

> Even before he fell the human being also had the spirit of this world, for he was from the world and lived in the world. So Adam was the chaste Virgin, understood the spirit, and so it was breathed into him by God. The spirit he had inherited from the nature of the world was the young man. These two spirits were now side-by-side in one arm. Now the chaste Virgin was supposed to be set into the heart of God and not to imagine, or set its sights on, anything else. It was not to allow itself to lust after the beauty of the comely young man. But the young man was on fire for the Virgin and desired to copulate with her. He said: "You are my dearest bride, my paradise and garland of roses. Let me

66. Ibid., 18.13.
67. Ibid., 11.22.
68. Ibid., 4.4–5.

> into your paradise and I will be impregnated in you, so that I will receive your essence and enjoy your charming love." ... The chaste Virgin said: "You are indeed my bridegroom and my companion, but you do not have my adornment. My pearl is more precious than you, my power or virtue is undying, and my mind is steadfast. You have a mind that is not steadfast, and your power or virtue is fragile. Dwell in my forecourt and I will be friendly toward you and do much good for you. I will decorate you with my adornments, but I will not give my pearl to you, for you are dark, and it is shiny and beautiful."[69]

Since the young man nevertheless persisted at dwelling in the Virgin and clothing her with his own attire, the Virgin turned to the heart of God and said:

> My heart and my beloved, you are my virtue and in you I am clear and bright. From your root I am eternally born. Deliver me from the worm of darkness that infects and tempts my bridegroom. Let me not be obscured in the darkness. I am your ornament and I have come that you would have joy in me. Why shall I then stand with my bridegroom in darkness? [And the divine answer was:] The offspring of the woman shall break the head of the serpent—the worm—and the serpent will strike the offspring in the heel.[70]

By the withdrawal of the Virgin, the human being became earthly, sensuous, and weak. For:

> When Adam was overcome and the Virgin passed into her ether, then the tincture (in which the fair Virgin had dwelt) was earthly, weary, stale, and weak. For the powerful root of the tincture, the source of its potency, without sleep or rest (and as the heavenly womb holding paradise and the kingdom of heaven), withdrew from Adam and went into its ether. It remained with its own proper worm in the third principle of this world.[71]

Despite all this, the Virgin cannot abandon the young man.

> The Virgin, as the divine virtue or power, stands in heaven and paradise, and mirrors herself in the earthly qualities of the soul, that is, as in the sun and not in the moon. Understand this as in the highest principle of the spirit of this world. For here the tincture is the noblest and brightest, where the human mind comes into being. The Virgin would have been happy in her place with the bridegroom if only the earthly flesh were not an obstacle to the earthly mind and sensibility. For the Virgin does not enter into the flesh. She will not let herself be bound within the earthly center. She spends this whole time in longing and calling out, in questioning and heartfelt seeking, while the woman Eve lives in her stead. But to those who are reborn she appears in a highly triumphant form, in the center of the mind. She also often delves

---

69. Ibid., 12.39–41.
70. Ibid., 12.47. [*Ed.*] See Gen 3:14–15.
71. Ibid., 13.8–9.

deeply into the tincture of the heart's blood, whereby the body, together with the mind and the senses, becomes so very excited and triumphant, as though it were in paradise, even directly getting a paradisiacal will. There the noble mustard seed is sown, the one Christ speaks of, which at first is small but afterwards grows as a tree—so long as the mind perseveres in the will. But the noble Virgin does not persist here, for hers is a far higher birth. Therefore she does not dwell in earthly vessels, but visits her bridegroom at times when he is desirous of her. Although she always respectfully anticipates his calling, and calls to him.[72]

The Virgin calls constantly to the heart of God, that it would deliver her companion from the dark worm. But the divine answer stands: the woman's offspring shall break the head of the serpent. That is, the darkness of the serpent shall be separated from your bridegroom. The dark attire with which the serpent has clothed your bridegroom, and has obscured your pearl and lovely crown, shall be broken and turned into earth; and you shall rejoice in me with your bridegroom. That was my eternal will, and it must stand.[73]

The Virgin herself speaks to us in the center of the light of life, saying: the light is mine; the power and glory are mine; the portals of knowledge are mine. I live in the light of nature, and without me you can see or learn nothing of my power. I am your bridegroom in the light, and your desire for my power or virtue is my withdrawing into myself. I sit on my throne but you do not know me. I am in you, and your body is not in me. I draw distinctions and you do not see that. I am the light of the senses, and the root of the senses is not in me, but alongside me. I am the bridegroom of the root, but it has donned a rough little coat. I would not lay myself in its arms until the root has taken it off. Only then will I rest in its arms eternally, and adorn the root with my power and give it my beautiful form. Then I will espouse myself to the root with my pearl.[74]

The Virgin as such is therefore the higher spiritual principle operative in the human being. It is the reason why the bond of the human being with God is not completely dissolved, but instead is renewed. If she is this bond, then how does she relate to Christ, the incarnate Son of God, and to what he does for the human being's redemption and rebirth? This is one of the more obscure points of Boehme's system, but one that also seems to have more light shed on it by looking back to related points in his system. In principle, the Virgin is none other than Christ himself, the female form of him. In this context Boehme sees the word of promise, about [Eve's offspring] striking the head of the serpent (Gen 3:15), as properly related to the Virgin.

---

72. Ibid., 13.9–11.
73. Ibid., 12.48.
74. Ibid., 16.3.

> The word God the Father spoke to Adam and Eve about striking the head of [or treading upon] the serpent, came forth from the heart and mouth of God, and it was the spark of love from the heart of God that had eternally been in God's heart. This word (counteracting the Devil's craftiness in the temptation[75]) imagined [i.e., created an image of] itself in Adam and Eve, in the light of life in its center, and espoused itself with the precious and worthy Virgin of chastity, in order to remain forever with Adam and Eve and to protect them from the Devil's fiery essences and darts. This word was to enlighten the soul and to be the soul's light when the body meets its end. It was to lead the soul through the gates of darkness and into paradise, before the manifest face of God—leading it into the second principle, into the element where there is no torment . . . The same word has been propagated by the first two human beings, from one to another, everywhere in the birth of life and the kindling of the soul, yet in the center. And the kingdom of God is near at hand, in the mind of every person. And they can reach it if they just will to, for God has given it to them by grace.[76]

Is this not clearly a consciousness of redemption that is inborn in the human being, a consciousness designated as the higher principle that was still in him even after the fall?

> Christ could only be the Virgin's son. He himself is a Virgin in mind, as the first Adam was in the creation. He is God and is born in the Father of eternity. God gives birth solely to his heart and Son. But when he conceives of the will to give birth to power or virtue, that conceiving is thus his word, which the Father speaks out of himself (out of the will, prior to willing). What is spoken or expressed, prior to willing, is the eternal wisdom of God, the Virgin of the chastity that has the powerful *fiat* of God as the instrument with which she creates everything and has created in the beginning. She beholds herself in all the created things, such that the wonder of all things is brought to the light of day through her. Out of this heart and word of God the Father, with and through God's chaste Virgin, there went forth from his eternal wisdom, from his omniscience, one who treads upon the serpent, in and with the word of God the Father's promise, and he has imprinted himself in the minds of Adam and Eve. He has espoused himself there eternally and has opened the gates of the heavenly kingdom to the soul. Together with the pure Virgin he has placed himself in the center of the light of life, in the portals of God. He has given the Virgin to the soul as a constant companion from which the human being has his wit and understanding, else these would be lacking. She is the portal of the senses, yet she abandons the natural counsel of the stars. For the soul lives within the stars' source or quality, and it is too coarse for her to be able to imprint herself in the soul there. Instead she shows God's way to the soul. But

---

75. [*Ed.*] Gen 3:1–5. In the text Baur references Boehme, *On the Election of Grace*, 7.17.
76. *Three Principles*, 17.104–5, 107.

if the soul becomes a hellish worm, then she withdraws within her gates and stands before God, before his word and heart.

But because the souls of Adam and Eve and all the children of humankind were too coarse, too wild, and too harshly tainted, by having the source and torment of hell within them, all were inclined toward evil. Therefore the word and the one who treads on the serpent did not form itself in the mind of Adam right away—not until the word became incarnate . . . But it was not at this time that the word becoming incarnate first came down from the high heaven beyond the stars, as the blindness of the world teaches. No, for the word God spoke in paradise about the one who treads on the serpent—whose self-image is imprinted in the gates of the light of life, standing within the center of the heavenly portals, and imprinted perceptibly in the minds of holy men—is waiting until this time. That same word is become human and is the divine word in turn in the Virgin of the divine wisdom, which was given to the soul of Adam along with the word, to be a light and a handmaid to the word.

The will of the heart of God in the Father is from the heart in the will of wisdom prior to the Father entering into an eternal espousal. The same Virgin of God's wisdom in God's word has, in the bosom of the Virgin Mary, presented itself in her Virginal womb and became as one with her, inseparably and eternally. Understand this with reference to the essences, and the tincture of the element that is pure and undefiled before God. Here the heart of God has become an angelic human being, as Adam was at the creation.[77]

If, according to scripture, Christ was conceived by and born of, a pure Virgin and as without sin, then, according to our knowledge, the pure, chaste Virgin who bore God is the pure, chaste Virgin in the presence of God and is an eternal Virgin. Before heaven and earth were created she was a Virgin, wholly pure and without any blemish. This same pure, spiritual Virgin of God had, in becoming human, put herself into Mary, and her new human being was in the holy element of God . . .

We cannot say that the heavenly Virgin, as she entered into Mary, became earthly. Instead we say that the soul of Mary has taken up the heavenly Virgin, and that the heavenly Virgin has put onto Mary's soul the heavenly, new and pure, garment of the holy element from God's spiritual Virgin (as received from God's mercy), as a newly reborn person. In the process she has become pregnant with the salvation of the entire world, and given birth to it in this world . . . The savior has of course taken on a body like ours, but not one intermixed with the holy Ternary. His is a body with the pure element, that of the purely holy, heavenly earth, one in which he was incarnate in his earthly life.[78]

---

77. Ibid., 18.20–24, 36–37.

78. Ibid., 22.29, 31, 37, 71ff. [*Ed.*] The last of these is not a quotation, but apparently a summary statement by Baur, enclosed within the quotes.

## Boehme's Mystical Theosophy as a Higher Way of Knowing God

These are the main passages that, midst all the twists and turns and repetitions, and with so many side comments from the wisdom of Paracelsus,[79] seem to set forth Boehme's ideas in the clearest way. Viewing them all together certainly underscores the undeniable fact that, while Boehme also has much to say about the incarnation, birth, and story of Christ as the account of occurrences in the external world, and seems to raise no doubts about the reality of this external history, his own mystical way of understanding and portraying this history is nevertheless simply another form of Gnostic docetism.

All that Christianity comprises is a principle laid down from the beginning in the history of humankind's development. It is implanted in this history and develops itself in tandem with this history. Christ is born in human beings' minds whenever the spiritual principle belonging to human nature—which indeed did recede so they were no longer conscious of it—can still never entirely and substantially be lost to it. The ideal and basic form of Christ's essential being (the heavenly Virgin) gains such power and life in a person that one's former self ("the old person") is reborn. The word becomes human, or incarnate, when the eternal word of promise, the faith in redemption, is so incorporated into one's consciousness, and so completely forms oneself internally, that it belongs to the being or nature of the person himself or herself. This is the same eternal birth of the divine being through which God himself is given birth, when the first principle opens up to the second principle, the Father to the Son, and in the Son the darkness and wrath of God is transfigured into love and light.

From this we see at once how Boehme's mystical theosophy positions itself in relation to the external words of scripture. Although he very much concurs with scripture, his theosophy alone contains the true key for understanding scripture. Hence here too it is simply the pictorial, mystical interpretation that brings what is given by speculation into agreement with the words of scripture, and in particular is what lifts off the covering that veils the face of Moses.[80] The divine spirit one shares in by being reborn is also the spirit of a higher enlightenment and knowledge.

> When the Devil is overcome in the flesh, then the heavenly gate is opened up in the spirit, and then the spirit sees the divine and heavenly being. In the fount or wellspring of the heart, the lightning flash rises up not outside the body, but rather in the brain's perceptive power, and the spirit engages in speculation there.[81]

---

79. [Ed.] Paracelsus, that is, Theophrastus Bombastus von Hohenheim (1493–1541), was a German physician and alchemist whose writings combined empirical medical science with alchemical speculation, Renaissance mysticism, and even elements from the Kabbalah. Boehme was attracted to his speculative views of nature and the elements constitutive of the natural world.

80. *Three Principles*, 17.36.

81. *Aurora*, 11.129.

Part Four: Ancient Gnosis and More Recent Religious Philosophy

This is the Virgin, who enters into the mind and fills it with her light.[82] In this con-

82. *Three Principles*, 16.47–51. Here we should remark about a few points with regard to the Virgin, who is so often spoken of in this section of our study. It is very obvious how much Boehme concurs with the Gnostics in his use of the image of bride and bridegroom. For the Gnostics Christ is the bridegroom and the soul is the bride, while for Boehme the Virgin is the bride who waits for the human being, her bridegroom, in paradise where she will be his bride and loving spouse when he has set earthliness aside (*Three Principles*, 15.18). But there is no essential difference between these positions. For Boehme, the Virgin stands above Christ, because Christ himself, in his supreme significance, is a masculine Virgin. He had to assume a male form, for internally he was in the likeness of a virgin, so that God's purpose could endure. [*Ed.* Boehme's Christ is androgynous, as are the fallen Adam and the second Adam. This point becomes clearer in the *Mysterium Magnum*, or *Explanation of the First Book of Moses*, a work of Boehme's more mature thought that Baur does not discuss.] For the attribute of the male, as of fire, shall rule, and the attribute of the female, as of light, shall soften his fire, and shall bring in the gentle likeness of God. (See *On the Incarnation of Jesus Christ*, pt. 1, ch. 7.13ff.) Like the author of the Clementine writings, Boehme also represents fornication as the greatest depravity, the greatest abomination, declaring it horrifying to heaven as he imagines it. Yet (in *On the Incarnation* and elsewhere) he views the worldly, earthly, sensuous element as being in the female aspect (according to one of the passages cited above, it is what dwells in the woman as it does in earthly life, in the same sense in which, regarding the status of the elements, the world is said to be womanish). Nevertheless for Boehme the highest state is virginity in which the difference of the sexes is superseded or transcended, a difference not originally present and only arising as a consequence of the fall, in the reproduction of animals. This recalls the way the Gnostics positioned Christ in relation to Sophia and to the Holy Spirit, inasmuch as the Spirit, as a female being, was said to be the mother of Christ. Boehme also certainly describes it as the Wisdom of God, which stands before God and reveals the wonders of God (as does Wisdom in the writings of Solomon and in the Apocrypha). She beholds herself in all the essences, and in this beholding what goes forth from the eternal element are the colors, the art and virtue, of God, and the sprouts of the lily of God, upon which the deity forever rejoices in the Virgin of the Wisdom (*Three Principles*, 14.87–88). – However, to me the remarkable parallels seem to present the Manichean myth of the figures of light and the heavenly Virgin, a myth I have treated in my treatise, *Das manichäische Religionssystem* [n. 1], 214ff. Just as the spectacle of the heavenly figures of light arouse the natural impulses of the demons, so that the longing of the darkness for the light sets the whole of nature in motion and expresses itself as sexual desire, so too Boehme has his heavenly Virgin acting upon nature in the same way. See *Three Principles*, 14.33: "For by the great longing of the darkness for the light and power of God, this world was born from the darkness, since the holy power of God reflected itself in the darkness. That is why this great seeking and longing for the divine power continues on in the spirit of the sun, stars, and elements, and in all things. All are in anguish and long for the divine power or virtue, and willingly sought to be rid of the Devil's vanity. But because that cannot be, all creatures had to wait until their mortal end when they go into their ether and gain a place in paradise, but only in figure and shadow. The spirit that has spent so much time here in such lust must be shattered. And here and now this lust must therefore exist, otherwise no good creatures would exist and this world would just be sheer hell and fury. But now, with the Virgin standing in the second principle, so that the spirit of this world cannot reach her, yet with the Virgin constantly reflecting herself within the spirit of this world, in its lust for the fruits and growth of all things, this spirit therefore is lusting and constantly seeks the Virgin. This spirit thus enhances many a creature with great skill and cunning, brought to the highest degree he can. He continually supposes that the Virgin should be given birth once again for him, the Virgin he saw reflected in Adam before Adam fell. This spirit also led Adam to fall, so that he could dwell in his virgin Adam. With his great lust he prevailed upon Adam to fall asleep. That is, he forcefully set himself within Adam's tincture or disposition toward virginity and sought to qualify, or have a common source, in her and with her, and to live eternally. In doing so the tincture became exhausted and the Virgin withdrew from it" (*Three Principles*, 14.33–34). "When the chaste Virgin found herself in Adam, with great wisdom, gentleness, and humanity, the external elements came to lust after what is eternal, to elevate themselves into the chaste Virgin and 'qualify' (find their vitality) in her. Seeing that Adam was drawn from them, from the

sciousness of a higher, direct knowing, Boehme opposed the theologians of his day who were biblical literalists, with the same conviction the Gnostics and the Manicheans held in opposing conventional Christianity—that they alone are the ones who truly know.[83]

---

*quinta essentia*, they desired what is theirs and sought to qualify themselves in it, something God had forbidden to Adam" (*Three Principles*, 15.17). "Because the spirit of the soul is from what is eternal, and had the Virgin in it before the fall, now the spirit of the larger world constantly seeks, in the spirit of the soul, for the Virgin, supposing that she is still there as she was before the fall. For the spirit of the larger world beheld itself in Adam's Virgin with such great pleasure and also wanted to live in the Virgin and be eternal. In feeling his fragility, and therefore being internally coarse, this spirit wanted to partake of the Virgin's sweetness and loving kindness and to live in her, so that he would live eternally instead of shattering once more" (*Three Principles*, 14.32). Just as the world-spirit (the Manichean demon, at least insofar as, like this spirit, it is the ruler of the stars and the elements) is drawn to the virgin by an external longing, as sexual lust, this same longing for the Virgin in Boehme's thought is also the cause of sexual craving as such. "The tincture has a longing for the Virgin. It is the divine inclination and continually seeks the Virgin, its playmate. The masculine aspect seeks her in the feminine aspect, and the feminine seeks her in the masculine. From this comes the great desiring of the male and female sexes, so that each desires to copulate with the other one. It is the source of the great, burning love that leads the tinctures to intermingle and enjoy each other with their pleasant taste. For each one supposes that it is in possession of the Virgin" (*Three Principles*, 13.39). – Based on the violent activity of natural phenomena such as thunder and lightning, in which the demon is dealt a blow by the sight of the Virgin, the Manicheans interpreted such phenomena as the work of the demon and not the work of God. At least on this latter point Boehme agrees with the Manicheans. See above, p. 359. See also *Three Principles*, 17.66: "Not without good reasons, Christ calls the Devil a prince of this world. For he is so according to the first principle, according to the kingdom of wrath, and he remains so eternally. But he is not so according to the kingdom of the four elements and the stars. For if he had full power in it, then there would be no vegetation or creatures on the earth. He cannot be involved in the issuing of the four elements, for he is in the original condition or source and there is an intermediate principle between him and the earthly realm. [By the very fact that the Devil is obstructed and bounded by the third principle, what takes his place in the existing world is the spirit of the larger world, which is why both Lucifer and the world-spirit together express the same thing as the Manichean demon or prince of darkness.] But when the heavenly bodies awaken in the elements the wrath of the fire in a thunderstorm, Lucifer is the master trickster here, and he enjoys it." This trickery recalls to some extent the Manichean fabrication of the Devil (*figmentum diaboli*), which is what Manicheans called the world. See *Das manichäische Religionssystem*, 396 and 399. In any event one can think of the impassioned actions of the prince of this world, in struggling to possess the Virgin, as gestures of a similar sort. The main idea these different positions share is always the struggle between light and darkness that has us beholding everywhere, in nature and in human life, a striving upward toward the light, a wrestling to gain freedom, a progression to a higher stage, but also everywhere a clash of form with matter. "For the soul comprehends the highest meanings. It beholds what God, its Father, does and what he works with in the heavenly forming of things. Therefore the soul marks out a model for the nature spirits, as to how they should shape a thing. Everything in this world is made according to this delineation. For the corrupted soul always works in such a way that it might construct heavenly forms, but it cannot do so. For it has only the earthly, corrupted *Salitter* on which to labor and work—indeed a half-dead nature in which it cannot construct heavenly figures" (*Aurora*, 15:51–52).

83. Boehme's account of the source from which he received his great spiritual gifts states that God has given this knowledge to him; that it is not the I or self Boehme is himself who is the knower; that it is God knowing it in him. He says wisdom is God's bride, and that the children of Christ are in Christ, are in the wisdom, are also God's bride. See, for instance, *Three Principles*, 3.4–5: "For the most part the theologians' books just describe history, what once took place, and they say we should be reborn in Christ. But what should I understand about this? Nothing but the *historia*, that this birth happened,

### The Relation of Christianity to the Mosaic Law

According to the underlying foundation of this worldview, the divine principle indwelling humankind can only develop itself successively in the series of specific moments and epochs.

Christianity is the great turning point with which the principle that of course already was present and expressing itself, albeit always in a constrained and delimited way, breaks through.

> In the death of Christ the covering over Moses' face has been removed. Before this the stars, together with the four elements, had been infected by the Devil and made hazy and cloudy for human beings, so that they did not see the Mosaic law clearly. Now the lily planted by the one breaking through the gates of the depths, and given into the hands of the noble Virgin, grows up, with its strong aroma, through Moses' engraved tablets and reaches into God's paradise.[84]

However, despite this typological relation of Moses to Christ, Moses nevertheless:

> has given his laws and strict teaching, in zealous and fiery form, via the spirit of the larger world, who is of the same root and quality as the fiery wrath of God.[85] . . . For then the issue was whether it be possible that a soul could be ransomed by the Father's clarity in the fire, if it lived within his law, which was sharp and consuming, and was very piercing to the soul.[86]

Indeed the noble Virgin, in the spirit of the prophets, likewise pointed to the woman's offspring, and the prophets have spoken from God; but "from his fierce wrath against sins, through the spirit of the larger world, he wanted to devour what he had made, because love was extinguished."[87]

Boehme did not make any further or more profound application of his ideas to history, however much he had prepared the way for doing so.

---

has happened again, and should happen. As much as they can, by persecution and calumny, our theologians make a big fuss about anyone seeking to investigate the deeper foundations of this. They say one ought not delve into divinity and investigate what God is. But so what if I speak in German, that is, plainly? Theirs is the dung and filth of the Devil. But the time is coming for the dawning of a new day" (*Three Principles*, 3.4–8).

84. *Three Principles*, 17.36. Allegory plays a major role in Boehme's thought too. His *Mysterium Magnum* is an allegorical interpretation of the book of Genesis.

85. *Three Principles*, 20.19–20.

86. Ibid., 18.32.

87. Ibid., 20.20.

## Schelling's Philosophy of Nature[88]

Presentation of Schelling's Position

Now we pass on from Boehme's theosophy directly to an epoch-making position in the most recent history of religious philosophy or Gnosis. It is nevertheless simply a recovery of Boehme's ideas after the long time span since Boehme's day, a recovery we can emphasize, for purposes of this investigation, as our next topic.

It is well-known how Schelling's treatise *Of Human Freedom*[89] is related, in its basic ideas, to Boehme's thought. We shall see this clearly in light of the foregoing presentation of Boehme's system. Without impugning the originality of this great thinker in the least, it may be maintained justifiably that the essential contents of the treatise *Of Human Freedom* are to be seen as a scientific reworking and thorough organization of the ideas Boehme brought to light initially, as subject matter in an unrefined condition and drawn from the mystical profundity of his own fertile spirit.

Just as Boehme drew a distinction, as I have indicated, between a first principle and a second principle, so Schelling distinguished from God as regarded absolutely, in other words from God inasmuch as he exists, the ground of God's existence that God has within himself—the nature in God, an essence or nature indeed inseparable from God but nevertheless different from him. The consequence of this distinction is that other things are both in God and distinct from God, inasmuch as they have their ground or basis in what is in God himself but is not God himself—that is, in the ground of God's existence. Therefore Schelling too speaks of the eternal one feeling a longing to give birth to himself, a longing that is not the one himself but yet is eternally coincident with him, and which wants to give birth to God, the unfathomable oneness. But inasmuch as it does not yet have the oneness within itself, the oneness thus regarded as for itself is also will, but will in which there is no understanding. For that reason it is not an independent and consummate will, not a conscious will. It is instead a will with a presentiment, the presentiment of the reason in which God realizes himself as the word of that longing. The eternal spirit who feels the word in

---

88. [*Ed.*] Friedrich Wilhelm Joseph Schelling (1775–1854). This heading will be misleading for Schelling scholars because what is regarded as his "philosophy of nature" proper is based on a number of treatises published during the years 1797–1800 and which consider the objects of human experience as real in themselves apart from the activity of the knowing subject. While Schelling continues to address issues from the natural sciences over the years following 1800, what Baur calls Schelling's "philosophy of nature" here is his speculative thinking about how nature is related to God and to the problem of evil in his 1809 treatise *Philosophische Untersuchungen über das Wesen der menschlichen Freiheit und die damit zusammenhängenden Gegenstände*. ET: *Schelling: Of Human Freedom*, trans. James Gutmann (Chicago, 1936); also *Philosophical Investigations into the Essence of Human Freedom*, trans. Jeff Love and Johannes Schmidt (Albany, 2006). See also above, n. 8, and below, n. 194.

89. Published in *F. W. J. Schelling's philosophische Schriften*, vol. 1 (Landshut, 1809). [*Ed.*] It was one of the essays in this volume (pp. 397–571). See *Friedrich Wilhelm Joseph von Schellings sämmtliche Werke*, ed. K. F. A. Schelling, 14 vols. (Stuttgart and Augsburg, 1856–61), 7:331–416.

himself and at the same time feels the infinite longing, being moved by the love that he himself is, speaks or expresses the word.

Since in God there is an independent ground or basis of reality, there are therefore two, equally eternal, beginnings of the self-revelation. The first beginning, that of the creation, is the longing of the one to give birth to himself, that is, the will of the ground. The second beginning is the will of love by which the word is spoken or expressed in the [divine] nature and by which God makes himself personal, a divine person. Hence the will of the ground cannot be free in the sense that is the case with the will of love. God sets himself forth as mind or intellect, as an intelligent principle, as light, the light in the dark ground, and brings forth the light locked up within the ground. This transfiguration of the dark principle in the light of course resists the ground. Because of it there forever remains a dark ground, and so there is a duality of principles in God. However love and goodness, as God's self-communication, must prevail, so there is a revelation. Accordingly, by making himself the ground of his own existence God extends himself via the creation, transfigures the dark principle in the light, and becomes an ethical, personal, truly intelligent being.

All this is not complete at the outset, because God is not merely a being, but is instead a life, a living being. Everything living has a destiny, a course to follow, and is subject to suffering and becoming. This too is something God has therefore freely subjected himself to, already initially by separating the light world from the dark world in his becoming a personal being. Being only experiences itself in becoming, and realization through antithesis necessarily means becoming. Therefore God subjects himself to becoming and to suffering. This is what makes a creature possible: the separation of powers, by which the concrete individual life emerges from the darkness into the light. In this constant transmutation of the dark principle into light, God himself first becomes God in the eminent sense.

According to Schelling as well, in this divine life process the vital center, the focal point of the antithesis, is the human being. For the elevation of the innermost center of all, into the light, occurs in no creature visible to our eyes except the human being. This is where both centers are found: the full power of the dark principle, the deepest abyss; and at the same time, the full power of the light, the highest heaven. God has loved the world in the human being alone, and the longing in the center has seized upon this very image of God when the longing came forward in opposition to the light. The word that is still suppressed and imperfectly present in all other things, the word expressing in nature the eternal spirit, is fully expressed for the first time in the human being. When the spirit then reveals itself in the expressed word, that is, God existing in actuality (*actu*), then the distinction between the human being's spirit and God as spirit consists in the fact that the oneness of the principles that is an indivisible oneness in God, must be divisible in the human being. This divisibility of the principles in the human being is the possibility of good and evil. The antithesis of good and evil is in itself none other than the very thing that forms the two principles.

The principle rising up from the ground of nature, the principle that separated human beings from God, is the selfhood in them, their self-will. When the self-will subordinates itself to the universal will, to the light, the rational principle, and with its combined powers makes itself subservient to the universal will, as basis and instrument for it, then the will is of a divine kind and rank, that is, good. However, when what the will is only in identity with the universal will, it strives to be as a particular will—when what the will is only so far as it remains in the center, it also wills to be at the periphery, that is, as a creature—then this very elevation of the self-will is also what is evil. This inversion of the principles, this false oneness, is the positive aspect in the concept of evil, the aspect that can be thought of as not simply negation and privation. But as for the actuality of evil, its universal actuality, the unmistakable, universal antithesis of evil to what is good, is only comprehensible from the fact that it is necessary for the revelation of God. Were the oneness of the principles in human beings just as indissoluble as it is in God, then there would be no revelation and activity of love. The ground may be effectual so that there can be love, and it must operate independently of love so that love might really exist. But the ground cannot operate without the oneness and by calling forth the antithesis. Hence in the initial creation the will of the ground stirs itself up with the self-will of the creature, such that when the spirit (the living oneness or identity of the principles) then goes forth as the will of love, this will of love might find an opposing element in which it could realize itself.

The initial creation is just the birth of the light in the realm of nature, in which the dark principle as ground had to be present so that the light could be raised up from it. But there must also be a second principle of darkness, which in the creation awakens the spirit of evil by arousing the dark ground of nature. That is, there must be an estrangement of the light from the darkness, one in which the spirit of love—previously the light of the initial nature's disorderly motion—now sets a higher ideal in opposition to the darkness. This ideal is the archetypal and divine human being, the one who was with God in the beginning, and in whom all other things are created, including human being itself. Hence evil is none other than the higher potency of the ground operative in nature, also coming to the fore in the realm of history. This potency, or power of evil, is the reaction of the ground to revelation, a reaction in which human beings apprehend themselves in their singularity and self-seeking. With this discord of the two principles, a different spirit jumped into the place where God was supposed to be—the inverse god, the being aroused to actualization by revelation, that which can never advance from potency to act, that which indeed never is but constantly wills to be, and therefore just by falsely imagining it but not itself having being, it takes on the appearance of true being.

This makes it self-evident how evil relates to God. Evil is necessary because without evil there would also have been no goodness. God can reveal himself only through the antithesis of the principles. Yet we still cannot say that, because of this, God has willed evil. For the willing of creation was directly just a willing of the birth of light, and with it, what is good. Evil does not come from God. Instead it is from the ground, which of course is the irremovable condition of the existence, or the personality, of God but is not God himself. Yet evil itself, as evil, does not come directly from the ground. For the will of the ground is surely just the awakening of creaturely life, and evil itself is not aroused selfhood as such, but is just evil inasmuch as selfhood has wholly broken away from its antithesis, the light or the universal will. This breaking-away of itself from the good is the beginning of sin.

However, just as evil, inasmuch as it comes from the ground, is not in itself what is evil, so too, when evil is wholly separated from what is good—that being the final purpose of the creation, and the complete actualization of God—then it no longer exists as evil. Evil could only operate through the good that was in evil itself and of which evil was unaware. But if evil becomes set apart by the death of all in it that is good, then evil is just a state of non-being, a condition of constant all-consuming activity; in other words a condition in which what is active in it is striving to be. Hence the ending or final revelation is the expelling of evil from what is good; the declaration that evil is complete unreality. In contrast to evil, the good raised up from the ground is conjoined in eternal unity with the original good; those born from the darkness to the light are linked to the ideal principle as members of his body, in which that goodness is perfectly realized and is then wholly personal being. As divine consciousness the spirit lives in the same way in both principles. God is All in All; the absolute identity of what is existent, with the ground or basis for existence, is realized in the spirit. This absolute identity, which is the result of the revelation of God, corresponds to the original indifference with respect to the opposed sides. In other words, it is the primal ground (*Urgrund*) embracing the duality of the principles but conditioning them, and dividing itself into two equally eternal beginnings.

## Its Relation to Gnosis and the Connection of Its Speculative Ideas to the History of Religion, to Paganism and Christianity

This brief account of the main ideas of Schelling's system, to the extent that it is contained in the treatise *Of Human Freedom*, also shows at once how this system is related both to Boehme's theosophy and to ancient Gnosis. There is an absolute knowing only to the extent that the knowing is conscious of its mediation. But in this mediation the knowing can only be conscious of itself in virtue of the fact that the knowing itself, the absolute, is known or recognized in accord with the different moments in which it goes outside itself in order to mediate itself with itself. This standpoint, which has been presented to us thus far as the characteristic position of Gnosis in all its forms, is also Schelling's position.

This is why Schelling also most emphatically resists the view he sets forth in his *Denkmal der Schrift von den göttlichen Dingen, etc.*[90] He criticizes those who "affirm a God who is once and for all complete, and for that reason a truly nonliving God, a dead God."[91] In other words, they hold "the concept of a stale theism that allows for no distinction in God, that describes the being in whom all fullness abides as something utterly simple—purely empty, devoid of substance, just barely perceptible."[92] If he is said to be a living God, then God must first give birth to his eternal nature, must have a life and therefore also a destiny. Hence he cannot be thought of merely under the abstract concept of being; he must also be thought of under the concrete concept of becoming. But every becoming presupposes distinctions, and moments in which the original one must go outside itself in order to mediate itself with itself.

The moments of this divine life process are, in Schelling's case, the same three main moments that all the Gnostic systems are occupied with. First, God in himself as absolute causality thought of in its purely abstract form; what Schelling calls the absolute indifference, or the primal ground. Second, the world or the creation, in which God extends or expands himself according to the real, dark, not yet intelligent aspect of his nature or essence, insofar as the ground is in him. In other words, God lowers himself by making himself—specifically, one part or potency of himself—into the ground so that creaturely being is possible; and in this act of his lowliness and condescension, the creation, he also subjects himself to suffering just as he subjects himself to becoming.[93]

This second moment is the same aspect of the revelation of the divine being that the Gnostic systems describe as a falling away from the Pleroma, a sinking down into chaos; as the suffering of the Sophia; as the light principle being bound by the power of darkness. It is the realm of creaturely being and life in which the Demiurge rules, real nature, the visible world that must take precedence as the ground so that the light principle could develop. The more one understands this dominant principle, this principle of creaturely being and life, in its pure being-for-self and in its alienation from the light principle, the more one is led to the concept of evil in the same sense in which, according to Schelling, evil has its root in the ground.

What remains is the third moment, the turning point in which spirit, in emerging from its being-in-itself and into the otherness or separateness of being, which

---

90. [*Ed.*] The full title of this polemical treatise continues with: *des Herrn Friedrich Heinrich Jacobi und der ihm in derselben gemachten Beschuldigung eines absichtlich täuschenden, Lüge redenden Atheismus* (Tübingen, 1812). See *Sämmtliche Werke*, 8:19–136. Hereafter *SW*. Friedrich Heinrich Jacobi (1743–1819) was a critic of Kant and advocated a philosophy based on feeling and faith. He utterly rejected the pantheism of Spinoza, and had criticized Schelling for his supposedly pantheistic tendencies. Schelling's treatise is a reply to Jacobi's *Von den göttlichen Dingen und ihrer Offenbarung* (Leipzig, 1811).

91. [*Ed.*] Baur cites *Denkmal*, but this may not be an actual quotation from it. See *SW*, 8:77.

92. *Denkmal* [*SW*, 8:62].

93. *Of Human Freedom* [*SW*, 7:403 (ET 84)]. See also *Denkmal* [*SW*, 8:71–72].

is the world, or nature, collects and concentrates itself, so to speak. Spirit does so in order to come to itself and to grasp itself within itself, in a center of light. In all these systems this center of light is the human being in which what is separate or individual is at the same time what is universal, albeit the universal with a concrete, determinate character. Thus for Schelling, as well as for the Gnostics, the human being is the one who in the depths glimpsed the hidden divine life, who beheld God when he grasped the will to nature.[94] In other words, and put in Boehme's terms, the human being is the one in which the center of birth is also a center of rebirth. What Schelling indicates succinctly about the human being, inasmuch as he is the pinnacle of revelation, as the archetypal and divine man,[95] directly comprises the entire christology and redemption doctrine of the Gnostic systems.

If, as Schelling says, the full might of the dark principle is posited in the human being, and at the same time the full power of the light is in him, then he likewise has in him eternally the principle of redemption as he does the principle of the fall.[96] The outward history of Christianity is then simply the manifestation of what the idea of the primordial human being comprises in itself.[97]

The three main moments we have briefly indicated in this discussion are elements all these systems have in common, howsoever much they may differ on other matters. But there is another noteworthy way in which Schelling's position is related to ancient Gnosis, and it serves at the same time to shed light more clearly on Boehme's relation to that Gnosis. For since Schelling is just expanding on what Boehme left in a still incomplete form, there is also the application Schelling made of his speculative ideas to the history of religion. The same relation existing between the two principles, when considered in speculative terms, is also presented in history.

The ground is what is antecedent, is the presupposition of God's [self-realization] as a personal and intelligent being; so too, in the history of spirit, love is not revealed right away. The ground initially had to operate freely; in other words, God worked only in keeping with his natural being and not according to his heart, or love. Hence the entire pre-Christian period was the time of the reigning deities and heroes, the time when nature was almighty and when the ground showed what it is capable of on its own. In those days understanding and wisdom came to human beings solely from the depths; for the influence of oracles issuing from the earth is what guided and shaped human life. All the godly powers of the ground ruled on earth, and they

---

94. *Of Human Freedom* [*SW* 7:399–400 (ET 79–80)].

95. Ibid., [*SW* 7:377 (ET 54)].

96. Ibid., [*SW* 7:363 (ET 38–39)].

97. This is the reason why Schelling too could express himself in *Of Human Freedom* about the relation of reason to revelation simply in the following way. "We are of the opinion that it must be possible to have a clear, rational insight even into the highest concepts. For only through us can they actually become our own, be assimilated, and become eternally grounded. Indeed we go still further and hold, with Lessing, that the development of the truths of revelation into truths of reason is utterly necessary if they are to be of use to the human race" [*SW* 7:412 (ET 94)].

sat on secure thrones as mighty princes. It was manifestly the time of nature's greatest glory, in the evident beauty of the gods and in all the splendor of the arts and practical knowledge, until the principle at work in the ground finally came forward, as the world-conquering principle, to subject everything to itself and become the foundation of a strong and enduring empire. But because the essential nature of the ground, for itself, can never generate or beget true and complete unity, the time had to come when all this glory dissolved and, like a beautiful body racked by a terrible disease, the world as it was disintegrated and chaos finally arose once more.

However, the end of the old world is simply the beginning of the new world in which, with the arrival of Christianity, the principle of the spirit and of love became the predominant factor. This principle was initially able to become predominant because the first principle increasingly disclosed its own impotence. The ongoing development is at the same time an ever-greater separation, and the antithesis of nature and spirit, of darkness and light, must also be regarded as the antithesis of evil and goodness. In the beginning of course, in the golden age, in blissful indecisiveness, there was neither good nor evil. But as the principle holding sway in the ground increasingly wanted to apprehend itself in its selfhood, those powers of the ground thus took on the nature of false spirits and imposed false magic and theurgy on belief in the gods. The higher light of the spirit that was in the world from the beginning—but was not comprehended by the darkness operative for its own sake, and was in a revelation still closed off and limited in scope—had for that reason to appear in a personal, human figure in order to confront the personal and spiritual evil. Only what is personal can heal what is personal, which is why God had to become a human being, so that human beings would once again come to God.

Thus Christianity marked the beginning of another kingdom, one into which the living Word entered as a strong and enduring center in the struggle against chaos, and there began a clearer battle, ongoing to the end of this era, between good and evil, a battle in which God reveals himself as spirit, that is, as actual in deeds (*actu*). Therefore paganism and Christianity are related to each other in the way the two principles that must be distinguished in the being of God are related to each other. Considered from a historical standpoint, these principles become the antithesis between two essentially different periods of world history and religious history, in each of which the deity reveals itself according to distinctive aspects of its essential nature. Each of these periods and each of the two religious forms corresponding to them has its own principle. Thus paganism is the original form as compared to Christianity, and although just the ground and basis of what is higher, paganism is not derived from any other form.

There is no mention of Judaism in particular in this speculative understanding of the history of religion. Judaism gets categorized together with Christianity in this major antithesis formed by paganism and Christianity. But it is indeed very easy, from the general indications provided, to locate the place where Judaism branches off as different in character from paganism. In the antithesis of paganism to Christianity, what directly stands out as more kindred to Christianity—a more definitive presentiment of, and prior receptivity for, the coming light for which the ground is continually longing—is something to which Judaism most especially and rightfully lays claim. Above all, however, according to the duality of the principles from which this entire way of considering things sets out, the only point that can be firmly established is the antithesis to Christianity. Therefore Judaism must be conceived of from the same perspective as paganism is, which is why Schelling, in a manner similar to that of the ancient Gnostic dualists, and as the foundation of his dualistic view, poses the following question to his opponent in his *Denkmal*.

> It is the case that the Old Testament antedates the New Testament. Why far earlier, in the Old Testament, does God, as an angry and jealous God, generally indicate his highest spiritual attributes by those of a more physical nature, whereas only after two thousand years has he revealed himself expressly to humankind and is found to be good?[98]

## Opposition to Schelling's Dualism

Everywhere this dualistic view surfaces anew, it must elicit the same opposition. It is also at once evident how closely the well-known polemic Schelling's system faced approximates to the ancient polemic against Gnosis.

Of course one could no longer repeat the arguments aimed at ancient dualism. This form of dualism in Schelling had already successfully overcome the penetrating arguments of the church fathers, and the more the Christian principle had permeated the religious consciousness, the less one could look askance at another dualism of a kind that also leaves room in turn for unity or oneness. This is a very essential moment in which the new religious philosophy that began its development in a new epoch, with Boehme, set itself apart from the ancient view proper to Gnosis—although of course even in this ancient Gnosis the dualism proper to it just manifested itself as one of the various forms into which Gnosis was subdivided.

Despite its difference from ancient Gnosis, the basic character of the new religious philosophy remained dualistic, and the ancient arguments aimed at dualism just took a different form. Whether one posits the principle that is distinct from God conceived in the absolute sense, that is, the real principle, as being within God or outside of God, in either case God is posited as dependent or conditioned, and that seems to conflict with the concept of God. And since as soon as one posits a duality of principles, the two principles, as related to each other, cannot be thought of as in a state of rest, but are instead just actively in motion—a motion in which the divine

---

98. *Denkmal* [SW 8.67]. [*Ed.*] This statement is presented within quotation marks in the *Denkmal*, and Schelling attributes it to Jacob Boehme there, but without specific citation.

being first gives birth to itself and realizes the concept of its being—then it appears that God is subject to the same laws of temporal development as those applicable to every natural being. Hence while Schelling's system can hardly be called dualistic in the ancient sense, the duality of principles it assumes still results in the same concept of the divine being. As soon as a duality of principles is adopted, whether the one principle be posited as within God or outside him, then God must first realize the true concept of his own being via a series of moments that, thought of as development or as struggle, subject the divine to a temporal process coming into conflict with the idea of the absolute.

This is the very point that most occupied the attention of the opponents of Schelling's position.

> There is nothing more objectionable than the idea of a God evolving from a dark ground, chaos, or nature that precedes him; a God evolving from a principle that, as such, is not intelligent and is not ethical, so as to first become in actuality the most perfect being; a God first becoming fully personal at the end of time. This assumption, making God into something that first comes to be in time, not only inherently destroys the concept of God, but also completely abolishes belief in an intelligent and ethical world governance and providence. For if God be declared fully personal, and most perfect in actuality (*actu*), only at the end of time or the end of the world—and as such God first attains a higher stage of perfection by creating the world, although he did not possess the utmost perfection at the time when he created it, so that the world is not the work of the most perfect of all wisdom, goodness, holiness, and personhood—then instead we have just a limited deity. This limited deity guides and governs the world as long as that process of God's evolution carries on, namely, to the end of the world. This leaves us in the sorry state of subjection to a being about whom we are at least dubious whether, limited in this way, it is mighty enough to know what is best at a particular time and can will to do it. We are unsure whether in fact it even knows and wills what is best of all; whether it be led to blunder in its creating and governing of the world, due to error or even moral lapses, thus making it incapable of serving and realizing the best purpose, on the whole and in individual cases.
>
> Put succinctly, this same doubt generally involving any theory of an independently pre-existing matter, or a chaos, as the ground of all things, also remains with regard to Schelling's theory. This is the doubt as to whether the nature given birth from chaos before the operations of intelligence would have made it impossible for the intelligence organizing it to make it an orderly place; in other words, made it impossible to construct such a world from this matter, in the way an intelligence still not fully evolved and most perfect of all would have wanted and wished for; that is, whether the chaos would not have presented such an obstacle to the organizer of the world that it even made it

impossible to completely realize the purposes willed by a wisdom and love that were still not fully evolved.[99]

According to this statement, therefore, we see ourselves returned to the standpoint of the first centuries, and it cannot be surprising that, on account of its dualism, this doctrine would even have been reproached as atheism and fatalism, as utter naturalism, as a doctrine doing away with any distinctions between reason and irrationality, right and wrong, good and evil.[100] However things may stand with these accusations or consequences, if that is what one wants to call them, it is nevertheless certain, and even conceded by the most fair-minded opinions of Schelling's position, that the main issue to which it takes us back is this: Could there conceivably be within God, and independent of God's spirit and personhood, some kind of root of life, and an effectiveness of the ground operating on its own? These opponents noted that:

> Although there is a difference among the qualities within God so that there is life and revelation, at the same time there must also be an inseparability of powers so that there is unity and perfection—a peaceful interwovenness and harmonious coordination of them in the eternity forever the same and excluding any temporal distinctions. Just as in endless space there is neither above nor below, so too in God's eternity there is neither before nor after. It is the same with the Trinity complete within itself; what we call the last is also in turn the first, and the first is the last. Hence in the Trinity no quality takes precedence over the others, and it is also not possible that in God anything at all is antecedent to the divine will or independent of it, least of all with reference to time. In this case speculation has taken a turn in which, with the object of seeking the root of evil, it loses sight of the idea of oneness, as is especially so in maintaining a long time passing with the ground alone at work,[101] and maintaining a universal evil, developed into a principle, emergent from the creation and everywhere in a struggle with the good. The reason for this is the predominant position of nature, the inclination toward the real aspect, the preference for the philosophy of nature, as well as the investigation into the spiritual aspect of all things. The prevalence of the ground in God has the consequence that this ground develops itself from the deep darkness to the blossoming of personal life right before our eyes, in organic fashion so to speak, and thus almost appears as a growing thing. That is also why the divine being, like a plant that, because it has roots, belongs to the night and heaviness, but in its flowering strives against it and to the light and freedom, yet is

---

99. Friedrich Gottlieb Süskind, *Prüfung der Schellingischen Lehren von God, Weltschöpfung, Freyheit, moralischen Guten und Bösen* (Tübingen, 1812), 59–60. (Published in the *Magazin für christliche Dogmatik und Moral*, vol. 17.)

100. This is the argument of Friedrich Heinrich Jacobi, in his *Von den göttlichen Dingen und ihrer Offenbarung* (Leipzig, 1811).

101. See *Of Human Freedom* [SW 7:404 (ET 84–85)].

not fully able to resist the necessity and the darkness and is not free from an advancing destiny in virtue of the whole.[102]

According to the principles of the system, this is in any event just an apparent dualism. However, as in Jacob Boehme's case, it indeed looks too much like a dualism as such.

## Schleiermacher's *Glaubenslehre*

### Its Task and the Subjectivity of Its Standpoint

Schleiermacher's *Glaubenslehre*[103] is the next remarkable phenomenon presenting itself in the domain we have undertaken to examine. The reason I set his work on Christian doctrine side-by-side with Schelling's doctrine of God finds its justification in the course we have already taken thus far.

Even if we let pass Schleiermacher's emphatic protest, in rejecting the assumption that his *Glaubenslehre* contains a philosophical grounding for the Christian faith, it must nevertheless be conceded, without hesitation, that this famous work commanding our attention here is epochal not merely in the history of Christian dogmatics, but also no less so in the history of the philosophy of religion. While the contents of the Christian faith should hardly be based on philosophy, a *science* (*Wissenschaft*) of the Christian faith (even one according to Schleiermacher) can only be accomplished in a philosophical way by the use of philosophical methods and certain philosophical elements, those which theology takes up within itself and works with. But this scientific procedure is completely the same as the one we have already become specifically acquainted with as religious philosophy, in other words, Gnosis.

We arrive at the absolute concept of religion only by becoming conscious of the moments of religion's mediation. Even Schleiermacher's *Glaubenslehre* therefore faces the twofold task of grasping the religious absolute in its purity, while at the same time, and in that very same way, becoming conscious of the moments through which the absolute concept of religion is mediated.

The distinctive feature of Schleiermacher's standpoint presents itself directly here in its decided antithesis to Schelling's standpoint. Here in fact the absolute itself does not mediate itself with itself. Instead everything of a mediating character just belongs to the standpoint of the knowing subject. There can be no more definitive way of

---

102. See Gustav Friedrich Bockshammer, *Die Freyheit des menschlichen Willens* (Stuttgart, 1821), 48–49.

103. [*Ed.*] Friedrich Schleiermacher (1768–1834), *Der christliche Glaube nach den Grundsätzen der evangelischen Kirche in Zusammenhange dargestellt*, 1st ed. (Berlin, 1821), 2nd ed. (Berlin, 1830), known as the *Glaubenslehre* (a term Schleiermacher used in the text). ET from 2nd ed.: *The Christian Faith*, ed. H. R. Mackintosh and J. S. Stewart (Edinburgh, 1928); *Christian Faith*, trans. Terrence N. Tice, Catherine L. Kelsey, and Edwina Lawler (Louisville, 2016). A comparison between Schleiermacher's *Der christliche Glaube* and Baur's *Die christliche Gnosis* is suggested in the next paragraph. As a "science," argues Baur, Schleiermacher's treatment of faith also entails (philosophical) knowledge.

pinpointing the subjectivity of Schleiermacher's standpoint than by its antithesis to the objectivity of Schelling's standpoint. Schelling had hardly any reservations about positing a duality of principles, and a real distinction, within the divine nature itself, and accordingly no hesitation about having the divine nature mediate itself with itself through a series of moments. In other words, and what amounts to the same thing, from this standpoint Schelling was apparently unable to avoid subjecting the divine nature to a temporal process of development. To the contrary, Schleiermacher strictly rules out all these determinations of the concept of the divine nature. For him, in the case of the idea of God one must steer clear of anything temporal and concrete, if what is of a purely subjective nature ought not be seen as something objective. In itself, of course, nothing seems more natural and necessary than this demand. However, the strictness with which Schleiermacher consistently enforces it must take us directly back to the opposite extreme of Schelling's position. Hence whereas Schelling is receptive to concrete determinations, in order to have a living God and not make the concept of God an empty concept, to the contrary Schleiermacher's God-concept, completely divested of everything concrete and humanly subjective, would be a mere abstraction, the abstract sum and substance of all those relationships that, based on the feeling of absolute dependence (*absoluten Abhängigkeitsgefühl*),[104] converge in the concept of an absolute causality.

The absolute is posited, to begin with, simply in the immediacy of feeling as the feeling of absolute dependence; and only on this basis do there follow the positive determinations that form the concept of God. The most distinctive thing about Schleiermacher's *Glaubenslehre* is that the divine attributes determining the concept of God are just the objective expressions corresponding to the various aspects and circumstances of the feeling of absolute dependence. Or, as Schleiermacher himself expresses it,[105] "All attributes which we ascribe to God are to be taken as denoting not something special in God, but only something special in the manner in which the feeling of utter dependence is to be related to him." For otherwise God himself has to be conceived as consisting of a multiplicity of functions, as is the case in finite life; and since if these are said to be particular functions, they are then respectively juxtaposed to one another and must in part exclude one another, so that in this way God would fall into the realm of antitheses.

This restriction also entails the fact that nothing can be ascribed to God that would have the divine activity appear, in human fashion, as alternating with states of

---

104. [*Ed.*] Schleiermacher prefers the adjective *schlechthinnig* (utter, simple) to *absolut* in the second edition (§4). He adds a note saying that the terms mean the same thing, but *schlechthinnig* avoids association with the philosophical absolute, an association Baur emphasizes. When Baur does use *schlechthinnig* it is translated as "utter."

105. *Der christliche Glaube*, 2nd ed., §50 [ET 1928, 194; 2016, 279]. [*Ed.*] Baur for the most part cites only page numbers of the German 2nd ed., whereas we instead cite proposition numbers. We also provide the ET page numbers for the two translations. With quotations we mostly follow the 1928 version; it has not been superseded by the 2016 version, which has problems of its own.

rest. Hence from this standpoint there can be no talk of a beginning to the world and a creation of the world. Instead the entire God-world relation is something we are conscious of only because of the feeling of dependence being related to our setting within the nexus of universal nature. For because our self-consciousness presents at the same time an awareness of the totality of all finite being, the same feeling of utter dependence that is a general constituent of our own self-consciousness also gets applied to the status of the totality of finite being.

Likewise, we cannot posit a distinction or antithesis of any kind within God because of the existence of sin. According to God's dispensation and will, sin is something real and necessary for human beings (inasmuch as, apart from God-consciousness and the recognition brought about by it, of a divine will that commands and forbids, there is no sin). Yet for God sins are not the same as the sorts of things we otherwise represent to ourselves as things simply to be rejected, thus as being things that are the same for God as they are for us—since for God there is as such no indirect knowledge. For God there is no sin in and for itself. For God there is sin only in relation to redemption, inasmuch as even redemption cannot be ordained by God if there were not at the same time sin ordained by God.[106] Therefore there is sin only inasmuch as it is at the same time subsumed under redemption. The entire antithesis of sin and redemption does not exist for God. Then according to this view the divine attributes are none other than the different ways in which the feeling of absolute dependence is related to an absolute causality, inasmuch as one cannot think of what is dependent apart from that on which it depends.

Of course, if we see the presentation of the one and undivided divine causality in a set of divine attributes as being just a human way of thinking,[107] then this view has its consummation in that every distinction regarding the divine being in the doctrine of the Trinity is also to be disavowed. The assumption that there are eternal divisions within the Supreme Being is not a statement based on a pious self-consciousness. Such a statement cannot derive from it, since it is not feasible to contend that the impression the divine made in Christ functioned to countenance such an eternal division in God as its basis.[108] Hence the divine in Christ refers just to the absolute divine causality as such, and thus in him too it just portrays a specific relation of the feeling of absolute dependence to that causality.

Since God-consciousness in the form of the feeling of absolute dependence can only be actual in connection with a sensible determination of self-consciousness, but the relation of sensible consciousness to God-consciousness can be one that changes in various ways, it must therefore be possible to have such a relation of the sensible consciousness to the God-consciousness in which the God-consciousness, as the higher form of self-consciousness, is forever steadfast. As this is a possibility belonging to the

---

106. *Der christliche Glaube*, §81.3 [ET 1928, 337; 2016, 504].
107. Ibid., §165.1 [ET 1928, 726; 2016, 1003].
108. Ibid., §170.2 [ET 1928, 739; 2016, 1022].

original perfection of human nature, Christ is therefore the consummated creation of human nature in virtue of the very fact that in him the God-consciousness accompanying his self-consciousness is an utterly powerful God-consciousness. Another way of expressing this constant power of his God-consciousness is to say it is an actual being or presence (*Sein*) of God within him. The oneness of the divine and the human, the God-man character (*Gottmenschliche*) as it presents itself in Christ, is therefore that very intensity of the God-consciousness in which the consciousness can simply be conceived of as a being [or a presence of God]. The standpoint from which this concept takes shape is—as we said in dealing with the divine attributes—the feeling of utter dependence. In other words, the divine element in Christ is nothing particular within God, but is the absolute divine causality itself to which the feeling of absolute dependence always takes us back, inasmuch as this divine causality fills and determines a human being's entire self-consciousness. So on the one side there is a being or presence, and on the other side there is a consciousness. But there is a being present only to the extent that the consciousness, for its part, presupposes the being, in the way the feeling of absolute dependence presupposes the absolute divine causality. If we wished to say that what is divine in Christ is the absolute at the point at which it attaches itself to the self-consciousness in the form of his human consciousness, that would simply be the objective way of looking at it. But this way of looking at it must instead be converted into subjective terms. Thus: what is divine in Christ is that very God-consciousness, or consciousness of the absolute, that, in the oneness of his own self-consciousness, has for its presupposition the being or presence of God, or of the absolute.

### The Relation of this Position to Pantheism

Therefore this position strictly excludes anything presupposing an objective distinction within the being or nature of God.

Very often people have designated the general view underlying Schleiermacher's *Glaubenslehre* as pantheism, and there is no denying the fact that in any event it is very closely related to pantheism. If it is correct to say that any view understanding the relation of the finite to the infinite as deterministic, and seeing the world as immanently related to God is pantheistic, then Schleiermacher's position must be assigned to this perspective. With an absolute divine causality and a feeling of absolute dependence that are simply counterparts, that leaves no room for freedom in an indeterminist sense. And when God and the world are, as Schleiermacher states,[109] in the final analysis only distinct in that God is of course the absolute, undivided oneness, and the world, although posited as a unity, "is nevertheless in itself a divided and disjointed unity which is at the same time the totality of all contrasts and differences and of all

---

109. Ibid., §32.2 [ET 1928, 132; 2016, 189].

the resulting manifold determinations," God and world do of course always remain two essentially different concepts. Yet they differ only in the way that the world must always be differentiated from God in Spinozism too.

Despite this, it is just as correct to maintain that Schleiermacher's standpoint is also in turn directly opposed to that of pantheism. Pantheism can only take up an objective standpoint and set out from the concept of the absolute substance as what is immediately given. All its specifications as to the being or nature of God inherently have an objective character. They are not merely abstractions drawn from the various relationships that may be differentiated within human beings' religious consciousness. Instead it is the absolute itself that reflects itself in human beings' consciousness, whereas Schleiermacher, in contrast, simply arrives at the concept of God based on the subjectivity of the feeling of dependence. Hence what for speculative thinking is the objectivity of the concept, is for Schleiermacher the immediacy of the feeling or the consciousness. Accordingly these are two opposed orientations and ways of looking at things, since one of them proceeds, so to speak, from above to below, only turning to subjectivity on the basis of objectivity, whereas the other goes in the reverse direction, from below to above, by arriving at objectivity on the basis of subjectivity. However, the point at which they meet is this same one of the individual being utterly determined.

### Christianity Is the Definitive Form of the Feeling of Dependence Developing Itself in the History of Religion, and As Such It Is the Absolute Religion, or the Religion of Redemption

Schleiermacher just holds firmly to the abstract concept of an absolute causality that rules out all concrete elements of life in God, so that in this context one can hardly speak of mediating moments. To the contrary, therefore, the manner in which his *Glaubenslehre* has the feeling of dependence, or the religious consciousness, mediating itself with itself explicitly expresses the very point we have to regard as the essential character of this religious philosophy.

In the idea of redemption, Christianity is understood to be the absolute religion. But the very concept of the absolute religion can only be attained in a critical way, that is, only by precisely distinguishing and defining the different forms the feeling of dependence adopts and traverses until, as the highest level of its development, it takes the shape of Christianity. This involves tracing the distinctively Christian element back to the general religious aspect, by analyzing the feeling of dependence in its various moments, in order to find the spot to be assigned to the Christian element as its special place. This endeavor will of course not, in a priori fashion, explain Christianity as a historical phenomenon based on the prior religious stages, although, in keeping with its genetic concept, the investigation will necessarily presuppose those stages. This way of considering Christianity, by placing it within the framework it shares with the history of comparable religions is, as such, one of the greatest and finest features of Schleiermacher's *Glaubenslehre*. It still has this feature now, although at present the cautious hand that has gone over this work in its second edition—in order to obviate the appearance of wanting to set philosophy above Christianity here, and in order to be able to recognize and separate out what Christianity has in common with other kinds of faith and in virtue of which it sets itself at their head—has removed everything said in the first edition (§§5–7) about the necessity of going beyond Christianity, and that it must take its standpoint beyond Christianity.[110] Only by holding strictly to this unitary perspective might one perhaps convey the view that the various forms of religion are the different moments in which the feeling of absolute dependence mediates itself with itself.

If religion, or piety, is defined as the feeling of absolute dependence, then every individual form of religion is to be considered as a moment in which that general concept seeks increasingly to realize itself. It is obvious that those religious forms that have not yet reached the stage of monotheism hardly play a part in this. As long as self-consciousness had not yet expanded to being a universal world-consciousness, the expressions of the religious life can only express absolute dependence with regard to an individual finite being, not with regard to the world as a whole. Hence the feeling of absolute dependence itself is then not as expansive as it must be if the absolute is said to be the absolutely determinative factor. Monotheism, the belief in one supreme God upon whom everything finite, the world to its fullest extent, is dependent, of course forms an important epoch in this regard. Indeed at this stage itself different forms present themselves, and they are different versions of this same function or mission.

If this monotheism still has a polytheistic form, it is just the monotheism of nature religion. For the multiplicity of gods it subordinates to the one supreme God has its basis in the manifold way in which natural life presents itself. The feeling of absolute dependence of course refers to one supreme being on whom everything finite is thought of as depending. However, the inadequacy of this view is that this dependent, finite factor is, in the first place, just the natural world; and there is not yet any consciousness of the difference between natural life and the ethical and personal life of a human being, and of how that human life is to be conceptualized.

---

110. [Ed.] Schleiermacher discusses these changes in his open letters to Friedrich Lücke. See *On the Glaubenslehre: Two Letters to Dr. Lücke*, trans. James Duke and Francis Fiorenza (Chico, CA, 1981), especially the beginning of the second letter (1829), where Schleiermacher writes, in response to Baur and others, that "some have concluded from the nature of the propositions in the Introduction that my *Glaubenslehre* is actually a philosophy and that it intends to demonstrate or deduce Christianity, insofar as my position can be considered Christian at all" (p. 56). Baur first advanced his interpretation in his inaugural dissertation of 1827–28 (see n. 119). His statement about taking a standpoint "beyond Christianity" does not mean that Christianity is not the absolute religion (for Schleiermacher and himself), but that such a judgment can be made only from a philosophical (not a dogmatic) standpoint.

When we proceed to Jewish monotheism, the theme of the feeling of absolute dependence concerns not merely nature but also human life as distinct from natural life. Yet just as what serves in paganism as the medium for this feeling is nature, in Judaism the medium is the state. So here too in Judaism there is another sphere that remains apart from the absolute element on which one feels oneself utterly dependent. This other sphere is the inner, ethical, and religious life. Inasmuch as Christianity first makes people conscious of this sphere and, in the consciousness of sin, discloses this innermost need for uniting consciousness of one's sin with God-consciousness, the feeling of absolute dependence is fully realized for the first time in Christianity. Accordingly, just as, when looked at from another angle, absolute spirit works its way through the use of various forms of religion, in order to mediate itself with itself and to arrive at a clear concept of itself, here the feeling of absolute dependence traverses the various moments in order, by the ongoing negation of these mediating moments, to become what is absolutely determinative.

These two different religious forms and stages appear to be related to one another in the same fashion when we characterize them according to the persons who are their founders. In addition to features it shares with the other religious forms, each religion [namely, Judaism and Christianity] is something original and distinctive. Thus it can come to the forefront of human consciousness simply all at once, as a whole. Hence the entire individuality of each religion presents itself directly in its founder. The characteristic feature of the religion of nature is that its religious consciousness is still largely intertwined with one's consciousness of nature and integrated with it, and one is hardly cognizant of a specific founder. But nothing is more characteristic of Judaism and Christianity than the originality by which Christ sets himself apart from Moses; in other words, Moses' standpoint relative to Christ, and Christ's absolute standpoint. Except that in this instance one may not overlook the inner connection existing between Moses' standing as prototype and the absolute, archetypal position of Christ.

Sin and redemption are the two elements through which the feeling of dependence mediates itself with itself. However, from the standpoint of Christian consciousness this antithesis is not something immediately given. Instead in turn it mediates itself. There is an aspect of the Christian feeling of dependence in which the antithesis of sin and redemption does not yet come to the fore, at least not in its starkest form. This is where God-consciousness affects us most superficially without our feeling inhibited by the incapacity owing to sin. It happens when we are awakened to realize our existence within the universal nexus of nature, so that our own self-consciousness includes the consciousness of all of finite things as being a totality, a whole. Thus self-consciousness expands to include a consciousness of the world as a whole. Therefore the presupposition for the antithesis of sin and redemption is the antithesis of God and world. This is why, in its first part, Schleiermacher's *Glaubenslehre* develops the feeling of dependence in its relation to our self-consciousness as expanded to include a world-consciousness, and then in the second part proceeds to the actual contents of

Christian consciousness, the antithesis of sin and redemption—the God-consciousness bound by sin and then in turn freed from its bondage. Here then is where we can first address in particular terms the relationship of this *Glaubenslehre* to the concept of religious philosophy, and to that extent also its relation to ancient Gnosis.

## The Concept of the Redeemer: the Distinction between His Archetypal and His Historical Aspects; Understanding the Archetypal Aspect as Something not Utterly Supernatural Is in the Interest of the Philosophy of Religion

According to Schleiermacher, Christianity is the absolute religion inasmuch as it is the religion of redemption. In other words, Christ is the redeemer.

Indeed Christ is the redeemer because the bondage of the feeling of utter dependence, which makes a liberating orientation of their God-consciousness impossible for all other people, is utterly abolished in him. That is why he is endowed with the power to redeem all those who, unlike him, can only be thought of as in need of redemption. This is the archetypal aspect that essentially sets him apart from all other human beings. In other words, it is the constancy of his God-consciousness, expressed outwardly by his infallibility and sinlessness.

But a question arises at once when Schleiermacher defines Christianity in more specific terms as the absolute religion, by saying that it essentially sets itself apart from other monotheistic faiths by relating everything about it to the redemption accomplished through Jesus of Nazareth.[111] The question is this: What is the justification for identifying this person, Jesus of Nazareth, with redemption in such a way that the very concepts one must have of the redeemer are also seen to fit the attributes of Jesus of Nazareth? Even if we grant that dogmatics would simply have to support itself here with auxiliary theses from apologetics, it is still self-evident that proving Jesus of Nazareth is the redeemer in the sense indicated can never be done by empirical means. For what evidence was history [i.e., the gospel account] supposedly able to provide that he is absolutely sinless? The only thing historical examination (*geschichtliche Betrachtung*) can ever show is what is best in a relative sense. But between what is best in a relative sense and what is absolutely perfect there is a gulf over which history can never leap.[112]

---

111. [*Ed.*] *Der christliche Glaube*, §11 (ET 1928, 52; 2016, 79).

112. [*Ed.*] No doubt an allusion to Lessing's famous "ditch" of which every scholar in Baur's day would have been aware. See Gotthold Ephraim Lessing, *On the Proof of the Spirit and of Power* (1777): "Accidental truths of history can never become the proof of necessary truths of reason" (*Lessing's Theological Writings*, trans. Henry Chadwick [London, 1956], 53). Lessing then states (p. 55) that going from historical statements about Jesus in the gospels to the claim that he is the Son of God, is of the same essence as God, is "the ugly, broad ditch which I cannot get across, however often and however earnestly I have tried to make the leap." We should also keep in mind that Baur's *Die christliche Gnosis* was published in the same year, 1835, as David Friedrich Strauss's *Life of Jesus Critically Examined* first appeared, and that Baur was deeply engaged with the issues raised by Strauss as well.

Therefore either Jesus of Nazareth is just called the redeemer in a very indefinite sense open to various interpretations; or, it is only the philosophy of religion, via the route of speculation, that arrives at the true and proper concept of the redeemer, and assigns this concept to the historical person, Jesus of Nazareth. If the latter is the only acceptable explanation, then it is the philosophy of religion alone that recognizes and secures for Christianity the stature and significance it has as the absolute religion. Since the concept of the redeemer is the truly dominant factor, the one whose normative and organizing influence extends across the entire contents of Christian dogmatics [e.g., Schleiermacher's *Glaubenslehre*], this shows us clearly how Christianity, as a historically-given religion, relates to the philosophy of religion. In other words, and what amounts to the same thing, it shows us how the historical Christ stands in relation to the ideal Christ.

In the Gnostics' case the results are similar: in part the separation of Christ from Jesus that we know they accepted in order, as it were, to split into two quite heterogeneous halves the one individual known from history; and in part that critical procedure by which they sought to expunge all the objectionable Jewish elements from the New Testament documents. The guiding idea in doing so was none other than the concept of the redeemer as it took shape for them in by no means a merely empirical way, but in part even in contradiction to the historical account. The analogy with Schleiermacher involves the relationship he assumes between the archetypal aspect and the historical aspect in the redeemer.

If this way of designating Christ is, in itself, favored far more than the usual formulation—according to which the divine and human natures are united in one person; the representation of a twofold Christ, an archetypal and historical Christ—then the specifications made about these two concepts also contribute to this picture. Schleiermacher strictly and consistently holds firmly to the idea of the archetypal feature of the redeemer, and carries through with it in order to place him above all others, as the founder of a corporate life or fellowship (*Gesammtleben*) comprising all other forms of pious association, such that everything existing outside this fellowship is an imperfect or incomplete religious life. But on the other hand the entire treatment of the historical concept of the redeemer very much intends to place him on the same footing as other human beings. Not only is the purely historical aspect of the person of the redeemer calculated to be a popular elaboration, to be conceptions suited to the religious domain (such as notions of angels and demons). Also all that concerns the person of the redeemer—miracles such as his supernatural conception, the resurrection, the ascension, the second coming and final judgment—are declared to be matters that must be set apart from the proper components of the doctrine of his person. Thus room is provided for thinking of the redeemer himself, in all these circumstances, as someone no different from ordinary human beings.

In general, this is the thesis that must hold good for the factors concerning the person of the redeemer. This position must be considered from a twofold point of view: first, with reference to the available New Testament testimonies on the subject; next, with reference to its dogmatic value.[113] This thesis leaves so much room open for ingenious criticism and exegesis, that the danger it may have posed on the path to the results of historical criticism—having a harmful impact on the standing of Christianity—can only be adequately prevented by assuming that the standing of the redeemer would in any event remain secure in its own proper domain, independent of the historical narrative. To be sure, what might result from recognizing, as the miraculous feature of the redeemer's appearing, the very fact that the man Jesus was said to have been archetypal, in other words that the archetype was said to have been historically and actually in him so that he would be the founder of a new corporate life? In this case there are two essentially different ways of looking at it, and they are never to be completely reconciled. That is because the ahistorical, archetypal redeemer forever hovers at a height not accessible to historical knowledge, by transcending the historical domain in a way quite analogous to how, for the Gnostics in their unsophisticated, unscientific way of treating it, the bond connecting the Christ with Jesus appears to be a very loose and external affair, indeed even one that is completely broken.

I am far from objecting to Schleiermacher's *Glaubenslehre* for the unavoidable conclusion it reaches [about the redeemer], but rather object to what his procedure entails. He should have openly acknowledged the undeniable role that the philosophy of religion plays in the entire internal organization of this *Glaubenslehre*, and he should have more clearly separated the speculative element from the historical element in his presentation. Hence we ought not let ourselves be deterred from further investigation of this *Glaubenslehre* along the lines of its philosophy of religion. For we contend—with this same interest in a philosophy of religion where speculative thinking is superior to a merely historical understanding—that when Schleiermacher spells out completely the concept of the supernatural element in the redeemer, his definition turns out to exclude what is utterly supernatural, what is actually miraculous, and the supernatural is always apprehended once again as together with the natural factor. Except that it befits the philosophy of religion to declare itself opposed to miracle in the proper sense, because miracle tears apart the context in which the concept must operate in the series of moments of its own self-determination, in accord with the immanent laws of its own movement.

Thus when it comes to the redeemer, the philosophy of religion can hardly be satisfied with some other concept than that of his archetypal character. But it would very seriously misconstrue its task if it were to seek to completely remove the redeemer from the realm of human development in virtue of that archetypal character proper to him, instead of endeavoring to capture his likeness within that realm. In the well-known thesis of Schleiermacher's *Glaubenslehre*, stating that the appearing of

---

113. [*Ed.*] Baur cites *Glaubenslehre*, §97.2, at this point, for this sentence paraphrases a sentence there (ET 1928, 403; 2016, 596), but he does not indicate that it follows a specific discussion of Jesus' supernatural conception.

Christ, and the establishing of a new corporate life through him, are to be regarded as the completion of the creation of human nature,[114] there is the most specific acknowledgment of this demand from the philosophy of religion [to treat the redeemer as being within the human realm]. Thus the appearing of the redeemer was indeed the first creation of humankind, although with this creation, implanted in humankind in nontemporal fashion, the incomplete or imperfect condition of human nature is what became evident. In this way the appearing of the redeemer within humanity is at once recognized as something that was necessary, since all other human beings just relate to the redeemer in the way that lesser degrees are related to the highest degree, which is perfect within itself. For, as Schleiermacher himself states:

> As soon as we grant the possibility of a continued progress in the potency of the God-consciousness, while denying that its perfection exists anywhere, we can also no longer maintain that the creation of humankind has been or will be completed, since undoubtedly, as advances are made, perfection is always still just posited as a possibility . . . [This is so] of course when perfection [of an essential life-function] is posited in the concept of it but is not a reality in the individual instance.[115]

Hence despite his archetypal character, which elevates him absolutely above all others, the difference between the redeemer and all other human beings is just a matter of degree, since he is set apart from them only in virtue of the fact that the same orientation of God-consciousness to what is absolute that presents itself in all others as merely relative, had become in him the absolute efficacy and constancy of his God-consciousness. Of course as highest, the highest degree is essentially different from all other (lesser) degrees, if only different by one degree. One can designate this as the circumstance of the redeemer's specific and relatively greater dignity or rank. In virtue of his specific dignity the redeemer stands alone of his kind, and indeed forever so in degree. But he is just *primus inter pares* (first among equals).

But the two concepts are not mutually exclusive, for each is completely true only in and with presupposing the other one. The specific dignity says that the difference in degree, which still always involves the possibility that a better one might come, with another religion, does not fully express the essential nature of the redeemer, for this essential nature is to be understood as something necessarily unique and remaining unique. However, the relative dignity, the fact that despite this uniqueness the founder nevertheless belongs to our species—and because in this species it is essential that each individual be pious—our piety relates everything to him, for it is all just different levels in the religious relationship, and ascribes the highest level to him.[116]

---

114. [*Ed.*] See §89: ". . . from that point of view the appearance of Christ and the institution of this new corporate life would have to be regarded as the completion, only now accomplished, of the creation of human nature" (ET 1928, 366; 2016, 553).

115. *Der christliche Glaube*, §93.2 [ET 1928, 378–79; 2016, 567].

116. See Alexander Schweizer, "Ueber die Dignität des Religionsstifters," *Theologische Studien und*

Surely this is the very view held by ancient Gnosis when it presupposes, in all those the redeemer draws to himself, a pneumatic principle related to the redeemer, and when the souls in which this principle has displayed itself in its perfect purity are said to be in the same relation to the redeemer as that of the bride to the bridegroom.

## The Archetypal and the Historical Factors, the Idea and Historical Reality, Are not Completely Unified in the Person of the Redeemer

Now we first reach a point at which the relation of Schleiermacher's *Glaubenslehre* to the philosophy of religion, or philosophical theology, must become fully evident and in its true light.

It is true that one does not acquire the idea of the absolute infallibility and sinlessness of the redeemer, or the idea of his archetypal character, in merely an empirical way. But it is likewise true that the idea of his archetypal character—when the creation of the human being is said to be incomplete—cannot merely be posited in the concept of him. For this truth must also be imparted in an individual. This raises the question: How are idea and reality related in this instance? Is the archetypal feature originally just given in the idea, and so lacks reality? Or, is it originally given in the historical reality, and so it simply has an empirical origin and lacks the significance of the idea?

Schleiermacher has not provided a further explanation of this issue where one would initially have expected him to do so.[117] Since he ascribes an archetypal character to the redeemer, and as a result of the historical account he considers Jesus of Nazareth to be the redeemer, these two points, taken together, presuppose that Jesus of Nazareth is both archetypal and historical. So there is no getting around this issue, and Schleiermacher has addressed it in his doctrine of the person of Christ[118] in this form: whether the archetypal [i.e., ideal] element (*das Urbildliche*) in Christ cannot also be thought of as being merely exemplary, a model or prototype (*ein Vorbildliches*)? Since the power or efficacy of the God-consciousness in the corporate life itself always just remains incomplete, then an exemplary dignity or role must certainly befit the redeemer. However, the archetypal character (*die Urbildlichkeit*) that in fact expresses the being or presence of the concept itself, and thus utter perfection or completeness, would not apply to him, since it would not be needed in order to comprehend the

---

*Kritiken* (1834), 503ff.

117. *Der christliche Glaube*, §11. See §11.4, where Schleiermacher speaks directly about the absolute superiority of Christ as redeemer, in comparison with Moses and Muhammad as merely the founders of religions [ET 1928, 58; 2016, 87].

118. Ibid., §93.2 [ET 1928, 378; 2016, 566]. [*Ed.*] The words "archetype" and "prototype" are often regarded as having the same meaning in English, but it is helpful to distinguish them when they translate the German *Urbild* (with the prefix *ur-* connoting what is original or ideal) and *Vorbild* (with the prefix *vor-* connoting what goes before). The 1928 ET translates *Urbild* as "idea" (thus not distinguishing *Urbild* from *Idee*) and *Vorbild* as "exemplar"; while the 2016 ET uses "prototype" for *Urbild* (thus not recognizing a distinction between "archetype" and "prototype") and "exemplar" for *Vorbild*.

always-just-incomplete result. Perhaps this would be the original hyperbole of the faithful when, in seeing their own imperfection, they consider Christ and incessantly pursue the issue of perfection in this hyperbolic fashion. For in all ages the believers have endowed Jesus with what they were able to understand as being archetypal in this domain.

Yet there are two points to raise in contrast to this view. The first one is that, by individuals subordinating their personal consciousness to the species-concept (*Gattungsbegriff*), the hope must emerge that at some time humankind, albeit just in its noblest and finest members, will surpass Christ and leave him behind; and that would obviously set limits to the Christian faith. The second point is that, if on the one hand we bear in mind that the creation of human beings could not remain incomplete, and on the other accept the fact that it must be very difficult to specify the difference between a genuine archetype (*Urbild*) and the kind of exemplary being or prototype (*Vorbild*) that has the power to bring about every possible enhancement of the whole [fellowship]—since of course the producing of this enhancement belongs to the concept of the archetype and not to that of the model or prototype—then this indeed shows that archetypal character alone would be the appropriate expression for the exclusive and personal dignity of Jesus.

It is easy to see that the main issue is raised by the second of these two points. What is at stake here boils down to whether or not the productive effect inherent in the concept of the archetype can also be attributed to the model or prototype. By equating the two concepts, archetype and prototype, in this way in the concept of productive efficacy, this productive effect, in other words the power of bringing about every possible enhancement, therefore cannot be located merely in the external, perceptible appearing of the redeemer. For it must be conceded that this very appearing, or perceptible presence, certainly in no way gives us the true concept of sinlessness or archetypal character. And if the entire concept of the redeemer just depends on his external presence as a phenomenon in history, then too the events of the resurrection and the ascension ought not be declared essential components of the doctrine of the person of the redeemer. For the efficacy of the productive power of the archetypal character would instead be conditioned by belief in the reality of these events, provided that the same argument should not be used to deprive of their significance belief in the reality of the redeemer's earthly life as such, to the extent that it is the object of empirical knowledge.

Here we are dealing with the concepts of being (*Sein*) and existence (*Existenz*), and the difference between the finite and the absolute with regard to these concepts. It belongs to the concept of God that God can only be thought of as existing; that the concept of God also includes God's being (*Sein*). So that must hold good for the absolute in each and every context. Only on this basis can Schleiermacher, in referring to Christ himself, call the divine element in Christ, the element that is precisely his archetypal character, a God-consciousness, one that is in fact a being or presence of

God [in him]. Therefore if the concept of the archetypal is conjoined, or synonymous, with the concept of the absolute, then existence cannot be linked in just a transitory way with the archetypal, for the concept of the archetypal also of course includes its being. Yet independently of its appearing outwardly in history, what is archetypal has its reality within itself. Hence it is not allowable to contend that creation is not completed without what is archetypal appearing in history in an individual person; and we are always left with the thought that humanity would at some point go beyond Christ.

If concept and being are identical in what is archetypal, then there is nothing to be added to it. The creation is completed in virtue of the fact that one can become conscious of the archetypal simply in a form presenting the essence of the human being. The archetypal human, in other words the God-man, has his objective reality in his concept. However, the reality is situated in the historical existence of a specific individual, and in virtue of that the reality becomes subjective. Hence the objective reality of what is archetypal occurs just in the sphere of consciousness; in other words, it has only an ideal significance. Previously, in order to get a closer look at the internal organization of Schleiermacher's *Glaubenslehre*, I have called attention to the fact that he understands that, of all the theses the *Glaubenslehre* has erected, some are descriptions of the conditions of human life, some are concepts of the divine attributes and modes of acting, and some express features of the world.[119] But in doing so he

---

119. See "Anzeige der beiden academischen Schriften von Dr. F. C. Baur," *Tübinger Zeitschrift für Theologie* (1828), no. 1, 220–64, and the scholarly writings noted there. In this same place I have also asserted, contrary to Schleiermacher, that the same three forms in which Schleiermacher elaborates the entire contents of his dogmatics, should also have already been made foundational in the Introduction. [*Ed.* They occur rather as §§32–35 at the beginning of the first major part of the dogmatic system.] Then it would have been made clearer where in fact in this *Glaubenslehre* the concepts of redemption and the redeemer have their place and their origin. In the *Sendschreiben* (Open Letters) about his *Glaubenslehre*, he too, as we know, is aware of this as well as of other matters. In *Theologische Studien und Kritiken* 2 (1829) [where the letters were first published], p. 515, he counters: "How could one expect that he has given rise to such confusion, which must necessarily lead to a host of other confusions? Why does one want to demand from the Introduction what can only have its proper place throughout the dogmatics itself, if one does not overlook the gap between the two?" In order to counter, once and for all, this distressing confusion, he directly announced the intention of indicating, in the new edition of the *Glaubenslehre*, the explanation of all he previously set about doing; of what the statements there involve when spelled out more precisely. In doing so he would then indicate, by the headings of the subsections, where those propositions that must precede the constituting of the dogmatic concepts, in fact have their proper setting. Then all that should precede and determine the schematic arrangement of the work would appear on its own and be more carefully clarified, and the Introduction would then be a more well-rounded whole. Schleiermacher himself is unsure whether such an Introduction would be an improvement. – I too cannot say that the second edition with its headings in the Introduction—propositions borrowed from ethics; propositions borrowed from the philosophy of religion; propositions borrowed from apologetics—strikes me as an improvement over the first edition. I very much wish that the *Sendschreiben* on the *Glaubenslehre* had left us no such legacy. Other critics have, with justification, called it an unscientific enterprise, a science wherein a principle all its own gets vested in piety and introduced by propositions borrowed from other disciplines rather than in its own terms. See, for instance, Karl Rosenkranz's criticism in the *Berliner Jahrbücher für wissenschaftliche Kritik* 109 (Dec. 1830) 366. In fact there can be no other way to describe it, and I do not see what can be said in reply to this. Either the Introduction is completely superfluous,

explicitly declares that the main thing for us is that the propositions of the latter two

or else it essentially belongs to the dogmatics itself. If it is superfluous, then it can be completely omitted, and it would have been far better to delete it entirely. But if the Introduction belongs essentially to the dogmatics, then what holds good for the dogmatics also does so for the Introduction. Hence what Schleiermacher has said in various places cannot be affirmed: that not a single thesis is to be found in the entire Introduction that is actually a dogmatic proposition. So are propositions that do not merely introduce the determination of the concept of what is dogmatic, but actually contain this determination itself, not dogmatic propositions? Is the doctrine of the redeemer, with the concept of the redeemer already spelled out in the Introduction, not a dogmatic concept? The main thing—and on its own it already suffices for showing that the gap pointed out between the introduction to dogmatics and dogmatics itself is nothing at all—is the undeniable fact that the entire contents of the Introduction actually organizes and sorts itself out, of its own accord, under those three forms of dogmatics. – The explication of the concept of piety, or of the feeling of dependence, and the derivation of the different forms and stages of religion in which this piety presents itself, belong to the first form [of the religious self-consciousness]. As Schleiermacher himself concedes (*Theologische Studien*, 514), it is no incongruity when the task of the Introduction is regarded as determining the proper place of Christianity among the different possible modifications of the general human, pious consciousness. This cannot take place otherwise than by the way in which the concept of piety, or the feeling of dependence, undergoes development. Each form of religion is a distinctive modification of the feeling of dependence; so the development of the concept of each religion is a description of a human condition. The concept of redemption as well, and the concept of the redeemer that Schleiermacher links directly with redemption, have their proper place here. For the concept of redemption is simply what distinguishes Christianity from other religions. Redemption is Christianity's own modification of the general human, pious consciousness. But when pious self-consciousness, in developing, also necessarily becomes a fellowship or community, or a church (on which see §6 [ET 1928, 26; 2016, 38–39]), then everything related to this fellowship obviously belongs under the heading of propositions expressing features of the world. With the same justification Schleiermacher himself uses later, in treating "The Constitution of the World in Relation to Redemption," what the Introduction to the whole work says about the religious community, or church, can be located under the same perspective. Accordingly, each modification of the general human, pious consciousness gets regarded here as a historically-given form of religion. Hence one can also speak here for the first time of the redeemer appearing in the person of Jesus of Nazareth, while, as a form and modification of the religious consciousness, the initial treatment of the redeemer cannot be historical in character, but only in general terms. – Of its own accord this likewise makes it clear what, based on the Introduction, is to be assigned to the third form. The concept of revelation applies in part to all religions, and in part to Christianity in particular. So one cannot spell out this concept unless dogmatic reflection turns back to God's absolute causality entirely in the same way as this is the case with Schleiermacher's *Glaubenslehre* in the third form as it concerns the divine attributes. This is also so with a related point when the Introduction mentions the specific difference between the redeemer and one who is merely the founder of a religion. For it involves that God-consciousness having become a being or presence of God as this is further elaborated in Part Two, and as God's absolute causality is presented with reference to the redeemer. If the Introduction had been organized according to these three main dogmatic forms, then the heterogeneous elements of Schleiermacher's concept of the redeemer would also have sorted themselves out on their own. Then it would have been clear that the entire historical aspect of the redeemer would just belong to the second form, and that mere analysis of the pious consciousness, as it could have been provided in the Introduction, simply in propositions of the first form, provides the concept of the redeemer distinctive to this *Glaubenslehre*. Then the historical concept of the redeemer can add nothing essential to it, for "the two other forms can only be understood in their dogmatic significance by means of the first form" [§30.2 (ET 1928, 126; 2016, 184)]. – Here, where pious self-consciousness is considered as something first becoming a fellowship and so nothing can yet be presupposed in the pious self-consciousness in itself—where it is something given only via the fellowship or the church and belongs to the second form—it would not have been possible to have interwoven, in the way this is done throughout all of Schleiermacher's *Glaubenslehre*, these two heterogeneous elements of his Christian

types contain nothing that would not also be contained in the first one. He says that, strictly speaking, the first form suffices for completing the analysis of Christian piety, and that it would be for the best to elaborate this form exclusively, since the others are just means for being able to understand it in its true dogmatic significance. He says that these other forms are not to be excluded from a Christian doctrinal structure, lest doing so would deprive it of its historical stance and therefore its ecclesial character.

I am also now convinced that this distinctive way Schleiermacher's *Glaubenslehre* is constructed affords us a deeper look into its inner nature. If the entire *Glaubenslehre* were reduced to propositions just describing the conditions of human life, then religious feeling would be regarded as just something developing purely out of itself and consisting of a series of inner states of one's soul or disposition. Also, the entire doctrine of the person of Christ is thus ultimately just the description of a condition of human life, namely, the condition of redemption, and the redeemer is none other than the idea of redemption thought of as personal in him and fixated on his person. In place of the historical Christ there is then the ideal Christ, the archetypal Christ, in whom the perfect God-consciousness, bringing about redemption, presents itself as being or presence, where human God-consciousness becomes a being or presence of God within human nature.[120] I too can see this view as not being ruled out, because of what Schleiermacher says as opposed to it. "If our aim is to make room in human nature before Christ, and apart from him, for the power of producing within itself a

---

consciousness: the form in which the general human, pious consciousness is modified to Christian consciousness by the analysis of consciousness itself; and what is given by historical Christianity in a concept of Christian consciousness that is not more specifically defined. But even this genesis for the concept of the redeemer is no reason for us to look down upon this *Glaubenslehre*. Hence in the Introduction, which is not yet dogmatics and also therefore does not yet separate out the dogmatic forms, there are the two elements to which these forms are linked and which, to give them their accurate names, are the philosophical element and the historical element. These two are still hopelessly intertwined. After the topic of Christian consciousness has once been introduced in this fashion, one can calmly set out to analyze religious consciousness, with the Introduction covering one's rear and letting calmly appear all that is of merely an ideal nature or belongs to the first form, as the archetypal Christ, as well as what belongs to the historical basis for Christian consciousness. – Nevertheless we should have thought that in the dogmatics one could not have spoken of the historical Christ without previously having spoken about the Christian fellowship or church. If the historical Christ is the founder of the Christian communion or church, then there can be no other way to know Christ than one mediated by the Christian fellowship. For in the dogmatic part of Schleiermacher's *Glaubenslehre* that is about Christ it speaks of the Christian church first of all and thereafter. Therefore what justifies this dogmatics, in presenting its Christ as archetypal, at the same time presenting him as the historical Christ? The dogmatics will point us back to the Introduction and what is said there about the religious fellowship. But this is the very reason why the Introduction itself must also be seen as an integral component of the dogmatics. So there cannot be another method for arranging and expounding the Introduction, different from that of the dogmatic part. Of course, therefore, as Schleiermacher insists, the gap between the Introduction and the dogmatic part is not to be overlooked. Yet this gap is simply due to the inconsistency of the method. Because of it this work, otherwise accomplished so skillfully and so impressive in its overall organization, rightly strikes us all the more unfavorably. But that can only be accounted for in the way I have done.

120. *Der christliche Glaube*, §94.2 [ET 1928, 388; 2016, 577–78].

pure and perfect archetype—then since there is a natural connection between reason and will, human nature cannot have been in a condition of universal sinfulness."[121] (As Schleiermacher points out in the first edition of *Der christliche Glaube*,[122] this view presupposes that, "in the way he is presented in faith, Christ is certainly archetypal. However this appearing of the Son of God has also everywhere just been a spiritual appearing in the souls of human beings. For in history the Son of God has not been able to appear in an external, individual person.")

At this point I must also refer in turn to Schleiermacher's concept of miracle, and thus I cannot be convinced that the remark made by Karl Nitzsch in opposition to me[123] is correct. He says such a procreation of the archetype through and within [someone of a] sinful orientation would not have been a linking of the natural and the supernatural, but instead of the unnatural with its contrary. The latter would then only have been the case if, as nobody maintains, the archetype was said to be begotten by the sinful orientation itself. However, Schleiermacher's concept of miracle necessarily entails that the sinful orientation is no absolute hindrance to the procreation of the archetype. As Schleiermacher says,[124] if the redeemer, inasmuch as he is the historical man Jesus, is to be recognized as a miraculous appearance because his distinctively spiritual substance cannot be declared to be from the substance of the human realm of life to which he belonged—but instead was just from the universal source of spiritual life, through a creative divine act in which, as an absolutely greatest act, the concept of the human being as subject of God-consciousness is perfected—then why should the same also not hold good for the archetypal nature of Christ, inasmuch as it is considered to be a procreation of the human soul?

The objection to be raised here is an entirely different one. If the archetypal character of Christ, or the redeemer, is to be considered a procreation of the human soul in the indicated sense, it nevertheless cannot be repeated as the same miracle in each individual soul in which it enters into consciousness. Instead it is a miracle only where it initially and originally arose. Hence one is always led back once more to a historical starting point. This is what Schleiermacher means when, in his second *Sendschreiben* on the *Glaubenslehre*, he remarks[125] that the feeling of the need for redemption is certainly a particular form of the feeling of dependence. But one cannot say, for that reason, that Christianity would be deduced from this feeling. Instead one can only say that, in virtue of the vitality of this feeling, Christianity arose when Christ had

---

121. Ibid., §93.3 [ET 1928, 380; 2016, 569].

122. [*Ed.*] Baur cites vol. 2, p. 184, of the first edition (§114.2), and quotes a passage to which nothing seems to directly correspond in the second edition.

123. In *Studien und Kritiken* 1.4, 851.

124. *Der christliche Glaube*, §93.3 [ET 1928, 380; 2016, 569].

125. *Theologische Studien und Kritiken* 2 (1829), 503.

appeared and was recognized in his glory and power. The Christ within always presupposes the historical Christ.[126]

Therefore, although the descriptions of the state of the human soul that constitute dogmatic propositions of the first form can simply be derived from the realm of inner experience, this experience is nevertheless considered at the same time to be an experience determined by the religious community to which the individual belongs. But if we go back to the beginning of this community and to its founder who in this capacity is the redeemer, we perpetually face the contention that, inasmuch as the redeemer is presented to us as a historical person, he cannot, in a historical or empirical way, be known as the subject of perfect God-consciousness, in other words, in his archetypal character and absolute sinlessness. What empirical proof was there supposed to be for this? What proof of this kind could a *Glaubenslehre* especially provide, one affirming that all the otherwise weighty proofs for it, such as miracle and prophecies, are utterly untenable? Yet on the other hand it remains no less certain that the idea of the redeemer is linked to his person and one only becomes conscious of it from his person as the intermediary. Then this contradiction can be resolved solely by accepting the fact that the idea of his archetypal character of course has its truth not in the historical phenomenon to which it is principally linked for us, but instead solely in itself. Yet as soon as we have become conscious of it ourselves, even as something true in itself, we must recognize the fact that it can enter our consciousness in no other way than through the mediation of that historical phenomenon.

Here ideality and historical reality are reciprocally related. But this is simply the familiar antithesis of the ideal and the real, the one in which we see ourselves situated in all our thinking and knowing. The idea has its truth within itself, is true not because of its being given externally but only through the reason that knows it, although we cannot become aware of it apart from the constant interrelation of the ideal and the real. Similarly, the concept of God of course includes God's existence, yet without consciousness of the world there would be no God-consciousness. But this does not mean that what is real and mediates consciousness of the idea, and is naturally and necessarily connected with it, is therefore taken up into the idea and that the two are united as one. It is no different when it comes to the archetypal Christ and the historical Christ. That is simply the reason why, with Schleiermacher's *Glaubenslehre* to the extent that we also have to take it as religious philosophy, it is like ancient Gnosis in that the archetypal Christ and the historical Christ hardly want to go together in a complete and indivisible unity.[127]

---

126. First *Sendschreiben, Theologische Studien und Kritiken* 2 (1829), 261.

127. In his comprehensive critique of Schleiermacher's *Glaubenslehre* (in the *Berliner Jahrbücher für wissenschaftliche Kritik*, Dec. 1830, 841ff, 865ff.; and Dec. 1831, 821ff., 924ff), which sheds light, in multifaceted and penetrating ways, especially on the subjectivity of its standpoint, Karl Rosenkranz finds (on pp. 935 and 939 and elsewhere in the latter issue) in Schleiermacher's christology a docetic tendency. It is an understanding colored by a docetic veneer because, owing to that wondrous being or presence of God in Christ, Schleiermacher sets Christ apart *specifically* from other human beings,

## Schleiermacher's Antinomianism[128]

In each of its forms this philosophy of religion also has the task of determining how Christianity is related to Judaism and paganism. The *Glaubenslehre* addresses this issue with its well-known thesis, "Christianity does indeed stand in a special historical connection with Judaism [because Jesus was born of the Jewish people]; but as far as concerns its historical existence and its aim, its relations to Judaism and paganism are the same."[129]

Of course several factors served to counterbalance Christ's Jewish ancestry. First of all, many more pagans than Jews converted to Christianity. Also, Christianity would not have been so well-received by Jews if they had not been receptive to

---

and in Kantian fashion makes Christ the ideal for them. Had he better understood the dogma of the two natures in Christ as originally expressed, he would not have had to devise such a torturous development of his christology. In it every impulse of the soul's lesser powers is sublimated in the predominant God-consciousness and, vice versa, every moment of God-consciousness ends up by usurping the sensory functions, where the uniformity of the God-consciousness gives rise to a rigid, unmoving state and takes away one's freedom. For, according to Schleiermacher (see especially *Glaubenslehre*, §93.4 [ET 1928, 383; 2016, 571]), "at every moment even of his period of development he must have been free from everything by which the rise of sin in the individual is conditioned." That is because that self-consistent consciousness of God in him ruled out any doubt or struggle on his part that would have put him on a par with us. Accordingly Christ would have been subject to what is good and true, and would not, as scripture teaches, have been subject to temptation just as we are. These remarks are undoubtedly quite correct, and it is also easy to see how such docetism is connected with the subjective standpoint for Schleiermacher as well as for Marcion. But as we said above (p. 397), one can just as well rebuke Schleiermacher for leaning in the direction of Ebionitism. Suppose we add in the fact that the feeling of dependence is actual only insofar as the self-consciousness is also sensuously determined. Then nature, as the principle of sensuousness and externality, and which gets negated by the God-consciousness, is necessary for religion, because otherwise religion could in no way become a reality. But the fact that human beings' world-consciousness is forever hindered from becoming entirely God-consciousness, and so the dissolution of the antithesis between sensuous feeling and godly feeling is forever prevented from realizing itself to the extent it wishes, then we are just left with an infinite or, more correctly stated, an endless approach to its realization. This is tantamount to saying that the resolution of this condition is never truly accomplished but is only something striven for. So the everlasting impulse said to operate from this side is not capable of clearing the way to the longed-for God (see Rosenkranz, 840ff. and elsewhere). Thus it is even more difficult to have a unitary concept of Schleiermacher's Christ for whom all of this must hold good. – The main concern as I see it is this: By what route does Schleiermacher arrive at his view of Christ? Before we can investigate whether or not the being or presence of God in Christ crosses over to a docetic view, we must ask, first of all: How is it justifiable to ascribe that presence of God to Christ? If Schleiermacher's Christ is said to be the historical Christ, then that puts us on the purely empirical path of the historical faith. However, if this is not the route we are to take, then it can no longer be maintained that the inner or archetypal Christ utterly presupposes the historical Christ. Then the religious philosophy referred to in the Introduction as expelled from dogmatics, like an enemy driven across the border, forcibly makes it way into the realm of dogmatics to claim a place for itself despite all the efforts to guard against that, and to establish its authority on the basis of those auxiliary propositions that dogmatics has to accept as its supporting structures.

128. [*Ed.*] This section really discusses Schleiermacher's treatment of (antipathy toward) Judaism. Antinomianism is not mentioned until the very end, in connection with Marcion.

129. *Der christliche Glaube*, §12 (ET 1928, 60; 2016, 89).

foreign elements after they were dispersed to Babylon. So these factors indicate that Judaism and paganism are related to Christianity in a fully comparable way, because each of them was said to provide converts to Christianity who were joining something different from what they left behind them. Accordingly, Christianity can no longer be regarded as continuous with Judaism, any more than it is with paganism. The elements in the Old Testament that are most decidedly Jewish have the least value. What we can find reproduced in Old Testament passages are just the kind of elicitations of piety that are of a more general nature and do not develop very distinctively Christian themes. On the whole they certainly remind us of similar and congruent points expressed by the nobler and purer elements of paganism.

In his second *Sendschreiben* on the *Glaubenslehre*[130] in particular Schleiermacher spoke in this same sense in opposition to belief that the Jewish people has a special inspiration and revelation from God, and against the view that belief in the revelation of God in Christ is in any way dependent on such a belief about the Jews. The conviction that the vitality of Christianity as it progressed is in no need of support from Judaism, is as ancient as Christianity's own religious consciousness. Hence the effort to prove Christianity from prophecy is never a happy undertaking. It can be simply attributed to a lack of renewed confidence in the inner power of Christianity when someone sets great stock in these external proofs. We—those of us who are in possession of a fuller understanding—should properly rid ourselves of dependence on the imperfect nature and meager elements of the Old Covenant.

I have intentionally reproduced these theses as much as possible in Schleiermacher's own words, since doing so lets us know very clearly the fundamental mindset on which this view relies. For Schleiermacher's feeling of dependence leaves Christianity with no other standpoint than that of subjectivity. Thus the only criterion can be immediate Christian consciousness, which determines the worth of all the phenomena of the religious life. So it is quite natural that, with regard to historical factors too, in the one antithesis of Christian consciousness everything is divided into what accords with this consciousness and what conflicts with it. From this standpoint what does not express full Christian consciousness is of course for that very reason not Christian. This also brings us to the point that the more the positive element belongs to the character of Jewish religion, and the more it distinguishes itself from the freer and more universal monotheism of [some] paganism, by its anthropomorphism and anthropopathism, the less congenial it can be for a theology whose essential nature is the avoidance of all objective specifications as to the nature or being of God.

Thus Schleiermacher's *Glaubenslehre* expresses a consistent antipathy to Judaism[131] and in the way it spells out the relation between Old Testament and New Testa-

---

130. *Theologische Studien und Kritiken* 2 (1829), 496ff.

131. In his first *Sendschreiben* on the *Glaubenslehre* (p. 282) Schleiermacher directly acknowledges that he has never needed any kind of rational theology to foster his piety or to understand it. The same is true for the sensuous theocracy of the Old Testament, for instead he has always developed his own

ment features. The history of the philosophy of religion has no noteworthy parallels it can draw to this, other than the antinomianism of Marcion, which rests on a wholly analogous standpoint.

## Comparison of Schleiermacher's Glaubenslehre with Kant's Religion within the Limits of Reason Alone

In this survey of the course of more recent religious philosophy, this is the most appropriate place to briefly refer to Kant's *Religion Within the Limits of Reason Alone*.[132] For it can be readily shown that consistency with regard to Schleiermacher's principles is ultimately rooted in a Kantian foundation and soil. So comparison of these two figures serves quite well to shed light on Schleiermacher's mystical obscurity with the help of Kant's intellectual clarity.

The two principles Schleiermacher distinguishes from each other as sensible consciousness and God-consciousness are what Kant calls, respectively, the evil principle and the good principle. Kant's evil principle, inasmuch as it indwells human beings as radical evil, as a natural predisposition or propensity (as Kant himself puts it), is not to be eradicated by human powers. Hence the way in which the good principle can gain the upper hand over the evil principle must appear to be incomprehensible, something surpassing human nature. So here we see right before our eyes Schleiermacher's entire supernaturalist position, but with one difference. From the necessity for moral transformation, and from the fact that the ethical inclination expressed, even in fallen humanity, by one's consciousness of the moral ought, is not eradicable, Kant concludes that such a transformation is possible. On the other hand Schleiermacher wants to regard everything that frees the God-consciousness from its bondage as something imparted to one, and so traces it back to the activity of the redeemer.

Yet because of the relative character of the entire antithesis, in the sphere in which Schleiermacher's doctrine of sin and redemption operates—because of the mutually opposed concepts of one's own deed and of what is imparted, the concepts of the God-consciousness as powerful and powerless, as capable and incapable with regard to uniting sensible consciousness with God-consciousness—we see repeatedly the angle from which we are to consider the situation. What he calls "imparting" is none

---

understanding further in the polemic against that method of doing theology. See also *Glaubenslehre*, §132, according to which: "The Old Testament scriptures owe their place in our Bible partly to the appeals the New Testament scriptures make to them, partly to the historical connection of Christian worship with the Jewish synagogue; [the following clause not quoted by Baur] but the Old Testament scriptures do not on that account share the normative dignity or the inspiration of the New" [ET 1928, 608; 2016, 853]. In opposition to this, see Rosenkranz [n. 127], *Berliner Jahrbücher* 118 (Dec. 1831), 943ff.

132. [*Ed.*] Immanuel Kant, *Die Religion innerhalb der Grenzen der blossen Vernunft* (Königsberg, 1793). Translated by Theodore M. Greene and Hoyt H. Hudson (LaSalle IL, 1934). See also the translation by Werner S. Pluhar, *Religion within the Bounds of Bare Reason* (Indianapolis, 2009).

other than the efficacy of the idea of the archetypal human being as this idea, along the lines of its objective reality, is implicitly contained in the religious consciousness of the human being. When this idea gets awakened in the individual's consciousness first of all simply in the communal life founded by Jesus, it is nevertheless not merely dependent for its reality on this origin in one's experience. That is because the absolute as such can never be merely something given empirically. Therefore, just as for Schleiermacher the general rule is that what is supernatural is nothing utterly supernatural, so too what is imparted by the redeemer's activity is nothing that is utterly imparted. Instead it is also in turn something original and natural.

We cannot link some other concept with the capacity imparted by the redeemer because even the concept of sin, which correlates with the concept of redemption, can hardly be thought of as an absolute incapacity. Schleiermacher explicitly maintains, about the concept of sin, that this concept is inseparable from the consciousness of sin. Therefore God himself is posited in the self-consciousness together with the factor of sin; except that the God-consciousness is not able to permeate the other operative elements and thus is not able to be determinative of this factor of sin. God-consciousness is indeed present, but as something lacking in power. As opposed to this powerlessness of the God-consciousness, in other words to the bondage of the feeling of utter dependence—the bondage constituting the essence of sin—redemption is its liberation. Redemption is the facility with which we are able to envisage the God-consciousness, to infuse it into the various sensible stimulations of the self-consciousness.[133]

But why should this facility be regarded as something imparted to us? For the God-consciousness is nevertheless always present and proves to be effective in human beings through the very fact that people are conscious of God. The state of sin differs from the state of redemption in virtue of the fact that, in such people, the sensible consciousness is prevalent and is dominating their God-consciousness. However, while the sensible consciousness is at once always posited together with God-consciousness, so too in the sensible consciousness the God-consciousness is never completely lacking, a nullity. Yet once God-consciousness is posited as an active power, then it is completely inconceivable why it cannot also prove to be something powerful to the degree in which it permeates the other operative elements and gains the upper hand over the sensible dimension. As Schleiermacher says,[134] it belongs to the human being's original perfection to attain these states of self-consciousness in which the God-consciousness can actualize itself. Thus this emergence of God-consciousness has its basis in human nature itself; and the fact that God-consciousness, being held back and bound by the sensible consciousness, must first be freed from this bondage, is simply a consequence of human development.

---

133. *Der christliche Glaube*, §66.1 [ET 1928, 271; 2016, 402]. See also §63.2 [ET 1928, 263; 2016, 386].

134. Ibid., §59 [ET 1928, 238; 2016, 345].

But for this very reason one also cannot contend that this state—the feeling of dependence having become free from its bondage, the facility with which we are capable of infusing God-consciousness into the different sensible stimulations of our self-consciousness—is just something imparted to us. In other words, that redemption is just based on the activities carried out by the historical Christ. As Schleiermacher says, if it is therefore actually the case that, "if both arresting the impulse to the God-consciousness and quickened development of it are to be equally the act of one and the same individual, and consequently opposites are to be explained by the same cause, then, in relation to the doer, the two must cease to be opposed."[135] There cannot be such an antithesis if sensible consciousness and God-consciousness are, in the same way, elements of the spiritual nature of human beings; in other words, if they are the moments of a spiritual development when indeed the same subject, inasmuch as the sensible consciousness dominates in him, is a person in need of redemption, but also, never being deprived of the God-consciousness in itself, is, on account of this power, someone who bears within himself the principle of redemption.

The circumstances are the same with the idea of the redeemer. Kant leaves us in no doubt as to the redeemer being the one pleasing to God, as the ideal of a humanity pleasing to God. He is simply a personification of the good principle in its absolute victory over the evil principle. As the preceding investigation also shows, this is the actual significance of Schleiermacher's archetypal Christ. The archetypal Christ, the God-man, that is, the absolutely sinless and perfect human being, is none other than the idea of redemption conceived of in a person. However, the redemption itself, to the extent it is thought of as realized in an individual—the God-consciousness in its absolute constancy and power—is something to which the God-consciousness of the individuals forming the Christian communal life is always just an approximation.

This obviously shows that there can be no essential difference between Kant and Schleiermacher when it comes to the relation of the redeemer to the individual, inasmuch as this person is the object of the redemptive activity. According to Kant, the individual is one with the redeemer or Son of God, inasmuch as a human being is a new person in disposition or character, and posits as unitary in his disposition what can in fact just develop successively. According to Kant the Son of God as redeemer, in other words that which is posited in the individual in virtue of his redeeming activity—the fellowship of the redeemer and the redeemed—is none other than the reception or acceptance of the good principle in one's disposition. To be changed for the better is to have the redeemer within one, in one's good disposition. What is said about the redeemer in fact holds good for the new human being, which is why for Kant the vicarious suffering of the redeemer is directly the suffering of the new person in place of the former one.

Schleiermacher's doctrine of the redeemer's activity amounts to the same thing, in that it is the acceptance of faith in the power of the redeemer's God-consciousness.

---

135. Ibid., §63.1 [ET 1928, 263; 2016, 386].

The redeemer produces his act within us, and his act becomes our act when the God-consciousness—which cannot be thought of as effective to some degree or other unless it is also assumed to have an absolute efficacy—gains predominance over the sensible consciousness, such that the God-consciousness and the sensible consciousness are related as positive and negative, and each plus of the God-consciousness corresponds to a minus of the sensible consciousness. The entire difference between the standpoints of Kant and Schleiermacher is just the difference between ethics and religion. What ethical consciousness is for Kant, namely the moral order of human beings conditioned by the victory of the good principle over the evil principle, is for Schleiermacher the God-consciousness, the religious order. What they have in common, the point from which both set out, is, however, the absolute dependence posited directly in consciousness. For Kant it is the absolute causation of the unconditional requirement of the moral law, while for Schleiermacher this absolute dependence takes us back to the absolute causality of God. Yet Schleiermacher's concept of God does not lead back to an objective reality independent of consciousness, any more than does the absoluteness of Kant's moral law. That is because Schleiermacher completely rules out all objective determinations as to the being of God. His concept of God is just equivalent to the indeterminate abstract concept of an absolute, original causality without which the dependence human beings are conscious of would have lacked the ultimate end point from which it derives. This abstract concept is no different from Kant's concept of the noumenon.

Here the concept of God is a completely lifeless concept, a sheer abstraction, which is also why the being of God in Christ cannot be a truly living and personal presence. Instead Schleiermacher's Christ-idea just completely parallels Kant's God-idea; and Kant's moral lawgiver derived from the absolute moral law, as the bearer of it, coincides with the idea of the moral order of the world, just as the archetypal Christ is simply the concrete expression for absolute God-consciousness. Given all this, we do not venture to contend that, in its major contents, Schleiermacher's *Glaubenslehre* is just completely carrying out the antithesis of the two principles Kant designated as radical evil and human beings pleasing to God. The difference simply lies in substituting God-consciousness for ethical consciousness, and in the skilful but untenable way in which the archetypal Christ is said to be conjoined as one with the historical Christ.[136]

---

136. The following statements indicate how far Kant is from making such an identification. (See *Religion within the Limits of Reason Alone*, Book Two, Section One B., The Objective Reality of the Personified Idea of the Good Principle [pp. 55–56].) "From the practical point of view this idea is completely real in its own right, for it resides in our morally-legislative reason. We *ought* to conform to it; consequently we must *be able* to do so ... Just for this reason must an experience be possible in which the example of such a [morally perfect] human being is presented (*so far, at least, as we can expect or demand from any merely external experience the evidences of an inner moral disposition*) [emphasis within the parentheses added by Baur]."

Put succinctly, the standpoint of Kant and of Schleiermacher is the same standpoint Hegel characterizes as that of subjectivity. Hegel says:

> All objective content vanishes and only what I posit holds good. I alone am what is positive, what is real . . . From this standpoint what is highest is not knowledge of truth, is not knowledge of God. All objective content has evaporated into purely formal subjectivity. From this contentless standpoint no religion is possible, for I am what is affirmative . . . All content, all activity, all that is living, remains on my side of things. I have only a lifeless, empty God, a so-called highest being, and this emptiness, this conception, remains just subjective. It never arrives at genuine objectivity.[137]

Kant also had not neglected to carry the principles of his philosophy of religion over to the domain of the history of religion.[138] Based on his standpoint, Kant saw Judaism simply set apart from the absolute religion by the widest gulf. (In any event he does not discuss paganism.) Schleiermacher stands very close to Kant on this issue too, and Marcionite antinomianism has found new friends in the two of them. Yet when considered from a higher standpoint, this antinomianism is itself none other than a higher, more spiritualized, form of Judaism. As I shall later point out, if Judaism is the religion of the antithesis, then also every form of religious philosophy that leaves in its wake a still-unresolved antithesis, on the whole stands on the same soil as Judaism. Thus for Marcion the antithesis of the visible and the invisible, of the law and the gospel, is irresolvable, because he is not able to comprehend what is visible as an element of the invisible, or justice as an element of love. Despite all its antipathy toward Judaism, Kantian religion itself is nevertheless simply a religion of law, for it can never do away with the conflict between the individual and the moral ought (in the way this conflict is essential to law). Also, as long as its redeemer always vanishes once more into an inaccessibly distant ideal, the divine and the human are never allowed to become truly one. It is no different with Schleiermacher's religious doctrines. The absolute always remains what is absolutely "over there," an abstract, contentless idea. Even within the redeemer's own self-consciousness the sensible consciousness can never harmonize with the God-consciousness so as to form a concrete unity.

---

137. G. W. F. Hegel, *Vorlesungen über die Philosophie der Religion* (1832), 1:110 f. See also 114, 118, 124. [*Ed.*] On this and subsequent editions and translations see n. 141. The quotation is assembled by Baur from pp. 110–18 (the last sentence being on the latter page). Cf. the ET, 1:297–300.

138. See *Religion Within the Limits of Reason Alone*, Book Three, Division Two, Historical Account of the Gradual Establishment of the Sovereignty of the Good Principle on Earth [pp. 115–28].

## Hegel's Philosophy of Religion

### Schleiermacher's Subjective Standpoint and Hegel's Objective Standpoint

The course of our investigation now takes us to Hegel's philosophy of religion, which adopts an objective standpoint as opposed to Schleiermacher's subjective standpoint.

Seen from a general perspective, the two standpoints are very antithetical, notwithstanding the fact that these two systems of religious philosophy, which have adopted mutually opposed standpoints, are in such close and reciprocal contact that this concurrent presentation of philosophical theology in these two forms, with each standing closely connected to the other, has contributed in a major way to giving a greater independent significance to the philosophy of religion, an importance that can no longer be denied. While Schleiermacher's subjective standpoint—that of an absolute feeling of dependence without an absolute that has objective content—involves of its own accord the necessity of proceeding on to the Hegelian standpoint of objectivity, it must also be conceded, on the other hand, that this transition can take place no more quickly and directly than from the standpoint of Schleiermacher's *Glaubenslehre*. Yet whichever of these two standpoints we adopt, by subordinating the other possible stance to it as apparently an unscientific position, we must always approach this as a philosophy of religion issue, if we are to be able to justify scientifically that the concept of the absolute religion undeniably belongs to Christianity as such.[139]

The philosophy of religion has gained this greater significance because of both Schleiermacher and Hegel. Yet the difference between the two also gets expressed in a remarkable way. There is nothing Schleiermacher seeks to distance his *Glaubenslehre* more urgently from than the assumption that philosophy would have anything to do with faith. In contrast, Hegel insists on nothing more emphatically than recognizing that it is philosophy's task to bring religion to the true concept of itself and to elevate faith to knowledge, since philosophy and religion coincide as one and religion's object, like that of philosophy, is the eternal truth in its own objectivity: the absolute, or God.

A distinctive feature of Hegel's philosophy is that it considers the philosophy of religion to be an integral part of philosophy as a whole. Since it regards the parts of philosophy as the links of a chain or the components of a circle, developed as connected and presented in their necessity, the necessity of religion is also a consequence of this connectedness. Hence the philosophy of religion is where religion first takes the form of a system complete within itself. Yet howsoever distinctive Hegel's philosophy may be, what at the same time comes to light, by the placement and significance

---

139. [Ed.] Since the word "absolute" (in German and English) derives from the Latin *absolvere*, which means to "loosen" or "absolve," it has a relational aspect for Baur and other Hegelians. The absolute, which is infinite, absolves itself of itself and goes over to its other, the finite; it includes this other within itself and thus becomes a "whole," or absolute spirit. For this reason both subjective and objective standpoints are essential. The absolute becomes a true or genuine absolute when finite subjects are conscious of it, and that can also be viewed as the self-consciousness of the absolute.

it gives to the philosophy of religion, is its very close relationship to ancient Gnosis, a far closer relationship than one would have supposed, given how far removed in time it is from ancient Gnosis and how very different is the route on which it reached its distinctive standpoint. This is mainly the perspective on the basis of which we also draw Hegel's philosophy of religion into the sphere of our investigation, a move that, by doing so, turns back again to the beginning from which we set out.

## General Overview of Hegel's System as a Whole; Its Relation to the Gnostic Systems

In going back to Schleiermacher's standpoint, so as to cross over from it to that of Hegel,[140] by making this transition we find ourselves caught up in the following passage in Hegel's *Lectures on the Philosophy of Religion*.[141] Hegel says that, in keeping with the aforementioned features of the subjective standpoint:

---

140. In his penetrating, critical endeavor dealing with Schleiermacher's *Glaubenslehre* [*Ueber Schleiermachers Glaubenslehre: Ein kritischer Versuch* (Berlin, 1824)], Braniss has investigated this aspect of it in particular, namely, the necessity it involves for crossing over from its subjectivity to a position of objectivity. See, for instance, pp. 138–39: "Our question is why Schleiermacher, who certainly gives a place to sensible feeling by positing a properly objective content in self-consciousness, nevertheless absolutely denies such a content to pious feeling or the feeling of dependence. If the reply to this is that there can be no objective content in the feeling of dependence—because it is God who is operative in it and God cannot be an object; for an object would always be something finite to which the I or self could react or reciprocate and by doing so would have annulled the absolute dependence—then this answer could carry no weight. That is so because the concept of the object of course involves specificity but does not essentially involve finitude, and on the other hand being essentially infinite only excludes being determined from outside it but does not utterly exclude all determinacy. The determinacy that rests on self-determination can always befit it without that in the least annulling its essential infinity. Hence in virtue of his self-determination, God can most certainly be present to the soul in an objective way, without that annulling God's character as absolutely infinite, and having that disturb in the least the emergent feeling of absolute dependence." [*Ed.*] Influenced by Schleiermacher and Hegel, Christlieb Julius Braniss (1792–1873), professor of philosophy in Breslau, developed his own speculative-mystical panentheistic system.

141. 1:116ff. [*Ed.*] Baur is quoting, here and elsewhere, and often directly, from the first edition (Berlin, 1832) of Hegel's *Werke*, edited by an Association of Friends of the philosopher. There the *Vorlesungen über die Philosophie der Religion* is contained in vols. 11–12, and edited by Philipp Marheineke. In his citations Baur refers to these as vols. 1 and 2, and we retain that numbering here. The translation of passages in the text are our own. A second, quite different edition, edited by Bruno Bauer and included in the *Werke* of 1840, came out after publication of the present book and so is not relevant for our purposes here; nor is the existing ET of that edition. Walter Jaeschke prepared and edited a three-volume German critical edition of these lectures (Hamburg, 1983, 1985, 1984) that separates into distinct texts the four lecture series on this topic by Hegel at the University of Berlin, in 1821, 1824, 1827, and 1831. The sources of this edition are extant manuscripts and transcripts, the second *Werke* edition of 1840, and the lectures of 1827 as reconstructed from earlier editions. The first *Werke* edition of 1832 plays a minor role, and it is not always possible to correlate Baur's quotations with the Jaeschke edition, which was translated into English as *Lectures on the Philosophy of Religion* (*LPR*), ed. Peter C. Hodgson, trans. R. F. Brown, P. C. Hodgson, and J. M. Stewart, 3 vols. (Berkeley and Los Angeles, 1984–87; r.p. Oxford, 2007). The edition of 1832 made slight use of Hegel's own lecture manuscript of 1821 and was based on transcriptions of the lectures of 1824, 1827, and 1831, woven

they must point to a transition in which the I renounces itself in its singularity. I must recognize something objective that in fact counts as truth for me, which I recognize as what is affirmative, as posited for me, something in which I am negated as this I, but something in which my freedom is at the same time retained. This involves my being determined as universal; I retain myself, simply counting myself as universal. This is none other than the standpoint of thinking reason. Religion itself is this action, this activity of thinking reason; it is, as an individual, positing oneself as what is universal and annulling oneself as individual, to find one's true self as what is universal. The universal object now has content within itself; it is substance moving within itself, not empty, but absolute fullness. All otherness belongs to it, and so I look upon myself as finite, the fact that I am one moment in this life, as that which simply has its particular being, its subsistence, in this substance. The finite is an essential moment of the infinite in the nature of God. Thus one can say that God is himself the one who finitizes himself, who posits determinations within himself. God determines himself in thinking himself and positing himself over against an other. God just is, but only by mediating himself with himself. He wills what is finite, posits it as an other to himself, something finite, for he has an other over against him. This other-being is his contradiction with himself. So it is the finite over against the finite, although the truth is that this finitude is just an appearance; that God has himself in it. The activity [of God] is creating, and it involves distinction, the moment of the finite. Yet this subsistence of the finite must also be sublated. For it is of God, it is God's otherness and it nevertheless exists in the determination of what is other to God. It is what is other and what is not other; it resolves itself, that is, it is not otherness itself but is an other and comes to ruin. For in this way the other-being has wholly vanished into God; and God himself appears through himself by receiving himself as his own result. God is the movement within himself, and because of it alone is he the living God. God is the movement to the finite and, by sublating it, is the movement to, or becoming of, himself. In the I as what sublates itself as finite, God turns back to himself and is simply God as this returning. Without the world God is not God.[142]

Here we have before us not merely the general standpoint of the system, but indeed also at the same time the essential elements that move it. So there can be no more definitive and direct expression of the entire difference between Schleiermacher's

---

into an editorially constructed text. All the sources for 1831 have now been lost except for excerpts made by D. F. Strauss.

142. [*Ed.*] Baur has assembled this quotation from pp. 116–22. Cf. *LPR* 1:306–8. The statement "without the world God is not God" is found only in the Hotho transcript of the 1824 lectures (1:308 n. 97), not the more reliable Griesheim transcript. As Baur explains later, ideal distinctions are found within God "before and apart" from the world, but they become real distinctions with the creation of the world. So the statement is not true with respect to the immanent or preworldly Trinity, but it is true with respect to the inclusive or worldly Trinity.

standpoint and Hegel's standpoint than this: Schleiermacher locates the entire content of religion in the feeling of the subject, whereas Hegel instead defines the essence of religion as the self-consciousness of God or absolute spirit. In other words, for Hegel religion is the idea of the spirit that relates itself to itself; spirit's relationship to absolute spirit; the divine spirit's knowledge of itself.

But this knowing of itself by spirit is mediated via finite spirit, that is, through the consciousness that, as such, is finite consciousness. So religion involves finite consciousness, albeit as sublated, for the otherness that absolute spirit knows is absolute spirit itself; so it is first absolute spirit from the fact that it knows itself. Therefore in order to be mediated by consciousness, or by finite spirit, it must finitize itself in order, by becoming finite, to become the knowing of itself.[143]

However, before spirit rises up to the religion in which it turns back to itself by knowing itself, it has to have already traversed an endlessly lengthy terrain. If we set out from the sensible domain, from the natural consciousness that has nature for its object, then spirit presents itself as the truth of nature, that is, nature gone back into its grounding, which is spirit as such. Nature is a rational system; it has within it the law of the vitality of things, but only within its inner being. Nature itself knows nothing of this law. The truth, the spirit, is thus in an existence not commensurate with this law. The spirit, the true existence of this law, what it is in itself, first goes forth from nature and shows that spirit is the truth, the foundation, the highest reality in nature. However, in its relation to nature as to something external, as finite consciousness of nature, as something set over against an other, spirit is, above all, finite spirit. As finite spirit it is conceived of as in contradiction with itself. By being in what is external it contradicts its own nature. Hence in order to free itself from this negativity and to raise itself up to itself, finite spirit goes back into its own ground, goes back to itself in its truth. This elevation of finite spirit is the initial emergence of religion, in which spirit knows about itself and, as the free, the absolute spirit, it has authentic consciousness of its own essential nature.[144] Nature and finite spirit are, accordingly, just the embodiments of the idea; they are specific configurations, particular modes of the idea's appearance through which the idea has not yet made its way in order to be as absolute spirit.[145]

But above the realm of nature and of finite spirit, as the embodiments of the idea, there stands the realm of pure thinking, the truth as it is in and for itself, without any veil or covering, and logic as the system of pure reason, as the realm of the pure thinking of its own essence, the pure essences themselves as they are in themselves, the realm of thinking spirit. Logic has for its contents the presentation of God as he is in his eternal, essential being, before the creation of nature and of a finite spirit.[146] Hence

143. *Philosophie der Religion*, 1:129 [cf. *LPR* 1:318, incl. n. 120].
144. Ibid., 1:61 [cf. *LPR* 1:119–20, also 320–21].
145. Ibid., 1:18.
146. Hegel, *Wissenschaft der Logik*, vol. 1 (Nuremberg, 1812–13), 35.

philosophy is, first of all, the logical idea, the idea as it is in thinking, in the way its contents themselves are the determinants of thinking. In addition, philosophy manifests the absolute in its activity, in what it produces. This is the way of the absolute, to become for itself, to become spirit. So God is the result of the philosophy by which it is known that this is not merely the result but instead it eternally produces itself, is what goes before. The one-sidedness of the result becomes sublated in the result itself. What is result is also in turn not result, not mediated through another, but is rather the foundation.[147]

Therefore the one that is, in equal ways, presupposition and result, is the absolute spirit mediating itself with itself. Hence the content of religion is the self-consciousness of God. God knows himself in a consciousness different from him. This is the consciousness of God that is in itself, but also for itself in that it knows its identity with God—an identity that is mediated by the negation of finitude. In short, God is this: distinguishing himself from himself to be object to himself, yet in this distinguishing, being utterly identical with himself.[148]

### The First Form of Absolute Spirit, or the Absolute, Eternal Idea of God: God in the Element of Pure Thinking[149]

This general overview of Hegel's system already puts us at a point where we see clearly how closely it is related to the systems of ancient Gnosis.[150]

When considered as to their general nature, all these systems, but above all others those that we deem to be representatives of the first and third main forms of Gnosis, the Valentinian and Pseudo-Clementine forms (while I have shown that the Marcionite form tends toward a subjective standpoint), bear on the whole the same inherent character. They have the same principle and the moments they traverse as they develop are the same. At the apex of the systems stands absolute spirit as it is in itself, in its pure abstractness and objectivity. In the Valentinian system the Aeons, in which the one Archon reflects himself, are none other than the pure thoughts, the pure essences, in which spirit thinks its own essential nature—the pure self-movement of the spiritual life that is existent in itself. In the Pseudo-Clementine system there is at least the Sophia who, as the soul identical with God himself, is thought of as bound to him; and the Marcionite system's distinctiveness is featured in positing the higher,

---

147. *Philosophie der Religion*, 1:18 and 61 [cf. *LPR* 1:119–20].

148. Ibid., 2:151 [cf. *LPR* 3:250 n. 3 (from the 1831 lectures)].

149. [*Ed.*] The three forms of absolute spirit or of the development of the idea of God are set forth in the third part of the lectures, "The Consummate Religion." See *LPR* 3:73ff., 185ff., 271ff., 361ff. They comprise a philosophical version of the Christian doctrine of the Trinity, as Baur explains in a later section.

150. [*Ed.*] Hegel was aware of Gnosticism as an antecedent to his system. See *LPR* 3:84–85, 89, 196–97, 219, 287–88, 315 n. 173, 364.

invisible God, lacking all objective content, as something we are conscious of in a merely abstract way.

Indeed in the Aeons of the Valentinian system, in their oneness, there is of course also difference manifesting itself—spirit's distinction from itself as the transition to other-being and to finiteness or perishing (*Verendlichung*). What holds good here is what Hegel says of God—inasmuch as God is considered in his eternal idea in and for itself, in the element of thinking, as it were before, or apart from, creating the world, that is, in his eternity as the abstract idea—that God of course eternally differentiates himself, but that what thus differentiates itself from itself does not yet have the shape of an other-being. For instead what is differentiated is just that from which it has been set apart. Spirit is just revelatory as itself, just differentiating itself for the spirit for which it is. Spirit is the eternal idea, the thinking spirit; it is spirit in the element of its freedom, is God simply inasmuch as he reveals himself because he is spirit but is not yet what appears, is just pure thinking for spirit. This is the theoretical consciousness in which the thinking subject relates to itself in a wholly undisturbed way; not yet posited in the process, but instead relating to itself in the wholly unwavering stillness of the thinking spirit (the Gnostic σιγή, or silence). For God is thought for spirit, and this is so in the simple conclusion that, via his own differentiation, which is, however, still just made in pure ideality and does not proceed to externality, God unites with himself. God is directly together with himself (the Gnostic Horos) in the element of thinking (the Gnostic ἔννοια). God is spirit, and no darkness, no shade or blending, intrudes into this pure light (the Gnostic *lumen paternum* or "light of the Father").[151]

God, or spirit, is of course process, movement, life—that is, self-differentiation, self-determination. However, the initial distinction is that he is as this universal idea itself. In this decision or division (*Urteil*) there is what is other, what stands over against the universal aspect as what is differentiated from it; there is God's whole idea in and for itself, such that these two determinations are also the same for each other, are this identity, the one. Spirit itself is this being the case; in other words, expressing it in the way it is experienced, spirit is eternal love. For love is a distinguishing of two who are nevertheless utterly not separate from each other (the Gnostic concept of the syzygies). Love is the consciousness, the feeling, of this identity, and God is love, that is, God is this distinction and the nullity of this distinction; a play of this distinguishing not taken in earnest, a play of love with itself that does not reach the seriousness of other-being, of separation and disunion. The difference is likewise posited as sublated, as the simple, eternal idea.[152]

---

151. See Irenaeus, *Against Heresies* 2.8.2 [*ANF* 1:368].

152. *Philosophie der Religion*, 2:177–204, and 206. [*Ed.*] Baur here refers to the whole of the "Division of the Subject" and the first major section of the treatment of Christianity, "God in His Eternal Idea, in and for Himself; the Kingdom of the Father," in the 1832 *Werke* edition. Cf. *LPR* 3:189–98, 275–90, 292 (on the play of love with itself).

Comparison of this position with the foregoing presentation of the Valentinian doctrine of the Aeons obviously demonstrates how precisely they agree if we separate the essential elements from the nonessential ones, the contingent form from the idea itself. What the Gnostics have in common [with Hegel] is principally that in their Pleroma, in the realm of the Aeons, the Gnostics too posit the absolute spirit's identity with itself as also indeed a distinction, but one that is directly annulled or sublated.[153]

## The Second Form: God in the Element of Consciousness and Representation

In that first form, corresponding to the Gnostic Pleroma, the kingdom of the Father as Hegel too calls this sphere, it does not reach the point of an actual distinction. However, the circumstances are different with the second form, where the absolute, eternal idea of God has, in the creation of the world, come to be in the element of consciousness and representation, or of difference.

What seems to be just a distinction in the initial, pure form of the idea, in the element of thinking, now comes into its own, and what had first been expressed only ideally, and as abiding in the oneness, is now grasped in the form of other-being, is saddled with otherness. That gives rise to a relationship. In being related to an other, spirit is not eternal spirit but is finite spirit, which is unreconciled, is alien. Here we have, as such, the creation of the world. What is created, what is otherness, splits internally into the two aspects of physical nature and finite spirit, with nature as the existent externality, as what is distinct with regard to God, in the determination of the manifold (*Mannigfaltigkeit*) serving as the sphere of finite spirit. So this created being is therefore an other, fully outside of God, separated from him. The idea has sundered itself, has fallen away from itself.[154]

In the Gnostic systems the ideal world, the light world, the Pleroma, sunders itself in the same way into the created, real, finite world, by the fall of Sophia-Achamoth, who, as the Sophia down below, is for that reason to be distinguished from her Mother, the Sophia above. That is because with her the distinction that was just a kind of playfulness in the Aeons of the Pleroma, a self-annulling appearance, has now become a very serious matter. In conceptual terms we may regard her on the whole as the being existing outside the Pleroma, as fallen away and separated from it, that is,

---

153. [*Ed.*] Within this sentence, in parentheses, Baur includes the Latin for Irenaeus' statement, in *Against Heresies* 2.7.3, that: "these being possessed of one nature, are of equal and similar properties, and exhibit no differences [among themselves]" (*ANF* 1:367).

154. *Philosophie der Religion*, 2:177, 204ff., 232. [*Ed.*] Pages 204ff. refer to the second major section of the treatment of Christianity, "The Eternal Idea of God in the Element of Consciousness and Representation, or Difference; the Kingdom of the Son," in the 1832 *Werke*. Cf. *LPR* 3:198ff., 290ff. On p. 232 Hegel says: "God is the creator, and indeed in the determination of the λόγος as the self-externalizing, speaking word, as the ὅρασις, the seeing of God. Nature is the existent externality, what is distinct in him [God] in the determination of the manifold. It is the sphere of finite spirit." No direct parallel in *LPR*, but see the excerpts of the 1831 lectures, 3:365. See also the version found in the 1827 lectures, 3:292–94.

according to the series of her changeable conditions. Thus she appears quite properly as the spirit answerable for otherness, and this other-being also directly splits here into two aspects: the external nature that in the Valentinian system unmistakably presents itself as spirit objectified in externality; and finite spirit that is the psychical element, which, according to its true concept, is finite spirit. The Demiurge, the principle of the psychical realm, taken together with human beings—who are just of a psychical nature to the extent that they are created by him—constitute none other than finite spirit, since the Demiurge's knowledge is limited to external nature, the sphere in which he operates and over which he stands as its ruler.

In the Pseudo-Clementine system we have the same element occupying this second form of Hegel's system, in part by transferring matter out of God, whereby the monad becomes the dyad and the antitheses, the chain of syzygies, begins to develop, and in part in the sudden reversal within the syzygies, whereby what is the worse member becomes the primary member. But in the Marcionite system this whole process—however much regarded as taking place ahead of time, beyond the range of consciousness, so the system itself has no knowledge of it—is simply posited as the antithesis of the visible and the invisible.

### The Third Form: Spirit in Its Return to Absolute Spirit, in Its Reconciliation

While the second form is the self-positing negation, inasmuch as in it absolute spirit appears as other-being, the third form is the annulling of the negation, is the negation of the negation.

It belongs to the essential nature of spirit to take back into itself what is alien, what is particular, what is posited as separate from it—to reconcile this with itself. Therefore as the idea has sundered itself, has fallen away from itself, what has fallen away has to be brought back to its truth, has to be turned from its appearing and back to itself. But this return of spirit into itself only occurs by spirit annulling finite consciousness as something finite; for it had only made itself finite in order to know itself by this becoming-finite. Thus spirit knows about itself as absolute spirit; it knows about its identity with God as an identity mediated through the negation of finitude. Just as God is the movement to what is finite, in the I, as what annuls itself as finite, God turns back to himself and, as this returning, is simply God.

In the Gnostic systems we have this same turning point in the fact that a human being is regarded as not merely psychical but also as a pneumatic or spiritual nature. For the difference between what is psychical and what is pneumatic consists in the pneumatic nature being self-aware of its identity with absolute spirit and, with this awareness, striving to overcome and cancel out the natural, finite consciousness within itself. Here too, accordingly, in the I as what annuls itself as finite, God turns back to himself. What Hegel says about the relation of finite spirit to nature—that it is nothing permanent; that finite spirit must annul this relation to nature by carrying out or manifesting this process in regard to itself, the fact that it is the divine spirit[155]—holds good in the same sense for the nature and characteristics of the pneumatic person of the Gnostic systems. And when finite spirit, conceived of as in contradiction with itself, simply because of this can free itself from this negativity and rise up to itself, to itself in its truth, so that it goes back into its ground, this going-back into the ground is clearly expressed in the Gnostic systems. For in the same relationship in which the pneumatic element, the light-seed imparted in a hidden way by the Sophia, frees itself from its bondage and rises up to be independent of it, the psychical element appears as what is untrue, as what in its nullity and negativity finally disappears, in other words, as what has its truth only in the pneumatic element.

Spirit's elevation to itself is the emergence of religion. The more that religion becomes receptive to reason, to thinking consciousness, the more certain spirit is of its reconciliation, of its freedom, of its returning to absolute spirit. This is also why pneumatic persons are those who, through Gnosis, religious knowing, the idea of the absolute, the absolute religion, are self-aware and form the community of the chosen ones, those the Sophia leads to their heavenly bridegroom, to union with the Pleroma, the realm of the Aeons, with which the ἐκκλησία, as one of the Aeons, is in itself one. They are the subjects who are within God's spirit, the community that is of course initially in the world but also rises up to heaven.[156]

## The Idea of the Process in Hegel's Philosophy of Religion, as in Ancient Gnosis

As we see clearly here, the kinship of Hegel's religious philosophy with ancient Gnosis accordingly consists, first and foremost, in the fact that in each case there is mainly the same process by which absolute spirit mediates itself with itself.

For Hegel it is a process of self-differentiation, sundering, and going back into self, as in the three moments of being-in-self, being-for-self, and being-with-self. In other words these are the moment of substantial, absolute oneness where the idea is affirmed as equal to itself, the moment of distinction or separation, and the moment of the distinct elements going back to an absolute affirmation.[157] The Gnostic systems

---

155. *Philosophie der Religion*, 2:232.

156. Ibid., 2:179, 258. [cf. *LPR* 3:187–88 (1824), 329 (1827)]. Tertullian directly expressed in a noteworthy way the fact that, also according to the Gnostics, in this return to himself, God is simply God. He writes, in *Prescription against Heretics*, ch. 7: "The same subject matter is discussed over and over again by the heretics and the philosophers; the same arguments are involved. Whence comes evil? Why is it permitted? What is the origin of man, and how does he come about? Besides there is the question Valentinus proposed: Whence comes God? He settles it by answering: from *enthymesis* [the operation of mind] and *ectroma* [abortion]" [*ANF* 3:246]. This means God is God only through his distinguishing from himself what, in his separation, he is in the *enthymesis* and the *ectroma* (the Achamoth), and, by taking it back into himself through the negation of the negation, mediates himself with himself.

157. *Philosophie der Religion*, 1:13?. [*Ed.*] The type is broken and it is not certain whether the final number is "4" or "1," but the reference is probably to p. 134.

also adopt the basic assumption that only in this process is God a living God, is absolute spirit, is thinking reason. That is because there is no life without movement, no thinking without mediating activity. In other words, true knowing is simply the concept itself inasmuch as it explicates itself in the three moments as the concept in itself, as the determinate concept, and as the concept coming from its determinacy to itself, by reinstating itself from its limited form.[158]

Thus without a world, also God is not God. Yet at the same time what this also shows is the vast difference between the purely logically spelled out concept of the process and the simply posited, just postulated, Platonic-Gnostic idea of a falling-away from the absolute, as it still has very essential and deeply rooted significance in the earlier presentation of Schelling's philosophy.[159]

## Further Development of the Major Moments of the System

The particular issue calling for our further attention at this point concerns the position and significance given to Christianity in Hegel's philosophy of religion. It bids us to go into somewhat greater detail as to the contents of this system.

## The Triune God in the Three Forms of His Self-Revelation

The same moments in which absolute spirit mediates itself with itself also determine the concept of the triune God. Because of the fact that, as absolute spirit, God eternally differentiates himself and in this differentiation is eternally one with himself, God is essentially the triune God, and the objective reality that in this way supports the idea of the Trinity in Hegel's philosophy of religion belongs to the characteristics of this differentiation.

The three forms of the divine self-revelation are therefore as follows.[160] 1. The kingdom of the Father is the idea in and for itself, God in his eternity before and apart from the world, in the element of thinking. 2. The kingdom of the Son is where God is for representation, in the element of his presentation as such; it is the moment of separation as such. This second standpoint maintains what in the first standpoint was the other to God (although there it did not have this *determination* as the other), so the pure ideality of thinking is not preserved here. Although according to its initial determination God just begot a Son, here he thus brings forth nature. Here the other is nature; the distinction or difference therefore comes into its own; what is set apart is nature, the world as such; and the spirit relating itself to it is the natural spirit. 3. The

---

158. Ibid., 1:32.

159. See in particular Schelling's treatise *Philosophie und Religion* (1804), 34ff. [*Ed.*] See Schelling's *Sämmtliche Werke* (n. 89), 6:38–42.

160. [*Ed.*] The reference to the three "kingdoms" of the Father, Son, and Spirit is found only in the 1831 lectures (cf. *LPR* 3:54–55), but the substance of the treatment in 1831 is similar to that in 1827.

kingdom of the Spirit sustains the consciousness that human beings in themselves are reconciled with God; that there is reconciliation for humankind.

Differentiating and spelling out these three forms is not facilitated by directly transposing into them the idea of the [theological] Trinity. Each of the forms involves all three moments: the one; the other; and the other as sublated, as identical with the one. Therefore in all three forms there is both oneness and difference, albeit in a different way in each case. Furthermore, if we start out with the Christian idea of the Trinity—where the Father is not yet what the Son is, and the essential being still closed off within the Father first opens out in the Son—then one is easily tempted to place the Son higher than the Father, as this is obviously done in the systems of Boehme and Schelling.

## 1. The Kingdom of the Father

The Father, as the principle of real, natural being, is the antecedent one. Thus the beginning in fact occurs with the differentiation, with other-being, but without our rightly knowing the basis for this otherness. Moreover, when the real aspect is very strongly emphasized, as in the other systems mentioned, then this creates the appearance of a dualism that is at least not adequately countered.

In Hegel's system this apparent dualism is nipped in the bud, for everything belonging to Boehme's and Schelling's first principle Hegel regards as the other-being, the other to God, and there is no differentiation apart from the positing of this distinction. Yet Boehme and Schelling are justified in holding that the moment of separateness cannot be divorced from the concept of the Father precisely because, as Father, he begets and creates and that plays a part in this moment, just as on the other hand the Son, as Son, is likewise the unity of the differentiation as well as the distinction itself. That is why Hegel also expresses the relations of Father, Son, and Spirit by saying: the abstract God, the Father, is what is universal, is the eternal, encompassing, absolute differentiation; the other, the Son, is the appearing of the infinite separateness or particularity; the third, the Spirit, is the [infinite] singularity as such.[161]

Accordingly the distinction or difference occurs only between the Father and the Son; and since Father and Son are one [in the third moment], it is also [equivalent to] the first one. If these aforesaid forms are therefore to be specifically distinguished from one another, then doubtlessly we must hold firmly to the following points. The all-pervasive distinction within the divine life, which is determined as simply an internal distinction in the first form—such that the process is nothing but a play of

---

161. *Philosophie der Religion*, 2:197–98. [*Ed.*] Cf. *LPR* 3:194–95. This citation is found in the third section, "Trinity," of the first part of what in the 1832 *Werke* edition is called *The Absolute Religion*, namely, "God in His Eternal Idea in and for Himself; the Kingdom of the Father." The structure is from the 1831 lectures, but this particular passage is found in the 1824 lectures.

self-maintenance, a play of self-confirmation[162]—becomes external in the second form and thus disperses to its full extent.

The most well-defined expression of this point is in the following passage from Hegel's *Encyclopedia of the Philosophical Sciences.*

> In the moment of *particularity* (*Besonderheit*), of judgment or primal division (*Urteil*), this concrete eternal being is what is *presupposed.* [Baur: What is in the moment of universality, in the sphere of pure thinking, in this eternal sphere, just brings itself forth as its Son, and it remains in original identity with this differentiated aspect.] Its movement [is] the coming to be of *appearance,* the falling apart of the eternal moment of mediation, of the only Son, into an independent opposition: on the one hand is heaven and earth, elemental and concrete nature, and on the other hand, standing in *relationship* to it, is spirit, which therefore is *finite.* Finite Spirit, as the extreme of inherent negativity, makes itself independent and becomes evil; it is that extreme by its relation to a nature that stands over against it and by its own resulting naturalness. Yet, amid that naturalness, it is, when it thinks, directed toward the eternal, but for this reason stands in external relationship to it.[163]

Nevertheless in this sphere, even if it is correctly called the kingdom of the Son, the antithesis posited in the Son's independence must be regarded as a superseded antithesis, since the Son, although an other than the Father, is, as Son, still one with the Father. For in this sphere the Son enters into the world, and we of course state this in the sense of the faith when we speak of this entry by the Son.[164]

Of course the divine appears outwardly in the Son. However, the distinction becoming manifest in the sphere of the Son is nevertheless superseded in the Son, because the distinction, that of the Father from the Son, is inherently superseded in the eternal sphere of universality, and is mediated in an eternal way. Of course if, in the context of the second sphere, the distinction posited in it is also in turn considered as superseded, then the third sphere, the kingdom of the Spirit, can only differentiate itself from the second and first spheres by the fact that the distinction is superseded not merely for faith but also for knowledge, for thinking self-consciousness. We are to understand it solely in this sense when the Spirit is called singularity as such. Singularity as such is the Spirit in the community, the collectivity of the subjects or persons who are within God's Spirit. Boehme distinguishes the Holy Spirit from the Son in this

---

162. Ibid., 2:199 [*LPR* 3:195].

163. *Enzyklopädie der philosophischen Wissenschaften im Grundrisse,* 3rd ed. (Heidelberg, 1830), 577. [*Ed.*] Part 3, Philosophy of Spirit, §568. Translation from *G. W. F. Hegel: Theologian of the Spirit,* ed. Peter C. Hodgson (Minneapolis, 1997), 145. Baur does not preserve (as we do) the emphasis in Hegel's text. The moment of particularity stands between the moments of universality (*Allgemeinheit,* §567) and individuality or singularity (*Einzelheit,* §569).

164. *Philosophie der Religion,* 2:183 [cf. *LPR* 3:190–91].

same way. Each of the three forms therefore of course involves this same mediation, although the way it functions gets regarded from different standpoints.

When it comes to ancient Gnosis, we are reminded here of the relation between the Sophia above and the Sophia below. Although difference will indeed be evident in the Sophia above, she is still always in an identity with the Pleroma. And however independent the antithesis is in the Sophia below, she too is still once again the superseded antithesis. She is raised up once more into the Pleroma, and it is of course the totality of pneumatic ones in which, as identical with her, what spirit has ultimately become is united with the absolute. This is the very embodiment of what is provided in the following account as a principal thesis of Hegel's religious philosophy—that the antithesis can only be superseded for individuals by it being superseded in itself, just as, according to the teaching of the Gnostics, all that is below has its archetype in what is above.

## 2. The Kingdom of the Son

Accordingly it is in the sphere of the Son that the distinction, having become external and manifest, appears to its fullest extent.

### Finite Spirit, or Human Being and Nature, as the Revelation of God

The now-independent antithesis reaches its peak in the human being. Finite spirit, with nature as its sphere of operations, is the human being. That is why we have to spell out here what human nature is and what is the vocation or destination for human beings.[165]

The two quite opposite characterizations—that human beings are by nature good, and are in harmony with themselves; and that they are by nature evil—can be balanced out in the following way. A human being is by nature good because of inherently being spirit and rationality, and being created with, and according to, the image of God. Just as God is goodness, a human as spirit is therefore the reflection of God and so is goodness in itself. This thesis is the sole basis for the possibility of one's reconciliation. However this very thesis, that one is good simply in oneself, involves the defect that it is one-sided. A person is good only in an inward way, according to the concept of what one is, but for that very reason not good according to what one actually is. The other side of the matter is that one is supposed to be for oneself what one is in oneself. As spirit, one must come forth from the natural state and immediate condition, and must overcome the disconnect between one's concept and one's immediate existence. This is the concept of spirit, and the divided condition or estrangement directly posited along with it.

---

165. [Ed.] *Philosophie der Religion*, 2:209–27. Cf. *LPR* 3:198–211 (1824 lectures), 290–310 (1827 lectures).

Because human beings are spirit, if they exist only according to nature they are evil; their natural being is what is evil. The absolute demand is that a person not carry on as a natural being. Inasmuch as one is good, one is supposed to be good by exercising one's own will. Hence one must become aware of the fact that one is not as one ought to be; that in oneself one is instead evil. So one must overcome a twofold antithesis: on the one hand the antithesis of the evil as such, the fact that oneself is what is evil—thus one's antithesis or opposition to God; on the other hand the antithesis to the world. The first form of the antithesis is the infinite sorrow on one's own part; the remorse felt because, as a natural being, a person does not measure up to the infinite demand of the good, a demand one is conscious of and causing a cleavage in a person that can only be an infinite sorrow or suffering. The second form of the antithesis is in how the I or self conflicts with the world—the unhappiness because human beings are not content in the world, the woes of the world.

These two moments in which the antithesis within the subject is most greatly intensified involve the need for reconciliation. What satisfies this need is the consciousness that the negativity of the antithesis is dealt with, is annulled; the awareness that the truth is not this antithesis but is instead oneness in virtue of negating the antithesis. Therefore the antithesis must be superseded. But the very fact that it is implicitly superseded constitutes the condition, the presupposition, the possibility for the subject, the person, to also supersede it for himself. One cannot bring this about on one's own, because one's positing only has a content that is not merely subjective when the presupposition for its positing is the unity of subjectivity and objectivity, this divine unity, the spirit. The substantial factor, the underlying basis for the subject's positing, is the presupposition that the antithesis is not existent in itself. That this is truly the case we see in the eternal idea that God, as living spirit, is the distinguishing of himself from himself, is the positing of an other and in this other remaining identical with himself by having this identity with himself in this other.

Hegel also expresses this point in the following way. The antithesis, the evil, the natural condition of human existence and willing, the immediate factor, is the incompatibility, the finitude incompatible with the universality of God, with the eternal idea. This incompatibility resides in the spiritual condition, because spirit is what differentiates itself, and because of that the incompatibility cannot vanish. If it were to disappear, then the primal division of spirit, its vitality, would have disappeared; it would have ceased to be spirit. But notwithstanding this incompatibility, a further factor is the identity of the two—the fact that the other-being, the finitude, the weakness, the fragility, of human nature is said to pose no obstacle to that oneness, which is the substantial feature of the reconciliation. This substantial feature is also present in the divine idea, for the Son is an other to the Father, and this other-being is difference, else there would not be spirit. However the other is God; it has within itself the entire fullness of the divine nature. This characteristic of otherness poses no obstacle to this other one being the Son of God, and thus God; and other-being likewise presents no obstacle in human nature. This other-being is what is eternally self-positing and eternally self-superseding; and this self-positing and self-superseding of the other-being is love, is the spirit.

Abstractly characterized, evil is what is other, is finite, negative, and on the other side [of the antithesis] God is what is good, is true. However this other, this negative element, also contains within it what is affirmative. One must also be conscious of the fact that the otherness contains the principle of affirmation; that the principle of identity goes together with the other side. Likewise, as what is true, God is not only abstract identity with himself but is the other, the negation; he is what posits his own essential characteristic as other to himself, a characteristic proper to spirit.

It is therefore only on this assumption that the antithesis in itself is superseded; that the subject as such, in its being-for-self, can achieve the superseding of this antithesis, can attain peace and reconciliation. But how does this take place? As long as spirit relates itself to an other, it is finite spirit. But with finite spirit we at the same time have nature. Nature is the arena for finite spirit. In nature, as in spirit, there is the sphere of alienation, of unrest, although the process is one of superseding this alienation. Its supersession begins with human beings seeing nature as a revelation of God, as a world in which one comes to know God. Finite spirit's consciousness of God is mediated by nature. Through nature, humans see God. Nature is still just the shell and untrue configuration by which a human being ascends to God.

## *The History of Religion as an Integral Part of Hegel's Philosophy of Religion*

This is therefore also the place where, in Hegel's philosophy of religion, we see the history of religion playing an integral part in the context of his system.[166]

A human being rises up to God by way of nature; in other words, finite spirit ascends to itself in its truth, and this ascension is where religion emerges. It belongs to the essential nature of spirit that it differentiate itself, and in this self-differentiation to be one with itself. So too the concept of religion can only be realized in the process of the self-producing spirit. The concept divides into its moments: its distinctions, its determinations, which it contains within itself and by which it mediates itself with itself. The historical religions in which religion exists as finite are just moments of the concept. That is why they do not express the concept, why it is not actually present

---

166. [*Ed.*] At the end of the discussion of human nature, Hegel writes: "The concept of the preceding religions has refined itself into this antithesis; and the fact that the antithesis has disclosed and presented itself as an actually existing need is expressed by the words, 'When the fullness of time had come' [Gal 4:4]. This means: the Spirit is at hand, the need for the Spirit that points the way to reconciliation." *Philosophie der Religion*, 2:227; cf. *LPR* 3:309–10 (1827 lectures). This provides the occasion for Baur's insertion of a summary of Hegel's history of religion at this point. The 1832 *Werke* edition followed the lectures of 1824 in dividing Determinate Religion into two main parts: immediate religion or nature religion, and the religions of spiritual individuality. The other lectures (1821, 1827, and 1831) all made a triadic division of Determinate Religion, differently configured each time. See *LPR* 2:88–89. In 1824 the triad was completed by the Absolute or Consummate Religion.

in them. The highest level to be attained, the certainty of the concept itself, where the limitations are abolished and the religious consciousness is not separate from the concept itself, is the idea, the completely realized concept, the absolute religion. The working of spirit has then set aside what is finite, for finite religion is in vain, and its emptiness has become evident to spirit's consciousness, to the free and therefore infinite spirit.[167]

Hence the three parts of Hegel's Philosophy of Religion are: 1. The Concept of Religion; 2. Determinate Religion; 3. The Absolute Religion. Determinate Religion is divided into two main forms, Nature Religion, and The Religions of Spiritual Individuality.

Nature religion is immediate religion, with the spiritual and the natural spheres as one, so that on the objective side God is posited [as this unity] and consciousness is caught up in natural determinacy. So in nature religion the spirit is still identical with nature, and to that extent it is the religion of bondage (*Unfreiheit*). The various forms of nature religion can essentially be reduced to three. 1. The Religion of Magic, which can be subdivided into the Religion of Magical Power, and the Religion of Being-Within-Self. 2. The Religion of Phantasy (Hinduism). 3. Nature Religion in Transition to a Higher Level, namely: a. The Religion of the Good or of Light (Persian Religion); b. The Religion of the Enigma (Egyptian Religion).

The second main form comprises The Religions of Spiritual Individuality. The subject's spiritual being-for-self begins at this stage; the idea is what is dominant and determinative. For the subject, naturalness simply becomes one's natural life, one's bodily being; in other words, it is what is utterly determined by the subject. At this stage once again, three forms come to the fore: 1. The Religion of Sublimity (Jewish Religion) is the reflection within self as the negation of oneness with nature, since it emphasizes spiritual being-for-self. It posits spiritual oneness within itself, like unto God and over against the natural sphere as something nonessential. 2. The Religion of Beauty (Greek Religion) unites what is natural and what is spiritual in such a way that the spiritual dimension is what is determinative in its unity with the bodily dimension, its instrument and expression in which it presents itself. It is the religion of the

---

167. "The labor of spirit over thousands of years has been working toward the concept of religion. This process set out from what is immediate and natural, and those features had to be overcome." *Philosophie der Religion*, 1:184 [*LPR* 2:514 n. 3 (1831 lectures)]. Hegel speaks in this same sense in the *Phänomenologie des Geistes* (1807), p. 24 of the Preface: "even the world-spirit itself has had the patience to pass through these forms in the lengthy process of time, and to undertake the enormous labor of world history, in which it bodied forth in each form the entire content of itself, as each is capable of presenting itself, and there is no less laborious way by which it could attain consciousness of itself." [Translation from *Hegel: Theologian of the Spirit* (n. 163), 99 (¶ 29 in the A. V. Miller translation of the *Phenomenology of Spirit* [Oxford, 1977]).] Compare with this [in the main text] the surprisingly similar passage from the *Pseudo-Clementine Homilies*, according to which the spirit of Adam or of Christ, that is, the divine spirit of humankind, "has changed his forms and his names from the beginning of the world, and so reappeared again and again in the world, until coming upon his own times, and being anointed with mercy for the works of God, he shall enjoy rest forever" (*Homilies* 3.20 [*ANF* 8:242]).

divine's appearing, of the divine's bodily, material, and natural manifestation. 3. The Religion of Expediency (Roman Religion) is the one in which the universal powers of nature, or even the gods of the Religion of Beauty, serve a purpose. The individual spirit in the gods just wills itself, its own subjective, finite purpose. This is the religion of external purposiveness, the Roman Religion, or in fact the Roman Empire.

## The Revelation of God in Finite Spirit: God's Incarnation

This second main stage of religious development, the religion of spiritual individuality, of course shows that revelation through nature and the world is only one mode of lifting human beings up to God. The other mode, the higher one, is through the finite spirit. Religion progresses by raising consciousness above nature; it is the advance from natural existence to spiritual individuality, to spirit's knowing its own truth.[168]

However, the highest stage in which God reveals himself within finite spirit is when the deity becomes known to finite human beings in an objective way, perceived and experienced by immediate consciousness. This is God's appearing in the flesh. God should be known as being for another, as present to human beings, and here "human being" refers to this singular human being [in whom God appears in the flesh]. Reconciliation is a present possibility only when the inherently existing oneness of the divine nature with human nature becomes known. Human beings can know themselves to be received into God only when God is not something alien to them; only when they are not merely something peripheral to God's nature but instead are received into God in light of their essential nature and freedom—received as subjects within God. This inherently existing oneness of the divine nature with human nature must be revealed in an objective way. This occurs via God's incarnation. God becomes a human being so that the finite spirit would have the consciousness of God's presence in the finite sphere itself. If there is to be a revelation to human beings of the nature of spirit, of the nature of God or of God as spirit, then God must appear as spirit in the form of immediacy, as perceptibly present.

But God's perceptible presence can have no other form than that of a human being. For in the perceptible, worldly domain the human being alone is what is spiritual. Therefore if what is spiritual is to be present in a perceptible form it must be present in human form. The oneness of the divine nature and human nature—human being in its universality; the truth that there is simply one reason, one spirit, that, as finite has no authentic existence of its own—is the thought of the human being from the standpoint of speculative thinking. But in the present case, from our standpoint, we are dealing not with the thought of the human as such. Instead we are dealing with perceptible certainty, with the fact that human beings would become assured that the divine nature and human nature are one; that for them it would take the form of

---

168. [Ed.] For what follows, see *Philosophie der Religion*, 2:228–56; cf. *LPR* 3:211–22 (1824), 310–28 (1827).

direct, sensible perception, of external existence. That is because human beings regard as certain only what one directly perceives internally or externally. Therefore if human beings are to be certain of that oneness, God had to appear to the world in the flesh.

Hence this is where the appearing of Christ as an event in world history finds its place in the philosophy of religion. We can consider this historical phenomenon in two different ways: directly and externally, as unbelievers too can deal with this account; or with faith and in the spirit. In the direct way of looking it, Christ is straightforwardly a human being, albeit simply one who embodied the truth in his life and died as a martyr for the truth. For the unbeliever, the external narrative about Christ is the same kind of thing as the story of Socrates is for us. But Christ's death commences the shift in consciousness, for it is the center about which consciousness revolves. Comprehending it involves distinguishing external understanding from faith, for faith considers it with the spirit. Faith is truth from the spirit, from the Holy Spirit. When they are compared in an external way, Christ is a human being like Socrates. But Christ thought of as having the divine nature revealed in him is a higher way of regarding him, for faith is essentially the consciousness of the absolute truth, of what God is in and for himself. But in and for himself God is this living movement, the Trinity, in which what is universal stands over against itself and, in doing so, is identical with itself. In this element of eternity, God is his coming together with himself, this closing or connecting with himself. Faith just takes hold, and is conscious, of the fact that in Christ we behold the course of this truth, which is existent in and for itself; and that this truth was first revealed through him.

The death of Christ is the touchstone by which faith stands the test. Christ's death has sidetracked the human circumstances of Christ, for what matters is understanding this death, in the sense that Christ was God incarnate. However his death, taken by itself, is the greatest proof of absolute finitude, for the negation itself is in God, although God preserves himself in this process. The process is the death of death, the negation of the negation. God is resurrected; God slays death in coming forth from it, and in his doing so finitude, his humanness and humiliation, is posited as something foreign to the one who is utterly God. This shows that finitude derives from what is other, from the human side that stands over against the divine process. This finitude—which at its most extreme point, in its being-for-self as opposed to God, is what is evil—Christ has taken upon himself in order to slay it by his death. Thus for those truly conscious of the spirit, the finitude of the human side has been slain in the death of Christ. In this way this death of what is natural has the universal significance of negating the finite, what is evil as such. Thus the world has been reconciled, for through this death what is its inherent evil has been taken from it. In truly understanding this death the subject feels its own estrangement, which Christ has taken upon himself by assuming human nature, but has negated by his death.

This marks the initial formation of the community. The [Holy] Spirit revealed that what were merely human relationships change into one that is transformed on the basis of the Spirit, for the divine nature pours itself into this relationship. The death is the passage or return to original glory, commencing with the narrative of Christ's resurrection, and his ascension to the right hand of God where the account becomes understood spiritually. This entire narrative gives people certitude about their idea of God, the assurance that the human being is directly present to God. The account indeed does so by how it understands spirit, by the very way it portrays the process in which what the human being is, is spirit. In itself God and death—this mediation whereby the human element is stripped away while on the other hand what is existent in itself returns to itself and only so is it spirit. The knowledge that God is triune takes shape from this understanding, and the [biblical] story is important because it is itself the story of God: sensible certainty passing over into spiritual consciousness.

## 3. The Kingdom of the Spirit, or, the Idea in the Element of the Community

This is the point connecting the second form to the third form where the idea exists in the element of the community, or in the kingdom of the Spirit. Passage from the sensible form into a spiritual element takes place in the community, the congregation.[169]

The individual, empirical subjects who have their being within God's spirit make up the community, as contrasted with the subject or person to whom the spirit has revealed what gives people assurance of reconciliation. For those people the divine account is an objective narrative. But they should also follow the course of this narrative with regard to themselves. The founding of the community begins with the establishing of faith, in other words the outpouring of the Spirit. The human being, the perceptible human phenomenon [i.e., Christ] who is the object of faith, is apprehended spiritually. After Christ is divested of his flesh the Spirit comes to the fore. Knowing God as triune, the consciousness of the divine and the human as identical, is God as Spirit, and this Spirit, as existing, is the community. Here we are not dealing with belief in the external, temporal narrative, which belief envisages in a sensible mode. Instead the sensible content gets transformed into a wholly different, spiritual, divine mode, and this content is posited in the element of consciousness, of inwardness, as a self-conscious knowing of it.

But the content of the belief should also be verified. Since the content itself is no longer perceptible, the verification also cannot be of the sensible kind. The sensible narrative is just faith's point of departure, for what matters is faith's returning into itself, its spiritual consciousness. This sheds light on the fact that the community itself produces this content of faith. The truly Christian content of faith is justified by philosophy, not by the historical narrative (*Geschichte*). What spirit does is no history (*Historie*); spirit only has to do with what is in and for itself; not with the past,

---

169. [Ed.] For the following, see *Philosophie der Religion*, 2:257–88; cf. *LPR* 3:223–47 (1824), 328–47 (1827). On the referents behind Hegel's abstract description of stages in the realization of the community, see *LPR* 3:34–35, 46–47.

but instead with what is purely and simply present. Hence the community begins with the fact that the truth is at hand, is known, and this truth is what God is—that God is the triune one, is life within himself, this process of his, this manifestation, in objectifying himself and being identical with himself in this objectification. God is eternal love, this objectification in its consummate development to the extremes of God's universality and of finitude; to the point of death and this return into himself in annulling the harshness of the antithesis. God is love by directly suffering, which is likewise salvific suffering.

However, with faith changing the sensible content into spiritual content, faith also gives this content a relation to the subject. Because reconciliation is accomplished in itself, in the divine idea, since the idea then has also appeared and human beings are thus assured of the truth, the subject is said to be a child of God, that is, to enter into this conscious unity, to bring it about within oneself, to become filled with the divine spirit, to place oneself within this oneness. The subject is only able to do this through faith, which is to say that reconciliation is accomplished in and for itself, and assuredly so, only by means of faith. The difficulty in this, however, is that the subject is not the same one as the absolute spirit. But the fact that God sees into a person's heart and knows his substantial will, his innermost, all-embracing subjectivity, what he inwardly, truly, and earnestly wills, is what removes this difficulty. Apart from this internal willing there is a person's externality, one's deficiency, although this externality, or otherness as such, one's finitude or imperfection, is relegated to being nonessential and is known as such. For in the idea the Son's other-being is a transitory, vanishing moment and nothing true, essential, enduring, or absolute. The evil human beings do is at the same time present as something in itself empty and under the power of spirit, such that spirit has the power to undo it. Faith itself is the divine spirit at work in the subject; it is the person's spirit acting in faith to counter his naturalness, to dispose of it, to dispel it.[170]

This is the concept of the community as such, the idea inasmuch as it is the process of the person in whom God's spirit dwells. The concept of the community realizes itself in the church as the concrete, enduring community in which the truth becomes the teaching of the church, and the supreme task is to bring persons to the truth. In the sacrament of baptism the church expresses the fact that by baptism one is born into a fellowship in which God is reconciled in himself, and in the sacrament of holy communion one gains, in a sensible, visible way, the awareness that one is reconciled with God.

But the spirit also realizes itself in the wider state of affairs, in the concretely subsisting community. At the same time this involves the transforming or reshaping of the community. Spiritual religion exists, first and foremost, in the heart and soul of the community, in its spirit. As self-contained and undeveloped, this heart and soul is feeling or sentiment. But the community also exists in the world, and that involves its

---

170. See *Philosophie der Religion*, 1:156 [cf. *LPR* 1:337].

being something set apart and distinct, such that the divine, objective idea confronts consciousness as something other to it, so the content of the idea, as the presence of feeling and sentiment, ought to develop and expand. Thus the community, as the kingdom of God, stands over against what is, after all, an objective factor. As the external, immediate world, this objective factor is, first of all, the heart with its interests. Another objective factor is that of reflection, of abstract thinking, of understanding. A third objective factor is that of the concept.

The heart finds reconciliation in religion by itself, although that then involves this reconciliation really taking place in one's life in the world. In this first external, objective factor, the first form of reconciliation is the unmediated one in which spirituality renounces worldliness and takes a negative stance toward the world. The community keeps to itself the state of being reconciled with God, by withdrawing from worldliness in monastic fashion. The second form is an accommodation to worldliness, where a worldliness devoid of spirit emerges as the dominant principle with regard to the church. [The third form,] authentic reconciliation whereby the divine realizes itself in the domain of actuality, consists of ethical and lawful life in the state, and this is the genuine form of disciplined worldliness.

The second external, objective factor, one that now also emphasizes the ideal element for its own sake, is the objectivity of reflection. In spirit's being reconciled with itself, the internal aspect knows itself as existing with itself, and this knowing is thinking. Put in wholly general terms, it is the freedom of reason that turns against what is merely spiritual externality, that is, spiritual bondage. When it first appears this abstract thinking seizes upon the concrete contents of the church's thinking by applying its own principle of identity. It holds that, if everything concrete is expunged from the concept of God, then that can be expressed by the thesis that "we cannot know God." At the same time, and from the same standpoint of subjectivity, it declares that "human being is by nature good." God's objectivity is negated, and with that all other objective characteristics vanish, so that God is absolutely one as in the Muslim religion. The antithetical position is that in Christ spirituality is concretely developed, and is known as trinitarian, that is, as spirit. So there are two extremes [of reflective thinking] in the further development of the community. One is spirit's thralldom, its bondage in the absolute region[171] of freedom; the other is abstract subjectivity, is subjective freedom devoid of content.

The third external, objective factor is that subjectivity develops the content from itself, but in accord with necessity. This is the standpoint of philosophy. The content takes refuge in the concept (*in den Begriff sich flüchtet*) and obtains its justification by thinking. This thinking is essentially concrete and not merely an abstraction and defining, according to the law of identity. The concept produces the truth, but at the same time the content is not something produced, but is recognized as truth existent

---

171. [*Ed.*] Baur writes *Religion*, but Hegel's text reads *Region*. Cf. *Philosophie der Religion*, 2:285 (*LPR* 3:344). Hegel is speaking here about tendencies in the Enlightenment.

in and for itself. So the objective standpoint is the justification of religion. Religion gains its justification from thinking consciousness in the philosophy that shows religion's rationality. Philosophy is theology inasmuch as it presents God's reconciliation with himself and with nature, by showing that nature, other-being, is implicitly divine; and by showing that finite spirit in part is in itself this raising of itself to reconciliation, and in part arrives at this reconciliation in world history.

## The Main Factors in Assessing the System

This is not the place for a comprehensive evaluation of Hegel's philosophy of religion, which in any event certainly cannot be divorced from his system as a whole. For our purposes it suffices to indicate briefly its general features that are most closely connected with the course of our investigation up to this point.

### 1. The Idea of the Process, the Views of Its Opponents, and Their Assessment

The first thing to note about the character of this philosophy of religion, or religious philosophy, is that in its main features it is demonstrably related to ancient Gnosis. So it is of course to be anticipated that, on the whole, we will encounter once again in this case the same objections that have been raised against this Gnosis, although in a different form.

The main point of contention concerns the general assumption from which this philosophy of religion sets out. It is that without an inner movement that is inherently part of his own essential being, God cannot be thought of as spirit, as thinking activity, as actually a living God. In other words, this is the idea of the process by which God, as absolute spirit, mediates himself with himself, becomes revealed to himself. The opponent maintains that this dialectical process on the part of the idea, this eternal self-estrangement and concurrent eternal sublation of it, this infinite process of God's becoming the world and God's incarnation, does away with the very idea of God. For just as the concept of the ground entails the further stipulation that self-manifestation and being actual is simply the consequence of the ground, the concept of such a God therefore involves his self-revelation, if one still wants to call this "revelation." It if be God's nature that he must reveal himself, and he is of necessity determined to do so, then God would be subject to fate; and in the necessary dialectical process into which everything is dragged, the whole thing would be mechanical.

The opponent says it would contradict the idea of God if he were to be the living God, the absolute spirit, only because of the movement through which he resolves on becoming finite, and finally turns back into himself through the I; in other words, only for spirit would God be spirit, be truly God. Leaving aside the fact that here God could be thought of as entirely like a human being—one who begins from a brutish and imperfect condition and only via a temporal life, and undergoing many changing circumstances and metamorphoses finally, with the help of another, that is, of finite spirit, reaches the higher stage of consciousness and fulfills his destiny—this view also precludes, and makes impossible, the thought of a personal God as creator, as well as the idea of a moral world order.

Furthermore, if God be spirit only for spirit, and only be a living God in his necessary manifestation in nature and finite spirit, then before the creation of the world he would have been neither spirit nor living. Therefore the ground of creation would in no way reside in a personal being. Instead it would reside in a chaotic darkness, in an obscure and blindly operating primal ground that would not yet be God, although, given time and under favorable circumstances, it could become God. The critic would add that, if the true God be simply the one turning back to himself from his self-divestment in finitude, then at no time would he be the true God. The divine consciousness would be a fragmentary aggregation ranging from the dimwittedness of animals all the way up to speculative thinking—all operating together. Since this entire creation, the divine being's self-divestment in nature and finite spirit, carries on eternally through the dialectical process, God never even attains fully infinite consciousness of himself. That would have been the case only if consciousness had illuminated all of this for itself as philosophical consciousness.[172]

There is no denying the fact that a doctrine of God as described in the foregoing criticism would not have been a very worthy idea of God, whether or not this is an accurate understanding of Hegel's doctrine. If this is the idea of the personal God that is counter-posed to Hegel's idea of God, then it must at once be conceded that nothing capricious and contingent can be in God as what is absolute, for instead what is free is also at the same time what is necessary; but what is necessary is none other than what is rational. As the activity of thinking, the positing of thinking, what reason, because it is absolute necessity, fittingly posits is not the necessity of fate but just the necessity of reason. This necessity is none other than the essential being of spirit itself. The dualism still so predominant and preponderant in Schelling's system, and somewhat pretentiously supporting the reproach of fatalism, can only be completely deflected by a system holding firmly to the idea of absolute spirit as the one supreme principle. Hence in and for itself that process, through which God first becomes a living God, does not do away with the idea of the personal God, as long as the process is just

---

172. See Immanuel Hermann Fichte, *Religion und Philosophie in ihrem Verhältniss* (Heidelberg, 1834), 5ff; Karl Friedrich Bachmann, *Über Hegels System und die Nothwendigkeit einer nochmaligen Umgestaltung der Philosophie* (Leipzig, 1833), 288ff. Bachmann (p. 289) even recalls the process of God's generation and the fermentation process within the chaotic aggregation of divine powers, about which Schelling, the poet of the philosophy of nature, has sung. [*Ed.*] In addition, C. H. Weisse and F. A. Staudenmaier published reviews critical of Hegel's "pantheism" and christology in 1833 and 1834. They are indicated by Walter Jaeschke in his edition of Hegel's *Vorlesungen* (n. 141), 3:xliii (ET 1:24), and mentioned by Volker Drecoll in his chapter on "Ferdinand Christian Baur's View of Christian Gnosis," in *Ferdinand Christian Baur and the History of Early Christianity*, ed. Martin Bauspiess, Christof Landmesser, and David Lincicum; trans. R. F. Brown and P. C. Hodgson (Oxford, 2017), 139 n. 31 (cf. 139–44).

thought of as one taking place according to the principle of absolute reason and necessity conditioned by the nature of thinking itself. And how was such a process, in and for itself, said to conflict with the idea of God, since the idea of the Trinity—however else it may be designated and with the only proviso that it not be dissipated into a merely subjective abstraction lacking any objective content—is not essentially different from the eternal process of God's mediation with himself?

Therefore what could have been justly held against Hegel was only that he carried the mode of thinking in human reason over to the absolute being of God. But if we do not want to allow this directly stated identity of divine and human reason, of divine and human spirit, with absolute reason, then every concrete concept of God falls by the wayside and we are once again returned from Hegel's standpoint of objectivity to the standpoint of subjectivity where God is a mere abstraction. This very standpoint of objectivity entails that finite consciousness can only be regarded as a moment of absolute spirit determining itself in what is finite. However, the opponents falsely conclude from this that God arrives at consciousness of himself solely in the finite consciousness of human beings. It is false because it is always simply the consciousness that, as finite, is lifted up or sublated, in which a human being knows of God or God knows himself in the human being; in other words it is God's self-consciousness as concrete consciousness, a divine-human self-consciousness, that of God incarnate.

But suppose one were to draw the further conclusion that, just because God's self-consciousness is a divine-human self-consciousness, it only develops itself gradually in time. Or what amounts to the same thing, that the God who, in returning to himself from his self-divestment in nature and finite spirit, and by sublating, in religion and philosophy, the finite element, would at no time be the true God. That of course appeals to the system's own being-within-one-another (*Ineinandersein*) of the infinite and the finite. Yet here again we encounter the same one-sided way of looking at it that just clings to the element of finitude. The spirit going forth into finitude—which in each finite form finds itself in contradiction with itself and, by the steady advance of this process overcomes this negativity and turns back within itself—is at the same time the eternal spirit identical with itself. Any instance of spirit's being-for-self necessarily presupposes spirit's being-in-self. Just as it is said on the one hand about God, that God cannot be God without the world, it is said on the other hand about the world, that "for the world, to be means to have only an instant of being."[173]

This being-within-one-another on the part of God and world, of spirit and nature, of the infinite and the finite, is certainly the characteristic feature of Hegel's system. From the standpoint of the idea of the absolute spirit, nature and finite spirit can only be conceived of as the necessary moments of spirit mediating itself with itself and, in this mediation, being identical with itself. Hence just as revealing himself, or as spirit being for spirit, belongs to the nature of God, so too it is only in finite spirit that absolute spirit determines itself as self-conscious spirit. It is in the nature

173. *Philosophie der Religion*, 2:207 [cf. *LPR* 3:293 incl. n. 124].

of consciousness that only at the boundary of the infinite and the finite can it branch out into the distinction of the subject from the object, the knower from the known, the perceiver from being. Without this distinguishing there is no consciousness at all. Therefore we either have utterly no concept of the divine consciousness, or else only the kind of concept that includes provision for what is finite. But the latter in no way detracts from the concept of God in itself.

If we say, as people so often do, that only a living, personal God who is distinct from the world can love and be loved—and therefore any doctrine that would do away with God's personal being, his eternal self-consciousness in which he knows himself as distinct from the world, his creation, would be caught up in an irreconcilable conflict with Christianity—then it is entirely a matter of distinguishing emotional (*pathologisch*[174]) concerns from speculative concerns, and of correlatively distinguishing the popular idea of God from the scientific form for presenting it. Anthropopathic and anthropomorphic concerns all too easily get intertwined with the way people so often place such great emphasis on the personhood of God. If God is absolute spirit, is absolute reason, then love would not have been an absolute attribute if God, as absolute spirit and absolute reason, were not also absolute love, absolute goodness and wisdom. Therefore people fear that, if the usual concept of God's personhood is dismissed, God's love will fall by the wayside too, and then the underlying assumption always is that God would not be thought of as spirit. However, if God is genuinely thought of as spirit, then either God as spirit is also directly what is personal, or else it is not evident what more needs to be added to the concept of God as absolute by the concept of the personal, unless it is that the personal God is the incarnate one, the God revealing himself in Christ.

When it comes to God's consciousness as such, of course his incarnate consciousness can only be one developing itself in successive moments of time. But since neither is God without the world, nor is the world without God, what is the justification for assuming that God's self-developing self-consciousness is just limited to the sphere of human history? What is the justification for assuming that an endless series of other phases of the world's development has not preceded the one known to us? In other words, how can we rule out here the possibility that some other kinds of beings were ones in which absolute spirit manifested itself as finite spirit? So how is that harshly maligned, and so often misconstrued, thesis that, as spirit, God would just be for spirit, anything other than the irrefutable statement that God beholds himself in all spirits; that the totality of finite spirits is the self-conscious reflection of divine being opening itself up, and mirroring itself, in them?[175] That in this sense "God is all

---

174. [*Ed.*] Baur uses this term not in a medical sense, referring to disease or dysfunction, but in a philosophical sense referring to emotions or sympathetic feelings.

175. [*Ed.*] Perhaps Baur has in mind here the conclusion of Hegel's *Phenomenology of Spirit*, where the lines of Schiller are quoted, "The chalice of this realm of spirits / Foams forth to God his own infinitude." From what we know about evolution today, there are certainly "other kinds of beings . . . in which absolute spirit manifested itself as finite spirit." Cosmology tells us that there are likely other

in all"? This alone is the true concept of God's immanence in the world. However, if one wants to call this position the logical pantheism of Hegel's system, at least what matters is not merely this term for it. Instead we simply have a different, and more satisfying, equilibrium between the interests of speculation and those of the Christian religion—one equally entitled to assert itself here.[176]

---

worlds in which this manifestation has occurred or is occurring. And the history of religions tells us that the "totality of finite spirits" includes many religions and cultures.

176. In similar fashion in the ancient church, Origen located God's consciousness in God's immanence in the world. Origen writes: "What is altogether without any beginning cannot be comprehended at all. However far the understanding may extend, the faculty of comprehension ceases to operate where there is no beginning" (*On First Principles*, 3.5.2 [ANF 4:341]). He also states, in his *Commentary on Matthew*: "It is not possible to comprehend in cognitive terms what is infinite in its nature. In virtue of its own nature, all cognition is of what is finite." Therefore God's power is conditioned by God's knowledge. Since God cannot be without the world, the world is of course as eternal as God. But God is always simply the creator of an infinite series of finite worlds that come to be and pass away. – Two especially energetic opponents of the allegedly blameworthy pantheism of Hegel's system are the two Catholic philosophers, Anton Günther and Johann Heinrich Pabst. See Günther, *Vorschule zur speculativen Theologie des positive Christenthums* (Vienna, 1828); Günther and Pabst, *Janusköpfen für Philosophie und Theologie* (Vienna, 1834). But the latest theory of creation, which wants to install itself as a barrier warding off this so-called pantheism, has for good reasons drawn the opposing rebuke that it rests on a dualism that sets out to establish, as an abstraction in its own right, the antitheses between God and world, spirit and nature, absolute spirit and finite spirit. See, in particular, the review of the *Vorschule* volume by Karl Rosenkranz, *Berliner Jahrbücher für wissenschaftliche Kritik* (August 1831), no. 35, pp. 284ff. and 291ff. See also the assessment of the *Janusköpfen* volume in the *Literarischer Anzeiger für christliche Theologie und Wissenschaft überhaupt* (1834), nos. 10–11, pp. 93ff. What this new creation theory affirms is in principle none other than the Pelagianism forever endemic to the Catholic Church and now applied in particular to the doctrine of creation—for time was when it was characteristic of this church that, in philosophy and theology, its real interests were those of Pelagianism. In contrast to this position, resting on overestimating the independence of what is human and creaturely, the view of philosophy in the usual sense may well be to consider Hegel's system, in which philosophy is at the same time theology, from the perspective of a preeminently theological system. – In more recent times the opposition to Hegel's system has chiefly focused on the doctrine of immortality, and certainly it must be a touchstone for establishing the truth of this system. I am very dubious as to whether the well-known treatise by Carl Friedrich Göschel in the *Berliner Jahrbücher für wissenschaftliche Kritik* (1834), nos. 1–3 and 17–19 [published as a book in 1835], which is intended to settle the matter, is as reassuring as people think it is. Logically the whole debate hinges on one thesis: just as absolute spirit eternally individualizes itself, so too there are eternal individuals. Yet I fail to see that individuals continuing to exist eternally as real subjects follows logically—and that alone is the element at issue in the sense of Göschel's treatise. But on the other side too, Immanuel Hermann Fichte makes no headway in his book, *Die Idee der Persönlichkeit und der individuellen Fortdauer* (Elberfeld, 1834). His investigation seeks to secure a broad basis by discussing monads, primordial arrangements, and other related factors. But he only knows how to apply to the main point what alone matters, the fact that the genuine fabric of the life of the self-revealing God is the infinite, ideal power of the world, in which a human being must accustom himself to all the forces subordinate to himself, in order to enjoy eternal life in this sense (pp. 169ff.). Yet this way of putting it makes it clear that he is abandoning the concept of immortality as an inherent feature of a human being as a person. Therefore if philosophy on the whole goes no further than this, then Hegel's philosophy too is not subject to the special rebuke that it does not know how to provide a convincing proof for immortality in the usual sense. – Even Schleiermacher's proposition §158 of *Der christliche Glaube* ("Belief in the immutability of the union of the divine essence with human nature in the person of Christ contains in itself also the belief in the persistence of human personality" [ET 1928,

Part Four: Ancient Gnosis and More Recent Religious Philosophy

*2. The Relation of Hegel's Philosophy of Religion to Historical Christianity. The Three Moments of Hegel's Christology; the Separation of the Historical Christ from the Ideal Christ; the Historical Christ*

Another major point calling for our attention here is the relation of Hegel's philosophy of religion to historical Christianity. Initially we may not have indicated how intimately this philosophy of religion is tied to Christianity, how earnestly it takes unto itself the entire contents of Christianity. Indeed it wants its entire task to be none other than the scientific exposition of Christianity as it is historically given.

For this philosophy of religion, Christianity is the world-historical turning point in which spirit, conceived of in its own development, first elevated itself to a clear consciousness of its own absolute nature, and decisively began to turn back from its self-divestment and to itself. Thus by apprehending the historical significance of Christianity it fully concurs with ancient Gnosis. This is also the reason why, as philosophy of religion, it largely adopts the same stance toward historical Christianity as ancient Gnosis did. Its doctrine of God is none other than the purely scientific understanding of absolute spirit and the carrying-out of its implications. So too its christology essentially differs only in form from that of ancient Gnosis. Those elements and tendencies already present in ancient Gnosis, but which could not yet be worked out in a pure form there, have now been elevated to their true concept. Succinctly put, what we therefore have here is the same separation of the historical Christ from the ideal Christ that ensued from Gnosis as the necessary result of its speculative understanding of Christianity, now emerging to its fullest extent in Hegel's philosophy of religion.

The doctrine of Christ's person indeed seems to directly provide the most obvious proof of how seriously intended is the effort of this philosophy of religion to take into itself the complete contents of the Christian faith and not leave out anything of

---

698; 2016, 967]) hardly provides a satisfactory guarantee. When he declares at the same time that "we must not continue to assert that this belief [in the survival of personality] and the God-consciousness are bound up together" [ET 1928, 700; 2016, 970], then there is no longer any basis for this belief even with regard to the person of Christ himself. Then why should "the immutability of the union of the divine essence with human nature in the person of Christ" be thought of as a personal continuation, inasmuch as the distinctive prerogative of the redeemer resides only in the distinctiveness of his God-consciousness? His God-consciousness in itself is not internally connected with belief in continuing personal existence. That belief in the immutability of the union of the divine essence with human nature in the person of Christ is therefore the belief that the consciousness that, through Christ, has become a being or presence of God within human nature, will always remain the consciousness of humankind—which is quite the same as Hegel's thesis that God's consciousness is always a divine-human consciousness; and that is also why the community of subjects existing in the spirit of God is forever an ongoing community. – On this matter philosophy is hardly able to elevate belief to its being knowledge. Nor does philosophy accede to belief in continuing personal existence. That is why philosophy simply is not based on sensuous concerns, is hostile to them; and only where someone wants to regard that inability as a disproof of the truth of philosophy's contents, must philosophy steadfastly hold that the recognition of absolute truth as such can never be made dependent on personal interest, and therefore not even on concern for continuing personal existence.

deep significance. Here we are not merely talking about some vaguely distant idea of humankind as well-pleasing to God; or of an archetypal relationship simply raising the human to the divine; or of a God-consciousness having become a being or presence of God. Instead it is that Christ is the incarnate one, is God become a human being, appearing in the flesh; it is that the unity, existent in itself, of the divine and human natures, had been revealed to people in objective fashion in a specific, individual subject. This is what is maintained here with the full weight given to it by the church. The greater the reality and objectivity of the idea of God in this philosophy of religion, the less it also seems that the full reality of its God-man may be subject to doubt.

But it is self-evident that everything depends on the sense in which Christ is God incarnate. A closer look at this doctrine of Christ lets us distinguish its three moments. The way of looking at it that is purely external, is merely historical, just sees in Christ an ordinary man, a martyr to the truth, like Socrates.[177] What follows from this *first moment*, where the person of Christ is still a figure for unbelievers, is the *second moment*, that of faith, where Christ appears no longer as an ordinary human being but instead as the God-man; as the one in whom the divine nature is revealed, in whom the divine is beheld. The question is: what mediates between the first moment and the second moment, the transition from unbelief to belief or faith? In asking it, we recall that faith arises from the outpouring of the Spirit, in which concern for what is immediate had become transformed into a spiritual destiny, what is sensible had become understood spiritually, and the man Jesus, as a human, perceptible phenomenon, had become linked to the consciousness of a spiritual content.

Therefore it is Jesus' death that brings about this crossover to a religious status. For Christ is God incarnate just because he has overcome death, has slain death, has negated the negation, and in doing so has negated the finite element, the evil, as something alien to him. Thus he has reconciled the world with God. What matters above

---

177. [*Ed.*] Baur's one-sentence summary of the first moment reflects the inadequacies of the 1832 edition of Hegel's lectures. This edition virtually ignores Hegel's lecture manuscript of 1821, where the teaching of Jesus is discussed in considerable detail, and statements are made that moderate the sharp distinction between history and faith. Here we are told that the words of Jesus confirm "the truth of the idea"; they confirm the truth of what he becomes for faith. The life of this teacher is "in conformity with" his teaching and "strictly adequate to" the idea of divine-human unity. The content of his life is simply the kingdom of God that he proclaims. By living it he brings it to life as a spiritual community. The kingdom enters into actuality through this individual, whose teaching of it constitutes his divinity. "Since it is the divine idea that courses through this history, it occurs not as the history of a single individual alone, but rather it is implicitly the history of actual humanity as it constitutes itself as the existence of spirit." See *LPR* 3:117–22, 145. None of this material is found in the 1832 edition. The 1827 lectures, which establish the distinction between "nonreligious" and "religious" perspectives on Christ, nonetheless seem to emphasize their congruence. The speech and activity of Jesus is that of a human being, yet it is at the same time "essentially the work of God—not as something suprahuman that appears in the shape of an external revelation, but rather as working in a human being, so that the divine presence is essentially identical with this human being" (*LPR* 3:320, a passage not found in the 1832 edition). All this can be said, according to Hegel, from the perspective of the first moment. Only faith can affirm that *God* is present in Christ, but history serves as a foundation (or "point of departure").

all in understanding this death is that it is the touchstone by which faith must stand the test. Hence the Spirit could not have come before Christ cast off the flesh, but only afterward, after he was no longer perceptibly and immediately present. In short, Christ is God incarnate only as mediated by faith. But what lies behind faith—and is the presupposition for the merely external, historical consideration [of Christ] having become faith [in him]—remains veiled in a mystery impenetrable for us.[178] The issue is not whether Christ in himself, as he appeared objectively in history, was God incarnate. Instead what matters is only that he had become God incarnate for faith.

Once faith is established, the object of faith can only be God incarnate. But from this it naturally and necessarily follows that, if the essence of faith consists of the historical account being understood spiritually, then the immediate, humanly perceptible appearance of Christ changes into a spiritual content, and the relation to him as merely a human being is transformed into a different relationship based on the spirit, in such a way that it sheds light on the nature of God. If the account of a perceptible Christ is just the point of departure for faith, such that the community of the faithful arising from the establishing of faith first produces this faith content in itself, then all that Christ is as God incarnate he is only in faith and in virtue of faith. God incarnate is of course faith's object, but is not the necessary presupposition of faith. What faith has for its presupposition is not Christ as God incarnate, but instead is merely the human Jesus as a humanly perceptible phenomenon. The divine and the human elements are still separate until faith, as the mediating link, is added to the picture. After Christ has cast off the flesh, the sensible aspect is transfigured into the spiritual aspect.

Here we stand at the same point where, in the Gnostic systems, Christ, the higher Aeon perceptible only to the eye of the spirit, descends upon the natural man Jesus. This is also where, in Schleiermacher's *Glaubenslehre*, the historical Christ merges into the archetypal Christ. Hegel fixes the death of Christ as the turning point at which the human condition of Christ was annulled and the transition to the religious and spiritual condition took place. That is because this is where comprehension of the phenomenon of Christ essentially became manifest. That happened only to the extent that the completely different spiritual and religious understanding of Christ's death superseded the merely external and historical way of regarding it (by going from the dead Jesus to a Christ who annulled death). This understanding of course contrasts with the minimal significance the Gnostics gave to the death, or that Schleiermacher gave to Christ's resurrection. Yet this difference is simply based on the fact that for the Gnostics, as for Schleiermacher, Christ's human appearance was already apprehended as both divine and human in nature, which is why there was no need for him to make the transition to a religious condition. However, the separation of the divine element from the human element is the same, in and for itself, in each of these cases. The difference is only that for Hegel it appears in an even more specific way, from the fact that he also fixes it externally, as indicated by the element of Christ's death. The critical

---

178. [*Ed.*] Baur is referring to the mystery of the resurrection.

basis for Hegel's doing so is that the account of Christ's death is only narrated by those who have already received the outpouring of the Spirit.[179]

Just as the second moment transformed and spiritualized the object of the first moment, so too the *third moment* is similarly related to the second moment, in that the separation posited in the second moment now first attains its consummation. With the second moment, of course via the mediation of faith, the spiritual content posited in the first moment, but in any event not yet consciously so, is that Christ is no longer merely a human being but is God incarnate. Yet in the second moment this spiritual content still clings to the external, historical phenomenon of Jesus, the one through whom it comes to be attested. This faith must therefore now first be elevated to knowledge. The spiritual content must be raised up from the element of faith into the element of thinking consciousness, where it is no longer based on the historical account as of something past and done with, but instead becomes justified by philosophy or the concept, as truth existent in itself, as absolutely present reality. For the truth existent in itself is absolute spirit, God as triune, the identity of the human being with God. Knowledge of Christ as God incarnate is therefore none other than the knowledge of this truth, the knowledge of the truth that the human being has true existence only in its universality, that the spirit does not have its true existence as finite spirit. In other words, this true existence is the consciousness of the unity of the divine nature and human nature. Hence in the first moment we have a human phenomenon, in the second moment we have the appearing of God incarnate, and in the third moment we have the pure idea, spirit in itself. And everything related to Christ's appearing and his life has its truth only in the fact that the essence and the life of spirit itself is what presents itself in him.

But what spirit is and does is no history in the usual sense. For faith it is of course a historical fact that the God-man, the incarnation of God, appeared, was born in the flesh. But from the standpoint of speculative thinking, God's becoming human is no solitary, one-time, historical event. Instead it is an eternal determination of God's being in virtue of which, in time, he becomes human (in each individual human being) inasmuch as God is human from eternity. The finitude and the painful humiliation Christ suffered as God incarnate is something God endures as human in every age. The reconciliation Christ accomplished is his deed occurring in time. But God reconciles himself with himself eternally, and Christ's resurrection and ascension is none other than spirit's eternal return to itself and to its truth. As human, as the God-man, Christ is human being in its universality. Not a singular individual, he is instead the universal individual.

Just as the advance from the first moment to the second moment, or the crossing over to the religious element, is carried out in Christ's death as the negation of the negation, in that his death sets aside his human circumstances and Christ emerges as God incarnate for faith, so too we find a comparable relation between the second

179. *Philosophie der Religion*, 2:249 [cf. *LPR* 3:323 n. 199 (1831 lectures)].

moment and the third moment. Christ as God incarnate for faith is also always at the same time still Christ appearing personally in history. The human circumstances of Christ are only absolutely abolished in speculative thinking where, as sublated, Christ simply is the universal human being; that is, where there is the identity of finite spirit with absolute spirit. Can there be any stricter and more decisive way than this of stripping away from Christ everything humanly personal to do with his appearing, even everything figurative and archetypal about his person? In its spiritual purity, the idea tears itself loose from every earthly, sensible shell. Thus all the narrated facts to which faith still clings seem to be the obscure reflection of the eternal process of spirit.[180] Considered from the highest standpoint, this reflection is just playing with the difference [between the historical and the ideal] in a non-serious way.

However, let us descend from these very abstract heights of speculation, far above the docetism of the Gnostic worldview, and go once again to that lower sphere in which the difference fittingly applies.[181] Here spirit is driven by the inner negativity of the idea, which carries out the never-resting labor of world history. At this level, and it is certainly of noteworthy significance, this philosophy of religion also takes up the historical appearance of Christ. Human beings should become conscious of the truth existent in itself, the unity of the divine nature and human nature. But with this consciousness spirit turns away from its self-divestment and finitization, and back to itself. This great turning point of world history occurs solely in the appearing of Christ. Only by faith grasping it as God incarnate could human beings become conscious themselves of the truth existent in itself. That is because everything they come to know for certain must have the form of their directly perceived experience, must exist outwardly for them; it must be manifested to them in an objective way. Also, Christ therefore retains a standing and importance no one else can share with him; and Christianity is by no means just one of the stages on the way to the absolute standpoint; it is the absolute stage or level itself. For the absolute stage is determined just as much by the content in which religion is identical with philosophy, as it is by the form that distinguishes religion from philosophy.

Hegel's philosophy of religion regards Christ as God incarnate only as this relates to faith, and without speaking specifically about which objective features of Christ's appearing faith in him actually presupposes. But how would faith in Christ as God incarnate have been able to arise unless he was, in some way or other, what faith took him to be? In any case the necessary presupposition is that the truth existent in itself, the unity of the divine nature with human nature, had become concrete truth, become known self-consciously, for the first time in Christ, and had been expressed

---

180. The facts of the story of Christ retain a figurative significance with reference to the nature of spirit, as they do for the Gnostics. See above, p. 82.

181. [Ed.] Here Baur distances himself from Hegel and hints at elements of his own view. See the next note.

and taught by him as the truth. This is also therefore the distinctive prerogative or preeminence of Christ.[182]

This directly raises the question as to how Christ knew the truth.[183] Did he know it in the only adequate form, that of the immanent concept? Or was it in the untrue form of the representation? The undeniable fact is that, in the New Testament accounts, the teachings and pronouncements of Christ lie before us in a form essentially different from the standpoint of speculative knowledge. So we find it necessary to deny the former possibility and to affirm the latter one. Doing so is to admit the consequence that, at least with regard to the form of knowing in this religious philosophy, although only in this one respect, it places the philosopher who knows God higher than the historical Christ. Except that, on the other hand, one does not see why this point is said to expose the most vulnerable and truly fatal position of this system.

Here the difference surely just involves the form of knowing, whereas the content remains the same. For according to the principles of this philosophy of religion, faith and speculative knowing, in other words religion and philosophy, of course differ in form but in content are said to be identical, always the same. This had to be the contention, first and foremost; and on the other hand it had to be shown that the faith would be absorbed by speculation, not merely as to its form but at the same time also as to its contents. Yet how shall a demonstration of this point proceed? For the

---

182. [*Ed.*] This statement provides an opening to Baur's own distinctive christology, which is summed up in the following passage from *Die christliche Lehre von der Dreieinigkeit und Menschwerdung Gottes in ihrer geschichtlichen Entwicklung*, 3 vols. (Tübingen, 1841–43), 3:998–99. See also *Die christliche Lehre von der Versöhnung in ihrer geschichtlichen Entwicklung* (Tübingen, 1838), 621–24, 735. "Idea and reality can never be joined together in such absolute unity that the idea does not transcend every manifestation given in reality, indeed every single individual; therefore the idea can actualize itself only in an infinite series of individuals. In every single individual the non-being of the idea must also be posited, be it only as a minimum . . . As certainly as the idea of humanity must actualize itself, and as certainly as it is established essentially in the unity of God and the human being, just as certainly can it be actualized only by virtue of the fact that it enters into the consciousness of humanity at a specific point in a specific individual. However, no matter how highly in other respects one may place this individual, in virtue of the idea of this unity that comes to consciousness in him, he must still stand in a subordinate relationship to the idea; and a God-man in the sense of the ecclesiastical doctrine embraces in itself an irresolvable contradiction." In Jesus Christ, the non-being of the idea is at its minimum, and he indeed is what faith claims him to be, but not in the orthodox sense because idea and historical reality exist in a tensive relationship, one of both unity and difference.

183. See Julius Müller's review, in *Theologische Studien und Kritiken* (1833), 1069ff. and esp. 1082, of Carl Friedrich Göschel's latest publication. While this treatise is of interest in various ways, what nevertheless stands out is when its author, in referring to passages such as 1 Cor 7:25, 40, and 13:9 ["For we know only in part, and we prophesy only in part"], is of the opinion that they must be devastating to all the philosophy of our time. Which philosopher from an absolute standpoint can also fail to acknowledge that his own perspective is a "knowing in part"? Were that not the case, how could this same Apostle Paul, who confessed that he too "knew only in part," proudly state that it has pleased God "to reveal his Son to me" (Gal 1:16)? We should not in fact disregard what is supposedly gained by such rejoinders, and overall by a polemic proceeding from assumptions that the opponent self-evidently cannot admit making, as long as the untenability of his standpoint as such is not explained to him. Hence if one does not go back to this standpoint, then this very harshly directed polemic may accomplish nothing.

philosophical system affirms emphatically the very thing that constitutes the content of Christ's teaching as God incarnate, namely, the oneness of the divine nature and human nature, as the truth existent in itself. So the difference is just in the form and is only to be found in the fact that faith regards the oneness of human nature with the divine nature as a truth just historically revealed and dependent on Christ's appearing in history; whereas for speculative knowing of truth existent in itself and given via the nature of spirit itself, one does of course become conscious of this truth via historical channels, but its content by no means coincides with the form in which it appears in history.

Therefore how could Hegel's philosophy of religion be concerned with a form that this philosophy, from its standpoint, can simply regard as a form required to meet the needs of perceptual certainty? How could it equate this form with truth existent in itself, and when for philosophy faith is rightly said to be a transformation of what is sensibly given into what is spiritual? Why should philosophy stop at this halfway house and not continue the transformation process to the extent that everything that, as mere form, can be distinguished from the content, is separated from the pure content of the idea, and then ultimately form and content become one? So whereas the contention on the one hand is that in faith itself the content and the form are of course two essentially different elements, the position firmly maintained on the other hand is that because knowing distinguishes the content of faith from its form, knowing has the content in a form different from that of faith, which is why it absorbs the content itself. So that it will not be swallowed up in this way, faith itself accepts no distinction of content from form. It regards form and content as inseparably linked, such that the truth of the content absolutely cannot exist in any other form than the original one, that is, the one given externally in history and from which faith has directly received its content. Any rising above this form to a higher level also instantly posits a disconnect between form and content. It sets the archetypal Christ above the historical Christ and, once begun, this process runs its course until, in the unadorned idea, the pure content is also ultimately the pure form.

The main issue we are dealing with here is always just this: are faith and knowledge absolutely antithetical, or are they just relatively opposed to each other. If this is an absolute antithesis, then all truth simply belongs to faith, for faith is the first to have the truth for its content. Then there is no knowledge differing from faith, and because of that there is no philosophy of religion. That is because, as philosophy about religion, the philosophy of religion, by its nature, has the content of faith in a different form than faith has it. But if faith and knowledge are only relatively opposed, then by the same token that acknowledges the form-content distinction. So then philosophy of religion cannot be deprived of the right to follow through with this difference and opposition to the fullest extent. Hegel's philosophy of religion is the consummate instance of doing so, and that returns us to the statement made above: that the separation of the historical Christ from the ideal Christ, a task the philosophy of religion made its own since its beginning, has been completed by Hegel.

The ideal Christ of Hegel's philosophy of religion is itself no longer the archetypal figure of Schleiermacher's *Glaubenslehre*. Instead it is the pure idea, the oneness of finite spirit and absolute spirit, as the truth existent in itself. Yet while the person of the incarnate God, in the way faith accepts his person as historical truth, separates into two completely opposite extremes—on the one hand the singular individual whose human circumstances are utterly set aside, and on the other hand the pure ideality of the truth—it for that reason leaves ample room for the historical Christ in this broad middle. If the incarnate God is, in itself, the unity of the divine and the human, is humanity at one with God, then the historical Christ is humanity in all its members who together are the living body of Christ, realizing the concept of religion, striving upwards from earth to heaven, uniting themselves with God. In his community, constantly growing and receiving the fullness of spirit within itself, Christ, the incarnate God ever-present in the living truth and actuality of history, celebrates life's eternal victory over death, the eternal feast of his resurrection and ascension. Therefore this philosophy of religion also does not lack a very concrete concept of the historical Christ.

## How Hegel's Philosophy of Religion Locates Christianity in Relation to Paganism and to Judaism

We still need to add a few remarks here about how Hegel ultimately locates the two subordinate forms of religion, paganism and Judaism, in relation to Christianity as the absolute religion.

Ancient Gnosis was always inclined to see paganism as negatively related to Christianity, whether that be paganism on its own or paganism lumped together with Judaism. Only in the Valentinian system and in the Gnosis of Clement of Alexandria does this relationship have a more positive side to it. In more recent philosophy of religion, paganism and Judaism are of course regarded by Schelling and Schleiermacher from a comparable standpoint, as the stages of development preceding Christianity. However they do so only in a general way and without more closely examining and spelling out this relationship.

Hegel's philosophy of religion has cast a very wide net in this part of its endeavors. Not only has it provided a very comprehensive presentation of the individual forms of religion; it has also assigned to each form the specific place to which it belongs in the context of them all, based on its character as an individual moment of the self-developing concept of religion. The result is that the placement of paganism and Judaism vis-à-vis Christianity follows of its own accord from the preceding presentation. However, what seems least satisfactory to me about this way of understanding the relations among these main forms of religion is essentially explained in the following pages.

## Assessment of Hegel's Concept of Paganism: Paganism or Nature Religion Is Religious Consciousness Mediated by the Consciousness of Nature

As for paganism, I cannot approve of Hegel's not applying the concept of nature religion to the full range of paganism.

Hegel's general definition is that nature religion is "the unity of the spiritual and the natural."[184] It posits the objective side, God, with consciousness [of God] still caught up in natural determinacy. This natural side is individual existence rather than nature as such, as a whole, as organic totality. Nature as a whole is of course a universal determination not yet posited at this initial stage. This individual, natural element, this heaven or this sun and so forth—thus an immediately existing natural thing—is known as God. But why should the concept of nature religion not also hold good where it is nature as a whole that determines the content of religious consciousness? What holds good for the part must also hold good for the whole; in either case consciousness is always caught up in what is natural, and in the same way.

According to Hegel, Indian religion (Hinduism) is in fact the only one belonging to the stage of nature religion.[185] But that definition of the concept of nature religion [as involving individual natural elements] is not even applicable to this religion. If nature-pantheism appears anywhere, it is certainly in Hindu religion. And how limited

---

184. *Philosophie der Religion*, 1:202 [cf. *LPR* 2:234 (1824 lectures), 519 (1827 lectures)].

185. [*Ed.*] To appreciate this statement we must understand the organization of Determinate Religion in the 1832 edition of the lectures. It is as follows:
Part I. Nature Religion. The Metaphysical Concept. The Representation of God. Various Forms.
   1. The Religion of Magic
      1. The Religion of Magical Power
      2. The Religion of Being-Within-Self (Buddhism)
   2. The Religion of Phantasy (Hinduism)
   3. Nature Religion in Its Transition to a Higher Level
      1. The Religion of the Good or of Light (Persian Religion)
      2. The Religion of the Enigma (Egyptian Religion)
Part II. The Religion of Spiritual Individuality. Transition. Metaphysical Concept of God. Division.
   1. The Religion of Sublimity (Judaism)
   2. The Religion of Beauty (Greek Religion)
   3. The Religion of Expediency or of the Understanding (Roman Religion)
This arrangement corresponds basically to the lectures of 1824, but it introduces the religion of the good from the lectures of 1831. If we consider the religions of the good and of the enigma as already transitioning to a higher level, that leaves the religions of magic (including Buddhism) and of phantasy at the level of nature religion. Baur may have thought that Hegel did not consider magic to be a religion in the strict sense, which leaves only phantasy (Hinduism) at the stage of nature religion. Baur by contrast wants to expand the category of nature religion to include all the so-called pagan religions, and to distinguish Judaism from them because it reorients divine mediation to history. The movement is from nature religion (*Anschauung*) to Judaism (*Verstand*) to Christianity (*Vernunft*). Hegel's scheme reduces Judaism's distinctiveness by treating it as one of the determinate religions.

the concept appears to be if defined in this way, especially when referring to Greek religion, when Greek religion is indeed said to belong to a wholly other domain, that of spiritual individuality! The essence of nature religion is spirit's being caught up in nature, but this captivity can take various forms. The general point concerns any mediation of the religious consciousness by nature—a being caught up in, or bound by, nature—as long as spirit essentially is in need of nature. But even so, this concept is still not spelled out sufficiently if the mediation via nature is not at the same time regarded as a figurative mediation.

We have the relationship of the figure or image to the idea, the figurative form related to a spiritual content reflected in it, when the governing divine power is envisaged as being in visible, natural phenomena. As the image or figure frames itself in manifold ways in its two main forms, symbol and myth, so the divinization of nature, which is proper to nature religion, has manifold forms as well. If nature is only one element in the process of spirit, then spirit must also be seen throughout nature. Spirit's shining forth through the hull of nature is what transfigures nature into being an image of the divine spirit that is the truth of nature.

It is an essential defect of Hegel's portrayal, a defect running throughout the whole, that nowhere does it give attention to the figurative or symbolic-mythic character of nature religion. So because of this state of affairs, Greek religion was not included under the concept of nature religion. For what Hegel calls "the spiritual individuality of Greek religion" is simply the mythic aspect of it. The mythical divine beings of Greek religion are of course spiritual individuals, personal beings each with a specific character. But if we look back to their origins we see that in some fashion their existence is rooted in the life of nature. What underlies them is some way of looking at nature that initially got grasped in symbolic fashion and then became personified in the myths. Thus they do not have a truly spiritual individuality. Instead it is just a figurative, ideal individuality. These are just personifications that always in the end just dissolve into an image, a figurative form; although it is indeed readily apparent how their individuality seeks to cast off the figurative, mythic hull and ascend to the higher region of free personality. Nonetheless one may call Greek religion "the religion of spiritual individuality" in setting it apart from the Oriental religions. Yet this is simply the distinction of symbol from myth, and it still always leaves us within the broader domain of nature religion.

If the task of more recent philosophy of religion also includes giving paganism a less restricted role than it has had, then that means understanding paganism as a religious form in its own right and as shaped by the general course of religious development. In paganism, nature is regarded as the mediatrix who envelops the spirit that, in the realm of nature, is rising to the stage of religion but of course is cloaked with nature's veil woven from so many colorful images, while at the same time also graphically setting forth in this veil the models or typology of the gods. This concept of paganism is very much the product of more recent philosophy of religion and of

### Part Four: Ancient Gnosis and More Recent Religious Philosophy

more recent knowledge about the ancient world. Only if the concept of nature religion is defined in this way is it broad enough to also accommodate the form of paganism that is described above in this book on pp. 30–34.[186] It is hard to say where to find a place for this within the organic structure of Hegel's philosophy of religion. It certainly belongs within the domain of nature religion, but only toward the side where the religious development is already striving to get beyond nature religion. In the form of nature religion that is further developed, the concept of matter appears in place of the concept of nature. Here matter is also conceived to be the necessary agent of spirit's activity, although matter itself is none other than nature thought of abstractly.[187]

186. [*Ed.*] Where Baur introduces Buddhism as resting on (quoting Schmidt) "the dualism operative through spirit (or mind) and nature (or matter), a dualism revealing itself in the phenomena of the world's formation" (p. 30).

187. See Karl Rosenkranz, *Die Naturreligion, ein philosophisch-historischer Versuch* (1831). Like Hegel, Rosenkranz also understands nature religion in a very narrow sense. For him it is even nothing but the religion of the people generally called savages, the shape of religion where spirit, first awakened to itself, is not yet living in spirit as such, or not aware of its own nature. Here spirit still lives outside itself, in nature itself. Nature religion is the lowest level of religion where, in order to make the thought of the divine an object for it, spirit takes up a still very indefinite stance and only gradually moves to make use of symbols. Rosenkranz sets nature religion apart in this sense from the symbolic and formative religions. He describes three stages of religion as follows. For the Negroes, the American Indians, and others, there is as yet no specific concept in play; they still just see the shape of the deity as arbitrary and coalescing with every sort of natural object. For the peoples of the Far East and for the Greeks, the Tibetans, and the Indians, and for those of the Near East, the Persians, Egyptians, and those of Asia Minor, this indeterminacy is no more and thinking seeks to arrive at an image of its own essence, within the natural domain. This image is the shape of deity although still mixed with natural configurations. Nevertheless this image at the same time allows the shape of self-conscious spirit, the human shape, to forcefully stand out. These are the symbolic religions. The Greeks, the Etruscans, and the Romans totally break through the limits of the natural domain, for they fashion the deity in human shapes in a definite way (p. 247). In narrowing the concept of nature religion so severely, Rosenkranz himself still concedes (in his Preface, p. vii) that, in all the pre-Christian religions with the exception of Judaism, nature constitutes the most important element for portraying the absolute, except that all of them do not approach nature in the same way. In one way spirit actually still resides entirely in nature; in another, nature becomes an ambiguous indicator of spirit, one in which spirit makes every effort to catch sight of its own essence; in another, nature as a human shape becomes the genuine image of spirit, self-consciously pervaded by spirit. But why then should that very stage of religion at which nature serves to make religion or religious ideas apprehensible in a figurative way not deserve most especially to be called nature religion? The main consideration can always simply be to see in what way nature serves to make religious ideas apprehensible in a figurative way; that is, to see how image and idea are related to each other. If the first stage may still be called the preeminently natural stage, inasmuch as spirit therefore still lives within nature and still has no inkling that nature has a merely figurative meaning for it, it in no way confines the concept of nature religion to this shape alone. – From this same perspective I also cannot be satisfied with the characterization of paganism by Isaak Rust in the second edition of his *Philosophie und Christentum oder Wissen und Glauben* (Mannheim, 1833), 53. In the intellectual tendency of spirit's self-development Rust distinguishes three stages. He designates the first one as the stage of feeling or immediate perception, the second one as the stage of understanding or intentionality, and the third one as the stage of reason, in other words of philosophy and knowledge. These three stages correspond to the three formative periods of religious development: paganism, or immediate ethical life; Judaism, or law; Christianity, or faith. While what he writes on p. 86 is correct as a general characterization of paganism, it in no way captures the distinctive principle of paganism. In addition to its one-sidedness in defining paganism chiefly from an ethical

## Assessment of Hegel's Concept of Judaism: Judaism Is Religious Consciousness Mediated by the Consciousness of the People and of the State

Hegel's philosophy of religion also leaves out much that calls for more specific treatment with regard to Judaism.

Hegel's general characterization is that the Jewish religion is the religion of sublimity (*Erhabenheit*). However, the concept of sublimity, which is the main thing Hegel pays attention to regarding God's relation to the world, is only a very one-sided way of designating the essence of the Jewish religion. When Hegel himself presents in detail what is distinctive about this religion—that in Judaism the divine wisdom has a very limited moral function; that obeying the law is not a spiritual kind of obedience; and that punishments are stipulated just in external terms—then it is not clear to what principle these features so characteristic of the Jewish religion are supposed to refer.

There is even less justification for Hegel's placement of the Jewish religion directly prior to Greek religion, so that the religion of sublimity can be considered to be simply the preliminary stage for the Greek religion of beauty. What these two religions have in common for Hegel is the fact that God has embarked upon free subjectivity, which has gained mastery over the finite as such, so that now the subject, the spirit, is known as a spiritual subject in its relation to what is natural and finite. In other words, what they have in common is the ideality of what is natural—that the natural has been subjected to what is spiritual; that God is known as spirit for itself, first and foremost as spirit whose intended purposes are rational and moral. But what can be the justification for saying this about Greek religion as well as about Judaism, when the Greek gods still so clearly bear within themselves the marks of their natural origin and of their dependence on the forces of nature?

But suppose one goes on to say, as Hegel does,[188] that ethical life is still the substantial being in Greek religion. This religion is the true being of what is ethical, but not yet the knowledge of what is ethical. That is because there is not yet a unitary subject present. The ethical contents are fragmented. Their foundation is the passions, the essential spiritual powers, the universal powers of ethical life. Because the ethical fragments into its particular determinations, what is natural appears opposed to these spiritual powers. Thus here too I see no superiority of Greek religion over Judaism. Instead the Jewish religion sets itself apart by its moral acts being tied to consciousness of a specific, morally-intended purpose that is uniformly based in God's will.

---

respect, as the natural life of practical spirit, it has the defect of locating the principle of nature religion just in feeling and not in a way of looking at things. It does not suffice to say the pagan spirit, which substitutes such an extensive polytheism for the absoluteness of God, conceives of its deities in earthly shapes, and also grasps them as temporal beings and makes their temporality a spatial existence, subjecting them to the eternal, natural power of fate. We still do not know from this what kind of beings they are, how they came about, and where they got their complexion and their shape. And we will never have correctly understood their concept if we do not take them to be symbolic, mythic beings.

188. *Philosophie der Religion*, 2:85 [cf. *LPR* 2:644].

But suppose one wanted to place less emphasis on all of this. The advance from polytheism to monotheism is still in itself so significant that this factor most decidedly exalts Judaism above the domain of paganism. Hegel too cannot fail to appreciate the significance of monotheism. For he finds monotheism to be necessary for the upward move to the religion of sublimity, since monotheism brings the separate spiritual and moral powers out of their isolation and together in a single spiritual unity.[189] So this makes it even harder to be convinced that Hegel's placement of the Jewish religion is correct. For Hegel himself this placement seems to be based on the fact that, whereas Judaism remains foreign to the unity of the ideal and the real, and regards God as being "up there," the Greek religion instead considers the natural domain itself to be the other aspect of the divine substance, as an essential element of it, inasmuch as it is essential for this substance to appear as free subjectivity within the finite as its manifestation. So the reason why Greek religion is the religion of beauty is that in it what is finite and natural gets transfigured in the spirit, becoming a sign of the spirit. In any event this is an aspect that ought not be overlooked when evaluating pagan religion, especially Greek religion, and its relation to the Jewish religion.

The great gap Judaism sees existing between God and what is finite is not a factor in this case, for God's immanent presence together with the world appears in place of that transcendent relationship. The divine is one with what is finite and natural. But as long as the oneness of the divine and the natural has not become the oneness of the divine and the human, then the consequence of that oneness is simply that the true idea of the divine gets lost in the natural and the finite. Without a doubt Judaism has the more refined idea of God. However, this Jewish God, who is thought of as purely supersensible subjectivity, must first come forth from his abstract being "up there." Paganism of course posits the oneness of the divine and the natural, but only as an unmediated unity, and the kind in which there can be no holding firmly to the pure idea of God.

If, as a result of these observations, we regard ourselves for good reason as justified in extricating the Jewish religion from the unnatural position into which it has been wedged, between Egyptian religion and Greek religion, then consideration of its true circumstances involves looking not merely at the individual forms of pagan religion, but at paganism as a whole. But this assumes at the same time that, by taking the entire phenomenon into account, paganism as a whole can be brought under one general concept. This will shed light on how, for Hegel, the two things are

---

189. Ibid., 2:39 [cf. *LPR* 2:669]. [*Ed.*] What Baur could not know, of course, is that, while the 1832 edition followed the arrangement of the 1824 lectures, in which the religion of sublimity precedes the religion of beauty, in the 1827 lectures Hegel reversed the order so that Jewish religion now follows Greek religion. And the passage Baur cites is from the 1827 lectures: "The necessity of the elevation of the religion of beauty into the religion of sublimity lies in what we have discussed already, i.e., in the need that the particular spiritual powers, the ethical powers, should be embraced within a spiritual unity." Obviously when such a passage is introduced into the 1824 arrangement, conceptual tensions arise.

interconnected—the placement given to the Jewish religion, and the limitations on the concept of nature religion. On the other hand, if this concept of nature religion be taken in the broader sense I indicated, then that must also give prominence to the relation of paganism and Judaism with reference to this concept.

Nothing is more pertinent for spelling out this relationship, therefore, than how decidedly the Jewish religion rejects any sensuous depiction of God's being, and because of that it draws a strict line between God and nature. It regards the oneness of God and nature that is characteristic of paganism as a denigration of God's being, since God's being and that of nature are entirely different in kind. But this separation of God from nature at the same time presupposes a positive concept of God that is defined quite differently. As distinct from nature, God can only be spirit itself, the self-conscious spirit, a self-determining, free, personal being. But human beings can be conscious of a personal God only inasmuch as they, as opposed to nature, have become conscious of their own being as persons. So whereas at the stage of nature religion, human beings' relation to God is in fact just a relation to nature, at the stage of Judaism it is the relation of one's free, personal being to the free, personal being of God: spirit's relation to spirit.

Nevertheless we should not also think of religious consciousness, defined in this way, as immediate consciousness. For Judaism also belongs to a stage of religious consciousness where religious consciousness has need of a mediating form. At the stage of paganism, nature is what mediates religious consciousness, for God-consciousness is consciousness of nature. What is the mediating factor for religious consciousness in Judaism? Briefly put, consciousness of the Jewish people and the Jewish state is what replaces nature-consciousness. Individuals know themselves and their communion with God only inasmuch as they know themselves as members of the people and the state to which they belong. In paganism God reveals himself in nature, while in Judaism God reveals himself in history. But Judaism does not consider history as a whole to be the revelation of God. Instead, just as the pagan's God-consciousness, as nature-consciousness, depends on individual natural phenomena, so too the Jews' religious consciousness is simply mediated by the history of a specific, singular people; and this history of a people begins with the history of a family [or tribe].

What the people or the nation is at a lesser stage, via a relation to nature, it is at the higher stage through the development of the state. The Jews could become conscious of their relation to God only to the extent that they had become conscious, above all else, of their relation to the state organized in terms of the Mosaic covenant. Everything providing the specific contents of their religious consciousness was given to them in and with this state. Therefore the state was the form of mediation that they required.

However, mediation of religious consciousness is rooted in a principle. In paganism this principle is a way of looking at or perceiving things [in nature] (*Anschauung*). In Judaism it is reflection (*Reflexion*), as the activity of the understanding (*Verstand*).

Reflective understanding (*der reflectirende Verstand*) expresses its activity both by distinguishing and separating different kinds, and by conjoining what is related and belongs together. Hence Judaism strictly separates God from nature. The image of God is not in nature. To the extent that there is an image of God, it is only in the human being as an intelligent and personal being. But reflective understanding always just sticks to a secondary sort of unity, to antitheses it does not know how to harmonize in a higher, internal unity. Therefore the Jewish religion characterizes itself as the form of religion belonging to the stage of reflective understanding, in particular because of how it positions human beings in relation to God. This relationship is like the relation between two free persons. Despite their being dependent, human beings are juxtaposed to God as completely free persons. They are entitled to assert their own will, as the Jewish religion expresses this point in its own conception of a covenant fully shaped as a contract concluded between two parties, with reciprocal rights and obligations. This relationship has a merely external basis.

The divine will is of course the standard governing moral acts. But human beings have not yet recognized the one absolute principle of their spiritual, moral, and religious life as residing in God. The divine will stands over against them as an external authority in the form of the law. Hence we are correct in calling Judaism not only the religion of reflective understanding, but also the religion of authority and of the law. For, as long as the law just stands over against human beings as an external authority, and has not yet gained an inner life within them in a higher principle, as faith has in Christianity, the law is just something to be understood. As first of all understood, the law should find its way into a person's heart and inwardness.

With the law being an external authority, there is also the external authority of an intermediary, a person through whom, as the fortuitously chosen instrument, God has revealed the law.[190] With all the good qualities it otherwise has, on this point the Jewish religion stands on the same level as Islam. In each of these religions, authority is the principle, and all the features of Judaism can be evaluated most confidently according to this principle. That includes the features in which Judaism is most antithetical to Christianity and the features in which it has affinity with Christianity and is most closely related to it.

Whereas the principle of authority, and the dominant tradition that arose as a natural consequence on this basis, produced a multitude of authorities utterly stifling the freedom of the spirit and transforming the religion into merely external, mechanistic observances, we see, in opposition to this, no more definitive carry-over from Judaism to Christianity than the prophetic announcement of a time in which the law will be not merely something external but instead an inner law, one not merely written on stone tablets but instead living in one's heart.[191] As soon as this had taken place the

---

190. [*Ed.*] Baur is referring to Moses, the law-giver, in whose succession came a "multitude of authorities."

191. [*Ed.*] An allusion to Jer 31:33: "I will put my law within them, and I will write it on their

principle of authority lost its power. The letter of the law had become the spirit of the law. The covering that veiled Moses' face,[192] and was the barrier that kept the spirit from ever attaining a living unity with the law, had fallen away.

### Christianity Is Religious Consciousness Mediated by the History and Person of an Individual

If paganism is the religion of looking at or perceiving things (*Anschauung*), and Judaism is the religion of reflective understanding (*Verstandes-Reflexion*), then Christianity can only be the religion of reason (*Vernunft*).[193] As the religion of reason it is also the absolute religion. But even from the standpoint of the absolute religion, religious consciousness as determined by Christianity still has its own distinctly mediated form.

In nature religion we have religious consciousness of the individually mediated form as nature, and in Judaism it is the theocratic state. In Christianity it is the history and person of a single individual (*die Geschichte und Person eines einzelnen Individuums*). However this single individual is at the same time the human being as such or in itself (*der Mensch an sich*)—the universal, archetypal human, the God-man or God incarnate. Accordingly, if at this highest standpoint the religious consciousness is a consciousness mediated by a specific form, it is itself not a random or external form. Instead it is an absolute form. Only philosophy of religion as Hegel defines its task can also make the connection between this form, the history and person of God incarnate as a single individual, and truth existent in itself. This is the main issue the philosophy of religion has to deal with from its most recent standpoint. The direction it takes in its further course of development depends on how it responds on this point.

### Concluding Remarks

At the conclusion of this investigation let us look back at the range Christian philosophy of religion has covered in its development up until now. In doing so we must in any event acknowledge that, throughout all these changing times, it has held firmly and most decidedly to the same course it adopted at the outset. That is also why what

---

hearts"; and to Prov 3:3: "write them [loyalty and faithfulness] on the tablet of your heart."

192. [*Ed.*] An allusion to Exod 34:33–35: "When Moses had finished speaking with them, he put a veil on his face . . ." And to 2 Cor 3:13–18, where Paul says that Moses "put a veil over his face to keep the people of Israel from gazing at the end of the glory that was being set aside. But their minds were hardened. Indeed, to this very day, when they hear the reading of the old covenant, that same veil is still there, since only in Christ is it set aside . . . When one turns to the Lord, the veil is removed. Now the Lord is the Spirit, and where the Spirit of the Lord is, there is freedom."

193. [*Ed.*] The puzzling distinction, at least to English speakers, between *Verstand* and *Vernunft* can perhaps be most simply explained as follows: *Verstand* makes things "stand under" (*ver-stehen*) externally related and merely "reflective" categories, whereas *Vernunft* as a process of reasoning grasps (and constitutes) the inner connection of things.

Christian philosophy of religion is from its latest standpoint is not just something concocted yesterday or today. Instead it is as old as the development of Christian dogma itself, the natural consequence of the course of development as conditioned by the nature of this particular subject matter.

Of course for that reason it was not, as so often happens, to be looked upon simply as a highly questionable and objectionable phenomenon wholly foreign to Christianity. If one believes, for good reasons, that the latest philosophy of religion most especially ought to be labeled as false Gnosis, then at least one should have been so charitable and consistent as to assign the same label also to what takes the same route it does and differs from it not in essence but only in form. Hence if, as a rule, it is allowable to draw a dogmatic conclusion based on a historical phenomenon of this kind—the latest philosophy of religion as the result of a course going back so far and, with all of it changing forms, remaining self-identical—then this conclusion can only be as follows. Either there is nothing that, as such, deserves to be labeled as Christian philosophy of religion; or, if one is not of the opinion that it is better to entirely abandon the concept of Christian philosophy of religion, then it can only be pursued further to its goal on the path that has already been trodden.

While there is no mistaking the identity and continuity of the course once taken and running throughout the entire history of the philosophy of religion, we can hardly overlook, on the other hand, the disparity when we compare the beginning with the end of the path running through so many centuries. So many antitheses first had to be overcome, so many inflexible and inadequate forms[194] first had to be stripped away. In

---

194. The systems of Boehme and Schelling in particular have many points at which they come into close contact with the form of the Gnostic systems. In the systems of the most recent philosophy of religion overall we can distinguish three forms indicative of the same progression of stages as we find in ancient Gnosis. In the systems of *Boehme* and *Schelling* the mythic and allegorical form still appears in part as very significant. Boehme's source-spirits and angels, but most especially his Lucifer and his Virgin, are symbolic-mythic figures wholly in the sense of ancient Gnosis. Like the mythical beings of the Gnostic systems, they repeatedly remind us to distinguish the form from the idea and to understand the whole system ultimately from the perspective of a marvelous allegory. This figurative form itself is scarcely foreign to Schelling's system. The well-known passages in *Of Human Freedom* (n. 88), where rigorous, abstract philosophy takes a back seat to the concretely visual character of the poetic presentations, show as much. See in particular the poetically animated depiction of the epochs in the struggle between the two principles (459–61, 493–96 [ET 51–52, 78–80]), and the descriptions of the efficacy of the evil principle that incline so heavily toward mythic, sensuous accounts (440, 441, 456, 474–76 [ET 33–35, 48–49, 63–65]). Here the evil principle is the aroused "eternal one" (441 [ET 34]) abandoning his peaceful dwelling place in the center and entering into the periphery, even straightforwardly taking the shape of the Gnostics' archon or Boehme's Lucifer. The ongoing struggle of the two principles, extending from one epoch to the next and endlessly unfolding, makes Schelling's system very similar to that of Basilides, whose "tedious storytelling" (as Origen speaks of it in his *Commentary on Matthew*) points back to the Zoroastrian religious system, as the template for all systems of this kind. – These systems therefore take the form of myth, more or less, although in the system of *Schleiermacher* the mythic form is portrayed in historical terms, since everything his *Glaubenslehre* contains is presented as a given, as fact, whether they be facts of external history or facts of inner experience. A strict line ought not be drawn between the two, because each one in similar fashion bears the stamp of something in itself objectively given.—The system of *Hegel* rises above this, for here

so many respects the process of spirit's mediation with itself first had to be removed from the externality of corporeal and material being and increasingly transferred to what is essential to spirit itself, as the express, innermost and freest labor of the spirit that, in all this, is simply striving for itself. In looking back to the beginnings of Gnosis, to all those original roots so deeply embedded in the soil of paganism, we see that the foremost task of Christian religious philosophy was in part to subject to itself the pagan element that was so prevalent, and in part to completely eliminate that element

---

logical form replaces the historical form. The form and method of Hegel's philosophy of religion is the self-explicating concept (see above, pp. 422–23). – While the first form (that of Boehme and Schelling) points back to the first main form of Gnosis, these latter two forms are at least analogous to the second and third main forms of Gnosis respectively. If external history is to be looked at, in the final analysis, as a mere form, then the factual element loses its reality more or less in the same way as it does in Marcionite docetism. However, the Pseudo-Clementine system for the most part has affinity with the logical system, inasmuch as the basic Pseudo-Clementine form is the monad expanding to the dyad, and from this expansion once again drawing back into itself (see above, pp. 200, 238). The essential thing here is that this is none other than the logical process of self-distinction and reuniting with itself by annulling the distinction. – The fact that all these systems differ in material ways and not just in a formal sense expresses something perhaps calling for attention here, especially also regarding the concept of the community. What Hegel calls the community is the Pleroma in the first main form of the Gnostic systems (see above, p. 422). The Pseudo-Clementine system speaks in the same sense about the world to come in contrast to the present world. In both kinds of Gnostic systems the image of the uniting of the bridegroom and the bride has the same significance in relation to the status it points to regarding the collective group of pneumatic persons, or true worshipers of God and Christ. – Only in Marcion's system do we find nothing corresponding to this. The idea of the world of Aeons or of the Pleroma remains foreign to him. Also the idea of a community rising up from the earth to heaven is not a topic about which he has anything particular to say. At least this topic did not have to have the same significance for him as it did for those other systems. This can be explained simply from the subjectivity of his standpoint, which confined itself to the individual's self-consciousness. A similar circumstance is evident when comparing Schleiermacher's system to Hegel's. Schleiermacher writes that "from our point of view we can have no doctrine of the consummation of the church, for our Christian consciousness has absolutely nothing to say regarding a condition so entirely outside our ken" (*Der christliche Glaube*, §157.2 [ET 1928, 697; 2016, 966]). He places all these contents under the ambiguous heading of a prophetic teaching that is "directly useful only as a pattern to which we have to approximate" (§157 [ET 1928, 696; 2016, 965]). – In Hegel's system, on the contrary the concept of the community certainly has its fully objective reality, in that what is "up there" and is "the world to come" is considered to be what is existent in itself and is present. Karl Rosenkranz expresses, in the most specific terms, in his "Kritik der Schleiermacherschen Glaubenslehre," *Berliner Jahrbücher* 118 (Dec. 1831) 946, this contrast between Schleiermacher's subjectivity and Hegel's objectivity: "Instead of recognizing that transferring the consummation of the idea from the visible world into an impenetrable and dubious 'up there' is simply an abstract notion of our consciousness, Schleiermacher goes halfway and sets up the consummation of the church as an ideal, as a state of being that of course was supposed to be realized but never developed so that it actually occurred. Instead the consummation has to ensue in some unfathomably distant future. However desirable that consummation might be, and however much God and human beings might do toward that end, the *concrete existence* of the church forever remains incommensurate with the *concept* of it. Representation will not do without its sensuous hues elaborated in spatial and temporal terms. Thinking that strives toward universality and necessity will hear nothing of the attractive appearance of representations and assigns them to the domain of fantasy and artifice. Dogmatics finds itself most actively thrust into this conflict with eschatology because eschatology is supposed to treat essential determinants of spirit as not yet existing. Yet as science, dogmatics cannot surrender the standpoint according to which everything essential to spirit, or everything through which it is definitely spirit, must exist and thus must of course exist now."

from itself. Christianity had to leave behind it all that is polytheistic and dualistic, the many different versions of the antithesis of spirit and matter, of a higher and a lower god, and the whole figurative, symbolic presentation of religious and speculative ideas. It had to rid itself of all this as much as it could, indeed at the initial stages of its own course of development. Judaism also was a force Christianity constantly had to deal with, one from which it could completely break loose only because it had attained a new religious standpoint. On the whole, however, the idea of absolute spirit—which took shape in all these forms so as to manifest its own proper nature in them, and through this mediation to grasp itself in its own eternal truth—is what first had to become conscious [of itself] in its freedom and purity.

But whatever one's verdict about the latest standpoint of philosophy of religion may be, it is nevertheless certain that spirit's labor, extending over thousands of years, can never be regarded as concluded. Just as Christian philosophy of religion was from the outset only able to develop on the basis of objective Christianity, this same foundation, from which it can never part ways, also provides the reassuring guarantee, for the future as well, that it can never regard its task as finished or its goal as reached, as long as all the interests that should get us to the true concept of Christian philosophy of religion and should be kept in balance in it, are not given their due.

# Index of Persons

Aaron, 200, 320
Abel, 100, 110, 116–17, 171, 188, 200–201
Abimelech (King), 228
Abiram, 171
Abraham, 23, 48, 110, 150, 171, 187, 200, 203, 214–15, 219–20, 300, 318
Achilles, 211
Adam, 23, 100, 103–7, 109, 115, 142, 171–72, 186–88, 200–201, 203, 214, 220, 233–34, 299, 305, 368–74, 377, 429
Adelphius, 263
Aeacus, 323
Aeneas, 267
Agricola, Johann, 339
Alexander the Libyan, 263
Allogenes, 263
Altizer, Thomas, xxv
Amelius, 263
Amos, 110
Anna, 139
Anaxagoras, 96, 284–85
Anaximander, 284
Anaximenes, 286
Anicetus (Pope), 246
Antiphanes (Poet), 284
Antoninus Pius (Emperor), 296
Apelles (Gnostic), 235, 241–45, 267
Apuleius, 84
Aquilinus, 263
Aristaeus, 323
Aristobulus, 322
Aristotle, 67, 133, 264, 324
Arndt, Johann, 343
Augustine, xviii, 337

Bachmann, Karl Friedrich, 436
Bardesanes (Gnostic), xvi, 59, 63, 65, 71, 121, 124, 137–38
Basilides (Gnostic), xvi, 8, 46, 55–57, 59, 61, 65–66. 71, 114, 121–34, 143, 154–57, 159, 177, 246, 266–67, 297–98, 300, 369, 456
Bauer, Bruno, 415

Baumgarten, Siegmund Jacob, xxxiv
Baumgarten-Crusius, Ludwig, 246
Baur, Ferdinand Christian, xiii–xxvi, xxviii, xxx, xxxv, 12, 29–30, 34–35, 40, 43, 64, 74–75, 134, 136, 162, 167, 179, 181, 184–85, 234, 240, 335, 340, 344, 376, 394, 396, 398, 402, 405, 444–45
Berdyaev, Nikolai, xxv
Bockshammer, Gustav Friedrich, 389
Boeckh, A. 90
Boehme, Jacob, xviii–xix, xxiv–xxv, xxxiv, 11, 342–79, 382, 384, 386, 389, 424–26, 456–57
Bohlen, P. von, 29–30
Braniss, Christlieb Julius, 415
Brown, Robert F., 344
Buddha, the, 264

Cain, 23, 100, 110, 115–17, 188, 200–201
Calvin, John, 341
Carpocrates (Gnostic), 46, 58–59, 62–63, 66–67
Cassian, Julius (Gnostic), 87, 304–5
Celsus, 114, 134
Censorinus, 92
Cerdo (Gnostic), 57, 59–60, 164–67, 169
Cerinthus (Gnostic), 66, 241–42
Cham, 134
Claudius (Emperor), 182
Clement of Alexandria, xviii–xix, 52–54, 63–65, 73, 79, 81, 85, 87–89, 92–93, 120, 123–31, 133, 159, 177, 180, 246, 265–67, 272, 278, 296–330
Clement of Rome (Pope), 178
Cotellier, J.-B., 218
Credner, K. A., 234
Creuzer, Georg F., xxix, 182, 251, 263–65, 267, 269–70, 276

Dähne, August Ferdinand, xxx, 100, 235, 327
Daniel, 110
Danz, J. T. L., 175

*Index of Persons*

Dathan, 171
David, 47, 235
Democritus, 96, 284
Demostratus of Lydia, 263
Deucalion, 200
Dionysius (Bishop), 241
Dositheus, 203
Drecoll, Volker Henning, xiii, xvi, 40, 64, 436

Elijah, 110, 150, 299
Elisha, 149–50
Eliot, George (Mary Ann Evans), xiii
Empedocles, 96, 285, 323
Enoch, 171, 203, 214
Ephrem the Syrian, 168
Epicurus, 262, 284
Epiphanes (Gnostic), 58, 66
Epiphanius, 8, 16, 72–73, 75, 81, 86–89, 100–102, 104, 107, 112–15, 117–18, 121–24, 152–53, 161–62, 164–67, 171, 174–76, 181–82, 184, 235–36, 240–43, 245, 269
Esau, 116, 171, 200
Esnig (Bishop), 162, 167–68, 175
Eusebius of Caesarea, 8, 165–66, 175, 183, 218, 224, 241–43, 245–46, 329
Eve, 103–6, 108–9, 112, 115, 117, 200–201, 305, 369, 372–74
Ezekiel, 110

Feuerbach, Ludwig, xxiv
Fichte, Immanuel Hermann, 436, 439–40
Frank, Othmar, 29

Gaius (Pope), 241
Gfrörer, A. F., 22
Gieseler, J. C. L., xxxiii, 5, 34, 37–39, 56–59, 61, 78, 95–96, 114, 123–24, 127–28, 132, 173
Glaucius, 177
Göschel, Carl Friedrich, 439, 445
Grant, Robert M., xxiii
Gunther, Anton, 439

Habbakuk, 110
Hadrian (Emperor), 246
Hagar, 321,
Haggai, 110
Hahn, August, 160, 164, 168
Ham, 117, 206
Harnack, Adolf, xxii–xxiii
Hector, 211
Hegel, G. W. F., xv–xxv, xxx, 11, 16, 35, 413–58
Hegemonius, 123
Hegesippus, 224
Heigl, Georg Anton, xxix, 251, 267, 269
Heinichen, 217

Helena, 181–84, 203, 242
Heracleon (Gnostic), 94–95
Heracles, 182–83, 210
Heraclitus, 134, 289
Herodotus, 182
Herder, Johann Gottfried, xxxiii
Homer, 284
Hosea, 110
Humboldt, Wilhelm von, 29
Hyginus (Pope), 246

Iamblichus, 92
Irenaeus, xviii, xxxi–xxxii, xxxiv, 16, 40, 51, 67, 71–74, 76–82, 85–87, 89–91, 95–100, 102–7, 111–14, 116–17, 122–24, 136–38, 143, 153, 162, 165–67, 171, 175, 181–82, 184, 196, 241, 246, 254, 268–70, 278–85, 300, 305, 330–31, 419–20
Isaac, 200, 203, 214–15, 219, 318
Isaiah, 110, 149
Ishmael, 200
Isidore (Gnostic), 126, 132–34

Jablonski, 182
Jacob, 23, 200, 203, 214–15, 217, 219–20, 325
Jacobi, Friedrich Heinrich, 383, 388
Jaeschke, Walter, 415, 436
Jeremiah, 110
Jerome, 181
Jesus of Nazareth, xxi, 25, 48, 81, 94, 111–14, 118, 131–32, 153, 156–57, 162, 185, 198, 215–19, 231–33, 302, 316, 324, 396–406, 441–42 (*see also* "Jesus" and "Christ" in the Subject Index)
Joel, 110
Johannsen, 191
John, the Apostle, 151
John the Baptist, 111, 145, 150, 203
Jonah, 110
Jonas, Hans, xxiii
Joseph, 23
Josephus, Flavius, 24
Joshua, 235
Judah, 217, 224
Judas, 116
Justin Martyr, 182–83

Kant, Immanuel, 383, 409–13
King, Karen L., xxiii
Köpf, Ulrich, xiii
Korah, 116, 171
Koyré, Alexandre, 343
Kühner, 137

Lazarus, 150

Leibniz, Gottfried Wilhelm, 342
Lessing, Gotthold Ephraim, 384, 396
Lewald, Ernst Anton, xxxiii–xxxiv, 37, 40, 56, 78
Lot, 23
Lucian, 182
Lücke, Friedrich, xxxiii, 36–37, 46, 55, 394
Luther, Martin, 339, 341, 343

Macrobius, 114
Mani (Manes), 123–24, 264–65, 335–36, 359–60, 366
Marcion (Gnostic), xvi, xxii, 3, 8, 12, 46, 56–61, 65–66, 68, 114, 124, 141–77, 179, 184–87, 189–90, 192–93, 196, 216, 226–27, 229, 236–38, 242, 244–46, 266, 278, 286–96, 302, 304–5, 335–36, 339, 413, 457
Marcus (Gnostic), 71, 89–90, 242
Marheineke, Philipp, xxx, 415
Markschies, Christoph, xxii, xxvii
Mary, the Virgin, xxiv, 81, 111, 113, 235
Massuet, René, xxxi–xxxii, 40, 90, 96–97
Matter, Jacques, xxxiii, 5–7, 38–40, 46, 58–61, 75, 81, 94, 104, 108
Maximus of Tyre, 134
Megethius the Marcionite (Gnostic), 164
Menander (Gnostic), 122, 180, 183
Messus, 263
Mestren, 206
Meursius, J., 90
Micah, 110
Miriam, 228
Mitteldopf, H., 167
Möhler, Johann Adam, xiii–xiv, xxv, 40–46, 94, 340
Moltmann, Jürgen, xxv
Moore, Thomas, 340
Moses, xxxiii, 24, 47–48, 110, 116, 118, 133, 139, 149, 188–89, 200, 203, 214–16, 218–20, 222, 235, 245, 316, 322, 339, 375, 378, 395, 400, 454–55
Mosheim, Johann Lorenz, xxxi–xxxiv, 3, 36–37, 55, 95, 103–4, 112, 114
Muhammad, 400
Müller, Julius, 445

Naaman, 150
Nahum, 110
Nathan, 110
Nathanael, 315
Neander, August, xxxi, xxxiii–xxxv, 3–6, 20, 39, 47, 55–61, 63–64, 66, 68, 75, 78, 87, 94–95, 103–4, 112, 114–15, 125, 127–28, 132–34, 137–39, 165, 173, 175, 234, 240–41, 245
Nebuchadnezzar (King), 189, 228
Neumann, Friedrich, 162, 167, 171
Nicodemus, 221
Nicotheus, 263
Nitzsch, Karl, 405
Noah, 23, 110, 171, 200, 203, 206, 214, 219
Noetus, 173–74
Numenius (Philosopher), 322

O'Regan, Cyril, xxiv–xxv
Origen, 65, 94–95, 102, 106, 113–14, 124, 130, 134, 177, 245, 275, 330, 439, 456
Orpheus, 37
Ovid, 292

Pabst, Johann Heinrich, 439
Pagels, Elaine, xxii–xxiv
Pantaenus (Philosopher), 329
Paracelsus, 375
Paul, the Apostle, xiii, xix, xxviii, 26, 49–51, 130, 138–39, 162, 166, 176–78, 228, 303–4, 455
Pearson, Birger A., xxiii
Pentheus, 329
Peter, the Apostle, 176–79, 183, 185–86, 203, 224–26, 228, 233, 246, 303
Pherecydes of Syros, 134
Philicomus, 263
Phillip, the Apostle, 113, 303
Philo of Alexandria, 4–6, 20–22, 24–27, 37–39, 44–45, 53, 65, 75, 100, 114, 235, 240, 316, 318
Philumene, 242
Pilate, Pontius, 82
Pius I (Pope), 246
Planck, G. J., 56, 339
Plato, 6, 20–21, 37, 41, 43–44, 67, 84, 88–89, 96, 106, 108, 260, 263–64, 274, 284–86, 302, 322–23
Pliny the Younger, 24
Plotinus, xxix, 251–77
Plutarch, 92, 125, 182–83,
Porphyry, 253, 254, 263–65
Praxeas, 173–74
Proclus, 92
Prodicus, 274
Prometheus, 200, 209, 324, 326
Prudentius (Poet), 167
Psyche, 84
Ptolemaeus (Gnostic), 71, 118–20
Pythagoras, 67, 90, 92

Quispel, G., 118

## Index of Persons

Rhodo, 165
Rosenkranz, Karl, 402–3, 406–7, 439, 450, 457
Rust, Isaak, 450–51

Salome, 302–3
Samson, 182–83
Samuel, 110
Sarah, 318
Saturninus (Gnostic), xvi, 56, 58–59, 61–36, 65, 71, 121–22, 124, 127, 132, 266
Schelling, Friedrich W., xv, xvii, xix, xxiii, 11, 342, 344, 379–90, 423–24, 436–37, 446, 456–57
Schiller, Friedrich, 438
Schlegel, Friedrich, 46
Schleiermacher, Friedrich, xiii, xv, xix–xx, xxiii–xxiv, xxix–xxx, 11, 389–425, 439, 442–43, 446, 456
Schmid, Heinrich, xxx
Schmidt, Isaak, 5, 30–33, 35, 126
Schneckenburger, Matthias, 235–36
Schweizer, Alexander, 399
Scythianus, 264
Semler, Johann Salomo, xxxiv
Seth, 100, 110, 116–17
Simeon, 139
Simon of Cyrene, 123
Simon Magus, 179–87, 203, 224–25, 227, 229, 241–42, 246, 340
Simut, Cornelius C., xxiv
Slenczka, Notger, xiii, 40, 340
Socrates, 106, 133, 431, 441
Solomon, 318, 376
Solon, 322
Soloviev, Vladimir, xxv
Spinoza, Benedict, 383
Staudenmeier, F. H., 436
Stesichorus (Poet), 182

Strauss, David Friedrich, xiii, xxv–xxvi, 396, 416
Süskind, Friedrich Gottlieb, 387–88

Tatian (Gnostic), 58, 307
Tertullian, xviii, 8, 67, 72, 84, 87, 100, 141–52, 158–61, 163–66, 169–76, 182, 187, 196, 235–36, 242–45, 269–71, 278, 286–96, 300, 324–25, 330–31, 422
Thales, 287
Theodoret, 73, 101, 108, 114, 134, 166, 168, 176, 340
Theodotus (Gnostic), 92
Theudas, 177
Thilo, J. C., 160
Tiberius (Emperor), 146, 152, 296
Tillich, Paul, xxv
Titus of Bostra, 165
Tobias (Prophet), 110
Triptolemus, 289

Valentinus (Gnostic), xvi, xxii, xxxiv, 12, 41, 46, 55, 59, 63–66, 71–73, 78–81, 83, 85, 87, 93, 95, 118, 126, 133, 154, 156, 159, 165, 177, 196, 246, 253, 272–73, 297–98, 304–5, 329, 422
Vater, J. S., 56
Virgil, 267

Walch, C. W. F., xxxiii, xxxiv
Weisse, C. H., 436
Williams, Michael A., xxiii
Wolff, Christian, 341–42

Zechariah, 110
Zoroaster (Nebrod), 37, 206, 263–64
Zostrianus, 263

# Index of Subjects

absolute spirit, 10–11, 15, 18, 20, 29–30, 83, 98, 174, 236, 283, 395, 414, 417–23, 435–40, 443–44, 447, 458
absolute substance becomes subject, 16, 254
Acts, Book of, 179–80
Adam, *see* Index of Persons
   and Christ, 200, 203, 214–15, 233–34
Adam Kadmon, 196
Aeons
   all things created in their image, 85
   and Christ, 82–83
   church fathers' critique of, 279–80, 284–85
   comprising an Ogdoad, a Decad, and a Dodecad, 74, 86, 89
   divided into male and female pairs, 86, 88–91, 121
   as emanations of the divine, mediating the transition from the ideal to the real, 3, 15–16, 73–76, 331
   Pleroma as joint product of, 81
   Plotinus' critique of, 267, 269
   as pure essences or thoughts in which spirit thinks its own essential nature (distinguishes and reunites itself), 418–20
   similar to Platonic ideas, 82–85
   total number is thirty, 74
Aletheia (Truth), 74, 86, 88–91
Alexandrian religious philosophy, 4, 20–23, 26, 63
Alexandrine theologians (Clement, Origen), 52–54, 296–329
allegory, allegorical, 5, 21–22, 25–26, 47–49, 52–54, 139–40, 177, 181, 209–11, 277, 316–19, 330–31, 378, 456
Anthropos (Humankind), 74, 86–89, 91, 136, 196
Apelles, a follower of Marcion, 242–45
Apocrypha, 22, 24, 38, 45, 121
archetype (*Urbild*), 84–86, 88, 157, 255, 272–73, 279, 398, 400–401, 405, 426
Asia Minor, 59, 141, 174, 450
Augustinian system, 337–38

baptism, 111, 131–32, 156, 220–21, 292, 433
Bardesanes, system of, 121
Barnabas, Epistle of, 47–48
Basilides, system of, 122–31, 132–34
Baur, Ferdinand Christian
   his authorship of *Christian Gnosis*, xiii–xv
   his concept of Gnosis, xviii
   and recent studies of Gnosticism, xxii–xxvi
   his treatment of religious history and religious philosophy, xv–xvii
   his treatment of Hegel, xx–xxii
   his treatment of Schleiermacher, xix–xx
   his use of the term "paganism," xvii–xviii
Boehme, Jacob
   angels in, 350–51
   on Christianity and the mosaic law, 378
   dualism and monism of his system, 359–60
   duality of principles in his system, 344–46
   on fall of human beings, 366–69
   Lucifer in, 351–58
   his mystical theosophy as a higher way of knowing God, 375–77
   on redemption, the Virgin, and Christ, 370–74
   seven source-spirits in, 348–49
   theosophy of, 343–78
   three principles or worlds in his thought, 354–69
   Trinity in his system, 347–48
   his use of mythic-symbolic form, 456
Brahmanism, 29
Buddhism, 30–35, 448
Bythus (Depth), 73, 75, 86, 87–89, 91, 98, 139, 253, 267, 280, 284

Catholic Church, 132, 152–53, 163, 175, 183, 222, 264, 341
Catholic Tübingen School, 40
Catholicism, 40, 338–40
Cerinthus, representative of Judaizing form of Gnosis, 241–42
Charis (Love), 73, 86–87

*Index of Subjects*

Christ
 and Adam, 200, 203, 214–15, 234
 apprehension of by history, faith, and knowledge (Hegel), 430–32, 441–47
 born in human minds (Boehme), 375
 church as bride of, 222–23
 conjoins male and female principles, 100
 and the Demiurge, 12, 17–18, 27, 39, 61, 81, 93, 161
 his descent into Hades, 171
 distinction between ideal (archetypal) and real (historical), 396–99, 400–407, 411–12, 430–32, 440–47
 docetic views of, 49, 65, 151–58, 229, 243–44, 294–95
 establishment of a new corporate life through him (Schleiermacher), 399
 forms a syzygy with the Holy Spirit, 75–76
 historical, 397, 400–407, 430–32, 440–47
 ideal, 391–92, 400–407, 411–12, 430–32, 440–47
 and Jesus of Nazareth, 112, 398, 441, 445
 Jewish Christ versus Christian Christ (Marcion), 149–51
 and Lucifer (Boehme), 366
 Marcion's view of, 145–46
 and Moses, 378
 and the Paraclete, 335
 and philosophy, 319–20
 the psychical, 80, 82, 94, 100
 as the redeemer, 72, 396–99
 as revealer of a new and unknown God (Marcion), 145–46, 148
 as revelation of God in finite spirit (Hegel's view), 430–32
 as the savior Aeon, 26
 and Simon Magus, 181
 and Sophia, 63, 107, 110–11, 121, 307, 376
 suffering and death of, 82, 161
 as an utterly powerful form of God-consciousness (Schleiermacher), 391–92
 and the Virgin (female form of Christ), 370–74, 376
*Christian Gnosis*, Baur's summary of, xxvii–xxx
Christianity
 as the absolute religion, 393–95
 as an ethical, positive religion, 35–36
 and Gnosticism, 25–26
 identified with Judaism and opposed to paganism, 178–247
 linked to Judaism and paganism, 71–140
 must attain to the idea of absolute spirit, leaving all else behind, 456–58
 as reformed, purified, enlarged Judaism, 216–22
 its relation to other religions (Schleiermacher), 393–95
 as religion of freedom from matter (Marcion), 158–62
 as religion of love (Marcion), 146–48
 its religious consciousness mediated by the history and person of an individual, 455
 separated from Judaism and paganism, 141–77
christology, 173, 233, 241, 294, 312–14, 384, 440, 445
church fathers (Irenaeus, Tertullian, Clement of Alexandria), 278–331
Clement of Alexandria
 Christianity as uniting all the separate streams of truth, 327–30
 christology of, 312–14
 as a Gnostic, 306–15, 327–30
 as an opponent of the Gnostics, 296–305
 his view of how Christianity is related to Judaism and paganism, 315–33
community (*Gemeinde*), 32–34, 403, 406, 422, 425, 431–34, 440, 442, 447, 457

death, and God, 431–32
Demiurge (world creator, distinguished from highest God) 5, 12–13, 16–18, 27, 29, 32, 44, 49, 56, 58, 61–62, 65, 78–82, 85–86, 89, 93–94, 99–100, 102, 117, 120–21, 136, 139, 141–46, 149, 151, 158, 161–68, 171, 192, 227, 237, 245, 261–62, 268–69, 273, 283, 383, 421
docetism, 32, 61, 140, 151–58, 173, 227–29, 235, 294–95, 304–5, 314, 375, 407, 444

Ebionites, 25, 61, 66, 178, 235–36, 240
Ecclesia (Church), 74, 86, 88–89, 91, 136
Egypt, 26–27, 39, 59, 71, 110, 134–35, 149, 176, 182–83, 318
Ennoia (Thought), 73–74, 86–87, 89–91, 101, 184, 238, 253, 282
eschatology, 457
Essenes, 24–26, 38, 45, 240
ethics, and religion, 402, 412
evil
 Boehme's view of, 343–46, 352, 355–56
 Hegel's view of, 425–28, 431
 Manichean view of, 34–35
 Clement of Alexandria's view of, 314, 316, 320–21
 as the Devil, 128, 142, 228
 distinction between Gnostic and Christian views of, 41–42
 Kant's view of, 409, 411–12
 as matter, 37, 41, 43, 57, 78, 94, 154

more profound awareness of in Protestantism, 340
Neoplatonic view of, 228–29, 261, 265
origin of, 8–9, 169, 189–91
Platonic view of, 44
power or principle of, 24, 63, 106, 122, 129, 164, 166, 191–92, 198, 456
Schelling's view of, 381–82, 384–85, 388
symbolized by the serpent, 109
Tertullian's view of, 293

faith
    Clement of Alexandria on, 297–98, 306–8, 320
    and deeds, 216
    different in form but identical in content with philosophy, 445–46
    as divine Spirit at work in the subject, 431–33
    Hegel on, 414, 431, 442–46
    and history, 441
    justification by, 148
    justified by philosophy, not history, 432
    and knowledge, 47, 53, 296, 306–7, 315, 318, 338, 414, 445–46
    and Protestantism, 340
    its relation to history and knowledge, 430–32
    Schleiermacher on, 389, 411
falling-away (*Abfall*) of the finite world from the spirit world, 9, 72–73, 327–28, 388
feeling of absolute or utter dependence, 390–92, 394–95
finite spirit, 77, 417, 420–22, 425–26, 428, 430, 435–39, 443–44, 447
First Corinthians, 49–51
flood, the, 117, 203, 206

Gieseler, J. C. L., classification of the Gnostic systems, 56–57, 61
Gnosis
    as absolute knowledge, 53, 306–7
    as the attempt to grasp nature (matter) and history as the series of moments in which spirit mediates itself with itself, 10–11
    church fathers' polemic against, 278–331
    concept of, xxvii, 3–18
    dissenting views on the origin of, 37–45
    first major form of, linking Christianity to Judaism and paganism (Valentinus, etc.), 71–140
    goal of is clear self-consciousness, 239–40
    meaning of the term, xv, xxvii, 46–52
    Neoplatonists' polemic against, 251–78
    origins of, 19–45
    practical wisdom of, 308–11
    as religious history, 8–10
    as religious philosophy or philosophy of religion, xxix, 8–10
    second major form of, separating Christianity from Judaism and paganism (Marcion), 141–77
    as spiritual, not ordinary, knowledge, 48, 50–54
    symbolic, mythic, and allegorical form of, 135–40
    third major form of, identifying Christianity and Judaism, and opposing both to paganism (Pseudo-Clementines), 178–247
    three main forms of (depending on how paganism, Judaism, and Christianity relate to one another), 61–68, 246–47
Gnostic names or figures are indexed separately
Gnosticism
    and Buddhism, 30–34
    Christian polemic against, 278
    classification of Gnostic systems, 55–68
    early views of as heretical, xxxi–xxxii
    historical and philosophical aspects of, 11
    history of research on, xxxi–xxxv
    modern (18th- early 19th century) treatments of, xxxii–xxxv, 3–7
    most original of ancient systems, 7
    and Pseudo-Clementine system, 199–203, 223–26, 236–40
    regarded as "Oriental philosophy," xxxii–xxxiii, 3–4
    and religious systems of the East, 26–27
    spirit's independence from matter in, 155–57
    traced to Philo and Alexandrian religious philosophy, 4–5
God
    as absolute spirit, *see* absolute spirit
    biblical views of, 22, 28, 50
    Boehme's view of, 344–78
    concept of as lifeless and abstract, 412–13
    as creator of the world, 193–98, 281–82, 292–93
    and death, 431–32
    divine life-process: identity, difference, return, 383–84
    divine process: going out from and returning to godself, 11, 16–17, 347–48, 418–38
    doctrine of in Pseudo-Clementine system, 193–98

## Index of Subjects

God *(continued)*
  Gnostic view of: highest God or primal being as distinct from Aeons, Demiurge, 5, 56, 62, 65, 79, 119–20, 133, 141–42, 163–67, 331
  goodness of, 290–91
  Hegel's view of, 414–59
  justice of, 292–93
  knowledge of, 288–89, 306–7
  Marcion's view of, 141–48, 163–67
  and matter, 10, 15, 94, 98
  monotheistic view of, 213–15
  and nature, 426–27
  oneness of, 287–89
  orthodox Christian views of, 279–95
  pagan knowledge of, 317–21
  personality and spirituality of, 438–39
  Platonic view of, 44
  Plotinus' view of, 256
  Schelling's view of, 379–88
  Schleiermacher's view of, 389–413
God-consciousness, 295, 391–92, 395–96, 399–401, 404–7, 409–13, 440–41, 453
good
  as divine or spiritual principle, 21, 122, 128, 141, 144, 148, 164–68, 173, 243, 252, 254, 274, 288, 290, 303, 409, 411–12
  and evil, 18, 34, 99–100, 108, 116, 122–23, 126, 135, 185, 188, 201, 235, 306, 344, 381, 385, 388
Greek mythology, 6, 184, 277, 323
Greek philosophy, 318, 320, 322, 324–25, 327–28, 331

Hegel, Georg Wilhelm Friedrich
  Baur's critique of, 444–45
  Baur's defense of, 436–39
  Christ viewed from the perspective of history, faith, and knowledge (philosophy), 430–32, 441–44
  Christianity as religious consciousness mediated by the history and person of a single individual, who is also the human as such, 455
  christology of, 440–47
  his concept of God (positing an other to God and sublating the difference), 416–18
  his concept of human being, 426–27
  his concept of Judaism, 451–54
  his concept of paganism or nature religion, 448–50
  his concept of the community (*Gemeinde*), 432–34, 457
  content takes refuge in the concept (*in den Begriff sich flüchtet*), 434
  critiques of by opponents, 435–39
  crossover from Schleiermacher to Hegel, 414–15
  his distinction between perception (*Anschauung*), understanding (*Verstand*), and reason (*Vernunft*), 455
  faith is justified by philosophy, not history, 432
  God and death, 431–32
  God and world, 416, 423
  God as process of self-differentiation, sundering, and going back into self, 422–23
  God as Spirit in its return to God, or reconciliation, 421
  God in nature, 426–27
  God in the element of consciousness and representation, 420
  God in the element of pure thinking, 418–19
  historical and ideal Christ, 447
  his importance to Baur, xxx
  incarnation of God in a human being, 430–31
  his judgment about Kant and Schleiermacher, 413
  kingdom of the Father, 424–25
  kingdom of the Son, 426–31
  kingdom of the Spirit, 432–34
  *Lectures on the Philosophy of Religion*, editions of, 415, 441
  location of Christianity in relation to paganism and Judaism, 447
  meaning of "absolute" for, 414
  moments of identity, difference, and mediation, 425–26
  objective standpoint contrasted with Schleiermacher's subjective standpoint, 414
  personality and spirituality of God, 438–39
  his philosophy of religion, 414–55
  relation of logic, nature, and finite spirit in, 417–18
  his relation to Gnostic systems, 415–22
  religion (faith) and philosophy (knowledge) are different in form but identical in content, 445–46
  religion as self-consciousness of God, 417
  religious consciousness mediated by nature, or people and state, or an individual, 448–55
  separation of the historical Christ from the ideal Christ, 440–47
  his system, 415–18, 422–23
  three forms of absolute spirit, 418–23
  treatment of the history of religion ("Determinate Religion"), 428–29

## Index of Subjects

triune God in the three forms of his self-revelation, 423–34
Hinduism, 429, 448
historical examination (*geschichtliche Betrachtung*) can only show what is best in a relative sense, 396
history of religion, 9–10, 14, 28, 67, 203, 213–14, 223–24, 315, 328, 332, 335, 338, 340–41, 382, 384–85, 413, 428; *see also* religious history
Holy Spirit
   Boehme's concept of, 347–48, 350–51, 357, 367, 369
   and Christ, 75, 214, 229
   faith is truth from, 431
   female principle for the Ophites, 101, 121
   in human beings, 300
   and the Trinity, 347–48
Horos (Boundary, Limit), 74–77, 81, 83, 86, 90–91, 138, 419
human being
   both spiritual and psychical, 421
   Christ born as, 111
   creation of, 79–80, 102, 105, 107, 122, 191
   divine life-process in (Schelling), 380–81, 384
   fall of, 130, 366–70, 384
   Gnostic concept of, 34, 42, 79–80, 100, 300, 421
   God had to become human so that humans could come to God (Schelling), 385
   God-consciousness of (Schleiermacher), 402, 405, 410–11
   as good and evil by nature, 426–27
   Hegel's concept of, 426–27
   human knowledge of God as God's self-consciousness (Hegel), 437
   image of God in, 193–94, 196–97, 200, 204, 299, 454
   as male and female, 237–38
   moral freedom of in relation to God, 297–99
   Platonic view of, 44
   as pneumatic (spiritual), psychic, and hylic (material), 93–94
   revelation of God in (Hegel), 426–28, 430–32, 441–44
   sinfulness of, 337

Ialdabaoth (evil founder of Judaism according to the Ophites), 57, 61, 102–8, 110–12, 115
ideal world, 15–16, 23, 27, 83, 88, 92, 279, 351, 420
ideal, 21, 44, 72, 85, 88, 91–92, 279, 365, 381, 406, 411, 413, 452
ideality, 406, 419, 423, 447, 451
immortality, 439–40

Irenaeus, arguments against the Valentians, 279–85

Jesus of Nazareth, *see* Index of Persons
   non-being of the idea as its minimum in him (Baur), 445
   proving that he is the redeemer cannot be done by empirical (historical) means, 396
   his teaching confirms the truth of what he becomes for faith (Baur), 441
   *see also* Christ
Judaism
   Alexandrian, 24–26, 48, 140
   in antithesis to paganism, 178–246
   distinction between God and world in, 276
   as ethical, positive religion, 35
   Hegel's view of, 447, 448, 451–54
   identified with Christianity, 178–247
   Kant's view of, 413
   linked to Christianity, 52–53, 71–140, 395
   one of the three main forms of religion, 8, 11–13, 61–67
   and paganism, 62, 63, 66, 145–46, 170, 223, 237, 328
   its particularism expanded into Christian universalism, 220
   Pseudo-Clementine view of, 213–15, 236
   as religious consciousness mediated by the people and the state, 451–54
   Schleiermacher's view of, 395, 407–8
   separated from Christianity, 141–77
   as true religion, 213–15
   two forms of (spiritual and sensuous), 21–22

Kabbalah, 38–39
Kant, Immanuel, Schleiermacher's work compared with, 409–13
knowledge
   and faith, 47, 52–53, 296, 306–8, 315, 318, 338, 414, 445–46
   and love, 50
   *see also* Gnosis

Lessing's ditch, 396
Logos (Word) 4–5, 16, 20, 23, 74–75, 86, 88–89, 91, 124, 133, 252–53, 271, 282, 308, 310, 312–15, 319, 322, 324–25, 327–29
love, 50, 144, 146–48, 150, 158, 186, 195, 197–98, 204, 225, 256, 290, 292, 298, 306, 309–10, 345–47, 349, 351, 353, 356–59, 361, 365, 370–71, 373, 375, 378, 380–81, 384–85, 388, 413, 419, 428, 433, 438

Manicheanism, 34–35, 335–36

467

*Index of Subjects*

Marcion
    his antinomianism, 141
    antithesis of law and gospel, 146–48
    Christ as revealer of a completely new, unknown God, 145–46
    Christianity as religion of freedom from matter, 158–62
    Christianity as religion of love, 146–48
    his critique of the Old Testament and its God, 141–43
    his docetism, 151–57
    his dualism, 163–67
    his hostility toward Judaism, 141–77
    imperfect nature of the Demiurge, 141–44
    importance for his time and reforming tendency, 174–77
    Jewish Christ and Christian Christ, 149–50
    polemic against by Pseudo-Clementines, 184–92
    profundity and shortcomings of his system, 170
    refuted by Tertullian, 286–95
    subjective nature of his standpoint, 168–73
    system of, 141–77
marriage, 159–60, 222–23, 301–5
Massuet, Réné, first scholarly interpreter of Gnosticism, xxxi–xxxii
material world, 10, 14, 16–17, 31–32, 94–99, 102, 132, 137, 154–56, 158, 192, 244, 361, 364–65
Matter, Jacques
    his classification of the Gnostic systems, 58–60
    his view of the origin of Gnosticism, 37–40
medieval scholasticism, 338
miracle, 323, 398, 405–6
Möhler, J. A., his view of the origin of Gnosticism, 40–45
monotheism, 193, 224–25, 227, 336, 394–95, 408, 452
Mosheim, J. L. von
    his classification of the Gnostic systems, 55
    traces Gnosticism to Oriental philosophy, xxxii–xxxiii
myth, mythic, 135, 137, 140, 158, 168, 177, 277, 316, 449, 451, 456

nature religion, as religious consciousness mediated by nature, 448–40
nature, philosophy of, 36, 341, 379, 388
Neander, August
    his classification of the Gnostic systems, 56, 58–59, 62–64, 66, 68
    early 19th c. scholar of Gnosticism, xxxiii–xxiv

Neoplatonism, 39, 41–42, 249–77
New Testament, 22, 46, 49, 139, 141, 166, 179–80, 219, 298, 316, 331, 340, 386, 397–98, 409, 445
Nous (Mind, Reason), 16, 73–75, 87, 89, 91, 106, 107, 109, 123–24, 132, 253–54, 282, 284

Old Testament, 4–5, 22–24, 39, 47–48, 52, 108, 115, 118, 120, 134, 137, 139, 142–45, 148, 158, 166, 171, 187–89, 193, 244–45, 288, 293, 298, 304, 307, 316, 322–24, 326, 328, 331, 336, 340, 386, 408–9
Only-Begotten, 16, 73–76, 83, 85–86, 89, 253, 314, 355, 370
Ophites
    Christian and pre-Christian elements in, 115–17
    main ideas of, 101–14
    system of, 100–120
Oriental (ideas, philosophy, religion), 3–4, 6–7, 14–15, 27, 39–40, 58, 184, 449

paganism
    critique of by Pseudo-Clementine writings, 204–12, 223–24
    its speculative character, 35
    linked to Christianity, 71–140
    one of the thee main forms of religions, 11–13, 27, 61–67
    opposed to both Judaism and Christianity, 178–246
    its philosophy comes from God via the Logos, 317–21
    its philosophy has a demonic origin, 322–26
    as a philosophy of nature, 36, 42
    plays an important role in religious history, 14–15, 28–29
    its religious consciousness mediated by consciousness of nature, 448–53
    separated from Christianity, 141–77, 317
    takes the antithesis of spirit and matter as its point of departure, 35
    truth of, 328
    use of the term, 12
    in the Valentinian system, 284–85
Paul, the Apostle, 26, 130, 138, 176, 228, 303–3
    his interpretation and use of the word *gnosis*, 46, 49–51
    polemic against, 228
    regarded as an apostate by Ebionites, 178
    regarded as the only apostle by Marcion, 176
Pelagianism, 341
Persia, 27, 38, 46, 176, 206, 286
Peter, the Apostle

children of, 303
in the Pseudo-Clementine Homilies, 179, 233
and Simon Magus, 179, 183, 185–87, 203, 223–25, 227
philosophy of religion, 20, 331, 342, 389, 396–400, 407, 409, 413, 414–55; *see also* religious philosophy
Platonism, 5, 20–23, 37–38, 41–45, 58, 72, 82–84, 88, 97, 120, 246, 251, 259, 264–65, 272, 277, 279, 330
Pleroma (fullness, completeness, wholeness), 75–86, 91–94, 96–100, 114, 138–40, 268–70, 273, 280–81, 283–84, 383, 420, 422, 426, 457
Plotinus
  doctrine of, 272–78
  his polemic against the Gnostics, 252–71
  and Valentinianism, 272–78
polytheism, 172, 199, 201, 204, 212–14, 224–27, 229, 273, 287, 394, 451–52
primal or supreme being, 73, 83, 86–88, 91, 105, 122, 163, 165, 226, 246, 297, 391, 394
prophecy, 199, 201–2, 204, 213, 217, 227–29, 232–35, 317, 408
Protestantism, 40, 338–41
prototype (*Vorbild*), 400–401
Pseudo-Clementine system
  Christianity as reformed, purified, enlarged Judaism, 216–22
  its critique of docetism, 227–28
  its critique of paganism, 204–12
  doctrine of God in, 193–98
  form and character of the Clementine Homilies, 179–83
  and Gnosticism, 199–203, 223–26, 236–40
  Judaism as true religion, 213–15
  its opposition to Marcion, 184–92
  prophecy in, 229–35
  relation of matter to God and origin of evil, 189–92
  when and by whom the *Homilies* and *Recognitions* were written, 178
Pythagorean number theory, 89–90, 97, 285
Pythagorean-Platonic philosophy, 12, 15, 25, 27, 135

real world, 15–16, 27, 88, 280, 295, 351
redeemer
  Gnostic view of, 72, 80–84, 93–94, 99–100, 111, 114, 117, 119, 121–22, 138–39, 153–58, 160, 285, 289, 300, 303, 310, 313–14
  Kant's view of, 411, 413
  Schleiermacher's view of, 396–406, 409–12

Reformation, the, 338–39
religious history (*Religionsgeschichte*)
  comprised of paganism, Judaism, and Christianity, 8–14
  essential element of Gnosis, 8–11, 24, 63
  Old Testament, 120
  Protestant, 341
  Pseudo-Clementine, 239
  and religious philosophy, 14, 342
  Schelling's, 385
religious philosophy (*Religionsphilosophie*)
  Alexandrian, 4, 26, 63, 139
  Boehme's, 343–78
  character of, 11, 14
  Christian, 455–58
  Clement of Alexandria's, 330
  continues to develop into modern times, 333, 342
  essential element of Gnosis, xxix, 8–11, 24
  Hegel's, 414–55
  Jewish, 23
  Kant's, 409–13
  more recent, 11, 343–455
  Neoplatonic, 250
  pagan, 34–35, 135
  and religious history, 9, 11, 28
  Schelling's, 379–88
  Schleiermacher's, 389–413
Rome, 59, 71, 165, 175–76, 242, 246, 266

salvation, 6, 80, 116, 127, 131–32, 161, 215–16, 221, 244, 290, 297, 314, 374
Saturninus, system of, 121–22, 132–34
Schelling, Friedrich Wilhelm Joseph
  application of his speculative ideas to the history of religion, 385
  critique of his system, 386–89
  his critique of theism, 383
  distinction between God and the (dark) ground (*Urgrund*), 379–80, 382
  divine life-process: identity, difference, return, 383–84
  God and evil, 381–82
  God as All in All, 382
  God as becoming, living, suffering, 380–81
  God gives birth to himself, 380
  his philosophy of nature, 379–88
  his relation to Boehme, 379
  his relation to Gnosis, 382–85
  use of mythic-symbolic form, 456
Schleiermacher, Friedrich
  his antinomianism, 407–8
  his attitude toward Judaism, 407–8
  Baur on the work of, xxix–xxx

## Index of Subjects

Schleiermacher, Friedrich *(continued)*
  comparison between his *Glaubenslehre* and Kant's *Religion within the Limits of Reason Alone*, 409–13
  his concept of miracle, 405
  dependent on philosophical methods and concepts, 389, 394, 398, 402–3
  distinction between archetypal and historical factors in the person of the redeemer, 396–406
  feeling of absolute or utter dependence, 393–95
  his *Glaubenslehre* (*Christian Faith*), 389–413
  primacy of the self over the world and God, 402–4
  his relation to pantheism, 393
  his subjective standpoint contrasted with Hegel's objective standpoint, 414
  subjectivity of his standpoint, 389–91
  three main dogmatic forms (self, world, God), 402–4, 406
Septuagint, 22, 45–46, 188, 322
serpent, 104, 106–10, 112, 114, 143, 210, 224, 304–5, 355, 358, 368, 371–74
sexuality, 159–60, 222–23, 301–5
Sige (Silence), 73, 86–89, 90–91, 184, 253, 267, 284
Simon Magus, 179–86, 203, 224–25, 227, 229, 241
Sophia (Wisdom), 15, 17, 57, 62–63, 74–78, 80–83, 86, 91, 101–5, 107–13, 115–17, 120–21, 124, 129, 131–32, 138, 165, 184, 238, 253, 258, 268, 270, 273, 376, 383, 418, 420, 422, 426
Sophia-Achamoth, 17–18, 24, 181, 237–38, 257, 268, 273, 276, 283, 420
speculation, the speculative, 8, 11, 22, 24–27, 35–36, 38, 40, 46, 57–59, 83, 140, 168, 173, 193, 230, 239, 245, 249, 267, 277, 278, 283, 296, 306–8, 317, 331, 337–38, 338, 342, 375, 384–85, 338, 393, 397–98, 430, 436, 438–39, 440, 443–46, 458
spirit
  its antithesis with matter, 10, 15, 18, 24–28, 30–31, 34–36, 44, 135, 154–55, 190, 236–37, 341, 458
  labor of, extending over thousands of years, never concluded, 458
  mediates itself with itself, 10–11, 18, 422–23
  *see also* absolute spirit, finite spirit, Holy Spirit
supernatural, 33, 156, 234, 396–98, 405, 410
symbol, symbolic, 135, 137, 140, 157, 449, 450–51, 456, 458
Syria, 5, 26, 59, 176
syzygy (pair of opposites), 74–75, 82, 85, 86–92, 101, 121, 124, 139, 140, 174, 181, 184, 199–203, 237–40, 253, 269, 328, 419, 421

Tertullian, his polemic against Marcion, 286–92
theology, 45, 192, 251, 267, 296, 329, 333, 341, 343, 389, 400, 408, 414, 435, 439
Therapeutae, 24
Trinity, 254, 331, 347–48, 351, 388, 391, 416, 418, 423–34, 437

Valentinian system
  belongs to first major form of Gnosis, 71
  Christian and pre-Christian elements in, 117–21
  development of its main ideas, 72–81
  its idea of syzygies, 86–93
  Irenaeus' critique of, 296–82
  matter, concept of in, 94–99
  Platonic foundation of, 72, 82–85
  relation of Plotinus' system to, 272–77
  three principles of: pneumatic (spiritual), psychical, hylic (material), 93
Valentinus, distinct from Valentinian system, 71
Vater, J. S., his classification of the Gnostic systems, 56

Wisdom of Solomon, 23

Zoroastrianism, 12, 15, 27–29, 37–38, 41, 43, 124–26, 128–29, 264

www.ingramcontent.com/pod-product-compliance
Lightning Source LLC
Chambersburg PA
CBHW060416300426
44111CB00018B/2869